The 18th New York
Infantry in the Civil War

The 18th New York Infantry in the Civil War

A History and Roster

RYAN A. CONKLIN

McFarland & Company, Inc., Publishers
Jefferson, North Carolina

LIBRARY OF CONGRESS CATALOGUING-IN-PUBLICATION DATA

Names: Conklin, Ryan A., 1985– author.
Title: The 18th New York Infantry in the Civil War :
a history and roster / Ryan A. Conklin.
Description: Jefferson, North Carolina : McFarland & Company, Inc.,
Publishers, 2016. | Includes bibliographical references and index.
Identifiers: LCCN 2016038836 | ISBN 9781476667164 (softcover : acid free paper)
Subjects: LCSH: United States. Army. New York Infantry Regiment, 18th
(1861–1863) | United States—History—Civil War, 1861–1865—Regimental
histories. | New York (State)—History—Civil War, 1861–1865—Regimental
histories. | United States—History—Civil War, 1861–1865—Campaigns.
Classification: LCC E523.5 18th .C66 2016 | DDC 973.7/3—dc23
LC record available at https://lccn.loc.gov/2016038836

BRITISH LIBRARY CATALOGUING DATA ARE AVAILABLE

ISBN (print) 978-1-4766-6716-4
ISBN (ebook) 978-1-4766-2651-2

© 2016 Ryan A. Conklin. All rights reserved

*No part of this book may be reproduced or transmitted in any form
or by any means, electronic or mechanical, including photocopying
or recording, or by any information storage and retrieval system,
without permission in writing from the publisher.*

On the cover: Staff officers of the 18th New York photographed
at Camp King, about Sept. or Oct. 1861. Pictured (L–R): unidentified guard,
Dr. Nathan P. Rice, Lt. Col. William H. Young, Lt. William H. Russell, Jr.,
Col. William A. Jackson, Lt. John H. Russell, Maj. George R. Myers,
the Rev. A. A. Farr, Dr. Alexander A. Edmeston, unidentified guard
(from the collection of the Schenectady County Historical Society)

Printed in the United States of America

*McFarland & Company, Inc., Publishers
Box 611, Jefferson, North Carolina 28640
www.mcfarlandpub.com*

Without my dear wife, Annie,
and bottomless cups of coffee,
this book would not be.

Table of Contents

Preface and Acknowledgments   1
Introduction   7

1. A Call to Arms: April 12, 1861–May 11, 1861   9
2. Birth of a Regiment: May 12, 1861–June 18, 1861   34
3. To the War Front: June 19, 1861–July 12, 1861   62
4. First Blood: July 12, 1861–August 3, 1861   79
5. The Makeover of an Army: August 4, 1861–September 30, 1861   106
6. Losing Time, People and Patience: October 1, 1861–December 13, 1861   131
7. With Winter Comes Changes: December 14, 1861–March 1, 1862   156
8. Making Moves: March 2, 1862–April 1, 1862   171
9. A New Campaign: April 2, 1862–May 3, 1862   178
10. Like Devils Incarnate: May 4, 1862–June 26, 1862   186
11. Battle of Gaines's Mill: June 27, 1862   210
12. A Change of Front Is a Retreat: June 28, 1862–August 24, 1862   234
13. From One Campaign to the Next: August 24, 1862–September 13, 1862   255
14. Battle of Crampton's Gap: September 14, 1862   264
15. The Worst Bloodshed Imaginable: September 15, 1862–October 31, 1862   284
16. No End in Sight: November 1, 1862–December 31, 1862   300
17. A Bleak Winter: January 1, 1863–April 26, 1863   316
18. Committed to the End: April 27, 1863–June 4, 1863   333

Epilogue: The Boys in Blue Fade to Gray   361
Roster   385
Chapter Notes   447
Bibliography   473
Index   481

Preface and Acknowledgments

Growing up in Gettysburg, Pennsylvania, it was impossible to ignore the monuments and markers that saturate the town. I benefited from the battlefield being my backyard, and the story of the Civil War's drama grew on me. My mind often drifts to imagine what life would look like for me if I was present during different times, so it was only natural that I thought of where my family was during the war. That's when I became aware of my great-great-great-grandfather, Robert Conklin, and that he was a volunteer in Company D of the 18th New York Infantry. Very little information existed about his regiment, but I learned early that they were not even present at Gettysburg. The question remained as to what exactly was their history if they existed and served for the first two years of the war?

My research into the 18th started in 1999, when I was just fourteen. The internet then was still unrefined and yielded little. My exploration through some of the most authoritative books on the war churned up mere mentions of the 18th; for example, they were present at the battle of Gaines's Mill, but any specifics beyond that did not exist. I just knew there was more out there, somewhere. One fact became abundantly clear to me at an early stage of my research, and that was that no one had ever written anything about the 18th New York Infantry, neither author nor veteran who knew their story best. I was disappointed to say the least, and somehow I took this shortfall in history as my burden.

These men were proud of their service, and most chose to permanently reflect their time in uniform by having their regiment etched on their headstones. The more cemeteries I visited, the more I saw this type of honor on non–government-issued markers. To me, the in-depth story of the 18th became a hostage to time, and reading "18 NY INF" on so many headstones was as if they were calling from beyond the grave for someone to find and share their story.

More than a century of silence is an outcry for a regiment of volunteer patriots that gave so much towards the preservation of the Union. Being a war veteran myself, I know that every soldier has a story to tell, and these men were no different. Aside from a photograph of Robert Conklin that I found in an old family album in my grandparents' basement, I came up short of anything relative regarding his military service. It was during this vain investigation that something unique happened. Robert was but one of 1,069 men who ever appeared on the rolls of the 18th, and I felt compelled to learn them all, and give my best attempt at telling the history of this seemingly "forgotten" regiment. Only then would I have the knowledge of what they did, and place my ancestor within their collective experience. I had always hoped of finding some historical gem about him which kept me energized. His pension record yielded little, but I learned he dealt with a camp illness in August 1862, but never left the line. When I first cracked open the *Complete Record of Officers, Soldiers and Seamen* for the town of Wallkill, County of Orange, I found an entry for Robert with words scribbled next to his name that explained he was "in all action in which the company was engaged." At first, I was not satisfied with this meager sentence, as I wanted more. Only after I fully understood the trials and ordeals that the regiment faced was how I came to appreciate the weight of those words, to have never left the regiment when situations in war pulled so many away, either death, disease, or desertions. I'm proud of his service and with my study of the regiment I'm proud of all of the members of the 18th.

My sixteen-year journey of collecting and researching anything and everything associated with the 18th could be best described as obsessive, but good historians must commit themselves in deep research if anything original and fresh is to ever surface. I've been to every hometown from which the companies hailed. I've exhausted the shelves and holdings of countless historical societies, libraries, and cemeteries across the country. I've walked every battlefield the 18th was ever on, the sites of all of their long-term encampments, and I've followed the trails of their marches. I had to make up for the loss of those eye-witnesses lost to time who could intimately describe the settings, so I needed to be there to know what they saw.

Before this sounds like a solo endeavor, there have been several people who have woven their way into my hobby, and I truly hope this attempt of mine to thank those I've met over the years can stand as my genuine token of appreciation.

If there's anyone out there that has shown a similar and unexplainable obsession with this regiment that I have felt, it would be Jeff Sauter, and I'm glad to have met him early in my research. He willingly opened his collection of photographs of numerous individuals from the 18th that he had amassed over the years, and without his images this historical record would not be what it is. Jeff also shared letters and ephemera from Captain Horatio Goodno and Captain John Mooney that proved their worth with anecdotes that historians yearn for. Of all the treasures and directions he's provided, his friendship is superlative.

At the Historical Society of Middletown and the Wallkill Precinct, I'm glad to have met Jerry Kleiner. Not only did he allow me the opportunity to give a speech on the history of the Wallkill Guards in Middletown on the 150th anniversary of their return to town, but he really encouraged me to take my work to the publishers and get over my fear that there could always be more information out there.

Before her passing in 2014, Helen Fox, historian for the town of Bristol, New York, helped answer numerous questions from afar, and was a great aid when I came to town, especially on several cemetery excursions.

Michael Maloney, librarian and archivist at the Schenectady County Historical Society, has been nothing but quick and cordial to numerous requests, and has come through every time.

Stan Maine of the St. Lawrence County Historical Association clued me into a fantastic letter written by J. C. O. Redington about Bull Run that I would have never seen had it not been for him. He should also be commended for his own work regarding local connections to the Civil War, especially with the 60th New York Infantry. Nancy Webster, great-granddaughter of J. C. O. Redington, has also been a wealth of information regarding anything Redington, and I applaud her preservation of local and family history.

An old family photograph album from Mary Helen Crans Lockwood, in the custody of Ann Cantrell, contained photographs of the very first volunteer of the Wallkill Guards, Sergeant Augustus E. Hanford and his cousin, Private Edward M. Hanford, both of Company D, which I am extremely grateful to have been allowed to include.

Marc Bodnar has been very helpful when it came to locating the final resting places of Civil War veterans in and around Albany and Schenectady. The same could be said for Kelly Grimaldi, historian for the St. Agnes Cemetery in Menands, New York, and I congratulate her ongoing efforts to restore worn down headstones for Civil War veterans buried there.

William A. Palmer, Jr., was most kind to take up my request to read part of Chapter 10 that dealt with the battle of Brick House Landing. His work on the history of Eltham's Landing during the Civil War is a worthy study, and I'm grateful for his contributions.

Ronald S. Coddington has generously shared photographs of Civil War soldiers through a series of publications, and I want to thank him for allowing me to use his image of Mortier L. Norton. Cathryn Anders of the Warwick Historical Society helped with several requests, and introduced me to Tom and Joan Frangos who were kind enough to allow me to use their images of Captain Robert A. Malone and First Lieutenant John S. King.

The artistic ability of Greg Trax is incredible. He was able to take an old photograph and breathe new life into his rendering of a snapshot of Company I. He makes what he does seem so effortless, a sign of his true talent.

Contemporary books on the topic of New York in the Civil War seldom emerge without the name of Jim Gandy of the New York State Military Museum and Veterans Research Center. He was extremely helpful in allowing me to peruse through the wartime diary of Dr. Frank Mattimore, and he obliged my requests to have various newspaper clippings that had mentions of the 18th to be copied and delivered. The Veterans Research Center is home to the largest set of photographs of individuals from the 18th, and their inclusion acts better than any words of mine can.

Maurice Klapwald, librarian, and Susan P. Waide, manuscripts specialist, both of the New York Public Library, complied to my hefty requests for camp inspections from the United States Sanitary Commission Records that dealt with the 18th. After having waited a couple of years to have these precious documents closed from the public to be scanned and preserved, they have been well worth the wait and proven essential to the understanding of camp life and conditions.

Although no member of the 18th had ever penned a concise record of the regiment's history for posterity, even when those kinds of books became wildly popular in the postwar years, this book has been indelibly shaped by their descendants. Over the years I have come in contact with dozens of them, more than I can name, and many times over they have provided personal glimpses of their ancestors that no library or public work could ever reveal.

One of the first descendants I came in contact with was Jill Palmer, great-great-granddaughter of First Lieutenant George Chapman of Company I. She opened up her family relics and shared with me original muster rolls, enlistment papers, Chapman's wartime diary, and even a photograph of him in his uniform. We forged a friendship over the years and I'll forever remember the breakthroughs we both discovered the more we studied Chapman's handwritten diary. Had she not mentioned it, I might not have ever discovered that George's son Arthur was the poet who wrote "Out Where the West Begins." One of my biggest regrets with this book was that I did not finish sooner, for she was one of my best cheerleaders of encouragement, but whose energy was silenced when she unexpectedly passed away in 2013.

The daily mentions of camp occurrences as recorded by First Sergeant Augustus W. Mowatt, Company C, became something I could always rely on to plug holes whenever other records fell short. I'm indebted for its inclusion, as well as a postwar image of Mowatt, which were one-of-a-kind items shared by his great-great-nieces, Susan Armentrout and Steph Graves.

Julie Jones O'Leary, great-granddaughter of Private Joseph C. Jones, Company G, was gracious enough to let an unrelated outsider read through a family gem that was his personal record of experiences from the war, written by both him and a son. Jones' memory, descriptions, and attention to detail added to the collective understanding of the common soldier at just the right moments and I can't thank her enough for sharing.

Brian Cooke and Richard Haarde, direct descendants of Colonel William H. Young, were both quick to answer my questions about their ancestor, and launched me in new directions to further my research. The same could be said with Charles W. Howgate and Margaret-Ann (Howgate) Bamberg, both descendents of Major William S. Gridley, who over the years provided a helpful understanding of the Gridley family. Another supportive Gridley relative equally knowledgeable on the family name was Tom Sisson, whose direct ancestor was the major's twin brother, Henry.

The Rev. A. A. Farr was the only regimental chaplain of the 18th, and had it not been for the images shared by his great-great-granddaughter, Sarah M. (Farr) Roach, we would never know his likeness. Barb Samans, great-great-great-granddaughter of Captain Peter Hogan, Company H, opened her records on her family history and provided wartime photographs of her ancestor and his background to better understand who he was.

William F. Potter kindly shared the last known photograph taken of his great-grandfather, Private Calvin B. Potter of Company B. Similarly, Donald LaMunion, Jr., provided an image of his great-great-great-grandfather, Reuben Miller, Company D. Bob Richford, great-great-grandson of James Richford, Company I, provided an image of his ancestor, and has been one of my longest supporters since I started this venture.

The only child of Captain Theodore C. Rogers, Company H, who was born just weeks after his death at Gaines's Mill, never knew her father yet she ensured generations after would never forget his sacrifice. Through Rogers' great-great-grandson, Daniel Rogers Carpenter, their family history was made clearer for me, and his painting of his ancestor became an item I cannot praise enough to have been honored to include.

Clark Hotaling, great-great-grandson of Captain Daniel H. Daley, Company A, took up a project that restored the cemetery plot of his ancestor, and in passing mentioned some old photographs he had that were passed down through generations. So grateful am I to have been allowed to use those that pertained to the 18th, which would have never been known about had he not reached out to me.

Gerard Mattimore was kind enough to share useful tidbits on his family history that pertained to his great-great-uncle, Dr. Frank J. Mattimore.

I'm very grateful to have crossed paths with David Griffith, and his mother, Marguerite (Whittemore) Griffith, and their generosity to have shared what they know on the history of the Whittemore family, and the letters written by her great-grandfather, First Sergeant Nathaniel G. Whittemore, Company I.

I would like to praise Elodie Pritchartt for her help sharing with me what has been passed down through her family regarding her great-great-grandfather, First Lieutenant Henry E. Munger, Company A. Although Munger "disappeared" somewhat after the war, I'm happy he could be "found" to have been included in his regiment's history.

Just before this book was finalized I came in contact with John P. Bartholf, a direct descendant of Dr. John H. Bartholf, and both he and Anne C. Clark were gracious enough to share a photograph of their relative to be included, of which I'm very grateful of their contribution.

Much credit is owed to Joan (Bantham) Byer, great-granddaughter of Sergeant John S. Bantham, Company F, and to her son Dave Byer, who allowed me to include a photograph of their ancestor, and to use passages of Bantham's wartime journal that were so helpful when it came time to describe the personal drama of battle better than I ever could.

I must also give thanks to my parents, David and Pat Conklin, for showing me early the benefits of learning and appreciating history, and that it's ever-present but up to us to go out and seek it. Your love is unconditional, your support knows no doubt, and for many things I thank you.

Lastly, I could not have written this book without the balance in life that is my wife, Annie Conklin. Like a champion, she put up with my times of seclusion slumped over a laptop longer than any spouse should. With the Civil War being a topic far outside her own interests, she daringly read the earliest drafts and was unafraid to call out my faults. Both in print and in life, she has an innate power to make me better. Thank you for all that you do.

Long before Colonel William A. Jackson became the first commander of the 18th, he was a student at Union College. In one of his school ledgers he kept in 1850, the seventeen-year-old scholar scribbled a note to himself that read, "A man should not write unless he is well informed." I was nearly the same age when I first read this, and only now do I feel I have lived up to his command.

Introduction

> "God grant that if it should be my lot to fall,
> I may be gloriously fighting in the ranks of the brave and true."
> —*Corporal Thomas Alexander, Company D, April 19, 1862*

On the eve of battle, Corporal Alexander looked at those he touched elbows with and felt they were worthy to fight and die for. Many in the regiment felt the same way, and some fulfilled this last full measure of devotion. They fought more for preservation of the Union, and less for bounties and bonuses. They fought for each other, their families, their hometowns, and cursed those who brought shame upon themselves. They were honorable in ways that are enviable. It was the adventure of a lifetime. It was duty defined. It was reminisce to the days of their Minute Men ancestors. It was war, yes, but its reality was not yet known.

Secession was new, and with it came a host of unknowns. In the North, states hastily scrambled together a volunteer force hell-bent to crush the insurrectionists of the South, and ultimately patch the country back whole. In New York, hometowns figured out on their own how to form companies of state volunteers, and how to align themselves to be picked up for a regiment. They came from Middletown, Albany, Fishkill, Canandaigua, Ogdensburg, Schenectady—all over the state men raised their right hands to enlist in the 18th New York Infantry. They signed up for two years of duty, yet no one believed the war would last that long.

History seemed to follow them from the beginning. The first military duty of the 18th was to escort the remains of the martyred Ellsworth. During the initial Bull Run campaign, the regiment was the first to suffer casualties on their approach after an ambush near Fairfax Court House. With an extended stay in Alexandria, Virginia, the 18th helped construct one of the many forts that encircled Washington, and their work on Fort Ward can still be judged with a visit to the protected landmark.

Civil War historians often overlook the battle of West Point (more accurately Brick House Landing), but the 18th was there and much can be learned from this largely ignored battle. Amidst a dense forest, the 18th cleverly hugged the ground in front of their enemy and shook tree limbs and screamed to deceive the Rebels into thinking they were on the attack. The tactic left the 18th as the only regiment in their brigade not to lose a single man. At Gaines's Mill the regiment was placed in the literal middle of the Union line to plug a dangerous gap, and they suffered terribly with heavy casualties. You won't just read numbers, but rather learn *who* the killed and wounded were, where they were from, and how exactly their loss affected comrades.

At Crampton's Gap, the 18th performed a bayonet charge that successfully punched through South Mountain, but again heavy losses darkened their spirits even after their first undisputed victory. Carnage earned a new definition when the regiment walked over the fields of Antietam and survived the day under a relentless barrage of artillery. Accounts from these witnesses, explained in their own grotesque imagery, will surely cast a new perspective for those who pour over America's single-bloodiest day.

The sting of defeat was just as miserable even without an enemy present, such as when the regiment trekked through the futile Mud March. Present at 1st and 2nd Fredericksburg, an amphibious landing over the Rappahannock and probes from enemy skirmishers kept the 18th hard at work. With just days left in their two-year contract, the regiment was committed to another campaign at Chancellorsville, and was close to being completely annihilated. Their contractual time ended in mid–1863, but men who were then considered veterans enlisted again in over 160 other organizations, and saw the war find its peace.

They served from the beginning of the war, and faced two years of hardships through grueling campaigns, tiresome marches, changing seasons, haunting combat, and torturous diseases. During their existence, 1,069 men attached their name at some point to become a part of the 18th. Nearly 500 men left early, either from resignations, transfers, deaths, discharges, and desertions. Forty-two men gave the ultimate sacrifice in battle, and 119 others proved they still had time to live after they were felled by wounds. Accidents claimed the lives of four, but disease was the predominant killer that left another forty-four men dead.

May this book break the 153 years of silence of the 18th New York Infantry, and serve as a record of their selfless sacrifice.

1

A Call to Arms
April 12, 1861–May 11, 1861

"I shall never say go, but I shall always say follow."
—Captain John C. Meginnis, Company D, April 22, 1861

The life of Samuel Hodgkins had always been spent in routine. Changing with the seasons, the twenty-one-year-old farmer had worked the same fields on his father's property, and still lived in the house in which he was born. His mother died when he was three which brought his maternal grandmother into the household to help keep house and raise him and his three siblings until he was thirteen. Through his grandmother's teachings he learned to view the world differently than his father, and he said he owed "what true manhood and patriotism I have ever possessed" to her.[1]

When the news of a federal garrison at Fort Sumter had been fired on by Southern insurrectionists on April 12, 1861, the news from South Carolina traveled at breakneck speeds to reach even the tiny village of Hodgkins' hometown of Oswegatchie, New York, in the northern regions of the state. The news shocked the entire nation, even after the widespread threats from the South, and their political differences that reached a fever pitch during the 1860 presidential campaign. Everyone knew that war had finally arrived. As allegiances divided the young country in two, Americans on both sides rallied together and braced for the aftershock.[2]

Hodgkins always concerned himself to stay current with the drama of politics, but his Republican views always clashed with his father's opinions. The household broke out in several fierce debates that mimicked the division of the country. In the 1860 presidential campaign, Hodgkins was very proud to have voted for the first time in his life. He voted for the entire Republican ticket for the national election that put Abraham Lincoln into the White House, but in doing so, "alienated myself from my father's good graces."[3]

War did bring a sense of unity as men put aside political ties and banded together in order to piece back the country, and Hodgkins said "every old fife and drum that could be found was brought into use." One of the first to point his finger at Hodgkins was his father, who made him feel that the vote he made created the mess the country was launched into. His father heckled him for his participation in electing what he called "that Black Abolition ticket" into the White House. Hodgkins was perpetually reminded by him that once Lincoln was sworn into office, war would soon follow. Now that his prediction had come true, his father challenged him to see if he had the "grit and nerve enough to go and fight."[4]

Hodgkins had already made up his mind that he was willing to offer his service to the country's calling. His own father must have forgotten that he himself was the son of a patriot, who under similar circumstances during the Revolutionary War joined as an underage teenager, and that sense of duty seemed inherent. Within days of Sumter's surrender, men and boys alike rallied in their hometowns and proudly signed their names to enlistment papers. A company of volunteers had already been started in the nearby town of Ogdensburg, but they had already left for the state capital by the time Hodgkins was made aware of its formation. He would not miss out on the next opportunity.[5]

As the patriot fever brought forth an endless supply of men willing to fight, a second company quickly emerged in Ogdensburg. On May 1, Hodgkins hitched a ride with his neighbor and traveled fifty miles to reach the town, and as soon as he arrived, he got right to business and located the colonel of the local militia who had the authority to enlist volunteers. With the official papers in his hand, Hodgkins proved to his father that he had the courage to answer his country's calling and took ownership of his vote when he proudly penned his name to a contract that attached himself to a company that would belong to the 18th New York Volunteer Infantry Regiment.[6]

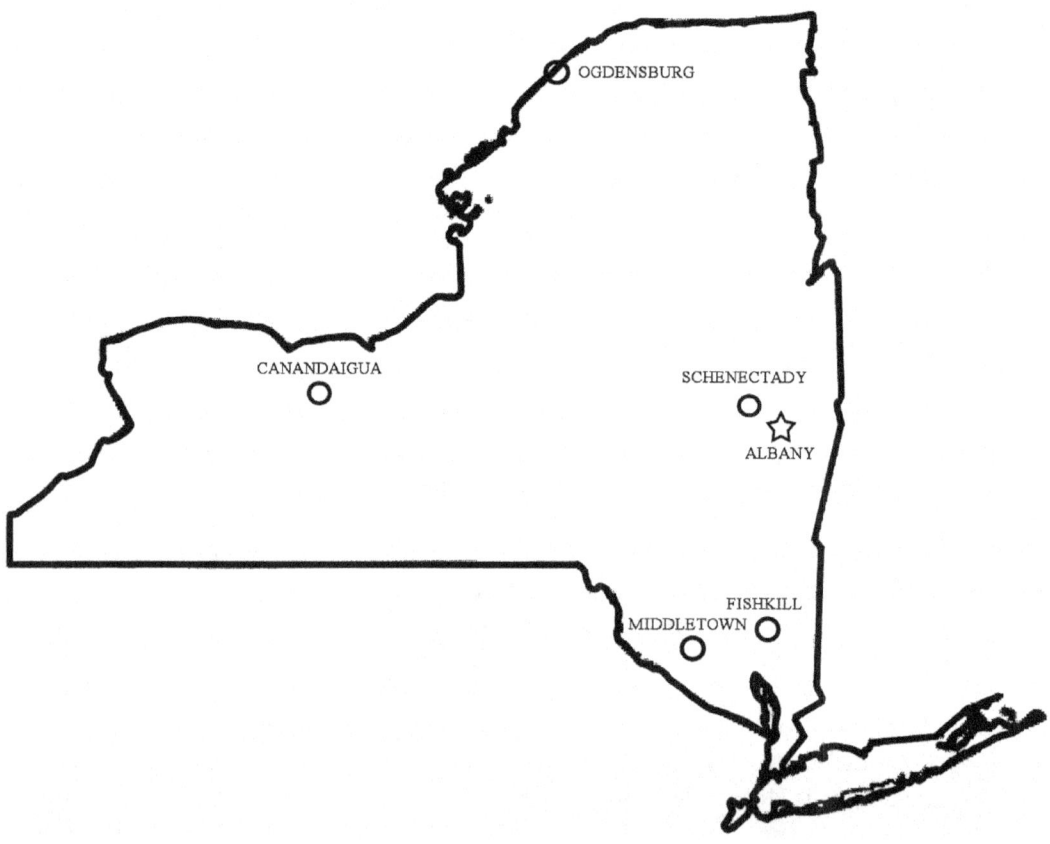

Map of New York showing locations of hometowns where companies were formed (author's collection).

Volunteers Needed

By April 1861, America was pulled apart by a divisive fault line of ideologies and principles that provoked the young nation to wage war against itself. Armed representatives of the freshly formed Confederate States of America turned their threats to realities when they fired upon Federal troops quartered at Fort Sumter in Charleston Harbor, South Carolina. The soldiers' refusal to surrender their fort to their unrecognized adversaries culminated into an inevitable revolution. At 4:30 a.m. on April 12, the bombardment commenced and the start of the American Civil War was scribed into the history books.[7]

Reports of the attack raced to Washington where President Lincoln immediately responded with a public plea. On April 15, he issued the call for 75,000 volunteers to quell the insurrectionists. As the bombs still fell upon Fort Sumter, New York Governor Edwin D. Morgan worked feverishly with the State Legislature to authorize funds for their projected volunteers. With impressive speed, both houses passed a bill on April 16 that authorized "the enrolling and mustering into service of the state, for two years, unless sooner discharged, a number of volunteers not to exceed thirty thousand men."[8]

Two days later, Governor Morgan issued his proclamation that called for seventeen regiments, comprised of 780 men each. By then, thousands of informed citizens throughout the state had already taken preliminary steps to organize companies and waited for their impending request to pass through the telegraph wires. Volunteers lined up by the scores in recruiting offices that popped up throughout every county. There were so many men ready and willing to serve that on April 25, Governor Morgan issued another proposal that asked for twenty-one more regiments.[9]

Word of mouth passed the news for the needed volunteers seemingly faster than telegrams or newspapers. Every conversation centered about the war and what it meant not only for the nation, but for their hometowns. From small agricultural hamlets to heavily populated cities, an outpouring of patriotic citizens, united behind a common cause, packed their local town halls and discussed what their next step would be.

Middletown

Middletown was a young incorporated village, the second largest in Orange County, and was centered in a region of clustered neighboring towns that was collectively known as Wallkill. Situated along the New York and Erie Railroad, Middletown had recently undergone an impressive growth during the 1850s from an industrial and transportation boom, and its population soared to approximately 2,200 by the start of the war. In 1859, Middletown celebrated their first building to be illuminated by gas-powered lighting.[10]

Like the rest of the country, Middletown residents had been polarized by political parties during the years that ramped up to the war. Republicans and Wide-Awake movements held their ground against Democrats who were further subdivided between Copperheads and War Democrats. Prior to the 1860 election, two Middletown printers with opposing political ideals started rival newspapers whose publications became a rhetorical slugfest that was absorbed by the locals.[11]

The most popular public meeting house and unofficial town hall in Middletown was

Built in 1852, Gothic Hall hosted Middletown's first war rallies, enlistments, and formation of the Wallkill Guards. This photograph was taken after the war, when Gothic Hall was owned by the *Middletown Evening Press*. The building was razed in 1940 (courtesy Historical Society of Middletown and the Wallkill Precinct).

Gothic Hall, which became flooded by residents to overcapacity during the evening of April 17. Erected in 1852, the hall could hold up to 500 people within its large assembly hall and basement. Prominent citizens of the town's city council temporarily set aside their political differences and focused on the importance of the country's unification and their necessity to answer Lincoln's plea. An aged veteran of the War of 1812 was made chairman and opened the floor for men to speak their minds in what became a series of extemporaneous speeches laden with patriotic sentiments, performed with the backdrop of a flag-draped portrait of George Washington that hung on the wall. Shouts of patriotic fervor ran rampant and feelings were almost spiritual. Encouraged by the audience to speak, one man caved to their requests and took the stand with exclamations that Middletown citizens must "stand by the Flag of our Country in this trying exigency, and to be ready, if need be, to sacrifice their fortunes and their lives in its defense." The people waited for words of this magnitude and emotions swelled to such a crescendo that the shouts and cheers could be heard outside the wooden confines of Gothic Hall. Passionate as they were, the crowd was reminded that very little, "if any, knowledge of the mode or the law under which companies were required to be organized." The energetic committee offered a motion that passed in which five nominated men instantly began to accept names of those who wished to enlist. One of these newly elected officials was twenty-three-year-old William E. Carmichael, who jotted down names of volunteers, to include himself, despite not having any official blank muster rolls to write on. At the conclusion of the meeting, someone in the audience overcome with excitement broke out with a rendition of "The Star-Spangled Banner" which the boisterous crowd took up in unison.[12]

Forty men from Middletown, Wallkill, Warwick, Monroe, and other surrounding villages signed their names to the newly created company at Gothic Hall's evening meeting. Nineteen-year-old Augustus E. Hanford of Wallkill, a machinist apprentice at the Orange County Furnace, had the honor of being the first man to give his name to the list. The company grew quickly and held nightly drill sessions at Gothic Hall. The Middletown Light Guards, a long-standing local militia organization, later joined the ranks and added to the size and expertise of the company.[13]

A committee of three prominent men from the town was formed that decided to tackle the formalities and legalities in order to protect those who chose to enlist. The "Military Committee" took full power of the company and collected the official roster of volunteers, raised funds for them, and organized for their upcoming travel to Albany for acceptance by the state.[14]

On April 22, another meeting was held at Gothic Hall for the purpose of electing the officers and non-commissioned staff who would formally lead the company. Everyone looked to thirty-three-year-old John C. Meginnis, an established engineer for the Eastern division of the Erie Railroad. There were at least a dozen railroad employees that joined the company and knew him well. Meginnis' own partner, Fred Eldridge, who fired his engine for the previous six years, was another who followed his engineer's lead. Meginnis soon found himself in charge of the young and spirited company of volunteers. The rest of the vacant positions were then filled, picked from a large collection

Nineteen-year-old machinist Augustus Emmet Hanford was the first to sign his name for Middletown's first roster for volunteers at Gothic Hall on April 17, 1861 (courtesy Mary Helen Crans Lockwood album, family collection).

of competent men. With the patriotic tunes that bellowed out from polished horns of the Middletown Brass Band, the company marched around the hall with their best military manners and officially presented themselves as a company under Meginnis' leadership. The newly christened Captain Meginnis addressed his men with the following words:

> You have conferred great honor upon me in electing me as your Captain. We have seen military companies formed in time of peace, but never before have we seen one formed as this has been for immediate service. Gentlemen, we go to defend our glorious liberties; and there is one thing I wish you all to recollect, I shall never say go, but I shall always say follow.[15]

Meginnis' address was immediately followed "by the most deafening shouts of applause." After the captain's words, the rest of the newly promoted officers were officially presented to the company and each took their turns with speeches. Following their words, the Military Committee unanimously voted to officially adopt the nickname, "The Wallkill Guards," which best reflected the area the company represented.[16]

After their first official drill, the Wallkill Guards and their brass accompaniment flaunted their success and paraded through their town streets. Flocks of people looked on and the spectacle may have been the deciding factor for any man who still wrestled with indecision to join. Word of mouth and advertisements that ran in the local papers helped increase the strength of the Guards rapidly. By April 30, 113 men appeared on the roster and the Guards were officially recognized and enlisted into federal service. Captain Meginnis' younger brother, twenty-two-year-old Samuel G. Meginnis, joined up that day after having arrived by train from Mechanicsburg, Ohio, where he was married two days before. The influx of men from the Wallkill and Middletown area continued to enter the ranks. By the time the company was to leave for Albany, which was one of the three main hubs for companies being raised in the state, the Guards' numbers stood at 128 and showed no signs of slowing down. The manpower of the Guards far exceeded the maximum limit for a company, and the State Military Board actually "declined to accept more than one company of 77 men." So many "rugged and patriotic men" desperate to enlist swamped the Military Committee that oversaw the Guards, and unfortunately the committee had to reject many just to keep numbers down. They even tried to discourage men with families from enlisting. Some were said to have "begged and plead for a chance of serving their country," only to be reluctantly turned away by the committee. With the company having the compliment of nearly twice its allowance, the Guards found it hard to eliminate their passionate volunteers who enlisted not for any special bounty or promise, but "only the privilege of doing and dying." The committee decided to send the oversized company as one to Albany, with hopes that they could split into two separate elements.[17]

On the evening of May 2, Captain Meginnis received the long awaited order which summoned the Wallkill Guards to Albany. He quickly prepared himself and his men to board the train the following morning. Before doing so, the Guards were ensured that they would have a proper sendoff by its citizens. They gathered the next morning at 7 a.m. with 135 members, and marched down the streets of Middletown to the town center—Franklin Square—where they were greeted by what seemed to be the entire village assembled. Friends, family, and countless patriotic well-wishers swarmed the streets and sidewalks during the Wallkill Guards' sendoff march. Flags and bunting adorned the facades of almost every building which created a very patriotic and colorful backdrop. The Ladies of Middletown worked for a week and made a costly but stunning red, white, and blue silk national flag for the Wallkill Guards. The women were under the impression that each company was required to carry a national flag and they were proud that they were able to put together such a priceless symbol for their first company to leave. On the women's behalf, local attorney and Middletown's "most public spirited man in town," James N. Pronk made the presentation. While the lawyer held the impressive banner in his arms, he spoke "an eloquent and impressive speech" to all who could hear. Pronk then transferred the flag to the accepting hands of Captain Meginnis who spoke a few lines in humble acceptance of the trophy. The captain then transferred the colors to his ensign, Second Lieutenant Roswell M. Sayer, who had just left his partnership of a successful local hardware store. The citizens made it known to the men that they planned to issue Bibles to each member of the Guards, but due to their delay in arrival they coordinated to have the books meet up with the men once they had an address in Albany.[18]

Following the presentation of their new flag, another prominent Middletowner—Charles C. McQuoid—presented Captain Meginnis with a sword and an equally beautiful sheath on behalf of the citizens of Middletown. McQuoid then concluded with a few remarks of his own to the Wallkill Guards and spectators. Meginnis had already received a new Colt revolver from a similar ceremony a week before, customized with all of the latest improvements by a local jeweler. After McQuoid placed the glistening new sword in the hands of Meginnis, he acknowledged the gift and stated that the sword "should only be drawn from its scabbard except in defense of his company's flag." This concluded the ceremony on Franklin

This undated photograph shows Middletown's Erie Station, scene of the send-off of the Wallkill Guards on May 3, 1861, en route to Albany. Built in 1843, this depot was eventually torn down and replaced in 1896 (courtesy Historical Society of Middletown and the Wallkill Precinct).

Square, as it neared time for the Guards to board their train. The excited yet tearful crowd followed the company as they marched down the street to the Erie Station depot where they swarmed the men as they filed into two overcrowded railcars. Last minute farewell shouts overlapped the cadence of the company's own drum corps. Friends and family hastily passed words of encouragement and goodbyes as the men squeezed into the two cars. The train slowly drifted away as the wheels worked up their momentum. Second Lieutenant Sayer waved the gifted flag back-and-forth from the rear platform of the train until the crowd was out of sight. The send-off was truly a "solemn separation" and another example of what happened in every town and city across America—for both sides. For some of these men this would be the last time they would ever see their home and loved ones.[19]

Fishkill

Thirty miles to the east of Middletown on the opposite side of the Hudson River, Fishkill and its close-knit villages forged together their own contingent to send to the state. Located in the southwestern corner of Dutchess County and chiseled by the Hudson River, the towns around are snuggled into high rocky mountains. Fishkill's name is a Dutch derivative of "Vis-Kill," meaning Fish Creek, which snakes through the center of town. Fishkill was a lot smaller than Middletown, with a population of a little under 10,000 in 1860. After the war's outbreak, Republicans and Democrats united under a common cause not seen since the days of the Revolutionary War. Passionate patriotic rallies bubbled up in and around Fishkill. Several different flag raising ceremonies emerged throughout Dutchess County, as townspeople banded together to display their support of the cause.[20]

Nestled along the banks of the Hudson River about six miles southwest from Fishkill was the neighboring village of Fishkill Landing, home of a local militia unit known as the Denning Guards. They quickly offered their services to the state and encouraged others from the area to follow them after they heard the news of the governor's request.[21]

Samuel Leith, a butcher from Fishkill Landing, was spurred to action and tried to raise a company. Leith had been orphaned when he was a boy, which forced him to grow up fast. Always the adventurist, when he was eleven years old he left his hometown in Scotland that shared his name and came to New York. He learned the butcher trade early and soon found work in New York. In 1858, Leith started his own butcher shop in Fishkill Landing until the events of war enlivened him. As soon as volunteers were called for, the twenty-one-year-old butcher bumped his age to thirty and quickly gathered men from the community that shared the same passion to become soldiers.[22]

With so many interested parties from the surrounding river towns, a formal meeting to cluster the volunteers was convened at Fishkill Landing on April 22. Sixty-six men from Fishkill, Matteawan [present day Beacon], Glenham, and Wappinger Falls fused around the existing Denning Guards and gained the numbers for a company-sized element to lend their service to the state. The day after the gathering, men reconvened and elected officers to head the company. The first and second lieutenant positions were given to John W. Birmingham and Samuel Leith, respectively. The choice of company commander was granted to Henry Wiltse, Jr., a twenty-seven-year-old lawyer from the area. Beginning his academic studies in 1850 at Rutgers College [now University], he earned his degree in 1853, and subsequently passed the bar from Albany Law School three years later. Wiltse's company was accepted by the state on April 25. That same day, the citizens of Fishkill raised $600 to support the families of the men that volunteered to leave their homes and fight. Rather than wait for any possible emergency funds to come from the state to help cover the travel expenses of the company to Albany, Samuel Leith generously put down his savings and paid for the journey. On April 26, the company exchanged their heartfelt goodbyes to their families as they boarded the train that would bring them closer to the warfront.[23]

Ogdensburg

At a stone's throw away from the Canadian border was the sleepy town of Ogdensburg, located on the northern edge of the state in St. Lawrence County. Dividing the two countries was the rapidly rushing St. Lawrence River, and Ogdensburg itself was split in two by the tributary Oswegatchie River. During the early morning hours of April 12, the Ogdensburg local newspaper did not yet have sufficient information as to what transpired at Fort Sumter, so that Friday morning paper ran just a small vague article about the possible seizure on page four. Moments after the paper was printed, the detailed dispatch that explained the attack reached the hands of one of the editors. He knew instantly that the story was big, big enough to trump anything that was just printed, so he took the news straight to the people. The editor ran outside and placed a dry-goods box on street corners and began to shout the contents of the dispatch. Crowds of concerned citizens gathered around him and listened to the shocking news of what had occurred off the Charleston coast.[24]

Word spread quickly and daily routines were broken as people pulled together as a community. The editor not only shared additional tidbits of the bombardment as reports trickled in, but he issued a notice to any man willing to volunteer for a six-month stint in a company could do so with one that would be raised in Ogdensburg. Applicants just had to sign their name on enrollment papers that he had drawn up and printed back in his office. Word of the list was shared throughout the nearby towns in hopes to draw enough men to comprise a company. Lincoln's April 15 decree that asked for men's length of service to be for the duration of two years made some individuals reconsider and names began to be scratched through. Soon, the editor's hasty attempt to raise a company dissolved. Despite this first attempt there were still plenty of interested men that held no hesitation to the president's mandate. Later that same evening, a second concerted attempt to form a company in Ogdensburg for the longer duration was implemented. The second try was swiftly filled with a long list of names.[25]

The Ogdensburg judge and several prominent men within and around the city convened at a conference within the Eagle Hall meeting house during the evening of April 17, and the Lyceum Hall on April 22. By April 25, Ogdensburg and its surrounding villages sent off their first company of sixty-five volunteers to Albany. Flag waiving and glory praising enthusiasts convened again in Ogdensburg and crammed the Eagle Hall later that night and continued their efforts to gather more volunteers for another company. Neighboring Depeyster citizens congregated at the Town House and added more names each night to their increasing roster of volunteers. The surrounding villages of Canton, Lisbon, Madrid, Gouverneur, and Potsdam similarly filled up with names and the men from St. Lawrence County soon had a second company under way.[26]

Fifty-year-old David L. Bartlett was a respected and established millwright throughout the Ogdensburg area. Bartlett was always an avid reader and taught himself many things through books. He apprenticed at the age of nineteen and became a millwright, and he engineered new mills throughout upstate New York, Montreal, Detroit, and even some in Mexico. Bartlett had moved his wife and ten children to Ogdensburg in 1850. Just a month before the Civil War's outbreak, Bartlett was the supervisor for a 100-man strong workforce whose mission was to seal a near-breach of the town's dam. He had already experienced a soldier's life long before his millwright days, and he never imagined a scenario that would see him back in a military uniform again. At the government's initial call for able-bodied men, Bartlett encouraged his son to volunteer in the first Ogdensburg company that was raised, and his son accepted the challenge. Bartlett immediately had second thoughts as soon as his son's company left town. He too was swept up in the overwhelming buzz of patriotism which prompted him to put an advertisement in the local paper on April 26. Bartlett wrote a few lines and stated that he refused to encourage his own son to venture down a path that he would not do so himself. So with that small public notice, Bartlett finished with a mention that he would become the first name for "Company No. 2" of Ogdensburg volunteers and encouraged anyone who wanted to join him, to meet him that evening. Bartlett was "a man of quiet tastes and kindly disposition," from what others said about him, and "while tenacious in his opinions, he granted the same privilege to others that he maintained for himself, and was on terms of cordial friendship with all." Several men were warm to the idea to have Bartlett as their commander, and many flocked to the residence of Schuyler F. Judd, the colonel of militia in Ogdensburg, to make it happen.[27]

Bartlett's company grew to fruition almost overnight. His straightforward naming of Company Number 2 immediately stuck by the people of Ogdensburg. The moniker lasted for the rest of the company's existence.[28]

On the evening of April 29, Bartlett and fellow volunteers held a meeting in Ogdensburg and chose their leadership of commissioned and non-commissioned officers for the company. Albert S. Seely was a twenty-seven-year-old express messenger in Ogdensburg that was chosen as Bartlett's second-in-command. Seely was more than likely acquainted with Horatio G. Goodno, who was chosen as the second lieutenant, as he too served as the express manager on the local rail line before the war. Fifty-year-old Goodno had moved to Ogdensburg from Vermont when the O. & L. C. (Ogdensburg & Lake Champlain) Railroad opened their traffic. After nearly six years on the line, Goodno left that job and opened a livery stable in town and kept up business until the war became his calling.[29]

David Leonard Bartlett, a fifty-year-old millwright, raised and commanded the second company from Ogdensburg (courtesy New York State Military Museum).

Ogdensburg's first company had already left for Albany and Bartlett did not want to miss an opportunity that could be afforded to them. In the early morning hours of May 1, Company Number 2 gathered at the Town House in Ogdensburg and prepared to leave for Albany. Bartlett's company was treated to several inspiring speeches from different citizens and closed with a blessing by a local pastor. The newly appointed officers worked within their new roles of their rank and formed the company into line. They were marched down to the rail depot where friends, relatives, and curious spectators had gathered to exchange their last goodbyes. The local brass band played familiar patriotic anthems as families bid their farewells to their men who were off to be soldiers. At 11:30 a.m., the train pulled away from Ogdensburg amidst cheers and tears as the music of the band faded away.[30]

The train shuttled the volunteers east to Plattsburg where the company disembarked and boarded a steamboat. The vessel was host to the first of several discomforts that plagued a soldiers' life when they were introduced to lice. Samuel Hodgkins was onboard with the company and suggested that the lice were left on the boat from the War of 1812 and "had teeth according to their age." Getting accustomed to their bites was just the onset of future aches.[31]

The steamboat ferried the men to Whitehall where they transferred back onto another train. When they passed through Fort Edwards, Bartlett's company was presented with a stand of colors by the well-recognized writer and publisher, E. Z. C. Judson. On May 4, Company Number 2 took their first meal together at the Pioneer House in Troy, eight miles north of Albany. In the afternoon, they finished the last leg of their trek when they entered Albany and added yet another company into the streets of the capital.[32]

Schenectady

As soon as the news of the Fort Sumter surrender reached the newspapers in Schenectady, located sixteen miles northwest from Albany, the news similarly enraptured the people. Reflective of its Dutch origins, a handful of towering church spires composed the city's skyline that could be seen from several miles out. Schenectady was a prosperous industrial city that would soon become a powerhouse that produced heavy machinery to the impending war effort, most notably trains. The city had a population of more than 13,000 near the start of the war, and its people leaned heavily Democrat. When President-elect Lincoln passed through the city on his way to his inauguration two months before the war, his reception was both hot and cold. When war broke out and the Union tore at the fibers, the people of Schenectady rallied together and contributed just as many devoted men to the cause than came from any Republican-rooted city.[33]

One of the first men to rise out of the city in its hour of need was William Seward Gridley. Both he and his twin brother Henry Seward Gridley were born on July 13, 1838, in Schenectady. Their father was a fervent "stump" speaker for the Whig Party and named his twins in honor of the twelfth Governor of New York—William Henry Seward. Eleven days after their birth, Seward attended a commencement ceremony in Schenectady at his alma mater—Union College—which allowed the opportunity for the proud father to present the newborns to a very appreciative governor that sparked a long lasting friendship. Seward would eventually ascend to become the Secretary of State in Lincoln's administration during the Civil War.[34]

Twenty-two-year-old William Seward Gridley let his passion and patriotism launch him to organize Schenectady's first company of volunteers within a week of war being declared (courtesy Margaret-Ann [Howgate] Bamberg).

Tragedy struck early for the young Gridley twins that tore the family apart. About a month before William and Henry's fifth birthday, their father, mother, and another sibling all died on the same day, most likely from a shared disease. This left William, Henry, and their one-year-old brother Nathanial orphaned, but they had a nineteen-year-old sister who took them under her care.[35]

Cleary's Saloon, as pictured in the 1870s, was Gridley's place of employment and where he summoned Schenectady's first volunteers, the "Seward Volunteer Zouaves," which eventually became Company A, to organize on April 19, 1861. The building was razed in 1884 (from the collection of the Schenectady County Historical Society).

Their stay with their sister was brief and she eventually gave the brothers up to be raised by the radical sect of Christian "Shakers" in Amenia, New York. As they grew older, the Gridley brothers shifted away from the cult and returned on their own to Schenectady. William Gridley began to study law and juggled work as a clerk and bartender at Cleary's Saloon, a hotspot eatery and bar located adjacent to the railroad depot in downtown Schenectady. With the rail lines just feet from its front door, the saloon also shared sides with the heavily frequented three-story Givens Hotel which was great for business. The saloon took its name from its owner, Thomas Cleary, who was married to Gridley's sister. Living just a block from his business, Cleary also opened his home to his brother-in-law to live in. Cleary was a socially connected proprietor held in high regard amongst the city elite and his saloon was a mainstay for them, which allowed Gridley ample opportunities to rub elbows and make acquaintances.[36]

In 1857, an eighteen-year-old Gridley penned a letter to the Secretary of War with a request to be appointed to the United States Military Academy. He expressed a desirous will to become a cadet and explained he met all of the criteria needed for the school. One thing he lacked, however, was legacy, in the sense that he did not come from an affluent family, nor did he have close relatives that ever attended the school. Try as he did, his letters were never successful and Gridley was not accepted.[37]

By the time the Civil War erupted, Gridley was twenty-two years old, and had etched himself as a military aficionado even without a West Point education. He served and held a position as a first lieutenant in the city's local company of artillery militia—the Schenectady City Artillery. He also helped spread and unite Republican ideals throughout Schenectady with the formation of several paramilitary Wide Awake companies, one in each ward, and one of which he led as their captain.[38]

When Lincoln and Morgan's immediate request for volunteers was publicized, Gridley wasted no time and utilized all of his resources and some personal expenses to form a company of his own. He placed an advertisement in the local paper on April 18 which called for the following:

> ATTENTION VOLUNTEERS: All young men who are in favor of forming a light infantry company and offering their services to garrison this state, or to the President of the United States, to aid and assist in defending the constitution and the Union of the United States against foreign or domestic foes, are requested to meet at Cleary's saloon, opposite the railroad depot, on Friday evening at 7:30 o'clock, the 19th inst. This means fight, and all who sign must go.[39]

The following evening, sixty men from the area answered the notice and attended Gridley's meeting at Cleary's Saloon. Gridley led the discussion of what was being asked of them as men, and soon patriots emerged from the crowd after forty-seven men in attendance committed themselves to their nation's call. Gridley's associations with the militia, bartending at the tavern, and the multiple Wide Awake companies had paid off. Men penned their names or made their mark to an application that Gridley formulated that asked for a company to be organized for military duty. Fittingly nicknamed the "Seward Volunteer Zouaves" in honor of his idolized Secretary of State, Gridley privately funded and controlled his small band of volunteers in which he was asked to be their captain. An election that same evening was also conducted that seated locals Daniel H. Daley and Edward W. Groot, to serve as officers to help command Gridley's company as his two subordinates. With the application of names in his hand, Gridley sped off to Albany to request his commission from the governor and put his company in service. Once he got to Albany, Gridley was given an order by the adjutant general to bring his company to the city for duty on April 22. Gridley backtracked to Schenectady and disseminated the joyous news to his anxious group of volunteers. As ordered, Gridley and his company went to Albany where they were inspected by an officer from the state militia, who also had to preside over another "official" election before his eyes to ensure the voting of officers was accurate. Captain Gridley and his two officers received their commissions, and the men expected to be picked up at any moment as Company A of the newly formed 3rd New York, but somehow that plan did not pan out as that position was filled by a different company. Regardless, Gridley's company of "Zouaves" were filled with pride to be Schenectady's first organized company for the war, and the fourth in the entire state of New York.[40]

Gridley's company was the first but not only contingent to be raised in Schenectady. There were several smaller groups that scrambled together on the heels of Gridley's, but only those that reached the proper size advanced as a company to the capital city. More than a week had passed before Stephen Truax, owner of a restaurant and ice cream saloon in Schenectady, reached his quota and formed his own faction of local men to become a company. Truax was also a captain of one of the fire houses in Schenectady, but most of his followers came from men that served under his command as captain in the independent militia unit from the city—the Schenectady Washington Continentals. The local paper printed a request from an anonymous recruit that begged one of the captains of the Continentals—Captain William Horsfall—to raise a company under his leadership. Horsfall did step forward to enlist but chose to follow Captain Truax's leadership and joined his company as second-in-command. When Truax's company reached seventy-seven men, they were inspected and enrolled into the state as an official company on May 2. The following afternoon, they loaded up on the cars of the train and took the short trek to neighboring Albany.[41]

Albany

By the time the second company from Schenectady had reached Albany, hundreds of other companies from around the state with similar origins had already descended upon the capital city. Companies rapidly fused together with other companies to form regiments and have their officers appointed in preparation of being accepted by the Adjutant General of New York. Other companies continued to be created throughout the state and spilled into the city at a steady rate.[42]

Albany was one of the nation's old cities of European settlement, having earned its charter as a city ninety years before the Declaration of Independence. Since then, Albany boomed with immigration, mostly from Dutch settlers, and when New York became an independent state, Albany was chosen as its capital. With its hilly cobblestoned streets, the city was progressive for its times and boasted an array of factories, streets lit by gas lamps, supreme ferry and rail lines, and a solid political system that was a strong arm for the entire country.[43]

Before Albany became the rendezvous destination of organized companies from across the state, the city busied itself to produce its own compliment of local volunteers. Men rallied behind friends to form companies and walked the streets to spread the word to encourage more to join. The "Call to Arms!" request appeared in Albany papers as early as April 15, when the state called for 30,000 volunteers, as part of Lincoln's first call. Saloon owner John Lawless held a meeting at his "Malta Saloon" on Maiden Lane as soon as he heard war had been declared. He quickly raised a sizable contingent of fellow Albany residents that shared the desire to go to war. On April 15, his company rallied under a flag held by Edward Fisher, a fellow volunteer and Mexican War veteran, and the company presented themselves to the governor. Lawless allowed the volunteers of his company to stay housed in his own saloon, which also doubled as his private residence, and the space filled quickly. His building filled up so fast that on April 17 he put a request to the hometown paper and asked for help to open other doors to quarter his fifty-two volunteers. By April 19, Lawless' company swelled to 102 men and became the first volunteer company in Albany to be raised and ready for duty. They were accepted by the state on April 22. The company paid tribute to their esteemed governor when they named themselves, the "Morgan Guards."[44]

Forty-two-year-old Harvey L. Rogers joined Lawless' company of Albany natives, yet he could consider himself a man of many hometowns. Throughout adulthood, Rogers chased many different business ventures and seemed to relocate every two to three years throughout New York in Albany, Buffalo, Troy, and New York City many times over. He followed the flock of prospective gold miners to the Sierra Nevada during the rush, but after eighteen months he moved on to his next location. He lived for several years in Chicago, New Orleans,

Charleston, and when war broke out Rogers was a resident of Whiskey Island, Mississippi. The citizens there were well aware of Rogers' strong Union sympathies, so when Fort Sumter was fired upon they gave him five hours to leave town. Rogers heeded their warning and hopped on the first boat northward and returned to Albany. He immediately joined Lawless' company on April 19, and his elder age secured himself a role as a sergeant, but what they did not know was that he shaved two years off since he was beyond the age limit cutoff.[45]

Local Albany resident John Hastings made a name for himself in the community through his work with the *Knickerbocker* newspaper, which was started by his brother. Hastings was born in Northern Ireland and arrived to America with his family when he was six years old. He was quick to form a list of willing volunteers after the outbreak of war and on April 22 Hastings opened his own recruiting hub at the Malta Saloon where Lawless' men were likewise housed. Forty men from the area immediately rallied behind Hastings' name, and still more volunteers stepped forward. Just two days after he started his drive, Hastings' company was accepted.[46]

William G. Weed, a thirty-eight-year-old Albany lawyer, called for a meeting of men willing to enlist in a company that he planned to organize. Weed was greeted with a large crowd of interested applicants and under his guide the company was nicknamed the "Albany City Volunteers." The company quickly voted Weed as their undisputed captain on April 22.[47]

By April 25, Albany had inspected, enrolled, and quartered thirty-two more companies to the existing 104 companies at large throughout the city. Like all infant companies that gathered in Albany, they would all bear witness to significant changes before ever being placed into a regiment. New recruits trickled in while others lost interest or were dismissed. Just a few days after his volunteers penned their names together to become a company, Lawless cut himself out on April 30 and left it leaderless. The captaincy was put to a vote two days later when the company settled on thirty-eight-year-old Albany harness and trunk maker, Michael H. Donovan. For military experience, Donovan had held every office in the city's local militia—the Albany Burgesses Corps—and he helped instruct tactics to many more local independent military organizations. When the war broke out, Donovan halted his trunk business and converted his downtown store into his very own recruiting center. His recruiting endeavors was also assisted by the untiring help from his friend, John M. Dempsey, a clerk and clothing store employee who embraced the ambition to defend the country and spread the interest in others. Dempsey's widowed mother and sisters were apprehensive to see him and his brothers so enthusiastic to join. Dempsey was a quiet natured man and he tried to coax a tearful sister when he said, "I shall not fall before God's appointed time." She pled with him and said that "there are those that can be better spared than you, those who are of little use at home." With a tear in his eye, Dempsey calmly replied, "Our army must not be made up of worthless men!"[48]

Several mini-companies fused themselves to reach their proper numbers in order to expedite themselves to be placed into service. This often led to arguments and disappointments when men who felt entitled to certain ranks did not receive the privilege, and there seemed a never-ending supply of those who felt entitled to commissions. As with Lawless' abrupt exit, just a few days before Weed's company was to be accepted by the state, Weed removed himself. He stated that he simply could not serve in the company and abruptly declined, and his second-in-command, Michael A. Nolan, elected as the company's first lieutenant, also declined to serve. After a quick election, forty-year-old Thomas J. Radcliff was voted to take charge of the company.[49]

Elected to fill Nolan's vacancy in Radcliff's company was a twenty-two-year-old volunteer named George Chapman. Chapman was raised by his extended family of uncles, aunts, and grandmother, after his mother died six months after he was born and his father killed in a mine collapse in California during the Gold Rush. As a resident of Amsterdam—nearly thirty-five miles northwest of Albany—Chapman had served in the New York State Militia for nearly three years prior to the war. When Chapman joined Radcliff's company his experience led to his election to become his second-in-command as a first lieutenant. Chapman was not alone with his decision and initially joined the company with two lifelong friends, David Hewitt and James "Jim" Chalmers, also both from Amsterdam. The three were the first men to leave from their hometown when they left for Albany on April 14, and joined what was then Weed's company five days later. Like many of the early volunteers, the trio were diehard Republicans.

Photographed in his uniform of the New York State Militia, George Chapman spent three years in the state's prewar military, which helped him earn a commission in what became Company I, and served as their first lieutenant (courtesy Jill Palmer).

For Lincoln's election five months before the war, Chalmers had organized a "Railsplitters" club of fifty young Republicans who voted for their first ballot. Forty-eight out of the fifty members served in the war.[50]

Also to join this new company as an officer was forty-two-year-old Charles Wesley Heald. He entered this new profession without any prior military experience, but he had a knack to reinvent himself in differing occupations. Born in Granville, New York, Heald lost his father at a young age which created a life of poverty for his widowed mother and several younger siblings. Despite hardships, Heald had an insatiable thirst for knowledge which kept him focused and after he exhausted the skimpy teachings given at the common school in Granville, he studied medicine twenty miles away at the Castleton Medical College in Vermont. Heald had to frequently leave his studies in order to work and make money to pay for his schooling, but he eventually graduated in 1848, at the age of thirty. He practiced medicine in West Haven, Vermont, before he moved to Albany for more lucrative opportunities, but he found little availability and soon lost interest in the profession. This decision was said by those who knew him to be, "his greatest enemy to success in life." Heald changed careers and became a preacher, but that was not his calling either. His attention then turned to study law where he graduated from the Albany Law School in 1857. When the war broke out, Heald again saw his venture path altered and he was among the first enthusiastic volunteers to offer himself for the cause.[51]

Canandaigua

Nearly 200 miles to the west of Albany, the village of Canandaigua worked tirelessly to fill up their rolls for able-bodied volunteers. Positioned at the foot of Canandaigua Lake, one of the collective Finger Lakes, the village and surrounding area boasted itself as a rich agricultural producer of fruits. The land was a never-ending series of ridgelines, valleys, and lakes, dotted with rolling vineyards and orchards. Men from Bristol, Bloomfield, Phelps, Clifton Springs, Victor, Manchester, and other towns rallied to Canandaigua, the largest and county seat of Ontario County, in order to form companies. In response to Lincoln's request, a twenty-seven-year-old lawyer from Canandaigua by the name of Henry Faurot spearheaded an effort to gather volunteers at the amphitheater at the town fairgrounds. A steady flow of volunteers added their names to Faurot's roster and Ontario County soon had their first company of volunteers.[52]

Faurot utilized his clerical skills and influence to prepare himself and readied his volunteers for their expected duty. He was also supported by his second-in commander, twenty-three-year-old James H. Morgan of Albany. Like Faurot, Morgan practiced law with the District Attorney in Albany until he accepted a position with more promise that brought him to Canandaigua before the war. On April 25, Faurot's company was enrolled at the headquarters in Albany the same day that ten other representatives from other companies filed for recognition. On May 7, the company was accepted by the state. Two days later, hugs and handshakes were exchanged between the citizen soldiers and their families as they bid farewell to Canandaigua and whisked away to Albany, where Faurot began in earnest to align his company into a regiment.[53]

The Adams House

With the hundreds of companies that constantly poured into Albany, their newly elected officers found out early the privileges and pains of their rank as they instructed the initial tasks to mold their men into soldiers. Concurrently, the political side of companies was about to take over as the hunt to form regiments began. With the search came the speculations and rumors within every company as to what regiment they would fall into and more importantly under whom they would be following into battle.

Like Elmira and New York City, Albany underwent a continuous influx of organized companies that flooded into the city. It took a great deal of organization and patience to control them at the rate they streamed in. The untrained volunteers had to look upon their elected leadership for more than just basic military training, but essentially everything. Food, lodging, and care for the sick were issues that company officers grappled with. If the respect was not present yet, it was about to be earned.

Any available building with space in the city filled quickly as companies from across the state rolled in. The flow never stopped which made the city's quartering of thousands of troops a logistical nightmare. Every boat and train that stopped into Albany at any given hour seemed full of volunteer companies, and city officials cooperated with military authorities as best they could with the influx. A lot of the clustering companies in Albany were temporarily housed in an aged and abandoned hotel known as the Adams House. It was located in the heart of the city on Broadway and stood adjacent to the Delavan House. This former hotel lacked luxury in every sense of the way and was missing several doors and windows. Most men slept on the floor with no bedding or furniture of any kind. Mattresses and blankets were at a minimum and could not satisfy the quantity of men that inhabited the old structure.[54]

Adding to the disparity at the Adams House, a drunken brawl that started over food complaints broke out there on April 29. Waiters were assaulted, chairs, tables, and dishes were tossed, and several windows not yet broken were smashed. Men fired pistols indiscriminately and some drew knives on each other, but injuries were surprisingly kept to a minimum, and the rowdy bunch was broken up by Governor Morgan who came loaded with police.[55]

Captain Wiltse's company from Fishkill had been housed at the overcrowded Adams House since the end of April. They were given a large room on an upper floor that luckily still had beds and blankets to sleep on, unlike most of their counterparts who arrived after them. Some of the earliest sessions of drill Wiltse's company conducted was done in the same room where they slept.[56]

Captain Truax's company of Schenectady men arrived into Albany around 4 p.m. on May 3. Shortly after their arrival, his company was treated to a "nigger show" at night. The antiquated term used by the men was a minstrel show where white stage performers blackened their faces and imitated African song and dance, popular during mid–nineteenth century America. The performance stretched late into the night and ended at 2 a.m.[57]

Those who stayed awake for the late night show had an early morning rouse on May 4 at five o'clock. Around 9 a.m., breakfast was served at the Adams House which consisted of bread, tough meat, potatoes, and a pint of coffee. Truax found shelter elsewhere at the newly constructed barracks being built on the edge of the city and eventually relocated his company there on May 7.[58]

The Wallkill Guards arrived to Albany the same time as Truax's company on May 3. The oversized company of Middletown volunteers similarly entered the Adams House and took up residency wherever it could be squeezed. The unsavory conditions at the billets disenchanted every newcomer upon arrival. John Smith King, a Middletown native and former printer for his hometown paper *The Whig Press*, wrote home to his former employer's paper that their "quarters are very poor, and a great deal of dissatisfaction prevails." To the families back in Middletown who followed the company's exploits through King's voice, they were displeased to read that their men were "leading a sort of wild life, so far as civilization is concerned. Indeed, I think we are almost semi-barbarous now." King was literal and unapologetic when he described the discomforts of the Adams House in a letter home:

> Our sleeping arrangements are—I don't know what. You can judge better what they are after I give you a description of them. Each man has a blanket, (that is if he is smart enough to get one early and hold on to it), and a straw tick. The ticks are large enough for one man to lie upon comfortably. At bed time, every man grabs one of the ticks, throws it upon the floor, jumps upon it, wraps the blanket around him, and is ready for sleep. The room where we sleep is just large enough for all the men to lie upon the floor. The ventilation is very poor, and the air is very stifling.[59]

Not only was the organization of regiments a priority for the State Military Department, but feeding the masses of soldiers was of top concern. King could at least comprehend that Albany was being overrun by volunteers like himself at an unforeseen rate and the city tried its best to orchestrate a system to ease their stay. He graciously complimented the city when others were so quick to scrutinize, and said that "the meals are pretty fair, considering the number that have to be served." But the food, if it came at all, continued to be stripped of anything special. Ever since the drunken brawl that started over food complaints, officers were encouraged to keep a watchful eye on the waiters in order to assure wholesome food was furnished. These temporary quarters became a window to the harsh realities of things to come with life as a soldier.[60]

Captain Bartlett's Company Number 2 from Ogdensburg entered the crowded Adams House on May 4, and found the abandoned hotel similarly underwhelming. Three days after leaving Ogdensburg, the company ate their second meal at 10 a.m. at their new residence. Luckily, Albany citizens were trying to ease the troubles of the ill-equipped troops by donating tin cups, plates, knives, and forks to the men at the Adams House. A generous meal was provided by the locals to the soldiers that consisted of a slice of boiled pork for each man and a fistful of bread. Coffee was served in large buckets usually reserved for horses to drink water from. After their meal, the company ventured throughout Albany in search of worn or unwanted blankets, quilts, sheets, or anything that could be used for bedding.[61]

The company began to see the semblance of order and normalcy in their situation. The most pivotal was the allowance of two meals a day for the men. The first meal consisted of pork and bread. The other was potatoes and bread. The potatoes were in ample supply and were cleaned, cooked, and carried over from the Delavan House across the street. There was outrage towards the proprietor of the Delavan House who charged his meals at the pricey rate of $3.50 per week by which some volunteers exclaimed was more fitting to be fed to pigs. Not only was it expensive, but its quality diminished quickly. Servings of sour hash were routinely served, and butter was denied until officers began to stand up to the proprietor. A company of thirty men once stood shoulder to shoulder and threatened to march for home unless the proprietor, or as one angered volunteer referred him as a "soul-less corpus," changed his cheating ways. During one of the deliveries of bushel baskets full of potatoes, one soldier from Company Number 2 spotted something join the food that proved not to be a potato. A large rat had been cooked into the cooking kettle prepared for the men. As bad as the miserable situation was for some, none were desperate enough yet to eat the rat. Instead, some men took the carcass and showed it to Captain Bartlett and even Governor Morgan to encourage action towards the food, but change for the better was gradual. Those who could afford spending money to board themselves elsewhere did so. Decades after the Civil War, Private Samuel Hodgkins of Bartlett's company reminisced about his time at the Adams House and summarized that he had "never suffered so much for something to eat or for a place to sleep, as I did the first seventeen days after I left home." Luckily, Bartlett befriended some workers at a local train depot that helped provide meals and lodging for some of his men.[62]

Problems for Bartlett's Company

With the food and housing problems aside, Bartlett was actively engaged to get his company aligned with a regiment. Many of the companies that were organized throughout St. Lawrence County had their officers in talks to create a regiment comprised solely of Northern New York men. On the evening of May 7, Bartlett and his two subordinates—First Lieutenant Seely and Second Lieutenant Goodno—met with the representatives of nine other companies from the northern regions of the state to voice their shared vision to form a regiment made wholly of Northern New York men. Their first meeting was brief, but they scheduled a follow-on meeting for the next day that would decide who would take command of this proposed regiment.[63]

Accordingly, thirty officers from ten Northern New York companies met behind closed doors on May 8 and expressed their ideas. Everyone seemed to abide by an unofficial agreement that the man who would become their colonel should obviously be a resident of Northern New York. Several names were optioned, one of which was one of the most influential men from upstate and a justice of the state's Supreme Court, Amaziah B. James. Another popular name brought up was West Point graduate Thomas A. Davies, a native of St. Lawrence County. New York's Attorney General, Charles G. Myers, was an Ogdensburg native with many prominent connections, but it was his son George R. Myers the men were interested in to fill the position of major.[64]

Those in attendance of the secret meeting eventually passed a few resolutions that narrowed the pool of candidates. First and foremost, everyone present made a pledge to keep all proceedings from this special meeting a secret to outsiders until the regiment was mustered into the government's service. The second resolution required any candidate offered must have had either a military education or seen active service of some kind. This provision ruled out the Republican-minded Judge James and left Davies, a known Democrat, as the foremost candidate which did not go over well with the trio of officers from Ogdensburg's Company Number 2. Just short of unanimous, Davies received twenty-seven votes because Bartlett, Seely, and Goodno dared not to vote for a Democrat. The three still opted for the ineligible judge, who they felt was unfairly excluded.[65]

The next morning, one of the officers who made their vote for Davies was approached by a congressman who accused the officer of bringing politics into their secret election for officers of their regiment. This was denied by the defensive officer but was more appalled at the reality that someone in their secret meeting had shared with an outsider. The politician was not present for the unmentionable meeting but seemed fully aware of what transpired the night before. This meant that someone had leaked the information which went against the first resolution that was unanimously agreed upon. The officers of the secret meeting quickly reconvened later that night in order to find the culprits that had violated their pledge. When asked whether anyone had broken the agreement, each officer individually denied the accusation. That all changed when the question was posed to the three officers from Company Number 2. Goodno broke first and responded to their question that, "It's none of your damned business, I do not intend to become the tail of a Democratic kite." Bartlett and Seely stood by Goodno, and the three knew immediately what effect their defiance would have.[66]

A resolution was quickly drawn up after the leak was identified and twenty-seven votes later, Bartlett's company was ejected from the Northern New York regiment. The vacancy was quickly filled the following day by another company from Clinton County, and the regiment was accepted by the state and designated as the 16th New York, under the command of Colonel Thomas A. Davies. One of Bartlett's volunteers searched for the positives and rationalized that, "after all I think it may be for our own good."[67]

After the officers were ostracized from their Northern New York neighbors, troubles mounted for Company Number 2 as men speculated if their leadership would ever lead them to be aligned in a regiment. Their current living conditions in the deplorable Adams House failed to improve. Other companies continued to filter in and overcrowded the dwelling. With hygiene hampered by crowdedness, some men began to see their first fight against disease. The men wanted to be moved to the developing Industrial School Barracks on Albany's edge where several other companies were transplanted and more adequately lodged. Rumors spread amongst Bartlett's men that if they were to relocate before they had been placed in a regiment, then the men would be split up and assigned to fill ranks in other companies. Their patience ran thin.[68]

About a dozen volunteers abandoned the company and headed for home. It got so bad that a sharp-tongued letter surfaced in a Democrat newspaper in Albany that compounded the actions of a few quitters upon the whole company and called them "girl-ant volunteers." This banter undermined the survival of the company, and Bartlett vigorously defended the majority of his men that were faithful volunteers and singled out those few who gave up. He needed to end the rumors that the company would be broken and dispensed to other companies, and the best way to ensure his words held true was that he needed more men to fill the vacant holes in his ranks. Luckily, First Lieutenant Seely had just returned to Albany from a recruitment drive back home in Ogdensburg where he not only was presented with a gift of a sword and epaulets from the proud townsfolk, but he was able to round up twenty-two men who volunteered for their company. A faithful soldier from Company Number 2 took it upon himself to exonerate the company's public image and published a list of names in the newspaper of those who quit. On the morning of May 11, Seely and his latest batch of volunteers proceeded to Albany where all but one passed the medical inspections. This helped bring the total number of men to eighty, which was two more than was required for a full company, making them eligible to be placed into a company whenever called upon. One of these galvanized Northern New Yorkers wrote, "I do not think there is one of us that is not anxious to see active service, and to strike a blow in the defense of our glorious stars and stripes."[69]

Men who missed the initial departure of a hometown company had to decide whether to stick around for another one to form or travel at their own expense to Albany and join a particular company that was still open for volunteers. Names on the rosters of companies increased daily. Before the lure of bounties and bonuses, these early volunteers were stirred by the calling of their nation. Some were drawn to the adventure of it all, while others buckled from pressures of being labeled a coward. For a worried government, luckily, having too many volunteers was better than too little, but the reality of war would soon dry this flood.[70]

Divide of the Wallkill Guards

The Wallkill Guards still had to face their dilemma of having too many volunteers. Days after they left Middletown, over a dozen more men from Middletown and Albany penned their names to the Guards and made their membership balloon to 170 men, which more than doubled the size requirement for one company. The discussion to split the Guards into two separate companies became an obvious idea, but going from talk to action came with resistance. The men rallied to preserve the company as one entity and keep the order of rank that was already in place. When the first call was made for men to voluntarily separate themselves into a different company, not a single man elected to leave. Captain Meginnis pressed the issue but without changing minds, he made the decision for them. On May 7, Meginnis had the recent volunteers pulled out of the Guards and placed into a skeleton company, and the men who left did not make their exit easy. Meginnis kept the same officers for his company and retained the nickname, but he still needed to drop more men. He decided to ask again for volunteers to leave and join the newer company, and his second effort paid off when thirty-three men willingly transferred.[71]

Nearly sixty men broke off from the Wallkill Guards, which were the most recent volunteers from Albany, but thirty-three men were from Middletown. The company did not limit themselves to accept only Middletown volunteers but continued to build their membership up with dozens of others from Albany who were in search of a company to join. One of these eager volunteers that drifted into the city one day was twenty-two-year-old Washington Irving Sawyer. He left his studies at the Hampton Institute in Fairfax, Vermont as soon as he heard that war had been declared. He returned to his hometown of Westport in upstate New York with every intention to enlist, but the crop of volunteers from his town rallied at a speed too slow for him. Despite urges that a company would be formed there, Sawyer left home and traveled nearly 125 miles to reach the capital city and joined this new company of Albany and Middletown volunteers on May 7. Sawyer's quick enlistment made him not only the first volunteer from Westport, but the first from Essex County.[72]

This hybrid company of Middletown and Albany men quickly reached a sufficient size, but they lacked leadership. They quickly secured the addition of Peter Hogan, a highly respected Albany native who had already collected his own swarm of local volunteers. When he and his men joined the company, they quickly made him their captain. Born in Bethlehem, New York in 1826, Hogan was an established civil engineer with deep family roots in Albany. His ancestors were not only among the first early settlers of Albany County, but they displayed a lineage of officers that served in the state's militia long before Hogan's birth. At age nineteen, he worked on the Reading Railroad in the engineering department, and remained employed there until America raged war with Mexico. At age twenty-one, Hogan followed in his family's patriotic footsteps and served as a lieutenant in the Reading Artillery and fought in several battles in the Mexican War, and was once wounded during the storming of Mexico City. After the war, Hogan returned home where he studied engineering at the Albany Academy, and earned recognition as a valued civil engineer until the outbreak of war in 1861 changed his course. Hogan did not hesitate to don the uniform again and seized the opportunity to command the group of Albany and Middletown men, and this company was quickly accepted by the state on May 7.[73]

Peter Hogan, a respected civil engineer and veteran of the Mexican War, headed the company of Middletown and Albany volunteers that became Company H (courtesy Barb Samans).

Hogan's company also had the recruitment help of twenty-one-year-old Theodore Caldwell

Theodore Caldwell Rogers walked away from a successful civil engineering partnership in Albany to join what became Company H as their first lieutenant (courtesy Jeff Sauter).

Rogers who had assembled several volunteers of his own from the city. Rogers came from a well heeled New York family as the eldest child of a Presbyterian minister. Through the different callings of the church that his father answered, Rogers lived at times in Connecticut, Massachusetts, Georgia, Pennsylvania, and lastly New York. He attended high school in Philadelphia and later graduated with a civil engineering degree from the Rensselaer Polytechnic Institute in Troy, New York. He was athletic, well cultivated, and a good speaker. After college he started a successful trade in civil engineering which most likely made him an acquaintance of Hogan. Just before war was declared, Rogers had secured a partnership from the most prominent commercial house in Albany, but the war changed his path and he faced a tough decision that only he could make for himself. Rogers did not jump at "the mere love of adventure, or the passion for military glory," as his friends would recall, but looked to prayer and felt God wanted him to do his duty as a Christian and patriot. Rogers walked away from his partnership and set aside his prospects of fortune in order to rally together volunteers for the war effort, and he became Hogan's right-hand man.[74]

The Waiting Game

The blend of New Yorkers from all over the state that invaded Albany provoked several unexpected reunions between old friends. Men would frequently roam the floors in the Adams House in search of former acquaintances in other companies to strike up conversations. Inactivity came in abundance for the men as they searched for ways to pass the hours. They debated current affairs and scrutinized the latest newspaper articles. Some men perched themselves out of a window of the Adams House and watched the hubbub of the street below. Friendships were being forged and camaraderie was in its infancy whether they knew it or not. If their officers were not orchestrating the minimal amounts of introductory drill, the men occupied their time reading or writing—if they were capable. Most men simply ventured throughout the streets of Albany and divided their time in saloons or churches. Some utilized their time to mend their worn out clothes if needed while others played cards. Gambling coincided with the army life throughout the entire war and was hard to avoid. Viewed as a moral taboo amongst most soldiers and their families, there were but a few men of the regiment who could say they never partook in card playing during their service. John M. Dempsey was one that refused to let the habit start. He was presented with a pack of playing cards during his stay at Albany but decided to send them home with a note that stated, "I shall have no use for these in the army"—and he never did.[75]

Soon, the long wait would be resolved as the building blocks of organization fused together a new regiment. Just before the 16th New York was formed, a separate complement of companies in the city were about to form as a regiment, but their efforts was abruptly halted when they unexpectedly lost Ogdensburg's Company Number 1 who broke to join their upstate brethren. Luckily for Ogdensburg's Company Number 2, who still looked for a home after being expelled from the 16th, answered an invitation and filled the vacancy of this new regiment.[76]

On May 10, the companies at the Adams House marched up to the Industrial School Barracks on the outskirts of the city and were met by another set of companies that fit the appropriate number for a regiment. The captains of these ten companies sat down and adopted a resolution that they would form into a regiment, and designated themselves with the next available number—18. The officers submitted their request to the Attorney General to hold an election for their field officers, and all seemed to be on track until their request to have their companies accepted by the state came back with one condition. The Attorney General mandated that Captain Bartlett's last-to-join company had to stand a full inspection, and submit paperwork of their passing with the regiment's official petition. Apparently the Ogdensburg men had made some waves in the military circles of the city, but their inspection went smoothly. This official meeting of the captains became the first formation of the ten companies that would soon fall under a unified banner and stand as a volunteer regiment from New York.[77]

2

Birth of a Regiment
May 12, 1861–June 18, 1861

"If rebels desire to lay their unhallowed hands on this flag,
they must prostrate our forms helpless for its defence."
—*Private John C. O. Redington, Company K, May 16, 1861*

Companies Form the Regiment

More than 1,000 volunteers quartered around Albany flocked to Tweedle Hall in the city for a special church service for troops on May 12. The Sabbath service centered around the topic of war and was very solemn at times, but impactful. Society was deeply rooted with Christian values and letters home from soldiers continuously expressed the necessity and importance of the Bible. An Ogdensburg volunteer in attendance said that the service "was listened to with much attention, all seeming gratified at the opportunity thus afforded them to attend such a service."[1]

A steady rain soaked the city on May 13 while the companies awaited their official orders to organize as an official regiment. The State Board granted their wishes and called for the state's next regiment, designated as the 18th Infantry Regiment of New York Volunteers, which had at that time 798 volunteers spread amongst ten companies. The newly commissioned company officers accepted the conditions and organized themselves in the following order:

Company A—Captain William S. Gridley—from Schenectady.
Company B—Captain John Hastings—from Albany.
Company C—Captain Henry Wiltse, Jr.—from Fishkill.
Company D—Captain John C. Meginnis—from Middletown.
Company E—Captain Stephen Truax—from Schenectady.
Company F—Captain Michael H. Donovan—from Albany.
Company G—Captain Henry Faurot—from Canandaigua.
Company H—Captain Peter Hogan—from Albany/Middletown.
Company I—Captain Thomas J. Radcliff—from Albany.
Company K—Captain David L. Bartlett—from Ogdensburg.[2]

Each company was authorized three officers: one captain at the helm, followed by one first lieutenant, and one second lieutenant. All of the company officers convened and discussed nominations for commissioned staff officers of their newly formed regiment. The most vital position needed was someone to lead their regiment, a gentleman with notoriety, education, and power was most desired. Military experience was ideal but not a deal breaker if one was a politician or had the sway of powerful friends. By May 13, ballots were made and tallied and their requests were sent to the men they voted for.[3]

William A. Jackson

The person the committee of officers called upon to serve as their colonel was the twenty-nine-year-old New York State Inspector General, William A. Jackson. Despite not having military service in the federal realm, Jackson gained military instruction from local militias and with his work as Inspector General. As a practitioner of the law and one of the most indomitable debaters regarding political matters, his skill sets were bar none.[4]

William Ayrault Jackson was born in Schenectady on March 29, 1832. He was the first of five children to Elizabeth (Pomeroy) and Isaac W. Jackson, and the family lived on the campus of Union College in the faculty apartment. His father was an alumnus of the institution and stayed on as a professor of Mathematics and Natural Philosophy, but was better known on campus as the ardent caretaker of an exquisite garden affectionately nicknamed "Captain Jack's Garden," of which his children would often be pressed to help water and weed.[5]

Given his father's tenure as a professor, Jackson benefited greatly with life on the campus and received personal instruction from him at home that prepared him for college courses. By age fifteen, Jackson started his freshman classes at Union College and established himself as a meticulous student with a high sense of discipline. He was an avid reader and made quoting Shakespeare a habit. He kept a diary of his school days in which he called his "common place book" that depicted a typical inquisitive adolescent who often seemed a bit dark and brooding, but often his insight shed light of a young man beyond his years. As an upperclassman, he worked at the campus library and kept it open beyond normal hours in hopes that other students would take the advantage to check out books. Few ever came, but Jackson took the opportunity to read dozens of titles in true tranquility. Jackson once wrote a note to himself that specified "a young man should read a good deal & write only when his mind is choking full." During his junior year, Jackson began to shy away from novels and concentrated more on the writings about government politics and speeches and found himself curiously addicted.[6]

Twenty-nine-year-old Col. William Ayrault Jackson left his office as Inspector General of New York to accept the commission as the first commander of the 18th New York (author's collection).

Jackson became a very skilled extemporaneous speaker. As a debater, Jackson knew no rival amongst his peers. He was the toughest amongst his classmates and never seemed to lose the upper hand in a debate, a skill that any budding lawyer would truly benefit from.[7]

In the summer of 1851, nineteen-year-old Jackson graduated with high honors from Union College. He dabbled in the engineering field with a brief job he held with an uncle as a surveyor for the Albany and Susquehanna Railroad for a few months. In December of 1852, Jackson made his most pivotal career move and moved to Albany and took lecture courses at the Albany Law School. His decision proved worthwhile and he eventually passed the Bar in April of 1853.[8]

Soon after his legal career began, Jackson formed a law firm in Albany with his second cousin, Frederick Townsend. The team worked together for a few years before they incorporated a former United States District Judge, Alfred Conkling, into their firm in 1857. Conkling, Townsend, & Jackson was short-lived after Conkling was terminated a year later, but the duo picked up Richard M. Strong, another prominent attorney. That same year Townsend was appointed to the governor's staff and served as the state's adjutant general. Jackson had surrounded himself with Albany's best and brightest and through these relationships his own power and prestige emerged.[9]

Jackson was a robust, healthy, and handsome man. He had thick chestnut colored hair that a friend described, "curled in dark masses about his low but broad forehead," and his dark brown eyes were said to look as if they were "full of fire." Jackson never married or was known to have had a courtship of any seriousness. He rather preferred a life focused in constant study of books, poetry, and laws.[10]

In the years that ramped up to the Civil War, Jackson let his deep interest in politics move him in new directions. He aligned himself with the newly formed Republican Party, and distinguished himself through his writings and "stump" speeches that he performed during the 1856, 1858, and 1860 elections throughout Albany County and the greater state. Jackson had "a bold and energetic character, and a quick, penetrating intellect, being an agreeable speaker and a vigorous writer," which helped gather many friends and admirers. Jackson's political addresses drew large assemblies anxious just to hear him speak and his energy always "elicited enthusiastic applause."[11]

John Meredith Read, great-grandson of George Read who signed the Declaration of Independence, spoke with Jackson during a speaking tour in 1860 and mentioned Jackson's oratory, "was easy and flowing and his voice well modulated … his conversation was agreeable and interspersed with anecdotes." Read himself was an admirer of Jackson and spent a lot of time with him during their lecture tour. Read once made a comment to Jackson about his envious robustness and strength, but Jackson laughed back and said, "Ah, my dear friend, you do not appear to enjoy very strong health, but do not envy me. I have a feverish tendency in my blood, and I shall die young from some inflammatory disease." Read never forgot those prophetic words as they would hauntingly resurface nearly a year later.[12]

Jackson also pursued an interest in military affairs and served as an officer in Albany's heralded militia—the Albany Burgesses Corps. Jackson and his law partners also served as founding members of the Albany Zouave Cadets, formed in the summer of 1860. This organization started as a highly proficient drill team inspired by the national craze set forth by Colonel Elmer E. Ellsworth and his Zouave drill team from Chicago. Their mix of acrobatics and military drill toured the country and when Albany was host of Ellsworth's show in July of

1860, some of the city's best young men became entranced by the military spirit of the escalating times and wanted to rival the stars. Answering their call, Adjutant General Townsend organized the Albany Zouave Cadets and acted as their leader. Many of the earliest to join were prominent attorneys in Albany who forged close friendships, but took military drill very serious. Far from a social club, the company drilled almost every evening and put focus towards their physicality. They performed all drills clad in full fatigue uniforms and upheld stringent rules and penalties for infractions. They were not permitted to smoke or drink, and any offense to these or obvious disobedience meant expulsion. Townsend eventually organized the company into the National Guard in December of 1860. Jackson's training as a cadet provided him with the building blocks of military instruction and how to ultimately become a leader. The Albany Zouave Cadets would soon see that their efforts before the war had essentially fashioned themselves as a grooming ground for some of New York's finest officers just months before the war broke out. With a company that stood close to a hundred before the war, nearly seventy-five cadets served as commissioned officers throughout the conflict.[13]

The partnership of Townsend, Jackson & Strong ended just a few months before the Fort Sumter bombardment as the men focused their attention to higher appointments within the State offices. Jackson followed his cousin's path and joined the governor's staff on January 1, 1861, and was appointed as the Inspector General of New York.[14]

Someone as fresh, energetic, and bold as Jackson proved himself a worthy candidate destined for military greatness when the war broke out. The arduous task to organize the influx of volunteers and companies that streamed into Albany by the thousands was a hefty job for Morgan and his staff. Jackson worked feverishly within his realm as Inspector General and was praised by the governor for his valuable knowledge and understanding of military organization.[15]

The first and most important approach for the Governor's Cabinet was to equip these civilian companies into armed and uniformed soldiers. The Albany depots like the Adams House became filled with unarmed volunteer organizations, with some men who took it upon themselves to shoulder their own muskets from home. Some militia units showed up in a vast array of uniforms, but most companies remained in their civilian attire, some of which looked quite ratty. The pursuit to procure and issue thousands of uniforms became the responsibility of Governor Morgan, who put the responsibility on the shoulders of Inspector General Jackson. After Lincoln's decree for troops, Jackson was among the first to be consulted by the governor on the best course of action to organize and equip the state's volunteers.[16]

Morgan formed the Board of Uniforms Committee which included Jackson and others to spearhead the acquisition of uniforms. In a meeting held at the Executive Chamber on April 22, Jackson reported a very detailed outline of the intended style, cut, and dye of uniforms that New York wanted to issue to its volunteers that would best represent the Excelsior State. Jackson stressed his concern that the United States Government would be unable to furnish their soldiers with accoutrements such as knapsacks, haversacks, and canteens, so he suggested that those too should be purchased by the state.[17]

Later that day, New York's Attorney General Charles G. Myers prepared a report for the Associated Press that asked for proposals to any interested manufacturer that was capable to mass-produce their order in an astonishing three weeks' time. Twelve thousand uniforms were requested and the applicant was asked to make their interest known at the Albany Capitol within twenty-four hours. A few companies responded, but all were quickly edged out by

Brooks & Company from New York City. They showed proof that they had already acquired an abundance of the requested broadcloth—a heavy wool fabric that was expensive to make and hard to find during the early weeks of the war. They created a monopoly and sapped all that was in the market and constricted the ability for others to gather enough broadcloth.[18]

On April 25, Jackson visited the Brooks Brothers in New York City to confirm their inventory and work towards a deal. The brothers were realistic with Jackson and informed him that it was impossible to obtain enough army broadcloth in the short amount of time asked, but they explained that they had the best chance to get close. Jackson was satisfied with the deal and presented them with a contract that same day.[19]

Soon after the deal was made, Brooks Brothers leveled with Jackson and explained that in reality it would take more than a month to acquire and manufacture enough army broadcloth to facilitate the requested amount. Brooks Brothers mentioned that they could use an alternative cloth that was "of equal value" to the wool used by the army, but it was of a different color and would be more expensive to produce. Jackson inspected the alternate wool and saw no problem with it, yet he still showed reservation and deliberated for more than an hour to make the command decision. Jackson's hesitation changed when a messenger who worked for the Brooks Brothers cleverly interrupted the meeting and stated that agents from Pennsylvania and Ohio were interested to buy their supply. There was still the overall fear that Washington was under threats of being captured and uniformed troops were needed. Jackson had to act fast so he sent an urgent telegram to Governor Morgan and asked for help. The governor replied immediately and sent a representative from the Board to oversee the situation. A final inspection of the new wool was made later that night, and by midnight the contract was granted to the Brooks Brothers. Jackson was still firm with the original agreement and affirmed that nothing would be altered to drive the price up. With the contract settled, Brook Brothers went to work to mass-produce 2,000 complete jackets, trousers, and overcoats per week with the price tag of $19.50 for each set. With Jackson's quick decision, the state became capable to equip their own troops at an eye-popping pace, but his hurried efforts and hasty timetable created shortfalls. The first shipment of garments was totally wrecked owed to the inferior wool used, along with other careless oversights by the manufacturer that were still sent out. Furthermore, state inspectors failed to keep pace and closely examine the gross inventory that was produced. Uniforms pushed out to troops were uninspected, many of which lacked buttons, had sealed button holes and open seams, and rotten wool with different shades. These oversights were so rampant that they popularized the word, "shoddy" to define their quality. This incident erupted into a blame game scandal that clung to Jackson's reputation. State officers battled with accusations against the company that only seemed to point fingers at all parties involved. Jackson felt he had acted in the best interest of the country given the enormous pressure placed on him, since uniforms seemed to be the hang-up of getting troops down to Washington. Brooks Brothers just could not keep up with the demanding pace, and the inspectors did not properly execute their duties. In the end, there was no winner, as Brooks Brothers had their money, but they were forced to provide an additional 2,350 suits at no charge.[20]

When the companies of the newly formed 18th New York asked Inspector General Jackson that they wanted him to become their colonel on May 13, he did not stall with an answer. Jackson penned a resignation letter to the governor immediately, and his vacancy as Inspector General was filled within days. Morgan seemed unsurprised that Jackson was offered a colonelcy and knew that it was more of a calling for him to resign from his staff. With just three-and-a-half months in office, Jackson helped put the state on track to organize its forces at the start of the war. Governor Morgan deeply respected Jackson, a man who "zealously and honestly performed" his duties. "His whole official conduct, so far as I have any knowledge and opportunity for judging," Morgan said, "was becoming to him both as an officer and a man." The news traveled fast to the regiment and from what little the men understood of their new commander, one volunteer proudly described that Jackson was "every inch a soldier and such a one as any man should deem a privilege to follow to the cannon's mouth." Jackson was quick to convert his uniform jacket worn in his former position and moved some buttons around to adapt it to his new rank of colonel.[21]

William H. Young

One of Schenectady's most prominent businessmen was thirty-seven-year-old William Henry Young who stepped up to his nomination and agreed to serve as the lieutenant colonel of the regiment. Young was born on April 22, 1824, in England. When he was twelve years old his parents brought the family over the Atlantic and settled in Schenectady.[22]

To develop a career, Young became an apprentice at the preeminent Schenectady foundry of Peter I. Clute & Son. His skills and professionalism quickly impressed his employers and he became a foreman and remained with the firm for several years. Young married into the Schenectady dynasty family of Barhydts and made Anna Alida Barhydt his wife in 1843. They had six children before the war, but two sons died in their infancy. In 1857, Young took a promotion to become the superintendent of the moulding department at Rathbone & Company's wide-ranging stove foundry in Albany.[23]

During the antebellum years, Young organized and served for several years in the local militia as captain for the Schenectady City Artillery. He was also in command at one time of another independent company from the city known as the Governor's Guards. Young also served and attained the rank of major in the 26th New York State Militia. Young was highly proficient in military drill and was an excellent instructor. After a city parade in 1856, Young was honored for his service with the militia, and he addressed the spectators with a message that stressed the importance of military drill and the benefits it had for the community. He also made mention of a possible conflict in the near future, but his foreshadowing sensed it would come from a European power rather than from within his adopted country. Young's leadership and esteem was immeasurable, and he set the stage for himself to become an instrumental drillmaster for a future volunteer infantry regiment.[24]

Pictured in 1861, Lt. Col. William Henry Young boasted years of leadership experience as an officer in the New York State Militia and as supervisor of a large stove foundry in Albany (courtesy Clark Hotaling).

In 1861, Young made a decision that would forever strengthen his personal character. Under the ministry teachings of the Methodist Rev. Alfred Augustus Farr of Albany, Young filled a void in his life and was baptized into Christianity. Inside a small upper room within the Broadway Mission, Young went on bended knee and "embraced the Christian faith, and humbly sought forgiveness for the past and grace for the future." His newfound Christian faith was described by others as "beautiful and symmetrical" and Young's "constant habit of prayer was wonderful, especially for one converted so late in life."[25]

The Rev. A. A. Farr

Young was lucky enough to continue to develop his spiritual growth under the guidance of his friend, the Rev. A. A. Farr, who decided to accompany the 18th and served as their chaplain. Born in Middlebury, Vermont on August 29, 1810, Farr attended common schools within his district, and took special pride and attention to become a bit of an English scholar, which helped him immensely in his future endeavors. As a boy of sixteen, Farr united himself with the Methodist Episcopal Church and began professing conversion to sinners. He held religious meetings throughout the neighborhoods around his home, and built his career from there. He received a local preacher's license but waited until he was twenty-nine before he accepted any appointments to a congregation. He eventually accepted his first probationary session as a junior preacher in 1839 in Troy, and from there he circulated, almost yearly, to a new congregation. Eventually he got to Albany which was where he was by the inauguration of war. With his unwavering trust and endorsement from Lieutenant Colonel Young, the Reverend Farr found a new congregation and exchanged his robe for a black chaplain's uniform and brought the word of God to the 18th.[26]

The fifty-year-old Methodist minister Alfred Augustus Farr left his congregation in Albany to bring the word of God to the 18th New York as their regimental chaplain (courtesy Sarah Roach).

George R. Myers

The last field officer needed for the regiment was the rank of major. Charles G. Myers, a District Attorney in New York and current Attorney General on the governor's staff and colleague of William A. Jackson, was not proposed the position, but his son was. George Ranney Myers was born on May 12, 1838, in Ogdensburg, the first of four children born to Charles and Frances (Ranney) Myers.[27]

As the son of a district attorney, Myers could tell his father had powerful connections. It was his father's persistence in February 1855 that got sixteen-year-old Myers nominated by his congressman who lobbied his name through Washington for an appointment as a cadet to the United States Military Academy. By all means, Myers was the perfect candidate for the institution. He was healthy, well educated, handled arithmetic well, he could read and write, and for his youthful age Myers stood at five feet eight inches. A year passed when then–Secretary of War Jefferson Davis wrote to both father and son on March 1, 1856, to inform them that the president had conferred young Myers an appointment as a West Point cadet. With the finest education and a military obligation in his future, the next eight years of his life were set before him, but something changed just two months after Myers celebrated his appointment. After what was puzzlingly labeled Myers' "mishap" by the same congressman who lobbied for his appointment, Myers reluctantly penned a letter back to Davis on April 26, and declined his appointment as a cadet. Instead, Myers followed his father's footsteps and studied law and soon found work as a lawyer in his hometown of Ogdensburg.[28]

Maj. George Ranney Myers of Ogdensburg turned twenty-three years old just five days before he was elected to the position (Roger D. Hunt collection, United States Army Heritage and Education Center, Carlisle, Pennsylvania).

In 1859, Myers' father was elected to the office of Attorney General for New York, a position he held for many years. His father was also a member of the Military Board that in April 1861 was the essential backbone to the state's call for volunteers and worked closely with Jackson.[29]

Myers was not the most desirous candidate to appoint for the third highest rank of the regiment, but he had been nominated before and was almost chosen by the 16th New York. He had just turned twenty-three only five days before his appointment. Since he turned down the opportunity to attend West Point, the only military experience he attained was from what little he received as a private in the Albany Zouave Cadets, an organization that led him to become acquainted with Jackson. Luckily, Myers' influential father made him a man of similar clout by relation. Second Lieutenant Horatio G. Goodno of Company K said Myers, "was considered one of the finest looking men in the regiment physically," but he had his critics who doubted his abilities to serve as an officer on account of his young age and inexperience, but that really could have been said to describe the entire volunteer force. Myers took this type of criticism and made it his goal to prove them wrong and make a name for himself.[30]

Appointments of the Field and Staff

Vacancies in other offices of the regiment's staff were selected by Colonel Jackson and put to vote. The first to be nominated and unanimously elected as adjutant was twenty-four-year-old Albany native, John H. Russell. Like Jackson, Russell had been a founding member of the Albany Zouave Cadets and was well acquainted with the colonel and major through the teachings of their paramilitary organization. He was immediately committed and resigned from the Cadets on May 17 and became the regiment's adjutant that same day. Although shy, Russell was described as "a good scholar and a very fine penman" and was eager to do his service.[31]

Jackson also appointed thirty-four-year-old William V. Horsfall, a Schenectady resident that assumed the regimental quartermaster with the rank of first lieutenant. Company G was very pleased with the selection of Isaac S. Green to serve as the fife major for the 18th. They knew him best as a music teacher and from his prewar tenure as the conductor of the Canandaigua Band.[32]

Special care and vigilance would be needed in the medical department to keep the men healthy, so proficient doctors were sought. Dr. James L. Van Ingen left his successful practice in Schenectady to take care of the New York recruits that were taken ill while in Albany. Dr. Van Ingen jumped at the chance to accept the position of surgeon for the 18th on May 14. He was a graduate of Union College in 1840, and after school he entered the naval service and demonstrated an impressive ability to care and fight dangerous diseases while stationed in the West Indies, almost at the expense of his own life. Like Lieutenant Colonel Young, Dr. Van Ingen also served in the 26th New York State Militia before the war.[33]

Also to be appointed to the medical department was Dr. Alexander A. Edmeston as the regiment's assistant surgeon. Born in Paisley, Scotland in 1830, he left his home country with his parents when he was ten and came to America where his father pursued the mercantile business in Amsterdam, New York. Education for Dr. Edmeston started at an academy that eventually led to his acceptance and graduation from the Albany Medical College in 1853. Dr. Edmeston started a practice in Albany,

The shy twenty-four-year-old John Henry Russell of Albany was described as "a good scholar and a very fine penman" and was handpicked by Col. Jackson to be the adjutant. Russell was wounded at Gaines's Mill, Virginia, June 27, 1862, and died a month later in Philadelphia (courtesy New York State Military Museum).

wedded in 1856, and walked away from it all when war came.³⁴

When the news of the regiment's leadership filtered back to the rest of the eager men in the companies, the response was a joyous and celebratory scene. The companies were now days away from mustering into the state's service, but they still took in new volunteers. Men who signed up for the opportunity to fight the Southern insurrectionists now knew that it was all coming together. Cheers throughout the companies were raised for Jackson, Young, and Myers, who they all believed to be qualified and competent for their new positions.³⁵

Demographics of the 18th

The 18th fused together as a regiment, but within they showed many variances from each other. Out of the 1,069 names that at any time belonged to the 18th, the average age of the men was twenty-four. Age only became an issue at enlistment for those who were either too young or too old to meet the requirement of being between eighteen and forty-five years old. In a time period where proof of age could be validated by a note in a family Bible or simply by their word, a simple twist of the truth was sufficient to bypass the age restriction in front of the recruiting officer. Dozens of boys enhanced their age by a couple of years, and those senior to the stipulation of forty-five likewise shaved off a couple years in order to get accepted. Officers were given special privilege to bypass the age restriction without penalty, four of which were forty-five or older. At least seventeen men joined the regiment when they were at least fifty years old or more. The oldest known to join the regiment was fifty-eight-year-old Private Francis Van Benthuysen of Company B, who pulled back more years than some of the men who enlisted were alive for, and stated he was forty. He only served for seven months before his vision and knees failed.³⁶

Born in Paisley, Scotland, Dr. Alexander A. Edmeston came to America with his parents when he was ten years old. A graduate of the Albany Medical College, he left his private practice in the city and enrolled in the regiment as the assistant surgeon (author's collection).

The younger youth were much more eager to march off to war despite their hindrance of age. The 18th was no exception and were laden with boys who defied the restriction. At least fifty-seven teenagers under the age of eighteen joined the regiment, but the number only reflects birthdates that can be determined, and the likelihood of an increase to this number is certain. Boys that were honest about being underage were still taken and made into musicians, like thirteen-year-old Joseph Napoleon Rockwell, who was the youngest known to join when he signed up as a drummer for Company A. Most of the youth were much more brazen and desired to shoulder a rifle instead of a fife or drumsticks, which is where the majority of age liars went. Private Cornelius Houghtaling was the youngest rifleman to lie about his age when he enlisted into Company B a few days after the outbreak of war at the tender age of fourteen. Sixteen-year-old Private William Henry Mayette bumped up his age to nineteen when he enlisted into Company K. He demonstrated a knack for the military life, and after a year-and-a-half of service he sewed on the first sergeant chevrons and became the senior non-commissioned officer of his company.[37]

Sometimes parents intervened and prevented their foolhardy children from enlistment if they were underage. Private Henry Levison of Company A was yanked from the regiment by his father just two days after he took the oath. Seventeen-year-old Private George E. Shannon added a year to his age when he enlisted into the same company just days after war broke out, but his parents found out and they pulled him out of the regiment on May 21. But the war would wait for Shannon and he eventually got his time in service with a cavalry regiment after he legitimately turned eighteen. Three others from the 18th would be similarly discharged by writ of Habeas Corpus before the regiment even left the state.[38]

Medical examinations at the time of their enlistments were substandard at best and rushed. This allowed men to keep their medical histories undisclosed which would have rendered an obvious disqualification. Smith Chamberlain, a seventeen-year-old fifer in Company I, was blind in one eye but for a musician this was overlooked. Somehow Private John Deanstatt of Company G was allowed into the infantry, despite the fact that one of his feet lacked toes from an attack of frostbite years before the war. During his stint in the prewar army, Private Samuel C. LaRue of Company A lost the tips of his index and middle fingers on his right hand. LaRue tried to corral his horse when his unit came under a surprise attack from Indians out West, but the rope wrapped around his fingers and cut them off. His five years of military experience weighed heavier than two missing fingertips and he was allowed to serve.[39]

The mixture of ethnicities that exemplified mid-nineteenth century America was mirrored in the regiment with 31 percent of the men being foreign-born citizens. Of the 1,069 names that ever once appeared on the rosters of the 18th, only the birthplaces of 109 are unknown. From the 960 birthplaces that can be determined, 299 of them are from outside the United States. Immigration was steady in the mid-nineteenth century as thousands of families throughout Europe and Canada flocked to America to escape famine, war, or to start anew.[40]

Nativity of Foreign Born Soldiers in the 18th New York Infantry

Canada	35
England	42
France	5
Germany	50
Holland	4
Ireland	142
Russia	2
Scotland	16
Switzerland	2
West Indies	1

Captain John Hastings' Company B held the highest percentage of foreign-born soldiers. Half of the company was born in a different country, and half of these immigrants were Irish.

Hastings himself left Northern Ireland when his parents came to Albany when he was six years old. As a high profile newspaper editor with the Albany *Knickerbocker*, more than two dozen fellow Irish-Americans signed up to follow Hastings. He was smart to have recruited in an ideal social setting where men congregated—a saloon.[41]

Although recruited simultaneously in Schenectady, Company A and E showed notable differences between foreign-born and native soldiers. The number of immigrants in Company A was 40 percent which doubled Company E's 20 percent. Company A also held the highest group of Germans in a single company with seventeen. Before the war, Schenectady had several Republican-obsessed Wide Awake companies, one in each ward, and one of which was made entirely of Germans which explains the bulk to appear in the company led by a fellow Wide Awake leader.[42]

Tucked into the hills and away from the larger cities, the villages of Middletown and Canandaigua yielded a markedly lower rate of immigrant soldiers. The Wallkill Guards of Company D were almost of pure New York stock, and held the lowest number of foreign-born men at 11 percent. In the western portion of the state, the generationally occupied villages around Canandaigua showed similar calculations with only thirteen percent of Company G being born outside the United States.[43]

In Company K, 45 percent of the men were foreign-born citizens. Being as Ogdensburg was separated from Canada by a mile-long river, Company K had the highest grouping of Canadians, with at least twenty in total, or 18 percent of the entire company.[44]

Foreign fighters proved they were just as loyal and willing to serve their newfound home as native-born soldiers were. Private John Van Bueren of Company A came to America from Holland with his parents in 1848, yet he "exhibited an ardent patriotism" for his new home and when his own mother tried to dissuade him from enlisting, he replied "that his heart was with his adopted country." He assured her and said, "Mother, you will be proud of me when I return home," but Providence would not allow him to keep this promise.[45]

Immigrant soldiers deservedly earned the same pride and respect as their fellow native-born patriots. Born in England and a member of Company G, Private John B. Roper would forever display his pride as a foreign-born soldier to future generations. With his tombstone, he had an epitaph inscribed that read, "He was proud to have served in the War of the Rebellion of his adopted country."[46]

Private Alexander Abercrombie of Company E was born in Scotland, but he had no idea where—or more importantly when. His parents died when he was about three and he was raised by an aunt in Dundee, Scotland who was also ignorant to his birth date. They eventually settled with March 1834. When he was about eleven years old, Abercrombie started to work at sea as a cabin boy, and after two years he entered the United States in 1847. Abercrombie found employment in Schenectady as a machinist in a locomotive shop, and worked there until the outbreak of war became his calling. When he signed up into Captain Truax's company in Schenectady, he was so excited that he never noticed the captain registered his name as "Alexander Abel Crombie." He would continually have to correct people when his name was called out as Private Crombie.[47]

Most of the native-born Americans could proudly trace their heritage to Minute Men of the Revolution, and some to the nation's earliest settlers. Of the 960 men from the regiment whose birthplaces can be determined, 661 were born in America. Native-born citizens born in the state of New York tallied to 565. Sixteen other states can be represented, to include the seceded state of Virginia, birthplace of Private Henry Clay of Company D, who was born in Princess Anne County [present-day Virginia Beach]. An untold number of the native-born Americans were actually first-generation citizens, which further perpetuated the languages, accents, and diversity that weaved throughout the regiment.[48]

Private Thompson H. Snyder of Company F had enlisted under the name Thomas and he had the singular distinction within the regiment to be of a race other than white. He may have appeared as fair as the rest of the all-white regiment, but his race was listed as "mulatto" in the 1860 U.S. Census and "colored" in the Schoharie County Town Clerks' Register. A year before the war, Snyder was listed in the census in Schoharie where he lived with his mulatto-listed mother and black grandfather. In 1861 America, African-Americans were still barred from the military, but could work as servants, and the 18th was not exempt to this rule. Several unnamed servants attached themselves to serve the companies and its officers, but Snyder's appearance to his peers was white enough to prevent any type of disqualification or discrimination.[49]

The occupations most of the men held before becoming soldiers were predominately structured around hard labor. More than a third of the regiment listed themselves as either farmers or laborers, which was the most common occupation in every company. Company I had nearly a dozen molders. Company D had a dozen railroad employees based on their notable network of rail lines throughout their hometowns. Other physically demanding jobs that men previously worked were as lumbermen, teamsters, and mechanics. There was a myriad of skilled workers that left careers as printers, blacksmiths, tinsmiths, hunters, salesmen, tailors, teachers, painters, shoemakers, clerks, and carpenters, all to become soldiers. A majority of the commissioned officers were educated with some sort of degree, most of which were lawyers. For some, military service became another social organization that expanded their *esprit de corps* first experienced in the service of local fire departments and militias. A few elder gentlemen had actually served several years of active duty in the regular army before the war, such as Private Samuel C. LaRue, Company A, Private Arthur W. Mills, Company B, and Private John Shirley, Company G. Among the prior service men, there were some veterans of the Mexican War. John Giffen signed up and became the drum major for the 18th, and under his belt he had previously served as a drummer in the 10th Regiment, United States Infantry during the Mexican War. Captain Peter Hogan, Company H, and First Lieutenant Edward Fisher, Company F, were also both veterans of Mexico. Some men even served for different nations, such as Private John Redman, Company K, who was an Irish native that served in Montreal in 1854 as a soldier in the British army's 26th Regiment of Foot. There were even a few Crimean War veterans, like Peter Sheehan, Company K, who had almost three years of service in the English army. Sheehan actually escaped from that duty when he deserted his regiment in 1857 while stationed in Montreal.[50]

Soldiers in the 16th New York quartered with the 18th at the Adams House were said to have stood at least one inch above the rest of the volunteers that came from all parts of the state. In one company, they had a dozen men over six feet tall, so it should come as no surprise that the 18th's tallest man was also from St. Lawrence County. Private David H. Gray of Company K took the honor to tower above the entire regiment with his height of six feet four inches. The thirty-three-year-old school teacher from Lisbon was jokingly nicknamed by his comrades as their "big Gray baby," and his size matched him to the height of President Lincoln.[51]

The Wands Brothers. First Lt. Alexander Hamilton Wands of Company B (right) and his brother, Qm. Sgt. Robert J. Wands (left), served in the 18th New York, but they also had three other brothers in different regiments (courtesy Jeff Sauter).

Many of the men who left their families joined companies that contained friends or family. Thirty-one groups of brothers whose kinship can be determined either took the oath together or joined at different dates. First Lieutenant Alexander H. Wands of Company B and Quartermaster Sergeant Robert Wands were brothers that served together, but they also had three others that served in separate regiments during the war. Like the Wands Brothers, Private Christopher G. Burn and Private Richard A. Burn—brothers in Company B—also had three other brothers that served in a separate Albany regiment. Privates Isaac, Simon, and William Van Kuren remained side-by-side and enlisted together into Company G, which was the same company that had another trio of brothers; Charles, George, and Lewis Dunkle. By the time Samuel Barry of Company D reached the rank of sergeant, his older brother George Barry commanded the company. Captain William S. Gridley commanded Company A which contianed his little brother, Private Nate Gridley, and his cousin, Private Joseph W. Gridley. Truly, William must have known Joseph was only sixteen when he enlisted, but he did not stop him. Sergeant Alfred M. Chesmore and his first cousin Private Nathaniel G. Whittemore both left their homes in Massachusetts to enlist in Company I. There were a couple of father and son pairs too. Sergeant Alfred Truax left his wife and children in Schenectady to join the company his father formed. Corporal Andrew D. Barhydt of Company E was a cousin to the wife of Lieutenant Colonel Young, whose own eldest son David W. Young eventually joined Company K in 1862. By the fall of 1861, Second Lieutenant Horatio G. Goodno would see his brother and fifteen-year-old son enter Company K. In the winter of 1861, Private William H. Hall joined Company F and was soon joined by his father-in-law, Private Joshua Pangburn. Some of the companies were raised in such tight-knit communities that a stranger amongst them was rare.[52]

Aside from Christianity, politics was like an addiction and pervaded their everyday lives. The 18th was a mixed bag of political allegiances, which undoubtedly sparked constant debates throughout the camp. Citizens were influenced heavily by the respect and allure of political and military figures, which can be reflected in the names of those that served in the regiment: George Washington Pollock, Thomas Jefferson Ketcham, Alexander Hamilton Wands, Horatio Gates Goodno, Henry Clay Mills, Andrew Jackson Smyth, Millard Fillmore Williams, Edmund Burke Hawley, Winfield Scott Hale, William Seward Gridley and James K. Polk Ormsby.

Gifts from Home

On May 16, a flag presentation at the State House was given at five o'clock to Company K. Attorney General Charles G. Myers was delegated by the Ladies of Ogdensburg to present the company with a beautifully constructed national silk flag. On their behalf, the Attorney General handed the flag over to the company and spoke a short but poignant speech and wished the company the best of luck and reminded them that the flag should, "suffer no disgrace at the company's hands, either in their conduct in camp or their action in the field of battle." Twenty-three-year-old Private John C. O. Redington, a musical instrument dealer and voice instructor for the public schools in Ogdensburg, took the opportunity to speak on behalf of the company. As the son of a preacher and a newly ordained minister himself from Middlebury College, Redington knew how to address crowds. With his deep-set eyes, he looked out to the crowd and paraphrased the symbolism that the Stars and Stripes represented and said, "if rebels desire to lay their unhallowed hands on this flag, they must prostrate our forms helpless for its defense." Redington finished to say their hearts, "shall inscribe upon this ensign the deathless sentiment, 'Don't give up the Flag.'" The company shouted three jubilant cheers in honor of Attorney General Myers and the ladies back home that promised never to forget them. Company K ended the ceremony and marched from the State House through State Street and Broadway, where they received a lot of attention from the citizens of Albany for the duration of their walk back to their quarters at the Adams House. Upon arrival, the men again gathered around their new trophy and sang the most fitting song they could think of—"The Star-Spangled Banner."[53]

The men from Ogdensburg were not the only ones who celebrated the cheerful reminders of loved ones back home. Six women in Middletown organized a committee at Gothic Hall in order to send food items to the Wallkill Guards after reading soldier requests from an article in the *New York Tribune*. Army rations were relatively new for the men and would become a staple diet, but it took little time to loathe the "detestably poor fare." The request for food drives for companies was taken further:

Hard bread and salt pork, or ham, day after day for every meal, is something that even the most heroic patriotism after a while rather revolts at; and I believe one cause that makes so many soldiers take to hard drinking is their much-salted and disagreeable food.[54]

The committee of Middletown women gathered on May 17 and forwarded four boxes filled with an assortment of goods for their homesick taste buds. Their purpose was to give them a taste of home and break the monotony of repetitive rations that the article said would "help out amazingly." The packages contained bread, biscuits, smoked beef, cakes, pies, jams, pickles, lemons, oranges, dried fruits, cheese, butter, sugar, tea, and plenty of writing paper with envelopes. The Express Company that shipped the goods were also kind enough to send the packages free of charge.[55]

Representatives in the City Council in Schenectady presented Captain Truax's Company E with a gift to lessen their financial burden that accumulated with their lodging in Albany. A resolution appropriated and distributed $100 for the purpose of paying their boarding bills.[56]

Mustering In

On May 17, the entire regiment was requested to be drawn up on the grounds of the Industrial School Barracks just outside the city for the purpose of being officially mustered into the service of the United States. The companies not yet quartered in the barracks started their march in the morning from the Adams House, through the city, and linked up at the barracks.[57]

Before the ceremony started, nine men in Company C were dropped from the regiment after they refused to take the oath and were drummed out of the camp and sent home. At 1 p.m., the regiment stood with its strongest number of 834 men who each answered their name when called, removed their hat, and raised their right hand. They were sworn in and took the oath of allegiance to uphold the Constitution, defend their government from foreign and domestic enemies, and to obey all officers who might be elected or appointed over them for the term of two years unless discharged sooner. As the immortal last words of the oath was read aloud, "So help you God," men tagged the ending with a shout for three cheers for the Constitution and three more for Colonel Jackson. The regiment was officially recognized into service as the 18th New York Volunteer Infantry Regiment, and earned the nickname, "The New York State Rifles." Captain Frank Wheaton of the United States Army—who was originally discussed to command the 18th until an order forbade regular army officers to command volunteer forces—had the job to inspect volunteer regiments when they mustered in, and complimented the 18th to be the best one he had inspected up to that time.[58]

Industrial School Barracks

Colonel Jackson's second cousin, Frederick Townsend, had similarly dropped out of public office to become the colonel of the 3rd New York, which was one of the first regiments to depart Albany for the seat of war. Their departure from the barracks on May 18 opened several vacancies. The six companies of the 18th still quartered at the Adams House packed up and marched together about two miles to the outskirts of Albany and were united with the rest of the regiment at the barracks. The Industrial School Barracks was a large brick structure that was the former Albany Industrial School, originally built to house impoverished and orphaned children. The building was also conveniently connected to the State Penitentiary. The barracks could accommodate multiple regiments simultaneously and had multiple floors with rooms that could house entire companies. More sanitary than the Adams House, these barracks were equipped with two bathrooms that were connected to the building. The barracks also offered the convenience to wash clothes and had a room suited for bathing purposes. The Hudson River was also close and occasionally captains took their companies down to bathe. The men slept in pairs, on bunk beds built three tiers high which were made out of thin wooden boards. With blankets to keep them warm at night, the men were quite content within their new home. More wooden barracks 500 yards from the Industrial School were under construction which soon allowed more companies to float in and free up the occupation of the city. As regiments relocated and vacated the wooden barracks, more came in their place.[59]

The food at the Industrial School Barracks was greatly improved in both quality and quantity when compared to the Adams House. Mornings had coffee readily available, noon brought water, and tea came in the evenings. The men were fed by contracted cooks outside of the military, and the menu was as good as what most boarding houses could offer. The food was cooked in the basement of their building and the men were waited upon by citizen waiters. For meals, the men dined on cold slices of beef or pork, sometimes mixed with beans, beef soup, potatoes, and bread that came with butter. No one could really talk about hard living at the Industrial School Barracks, but Private Edward M. Tilley of Company K said it best when he stated that, "there will naturally be some complaint somewhere." Nearly 9,000 meals were prepared each day to feed the four regiments quartered at the barracks. If the men complained about anything regarding their meals, it was the times in which they were served. Breakfast was supplied at nine in the morning, dinner from two to three, and supper was given between eight and nine o'clock in the evening. Regiments were served based on their seniority at the barracks, meaning those who had been there longer were cycled through first for meals.[60]

There was a large tract of land within the barracks which was not the most level ground, but was adequate enough for the purpose of drill and parade reviews for the regiments. Opposite of the 18th's side of the green was the 14th New York who similarly shared the drilling space between the regiments. The barracks was surrounded by a tall wooden fence that was guarded on the outside by the colorfully garbed company of what was left of the Albany Zouave Cadets militia. Dressed in their French-inspired uniform of red pants and a blue shell jacket that dripped with buttons, they presented a sharp and inspiring appearance to the men who still waited for their issuance of uniforms.[61]

Between training sessions, there was little or nothing to do. "One day is like another pretty much," wrote Sergeant Augustus Mowatt of Company C. Some men would stir up games of "pitching quails," which was a rudimentary version of baseball. Large religious services were held every Sunday at the barracks and every man was required to attend. Leaving the compound was off-limits without a pass, so most men would casually stroll around the enclosed grounds. About two men from each company a day were ever given passes to go into the city. Men risky enough to outrun the Albany Zouave Cadets that patrolled the exterior did so to have their fun downtown. Punishment was always dealt to those individuals on their return—if they returned. On one Saturday—May 18—the daily limit of passes was bumped up to five.[62]

Hours of daily drills and dress parades was initiated as soon as the regiment came to be. Every day, companies would be drilled by their officers. In the afternoons, the companies would collaborate to be drilled as a regiment for dress parade in front of the barracks. The Albany Brigade Band likewise quartered within the area frequently played the patriotic melodies of popular tunes. The sight of these regiments converting citizens-to-soldiers was a spectacle that often drew large crowds of interested Albany residents curious enough to watch. A few regiments even drilled together for a battalion-size drill at the Washington Parade Ground [present-day Washington Park] on May 19.[63]

Along with their constant drill, the regiment began to see improvements to correct their undisciplined few. Some men implemented measures to ban alcohol, as quite a few abused it when in the city on pass. A temperance pledge was started in camp that achieved minor success.[64]

At the barracks, the men were officially paid their first sum of money from the government. They were given gold and silver coins according to their rank. The rank structure dictated how much each man was paid, increasing as the rank got higher. Privates started off getting paid a total of $11 a month whereas a colonel would be paid roughly $654. Still, for most of the privates, this was more money than any of them had ever seen. Private Samuel Hodgkins of Company K spoke on behalf of all the privates in the regiment when he said, "we surely all felt rich, had more real money in our pockets that we could rattle, than any of us had seen for many a day … real money that would make a noise in one's pocket was something very strange, and mighty good to have."[65]

The Industrial School Barracks was an improved environment with cleaner conditions, but living in close quarters with so many men always opened avenues for disease. After a small outbreak of measles which sent a few men to the hospital, Lieutenant Colonel Young ordered all of the companies to be vaccinated on May 21.[66]

Uniforms

The men finally received their highly anticipated uniforms on May 22, which completed their physical transformation to soldiers. Before they received them, the Articles of War were read to each company that outlined the overall rules that a soldier would adhere to and live by from that day forward. At the commencement of the reading, the men were finally handed their blue suits.[67]

Despite the wool being of poor quality, of which Colonel Jackson was well aware of, the uniforms were the standard issue 1861 New York State pattern. The jacket consisted of dark blue wool, but so deep was the dye that the men viewed them closer to black than blue. The jackets were trimmed with light blue piping that outlined the epaulets, collar, and a belt loop. Lined down the front were eight golden buttons printed with the New York State Militia emblem. The trousers were of light blue dyed wool and were the standard issue for Federal troops. The weighted woolen overcoats issued to the 18th were different than the blue ones that most regiments received. Instead, they received ones of gray colored wool that came with a cape attached at the neck. When they donned the gray overcoats, their differed appearance from other regiments was complimented by an Albany reporter who said they presented, "a pleasant contrast, and is much prettier than the heavy dark blue overcoats." Four months later they exchanged their gray overcoats for the lighter blue kind prescribed by infantry regulations. Other items issued to the men consisted of ordinary dark blue fatigue caps, two pairs of thick flannel drawers, two pairs of woolen socks, two flannel undershirts, a wool blanket, and one pair of black hard cowhide shoes.[68]

The uniforms came as a huge moral booster for the men, but there seemed to be a universal complaint that they were made way too large. Private George W. Royce, Company G, sarcastically exclaimed that the uniforms were "large enough for two common sized men." Luckily, there were plenty of men in the regiment handy with needles who went to immediate work with alterations for their comrades. One thing men from Company K did not complain about was that they were supplied uniforms before their counterparts in the 16th New York, whom they continued to mock in spite.[69]

Officers of the regiment had to buy their own uniforms and accoutrements, but were most often gifted these items. Family, friends, churches, and other benevolent societies and charitable people pulled together funds and dressed most of the officers of the regiment. Several small presentations of swords and revolvers occurred. Newly commissioned First Lieutenant Theodore C. Rogers of Company H received more than he expected. His friends provided his full dress uniform, a sword, belt, sash, epaulettes, and a revolver, and the adoring ladies from his father's church congregation presented Rogers with a purse that contained $500 in gold.[70]

Drill

The men had the appearance of soldiers, but they had much to learn until they could fluidly move in formations and snap to orders. Their first full day in uniform, Colonel Jackson drilled the regiment twice, for about two hours each session. Private Joseph C. Jones of Company G remembered, "We learned to mark time to the right and left face and tried to keep in line and right and left wheels, which was very hard to accomplish. We got those things down fine later." Jackson himself had a lot to learn. He was not overly confident as most in his position were in those early months of the war, but like everything he ever pursued, he did so with a hunger to learn. With his determination and discipline in reading manuals, combined with his suitably experienced staff, the cohesiveness of the regiment began to formulate into a drilled machine. Drill was performed whenever the weather cooperated. Eight-hour drill days was started and lasted for ten consecutive days.[71]

They were instructed through countless repetitions of the manual of arms both with and without rifles. Naturally, the men were sloppy and sluggish before the reactions to commands became muscle memory. They shared a stock of some of the most decrepit and well-used rifles that were hardly serviceable. More like props, they served their purpose to practice the manual of arms with. Private Joseph C. Jones recalled the practicality of those rifles:

> You ought to have seen us with those old queen muskets. We must have made a hostile appearance indeed.... The parts would not stay together. A bayonet would be missing and then the ramrod; the lock would be put out commission. The barrel would be bent so it would shoot around a hill, I presume.[72]

Reminders of Home

The closer the days got to their rumored move, the influx of supplies donated to the men trickled in. Several hometown organizations emerged that searched for ways to help their men, and many answered the flood of requests for havelocks. A British army design, havelocks were a headdress made of heavy white material that draped over their caps in long flaps and covered the necks of the soldiers to help prevent sunstroke. The Ladies of Albany promised to sew enough havelocks to supply the entire regiment by June 13. Company K received a large box from the Ogdensburg Volunteer Aid Association whose package was received with a unison cheer by the men. The box was full of more havelocks and towels that they were allowed to keep. The Ladies of Schenectady eventually did the same with a box of havelocks that reached their two companies by mid–June, as did the Ladies' Association in Middletown. These seamstress societies sent enough havelocks for each man in the regiment to cover their caps.[73]

Patriotic Christians of Albany were able to donate New Testament booklets to the men on May 23. Anyone that desired a copy took one, and a majority did so. The Ladies of Albany also contributed three needle books for each company. Local newspapers from their hometowns trickled into the city and became cherished gifts. One soldier not from Albany stated that he "would rather have one paper from home than a half dozen of these city ones." Eighty rubber blankets were delivered to Company E from the Ladies of Schenectady near the end of the month. Each man in the company also received a small strip of paper containing an appropriate quotation from Scripture, and a small sewing kit which contained a dozen needles, two skeins of white and black thread, and about two dozen buttons. Captain Bartlett of Company K wrote home and applauded the philanthropic donations of their townsfolk and promised that their gifts would "strike hard in defense of our glorious country, while 'thinking of those whom we have left behind.'"[74]

Ellsworth's Funeral

While the 18th performed endless drill sessions in Albany during their first week as a regiment, the threat on the nation's capital escalated. Virginia seceded from the Union on May 23, which heightened the fear of Washington's possible capture. Union regiments streamed into the district, but the request for more only increased. In the afternoon of May 24, Governor Morgan informed the officers of the 18th that their regiment might be ordered to Washington within twenty-four hours. Immediately, passes were revoked for everyone as they prepared to depart Albany within the expected time frame.[75]

Earlier that same morning a pivotal clash near the nation's capital unfolded. Elmer E. Ellsworth, colonel of the 11th New York (1st New York Fire Zouaves), moved into Alexandria, Virginia, and was tasked out to disable some railroad lines that led to Richmond. The Marshall House in downtown Alexandria flew the Secessionist's flag which was something Ellsworth could not stomach. He grabbed a couple men from his regiment and entered the boarding house and took down the flag himself. During their exit of the house the proprietor, James W. Jackson, fatally shot Ellsworth on the stairs. One of Ellsworth's Zouaves, Francis Brownell, sprung into action and deflected another shot and was able to kill Jackson with a gunshot and several bayonet thrusts. Instantly, two martyrs for both causes were born.[76]

Ellsworth's death sent a shockwave of mourning throughout the country still loyal to the Union. Ellsworth was a personal friend of President Lincoln, and this connection seemed to be received just the same by the rest of the Union. A viewing in the White House was the first of many stops of Ellsworth's body on his long journey home. His body finally reached Albany by steamer early on May 27.[77]

The 18th had fully expected to be far gone from Albany by the time Ellsworth's remains reached the city. The body of the nation's newest hero lay in state at the Capitol all morning until 9 a.m. and was visited by thousands. The body was then removed for a funeral procession through the streets. Since the 18th and 14th New York were the only two uniformed regiments at the Albany Barracks at the time, they were easily conscripted into the sad duty to escort Ellsworth's remains. Both regiments left the barracks in the morning and entered the city to await their spot in the procession. At 9:30 a.m., the order was organized to escort the coffin from the Capitol to the steamboat landing via State Street and down Broadway. A large number of civilians lined the streets as a band led the procession. Two companies of the Albany Zouave Cadets, who owe their existence to the influence of Ellsworth's prewar Zouave demonstrations, marched in black pants instead of their customary red and their muskets reversed over their shoulders. The horse drawn carriage with Ellsworth's remains slowly rolled down the street as the curious and saddened citizens looked on. Following behind the remains of their colonel walked five members of his regiment, including Sergeant Francis Brownell, nicknamed "Ellsworth's Avenger." His bayonet was still stained with the blood of the colonel's killer. Governor Morgan and members of his staff followed closely behind with a carriage that had Ellsworth's family aboard. Behind them came the fire department, another band, and the 14th New York. The 18th brought up the rear and marched slowly in formation. Both regiments were uniformed to their fullest with winter overcoats. Cannons were fired in honor of the slain hero throughout the procession. Bells tolled and flags had all been placed at half-mast. The procession continued to the railroad station where the flower-covered coffin was transferred and sent to Ellsworth's final resting place upstate. Almost sixty years after the affair, a reminiscent Samuel Hodgkins recalled his participation in the procession of Ellsworth's body as, "the first military duty I ever had the honor of performing for my country."[78]

Waiting to Move

With the alert to leave Albany now several days passed, Ellsworth's funeral knocked the regiment off their routine of drill. They got back to it with daily sessions that lasted for eight hours. During the afternoon of May 29, Major Myers took his try to drill the regiment at the barracks during dress parade, which he performed superbly in the eyes of the men. In just a week and a half of drills together, the lines of the performing troops grew crisp and were said by one member of the 18th to be "geometrically beautiful, having unavoidably, all degrees of curvature."[79]

Men constantly sought for insight on where and what their destination and duty would be, but unfounded rumors was all they found. Some men overheard talks that they were to be garrisoned in Brooklyn. Others heard they would be moved to Long Island, Elmira, or even down to Fort Monroe near Hampton, Virginia. New barracks being built three miles below the city was mentioned in the papers to be occupied by Jackson's regiment for an unspecified time. The uniformed yet unarmed 14th and 18th regiments reluctantly expected to be sent there to spend their life as garrisoned soldiers stuck in camp life which terrified the men. It was also believed that these two regiments were not expected to be sent south for at least three months. These rumors were less than desirable to the men who were hell-bent to get down south. Private Tilley wrote, "the boys do not like the idea of going North any farther until they have had a brush with Jeff Davis' minions in a more Southern clime." The field officers knew as much as their men, yet they performed their duties and remained positive and assured the anxious soldiers that, "Uncle Sam has the direction of our movements," and that they would not be sent to the new camp a few miles down the river.[80]

On June 1, the 18th did move, but not to the location initially thought. The freshly built barracks 500 yards next to the Industrial School had been vacated earlier in the day by the 16th and 28th New York who transitioned to a newly constructed encampment three miles below the city. The 14th and 18th New York quickly took possession of the spacious wooden barracks in the next lot immediately after they were emptied. The new barracks were of newer construction and were more spacious and easier to keep clean than their previous billets. The men still slept in bunks that were built three tiers high and were stocked with good beds and blankets.[81]

The grounds that surrounded these barracks were noticeably more level and larger than inside the Industrial School Barracks compound. When weather permitted, the 14th and 18th performed dress parades every afternoon on the small patch of land that separated their two barracks as the Albany Brigade Band played on. The 18th had one large tent that was erected in their space which the men used for various purposes. Prayer meetings were held every Sunday and Wednesday evenings with heavy attendance, and on Tuesday evenings the tent was home to a debating society. Church services were still held every Sunday at a chosen spot in front of their former quarters at the Industrial School Barracks and large crowds of citizens continued to show up to partake.[82]

Presentation of Flags

The same day as their shift to the newer barracks, the 18th was also presented with their official regimental colors. This meant that the flags previously presented to Company D and K by their hometown admirers were no longer needed as the regimental colors superseded any other flag. Around 4 p.m., on June 1, the entire regiment concluded their dress parade at the Industrial School Barracks but remained formed up for the presentation. A large crowd of men and women had gathered to watch as local Albany lawyer Jacob I. Werner presented on the behalf of the Ladies of Albany to Colonel Jackson, two beautifully constructed flags, both a state and national flag. The national flag was made of red, white, and blue silk, and personalized with the inscription of "Rally around it" and "18th Reg. N. Y. V." Both staffs had a silvered plate which was engraved, "Presented to the 18th Reg't, N. Y. S. Vols., Col. Wm. A. Jackson, by his lady friends of Albany, June 1, 1861." Werner's lengthy speech touched on the importance of both kinds of patriots currently called up for service. The citizens at home who were needed to furnish the material aid, or what he called, "the sinews of war." The other and most important patriots required for victory was the main audience in front of, the men of the 18th. Werner continued to explain that their destiny would soon lead them to the "barbarous" enemy and reminded the men to never forget their loved ones back home who would continue to encourage and pray for them. He finished with:

> Take it, and in the language of the motto inscribed upon its ample folds, "Rally around it" rally nobly around all that is represented by it, and return with it only when your country is one and united forever.[83]

As the cheers and applause subsided, Colonel Jackson addressed all who were present and spoke the following words in humble thankfulness:

> Sir, I thank you for your kindly words, and for myself and my command I thank through you, the ladies who have given us this beautiful flag. I can simply say that the Eighteenth regiment here pledges itself to maintain the honor of this flag, and to bring it back unstained by aught, except the smoke and dust of battle. Ladies, this token of your regard will be very dear to us. In the spirit which prompted its giving, we recognize that noble trait which, in all ages, has characterized woman's loyalty to her land. We will never forget the motto you have inscribed upon the broad folds of this flag, and by God's help, we will, "rally around it" where the crash and din of battle is loudest, remembering that we strike for the fair hands that have given it to our keeping and the warm hearts that are praying for us at home.[84]

Run the Guard

Aside from the regular drill duties performed in their previous barracks, very little change was adopted in their new space except the concept of having to perform their own guard duty. The Albany Zouave Cadets turned the duty over to the regiments within and left after a few days. An equal number of men from each company from the 18th took turns at a rotating guard with eight-hour shifts that performed round-the-clock protection inside and outside of their barracks.[85]

Since they pulled their own guard rotations at their new barracks, more men took the opportunity to "run the guard" and wandered downtown. There was very little fear to run passed the sentries from their own regiment since they still shouldered the comically worn-down and busted muskets. Private Joseph C. Jones claimed their decrepit condition "was one thing favorable about these arms" which allowed them to run the guard free from danger. Furthermore, guards were not even allowed to have loaded muskets which basically rendered sentries on guard duty powerless.[86]

After two and a half weeks of being housed as a regiment at the barracks, life there had quickly slowed down. Days were monotonous and little occurred to write home about. They became anxious to move, and many could just not sit tight, so men habitually snuck out of the barracks and frequented the city establishments. Some would go unnoticed and returned without penalty, but most would have a guard in close pursuit on their heels that scoured the city for runners. If they were caught, they were placed under arrest and locked in the guardhouse at the barracks. In one instance, two Company K soldiers successfully escaped the guards and had their fun in the city, but with every intention that they would return to the barracks when they were done. Their revel was cut short when a guard caught up with them downtown. Their pursuit of a good time turned into confinement in the guardhouse, where they lived on bread and water for an unspecified length.[87]

Private Joseph C. Jones related another incident where he and a few men from Company G decided they would take their chance to run the guard in order to bathe in the Hudson River. They picked out a point between guards and made their break for it, but they did not go unnoticed. Private Morton P. Pittenger of the same company was one of the guards, and he happened to see the mad dash escape. Pittenger yelled out, "Halt there!" The men ignored him and kept running until Pittenger fired a pistol shot in the air that jolted the runners into a panic. Private William "Billy" Matteson was one of those surprised sprinters, and after the crack of the pistol he stubbed his toe and flew to the ground. The timing was perfect as the group of runners "all thought he was shot and gave ourselves up then and there. We were green!" The men were placed in the guardhouse for just a few minutes until Lieutenant Colonel Young entered, prepared with a short lecture. Jones would never forget what Young told them when he said, "Boys, I am going to let you off this time, but you will find out when we get on the lines this business will be played out." Young made an impression on this group and no further problems from them ever took place.[88]

Young's mercy had its affect on these few, but the regiment was much larger and harder to control. On June 2, an astonishing herd of nearly 150 men from the regiment ran the guards after dusk and spent that Sunday night in the city. Most returned the next morning before daylight, but about seventy were corralled and placed in the guardhouse together. Private Tilley stated that every day the guardhouse was "filled with these unruly volunteers." On the night of June 4, Tilley noted the number of men on guard was doubled and orders were given to "stop all passers at all hazards," in an attempt to cease the party-goers venture in the city. Regardless, men still found methods out, and the continuous cat-and-mouse game continued.[89]

Earlier that day, the regiment seemed to be on the brink of mutiny. Wages from the state to cover their service previous to being sworn into the government was a few days overdue and several men began to believe it would never come. When the daily call of formation for drill was given, a large portion of the regiment refused to drill until they received their pay. Soon, several men armed with sticks formed their own line with a fifer at the helm. The irritated assemblage marched around the grounds and yelled "no pay, no drill" in order to draw attention. They got what they asked for when Colonel Jackson took notice and intervened immediately. He approached the mob and convinced his soldiers that of anyone else around, he was one that knew firsthand of the management woes within the state and guaranteed the problem would be remedied quickly. His convincing plea was enough to satisfy the displeased soldiers and reassured them that the issue would be resolved. The regiment was paid their due sum six days later, where each private received an average of thirty-six cents for each day served before May 17, with a marginal increase for those of higher rank.[90]

Final Equipage, and Dealing with a Thief

All of the officers received their tents on June 7 and they wasted no time to pitch them right in front of the barracks. The enlisted men would have to wait for their tents, but until then the erected ones from the officers gave their residence an appearance that looked more like what an encampment should. The most sought after missing piece for the soldier was what they needed most—guns. Governor Morgan received a dispatch that told of the arrival of a regiment's worth of Enfield rifles that had arrived in New York City, and he promised his longtime friend Colonel Jackson that he would have them.[91]

On June 10, the regiment was issued their basic load of equipment required for a fighting soldier. Each man was issued a knapsack, haversack, bayonet and scabbard, canteen, cartridge box, cap box, and belts. The arrival of equipment ushered in new rumors of their future movement. From all that was said, the men at least agreed that they would be leaving somewhere within a week.[92]

The regiment tried their first dress parade drill with donned equipment later that evening and instantly felt the temperature rise. The summer sun struck three soldiers down with heat-related injuries and had to be carried off the field. As a lesson from this, drill practices were conducted during the cooler hours in the mornings and evenings, and havelocks sent from home were allowed to be worn.[93]

At that same evening dress parade on June 10, another example was made in front of the men at the expense of a private who was convicted of thievery. Thirty-year-old Private John Connors of Company B was caught stealing clothing and was confined to the guardhouse. The 18th was formed into line as the thief was escorted out of the shack and marched to the head of the regiment. With two guards on either side of him, Connors wore a placard with the word "thief" draped over his chest and back. The regiment's drummers and fifers played "Rogue's March" throughout Connors' public humiliation. As an example for the whole regiment to witness the intolerance of thievery, Connors was drummed right out of camp and discharged from the service.[94]

Leaving New York

Major Myers received a letter on June 11 from his father in Washington that brought the news everyone had been waiting for. After having left a meeting with President Lincoln that confirmed the Secretary of War's acceptance of the New York Volunteers for a period of two years, Governor Morgan and Attorney General Myers sent word back to the state to send regiments to Washington as soon as they got uniformed. Attorney General Myers tipped off his son that he should get the 18th prepared to leave at an hour's notice for a trip to the nation's capital. The attorney general expected marching orders to be issued to the regiment at any moment.[95]

Colonel Jackson separately received the same flood of messages through his connections. The news was supposed to be kept quiet from others in case plans fell through, but being the most convincing news yet to be received, the information was shared with the men of the 14th and 18th New York after their dress parade on June 13. Though they were instructed not to celebrate at the telling of the news, the men in both regiments could not suppress their elation. Private John C. O. Redington described "a scene of enthusiasm unparalleled in military discipline was witnessed." Private Tilley mentioned "cheer after cheer went up higher than the hundreds of caps which were in the air at the same time" and the celebrations kicked back up when they returned to their quarters. No one knew when exactly they were to leave, but the order to immediately pack all their belongings was enough to satisfy them. Telegraphs were dispatched to inform those officers who were home on furloughs or recruitment duty to return to the regiment at once. All passes were cancelled and extra guards were again posted at the barracks to prevent those daring few who needed their last round of frivolities in the city. Guards were also sent down to comb through Albany in an effort to collect those who had already slipped out without permission.[96]

Elation carried into the following day, and a few men took things too far. Six members of the 18th found themselves jailed in Albany for being drunk in public. As their fellow comrades prepared for the regiment's departure, these six men were being brought down for trial where each pleaded guilty. Luckily, Colonel Jackson was able to convey to the judge of his regiment's immediate departure of the city and stressed the importance to have every man in line. The soldiers escaped doing time in the penitentiary and were all released back to the regiment.[97]

Colonel Jackson had a lot on his mind as he readied his men to move south and enter the war. An additional headache that never seemed to disappear from the New York papers was the scandal over the Brooks Brothers contracts for shoddy uniforms. So many complaints had been raised from New York troops about the inferior quality of uniforms that a few members in the State Cabinet—to include Attorney General Myers—left for New York City on June 4 and began a formal investigation on the manufacturers of the uniforms. Being the former Inspector General that struck the deal, Jackson was the highest person-of-interest in the investigation. Just as Jackson readied the regiment to head south, he was forced to revisit the whole ordeal and provide his testimony in a court inquiry on June 15. Jackson's statements, along with seventeen others all seemed to explain the same cycle of events, and again fault was found to be shared by so many players that no one seemed to take the brunt of the blame. There was a heightened focus to find if anyone profited personally from any private deals, but with no admission from anyone there was little to add to the scandal. Jackson did what was asked of him with his testimony, but his focus was on more important duties and did not get avidly involved in the manhunt to defame someone's character.[98]

With time winding down on the regiment's expected departure for "the seat of war," Captain Bartlett succeeded in one last jab at the 16th New York that just weeks before had denied his company. Bartlett initially intended to procure his son and have him transferred to Company K, but his son's company commander did not broker the deal. Bartlett "brought the arm of civil law to hear" and was successful in getting his son discharged from their regiment by writ of habeas corpus on June 2. A separate swap was mutually successful by Bartlett and the 16th New York by the transfer of Private David C. J. Russell out of the 18th and into the 16th, in exchange for Private Arthur M. Grant on June 15. Grant would join Company K on June 24 to serve alongside his younger brother Ralph.[99]

After a month in service, forty-seven men were listed as deserters from the 18th, and most were never heard from again. Some were sick and sent either to hospitals or their homes where they made their escapes. Whether the skepticism of not being sent south or its reality was the genesis of their flight from the service, their decision remained a blemish on their personal characters in the eyes of those who knew them. Musician William Pitt Whitcomb was promoted to drum major shortly after his enlistment and was sent home to Ogdensburg on June 5 on furlough, but he never returned. Men had grown anxious that their new drum major might not ever return, especially those from Company K who knew Whitcomb best and were confused by his flight. Colonel Jackson issued a request for Whitcomb's arrest on June 14, but he was never apprehended and actually pulled the same stunt in a Pennsylvania regiment months later. The night before the regiment's departure for Washington, twelve men took their last opportunity to flee. The local paper tried to instill fear in these deserters and decreed that, "they will be followed up and punished." An officer from the regiment was detailed to remain behind about a day or two for the purpose to wait with those still sick in the hospital that were not yet fit to travel south.[100]

Just as soon as the expectation to leave the state settled in, one officer decided he would not make the trip. Forty-three-year-old First Lieutenant John W. Birmingham of Company C resigned from his position on June 16. That same day his position was filled by a musician from Company E that was half the age of Birmingham, but fully capable to handle the job. Andrew Barclay Mitchell, a red-headed student from Union College who tended to reduce his first name to an initial, transferred companies and was commissioned as their first lieutenant. For a musician from a different company brought into one made wholly of Fishkill area men, the transfer had its ripple effects, especially with their second lieutenant.[101]

With another ten holes created from those who were legitimately discharged for medical reasons, the steady pace of men that enlisted into the regiment balanced the vacancies. Thirty-five men joined between May 18 and June 18, and by the time of their departure the regiment stood just over 800 strong.[102]

On June 17, the 18th was drawn up in line and cheered their neighbors of the 14th New York as they vacated the barracks to begin their travels to Washington. The ovation was genuinely for them, but the men of the 18th saw their exit as proof that their turn was next.[103]

The following day, the 18th packed their equipment and moved based on their marching orders and officially ended their residency at the barracks. Before they left, each man was given essential items such as a tin plate, knife, fork and spoon. They received a quick class on how to properly roll their blankets and overcoats and how to pack everything neatly into their knapsacks. Lastly, each man was given a chunk of cold boiled meat and a loaf of bread to tie them over during their travel. At 2 p.m., the regiment was ordered to form a hollow square, of which Governor Morgan and his staff stepped into and addressed the men. The chaplain of the barracks gave a short address and offered spiritual guidance. Captain Stephen Truax, Company E, recalled the chaplain's words of encouragement:

> [The chaplain] then made a few remarks reminding the men that it was their privilege to protect the institutions which their fore-fathers founded; that to do it some sacrifice must be made, many hardships endured, but that in the end, when the government is sustained, every soldier can return to his home with the proud satisfaction of having upheld the government which protects him in his right.[104]

After ending with a short prayer that asked for God's protection, the men that surrounded the chaplain responded with a cheerful applause. The last to address the regiment was Colonel Jackson who carefully chose words that motivated the men. After Jackson closed the show, he reformed the regiment and marched them out of the barracks at three o'clock in the afternoon. Their march was chaperoned under the escort from the Albany Zouave Cadets, and together they marched to the wharf. Thousands of citizens came out and clogged the route of travel to cheer them along their last march through Albany's streets. "Every street was packed with cheering crowds," wrote Private John C. O. Redington of Company K, "sad, yet firm in giving up their dear ones." Countless cries of "God bless you" pierced through the claps and cheers, and some even broke into the columns of troops in order to grasp one last handshake from their heroes. Bouquets tied with patriotic colored lace sailed through the air and landed sporadically in the ranks of the soldiers. Flags and handkerchiefs were vigorously waved. Men and women, old and young, shed plenty of tears and hollered the cheers that drowned out any command barked by the officers. Redington viewed the event with a broader perspective when he wrote:

> The scene was mightily beautiful and impressive, and nerved anew, the soldiers' determination to strive to be worthy of the immense ovation. And yet this, as well as multitudes of other popular expressions of sympathy along the route of march, were not given to the soldier, but to the cause.[105]

After a slight delay through the crowded streets, the men reached their destination and embarked on the steamer *McDonald* which also had two other barges fastened to its sides. Eight horses were assigned to the regiment for the officers and were likewise brought aboard. Once everyone was on, the infantrymen immediately stripped off their knapsacks and accoutrements of which they had carried for the past three hours. Afterwards, the men sought out their assigned quarters and received a supper that consisted of a single cup of coffee and a hearty sandwich. Most of the men proceeded to sleep by the time the ships set sail at 6 p.m. The flotilla steamed down the Hudson River and finally fulfilled the wishes of the spirited yet naïve patriots.[106]

The day after the 18th departed Albany, two members labeled as deserters from the regiment were caught and arrested in the city. One of them was Albany native Private Edward Ryan of Company I, who was caught and arrested while he attempted to buy some eggs for breakfast. Both deserters were immediately sent off to be reunited with the regiment where they kept their place in line and served honorably.[107]

3

To the War Front
June 19, 1861–July 12, 1861

"Both officers and men are, to use a common phrase, spilling for a fight."—*Private Edward M. Tilley, Company K, July 2, 1861*

Displays of Praise

The advance towards the seat of war had finally begun and for most this adventurous journey drew them out of their state boundary for the first time. Still feeling scorned by the 16th New York, Company K congratulated themselves for having left the state before them. The flotilla slowly churned through the Hudson waters until the steamer stalled on a sandbar close to midnight near Castleton, which held them up for nearly five hours until the tide rose. When the men awoke the following morning, they were surprised and disappointed to learn their steamer was only located some ten miles above Poughkeepsie. With the coming of daylight, men congregated on the upper decks of the ship to gain the best vantage of their voyage. As they sailed passed the edges of Poughkeepsie, Newburgh, Yonkers, Rondout, and other smaller villages along the way, they were cheered by handkerchief waiving citizens gathered along the shores and banks. Celebratory cannons saluted with blasts and church bells rang over the water. The vessels eventually coasted beyond state lines and reached Jersey City, New Jersey, shortly after noon on June 19.[1]

As they shuffled off the steamer and onto the Jersey City pier near 1 p.m. they first turned in their state issued blankets in exchange for new ones, but it was not an even swap as the newer blankets had not yet arrived. Each man then received three days rations though.[2]

More importantly to the men, they had their rifles waiting for them at the pier. Crates of encased muskets were hoisted from the hold of the steamer and cracked open for distribution. The men received their rifles by company as they disembarked and they were pleased to find they were the British 1853 Enfield Rifle-Musket. These were slightly lighter and more accurate than the common rifled Springfields or clunky smoothbore muskets still in circulation at the time. The ones they pulled from the crates and given to the men were not of a uniformed color, but they were brand new. They were recent arrivals from England, procured from a government business deal by the famous "Pathfinder" John C. Frémont, who purchased 10,000 Enfields that were slated to be bought by the Pope to arm the Papal Army. The men benefited from the relationship that Colonel Jackson had with Governor Morgan after he had procured them and promised his former inspector general that his regiment would be the first to receive them. Several individuals felt compelled to boast that they were the first to be equipped with Enfields. In fact, out of the first forty-six New York regiments organized in the first three months of the war, the 18th and the 3rd New York were the only two to be equipped with Enfields. It's all too fitting that Jackson's cousin, Frederick Townsend, colonel of the 3rd New York, had also served as a staff member for Morgan. The 18th took up a nickname that made sense—New York State Rifles—but the name was seldom used.[3]

From Jersey City, the newly armed men were joined by civilian volunteers that helped pack them and their baggage into a twenty-four car train on the Camden & Amboy rail by 5 p.m. Some members of Company G took notice of a wooden barrel that was rolled into their car that had its top knocked in. They thought and wished that it would be full of soda crackers, but inside was hardtack to be issued by the commissary sergeant. The hardened squares of bland dough was somewhat of a novelty, but as Private Joseph C. Jones of Company G recalled his first taste from this initial issue, "well, one bite was sufficient. We weren't hungry." Several more barrels were rolled aboard and traveled with the men. Within time, this bounty of bottomless hardtack "would have been worth their weight in gold," but as Jones later recalled, "we had not got to that yet."[4]

The 14th New York had passed through Jersey City moments before the 18th and were cheered wildly by the townspeople. The 14th dropped hints to the crowd to stay on hand and bid the 18th a similar farewell. Citizens swarmed the regiment while they boarded the train and tossed bouquets that were caught by overjoyed soldiers. Private Edward M. Tilley—the newly appointed regimental clerk—received two bouquets, one of which had a note affixed to it with the following message:

> Remember them that are in bonds, as bound with them. Don't send back fugitive slaves, but help them to freedom. God speed the right, give us the victory, help you to your duty, nobly and well, and bring you safely to your home and friends, when this great contest is over.
> Yours, for the right,
> Mary Hathway.[5]

Private Tilley was not too optimistic on the prospect that fugitive slaves would find respite from the 18th. His assumptions were based on Colonel Jackson's open opinion on the issue when he said that the colonel was "not the man who desires the occupation of slave catching, and I think it will be very few of the poor darkies whom he will send back into slavery."[6]

The trains pulled away from Jersey City around 6 p.m., but the well-wishing from grateful citizens was far from finished. Similar merry events continued along their journey through New Jersey along the tracks to Philadelphia. Each momentary stop at various stations brought out people eager to encourage the volunteers. They were surprised each time, some speechless, but Private Tilley was able to gather his thoughts about their receptions:

> At Jersey City the young ladies were very generous with their kisses, of which privilege of volunteers availed themselves quite extensively. At Newark, Elizabethtown, and New Brunswick, the ladies turned out en masse to greet, and bid us "God speed" on our way. Bouquets with notes, and in some cases strawberries, pincushions... were distributed among the men, and when we left they would cluster around the car windows to shake hands, and wish us a safe return home again. Little children were raised by older hands to the car windows to kiss the men, and in one case, I saw two men lift up a cripple to shake hands, he wishing to do his share towards encouraging us.[7]

Their treatment as heroes had lasting effects, and Private Joseph C. Jones later recounted his perspective of the train ride of praise:

> All the way through Jersey it was a perfect ovation. Every station we stopped at the people vied with each other to cheer us on our way. We were showered with bouquets of flowers ... flags ... the air fairly blossomed with cakes, pies, fired chicken, lemonade, cigars. One man came lugging in a jug of brandy. He wanted to keep the boys spirits up by pouring spirits down, I suppose.[8]

After a few hours on the trains, the 18th arrived to South Amboy, New Jersey, at two o'clock in the morning of June 20. Nearly an hour later they pulled into Philadelphia. Through a slight rain, the regiment switched rails and marched to the Broad and Prime Street depot and had to wait nearly an hour for their large quantity of baggage to be switched onto their next train bound for Baltimore.[9]

After two days of travel with hardly an opportunity for good sleep, the fatigued men had similarly forgotten the last adequate meal they took. Luckily for them, Philadelphia welcomed the regiment with the surprise of a considerably well prepared breakfast at a nearby cooper shop—free of charge. The Union Volunteer Refreshment Saloon, along with its friendly rival Cooper Shop Refreshment Saloon, both popped up a month before by a handful of charitable men and women of South Philadelphia who had grown sympathetic to the thousands of hungry troops that swarmed the depot while they waited for transportation south. Their objective was simply to treat any passing Union soldier a free meal fit for a king at no expense. The 18th shuffled through the darkened streets near the depot and entered the gas-lit chambers of the Union Volunteer Refreshment Saloon. They first cycled through a wash room and then entered a large extending hall where they seated themselves behind two long stretched tables, 150 feet in length that filled the long corridor, and continues enough to feed about 500 men at a time. The volunteers of the saloon took a head count of 813 men belonging

Philadelphia lithographer James Fuller Queen created this wartime print of the exterior of the Union Volunteer Refreshment Saloon, located on the southwest corner of Washington Avenue and Swanson Street, in Philadelphia (The Library Company of Philadelphia).

Another Queen lithograph shows the interior of the Union Volunteer Refreshment Saloon. The 18th New York was treated to a generous free breakfast here on June 20, 1861, for all 813 men, at 4 a.m. (The Library Company of Philadelphia).

to the 18th, and even at 4 a.m., they had no problem to fill each man's stomach. The feast consisted of bread, butter, cold boiled ham, herring, pork and beans, cheese, coffee, and milk which was all readily available and served to the soldiers by waiters who encouraged the men to eat as much as they could. The food was a delightful change of pace against the regular rations of salt pork and bread that they were supplied with since their departure from Albany. It was an unforgettable treat to all who passed through and the men would be forever grateful. Private Samuel Hodgkins of Company K wrote decades later about its lasting impact:

> A fine supper was served to the entire regiment, a bunch of tired, hungry, appreciative men, who enjoyed it immensely. These wealthy society women performed this kind of service for every regiment passing through Philadelphia all during the war, a service greatly appreciated by men so far from home, many of them entering a large city for the first time in their life.[10]

Ammunition was also supplied to the regiment while in Philadelphia, but was not issued to the individual yet. Private Tilley was put in charge by Colonel Jackson to supervise the ammunition car that contained 25,000 cartridges and 40,000 percussion caps.[11]

After their breakfast, the men waited outside in a light rain for two or three hours with nothing to do. The regiment eventually embarked on their new train at about 7:30 a.m. and continued their journey south towards clearer skies. As they passed by Wilmington, Delaware, citizens and even some of the railroad mechanics lined their passage and continued the displays of praise. As the land leveled and the evenness of the crops drew their attention, some men caught their first glimpses of slaves hoeing half-grown corn and hay. Sightings of national flags and cheerful townsfolk continued to be spotted during their brief trek through Delaware. The route eventually crossed into the border state of Maryland, and at about 1 p.m., they passed their first of many guard squads stationed at Havre de Grace. The cars of the train crossed the river here on a large ferry boat so massive that it could shift twenty-one cars at once.[12]

Through Baltimore

As they neared a mid-afternoon arrival in Baltimore for another rail line switch, some of the men prepared themselves that their reception would not be so warm. Just two months before, Baltimore was the scene of a violent protest that caused some of the earliest casualties of the war. The 6th Massachusetts Militia were similarly changing trains when rioters clashed with the Bay State men that escalated into rifle exchanges which left dozens of dead and dying, both soldiers and citizens alike.[13]

Every regiment that marched through the shifty city afterwards did so at extreme caution. Regiments slipped through Baltimore unmolested but did so under the same angered gazes from protestors that tested each man's nerves. The 18th were well informed by the gossip and progress of the war and puffed their chest at their first obstacle. They scoffed at the potential animosity they could be encountered with and liberally spread the watchword, "Through Baltimore!" For added assurance, Colonel Jackson ordered that ammunition for the individual soldier to be finally dispensed as a precautionary measure shortly before they arrived, but his order was explicit, as he only allowed ten designated men in each company to load their rifles before everyone exited the railcars.[14]

With the rampant rumors, the men had fantasized a city turned upside-down. As their train pulled into Baltimore at 4 p.m., their expectations were changed. They were greeted with the sight of two immense Union flags at the depot, which squashed fears that their coming was to be unwelcomed. Next to the depot was a large machine shop factory that emptied with cheering mechanics. They were quickly joined by a gaggle of women that cheered in support and vigorously waved their handkerchiefs.[15]

After their locomotive crawled to a halt, the New Yorkers poured out of the cars and assembled themselves in a formation for their brief march to the Camden Station that would take them to Washington. Shouts of hurrahs continued to be echoed by the mechanics, and as soon as the regiment stepped off the cars they were quickly surrounded by a cordon of local police who were brought in to ensure the regiment passed through the city without incident. Based on their inability to prevent the riot two months before, the officers of the 18th were timid to rely on the police. The companies quickly fell into columns of four deep next to the cars and filled the street from curb to curb. The drum and fife corps—about twenty strong—assembled to lead the regiment. On Colonel Jackson's order, everyone affixed their glistening bayonets to their new rifles for the first time. Before the regiment advanced, Colonel Jackson took a moment and gave a short impromptu message and said, "No matter boys, what they say, but if any violence is used—defend yourselves." The men responded with a resounding cheer. Several men made brash comments that they actually hoped that they would be challenged so they could finally use their brand new rifles.[16]

The path of the regiment was lined by a gauntlet of citizens that gathered along both sides of the street. The earlier cheerful welcome by the locals had grown to an eerie hush. The color guard unfurled their flags and the bugle signaled the regiment forward. The walls of people glared with suspicious gazes, yet remained eerily silent. One Northern New Yorker was surprised to see such a large proportion of the crowd to be "colored people, of many varied shades of appearances." Occasionally, a supportive cheer popped through the silent onlookers, but the regiment remained stone-faced. Supporters were mostly found to be adolescents who were ignorant to the attitudes of their elders. Sergeant John S. King of Company D mentioned that "women in some houses waved us a God speed, but most of the people were silent." The regiment kept their lips sealed and let the rhythm of their footsteps resound like a heartbeat. The band kept quiet which impelled one Baltimore man to yell out to the colonel to ask where his music was at. Never short of words, Jackson promptly retorted, "in the boys' cartridge boxes."[17]

"If looks counted," Private Joseph C. Jones stated, "they had us paralyzed." Private Tilley concurred and poetically described the facial expressions of the citizens to be, "many a contemptuous sneer, scowling visage or Plug-Ugly bravado declared unmistakably the secession devil within, kept in check only by the bristling steel and the fear of leaden hail." As they continued their intimidating march to the depot, an unseen bystander threw a stone at the drum corps. Drummer Thomas Riquer of Company K instantly dodged the stone that would have otherwise pegged him in the head. Luckily, this was an isolated incident and the march was void of overt danger, but the episode gave the men something to write about back home to their interested friends and families.[18]

Having walked nearly two miles, nerves settled when the men reached the Camden depot. They boarded their train which would be their last shortly after 4 p.m. Less than an hour later the cars pushed out down the tracks and left Baltimore. Just eight miles out of the city, the train was halted and delayed for nearly an hour at the Relay House, a junction of the Baltimore and Ohio Railroad and the line of tracks that led to Washington. The 18th's train eventually traveled over a bridge that had recently been rebuilt after secessionist arsonists set it ablaze. Since that incident, the new bridge was under the occupation of a company of Northern soldiers. The men peered out of the windows and doors of the cars and began to see more signs of a nation at war with itself. The copious amounts of national flags had significantly lessened. Pickets were posted throughout the rail line and at every bridge, and the 18th exchanged cheers and hand waves as they passed by their posts and encampments. Signs of slavery also increased the closer they got to the nation's capital and became chiseled into the memory banks of those who had never been exposed to the peculiar institution.[19]

Washington

The gears of the train screeched loudly as its momentum rolled to a halt in downtown Washington shortly after 10 p.m. on June 20. After two days of solid travel, the routine of train hopping had come to an end. The men disembarked the cars, assembled into a formation, and shuffled through the dark streets towards Capitol Hill. The night was warm, but the darkness hid Washington's spectacle for the majority who had only known second-hand accounts of the city's splendor. Closing their eyes was on the forefront of their minds as the persistent travel hardly allowed for suitable sleep. The regiment marched to the upper part of the city to reach Capitol Hill and sought refuge near the Capitol Building in a large unoccupied brick structure known as Woodward's building, near the corner of 11th Street and Pennsylvania Avenue. The men were still without tents, blankets, and adequate supplies to form a camp outside, but the inconvenience bothered little on account of their fatigue. They filtered into Woodward's building and collapsed upon tables, benches, and anything else available, but most settled for the floor. Wherever they could find room, the men wasted no time to fall asleep. Their exhaustion outweighed the fact that supper never happened. Sergeant John S. King chalked up the night to be "the toughest one we have experienced since we volunteered." Enjoying the perks of holding a commission, the staff officers of the 18th spent the night quartered at Clay's Hotel.[20]

First call started the next morning at 5 a.m., and the drum rolls barely jerked awake the deep sleeping New Yorkers. As the morning sun rose over the unfinished dome of the Capitol on June 21, the soldiers ventured out of the makeshift billet and gathered in the streets before it. From the vantage of Capitol Hill, the soldiers were able to survey the lively landscape and feel the pulse of the nation. The heat was also there, because by 7 a.m. the temperature had already registered seventy-five degrees, and the afternoon bumped up by twenty. The annoyances of flies prevalent among the soldiers earned the moniker of "secession flies" and were alleged by Private Tilley to "stick like Spaulding's Glue."[21]

Colonel Jackson and his staff had a lot of logistics to hash out in Washington, most importantly how to acquire equipment, provisions, and where to set up an encampment. While these questions waited to be answered, the men were granted permission after breakfast to venture out and take in the sights of the city. Washington was still regarded as an unrefined city, a mini-metropolis of a few widely scattered government buildings, strewn with statues of war heroes and forefathers. The unfinished obelisk of the Washington Monument in a way represented a nation that was truly a work in progress. Companies split into small parties and fanned out in different directions along Washington's wide avenues and cross streets. Some conquered the endless staircase of the Capitol and obtained a breathtaking view of the city, Arlington Heights, Alexandria, and the numerous camps strewn in every direction. Amid construction of its iconic cast-iron dome, men entered the Senate Chamber and Hall of Representatives. The Capitol corridors were sprinkled with statues and painted artworks that were mentioned by First Sergeant Robert A. Malone of Company D to be "beyond description." Down at the Navy Yard men were able to see the fitting of a vessel bound for the war front. Many probing minds were satisfied with the inspection of "curiosities and scientific articles" housed at the Patent Office at Seventh and F Streets. Others headed straight to the nucleus of power and drifted through the public rooms and hallways of the White House. Those who perused with wide-eyed interest of its large mirrors and flowered carpets actually had the pleasure to speak and shake hands with President Lincoln and Secretary Seward, both of which gave words of encouragement for what would soon be asked of them.[22]

Camp Harris

Colonel Jackson spent this time with General Joseph K. F. Mansfield, commander of the troops in Washington, who assigned him a place of real estate for his regiment north of the city. When the expected orders were finalized and shared with company officers later that evening, the regiment reassembled at the Capitol Building at seven o'clock and prepared for the march to their encampment. They left half an hour after sunset and marched in columns down Pennsylvania Avenue. They turned north on 14th Street and continued straight on this path to Meridian Hill, opposite Columbia College [near the present-day Columbia Heights Metro Station]. This is where the regiment halted their march as night set in after nearly four miles. They were immediately issued tents of the common "A" pattern and their camp began to take form. Some men commenced to set them up, but as late as it was most decided to just sleep on the ground and wait until the morning light could aid in their task.[23]

The 18th's camp was established on a dry flat tract of land in the middle of a greater open field that encompassed nearly twenty acres. Its openness made it ideal for drill purposes, but with one tree meant the ground was void of any shade for the men. They named their new settlement, Camp Harris in honor of Senator Ira Harris from Albany.[24]

Their first full day at Camp Harris—June 22—allowed the men plenty of time to adjust and settle in. Their first task was the assembly of the tents if they had not done so the night before. On average, each company received nineteen tents, two of which went to the commissioned officers, one for the sergeants, and fifteen tents assigned to the corporals and privates. About four to five men were assigned to a single tent, so they made them as comfortable as possible.[25]

Each company cook received a tent to themselves, although the position was by then still unassigned, but

Capt. Peter Hogan (center, behind table) and two officers (presumably also from Company H) enjoy a catered meal at Camp Harris in Washington, July 1861. Only Hogan is identified, but author believes the officers are 2nd Lt. William E. Carmichael (left) and 1st Lt. Theodore C. Rogers (courtesy Barb Samans).

interested applicants within each organization quickly stepped up to the job. Cooks began to prepare meals for the men in their sheet-iron kettles for the first time. Their first meal at camp was breakfast that consisted of bacon, bread, and coffee. Some men still showed reservations to forge a liking of coffee without milk, but the drink was the most important staple for a soldier. The menu for their afternoon meal brought forth pork, bread, and salt pork soup. Evening supper was just a rehash of breakfast. Rice and fresh beef would eventually be cycled into the menu. Tables were gone for the common soldier who had to quickly acclimate themselves to take their meals on the ground. Most of them seemed quite optimistic and complained very little as they acquainted themselves with a soldier's life. Private Hodgkins spoke of his own happiness of their camp that can speak for the majority:

> But every one was happy and was doing his best to have a good time and make the best of everything, so all went as merry as a marriage bell. I thought of the eleven dollars a month, beds and food furnished, and all room we wanted for a tent, and who wouldn't be a soldier under such favorable conditions.[26]

Camp Drills

The government issued meals gave relief to those who feared food from locals could be poisoned. Upon their arrival to Washington, the officers issued warnings to their men not to accept any food from citizens that may be offered to them. Captain Stephen Truax said that during their first day at Camp Harris, "a couple of secessionists were detected in an endeavor to poison the well for which ours and Col. McQuade's [14th New York] regiment procured water." Truax also mentioned that four men from a nearby Maine regiment were poisoned after they consumed pies that contained pulverized glass. The men were in a peculiar atmosphere of citizens that were at the fault line of the country's division and they had to resist the temptations of homemade goods.[27]

During their first evening in camp, a lot of the men gathered to watch the neighboring 14th New York perform a well drilled dress parade. They had taken up the tract of land to the left of the 18th, on the opposite side of the road amongst a patch of woods. Later that night, Colonel Jackson took his opportunity to run the 18th through a dress parade, and drilled them under the light of the moon.[28]

Around 1 a.m. on June 23, the calm camp was ruptured by the sound of four guns being fired, followed by a long roll of a drum from the 14th New York camp. Preached but not practiced, the drum roll was an alarm used to signal an attack. This came as a complete surprise to them. Immediately, half-asleep men from every regiment within earshot shuffled awake in their tents and hastily grabbed their gear in the dark. "Fall out! Fall out men! For God's sake fall out, the enemy is upon you!" screamed both Lieutenant Colonel Young and Sergeant Major Thomas M. Holden as they passed the company streets. The rows of tents filled with scrambling men in all sorts of dress and equipment. The companies fused together quickly in the darkness and in an unimpressive fifteen minutes, the 18th was formed.[29]

"To arms, to arms, they come!" shouted the officers. Acting accordingly with the alarm, the surrounding regimental camps throughout Meridian Hill also came alive. A neighboring New York regiment deployed as skirmishers while an artillery battery rolled out near a crossing looking over the Potomac River. Wide-eyed men became fueled by adrenaline. War had come, or so they thought. Sergeant George Blake of Company H took a moment to study how his peers looked during this frantic episode:

> The men look rather peculiar at first some had left their coats other their caps pants belts & even their guns in their tents, they were so excited they hardly knew what they were about, that is as true of the Officers as of the men. I mean the Commissioned ones.[30]

The men stood firm for nearly an hour until Colonel Jackson instructed everyone to return to their tents. Those fully dressed were told to remain so, and those missing articles grabbed what they forgot. Company B was pulled aside and detailed for picket duty. Sporadic fire, sometimes with intensity, was heard throughout the neighboring camps which put everyone on edge, and false rumors of secessionists infiltrating nearby camps ran wild.[31]

Further orders never came down and minds began to wonder. After several hours passed and daylight crept in, the regiment's readiness was put to rest when Colonel Jackson addressed them with news that the alarm was a false one. Jackson confirmed to them that the drill was an exercise "to see how rapidly they could fall out." The naïve men actually felt disappointed that they were not under attack, having convinced themselves that they were ready and willing to engage their foe, but instead were instructed to return to their quarters.[32]

Lessons were learned during the early morning exercise and Colonel Jackson regrouped his thoughts and outlined room for improvements. He addressed the men later that in the day during their evening dress parade and read orders to them that centered on the importance that everyone "must hold ourselves in readyness to march at any moment." Knapsacks were to be packed and buckled and "ready to put on so that if orders should come we could form in line of battle in less than 10 minutes & be ready to march." Jackson then formed the regiment in a square and finished the drill with a run through of the manual of arms. Being that it was Sunday, at the conclusion of the drill Chaplain Farr led the men in prayer, and together everyone sang a hymn and recited the benediction.[33]

Three nights later, the same middle of the night drill took place, but this time the 18th shaved their formation time down to nearly five minutes. Jackson's words had worked. Private Tilley took notice of the anxious attitudes of the regiment and mentioned:

> Both officers and men are, to use a common phrase, spilling for a fight, and if the enemy will give us but half an opportunity there will be a good square American fight, and the stars and stripes will not be lowered while a son of New York remains to give them to the breeze.[34]

Aid Problems for Families

Complaints from a few members of Company K surfaced after questions rose about their initial terms of enlistment. Apparently, a number of soldiers in the company enlisted under a misunderstanding or interpreted false representations concerning bounties that were to be earned upon enlistment instead of at the end of their service. Several from the company also grumbled that their families were not being cared for back home. Forty-three-year-old Private Peter Sheehan enlisted at Malone in May, and did so after he shaved eleven years off of his age. He volunteered on the promise that Ogdensburg would provide care for his wife and daughter in his absence. Sheehan's wife, however, was denied at Ogdensburg and was told that the nearby town of Malone would help her, but she was turned away there too. Sheehan did not stand for this, so he began a successful battle for a discharge.[35]

Another misinformed soldier from the same company had a similar but larger issue at hand. When Private Thomas H. Buckley traveled from his home in Burlington, Vermont, to enlist in the company, he was promised that his wife and two children would be cared for while he was gone. Buckley's family relocated to Ogdensburg but were similarly refused aid from the town. With no alternative, his wife took her children and traveled to Albany and attached herself to her husband's company. When the regiment left for Washington, Buckley's family similarly traveled south and arrived at Camp Harris on June 26. No one knew what to do with Private Buckley and his family since they had no friends, having emigrated from England two years prior. To make matters worse, his eighteen-month-old daughter contracted consumption during her mother's fruitless journey and was unlikely to recover. Colonel Jackson took pity upon Private Buckley and wrote to General Mansfield, commander of the troops in Washington, and had him discharged.[36]

Negligence with Rifles and the Death of Gale

Like all of the inexperienced regiments were at the time, several mistakes and accidents occurred throughout the ranks. Hydration was always important, but some men either simply forgot to drink, or consumed too much water and suffered pains. Weapons remained the culprit of most accidents, which put the citizens of Washington in constant fear of the volunteers. Men fired their rifles indiscriminately in any direction they pleased. Target practices were set up at random throughout the city limits of Washington without much thought as to where bullets fell. Sergeant John S. King recalled a time when he stepped out of camp and had "a bullet sing pretty close to my ear" when it passed his head by about a foot before it lodged in the dirt bank next to him, "making the dirt fly." He assumed a company was nearby in the middle of a target shoot drill.[37]

Former militiamen and hunters were comfortable with muskets, but revolvers were somewhat of an oddity that many had little to no experience with. Some of these negligent early volunteers viewed small arms as playful toys, dropped them often, and even used them to kill flies when they fired just the caps. As expected, many casualties were created from these acts of carelessness.[38]

Colonel Jackson tried to stifle the problem when he mandated an order near the end of June that forbade his men to independently discharge a firearm or cap. Just days later, this order was directly violated which claimed the life of the first soldier of the regiment. On June 28, around 8:30 a.m., nineteen-year-old Private Alonzo Richardson of Company F was in his tent at Camp Harris when he noticed a spider had crawled up the side of his tent. He grabbed what he thought to be his unloaded rifle from a stack in his tent and decided to snap a percussion cap to stun or kill the spider. Turns out, the one he grabbed belonged to his tent mate who had just returned from guard duty and had left the rifle loaded and placed amongst the stack. Richardson pulled the trigger and was stunned when the rifle fired which left a hole through his canvas tent. The lead ball passed through Richardson's tent and into an adjacent one which was occupied by Private John H. Gale of Company A. Gale had felt sick earlier that morning and was on bed rest in his tent when the unexpected bullet tore clean through the canteen he wore and into his right arm. It had enough velocity to pass into his chest down near his sixth rib where it stopped within a half inch from the surface of his left side, just below his ribcage. Richardson instantly sank in disbelief, completely overtaken by sorrow for what he did. Richardson had directly violated Colonel Jackson's recent order designed to prevent such accidents and was immediately placed under arrest. Private Gale, a twenty-eight-year-old man with a wife and two children he supported back in Utica, struggled for his life and lingered for hours in painful agony, but his wound was mortal. Gale died that evening at 4 p.m. His comrades of Company A gave him a soldier's funeral and buried him in Washington. With the incident chalked up as a regrettable mistake, Richardson eventually returned to the line without any repercussions.[39]

Camp Life and Drill Continue

Company and regimental drill occupied most of the men's time. Sergeant John S. King wrote on June 28 that "we drill early and late, and are getting quite proficient in the use of arms." The skirmish drill tactic was also rehearsed countless times. Their first trial with target shooting with their Enfields began which turned into a routine. After every evening dress parade held in the field around their camp, the chaplain ran through religious exercises of prayers, sermons, and songs. The 18th was very lucky with their choice of grounds in which they encamped, as others around them were lodged in the woods and found it much harder to drill. Nearly every day, the men bathed in the nearby Rock Creek which also served as a prime location to wash clothes.[40]

The daily grind at Camp Harris was manageable and embodied the quintessential camp setting. Quartermaster William V. Horsfall, referred by the men as "a tip-top fellow," supplied the food the men ate. Others regarded Horsfall more cynically, like when First Sergeant Malone called the quartermaster, "a very bad manager, or else he intends making enough out of us to keep him the rest of his days." Malone mentioned their "provisions are very bad and also scarce, hardly sufficient to keep us alive." Their "grub" consisted of a sliver of hardened salt pork or salt beef—which was mostly all fatty portions—along with a small piece of bread and coffee for breakfast, yet bread failed to appear at one or two meals. Dinner was comprised of beef or bean soup, bread, and water. A later supper consisted of bread, beef, and coffee, but sometimes the menu varied by the addition of rice or potatoes, if available. They received this daily staple in stride at Camp Harris and took all they were allowed upon their shiny tin plates. A few times the food ration was unexpectedly halted which left coffee as the only vittles available for days on end. One whole weekend saw bread replaced with ten small crackers for each man. The grumbling men yearned for some of the "contraband goods" that would be more accessible once they were in Virginia. Soldiers spent what little income they had on food from vendors and sutlers until that ran out, but they expected to be paid soon and planned on continuing their purchases. Malone remained quite the optimist:

> We do not blame the Government, for we think it is the fault of the Commissary Department, and that they are plundering and enriching themselves on those who patriotically leave their families and homes to respond to their Country's call for protection. They are still devoted to their Country, and will never desert their glorious flag; but still it dampens their ardor and their honest manliness to think that they should be treated worse than they would treat a dog, by these greedy pilferers who have the charge of their provision.[41]

The June heat in Washington was compared by some men to be similar to sultry summers accustomed to in New York. The summer days bore stifling afternoons that often reached or surpassed the mid-nineties. One overheated soldier collapsed while on guard duty, and his life was saved with prompt medical attention. The homemade havelocks adorned on their caps continued to be field tested to see if they could shield the sun's power to prevent sunstroke. Sergeant King made a mention of them in a letter to the Ladies Association of Middletown who gifted them and exclaimed that the havelocks had prevented men to be overpowered by the sun, and "any person who does not believe it, come down and drill four or five hours in a scorching sun." Others in the regiment hummed a different tune, and even Colonel Jackson did not buy into their effectiveness. They were deemed useless, acting more like hoods that trapped the heat, and Jackson limited their appearance. In short time, the garment disappeared completely.[42]

The open plains that surrounded Camp Harris did not go unoccupied long after the 18th's arrival. They were quickly settled by more than a dozen newly arrived regiments. Within ten days of the establishment of Camp Harris, these new regiments moved within the lot and encircled the regiment which gave the illusion that everyone was part of one large encampment. Sergeant King mentioned that the tents from the camps that surrounded them could be seen to "stretch out as far as you can see." Private Thomas W. Nutting of Company D wrote in awe of the canvas cities and said that they embodied "much more of a warlike appearance than anything I have yet seen."[43]

Sundays were not a day of rest unless bad weather permitted it so. They had a lot to learn and perfect, which left little time for leisure. On June 30, a regimental inspection of the men's weapons and equipment was all that was performed that day. A gentle rain commenced after the inspection which sent the soldiers to retreat to the protections of their canvas shelters for the remainder of the day. The precipitation also helped greatly lower the temperature for a change.[44]

The overall health at Camp Harris was good, but the first of many shared sicknesses ran through the tents near the end of June. Several men in the regiment shared similar symptoms of common diarrhea and were treated accordingly. Sickness was an excusable pass out of drill, but Lieutenant Colonel Young preyed on those who played "old soldier" in order to get out of drill. The game was easy for Young who could immediately pick out those that shammed "on account of their awkward maneuvering," and set them aside "for separate drill during the hours the others are at rest or off duty."[45]

Men from the color guard cut and erected a wooden flag pole on July 1 that waived the regiment's national flag. The pole was tall and dominated over Camp Harris. The patriotic exercise coincided with a visit from the camp's namesake, Senator Ira Harris. Unfortunately, the ceremonial flag raising and Harris' visit was cut short on account of foul weather. During the day a thunderstorm mixed with heavy rain and winds swept above the camps on Meridian Hill. Harris made a promise he would return to the regiment the following day. During the deluge, men huddled inside shaky tents and hoped their stakes would hold their corners down from the uprooting winds. Once dry, Private Tilley recorded the event:

> Although myself and comrade had our hands full to hold up our own tent, yet we could but help laughing at the scene spread before us. While some were using their utmost exertions to keep their tents from being blown down, others, for the first time in their life, perhaps, were digging trenches around to keep the water from running in. Quite a number of our regiment slept on damp beds that night, but bore it all without grumbling, making up our minds to take such events as part of a soldier's life. We were much more fortunate than some of the neighboring encampments, which being in lower ground, and in the woods, were overflowed to quite a depth, and were obliged to empty their tents the next day to get them dry. We have now been in camp ten days, long enough to get somewhat used to its peculiarities, and in most cases I think the boys like it well.[46]

July 4th Review of New York Troops

As the eighty-fifth anniversary of the birth of American Independence neared, Major General Charles Sandford—commander of the New York troops in the District—called for a Grand Review of all the state's troops currently encamped around Washington. President Lincoln, General Winfield Scott, and their staff were the honored guests to oversee the passing troops in Washington's first parade of troops. The day before the march, everyone in the 18th pulled together and worked tediously all day to prepare. Uniforms were brushed clean, bayonets and swords were polished, and all leathers were burnished to a shine.[47]

The dawn of July 4 started with the bugle tune of "Reveille" that woke Camp Harris to life at 4:30 a.m. As the sun began to illuminate Meridian Hill, the songs of "Hail Columbia" and "The Star-Spangled Banner" bellowed from neighboring camps. Several brass bands within ear-shot of the 18th began to play off each other which filled the air with the most patriotic atmosphere a soldier could wake to. At day-break, national salutes were fired to herald the commemoration of the birth of America.[48]

The 18th left their camp at 6:30 a.m. and marched to 16th Street opposite the White House and waited for all the Excelsior State's regiments to take their place. Regiments fell into sequential order in the early morning hours and were divided into four special brigades. The 18th became the leading regiment for the second brigade and formed their line at 7:30 a.m. near Lafayette Square. The regiment waited for over thirty minutes and surveyed the scene of mass troop movements finding their starting positions. In the distance, the striking statue at Lafayette Square that depicted General Andrew Jackson saddled atop a rearing horse seemed to jump out above the sea of troops and their flags, with the White House in its backdrop. Once the order of march was organized, twenty-three New York regiments—more than 20,000 men—stepped off and launched the Grand Review at 8 a.m. Marching around Lafayette Square, the unison boots of the 18th took their turn down Pennsylvania Avenue. As they neared the White House the cheerful crowds of people in attendance swarmed. Above their heads, a raised platform erected on the sidewalk in front of the White House soon came into view. Beautiful silk flags and bunting draped around the canopied suite where President Lincoln, General Scott, and several members of the Cabinet and military stood and viewed the passing soldiers. Sergeants called out the cadence to keep their men in step. As the 18th marched in column and passed the platform of the honored guests, officers and sergeants rendered their salutes and received them in ceremonial fashion. First Sergeant Malone mentioned that "the streets were rather crowded just there, but in other parts of the city there were not so many people as we expected to see." The 18th continued their march down Pennsylvania Avenue and through several other city streets before they eventually arrived back at Camp Harris. In all the day's festivities, the men had marched about twelve miles under an unforgiving summer sun, trapped in wool suits. The day seemed cooler than others due to a welcoming breeze, but the respite was minimal and the men were exhausted by the time they arrived back at camp. Malone mentioned another added pain felt by the men was the refusal of canteens. He stated they "were not allowed to taste a drop of water all the way." One could not simply drink freely from their canteens while on the march unless ordered to do so. Lessons were being learned by all.[49]

The festive mood was still in full swing throughout Meridian Hill which stretched on into the evening. Several camps gathered around huge bonfires and provided the lyrics to hymns sung over the chords of nearby bands. The men of the 18th even put on a display of fireworks within their camp. July 4 was a day of jubilee in Washington, and the celebrations were undoubtedly heard across the Potomac to the ears of the looming Confederacy.[50]

For some, the holiday spent away from home jerked memories of hometown celebrations, which could lead to feelings of homesickness. Sergeant George Blake wrote home to his cousin with multiple reasons for this emotion:

> The 1st & greatest one is my being away from home 2d my employment being different & 3d traveling 4th living in tents 5th my companions, O Dear, I find the more reason I write the more come, so I will quit here & you can see that they are all caused by my not being at home "Home, Home Sweet sweet Home." I do not wish you to think from the above that I am sorry that I am here far from it. I enlisted to defend the rights of our government & I feel as willing now as then & even more so to meet the enemy on the field & show them & the world what the government can & will do when their rights are tampered with.[51]

Promotions and Discharges

A few more days passed and the regiment neared closer to the inevitable movement into Virginia. Colonel Jackson shared with the regiment that he had talked with the president on July 4 and could pass news that they should likely head out in less than a week. Before the advance, some companies needed to be restructured after three first sergeant positions became vacant. When the regimental adjutant, First Lieutenant John H. Russell, read aloud orders during dress parade on July 8 to the regiment that they were to move the following day, First Sergeant John T. Morgan, Company I, quickly made his escape and deserted. Company B's First Sergeant James Barron was reduced in rank and his position filled by Sergeant William B. Purdy. Barron would later desert from the regiment in August. Company K's First Sergeant Richard "Dick" Montieth, was replaced by Sergeant Freeman F. Huntington. With each promotion, other vacancies opened and were filled by appointments from their company commanders. The regiment lost four men to desertion while at Camp Harris, and another soldier hospitalized back in New York decided to disappear.[52]

Six more soldiers were also discharged for disabilities, mostly attributed to illnesses that rendered them unfit for military duty. The health of Private John Gowan of Company K quickly sank when he contracted a cold that settled in his lungs. The forty-one-year-old store keeper from Scotland was sound and healthy at enlistment, but with a few weeks of camp life exposure, pneumonia got the best of him. He was discharged on July 8 and returned to his home in Crysler, Ontario, Canada, to his wife and three children, but he brought his disease with him. He dealt with severe coughing and fluid in his lungs for several months until he died from the disease on January 19, 1862. Despite his illness being connected to his service, Gowan's death was never included in the summary of regimental casualties because he was already medically discharged and off the books.[53]

Cleanliness of Camp

During the three weeks that the 18th spent at Camp Harris, Colonel Jackson was visited by his father who wanted to spend some time with his son. Being the inquisitive professor that defined him at Union College, Isaac Jackson took up an interest in sanitation issues the army was faced with. He wrote an op-ed that appeared in the newspapers which called attention to matters that dutiful soldiers, such as his son, were "influenced by an esprit de corps which almost exclusively deters them from making statements that may be supposed dishonorable to their commands." With no repercussions to use unabashed words, Isaac started a dialogue that volunteers needed greater care, materials, and provisions in order to preserve their spirit and promote better health.[54]

Isaac Jackson was not the only forward thinker regarding the health and camp conditions of the volunteers. In fact, the wheels were already in motion of a civilian organization that came to be known as the United States Sanitary Commission, which quickly received the official endorsement by the government to aid and advise the health of volunteers. One of these newly appointed civilian officials paid a visit to Camp Harris on July 11. His inspection found that after nineteen days in camp, the 18th was in no ways living abnormally unhealthy when compared to other neighboring encampments. Still, a lot can be learned from this surprise assessment that highlighted their conditions. The 18th had 791 men on their books, with nearly a hundred cases of mumps, and many more cases of diarrhea, fifty men of which were listed sick enough to be placed off duty. With an average of five men to a tent—which were placed six feet apart—it is hardly surprising to see the trend of diseases that jumped from one host to another. Drinking water was in good supply from a nearby spring and food remained the standard army issued rations. There were no dried fruits available at the time, and vegetables came when they could. Bread was daily and fresh meat was cooked three times a week. Two unskilled cooks for each company made meals, and one company pulled together a fund and hired an outside cook for $22 a month.[55]

Leaving Washington

When the neighboring 16th New York left their camp on July 11 and crossed over the Potomac and entered Virginia, there was little doubt that the 18th would soon follow. Several other neighboring regiments had made the similar move and began to flood the city of Alexandria. The 18th's order from Washington to cross arrived later that night at 10:30 p.m. When "Reveille" was bugled the next morning at 3 a.m., July 12, the men awoke to a camp that disappeared almost in the blink of an eye. The art of tearing down their camp was a marvel in itself and documented by Private John C. O. Redington of Company K:

> The "striking" of the tents of an encampment is a novel sight for a civilian. At every tent stand two men, who throw the thing over when the drum give the signal; and a couple of acres of houses, numbering between two and three hundred, fall simultaneously and similarly, changing, as with a mangle wand, the entire appearance, from the populated to the deserted.[56]

By 10 a.m., the regiment had slung their weighted knapsacks on their backs and bid farewell to Camp Harris. As they pulled away from Meridian Hill, their former neighbors of the 14th New York cheered them wildly, having been drawn up for a battalion drill at the time the 18th made their exit. Private Patrick Percell of Company H must have seen their march to the wharf as a point of no return, so he elbowed himself out of the formation and deserted the regiment. The 18th walked a distance of nearly four miles to the steamboat landing and embarked on two steamboats—the *Baltimore* and the *Philadelphia*. Soldiers from the 71st New York State Militia were also on hand to guard the steamers and helped with the baggage transfer which created a slight delay. Once the steamers were loaded, the 18th began the eight mile drift down the Potomac River. With wishes granted, the anxious men were about to step foot on enemy soil.[57]

4

First Blood
July 12, 1861–August 3, 1861

"If I am shot tomorrow, it will be in the struggle
to protect that same flag I have sworn to protect."
—Second Lieutenant Edward W. Groot, Company A, July 18, 1861

Alexandria

After an eight mile drift down the Potomac River, the two steamers that carried the regiment anchored and tied into the Alexandria wharf at 1:15 p.m. on July 12. "Virginia's 'sacred soil' has again been desecrated," penned Private John C. O. Redington of Company K soon after he stepped foot in the city. Corporal Henry Schermerhorn of Company E wrote that, "Alexandria is a very nasty, dirty looking place. The [11th New York] Fire Zouaves have turned some of the houses inside out." After the death of their martyred commander Ellsworth, the Zouaves had retaliated harshly to the buildings and residents of the city.[1]

As the 18th marched about the city on their way to establish a new camp, animosity could plainly be felt between the New Yorkers and the citizens of Alexandria. The tension was not subdued but exacerbated—especially by Company K—who antagonized the disgruntled residents when they sang Union hymns loud and proud through the streets. Their songs were also punctuated with requests by other soldiers for "three cheers for the red, white, and blue." Private Redington was greeted by a well dressed woman who drew a revolver on him while he sang, but no harm was done. He stated that "perhaps [Company] K merited all this, for no company sang more heartily through those dingy streets." Elsewhere in the city, sixteen-year-old Private William Henry Mayette of Company K was separated from the rest on a detail as a guard for the regiment's baggage. His independent singing was similarly interrupted by an unarmed, but defiant Alexandrian who advised the young soldier, "You'd better not sing those songs here." Mayette then began to load his rifle and asked the local if he was going to make him stop singing. Without a response back, the chagrined man walked away.[2]

Camp Myers and Hunting Creek Bridge

The 18th marched about a half mile south from the Alexandria wharf and set up a new camp in the southern suburbs of the city along the bank of Hunting Creek and its intersection

This wartime photograph of Alexandria, Virginia, shows the western edge of the city from the southern side of Hunting Creek, which flows at bottom. At center is the roundhouse depot of the Orange & Alexandria Railroad (Library of Congress).

with the Potomac. Their camp was an open field surrounded by woods near the Hunting Creek Bridge. The 18th bestowed the name Camp Myers for their new camp in honor of Major Myers' father, Charles G. Myers, the Attorney General of New York. The men went to immediate work and set up their tents. A late night rain that lasted until the following morning made their first sleep at their camp a soggy one, and those who failed to set up their tents in a timely manner learned a valuable lesson.[3]

While the rest of the regiment assembled Camp Myers on their first night, Company A was tasked out for picket duty. After he received his orders, Captain William S. Gridley led his company to the Hunting Creek Bridge. The bridge ran over a half mile wide section of Hunting Creek—a tributary of the Potomac River. The bridge opened a road system that connected a vital path south that led to Mount Vernon and Fairfax Court House. To the 18th, this meant it could serve as an avenue for the enemy to enter Alexandria. Gridley's orders, and for other companies that followed, was to guard the bridge and prevent an incursion if the Rebels felt so bold. Enemy pickets were expected, and if they proved to be too strong, Gridley was instructed to burn the bridge and retreat back to the regiment.[4]

When Company A arrived they found a company from the all–German 29th New York already posted on the bridge. Gridley relieved the Germans and took possession of the bridge. Gridley split his company in two and sent one half south across the bridge, where twelve men were then posted on each of the three roads that branched off from the bridge, covering all avenues of approach. First Lieutenant Daniel H. Daley supervised this half from a nearby barn. Daley also kept a small contingent in the barn with him as support if needed. Gridley

First Lt. Daniel Hennison Daley of Schenectady was twenty-one years old when he joined Company A on April 22, 1861. He was severely wounded in his right shoulder at Crampton's Gap, Maryland, September 14, 1862, which crippled his arm and eventually claimed his life in 1866 (courtesy Dale Hotaling).

remained on the northern side of the bridge with the first half to act as another safety net if Daley was hard-pressed. Gridley also deployed twelve men down the banks of the creek to act as skirmishers and to ensure that no boats came up the river. The men were very eager and vigilant to be doing the work of a soldier, especially something other than drill. At one point in the night, some of the men on Daley's side of the river heard the unmistakable sound of movement in the bushes near their position. Suspecting it to be Rebel pickets, a group of them fired a volley in the direction of the sound. Before the smoke of the rifle disappeared, the grunting of a wounded hog cleared suspicions. Soon after, a half a dozen other wild hogs poured out of the bushes. In a letter written home a few days later, Gridley lightheartedly remarked to a friend back home, "you can make up your mind that the boys had fresh pork for dinner next day."[5]

The Army of Northeastern Virginia

On July 13, the 18th was organized into the newly formed Army of Northeastern Virginia, commanded by Brigadier General Irvin McDowell. McDowell initially wanted to dedicate more time with his infant army before he advanced on the enemy. Lincoln disregarded the Union commander's hesitance and explained, "You are green, it is true; but they are green also. You are all green alike." Without time to spare, McDowell followed Lincoln's mandate and quickly greased the gears of his inexperienced army towards a meeting ground. The 18th was placed into the Fifth Division, under the command of Colonel Dixon S. Miles, of the 2nd United States Infantry.[6]

At the age of fifty-seven, Miles had spent most of those years in a soldier's uniform. Graduating from West Point in 1819, he served in the Seminole campaign in Florida, the war with Mexico, and throughout the Indian campaigns on the frontier in the antebellum years. Camp Myers was chosen as the headquarters for Miles' division. His new division consisted of two brigades, the second of which was home to the 16th, 18th, 31st and 32nd New York regiments, and placed under the command of Colonel Thomas A. Davies of the 16th by virtue of him having the earliest commission. Davies' brigade was also augmented by the addition of Battery G of the 2nd United States Artillery—known as Greene's Battery—commanded by First Lieutenant Oliver D. Greene. With about ninety men, a hundred horses, and four 10-pound Parrot rifles, the battery added essential muscle to the brigade.[7]

Left: Col. Dixon S. Miles was testy with his subordinates during the battle of Bull Run, and his actions during the day would forever blemish his career after accusations of being drunk mounted against him (Library of Congress). *Right:* Col. Thomas A. Davies of the 16th New York was a native of St. Lawrence County. During the Bull Run campaign, Davies commanded the second brigade of Miles' Fifth Division, of which the 18th New York was part (Library of Congress).

Awaiting Orders

Life at Camp Myers was kept busy and routine. Companies took their turns through shifts of picket duty around the bridge, and drills in camp were done at the company and regimental level. Food returned to daily rations of a single loaf of bread, salt pork, bacon, rice, coffee, tea, and occasionally, fresh beef was delivered.[8]

Inspection of their arms and equipment was conducted on Sunday, July 14, followed by the regiment's Chaplain A. A. Farr, who preached what Sergeant Mowatt of Company C called, a "good and appreciated sermon" to the men. Talks around camp always regurgitated the latest news reports or rumors, and the men were assured that they would soon meet the enemy that had concentrated around Manassas, less than thirty miles away. The certainty of battle made these divine moments with the chaplain much more significant.[9]

Orders for the army's advance westward toward the Confederate lines came down on July 15, and the 18th prepared to march the following morning. Ammunition boxes were inspected to ensure that each man had at least the proper allotment of forty rounds per person. Men who were capable of writing quickly scribbled either a letter home or a note in their diaries that told of their fully expected victory that they would soon be granted with the battle they anticipated. Captain Gridley penned home a letter that said, "I think we will smell gunpowder before 2 o'clock tomorrow—all the moves around here look like it." Gridley's prediction did not hold true after orders trickled down to the line officers that called for a 3 p.m. departure.[10]

As the packing continued into the evening, each man in Miles' division was directed to pack three days worth of cooked rations in their haversacks, which consisted of about fifteen "hardtack" crackers and a half pound of bacon. They were ordered to withhold coffee, sugar, beans, and rice due to the lack of camp kettles and mess pans that were also ordered to be left behind. A lieutenant in charge of the Commissary Department stated that he only observed Miles' Fifth Division to have solely "obeyed the order literally."[11]

Advance on Manassas and the Baptism of Fire

The morning of July 16, the entire Army of Northeastern Virginia made their moves to march towards Fairfax Court House in pursuit of the Confederate forces massed at Manassas Junction. All morning, the men packed up their belongings and were checked by their officers that they had their ammunition, food in haversacks, and canteens topped off. Shortly after 3 p.m., the 18th left Camp Myers in light marching order and began their advance west on the Little River Turnpike. Their tents were left standing and knapsacks were tucked inside. A small detail of soldiers, mostly those too unfit to march, guarded the camp and property under the command of Second Lieutenant Horatio G. Goodno of Company K. Despite his pleas for the privilege to be with the regiment, someone had to stay behind as the officer of the camp, and Goodno was their man.[12]

Being as they were positioned on the right of the brigade, the 18th was first in column and led the way with their division. They marched westward on the hot dusty road "with buoyant hearts and spirits" as Sergeant John S. King of Company D exclaimed. The men marched for about six miles until they reached their destination where the Little River Turnpike split into the old Braddock Road, two miles shy of the town of Annandale. They reached this point about 11:30 p.m., and the entire division encamped for the night in a large open field. Without any tenting supplies, they settled on the ground and wrapped themselves in their blankets and slept as best as they could. Heavy dew set in that soaked their blankets entirely which made for a chilly night.[13]

At some point during the night, Major Myers' horse broke loose and jumped over its fence and stampeded through the camp as the men slept. Several soldiers were stepped on and pained, but none worse than twenty-year-old Private John B. LaQue of Company A. The horse trampled him as he slept which broke his right shoulder blade, and was followed by a

84   The 18th New York Infantry in the Civil War

swift kick to his head with a lacerating effect from its metal horseshoe. The animal was eventually corralled, but LaQue would miss his place on the firing line, being relegated to camp duties for several weeks until he recovered.[14]

Strictly adhering McDowell's order, Miles awoke his division the next morning before daybreak. At 4 a.m. the long drum roll awoke the soldiers who instinctively consumed a quick breakfast before they shouldered their rifles. The strong southern dews not only made for an uncomfortably wet night, but caused their rifles to be heavily rusted. Private George W. Royce of Company G characterized the rust levels on the guns to have "as much as they would have been had they been out in a 24 hour's rain."[15]

After the morning coffee was consumed and everyone formed back on the road in the same order as the day previous, the division resumed their march and pressed down the old Braddock Road by 6 a.m., on July 17. Companies A, B, G, and K from the 18th were sent 200 yards in front of the entire division to act as the front line skirmishers, supervised under the command of Lieutenant Colonel Young. Nearly 100 pioneers trailed behind them about a half mile, armed with muskets, axes, and spades in the event they were needed to clear the roads of any barricades. One man per company from the brigade was drawn to make up the

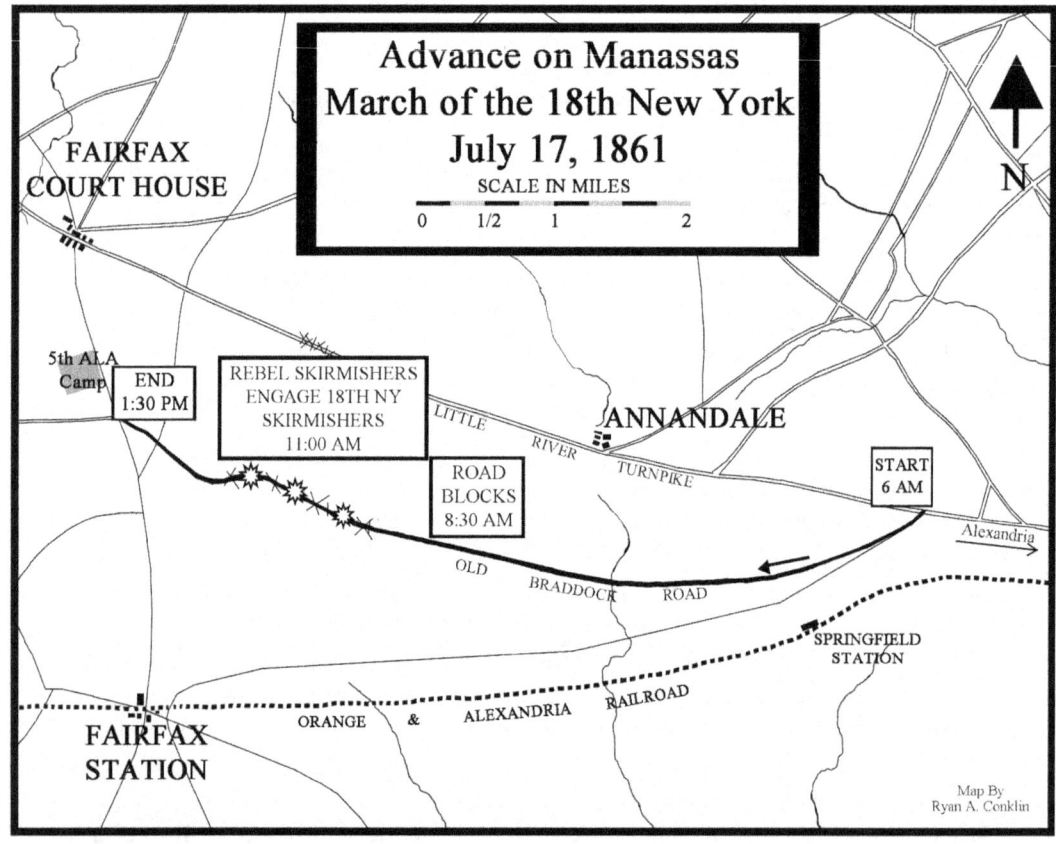

Route of the 18th New York as they advanced west on the old Braddock Road, July 17, 1861. Companies A, B, G and K were out front, skirmishing for the entire division, and first came under fire around 11 a.m. (author's collection).

pioneer corps. Behind the pioneers rolled the guns from the battery, followed by the second and first brigades of infantry.[16]

Virginia was secession country by the full understanding of the men, but two incidents occurred along their march that surprised their assumptions. Private Royce recalled that during their morning hike they came across "a few loyal citizens in eastern Virginia," and when they passed one particular house, two women waved handkerchiefs from their yard in a display of solidarity to thank them. As each company passed, men responded with three hearty cheers to thank them. One man in Royce's company hollered at the women and asked them to "show the stars and stripes." One of the ladies responded, "We have not got them or we would." Farther down their morning march they made a momentary pause at another house that had adequate water resources to fill up their canteens. Royce noticed a woman come out of the house who said the sight of Union troops was "the happiest day she had seen in her life but she wished to God that we had come sooner, for that morning the rebels came there and forced her husband and two sons to go with them. The youngest son was but fourteen years old."[17]

By 8:30 a.m., the march was brought to a sudden halt by undefended obstructions that covered the road. Multiple obstacles of bushes, fence rails, cuts in the road, and recently felled trees hacked down by the Confederates were strewn across the old Braddock Road. Some of these barricades were quite extensive, and the Confederates were successful to slow the Union advance without a fight. The pioneers worked feverishly to remove the obstacles to make it possible for Miles' division to slip through and continue their march, although behind schedule. So great were the blockades that the division could only manage to travel merely one mile per hour.[18]

Slow but steady, the division marched on and braced for enemy contact. Within about five or six miles from Fairfax, the sound of rifle fire was heard up ahead and the men anticipated an engagement. With nearly three miles to go until they reached Fairfax Court House, the division was again halted around 11 a.m., after more obstructions spun the pioneers to work. Without warning, the 18th's skirmishers suddenly received their baptism of fire. Muskets from Confederate pickets hidden behind felled trees opened with a volley just fifty yards ahead of them. The staggered line of New Yorkers were under the same cover of woods so the bullets aimed either smacked into tree trunks or were aimed too high. Their opposition was two thinly stretched companies of the 5th Alabama. After their futile volley against the New Yorkers the Rebels retreated down the road, but not before some Enfields from the 18th answered back. The Alabamians disappeared without the loss of a man. The Southerners retreated farther west down the road and rallied to a masked battery and concealed themselves behind trees, fences, and other structures to await the next hit. As the 18th skirmishers closed the gap and pushed down the road, the Confederates again opened fire with another volley once they got in range. Reloading on the run, the Rebels leapfrogged back to their next line of defense. The guerrilla fight lingered in this fashion three or four more times through another mile.[19]

During a lull in the fight, twenty-six-year-old Sergeant John S. Allen of Company K sprang ahead of the skirmish line and led eight others from his company forward and harassed the Rebels with musket fire. The former bookkeeper advanced his squad to the top of a hill enclosed in a narrow cut in the woods near the roadway and could plainly see a large gathering of Alabamians. Allen fired a round at their line and began to reload by the time the Confederates responded with a concentrated volley towards their position. The squad dove for the ground, but four men were pegged by musket balls. One pierced into Allen's left arm and ricocheted into his side just under his lungs. As the wounded sergeant fell to the ground, he shouted to those around him, "I'm shot but go on boys." Allen was placed in a blanket and was hauled to some woods nearby where the surgeon quickly began his profession. When the litter team passed a friend of Allen's from the 16th New York, he asked Allen if he wished to send a word home to his family. Allen simply replied with, "if I die, tell my Father I die for the cause." Though pale, bloody, and weak, Allen toughed out the pain rather calmly, but the fight for his life had just begun.[20]

Also hit from this volley was Private Hugh McKinley, Company K, who received a slight wound from a bullet that traveled through his thigh. Sergeant John Waterson of Company A was similarly struck in his thigh but his wound proved more serious than McKinley's. Thirty-nine-year-old Private Thomas Territ of Company K had a narrow escape from being wounded when a bullet sliced through the blanket he carried. His close call was just another story for a man that had already served twenty years in the army and navy.[21]

Second Lieutenant Edward W. Groot of Company A was the fourth to be hit. Considered "a brave boy" by his men during the volley exchanges on the skirmish line, he found inspiration from his men's prowess. "I had no idea the boys would fight as they did," Groot wrote in a letter the following day from an infirmary in Washington. His left hand was badly shattered by a bullet that passed through. Fortunately, his hand was saved from amputation.[22]

The skirmishers from the 18th had received about fifteen volleys from the Alabamians. As the men pursued the bounding Confederates, the enemy grew in size. The two companies of the 5th Alabama had fallen back and reconsolidated themselves with the rest of their regiment. Soon, the 18th was up against more than 200 rallied Confederates that gathered behind a raised embankment, reinforced with fallen trees.[23]

With their tactic to fire and run, the Rebels hardly allowed themselves to be easy targets. "They retreated so fast that it was hard work for our boys to get a shot at them," complained a member of the 16th New York. Only two Alabamians were shot; one in the leg, and one in the ear. Both evaded capture and were carried off by their comrades.[24]

The Confederates were successful to nab a couple of the advanced New Yorkers. Private John W. Browning of Company G was one of the five to be wounded, shot in the right foot and helpless, which made him easy bait when he was captured and brought behind enemy lines. The same happened to McKinley who had nowhere to run after his thigh wound and was captured. Private Calvin B. Potter of Company B felt that the Confederate cavalry had seemingly come out of nowhere when they surrounded him and made him their prisoner. During the early afternoon, two others were captured—Corporal Chester C. Shaw of Company H and Private Abram Crozier of Company B. Rebels quickly interrogated two of these captured men and learned what effect their firing had done. They passed grossly overstated reports to the Rebels that they caused casualties to be fifty killed and wounded, whereas the other stretched that number to seventy. Confederate reports certainly boasted these numbers with pride, but the word from their captured Yankees was extremely inaccurate, if not wholly done for their own comic relief.[25]

As the first two wounded soldiers from the 18th were rushed back to the rear, the rest of the regiment not on the advanced front was ordered to form in battle line. The 16th New York was also called up and similarly formed their attack line, and together both regiments advanced to flush out the enemy pickets. "Forward up the Eighteenth!" was shouted. "Forward,

Eighteenth," Colonel Jackson hollered to his men, "double quick!" Jackson aligned his wing of companies to the left of the 16th. Together, both regiments advanced in good order through the thick Virginia woods but the Confederate pickets had by then withdrawn and moved on out of sight.[26]

Lieutenant Colonel Young continued to advance his skirmishing companies ahead of Jackson's elements and the 16th. They eventually caught up and melted their lines and made the 18th whole, and the two regiments pushed forward together. From tree to tree, men used what was thickest to shield their bodies as they crept forward. After about half of a mile, the 16th and 18th pushed through the emptied woods until they came upon the view of a masked battery and entrenchments looking down the road which prompted Jackson to call for a halt. The parapet before them sat upon the brow of a hill, fortified with about six-foot thick dirt mounds and framed with poles, and it held a commanding view of the road that had Companies D and F split on opposites sides of the woods. Everyone paused for a moment and peered around the trees and stumps they hid behind, hoping to see some enemy activity. After ten minutes passed without any sign of Rebels within, Jackson gave the nod to advance the line. Company D was the closest to the parapet, and approached it head-on. There seemed to be little worry, as Sergeant John S. King noticed the men in his company hastily grabbed blackberries from the bushes they pushed through as if there was no masked battery before them. Their intuition was correct and the battery position was abandoned and seemingly never had a gun. The entrenchments and breastworks that stemmed off from the parapet stretched to nearly 500 yards in length and were similarly empty. Although fortified with sandbags and mangled heaps of green brush piles a couple feet thick, Miles would later survey these deserted earthworks and viewed them as "badly constructed, but capable of considerable defense." Several signs pointed that their former occupants had fled their defensive position in a hurry. Sergeant King found warm bread in a nearby ditch and a knapsack with "Tuscaloosa Volunteers" painted on its canvas. King sifted through the pack and found two letters that he took and intended to send home as souvenirs, but he lost them before he had the chance.[27]

The two forwarded regiments pressed on for a short distance until the sound of nearby musketry was heard on their right. The command of "Rally on the right" was given and the 16th and 18th closed up and merged back onto the road. They prepared themselves to repel a charge from Confederate cavalry that was somehow assumed to be the cause of alarm. It was indeed a false one as it turned out to be a Union element from another brigade that had entered Fairfax from a different direction.[28]

The two regiments walked up the road and continued a quieted march that neared Fairfax Court House. About a mile out from the village, the regiments stumbled across the abandoned camp of their enemy that showed more signs that they had been surprised and unprepared to leave. More papers and personal letters from its former tenants identified the camp belonged to the 5th Alabama. The 18th eventually broke ranks and perused the enemy encampment. Campfires still burned and abandoned ovens still contained freshly baked bread ready to eat. A regimental banner from the Southern regiment was found but did not last long. Sergeant King watched the flag get "torn to pieces in a jiffy" by trophy hunters from the 18th, with him being one of them. Corporal Frank Seymour, Company E, mentioned, "we, of course, appropriated everything to our own use, and your humble servant nabbed two-hundred and fifty cigars of the 'contraband.'" A soldier from the 16th looked upon several hundred barrels of provisions, hams, dressed chickens, tobacco, cigars, flour, tea, and sugar before him and said that these were "articles better suited for a picnic or a party in a summer house than to soldiers in the field." Men from the 16th seized "all of the tobacco and cigars before we knew anything about it, so we did not get any of them," mentioned a saddened Private Royce. He eventually found a suitable souvenir when he found a six-shooter revolver with two loads left inside that he nicknamed his "converted secessionist." His find was prized by his friends and "two or three of the boys in our company offered me five dollars for it before I had had it an hour." Some members of the 18th were quick to stash the booty from the quartermaster's stockpile of the 5th Alabama, which was full of shirts, shoes, boots, cigars, and southern tobacco. Amongst an endless scattering of bush tents, the camp was strewn with other valuable equipage such as overcoats, knapsacks, mess chests, camp furniture, kettles, bowie knives, pistols, and even a box of muskets. One soldier from Company A stated that, "our boys soon made a meal, for this living on crackers for three days is not very nice." Miles' entire division had traversed more than ten arduous miles in less than a day under light marching orders and took full advantage of the bounty earned. Six Alabamians were also added to the list of acquisitions by Miles' division. Some of these captured Southerners were sick and feeble, and intentionally left behind for the New Yorkers to inherit.[29]

The camp was near the intersection of the old Braddock Road and the path which connected Fairfax Court House to Fairfax Station, a little more than a mile south of the court house. This was Miles' objective outlined in McDowell's plan, and he arrived to this destination just before 1:30 p.m. on July 17. This was, of course, several hours behind the intended hour of arrival, but the mixture of sporadic skirmishing which lasted nearly four hours alone, and the added road obstructions delayed not only Miles' division, but almost all of the divisions during their movements throughout the encompassing area. The 18th sustained the only casualties of the day, with five wounded, two of which were captured. Four others from the 18th without injuries were also captured.[30]

Shortly before they reached this vital intersection, a company of cavalry from McDowell reached Miles' division with news of the successful seizure of Fairfax Court House. McDowell desperately wanted to continue their pursuit, but his soldiers needed rest after their long day on the obstructed roads. Miles' division spent the night encamped within the vicinity of the old Braddock Road intersection. The 18th remained for the night in the woods closest to the abandoned camp. The tired and tested troops earned some much needed rest. Companies C and I of the 18th spent the night on picket duty to ensure the Confederates did not encroach on their gained ground.[31]

The wounded soldiers not captured from the day's skirmish had since been shipped to Washington for hospitalization. Updates returned to the line that the injured had demonstrated improvement, but uncertainty always prevailed with news that traveled by word of mouth. Two of the wounded would eventually take a turn for the worse. As soon as Second Lieutenant Groot got pen and paper at his hospital, he jotted a letter to friends back home to state his injury to his hand was not life-threatening. He also made claim that he would rejoin the regiment after his letter was finished and before the expected battle, but he was not allowed to leave his hospital bed. "If I am shot tomorrow," Groot poetically concluded in his letter, "it will be in the struggle to protect that same flag I have sworn to protect."[32]

McDowell continued to push the next morning—July 18—and drew up orders for his divisions on their intended movement. While the divisions waited for the resupply wagons, the men prepared themselves to continue their march westward. The 18th, with the rest of their division, resumed their route on Braddock Road at 9 a.m. towards Centreville, about eight miles distant.[33]

Centreville

The landscape during the course of their march was absent of the hills and valleys that the men were more accustomed to back home. The dwellings they marched passed as they neared Centreville were few in number. Their deserted appearances prompted Private John C. O. Redington to write that, "most of these are shut up and others have only slaves to watch over them while the pious proprietors are fighting against their native land."[34]

Though the march was void of any enemy attacks, an unforeseen problem surfaced when the men drank their canteens dry and resupply became a concern. The 18th and other regiments found water very hard to come by. A few desperate individuals literally discarded their canteens, which quickly proved to be a massive mistake that a green soldier would make only once. Their inexperience as soldiers was further revealed after others made a personal decision to toss their blankets that they felt was too heavy. Men had to be instructed to limit their intake of water to sustain themselves from the sizzling summer heat of Virginia.[35]

Their destination of Centreville was a small country village with a population of about 200 inhabitants. Centreville sat atop the western side of one of the long ridges characteristic of the area, with a scattering of domiciles mostly constructed of stone. The men arrived there later that afternoon without any surprises or mishaps. Private Royce scoffed at Centreville being referred to as a village, because "I could see no village, there being but one or two houses in sight, and they were nearly a mile apart." Before Miles' division neared Centreville, a brigade from First Division had already cleared the village by nine o'clock that morning and found it completely undefended. McDowell claimed Centreville as his hub to regroup his divisions and prepare for his next intended advance, which would be a movement of attack. After two days of solid marching that spanned more than twenty miles, the 18th set up a camp just below Centreville Heights, about a mile from the village. The men were still without tents which prompted them to get creative with what nature provided. In about two hours, the 18th fashioned a "regular paradise" of shelters made of vines and branches. Private Redington accepted the regiment's shortcoming when he said, "after the day's work, the dry or damp Heavens above form the only roof."[36]

Within the hour of the 18th's arrival to Centreville, the sound of heavy cannonading echoed from the south. The firing increased with musketry and the exchanges carried throughout the late afternoon for more than an hour. The sound of battle ensured everyone that the Confederates were close at hand and willing to fight. The clash pitted a brigade from First Division against Confederate Brigadier General James Longstreet's Virginians at Blackburn's Ford, three miles south of Centreville. Hoping that Blackburn's Ford could provide an easy avenue into enemy lines, the Union brigade pressed three times but was repulsed by Longstreet's stiff resistance and superior strength. Both sides sustained minimal casualties and retired without any major land exchanges. Miles' division held his forces at bay in Centreville while the small battle ensued a couple miles south. They awaited the rest of the divisions to arrive, albeit impatiently. Several curious soldiers of the 18th were able to obtain an elevated observation of the battle from the top of a neighboring hill. The consensus was agreed upon that the enemy was much larger than rumors had led the men to believe. They could even listen out and hear the rumbling of the railcars from Richmond reach Manassas with more fresh troops whose own cheers echoed over the land. With all of the divisions of their own simultaneously converging on Centreville, everyone was certain that a large battle was about to unfold. In the words of Corporal Frank Seymour, "There will be some rough work before long, you can 'bet high on that.'"[37]

The Fifth Division received a resupply of provisions at Centreville their first night and prepped another three days' rations into their haversacks. Corporal Seymour wrote about the rations as being "insufficient" and of the "poorest quality" which created "a vacuum in every man's stomach."[38]

Private Edward M. Tilley—acting regimental clerk—brought up a supply of ammunition for the regiment that same day in Centreville. He had been left behind in Alexandria when the regiment launched their march, detailed for the acquisition. With the roads from the city since cleared Tilley made the journey to Centreville with his supply in one day. He was determined not to miss the impending battle.[39]

McDowell's army regrouped the next two days in and around Centreville and anxiously awaited orders to advance on Manassas Junction where the enemy was expected to be centralized. Just days before, Confederates were welcomed occupiers of Centreville, but now their abandoned encampments could be seen dotted around the land, some since filled by Federal troops. Corporal Seymour surveyed the land and felt they were amongst an endless massing of blue uniforms that stretched "about us for ten miles." Centreville's sudden reversal of occupiers did not go over well with the Southern sympathizing locals. One rebellious woman was openly abusive to the troops in her village which prompted Corporal George W. Shook of Company F to steal her small silk Rebel flag from her. He eventually mailed the banner home.[40]

Captured Confederates began to increase amongst the divisions in Centreville. The 18th saw eleven brought in on the morning of July 19. They also started to see the dead and wounded from the skirmish at Blackburn's Ford pass through which was always a sobering sight. Sergeant King watched with curiosity the burial of a soldier from a Massachusetts regiment wrapped in a carpet to serve as a coffin.[41]

At 5 p.m. on July 20, the 18th received orders and prepared to close in on the enemy. McDowell's intent was to move several columns closer to the Junction in order to shorten the following day's march, but only if he left immediately that evening. Closer to 6 p.m., the regiment was all formed up and ready to march when all of a sudden an order came that ended all plans. A nearby creek named Bull Run was paramount for drinking purposes by both armies, but reconnaissance showed that the crossings over the creek were heavily guarded by Confederates. McDowell had already devoted his two days in Centreville strategizing with this information. The new order asked the regiments to stay steadfast, but not to step off until early the next morning. The men broke ranks and were instructed to thoroughly clean their rifles, pack four days rations into their haversacks, and stuff forty rounds of ammunition into their pouches. Joyous as they were at the prospects of a fight, things got better when mail call arrived. For some who understood the gravity of their situation, they poured over these letters and hoped it would not be the last they would hear from loved ones. Adjutant John H. Russell felt the "most singular depression of spirits" when the thought crossed his mind after having read a letter from his brother. Russell mentioned that "many of my brother officers were similarly affected and spoke of it." Sad but true, "the conviction settled on the minds of many that it was their last night on earth."[42]

Miles' division was ordered for the following day to be held in reserve on the Centreville ridge and demonstrate against Blackburn's Ford to prevent any enemy assault that may come from that wing. With Miles' two brigades, they were reinforced by the addition of a brigade from First Division under the command of Colonel Israel B. Richardson, fresh from the battle at the ford three days before.[43]

Battle of Bull Run (Manassas)

On Sunday, July 21, the 18th was roused at two o'clock in the morning in preparation for McDowell's divisions to step off their march at 2:30 a.m. Very few of the men were actually awakened, as most stayed up through the night and talked in groups about the coming day. The regiment formed by the flickering glows from the burn piles of boughs used for their shelter. Men could see the same fashion of high-flamed fires dotted throughout the surrounding land as other regiments prepared for the march. The darkness of the early morning prompted significant delays in the orchestration for divisions to get out onto the road. First Division was slated first in the order of movement but their setback by the jungle of troops delayed the rest of the divisions by two to three hours behind the appointed time. This was the first of many blunders that plagued the army on that fateful Sunday.[44]

After daylight, Miles' two brigades formed and found their starting place at 5 a.m., but were still jammed by the other bottlenecked divisions that blocked the road. First brigade moved in column through the congestion and proceeded to Centreville and occupied the entrenchments initially built by Confederates. They wasted no time and strengthened their given fortifications. Miles set up his command staff at the same location. Davies' brigade was still stuck amongst the columns of the other divisions as they attempted to unite with Richardson's brigade already in place near Blackburn's Ford. Miles found a path for Davies that allowed them to bypass the congestion, so they crossed left off the road through fields and towards the ford. With Greene's Battery in advance, the brigade traversed over farm fields for a distance that ensured him he would not again be blocked by the mess of columns. The 18th, with the rest of their brigade, re-entered the road that led to the site of Thursday's battle at Blackburn's Ford. They proceeded to Richardson's location near the ford and connected to the left of his line. Like Centreville, their position three miles south near Blackburn's Ford was elevated, wooded, and offered visual superiority to track enemy troop movements from afar. Davies ordered the 18th to push out their line of battle into a clearing and get in front of the Union battery and protect their left flank in case the enemy showed intent to capture the pieces by a flank maneuver. From atop his saddled horse, Colonel Jackson looked over to his second-in-command to again advance a force of skirmishers. Lieutenant Colonel Young pulled two companies from the 18th and two from a Massachusetts regiment in Richardson's brigade and deployed them as skirmishers in front of the line. On the road to their rear, the 32nd New York was held in reserve. The 18th had reached their designated position by 8 a.m. in the open field and braced for the unexpected. The men went to task to strengthen their positions with logs and crudely sharpened tree limbs.[45]

The 18th saw its first victim early before major hostilities broke out, owed to another

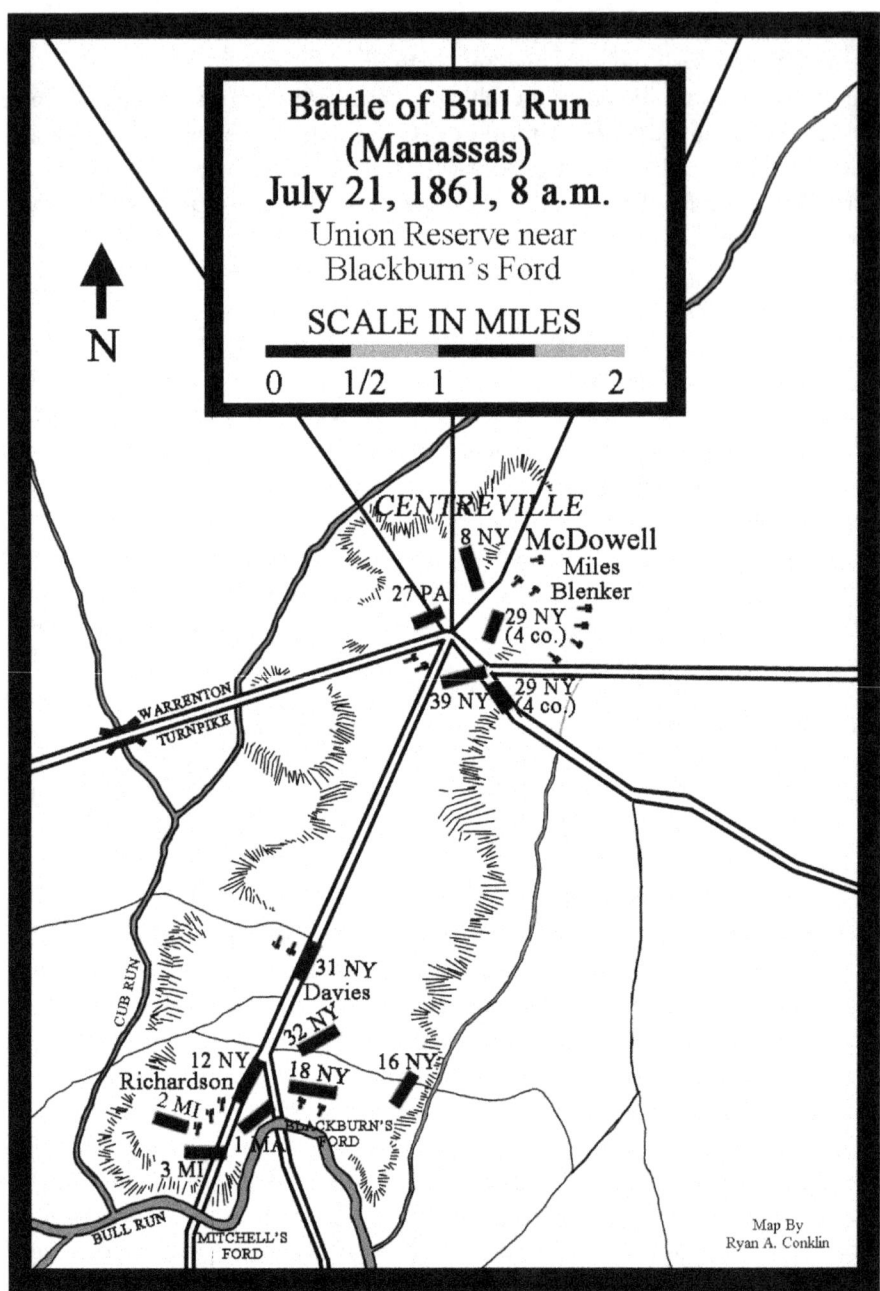

Arrangements of the reserve regiments around Blackburn's Ford and Centreville, around 8 a.m., July 21, 1861 (author's collection).

self-inflicted wound. Just one week after his promotion, First Sergeant Freeman F. Huntington of Company K exemplified what not to do when he accidentally discharged his musket into his right hand. His index finger was over the tip of his muzzle just when the loaded rifle accidentally fired which resulted in the loss of half of his finger. Huntington overcame his blunder and served his time in the regiment with an exemplary record.[46]

Before the 18th had taken their initial position, the opening salvo of a distant battery behind them roared open at 6:30 a.m. The cannon blast was a signal from the First Division that they were ready to attack. The armies were set and soon each man would have their curiosity about warfare answered. Requests to God and thoughts of home ran off the lips of many anxious participants. For the next several hours, the First, Second, and Third Divisions of McDowell's army along the Warrenton Turnpike leveled their muskets and took aim at their Southern brethren and launched the first large-scale battle of the war. Being as most of the day's fighting occurred around a large slithering creek named Bull Run, Union troops dubbed the fight as the battle of Bull Run, but the Confederates tended to name fights after the nearest town and christened the battle of Manassas. Dozens of interested citizens and politicians, some having made the trip from Washington, picnicked along the surrounding heights to observe the contest between the two armies with insatiable curiosity. They became first-hand witnesses to a rude awakening that the rest of the country would soon learn.[47]

Six miles away from the engaged divisions, the positions of Davies and Richardson at the ford stood as the extreme left of the Union army. With Miles planted at Centreville with his first brigade, Davies kept command three miles south of both his and Richardson's brigade. The men of the 18th understood that their position was one of reserve for the rest of the army, which many naïve men found disappointing, but at least the days before gave most a taste of combat. Private Hodgkins of Company K explained this sentiment when he said, "we were all terribly afraid that the war would be over before everybody could get a chance to take part in a battle."[48]

In accordance to McDowell's outlined plan, Davies moved forward two artillery pieces commanded by Lieutenant John Edwards, Battery G of the 1st United States Artillery, who were attached to Richardson's brigade. Davies emplaced them into an open field about eighty yards from the Centreville Road, and faced the ford. They were to protect the army against any possible assaults from that wing. The positions of the cannons were almost identical to where they were set a few days before during the clash at the ford. The battery was to make a demonstration—merely a deterrent—to the Confederate batteries located about 1,500 yards ahead of them on the other side of the ford. After the artillery signal from the First Division ushered the day's events, Edwards' battery of two 20-pounder Parrot Rifles opened up a rapid and sustained fire at 9 a.m. and sent whistling shells over the heads of the 18th and into the fords out to their front. Many landed near Confederate positions who occupied the opposite bank of Bull Run. After about two hours into the artillery demonstration, the deployed skirmishers under Lieutenant Colonel Young's command were recalled, and the 18th became whole again, and were pulled back to the road to protect the left flank, near a building used as a hospital.[49]

Not far from the 18th's position was a dirt road that intersected the Centreville Road and led all the way to the enemy's position at McLean's Ford. The local guide that accompanied Davies informed him that the road [present-day Compton Road] was without obstruction and offered the enemy a quick avenue to separate his command from Miles and outflank his vulnerable brigades. He plugged this path when he advanced his 16th New York onto the road, about a half mile to the left of Edwards' battery that the 18th supported, both regiments of which remained within eyesight of each other. The 31st New York remained behind the 16th at the junction with this unobstructed road and Centreville Road. The brigade was set.[50]

Edwards' batteries fired incessantly without a reply from the enemy, and by 10 a.m., their ammunition neared a dangerous low. Having felt that they had demonstrated enough based on the enemy's rearward movement that put them out of their range, Davies ordered the batteries to cease-fire. About an hour later, Miles rode down from Centreville to check up on Davies' progress. He immediately disagreed with what he saw and quickly reorganized the positions of the regiments. Miles was irritable to begin with. Since the initial departure from Alexandria five days prior, Miles had suffered harshly from dysenteric diarrhea. After his first prescription of opium and quinine pills failed to improve his condition, he resorted the second day to his physician's authorization to use brandy. If there was anything that Miles was notorious of before the battle of Bull Run, it was his fierce temper, cruel speech, and heavy drinking habit. His intake of liquor that Sunday far exceeded any dosage any physician would have prescribed and his drunkenness was outwardly noticeable. When he arrived to Davies' position, Miles quickly ignored their defensive orders and sent forward several companies from the 16th and 31st New York to feel for the enemy's strength closer to the ford. Miles then took another battery from Richardson's brigade and positioned them next to Edwards' battery. Disregarding the limited ammunition, Miles ordered that both batteries resume their rate of fire. He then sent the 18th farther back about a mile into the woods on the Centreville Road as a reserve, all at the double-quick in fear of another anticipated enemy movement. The 32nd New York's position was the only placement that Miles did not rearrange.[51]

As soon as Miles returned to Centreville, Davies sent back the brigade corps of pioneers to the road the 16th had earlier occupied. The pioneers felled trees and blocked the road coming from McLean's Ford so as not to give the enemy an opportune chance to fold the Union's extreme left and get in their rear. Under Miles' orders, the 16th and 31st were pushed deeper into the woods closer to Bull Run and received some unnecessary shots from the enemy posted near the creek. After the wounding of three men, the two regiments were quickly withdrawn since orders outlined that no engagement should be brought on.[52]

While the 18th remained in their reserve location, the speculation of the day's events was impossible to be accurately judged from their inactive position. Other than the constant rearrangement of positions, the rest of the units near the 18th had very little excitement. The Union batteries continued to sporadically drop shells upon moving Confederate columns based on dust clouds that formed above tree lines, but they were at great distances.[53]

While the Fifth Division passed the afternoon in great inactivity, the same could not be said for the other divisions on the front lines to the west. The First, Second, and Third Divisions had fought several hours with a worthy adversary that fought from a hard defensive position. A culmination of violent combat, little sleep, a shortage of water, and an even larger lack of confidence in themselves, McDowell's troops broke at their seams. Several times the momentum changed for both armies and the projection of a clear winner was hard to judge. Casualties mounted heavily and confusion with identifying friend-or-foe occurred on both sides as uniforms ranged in endless variations of colors, shades, and styles. The battle of Bull Run became an entangled mess throughout the afternoon, but was worsened for McDowell's troops as soon as the Confederates gained the addition of much needed reinforcements at the right time. As soon as McDowell's troops had just pushed for yet another shove by the time the fresh Rebel reinforcements emptied a crippling blow of concentrated musketry into them. Scores of tired, scared, and undisciplined men on the Union line broke and ran for

4. *First Blood*   95

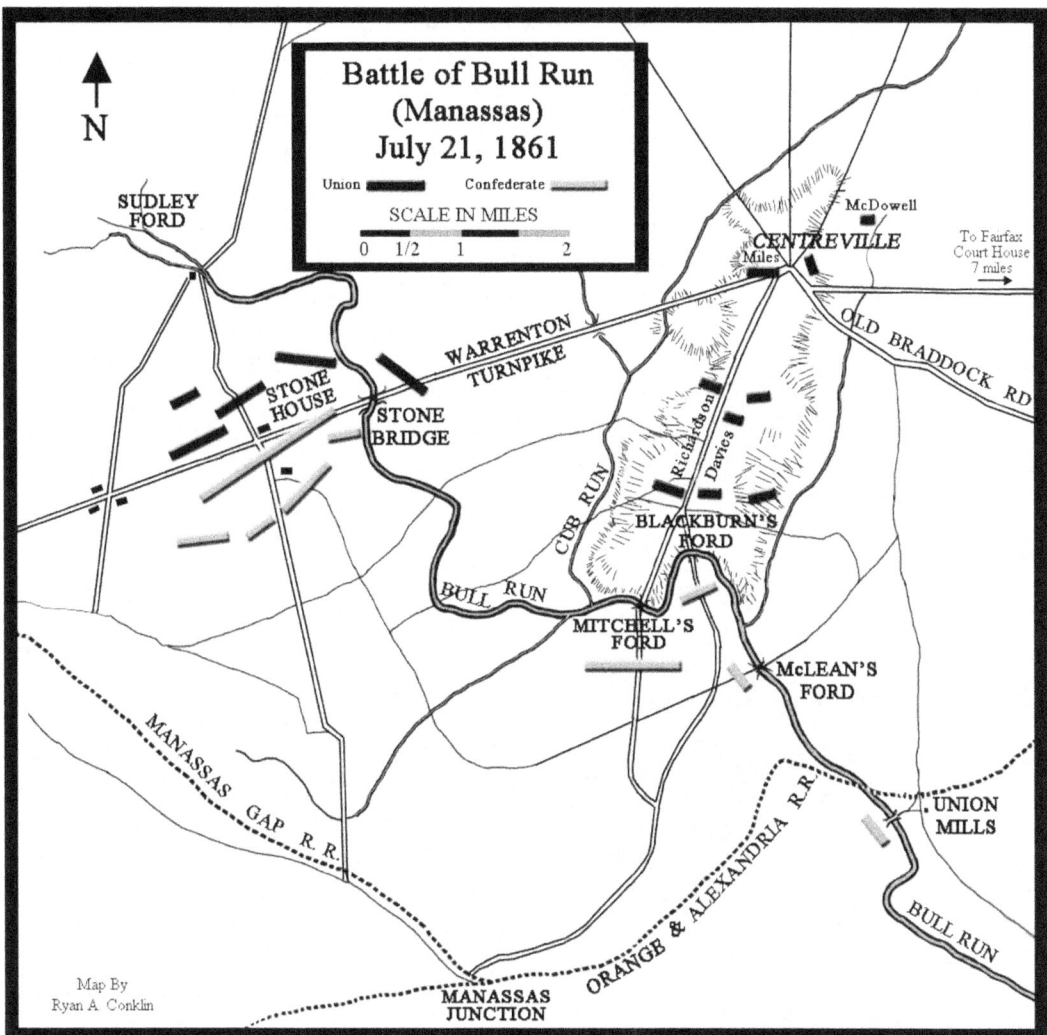

Battle space of both armies, shortly before the retreat of the First, Second, and Third Divisions near the Stone House (author's collection).

their lives. Officers tried feverishly to control the melee but to no avail. The more men that turned spread the feeling of panic to others, and chaos soon followed. The day had been lost as McDowell's divisions morphed into an intermingled horde that sprinted as fast as each man could exhaust themselves. McDowell instantly realized the improbability to regroup his panic-stricken men, so he ordered those who stood firm to leave the field in an orderly fashion. McDowell's attention then shifted towards covering the embarrassing retreat.[54]

"The Generals who ordered the battle are the ones to be blamed," complained Private John C. O. Redington, "not the soldiers whose duty it is to obey the orders." As an ordained minister, he found it foul to be fighting on the holiest day of the week. Detailed as the clerk at Fifth Division Headquarters, Redington's experience away from the 18th allowed for an opportunity to witness the day's fierce combat and subsequent demise up close. He was torn whether it was right to fight on a Sunday, so he put the decision to God through prayer and decided that since the battle was already under way and the enemy had overwhelming numbers, his duty was necessary. After he obtained a leave of absence from his clerk duties, Redington grabbed his rifle and ammunition and walked to the front lines around 12:30 p.m. He walked over four miles, amidst a path of dead and dying troops, all of which vanished the last mile as men traversed through the woods to avoid the rain of shells. Redington stopped a few times to pray, and once to drink from a brook which he shared with about thirty southerners who were either ignorant or unthreatened by his allegiance. His uniform, buttons, and accent left no doubt he was a Northerner, but Redington owed his unchallenged passage and friendly interactions with them as a miracle from above. When the Union army lost the fight and fled in a panic, Redington joined in the retreat and disarmed himself in order to help carry wounded troops back to Centreville. At one point, a company of Confederate cavalry spilled out of the wood line near Redington, and one trooper took a shot at him. The bullet missed Redington's face by six inches and fanned his cheek as it passed. He again felt shielded by his Savior, but he knew the defeat of the Union army, "was God's retribution for breaking his day."[55]

Photographed in August 1862, John C. O. Redington, formerly a private in Company K, left the 18th New York a year before after he was sent home to recruit for the regiment, and did so well that he amassed a company of volunteers which earned him a commission as captain in the 60th New York (Library of Congress).

More and more panicked and demoralized soldiers rushed through Miles' entrenched brigade in reserve in Centreville after the battle was lost. The frenzied extraction of fleeing soldiers destined for as far back as Alexandria was further mixed with the addition of terrified civilians who naively intended to watch the day's foray. Roads became choked with people and horses, and government wagons were left recklessly abandoned. Soldier equipage of all sorts littered the path after their owners carelessly stripped themselves in order to run faster. Corporal Frank Seymour comically recalled seeing, "one long legged dandy, traveling at a rate of speed which would compare favorably with running time on the Central Railroad." Miles tried in vain to rally the passing troops but found it impossible. The victorious Confederates continued their efforts to demoralize the troops and made a push through the left flank of the army, where Davies troops were still positioned. Word of the day's outcome reached Miles' attention and he hastened to regroup his brigades back onto the Warrenton Turnpike at the bridge.[56]

Greene's Battery—attached to Richardson's

brigade for the day—had set up a new position on the crest of a hill that granted them a large panorama of the land. The 18th was still held as a reserve for Davies' brigade and remained near to Greene's Battery. An aide from Miles rode down to Richardson's position with orders for all units to rally back to Centreville and begin to cover the retreat of the army. Richardson quickly regrouped his brigade and proceeded back closer to the village. When the aide reported the news to Greene, he sternly responded, "Who in [the hell] are you? Get out of here!" Greene refused to obey the order and would not fall back until a more authorized person other than an aide instructed him to do so. The four regiments that were Greene's support now dwindled to be just the 18th. Greene looked at Colonel Jackson and asked him, "Will you stay and support my battery?" Colonel Jackson similarly refused the order from Miles' aid and offered his regiment to support Greene, and stated that the 18th "should remain by [your battery] as long as there was any fighting to be done there." The same runner again appeared before the defiant duo and declared that "all was lost" and he ordered Colonel Jackson to form his regiment in column of division on Greene's right and both move back to Centreville. Again, both refused.[57]

To the left of Greene's position, a strong contingent of Confederates was seen to advance on the crucial road that Davies earlier predicted, now obstructed. In fact, from where the 18th were first stationed in the woods during the morning, they were said to have been within 600 feet of a masked Confederate battery, unbeknownst to them. Sergeant King assumed that the reason the Confederates did not attack when the 18th were in position must have been due to the intimidation of their Enfields. It was only after the 18th relocated to their alternative position down the road that the Confederate flanking attempt began. Near five o'clock on that sweaty evening, three Confederate infantry regiments approached Davies' direct left. They filtered down a gorge that led into a valley, a distance of about 500 yards from Davies. Originally believed to be their own troops, the questionable force unloaded a musket volley towards Davies' line that erased the speculation on their allegiance. Davies immediately ordered all six pieces of his batteries to change front to their left and hold their fire. The 16th and 31st New York filled the gaps between each gun and were instructed to lie down on the ground to prevent the Confederates from possibly shifting away from Davies' new front and attempt a flanking maneuver.[58]

Nearly a mile away, the 18th heard this firing and knew it originated from where they were stationed at during the morning. An officer rode up to the regiment and confirmed their conclusions and requested them to hurriedly join the battery and support them. Jackson moved the men at the double-quick through the woods to a position on a road about a mile back from where they had earlier been.[59]

The flanking maneuver from the Confederates was bold, but their execution was flawed. The 5th South Carolina and 17th and 18th Mississippi regiments filtered into the valley at the base of Davies' front and moved in quick fashion with their muskets at the right-shoulder-shift. They stumbled upon the obstructions on the road that Davies had earlier instructed the pioneers to clog. Davies waited until the last enemy column entered the valley before he unleashed his breath of fire. When their end came into view roughly three-quarters of a mile, he instructed Edwards to fire a solid shot from his 20-pounder. The mouth of the brass gun sent a cannonball forward that smacked a direct hit on a horse and rider that propelled them both into the air. The artillery contingent then followed with a gruesome succession of blasts that poured walls of grape and canister towards the Confederates. As the rounds sprayed down on the enemy, the howls of the Southern wounded screamed almost as audible as the artillery that boomed.[60]

Another aide from Miles reached Davies with instructions for him to again pull his brigade back towards Centreville. Realizing the impending doom if he were to pull out and expose a back door entrance to their own retreating troops, Davies sent the runner back with a request for reinforcements. The Confederates fired several volleys into Davies' men atop the hill with little effect. While prone between the guns the infantrymen watched the bullets from the opposite side of the slope safely pass over them. In less than fifteen minutes, the artillery barrage broke the flank-attempting Confederates. They withdrew and ran in every direction towards barns, trees, and bushes as they gave up the possibility of entering the Union rear. Davies' artillery had successfully repelled the roundup of his flank with minimal casualties, and without the necessity of musket volleys from the prone infantry. One officer was killed and two privates were wounded from the Union batteries. This was incomparable to the Confederates they turned away, who lost fourteen and another sixty-two wounded, some of which came from their own unfortunate friendly fire incident.[61]

After the fighting broke off, orders from Miles again reached Davies that instructed him to act like the rest of the Union troops and fall back to Centreville. The day neared 6 p.m. and the men were exhausted. As the 31st, 16th, and the batteries cleared off the hill, Davies headed towards Richardson's line but found that they had already left per Miles' request, unbeknownst to him. Surprised and somewhat perturbed at his commander's executive decisions, he rallied what was left of his own brigade. The 18th had made it about halfway down the road when they were unexpectedly reunited with Davies and his forces already in retreat after repelling the Rebel flanking attempt. A heavy reluctance was felt by those in the 18th who played out scenarios in their minds that had they not been ordered away from their former position in the woods where the attack was made, the Rebel attempt at their rear could have been altered, or entirely prevented, although the standoff was successful in the end. The feeling was mutual when the battery commander approached Colonel Jackson and told him, "My God, Colonel, I wish I had had your regiment there." Davies ordered Greene's Battery, the 18th, and the 32nd back to Centreville, which the entire second brigade executed quickly and orderly. Nearly a half mile into their march, a column of Confederate cavalry spilled out of the woods behind them and onto the Centreville Road. Greene was prepared, and when the cavalry came to about a hundred yards his battery fired four shells straight towards the head of their column. The barrage was enough to shock the cavalry who smartly dispersed in every direction. The 18th continued their retreat and became the last regiment to bring up the rear of the Union army to Centreville. They reached the heights of the village and neared their former camp close to 9 p.m. and halted along the roadside. Corporal Frank Seymour described the mood of the regiment when they took their guarding position at Centreville:

> We then picked out a place on the roadside which was protected by nature from the assaults of the enemy, and with our arms by our sides, and many unhappy reflections as to the results of the day in our heads, we lay down, not to sleep, but to rest our wearied bodies.[62]

They too were just as exhausted from the day's confusion, orders, and rapid repositioning, and when given the opportunity of rest the men remained in their battle line and dropped to the ground, but they had to remain awake. Davies had preserved the left flank stationed at Centreville Heights and protected the Union rear. Davies was then under the direct orders from McDowell himself, after Miles had been shamefully relieved of his command. This was the first time the men of the 18th had seen McDowell during the course of the day.[63]

After nearly a half hour of rest, Confederate cavalry elements appeared down the road, but Federal artillery on the heights cleared them quick and that was the last of the enemy to be seen. As the rear guard for the Union army, the men's rest lasted about an hour. The scene before them was deplorable. Defeated troops continuously streamed through Centreville and the 18th could do nothing but stay awake and watch.[64]

During the course of their rest, a glimmer of hope rose amidst a day of tragedy when some merciful members of Company K stumbled upon a wounded dog. Just behind a stone wall that the Northern New Yorkers leaned against, they found the pup in a weakened pant. One of the men approached the animal and found it to be bloodied with its left foreleg dismembered about three inches below the shoulder, an unintended victim of the day's carnage. A couple of the guys called out to Dr. Edmeston—the regiment's assistant surgeon—who came and dressed the stump, and the dog was said to look every bit grateful for the aid. Some of the boys chipped in a communal pot of rations and fed him, and "others gave him water from the scanty supply in their canteens." They were smitten with the dog, one that they fittingly named, "Bull."[65]

After Lieutenant Colonel Young, Chaplain Farr, and Adjutant Russell canvassed the position of the regiment posted along the hills, they sat down together in the grass by the roadside and tried to figure out where and how the day went so wrong. Though they could not admit the notion to their men, they all confided to each other that the sun they saw set would surely be the last one they would see. Rumors had gotten the best of them and they felt completely defeated. Russell explained what they heard that made them so depressed:

> Nor could we glean the slightest hope to cheer our drooping hearts and wearied bodies, as rumor after rumor reached us, each confirming the previous one, that our retreat had been cut off, that Alexandria was in possession of the enemy, and that they were already on their way in force to attack Washington! The thing was so plausible that we could see no reason to doubt it.[66]

Retreat to Alexandria

Late in the night, McDowell gave the reluctant order to withdraw all troops from Centreville and move back to Fairfax Court House and ultimately, Alexandria. Davies formed his brigade and placed the 16th in front, followed by Greene's Battery, the 18th, 31st, and lastly the 32nd New York in the rear. What was left of the 1st United State Artillery, under the command of Second Lieutenant Edward Bayard Hill, attached themselves to Greene's Battery, but they barely had the manpower to keep the pace to move their guns. They were in the thick of the day's fight and were nearly decimated by a cavalry charge. Colonel Jackson sent nine men from the 18th to temporarily act as teamsters for the battery that helped escort their equipment on the march back. The brigade left Centreville at around 11 p.m., and in the process they left behind one of their sick soldiers in a makeshift hospital in the village that was abandoned. Sergeant Henry B. Stall of Company A was captured shortly thereafter by the enemy. The regiment pushed on through the dark for a quick-paced and lengthy march, guided by the grey glow of the moon. After about two miles on the road, the second brigade passed through the gauntlet of first brigade who had split to both sides of the road and stood at parade rest. The commander of this brigade informed Davies that they had specific orders to remain the rear guard for the retreating soldiers in order to prevent from a possible attack from their rear.[67]

The downtrodden soldiers of the 18th lumbered on for nearly eight miles on their exhausting journey back to Fairfax Court House, fumed by the sting of defeat and humiliation that the entire Union army wallowed in. The lengthy night march was conducted over dry roads of which continual boot-pounding kicked up a clay-powder dust that choked the breathable air. The roads were also encumbered with exhausted stragglers, hobbling wounded, strewn army equipment, and rotting food. Corporal Seymour counted "no less than ten of our army lying dead, and as many as one hundred wounded" that blended into the sea of federal property tossed from overturned wagons at the wayside. The men marched on in their sweat-soaked uniforms and yearned to cap off their canteens with a fresh supply of water.[68]

The men of Company K who tendered care for their wounded dog Bull, decided to keep the pup and took him on the march. They took turns and carried him in their arms, but eventually Major Myers took notice of the regiment's newest member and offered to help. He placed Bull on his saddle in front of his lap and gave the dog a free ride for the remainder of the march.[69]

The brigade reached Fairfax Court House around 3 a.m. on July 22, after a swift double-quick march under the cover of night. The regiment had done well to stay together up until this point, but the march was taxing. The tired and foot sore soldiers paused for about forty minutes near their former camp, and before anyone wanted to hear the expected command, the call to continue their march towards Alexandria was given. Adjutant Russell mentioned, "the men were well nigh beat out, and this

Pictured in 1861, Maj. George R. Myers (left) and Adjutant 1st Lt. John H. Russell pose together in full dress uniforms (author's collection).

order was a little too much for them." Russell himself had just unsaddled his horse and wrapped himself in a blanket on the ground when the call came. He sprang up and fixed his saddle, but the next thing he remembered after that was being awakened by Lieutenant Colonel Young. Russell had blacked out by his horse's side with the bridle still in his hand. Russell admitted that many of the officers on horseback fell asleep in their saddles during the march and their auto-pilot horses kept them with the regiment. For the men who had to make the grueling journey on foot, there were several in the regiment that could no longer maintain the demanding pace for the last leg back to Alexandria. The regiment shed many stragglers and thinned their number as they struggled to press on. Some went to rest on the wayside for a breather, while others cooked coffee or searched for anything to satisfy their unquenchable thirst. Forty-two-year-old Sergeant Harvey L. Rogers of Company F stumbled with the regimental colors he carried, and broke his right hand in his fall. His comrade, Private Lewis Spawn, wrapped Rogers' injured arm and wrist into a makeshift flannel sling. Rogers' injured hand brought an end to his budding service a month later.[70]

Seventeen-year-old Private Kinsley Kingsland of Company C broke down and fell out during the hasty march. He failed to return to the regiment for some time and was eventually listed as a deserter. At five feet, four inches, and barely 118 pounds when fit, he could not hide his weakness. When Kingsland later attempted to limp into Washington on his own, he was refused by a provost marshal who stated, "such men were not wanted in the Army." Kingsland was redirected back to the surgeon of the 18th who had him discharged in November.[71]

Morning daylight rolled up to illuminate their journey, but with it came rain that doused the men and literally soaked whatever motivation they had left. After a grueling march from Centreville to Alexandria—nearly twenty-eight miles in eleven hours—the leading bulk of the regiment that kept pace chiseled to about 200 and finally reached Camp Myers at 10 a.m. on July 22. The tents of their camp came as a welcoming sight to the drenched, worn-out, and hungry soldiers who continued to stroll in throughout the day. After having spent the past few days glued in the saddle, Colonel Jackson finally dismounted his horse and penned a letter home telling of the universal ache his regiment experienced: "From half past two Sunday morning until Monday at midday, we neither slept nor rested." Like everyone else, Russell was glad the ordeal was over and the reality of the campaign settled in, "My heavens! I shudder now to think of what I have gone through with, both bodily and mentally; but it's over with, thank Heaven." The wait to rest would be longer for Company D, for when they returned they were all posted on picket guard, and the only sleep they could get was what they could steal without getting caught.[72]

As comfortable as the men wanted to get within their camp, they became paranoid with the constant notion that the Confederates were on their heels and bound to attack at any given moment. Privates Alvin Barringer, Company D, and Edward Schufeldt, Company H, felt they had seen enough and both walked passed Camp Myers and deserted the regiment. As unprepared as the devastated Army of Northeastern Virginia truly was, some prideful soldiers discounted the army's vulnerability and begged for another fight. Private Tilley wrote that day that, "The boys feel bad at being defeated, but wish to get at them again to endeavor to repay them in part for the trouble they gave us." Another soldier boldly spoke on their behalf and said "the 18th regiment is longing for a brush with the rebels, wherein they may have an opportunity to use their rifles, before called upon to run."[73]

Sporadic groups of stragglers returned to Camp Myers throughout the day, yet a large bulk that fell out "took it easy" and made it back by 4 p.m. Sergeant Lot Reznor and another comrade of Company G returned to the camp later that night after they had gotten separated from the regiment. The two were never awakened when the regiment left Centreville and remained asleep in the open field where they rested. When they awoke, they realized their regiment was gone and replaced by Confederate cavalry. When the chance arose, the two sprinted for the woods and sparked a couple potshots from the enemy, but they evaded capture and made a hair-razing journey back to the safety of their camp.[74]

The men of the 18th slept well their first night back on account of how exhausted they were. The next morning's agenda at Camp Myers involved a thorough cleansing of their rifles which were highly rusted from the rain during their retreat. At one point in the day, the regiments of their brigade were called up to repel a possible enemy attack after rumors swelled that the enemy was within five miles. The men welcomed the chance that they would be attacked, but such an event never occurred. The regiment resumed a rotating guard at the Hunting Creek Bridge.[75]

Contrabands

Rumors of an imminent Confederate attack eventually fizzled out, and a sense of normalcy returned to Camp Myers. The only people that actually ventured in or near Camp Myers were runaway slaves. Commonly referred to as "Contrabands" in reference to the fact that they were property of the enemy, these escaped slaves streamed into Federal camps. The Union army was somewhat baffled on the proper way to receive them. Colonel Jackson had made it known that he was not ambitious to start a crusade of slave catching. Others like Second Lieutenant Charles W. Heald of Company I were more vocal on the topic and denounced slaveholders when they came to their camp in search of their runaways. Union commanders initially wanted to avoid the subject and instead respect the way the people lived in the seceded state. Others knew that some slaves that fled not only did so to escape bondage but to avoid conscription into the Confederate army. Many were also willing to help Union troops and were put to work throughout the camps to help cook, clean, care for livestock, and perform manual labor duties.[76]

On the night of July 23, Second Lieutenant John Vedder of Company E captured a yard boat on Hunting Creek which contained three runaway slaves. The next night, four of the regiment's companies were out on picket duty when seventeen fugitive slaves—men, women, and children—left their masters near Manassas and surrendered themselves to the 18th. Private Royce mentioned that "they are all in good spirits and feel 'bully' over their escape." Captain Gridley commanded the companies on picket that night and welcomed the escaped slaves, one of which related to the captain that he had been a servant to a Rebel officer and fled the day of the battle. Gridley congratulated him and said he was, "a right smart dark" for doing so. Without strict orders to prevent it, the New Yorkers welcomed them into their camp.[77]

These episodes pervaded the Union army, and generals remained indecisive. Were they property of the government? Were they free? These questions flooded the War Department after the Bull Run mess. Republicans eventually convinced Lincoln to sign the first Confiscation Act of 1861, which meant escaped slaves could be considered contraband and received as such if they had been in the employ of the Confederate army. This act was very vague and lacked a definition to say if this meant they were also free. A big win for Abolitionists, this act sent shockwaves to those who felt state's rights were imposed, but it helped ratchet the focus on broader issues that the war had only begun to unveil.[78]

The First Casualties

The three wounded 18th soldiers shot on July 17 that stayed in safe hands were all since lodged in Washington hospitals. John Waterson's grueling gunshot wound in his thigh was too much for his body to take. He lingered for a week before his eventual death on July 23. The twenty-three-year-old earned the unwanted distinction to be the first soldier from the 18th to die from an enemy bullet. Waterson's body was shipped back home and buried in the Albany city cemetery.[79]

Second Lieutenant Edward W. Groot's gunshot in his left hand mangled his hand, but not enough to require an amputation. He concentrated on recuperation and vowed to return to the regiment, but his condition would eventually require a forced discharge in December. Groot remained devoted to the cause and eventually joined another regiment before war's end.[80]

After a ball pierced through Sergeant John S. Allen's left arm and sliced into his side during the skirmish, he was rushed to the rear where the surgeon went to immediate work on his wounds. In order to save his life, the surgeon informed Allen that he needed to amputate his arm close to the elbow. Allen accepted the decision but because of his open wound in his side the surgeon had to also forego chloroform. The surgeon explained the threshold of pain would be great, but Allen "sat coolly" and watched the saw blade slice through his arm, "without a groan." A letter written by the surgeon stated:

> [Allen] exhibited the greatest fortitude, remarking it was too sad he could not go to the [Manassas] Gap. He could fence, and use a revolver and could go yet. When the operation was over he said "Let me see my arm" and when it was shown him said "Good bye, good bye."[81]

Allen was hospitalized in the Washington Infirmary where he received daily care and was monitored closely after his amputation. Many comrades and friends paid Allen a visit in the hospital and always found him in positive spirits. Allen wrote letters to his family back in Ogdensburg, and even penned a letter to Captain Bartlett that expressed his optimism that he would recover soon and visit the boys at Camp Myers. A patient from another regiment who occupied a cot next to Allen recalled that when a man informed the one-armed sergeant that his service as a soldier was done, Allen simply replied with, "That is all that troubles me." On August 8, Allen was visited by New York Senator Preston King, an Ogdensburg native and family friend, who provided some encouraging news to family back home. King later shared Allen's story and desires with the Secretary of the Interior who was impressed by what he heard. The secretary quickly offered Allen a clerkship in his office once he was cleared by doctors.[82]

The news of his possible appointment seemed to reinvigorate Allen's spirits, but fate had other plans for he never left the hospital. The day after King's visit, Allen's health plummeted during the early morning of August 9. He passed away during those early hours in his hospital bed and became the first Northern New Yorker to die in the war. Allen was buried at the Soldier's Home cemetery two miles from the capital city of the nation he swore to protect and gave his life for. Allen was a much-loved son, husband, father, and friend. His two-year-old son would never see his father again. His wife was eight months pregnant when she entered widowhood, and twenty-six days after her husband's death she gave birth to a boy—John S. Allen, Jr.[83]

The Aftermath of Bull Run

The loss at the battle of Bull Run made it clear that the war would not be won so swiftly. Underestimating the Southerners was hard to admit. The thought that a mighty demonstration against the defectors would be enough to straighten out differences vanished overnight. "We got badly licked," wrote one disheartened soldier from the 18th to a friend back home in Schenectady, "and I'm afraid we will get it again, for the reason, that the Southerners are fighting for their homes." The fantasy of heroics seemed to fade from this dejected soldier who continued to write to his friend, "you have seen me for the last time, if we have another engagement. We have been fooled like h[ell], and we are stuck for three years as sure as you live…. I think when you stayed at home, it was the wisest thing you ever done in your whole life."[84]

One to put his worries to paper was Adjutant John H. Russell, who wrote a letter to his brother that explained his fear of the skilled enemy and the embarrassment felt from the sting of defeat:

> The South has been tremendously underrated by us Northerners; that they have a *splendid* army, of enormous strength, splendidly equipped, well cheered, well provided for in every way, clothed, fed and armed, and what is still more, they'll fight *for* the South, all the stories to the contrary notwithstanding. I have seen and talked with prisoners from their forces who have been brought into camp by our pickets, and with precious few exceptions they all vow fidelity to their cause, being as much impressed with the belief that they are *right* as we are. The only thing in which they seem misinformed is regarding their treatment *by us*, as they all have the idea we are here to rob and murder them,—a thing that has doubtless been drummed into them to arouse them to desperation.[85]

The battle did give the men the experience they yearned for and had a better understanding of what their decision to serve meant. First Sergeant John M. Dempsey, Company F, demonstrated his grip of expectations and tried to be positive to worried family back home after the battle and said that he "did not expect, before me, a path strewn with roses, so I meet with no disappointments."[86]

From the Union army's perspective, the battle of Bull Run was filled with multiple flaws and mistakes that culminated to their self-destruction. With nearly 3,000 Union soldiers listed as killed, wounded, or missing, the tally stacked higher than the Confederates. Despite the defeat, the volunteer army showed promise and could no longer be considered green. Corporal Seymour spoke very highly of the competence of the regiment's officers, but as for the higher-echelon commanders such as Miles, McDowell, and a few others, the sharp-tongued soldier referred to them as "inexperienced, and possessed no more military knowledge than a superannuated poodle." A long list of problems rose that required keen attention by both armies as each strived towards the road to victory.[87]

By July 25, the missing men from the regiment were listed at eleven, and six of these were understood to be prisoners. This number was minuscule when compared with the other regiments that were shredded upon the open field in the thick of the action. The march and skedaddle of the army had lost a lot of their organization, and dazed and confused men sought safety before reunion with their regiments. Private Joseph Baker and First Sergeant Freeman F. Huntington, who had just had part of his finger amputated from his self-inflicted accident, both appeared on the missing roster until they returned back into camp several days after the battle.[88]

Bull the dog made it safely to Camp Myers atop the saddle of Major Myers. The three-legged pup was shown to the colonel who declared him to be the pet of the regiment, and with attention from the medical staff Bull made a quick recovery. Private Jehiel J. Stevens of Company K mentioned the mascot became "the pet of the boys, any one of whom would fight at the drop of the hat if anyone attempted to impose on or abuse the dog." Bull remained with the field officers of the 18th but really had the entire regiment as caregivers. He proved himself to be "a most efficient guard at Headquarters." Throughout the rest of the existence of the 18th, to include all of their hard marches, Bull would be there.[89]

5

The Makeover of an Army
August 4, 1861–September 30, 1861

"I have not the least doubt about it that they
are drilling us so that we will be all ready to march."
—*Sergeant George Blake, Company H, October 30, 1861*

Reorganization from Top to Bottom

While the commanding staff of the Union army licked their wounds clean from Bull Run, major changes to its infrastructure began immediately. Major General George Brinton McClellan was appointed to the overall command of McDowell's army on July 27, and christened the new army, the Army of the Potomac. He was a West Point graduate and tested his mettle on battlefields during the Mexican War. At thirty-four years old, McClellan was then the youngest general with also the most seniority in the United States Army. Fueled by popularity, there was no argument that McClellan did not exude anything less than the definition of confidence, and his sheer presence before the troops acted like magic to instill the much needed ingredient of *esprit de corps*. Newspapers dubbed him the "Young Napoleon" and in time his troops fashioned a deep-seated trust and respect for the leader they nicknamed "Little Mac."[1]

McClellan overhauled the army with the reinstatement of divisional structure and reorganized the regiments in a way he felt was a better model for command and control. On August 4, McClellan appointed his close friend Brigadier General William Buel Franklin as the new commander of the brigade that the 18th belonged to. Franklin was a Pennsylvania native and graduated as the top cadet of his West Point class in 1843. Franklin had recently served in command of a brigade in McDowell's Third Division at Bull Run. The units that now comprised Franklin's brigade consisted of the 15th, 18th, 31st and 32nd New York regiments, a battery from the 2nd United States Artillery, and a cavalry contingent of the 1st New York Cavalry.[2]

The same day General Franklin entered the brigade, two officers transitioned out of the regiment. Captain David L. Bartlett—the organizer and commander of Company K—regretfully resigned his position and returned to his home in Ogdensburg, never to put a military uniform on again. He had turned fifty-one years old shortly before the regiment moved south and his age worked against him with the hardship of a soldier's life, and the southern summer

Left: A dependable and competent gentleman, Capt. Albert Sykes Seely took over Company K after Bartlett's early resignation, but sickness would eventually force his resignation before the regiment mustered out (courtesy New York State Military Museum). *Right:* Brig. Gen. William Buel Franklin (pictured as a major general) of Pennsylvania graduated top of his West Point class in 1843. Through continual reconstructions of the Army of the Potomac, Franklin earned promotions and at times commanded over the 18th New York as their brigade, division, and corps commander (Library of Congress).

clime was also a contributor. First Lieutenant Albert S. Seely took charge of the company which enabled every subordinate officer in Company K to be bumped up a rank. Seely was already viewed as a dependable and competent gentleman to lead the company in the eyes of his neighbors. Back when the company was in its infancy in May, the citizens of Ogdensburg presented the young lieutenant with a sword and epaulets in a gesture of their admiration for him. He seemed weary to make a promise to his townsfolk's expectations that he was the right candidate to wield the sword in a battle. Instead, Seely felt that the only test there was, was to face the enemy in battle which would prove to them—and more importantly to himself—that their confidence would not be misplaced.[3]

The other resignation was a forced one from the regiment's surgeon which came as a godsend to the men. Dr. James L. Van Ingen had the distinction of not having lost a single soldier to disease under his watch, but he lacked the confidence from the regiment caused from his own drunkenness. He was unpopular and complained by the men often for his "intemperate habits." Before their first brush of battle, First Sergeant Robert A. Malone of Company D was unequivocal in a July 8 letter to his hometown paper that condemned the surgeon's actions:

> [Van Ingen] is not at all the man for such an office—he is scarcely ever sober, and always unfit to attend to his business, besides being a most tyrannical, arbitrary man. I don't think he would hurry himself in the slightest degree to assist a wounded man, and I have no doubt if we go into action that many lives will be lost from his neglect.[4]

Lieutenant Colonel Young solicited Dr. Van Ingen to resign, which he did on August 1. General Mansfield, commander of the Department of Washington, must not have known about his habits and suggested the doctor to reconsider his resignation. Heed to his suggestion, Dr. Van Ingen tried to redact his forced resignation and penned a withdrawal the day after, but he was too late. His resignation had already been finalized and he was out of the regiment on August 4. Dr. Van Ingen was quickly picked up by the 5th New York to become their surgeon, but the same complaints and two court-martials sent him packing less than six months later.[5]

Two weeks after Van Ingen's exit, his replacement was found with the appointment of Dr. Nathan Payson Rice as the 18th's new surgeon. Born in Boston, Massachusetts, on May 26, 1829, Dr. Rice earned an education from Harvard University, and graduated from their medical school in 1853. He started a practice in New York City and gained notoriety among medical journal readers as the author of articles about the early uses of anesthesia.[6]

More Drill and More Mishaps

As the command structure was being rearranged around the army, Colonel Jackson retained the same intensity and routine of daily drill to his regiment. As more escaped slaves entered Camp Myers, they became the audience to the regiment's drill practices. Except for Sundays, battalion drill was conducted everyday at 5 a.m. Company drill commenced at 10 a.m. and the daily dress parades were performed at six o'clock in the evenings. The daily routine of drill was mandatory and cancelled only if the weather did not cooperate. With the time off between drills, the men caught up on correspondence, washed clothes, bathed in the nearby creek, or simply lounged under the shade of the trees to escape the day's heat. With the occasional inspection of arms, Sundays were still mainly a day of rest. The men regularly attended church services with Chaplain Farr and spent the remainder of the day resting, if their company was not posted on picket duty, that is.[7]

Drill was still paramount and their attention to details was still needed to be preached to these citizen soldiers. Despite the warnings, men like Private Alexander M. Wallace of Company A made heads turn when he accidentally wounded himself in his right hand while he was on guard on July 28. He would do little to no duty after the incident and was discharged in January. The night after Wallace's injury, a fight broke out in camp between a few quarrelsome soldiers that was brought to an end after an officer indiscriminately fired his pistol and wounded one of the fighters in the leg. Forty-nine-year-old Private Charles Peterson of Company B was a bystander but was struck in his right arm from one of the officer's stray rounds. A former blacksmith, Peterson was sent home with a lame hand before the end of the year. On August 4, a soldier on guard duty shot a musket ball through his hand. Two days later, a sergeant in Company H became the sixth self-inflicted accident since the regiment left Albany when he shot off his finger with his pistol in camp. One cannot but wonder whether some of these accidents were true mistakes or desperate attempts to get out of the service. The sergeant who lost his finger called it an accident, though some questioned his misfortune. Either a case of mistaken identity or he was caught breaking the law, another dark incident occurred on August 10 when Corporal Charles H. Thompson of Company B was shot and killed by one of the provost guards stationed around Alexandria.[8]

The food at Camp Myers remained the standard camp-prepped provisions made available to regiments. "A small piece of dry bread and a half a pot of unsweetened coffee," was all that Sergeant Mowatt of Company C could write about each morning in his diary. Talking like a true veteran, he took it in stride and used it as a preparation for future discomforts by writing, "Hard living and hard times in Old Virginny and no doubt worse a coming." Days where the weather would not cooperate did more than just soak the men's spirits, it ended the chance for a warm meal. During a rain storm on August 1, Mowatt wrote that the rain put "a stop to all outdoor cooking in the midst of plenty suffering with hunger, such is soldiering, in the times of war, learning by experience." Within the first couple of days in August, the catch-up game to acquire better rations slowly picked up but retained no regularity. Sometimes the rations would be larger and of better quality, and the next it could be nothing but bread. In Mowatt's words, "so it goes, a feast one day and a famine the next."[9]

Front and back of an identification disc for Pvt. William H. McKinney, Company E, most likely made by a nearby sutler in the early months of the war. Note the name "War of 1861" as the conflict was then called before the new year. Discs like these were personal purchases during the Civil War, as the War Department was still decades away from the concept akin to the modern "dog tag" (author's collection).

The men received their long awaited gold and silver pay up to the end of July on August 7, and the payment was a relief to their worries. Mustering for payment was always one of the happier days in camp. Not only was it good for the men to be given their due earnings, but with it came peddlers that swarmed the camps and thrived on the newly paid soldiers. Tired of the same dry bread that constituted meals, men spent part of their pay on personal effects and stocked up on fruits and vegetables and indulged themselves with cakes and pies.[10]

Company F Turns on Captain Donovan

Major grievances had reached a boiling point in Company F that threatened to break down the order of the company against their captain. Since Captain Michael H. Donovan's reign as their company commander, the men saw a darker man emerge than the one they elected as their captain. First, Donovan ignored the company's mutual agreement to elect their own non-commissioned officers without interference, but that is exactly what he did when he self-appointed several to positions of authority that were not offices at all. Colonel Jackson had to interfere and keep them off the rolls of the company. More importantly it was Donovan's attitude that turned his men against him. Second Lieutenant John Mooney recalled a time when Donovan drew his sword upon "one of the most harmless men in the Regiment." In the presence of his company and several companies who looked on, Donovan knocked the soldier out of his formation with his sword, "without just cause or provocation." He continued to beat the soldier with the edge of his sword and threatened to "run him through." The astonished onlookers from the company could only watch in horror and listen to Donovan's incessant cursing amidst the beating. Men felt helpless. Donovan turned the threats

Capt. Michael H. Donovan (far left) and his Company F, pictured in camp. Donovan's harsh style of command once put the company on the brink of mutiny, but through the use of court-martials the men quieted down. Donovan was one of two captains who held their position as company commander for the duration of the regiment's existence (from the collection of the Schenectady County Historical Society).

upon them and yelled that he would "blow the first man's brains out who dared to dispute his authority." The men eventually united against Donovan and looked to Lieutenant Mooney to draft a petition that requested the help of Colonel Jackson. Mooney penned a four-page draft that highlighted their grievances, and asked for a more qualified man to lead the company. It remains unknown if Jackson ever received the petition, as the letter remained in Mooney's possession and Donovan's office was never threatened.[11]

Companies continued to cycle through guard duty around the camp. Boring as the task was, the job was important, yet it was easy for some men to grow tired of the repetitive chore. When Company F caught wind that their disliked captain was going to commit them to a stint of guard duty on a day outside of the normal rotation, they gathered on the evening of August 8 to air their grievances and to persuade the company to not turn out for guard duty the next morning. First Sergeant John M. Dempsey did what was expected of his office and immediately reported the situation to Captain Donovan. The captain took this bit of information and went up his chain of command and reported the rumor to the colonel, "that he might expect trouble with my company the next day." The following morning, Dempsey attempted to form the company at 9 a.m. but as expected they refused. Dempsey approached Donovan just as he had the night previous and reported the company's refusal to form for guard duty. Donovan trekked down to the mutinous company grounds and took a hold of the situation. He found the company of twenty to thirty men seated on the ground near some trees and not in line like the first sergeant had ordered. "No guard duty to-day," joked Private Daniel Stillwell to his captain. Donovan was not in the joking mood and quickly stared the company down and forcefully ordered them to form. Minds were changed and most of the men began to form up. The group that sat under the trees slowly saw their party dwindle. Private James Slattery stuck to his guns and looked towards those who complied with the order and called them cowards. Donovan looked at him and others like Private Edward Adams who similarly laughed and scoffed at those that formed. Donovan repeated the order multiple times to persuade the men of his seriousness. Private Walter Allen walked a leashed dog— possibly Bull—around the camp towards the company when Captain Donovan appeared, but he immediately turned around when orders were yelled. Donovan noticed Allen turn away and said he continued to walk away and even "looked at me over his shoulder sneeringly just as though he did not care for the order, and did not intend to obey it." Private Alonzo Richardson did a similar thing and just walked away from the whole incident. Donovan was surrounded by both compliant and mutinous men. Donovan was certain he heard Adams remark, "There goes old Buckfart," which was directed towards Private Francis Noonan after he gravitated towards the obedient formation. Adams seemed to be the most ardently incensed by the failed mutiny when he addressed loudly for the crowd to hear, "Those are fine fellows to make an agreement one day and break it the next." Just a small handful ended up ignoring their captain's order and walked away. After five minutes had passed and Donovan's command to fall in was given fifteen times, he tasked Sergeant Michael Daniels to round up the defecting few and had them arrested. This quickly changed their stance and Privates Stillwell, Slattery, Adams, Allen, and Richardson plead ignorance and apologies for their refusals, but they went unheard and they were placed in the guardhouse.[12]

More than a week later these men were made an example of and their actions were subjected to the regiment's first round of court-martial trials. With a panel of thirteen of some of the most senior-ranking field officers from the area, one of which was Major George R. Myers, the court heard their cases. All of the men stirred up stories that they were sick or never heard the order, and that they would have certainly complied had they heard Donovan's instruction. Their alibis were even corroborated by multiple witnesses that demonstrated there was more devotion to each other than to their captain's words, yet all five were convicted and outrageously sentenced to death by musketry. The officers of the court initially settled with a not-guilty sentence for some, but the court reverted towards a universal guilty to all parties and sentenced them to death to serve as a demonstration to the army that violations of the Articles of War would not be tolerated. The men were mortified to say the least and hauled off to the guardhouse for an unspecified time.[13]

The Blame Game, Court-Martials of Commanders

Court-martials were in high demand throughout the ranks of the Army of the Potomac in early August. Several accusations of incompetent or drunk officers during the battles at Blackburn's Ford and Bull Run surfaced that led to many investigations and court inquiries. Colonel Jackson had to sit as president for one on August 5, in which both officers were exonerated on charges that they ordered their regiment to retreat from the battlefield.[14]

Jackson himself seemed to be caught in the finger-pointing after the battle. A three-page paper in Jackson's compiled service records at the National Archives shows charges were made against him with accusations of being drunk during the battle. The specifications are quite detailed and seem to have been made by a senior officer, most likely Colonel Davies of the 16th New York. The affidavit said Jackson had a one-gallon flask strung around his neck that contained a liquor-and-water mixture that he drank from and offered to others during the battle and the days that led up. Jackson was further accused of using foul language against the regiment when the 18th was ordered to a reserve position to protect a battery, which was considered "conduct unbecoming of an officer and a gentleman." The accusation specified that Colonel Jackson yelled, "God damn your souls to Hell! Jesus Christ!" and "God damn you why don't you form?" Lastly, the third charge was a "positive & willful disobedience to orders" in which Jackson disregarded Davies' orders to send out six companies in the evening of July 24 and relieve the 80th New York at the junction of the Richmond and Fairfax Roads. All of these accusations never seemed to go anywhere, as Jackson was never charged or reprimanded.[15]

The same could not be said for Colonel Dixon S. Miles, whose overwhelming accusations of his sobriety during the battle of Bull Run became headline news. A court inquiry began on August 10, but the trial and investigation waged for several months to allow time for officers to tend to their regiments. The oaths from dozens of officers present at the battle that came in contact with Miles were gathered. Equal amounts of testimonies that supported both sides of the allegations are what prolonged the case. On the seventh day of testimonies, four officers from the 18th took the stand. Colonel Jackson, Adjutant John H. Russell, Captain Thomas J. Radcliff of Company I, and Captain Henry Wiltse of Company C, all testified and adamantly defended Miles to say he did not appear intoxicated on the field, or as Jackson put it, did not see Miles "drink a drop that day." Had Miles not suffered at the time from an illness and been prescribed medicines from a doctor that intoxicated him, Miles would have certainly been cashiered. Under these extenuating circumstances, Miles was essentially acquitted at the end of October, but was removed from the Army of the Potomac and transferred to command the federal arsenal at Harpers Ferry.[16]

A Private on a Pass

Oftentimes men from the 18th were granted passes to Alexandria where they could take a break from their duties, but sometimes this ushered trouble. Private John LeFleur of Company I was on one such pass in the city on August 12 and went straight to a saloon on King Street. After having one too many drinks, LeFleur attempted to enter a private apartment in search of more alcohol. A male occupant met LeFleur and made him leave. Once outside, LeFleur flipped and called him "a secession son-of-a-bitch" several times. LeFleur then raised his rifle and leveled it at the man and yelled, "I'll shoot you, you son of a bitch, anyhow," just as the man jumped inside and slammed the door. LeFleur was hell-bent and attempted to enter another door but was met by a group of men who overpowered him and took away his gun. He struggled a bit and yelled that the gun was not loaded. The men that took down LeFleur brought him to the authorities and had him detained. More than a week passed when LeFleur had to relive this night through a court-martial testimony and was found guilty on several charges. He was sentenced to wear a 32-pound ball and chain affixed to his left leg while he performed hard labor. The punishment would last for ten hours every day for ninety days. Luckily, Second Lieutenant Charles W. Heald of his company testified in defense of LeFleur's character and said that he had been a good and faithful soldier, and always "considered him one of the best men in the company." Heald also stated that "the few times that [LeFleur] has been in liquor, I have found him easily controlled." With this and the compassion of General McClellan, LeFleur's sentence was later lessened to rid the ball and chain.[17]

Camp Misery

With the influx of regiments and new forts built around Alexandria, troops once on the front soon found themselves tucked inside friendly lines. Time came for the 18th to cease their guard of the Hunting Creek Bridge and pack up their camp for a move west closer to the enemy lines. At 7 a.m., on August 15, the tents were struck and Camp Myers came to an end. They were formed in columns for their march to their new location and trekked through Alexandria. They turned west down the Leesburg Turnpike [present-day Leesburg Pike] about a mile out of the city where they set up their bivouac on the slope of a dominating hilltop locally known as Shuter's Hill. An artillery battery from Maine occupied the crest above them on a base called Fort Dahlgren, which was also linked to Fort Ellsworth [present-day George Washington Masonic National Memorial]. Shuter's Hill held a commanding view looking over King and Duke Streets, and both were a part of the long-stretched defensive ring of forts that surrounded Washington. The men spent the afternoon pitching their tents and made them as comfortable as circumstances and terrain could allow. The following morning of August 16, the rest of the remaining regiments assigned to Franklin's brigade similarly relocated and drew in closer to the 18th.[18]

The ground of their hillside encampment was marred by excessive mud. Two nearby abandoned homes believed to be owned by secessionists were stripped to their skeletal frames almost instantly by the soldiers. The wooden siding was repurposed for the men to act as floorboards to stay above the ankle-deep mud. Corporal Andrew D. Barhydt of Company E described a floorboard he built to be four inches tall, but its stiffness ushered obvious back aches when it came time to sleep on them. A heavy rainstorm showered on the camp on August 19 and stirred up the grounds. The torrential downpour lasted for more than twenty-four hours. Being encamped on the hillside of Fort Dahlgren, the 18th saw most of the rain pour down the hill which created excessive mud throughout their camp. The conditions worsened for the 15th New York who were encamped below the 18th. The rush of mud and rain washed down the hill and flooded out the 15th and forced them to pack up during the storm and relocate their camp to more suitable ground, but there was hardly a better spot. The rain-soaked soldiers of the 18th despised this short-lived mud-covered camp under the guns of Fort Dahlgren and Ellsworth, which affectionately earned the nickname "Camp Misery."[19]

With impeccable timing at such an abysmal encampment, the Sanitary Commission made their second inspection of the regiment's condition on August 20. The regimental surgeon provided numbers for the inspector and explained the general health of the 18th had improved, yet the regiment looked like they were under hard times. The regiment stood at

760, but eleven were hospitalized elsewhere in the city, nine were in the regimental hospital, and thirty-nine were confined to their own tents on that particular day. During the last two weeks before the inspection, the 18th had a daily average of forty men on the sick list, but no deaths. Malaria seemed to be the biggest plague, blamed on a nearby swamp. Privies were dug 100 yards from their camp, but were since filled in by rain. There also was no adequate place for the men to bathe, so they skipped baths. Tents were placed closer together than their last encampment, being three feet apart. An average of four to six men shared a tent. The camp streets and drains along the edges of the tents and the space between them were cited by the inspector to be neglected and littered with food, bones, and other rubbish. Only one company was said to have had rubber blankets which helped deflect the wetness, but most men slept on the bare ground. The inspector counted 450 men to be without blankets, but at least they all had good overcoats. It was clear that moral was not stellar, and the regiment lacked any organized games, amusements, or mutual benefit societies. Colonel Jackson had appointed a regimental sutler for the men, but the crooked businessman ignored fixed prices on items outlined by army regulations and set them high. The sutler did offer spirits, but they could only be sold at times when Jackson allowed. Men in the regiment still found other ways to procure alcohol, yet intoxication was not a rampant problem. Averages of five men daily were placed in the guardhouse for random offenses, and seldom for infractions of being drunk. The food rations still seemed to be good, although there was always a want of more. Fresh meat was available three times a week, but the unskilled company cooks were said to have cooked food badly. Rations of tea were often served instead of coffee, and a surface spring provided drinkable water. Fresh soft bread came from a general bakery in Alexandria.[20]

The heavy rainclouds eventually passed which allowed the familiar August sun to dry up the mud for several days. The summer heat lingered in Alexandria which made canvas tents feel like furnaces. Only a few trees in close proximity to the camp offered respite from the concentrated rays of the sun. Even before the ground had time to harden, drill still prevailed. With the welcoming of better weather, so too did the peddlers return who lined up along the limits of the camp on the roadside and offered the temporary relief of refreshments.[21]

The regiment's poorly constructed uniforms were well worn out by August and literally tore at the seams. A majority of the men had been without socks for weeks, and most had but one shirt apiece. Luckily, the men had the benevolent ladies associations of their hometowns to raise funds and clothing and forward the articles to their camp. Company D received a large box of clothing that contained dozens of shirts, handkerchiefs, socks, sheets, drawers, and other essential garments. The government supplied to the rest of the regiment more clothes just before they left Camp Myers. Every man in the regiment received a new woolen shirt, two new pairs of wool socks and two pairs of cotton drawers. Most importantly, each man received a new fatigue cap that came with gold letters and numbers that denoted the company and regiment on it. This now made it easier to identify soldiers with their proper affiliation.[22]

With better weather, the regiment also partook in their first review of Franklin's entire brigade by General McClellan, which was conducted on August 24, about a quarter of a mile from Camp Misery on a spacious level field. From the eyes of the 18th, they felt McClellan, "expressed himself well satisfied" as one 18th member summarized. McClellan also took notice of the disheveled appearance of the regiment who extended their exhausted uniforms by the efficiency of needles and thread. Private Samuel Hodgkins of Company K recalled how the regiment uniquely acquired replacements:

> We were inspected by our new Commander in Chief, General McClellan. By this time the 18th was destitute of clothing, not having had any issued to us since receiving our first suit in Albany, and that had not been very good. We went out on parade all cleaned up but very ragged, some were barefooted, some without pants, just drawers, some without coats and some with straw hats, etc. After we had passed the General, he called the Colonel back, and asked what regiment that was. [The colonel] answered "The 18th New York Volunteers of Albany." The General said, "You have a fine regiment of men, I see you have them well drilled and I will see that they have better clothes."[23]

Adding to the adverse conditions of a swampy camp, several men in the regiment began to contract and spread diseases. At Camp Misery, Corporal Barhydt recalled "a good many of the Reg. are getting the Fever Ague." Flu, measles, mumps, and fevers passed through the ranks and affected several men. The daily sick list rose and fluctuated from 75 to 150. A few soldiers were so afflicted that they had no hope for a speedy recovery and were given medical discharges and sent home.[24]

Near the end of August, a handful of the older men from Company K were sick and sent home. One of them was forty-three-year-old Private Peter Sheehan, whose exit came more as a relief to the company. Since the battle of Bull Run, Sheehan seemed to do all that he could to get himself out of any type of duty. He went as far as to curl himself into a ball, and performed several fits which he said were attacks of epilepsy. Sheehan was an Irish immigrant who served in the English army before the Civil War, but the men were quick to learn that he had deserted that outfit which led him to settle in New York. Sheehan maintained his epileptic episodes with the hospital staff, which eventually led to his medical discharge on those grounds. Tired of seeing him sham duty, his peers were glad to see him go. His company officers certainly did not fight to keep him either, for they attributed his epileptic fits were merely a result of his insatiable appetite for whiskey. First Lieutenant Horatio G. Goodno went as far to say Sheehan "was drunk most of the time" and "was a worthless soldier."[25]

Officers in ill health fared better than the enlisted men and were often granted furloughs, such as the one Captain Stephen Truax of Company E took on August 6 for a thirty day leave in Schenectady after having contracted a fever and diarrhea. Even Colonel Jackson needed to take a leave of absence on August 25 to return home and recuperate for a few days after he contracted a serious bout with the flu. He left Lieutenant Colonel Young in his absence with full command of the regiment for the first time.[26]

Lieutenant Colonel Young took on the interim command with ease. The same day Jackson took leave, Young conducted the standard inspection of arms usually held every Sunday. Rifles, knapsacks, cartridge boxes, bayonets, and belts were all visually inspected by Young's keen eyes, just like Jackson would conduct weekly. Once satisfied with what he saw, he dismissed the parade and complimented Company E "as bearing the best inspection" on that particular day. This was a feat that every line officer in their respective companies strived to achieve during Sunday inspections. The best presented company—and in this case Company E—was accompanied by the drum corps and regimental colors and marched to the colonel's tent where they saluted him with their rifles before they retired back to their tents to gloat until the next Sunday inspection.[27]

Understanding that soon the regiment would be tasked out to begin construction of a new fort, a heightened focus on drill prevailed at Camp Misery. The 18th conducted six hours of drill daily, but no drills were ever held before breakfast. A break from training seemed only to come when companies were tasked out for guard duty away from the camp.[28]

Camp King

The unfavorable location of their swampy and despised hillside camp was resolved when the 18th was instructed to pack it up on August 27. Young's command to strike the tents around noon came as words of mercy. A soldier in Company A exclaimed, "Never was better news received by us, who had been camped in a very unhealthy place for some time," After the usual delays incidental to a march, the regiment traveled about two miles northwesterly down the Leesburg Turnpike, and stopped about two and a half miles from Bailey's Crossroads in which the enemy pickets were expected to be posted. The 18th formed their camp in a field right off the turnpike, a short distance from the toll gate and Fairfax Seminary [present-day Virginia Theological Seminary]. The other elements of Franklin's brigade would also follow their lead and settled within the same neighborhood.[29]

The 18th's new camp was given the name "Camp King" after New York Republican Senator Preston King from Ogdensburg. This new camp [near the present-day T. C. Williams High School] was far superior to their previous swampy one, and sat atop high lands with a splendid view of the greater landscape around them. The camp did seem to lack an ample water supply, but a small house nearby converted into a hospital for the regiment had access to a large well near the roadside which the men drew water from. More trees in the area offered lumber and shade.[30]

Used as a hospital for nearby Union troops, Aspinwall Hall dominated the campus of Fairfax Seminary (present-day Virginia Theological Seminary) near Alexandria, Virginia (Library of Congress).

Camp King, about two miles northwest of Alexandria off the Leesburg Turnpike, was the longtime encampment of the 18th New York during the fall of 1861 and following winter. Above the tree line can be seen the spire of Aspinwall Hall (from the collection of the Schenectady County Historical Society).

Bailey's Crossroads and Munson's Hill

With the relocation and establishment of Camp King, the 18th was now closer than ever with the enemy, and strict discipline was continually enforced throughout the camp. Just two more miles down the Leesburg Turnpike from Camp King was a road junction known as Bailey's Crossroads, which was hotly shared by pickets from both sides, with each about a quarter of a mile from the crossing. A half mile behind Bailey's Crossroads on the Confederate side stood a dominating land feature called Munson's Hill that had just been claimed by a Virginia regiment from Confederate Brigadier General James Longstreet's brigade on August 28. The pointed hilltop was roughly eighty feet above everything within the surrounding area which provided the best natural observance of most hills, valleys, roads, encampments, and even Washington. The occupied hill became the enemy's advanced outpost nearest the Potomac, which made the site a savory tract of real estate for Union troops. Confederates went to immediate work to reinforce Munson's Hill and threw up meager-looking breastworks that wrapped around the crown of the hill, and surrounded by a ditch for added protection. It was the quick arrival of artillery pieces that immediately worried the Federals and prevented an unplanned seizure of the hill.[31]

Just as soon as pickets from a New Jersey regiment were pushed away from Munson's Hill and farther back from Bailey's Crossroads when the enemy moved in, Franklin's former brigade made their appearance near the line to help bolster the buffer zone. Sporadic companies from the 15th, 18th, 31st, and 32nd New York left their camps at 10 p.m. on August 27, and established a new line of pickets near the crossroads. Company D was the contingent

Unidentified Union troops pictured in the middle of Bailey's Crossroads at a more peaceful time (Library of Congress).

from the 18th that night. They fanned themselves out along the line in search of enemy pickets. Their position varied to within 300 yards of Bailey's Crossroads, and their neighbors on the picket line were a couple of New Jersey regiments and the 2nd Michigan.[32]

The sunrise that crept in on the morning of August 28 illuminated the land and provided the confirmation on just how close each side was to each other. Most were within 300 yards of each others' pickets. Officers paced along the line and urged their men not to fire on the enemy pickets unless done so in self-defense, all in an effort to conserve ammunition or deter the provocation of a bigger fight. Oftentimes the lines were so stretched thin that this order was merely an overlooked formality.[33]

Without deliberately opening fire yet still having the want to harass their enemy, the men on the picket line got creative. August 28 was Company D's first day on the line and the only from the regiment, and a part of their line joined forces with a portion of pickets from a neighboring New Jersey regiment. Together, they decided to play a little trick on the Rebels with some foraged materials that were nearby. This handful of New Yorkers and Jersey men grabbed a heavily used black stove pipe that they found in the road and took the top off of it. "Borrowing, or rather taking a wagon," as one put it, they then emptied the wagon, and stripped two of the hind wheels. They then affixed the stove pipe tube to the center of the axle on the wheeled wagon cart that together formed a crude semblance to an artillery piece, especially from a distance. When they wheeled the "thing" out into the road and in clear sight of just under a mile of the Rebel fort, the men went through the act to unlimber and charge the pipe like a real cannon crew. Immediately, the Company D pickets saw the Rebels scramble upon their breastworks and peer out with their field glasses. Nineteen-year old Private Rodney S. Vedder, a former student of Union College who left school in order to join Company E, described the enemy's panic, "all the 'stir' imaginable was observable in the fort." The Yankee pranksters then rammed down some wet paper down the pipe, and instantly the Rebel pickets before them "were seen running 'helter skelter' into the fort." Before they had finished the "load" of the pipe, the Confederate battery in the fort answered first with a six pound cannonball that struck about thirty feet in front of the "32 pounder stovepipe." Private Vinson H. Clark, Company D, said the cannonball "made the boys bounce some, and came very near putting the Lieut. Col. of the 31st hors de combat." Having escaped any injuries, the faux artillerymen went back at it and maneuvered the sheet iron gun, which caused more fire to come their way. Private Vedder said the firing ceased when one of the men "raised the stovepipe in his hand, while another waves the Stars and Stripes, and then, to the dismay of the rebels, beat a retreat." The enemy had fired a total of five shots, but none were as close as the inaugural ball. Clark went on to comment that "all the damage done was against themselves, they having succeeded in putting two shots straight through a secessionist's house, and scaring the family, baggage and all, on double quick for safer quarters." Sporadic musketry exchanges continued in fashion throughout the day, and tapered off a half hour before darkness settled. This "stove pipe affair" would make its appearance in New York papers, but when the men present read that the credit was given to the 2nd Michigan—neighbors on the picket line more than a mile from the incident—prompted Clark and Vedder to reach out to their hometown papers to clear the air in print and bestow proper honors "on whom honor is due."[34]

The same day of the stove pipe affair, Company D Privates Henry Hayden and George House were taken by the Rebels. Their capture was a testament on how intermeshed the lines tended to be. Both were forwarded to a Richmond prison, but their comrades could only speculate their outcome and were unsure if they were alive or dead. Hayden and House were said by Clark to be "both good fellows," and added that their loss spread "a gloom over the whole company." The incident certainly highlighted to others of the importance to stay vigilant and disciplined on the picket line. Two weeks would pass until a letter brought news that they were alive and well, although prisoners of war.[35]

Numerous companies from the regiment manned the line concurrently, regardless of what weather had in store. The line was also shared by other companies from nearby regiments. By then, corn was in season and abundant and the smell of it being boiled and roasted permeated both sides of the picket line. Frequent potshots were exchanged around Bailey's Crossroads almost on a daily basis while both sides maintained their checkmate of each other. So close were they to the enemy fortification that Private Rodney Vedder said they could "easily distinguish the negroes at work on the entrenchments, and the troops drilling." From his forward position on the picket line, another soldier from the 18th described the view of the Confederates before him:

> The rebels still hold Munson's Hill, and their entrenchments and sentry walking his rounds can be plainly seen from our camp with the naked eye, it being only about two and a half guns and felt so disposed, they could shell our camp, it being in plain sight of them. They have breastworks thrown up, commanding the approaches from our side. It is not yet, however, constructed with a view of permanency, and I should judge not very formidable. There is no ditch outside, or at least a very shallow one. In fact, it is an embankment of the simplest kind, and could be easily taken by our boys, who wait anxiously for such orders to come. I presume however, that Gen. McClellan has good and sufficient reasons for not molesting them at present. Groups

of rebel soldiers may be seen most any time during the day sitting on their embankment and watching the interchange of shots between our pickets and their own, which is constantly kept up. Some months since, our men at the report of a gun would have jumped to their arms, but they are now getting so accustomed to this kind of warfare that they pay no attention to it, at least only those who are particularly interested, being the party shot at. It is getting to be an every day affair, and each one has their turn at it, as they are placed as pickets upon the advanced posts.[36]

McClellan's reluctance to seize the hill was less strategy than it was hesitation which defined the young general. The best assumption made from the perspective of the 18th was that the breastworks atop Munson's Hill seemed poor and able to be taken. The newly promoted Second Lieutenant Edward Tilley of Company K flatly stated that the Rebel's bastion was simply, "not very formidable." The high ground greatly favored the Confederates who could theoretically sweep any assault on Munson's Hill with lethal artillery, upon an army that still searched for confidence within themselves. Rumors spilled out amongst the Union camps that Munson's Hill was occupied by as many as 25,000 Rebels, which was a number grossly overstated. What was not known by the Federals was that the occupation consisted of just one brigade of Longstreet's infantry, J. E. B. Stuart's Cavalry, and one functional battery, an aggregate force that was exceedingly less than Union assumptions. To the men at the bottom of the hill it looked as if the Rebel artillery displayed a mass array of differing calibers, and its dominance above the land made Alexandria and Washington worry. Just as the Union pickets had once done, Longstreet's men pulled a similar trick out of the manual of deception and utilized an abundant supply of crafted logs and stove pipes.[37]

Within time and rotations, everyone had gained familiarity with the enemy and their practices and could write home about what a real Rebel looked like, and citizens of the North were fascinated by tales from the front. Lieutenant Tilley received his brother as a visitor to Camp King at the end of the month, and he came with a curiosity to see a live Rebel. On August 31, Tilley requested and was granted permission by the colonel to proceed with his brother toward the picket line that the regiment occupied nearest the Confederates at Munson's Hill. The Tilley brothers armed themselves with rifles and revolvers and trekked through the woods until they met up with some pickets from Company D. Other soldiers from the same company were closer to the enemy, but Tilley felt near enough to satisfy his brother's request. As soon as the two showed up, a few scattered shots rang out from the Confederate pickets which prompted them to take refuge in a nearby ditch which already housed some fellow soldiers from Company D. About 500 yards to the front of their ditch, the appearance of Confederates "walking about very coolly" in the road apparently felt that they were out of accurate firing range. A barn nearby the Confederates also housed enemy pickets who routinely fired a few rounds to ensure that the pickets from Company D kept their heads down. Picket duty often went in this back-and-forth pattern. The Tilley brothers, along with several other Wallkill Guards, fired a few shots of their own towards the nonchalant Confederates which were accurate enough to force the Rebels to dodge into nearby bushes and seek protection. An enemy ambulance from the fort made its appearance and prompted the Confederates to pick up the rate of fire, possibly pending for an attack. But no attack was made and the typical harassment of picket duty ensued. Several exchanges were made from along the picket line by both Captain Meginnis and his men and the Confederates down the road and barn. Eventually the potshots lessened and the satisfied Tilley brothers withdrew to their camp and left Meginnis and his men to persist their usual picket presence.[38]

New Responsibilities for Franklin and Newton

Newly organized regiments continually streamed into Washington and Alexandria which forced General McClellan to routinely restructure his command. One major change McClellan made to the Army of the Potomac was when he reinstituted the divisional structure. On August 28, General Franklin was elevated from brigade commander to become the commander of a division, in which the 18th's brigade would still fall under. His headquarters was just a short distance from Camp King which allowed his former brigade to continue to witness his untiring efforts to do good for the men. Franklin made his rounds on horseback through all of his regiments and ensured that they remained prepared to thwart off any attack. Franklin's vacancy as the brigade commander was given to newly promoted Brigadier General John Newton. One of the few Virginians to stay loyal to the Union, he graduated from West Point a year before Franklin and was classmates with Confederate General Longstreet, his rival on Munson's Hill. Newton had nearly two decades of unblemished service in the regular army as an engineer.[39]

Virginia native Brig. Gen. John Newton (pictured as a major general) was one of the few loyal regular army officers who kept their allegiance to the Union instead of their seceded state. After Franklin was promoted to divisional commander, Newton was given his former brigade that the 18th New York belonged to (Library of Congress).

Building Fort Ward

Leesburg Turnpike was a critical approach to Alexandria from the northwest, and the Confederates had the upper hand to command the road by the reach of Munson's Hill. To combat this, another Union fort beckoned to be built to keep the Confederate hilltop in check and add to the defensive perimeter of Washington. The first order of business for Franklin on the day he was promoted were orders for this new fort's construction, and with the 18th nearby they were obviously looked upon to help build it.[40]

Since the secession of Virginia, the threat of an invasion on Washington was more than just paranoia. Thousands of soldiers filled throughout the epicenter of the capital city and busied themselves with the construction of a ring of forts on seemingly every hilltop with sizeable elevation. It was only a matter of time before the 18th dropped their rifles and picked up shovels to help. They received their first introduction in the fundamentals of fort construction on August 17, where they inspected the interior and exterior of Fort Ellsworth.[41]

The tract of land that was soon to be shaped into a new fort was situated about a mile west from Camp King, on the left side of Leesburg Turnpike. The land chosen was on the brow of a hill that provided a great view of some sixty miles all around. The property was

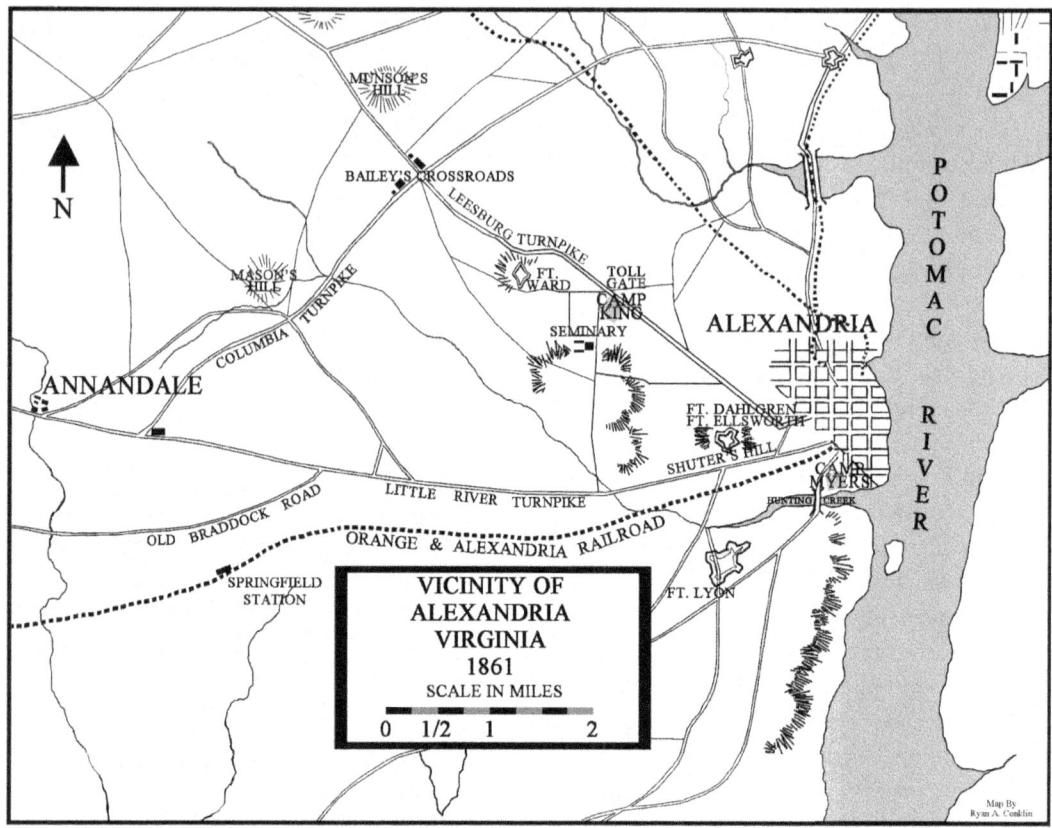

This map of the vicinity around Alexandria, Virginia, highlights many key landmarks pertinent to 18th New York in 1861 (author's collection).

owned by Cassius Lee, cousin to the Confederate General Robert E. Lee. Just a few miles farther west down the Leesburg Turnpike stood Munson's Hill, and its Confederate occupation could be easily seen from their new location since it was about forty-five feet taller than their elevated spot. Both lines now fell within artillery range of each other which stressed the necessity to finish the new fort as quick as humanly possible.[42]

Eleven days after their crash course lesson on fort construction, the 18th rolled up their sleeves and broke ground for the new fort on September 1. The enormity of the job became immediately clear, and as one Company A soldier looked at the job ahead, he said, "For a while our boys will have all and more digging than they want." The regiment was detailed for six consecutive days digging trenches, followed by five days of chopping down the forest that surrounded them. From then on, fatigue parties of men from the regiment would make the short trek day after day to dig deeper pits and trenches. From dusk to dawn, the men tediously chipped into the Virginia soil and created deep trenches, pits, and parapets for future artillery pieces. Considerable digging was also required to hollow out pockets in the ground for powder and magazine storage rooms. Sometimes several companies at a time were tasked, when other days asked for only a select number of men from each company to be grabbed and sent forward to dig. With the enemy on nearby Munson's Hill, even Sundays begged for continued work. Sergeant Mowatt of Company C griped one Sunday that the men "were sent out to work in the trenches, which hardly seems right on the Sabbath day, but rendered necessary by the vicinity of the enemy." The only way to dodge trench work was to either be on picket duty or sick in the hospital.[43]

There was no regularity as to when, how long, or how many men would be tasked out on any given day to work. A mid-day break for lunch was a welcomed rest when they got it. The only thing that was routine was the 5 a.m. wake-up, breakfast, a short march to the fort, and a guarantee that the day would be full of hard labor. Once they got to the fort, they would be given what Private Rodney Vedder eloquently called their "implements of peace—the axe and the shovel" and started their day's work. Some days men would work for half of the day and trade off with a new set of detailed men in the afternoon. For some companies that spent the required guard shift overnight, they were only given a few hours in the morning to sleep before being called up to march to the fort and join their brothers to dig.[44]

The 18th was not the only regiment that pitched forth details of men during the construction of what would soon become Fort Ward. Men from the nearby 5th Maine and 15th, 31st, 32nd, and 40th New York regiments shared the sweat, aches, and pains that were brought on from the laborious work.[45]

For those not on the picket line or fort construction, military drill took precedence at Camp King. Slight changes in routines took place that the men had to adjust to. The drum corps would usually drum the regiment awake at 5 a.m. The changing of the guards was done at 8 a.m., which was an hour earlier than usual. Company drill was changed to be conducted before breakfast, and battalion drill commenced after their morning meal. Dress parade was still held nightly at 6 p.m.[46]

Acquisition of goods proved more streamlined at Camp King when compared with previous camps. Rations started to come more "regularly, promptly, and bountifully" according to Captain Seely, and the stoves the companies had were quite good. The stoves were thirty inches in diameter and four feet high, and had different compartments that Private Rodney Vedder said could "hold a frying pan, a large boiler, two six-quart pans and a gridiron." Confidence was restored in their appearance in early September when the regiment received the much needed second issue of new uniforms that McClellan had promised them after an earlier review. They also traded in their gray overcoats for the light blue standard issue. Sergeant Mowatt wrote that the men made "a very fine appearance with our new overcoats. The regiment never looked better than at the present time." Captain Truax was also gifted fifty books for the company that quickly made their way through the hands of the regiment.[47]

Food seemed easy to come by, and the prosperous sutlers were always willing to oblige a hungry soldier with money. Private Rodney Vedder penned in his journal for September 3 that described how easy and plentiful food was to come by within the area. His entry also sheds a glimpse on how much freedom a pair of privates could have to freely walkabout outside their normal boundaries on the picket line:

> In the morning, we, together with the next "squad of four," made a rousing fire and boiled us some corn and potatoes. Lieut. [John] Vedder bought a dozen of eggs, and these, together with some "Carolina" potatoes, boiled beef, bread and butter, made an excellent meal. After breakfast, "Chum [William] Harris" and myself proceeded on a scouting adventure, in a southwesterly direction. Leaving our woods, we proceed through a cornfield and suddenly came upon a band of [39th New York] "Garabaldis." They exhibited the same plundering propensity they are so noted for. Passing through an almost impassible swamp, we came to a beautiful stream; following this up until we came to a temporary bridge made by felling a tree, we attempted a crossing. My "chum" succeeded, but I made a false support of my gun, and it went into the water. Pulling it out as

quickly as possible, I reached the shore, and after snapping two or three caps on it succeeded in firing it off. Traveling on we came to the Loudon & Hampshire RR crossing, where we entered a house occupied by a Dutchman and his wife, and inquired for something to eat. They furnished us with a quarter of milk—price, nine cents. But what excited my curiosity the most, was to find a stove, "manufactured in Schenectady, in the year 1840, by "*Clute & Brothers*".... In coming back, we noticed the "Garabaldians" were building a fort at the junction of the rail, and two cross roads. Arriving at our picket station, we rested a few minutes, and then tramped towards the cross roads and came to a house occupied by three secession families. In conversation with them, we found that they had left "Bailey's cross roads," that being in too close proximity to where the balls were flying. Before leaving, we had a quart of milk, a pint of buttermilk, and seven apple dumplings with syrup. At 5 o'clock, we were relieved by the 32d [New York] regiment.[48]

Continual work on Fort Ward was persistent and eventually began to assume the semblance of a fort by mid–September. Even the landscape around them in every direction had morphed into a barren land of cut trees from those used to build forts. After two weeks of solid hard work on Fort Ward, Lieutenant Tilley paused during some down time and penned a letter to his hometown newspaper that described the fruits of their labor:

For the past two weeks we have been doing a great deal of hard work in the digging line. The results is an addition of one more to the long line of forts, between here and Chain Bridge. It is one of the strongest kind, and I think will surpass all others in durability and size. The ditch, by which it is entirely surrounded, is one of the most perfect I ever saw, and I should judge that it was almost impassable. Its width is eight feet and depth about the same, the bottom being filled with long, sharp pointed sticks will give those a sharp reception who should be unfortunate enough to fall into it. The fort is to be manned with some forty odd guns, some of them of the largest caliber. The men are busy at work getting ready for the armament and building magazines and bomb-proof casements to shelter them in case of an attack. When this fort is finished and properly armed and manned, I think it can be successfully defended against the assaults of 50,000 men, and to take it at all, must cause an immense sacrifice of life to the assailing party. The Jersey brigade is building a fort within a short distance from this one, and still further on, the 16th and other regiments are just commencing another. These will all be finished in a short time and then a few thousand men will be enabled to defend Washington against a very large force. After that, we hope, if the rebels do not attack us before, to receive orders to advance, and will endeavor to show what Northern mud-sills can do when led on by competent officers and in good fighting trim. The next time, I think our boys will not retreat until they find out which side is whipped, and will go near enough to ascertain this fact.[49]

The work at Fort Ward continued with great success. More than 3,000 soldiers from different regiments had taken part in Fort Ward's construction. A national flag was erected above the fort at noon on September 4 for the first time as an intentional jab to spite their enemy. The band of the 15th New York belted out songs for the occasion as the Stars and Stripes was hoisted up the mast. Men climbed atop the ramparts and screamed their throats dry in nine unison cheers, all in an effort to attract the attention of the enemy on Munson's Hill to bear witness to their achievement. The New Yorkers expected to get a response from the enemy's artillery, but the hill remained silent.[50]

On the evening of September 6, First Lieutenant Daniel Daley of Company A was put in charge of a hundred men from the regiment to go and guard Fort Ward. Daley, along with Second Lieutenant John Vedder of Company E, made their rounds of areas at the fort that the soldiers were to stand guard. Around midnight their attention was drawn to what Daley described as "a man making a great noise." They moved to find twenty-eight-year-old Private Philip Cullen of Company I drunk at his post. Cullen had been placed as a sentry to guard a wagon, but the Irishman was so drunk when Daley found him that he had to be taken off his post. Daley looked around the wagon and found a barrel of whiskey underneath that had a hole knocked into it made by a pickaxe. The next morning the barrel of government whiskey was found to have been leaked of thirty gallons. Cullen had no rank to be stripped of, but three months later he would relive this night in a court-martial that sentenced him to have half of his pay forfeited for six months, and worked at hard labor with a ball and chain to his leg for thirty days.[51]

The whole regiment turned out together by daylight on September 8 and grabbed their axes and shovels and split itself into wings, where one dug out entrenchments while the other worked in the woods. Six days later, the right wing dug out bomb and magazine shelters at the fort, and the left wing occupied the picket line.[52]

On September 19, the regiment took a pause in their work and watched a large military funeral of a captain from the 15th New York who died the day before from a skull fracture after being thrown from his horse. During the construction of Fort Ward, the 15th was pulled from the brigade and sent to Washington to receive instruction on engineering. The organization was converted into a sapper and miner regiment and would remain in that form for the rest of the war.[53]

Either a devised drill or officers received information that spooked them, orders came down to the regiment at 9 p.m. on September 20 to prepare for an attack. Companies quickly fell into line and officers tossed out ammunition to their men. Fantasies and worries of a fight played out in the soldiers' minds as the regiment was swiftly marched to the fort. Expectations soon dissipated as the night remained calm without any alarms.[54]

War and Peace on the Picket Line

The skirmishes around Bailey's Crossroads remained frequent and unpredictable. Through predominantly bloodless rifle exchanges, both sides understood that neither opponent was willing to lose ground. If anything, the time on the testy picket lines provided an opportunity for the men to familiarize themselves with their enemy and their routines. For others, it was an opportunity to sharpen their aim with real men as targets. Private Ira Fisher, Company D, was on the picket line when he noticed a man perched in a tree that made him suspicious. Concealed by a cornfield, Fisher neared closer and discovered he was looking through a telescope towards his camp and taking observations. With enough to believe he was a Rebel, Fisher drew his rifle and shot the man, and down fell a Rebel officer. Private Samuel Meginnis—brother of Company D's captain—was said to have similarly shot a Rebel picket out of tall tree. Private Vinson Clark claimed Private James Dailey, also of Company D, was seen to have "brought one to the ground and wounded some more," all of which must have assuredly been, "in self-defense."[55]

The picket lines still continued to be a constant point of harassment with the enemy. Men kept watch for glimpses of the enemy atop Munson's Hill, and shared closer views through officer's field glasses. Being within shouting distance, men on both sides tried small talk or shouted playful banter back-and-forth to each other. Captain Gridley of Company A recalled one such interaction on the line:

> They are so near together that they talk to each other, call each other names, and they ask each other "how they like Bull's Run." Our men told them that "they would give them Bull Run inside of thirty days." One fellow calls out, "O you son of a gun, you work for ten dollars a month." "Yes," says our man, "we work for ten and get fifteen, and you work for nothing, and get paid off in shinplasters, while we get the shining gold," at the same time showing him the gold.[56]

As near as the lines of pickets were, there were one attempt at temporary peace which allowed both sides to meet face-to-face. During the morning of September 13, a Confederate captain and six of his pickets appeared in the center of Bailey's Crossroads and waved a flag of truce. Men from the neighboring 2nd Michigan approached them first and halted the squad and asked what they wanted. When the Rebels showed they were unarmed and interested in a friendly sociable chat, two officers from the Michigan unit obliged to their parley. They were then joined by Second Lieutenant Edward W. Groot of Company A and First Lieutenant A. Barclay Mitchell of Company C, and the two small groups chatted in the open. They talked a good bit with the men who introduced themselves as members of the 5th Virginia. Their talk centralized on how both sides felt each other's pickets were getting too zealous with their firing. One of the Yankee officers divulged McClellan's standing order that they were not to fire unless fired upon. Once they forged a verbal agreement to ease up the firing, their talk naturally turned to the war, and for a brief moment in time there felt a sense of peace. The four mutually agreed to stop the picket firing between each other for twenty-four hours. Both pairs parted ways with handshakes and returned to their respective boundaries on the line with the prospect of peace. For awhile all was quiet, with each side wondering whose pickets would be the first to break the verbal agreement. Despite the temporary compromise, less than thirty minutes later Confederate pickets fired towards the direction of the 18th's surgeon and other officers grouped together on the picket line. No one was harmed, but anger and distrust in the enemy was restored. "This is a game that two can play at," wrote Lieutenant Tilley, "and our boys, although they will not fire first, are not at all backwards in accepting the challenge when they commence it."[57]

For others, time on the picket line allowed the men an opportunity to be alone which was hard to find amongst the crowded camps. While alone out on his post on September 14, Sergeant Blake of Company H took the opportunity to enjoy a short communion with his Savior. Even on the picket line he never truly felt alone, "for I do not know what moment someone will come to the spot that I am at." He walked out about a quarter of a mile from his position and into some woods and went ahead with his ritual, but his constant worry that "someone was near or would come so that the great pleasure of being by myself for a few moments was spoiled by fear."[58]

After some disagreeable weather over a five-day picket stint near Bailey's Crossroads in September, Private Charles H. Brandow of Company G developed a cold that quickly turned to typhoid fever. The twenty-one-year-old lost his strength so rapidly that his comrades had to carry his gear back to camp when their rotation ended. Even without his accoutrements, Brandow fell out of the company unnoticed midway to camp and dropped by the roadside and fell asleep. He stayed there alone overnight amidst a heavy rainstorm with no coverings. The next morning, two comrades realized Brandow was missing in camp so they backtracked their last march and found their friend along the roadside in dire shape. They rushed him back to the regimental surgeon who had him shipped to a general hospital in Alexandria the next day. "Everything was a blank to me," Brandow later remembered, "for about six weeks from the time I entered the hospital." Private Jesse Parshall—Brandow's brother-in-law and boyhood friend who both joined the company together—became a frequent visitor to the hospital. One night, fever overpowered Brandow's senses so much that he unknowingly walked out. Parshall was surprised to be visited by Brandow that night at his tent amidst a rainstorm. With an obvious look of confusion, Brandow was barely clothed in underwear and dragged a mud-covered blanket. Parshall took instant pity on his friend and gave him shelter that night, and brought him back to the hospital the next morning. Brandow's fever eventually broke, but his rheumatism never ceased and his muscles always seemed clenched. His suffering in the service ended when he was medically discharged in December.[59]

Story of a Sacked Quartermaster

The Whig Press newspaper in Middletown ran a story on September 4 that told the tale of how a regiment's quartermaster shamefully lost his job. Void of names except for McClellan who was said to have been dressed in civilian clothes, the general made a surprise visit to the quartermaster who was derelict in his duties and viewed as a drunk and a cheat. Soldiers of the unnamed regiment were done with the malcontent, and so was McClellan who was said to have relieved the quartermaster on the spot. *The Whig Press* published a follow-up article a week later that confirmed that the story belonged to the 18th New York. If true, this would explain why the regiment's quartermaster, First Lieutenant William V. Horsfall, suddenly and unexpectedly resigned on September 16 under the terms that he could no longer adequately serve within his role. He had been in ill health for months with complaints for shortness of breath and fatigue, but he had also cited he had other business ventures to pursue back in Schenectady. Unable to validate all of the particulars of the story, the article now as it did then was certainly entertaining gossip around the embers of campfires. Horsfall later died in 1868 from an overdose of the addictive laudanum that he took for his heart disease.[60]

Following the example of his brother, William H. Russell, Jr., joined the regiment on September 21, 1861, to become quartermaster, but that appointment was short-lived when he was made aide-de-camp for the brigade (author's collection).

Horsfall's vacated position was quickly filled by Adjutant Russell's younger brother, William H. Russell, Jr., who was brought into the regiment on September 21 as the newest quartermaster. Before the war, Russell had served as a founding member of the Albany Zouave Cadets alongside Colonel Jackson, Major Myers, and his brother. Russell had stayed with the company through its mass exodus at the outbreak of the war when men resigned to join the volunteer force. Through countless correspondence with his sibling at the warfront, William had a change of heart and joined his brother, and like him, William soon impressed and won the respect of the officers for his meticulous approach to his office.[61]

Payday and Whiskey

Covering the months of July and August, the 18th received another installment of payment from the government on September 21, this time in the form of treasury notes, with the odd change issued in gold and silver coins. Money in hand was a joyous occasion in camp but many hardly made it last. Groups of friends gathered in tents and played round after round of card games and gambled away their earnings. Sergeant John S. Bantham of Company F had just joined the regiment earlier that month and was not included for payment, but he painfully looked at those that were when he said, "in a short time all the money paid will be in very few hands so foolish are they, who, suffer hardships & privations & when an equivalent comes in the shape of money, they squander it away."[62]

A worse vice that coincided with payday for many men in the 18th was excessive purchases of alcohol from sutlers. Several fights broke out in camp throughout the night between soldiers who, as Bantham put it, "got beastly drunk" from too much whiskey and made the night of sober troops hard to fall asleep. A heavy and windy rain shower that night did not help much either. Someone got the idea to cut the ties of two or three tents in the middle of the storm which made them fall down. The occupants within were quickly exposed to the storm and screamed such obscenities as "Where is the son of a bitch who cut my tent" and other choice sentences.[63]

First Lieutenant A. Barclay Mitchell of Company C recognized the pattern best exemplified by Private John Thompson of his company. Mitchell spoke about him and stated that there was "no better in the regiment when sober," yet Thompson was "bad when intoxicated," and yet he seemed to repeat in this pattern of drunkenness at each pay day. Captain Michael H. Donovan of Company F, first met Thompson when he had to break up a fight he was in. Even Donovan could attest to Thompson's unflinching duty as a soldier, yet quarrelsome when drunk. Thompson was by no means a rarity for this type of action on payday.[64]

Deserters, and the Capture of O'Dell and Ireland

Between the aftermath of Bull Run and the end of September, twenty-eight individuals deserted the regiment, three of which were quickly arrested and returned. Sergeant George Craig of Company F fled on August 10 and left an unpaid debt to a nearby sutler of $4.15. One month later, Private John Craig of Company B—possibly a relative—deserted camp while he too was indebted to a sutler with a balance of four dollars.[65]

With pay in their pockets, the time was right for Private William H. O'Dell and Private William C. Ireland of Company C to desert. They left the camp unnoticed on September 21 and swapped their uniforms for civilian clothes. Two days later they had made it to the docks of Alexandria and waited for a scheduled boat for Washington. The duo must have felt their plan was foolproof, but they had no idea they were being followed. A sentry from the 17th New York on guard near Alexandria noticed them, and although they were dressed as civilians, their rugged appearance differed from the typical Alexandrian attire which made them look suspicious. They looked like they had traveled a great distance and the guard believed them to be secessionists, and possibly spies, so he grabbed a partner and followed the duo at a distance. While O'Dell and Ireland waited for the next boat to leave at the wharf, the two guards sprung up on them. O'Dell and Ireland dished out a story that they were tourists, "looking over the encampments around the seminary," and were quite cooperative with the guards. When asked to show a pass that would have gotten them to the seminary, they continued their lie and said they did not have one. O'Dell was adamant that he lived in Alexandria and the guard promised that if the story checked out that they would be allowed to return home. Under guard, O'Dell and Ireland were brought to the headquarters of the 17th New York where they broke down their fabrication and confessed to a captain that they belonged to the 18th New York. They were taken to the Slave Pen in Alexandria and locked up. The two were released back to the regiment on September 24 and had their day in court two weeks later. Their court-martial convicted them both guilty of desertion. O'Dell and Ireland were sentenced to have their heads shaved and branded with a two-inch long letter "D" to tag them as deserters on their left hip. Lastly, they were both drummed out of the regiment and confined in the District of Columbia Penitentiary. A special order from the headquarters of the Army of the Potomac was issued in January that remitted their punishment of being branded and shaved, but their desertion charge stayed and they were dishonorably discharged.[66]

Even their court-martial in camp was not enough to deter Private William H. Potts and Private Michael Scanlin, both of Company I, to desert the day after the proceedings began. They were more successful than their counterparts and were never seen or heard from again.[67]

One method deserters at this time used to slip away from the 18th was to volunteer themselves to go collect water outside of camp boundaries—which was out of sight of others and a perfect avenue to get a head start. To curb this problem, an extra guard from each company was added on September 24 to guard those who fetched water.[68]

Confederates Withdraw from Munson's Hill

The days of face-offs on the picket line came to an end when the Confederates unexpectedly withdrew from Munson's Hill on September 28. For the Rebels, the decision to withdraw was one of necessity in order to consolidate their forces. The advanced outposts on Munson's, Mason's, and Upton's Hill were too risky for them and they expected McClellan would soon launch an attack upon their thinly defended hills. The men in the 18th had always felt Munson's Hill before them was poorly defended and had wanted for some time to cleanse that hill of the revolting Rebel flag. General McClellan demonstrated extreme caution with the fort, unnerved by their heavy caliber gun and troop strength that he assumed to be larger than truth. This kind of hesitation and overstatement of enemy numbers would begin to be a flaw of McClellan's leadership that resurfaced time and again. The hill's sudden abandonment made Union troops scratch their heads, and when word reached McClellan, he quickly dispatched troops to inspect the area. Federal soldiers found Munson's Hill empty as expected.

A shaved and painted "Quaker Gun" log like this topped the Confederate-occupied Munson's Hill and cleverly deceived Union troops, keeping them distant (Library of Congress).

The fortification was stripped of any valuables and the abandoned Confederate cannon that kept the Yankees at bay for so long turned out to be a hoax. McClellan and others had been embarrassingly fooled by a "Quaker Gun," which was nothing more than a peeled log painted black. The lack of heavy artillery demonstrations finally made sense. Regardless of the blunder, the exit of the enemy was still a win for the Federals. Lieutenant Tilley proudly explained, "the rebel flag no longer floats defiantly in our sight." Munson's Hill remained in federal control and Camp King no longer felt threatened. Picket duty switched to new locations nearby, but were void of a lurking enemy.[69]

6

Losing Time, People and Patience

October 1, 1861–December 13, 1861

"The Colonel always labored to please his men, and the men all loved him."—Sergeant Rodney S. Vedder, Commissary Sergeant, November 11, 1861

Drill and Camp Life

By the start of October, the work at Fort Ward continued but its intensity lessened. Whole companies on fatigue duty dwindled down to small detachments. Eventually the work happened a few times a week. As some of its final touches for its defenses, ten large cannons were moved into the fort on October 7, six of them being the heavy 32-pounder guns.[1]

With less time devoted to the construction of the fort, more time was committed to the instruction of drill. The practice was always a necessity, but especially with the recent additions of new recruits that seeped into the regiment throughout September. The 18th focused their time and attention to both skirmish drill and battalion movements.[2]

After having gone nearly two months without an accident in camp, Private Michael Martin of Company H ended that streak on October 1. While he cleaned his rifle in his tent, he shot himself through his left hand. The ball passed through his palm and forever lamed his index finger and was unable to make a fist. Martin tried to return to the regiment but had to be discharged just before Christmas.[4]

On October 3, General Franklin moved on the news that a train at Springfield Station was full of wood and sleepers that he wanted, but to get to them his troops would have to push away enemy pickets at Springfield. Under the command of the colonel of the 31st New York, 800 men from Newton's brigade were used for the job. The right wing companies of the 18th were part of this detail and together they marched out of camp at 11 a.m. They tramped in a southwesterly direction for several miles until they reached Springfield and were met by some enemy pickets, but they were easily driven away without a single loss. At the Springfield Station depot, Newton's men were able to unload thirty-two car loads of wood and sleepers. The companies of the 18th stood guard all day of the wooden train on the Orange and

Alexandria Railroad. Without any serious harassment from the enemy, the group returned back to camp near dark.[5]

The overall health at Camp King was slightly better than others around them. Second Lieutenant Edward M. Tilley of Company K regarded this triumph was due to the neatness in camp, and how all the garbage was regularly collected daily in one mass pile and either burnt or carried off. To promote further cleanliness the surgeon ordered the regiment to strike their tents on October 5 in order to clean the grounds, and then they pitched them back in place later that afternoon. Still, a disease-free camp was unobtainable, but it was better than others.[6]

During the divine services on Sunday, October 6, Chaplain Farr read aloud the Articles of War to the men for their second time after their afternoon dress parade. In October, Farr received a large shipment of books from the benevolent United States Christian Commission to jumpstart a circulation of books for the regiment. The men were ecstatic by the gift of a vast array of miscellaneous books. Farr penned a letter of sincere gratitude to the Christian Commission and applauded their efforts. "If you had been present and seen for yourself the joy of the soldiers at this increase of their library," Farr wrote. "The men love to read" and he willingly took up the responsibility to get the men reading. "Intelligent men are what we want," Farr said, "and it is my desire to cultivate this fondness for books."[7]

The left wing took their turn out on the picket line on September 30 at Bailey's Crossroads. When Company B got there to relieve a company from the 31st New York, Captain John Hastings was puzzled when he could not find any of their officers. Hastings waited nearly fifteen minutes before he was approached by a first sergeant of the 31st who pointed out where the captain could be found. They looked over to see two privates trying to wake their sleeping captain who looked every bit sloshed. Hastings was appalled and left to seek out Major Myers since he had no officer to relieve. Myers told him to take the orders from the first sergeant of the 31st, so Hastings trekked back up and began to throw a squad of his own men across the road.

Nearly a half an hour had passed before Hastings noticed that the drunken captain was awake. He was unsteady on his feet and began to yell in German at his own men. Fights broke out amongst them which the drunk captain settled after he brandished his pistol at them. Hastings and his subordinate, First Lieutenant Alexander H. Wands, were both bewildered by what they saw. They perceived most of the 31st's company to be drunk, and heard two or three privates declare in broken English that "they would have nothing more to do with [their captain]." The company eventually left the picket line and gave the men of the 18th something to laugh about, but back at Camp King drew up charges for the drunk captain which eventually fell through on the technicality that he was not drunk, but rather misunderstood owed to his German dialect and wobbly from lack of sleep.[8]

The war proved itself to be slow, but the citizen soldiers adapted to camp life rather quickly. "Some of the men who at first took camp life very hard, now being used to it, feel quite at home," wrote Lieutenant Tilley in a letter home, "The men are all well fed and clothed, and I presume three-fourths of them are in these respects better off than they have ever been before, which is, I know, saying much." Reading and writing letters still trumped a soldier's desire. Sergeant George Blake of Company H read a letter from home during a rainy afternoon and said, "I did not mind having my feet 3 or 4 inch in water as long as the letter lasted." Tilley explained, "There is nothing which a soldier prizes more than a letter from home and next to a letter a newspaper." Newspapers from the men's individual hometowns were always a desired commodity and allowed the men to keep tabs with the news and gossip of folks back home. When Private Francis Christiance of Company E got a hold of a copy of Schenectady's *Evening Star and Times* on October 7, he was shocked and outraged by an article that was specifically written about him. The story explained that he had been sentenced to be shot as a deserter, "and perhaps met his faith at noon to-day." Christiance was without words and he must have read the article a few times to wrap his head around the text. He could not prevent his mind to race back home and think of the ramifications of this spun-out falsity had to have done to his wife and children. Later that very afternoon, Colonel Jackson received a letter from Christiance's wife that requested his body be shipped to her. Everyone in camp surely had a good laugh at it all, as Christiance was a soldier in moderately good standing. He had previously lost his rank of corporal after an infraction of disobedience back in May, and a few days before the newspaper article he had faced a court-martial for an undisclosed offense,

An undated photograph of Company B at Camp King, with Capt. John Hastings (officer at left) and 2nd Lt. Mortier LaFayette Norton (tall officer at center right). The unidentified female next to Norton could be someone's wife, but there has never been any mention of any such woman ever being attached to the regiment (from the collection of the Schenectady County Historical Society).

but he was very much alive and was not sentenced to be shot. Christiance was furious with the newspaper editor who chose to publish a baseless rumor, but his main concern still went to his wife. He sent her a letter and assured her that he was not shot, nor would be, and he was not even near a situation that would require such a penalty. He then closed his letter as, "truly your loving and yet living husband."[9]

One noteworthy letter to arrive in camp brought good news from one of the seven men from the regiment that were made prisoners during the Bull Run campaign. There had been no communication from any of them, and rumors on their conditions abounded. When Private Calvin B. Potter of Company B penned a letter from a Richmond tobacco factory renamed Libby Prison to his lieutenant on October 4, Potter had all but rose from the dead for his friends at home that had by then already mourned his death. Second Lieutenant Mortier LaFayette Norton received the letter and was similarly surprised by the correspondence and excitedly forwarded Potter's letter to be republished in the Albany papers to tell of his existence. A New York native, but raised in Wisconsin, Potter was a recent 1860 graduate of Albany Law School and began to practice just before the war, but at its outbreak he walked away from the books and picked up the gun. He had the qualifications to earn a commission, and would have at least gained some rank had he not been captured. Potter was understandably embarrassed to be taken at the regiment's first engagement and was heartbroken that the war would end before he had a chance to get back into it. He wrote to Norton, "I have been here so long without hearing from anybody that I want you to write me, if only six lines." Potter was in company with the majority of the Union prisoners from Bull Run—to include the six others from the regiment captured during their first skirmish. No beds or items of comfort were available for the near 500 men from Potter's count, and their diet was small and repetitive. Potter also explained that "we are treated well here, and get on well enough," despite the excessive boredom. There was a lot of that going around for both imprisoned and free soldiers.[10]

On October 10, an inspector from the Sanitary Commission made a third visitation to the 18th, and conditions at Camp King seemed to be the best encampment yet. Lessons from previous camps and a vigilant surgeon helped keep the camp fairly clean. Camp streets and tent drains were tolerable, but there were still signs of food scraps and garbage. There still was no systematic disposal of food and slops in place for the regiment. Tents were struck weekly and were cleaned and aired. Most men slept on wooden floors within their tents, and finally the regiment could boast that each man had a blanket. Men washed clothes weekly, and morning inspections ensured the practice was done. Officers also looked over their men and made sure they bathed once a week, and washed their head and neck daily, but feet seemed to be ignored. A privy trench was in place about 100 yards from camp, equipped for a rail for men to sit on, but no screen for privacy was erected. No earth was regularly thrown to cover the pit, but lime was often dropped as their attempt to disinfect. Men were not allowed to relieve themselves within their camp, yet many did at night. While the inspector was in camp, four soldiers were punished for violating this rule. The morale of the men was generally good. The sutler appointed to the regiment was about to lower his prices to match regulations. The sutler no longer sold spirits, wine, or beer, but officers informed the inspector that the men freely obtained liquor from the nearby camp of the 39th New York. Still, intoxication was not an epidemic in camp. The 18th stood at 728 strong that day, with 10 patients in general hospitals, 9 in the regimental hospital, and 39 sick in their tents, which reflected the daily average. The well near Camp King continued to provide the men with clear drinkable water. Rations were still of a good quality and quantity. Fresh meat was served every four days, and both fresh and dried vegetables were dispensed daily. One company cooked their meals in a portable stove, while all others used a trench. Their supply of bread still came fresh from an Alexandrian bakery. Life at Camp King seemed quite tolerable.[11]

The fall weather at Camp King continued to chill throughout October. "Cold weather is upon us and we are reminded of it, much more forcibly here in our thin tents, than you are at home in your convenient houses," wrote Tilley to friends back home. Frosty morning reveilles saw more men awake and bundled around campfires before the drums ushered in the day. "The soldiers feel the change and complain somewhat of the thinness of their blankets," remarked Tilley, "but by building large camp fires, which they keep burning through the night, manage to keep warm." Around the embers, the men would amuse each other "with 'huge stories' and conversation." Others looked upon the escaped slaves within their camp who were called up to entertain the men with "songs and genuine African talk." Cooks cried out, "there is your nice coffee fighting hot" when the staple was ready to be dealt out. During the daylight hours, the men could be assured of comfortable "Indian summer" days. With the changing season came rumors that the troops could go in winter quarters, which meant more inactivity that seldom few wanted. Though winter weather was new for both armies, what Virginia had to offer would not be as pleasant as some expected. Tilley jokingly added that "if we stay in these parts much longer, we shall want to make acquaintance with the army stove."[12]

The 18th got to see the trials of aeronautics prove itself as a military asset from the comfort of their camp. Balloon enthusiasts and entrepreneurs, Thaddeus S. C. Lowe and John La Mountain, made several ascents in the skies above the Union camps and pitched their importance to generals in hopes of having their inventions bought by the government. La Mountain was attached to General Franklin's division, and in the early fall he launched his balloon *Saratoga* near Camp King on several occasions throughout October. One of La Mountain's reconnaissance-gathering demonstrations was even viewed by President Lincoln and his wife, who afterwards drove through Camp King.[13]

Discharges and Deaths

Disease, aches, pains, and accidents continued to take its toll as the regiment's manpower was scaled back. An additional thirty-six enlisted soldiers and three officers were discharged throughout September and October based on disabilities that hindered their job performance. Dropping out of school to join the 18th, Private Henry Carbino of Company K was one of those spirited youth who lied about his age and had only turned fifteen the previous July, but his brief service was mostly spent in hospitals. He had done little to no service between three hospitalizations for tonsillitis and fevers, and his overall youth and feebleness culminated to him being ousted from the 18th. As an infantryman, Corporal George W. Shook of Company F fell out of almost every march by reason of his weight. At five feet six, the twenty-eight-year-old Albany bartender weighed in at 230 pounds and his size caused difficult breathing and irritation between his thighs during marches that prevented him to keep pace. The colonel supported Dr. Rice's recommendation and discharged Shook from the regiment in September.[14]

Most of these discharges were based on genuine health concerns, principally diseases that wreaked havoc on their immune systems. Some got so bad that death was certain if they remained in the service. Private William C. Dunning of Company H died in camp from unexplained circumstances, most likely disease, on September 21. The following day, the ill-stricken Private Stephen Hogeboom of Company I was discharged from the regiment, but was too ill to be shipped home. He remained in a hospital in Washington and continued to battle his disease in vain. Hogeboom died two-and-a-half weeks after his discharge in a Washington hospital on October 15.[15]

Captain Henry Wiltse, Jr.—founder and commander of Company C—parted with the regiment by reason of dismissal, urged by the officers above him. Since the battle of Bull Run, Captain Wiltse had absented himself from the regiment and took up residence in Alexandria where he claimed to be too violently ill that he could not move. By September, Wiltse had only appeared in camp but one day, and Colonel Jackson needed him to be present to handle the matters of his company. Jackson sent several pleas that asked for Wiltse to at least make an appearance at his headquarters, but Wiltse disregarded them and stated that his illness prevented him to travel, yet he was spotted by others to having regularly frequented Washington on Sundays. Wiltse's lieutenants even felt compelled to complain to the colonel that they questioned why they should "be compelled to do the duty of man who is as well, and fit for duty as many officers of the Regt." Enough was enough for Jackson, and on September 9 he started the paper trail to his superiors that outlined Wiltse's shirking of duty and prefaced, "his prolonged absence from the Regiment has had a deleterious effect upon the discipline of his company." Though it took several weeks to gain the desired signatures, Wiltse was dismissed from the service on October 19, still without having made an appearance in camp. Wiltse remained in Washington as a civilian and in a strange twist of fate, seven months later Wiltse did become very sick with a four-day fight from inflammation of the bowels which killed him on May 7, 1862.[16]

After seeing so many chances of promotion come and go, Second Lieutenant Samuel Leith of Company C was tired of being passed up for what he felt was entitled to him. Even as his captain was bound to be cashiered, no talks hinted at Leith's elevation in rank. Leith had seen it happen before when a musician from another company was transferred to a position above him. He felt compelled to resign, but not on the grounds of being overlooked, rather he complained of chronic rheumatism that made him unfit for duty. He penned his resignation to Colonel Jackson on October 9, but his paperwork was handled slowly and he continued his service for a few more weeks, but he eventually left when paperwork was approved on November 29. Not long after some time at home, Leith recruited a new company for a different regiment and eventually attained the rank he felt was right before war's end.[17]

The loss of officers gave rise to promotions as men moved up the pecking order. While awaiting Leith's resignation to be confirmed, Second Lieutenant John Mooney of Company F was transferred to assume his office in Company C on October 19. The transfer brought minor relief to Mooney given his noted disdain for Captain Donovan. Mooney's vacancy in Company F was filled internally by the promotion of First Sergeant John M. Dempsey to second lieutenant which came with great enthusiasm by the men of the company. Dempsey helped form Company F and was then, like Leith, under the impression that a commission

6. *Losing Time, People and Patience* **137**

Left: When 2nd Lt. John M. Dempsey of Company F became a commissioned officer on October 19, 1861, his company gifted him with a new sword, sash, and belt (courtesy New York State Military Museum). *Right:* A butcher from Fishkill Landing, 2nd Lt. Samuel Leith of Company C resigned from the regiment in the fall of 1861 (author's collection).

would be granted, but due to the consolidation of thinned companies others were bestowed the rank before him. Dempsey was not discouraged and had "a spirit of pure love for his country" and gladly served in any capacity he could. The kind-mannered soldier quickly won the esteem of the men in his company, and when he was promoted they presented him with a new sword, sash and belt.[18]

Recruitment

As the romance of a short war faded and numbers thinned throughout the regiments, a hard push towards recruitment held the 18th together. Several commissioned and non-commissioned officers were selected from each company as representatives. Throughout September, they were sent to their respective hometowns for a couple of weeks to recruit and entice those who felt they may miss the war. These recruiters held nightly meetings in public spaces and answered questions from anyone who approached them.[19]

The recruiting drive throughout September and October was successful and helped restore fit men to the regiment. Despite falling far from their goal to restore the roster of the regiment to reach 1,000, all of the representatives from the 18th sent back home had acquired handfuls of willing men. The recruiters saw competition from brand new regiments that required their men to serve for three years. To entice volunteers to gravitate towards the 18th, recruiting officers emphasized that the regiment had just eighteen months left in service, and recruits would be entitled to the same 160 acres of bounty land, $100 in cash, on top of their regular base pay. For the same benefits for less time than was asked for the three-year regiments, the deal was inviting. Some recruiters advertised that any man who enlisted in a regiment already in the field was ensured to be discharged with the regiment on the date of their scheduled end. The recruiters also nudged how every man in the 18th carried the celebrated Enfield rifles, and that one would be supplied to any man who enlisted.[20]

Recruits quickly left home in packs and were escorted down with the recruiters, who were by then aptly referred to as "veterans." of the 18th. Private Charles W. Huston enlisted in Ogdensburg for Company K on October 15, and left home with nineteen other recruits five days later. His journey to the regiment mimicked the route that the original members made several months before them. These recruits were even treated to the same bountiful feast in Philadelphia at the Union Volunteers Refreshment Saloon, and were cheered when they entered its dining hall. Thousands of citizens still gathered along train tracks and waved flags and clapped as they passed. Even as thousands of Northern troops passed through Baltimore on a daily basis, the citizens still turned out to display their disgust. "Everything looked black," as Huston described Baltimore, "the inhabitants, with few exceptions, looked at us with frowns and scowls upon their faces, as if they would have seen us sunk into the depths of the earth." Most of the antagonists were tightlipped, except for an old woman who looked at Huston's squad and "had the pluck to tell us that she wished we might all be shot." Once they got to Alexandria and made the march to Camp King, they were welcomed into the encampment with open arms. As Huston described their reception, "we were received like brothers by the boys, every one offering us a share of what he had."[21]

By the end of October, the regiment was able to enlist and deliver fifty-six raw recruits to the thinned companies. One bold man who enlisted purely for the money was fifty-two-year-old John Harden. The Irish-born immigrant enlisted on October 14 in Ogdensburg, but two days later he escaped the watch of the guard in Watertown and fled to Canada and lived out the rest of his unfulfilled

Riflemen Wanted.

50 ACTIVE YOUNG MEN for Co. "G," 18th Regiment New York State Volunteers, 5th Brigade, Army of the Potomac.

The men are enlisted for the term of two years, dating from the 17th day of May last, leaving only about one year and a half to serve.

Pay $13,00 per month with rations and clothing. Each man's pay and rations will commence as soon as he is sworn in. At the end of the term of service they will receive a Bounty Land Warrant of 160 acres of land and $100 in cash, the same as the three years volunteers.

This Regiment has had five months active service in Virginia, is thoroughly organized and in a high state of discipline. Its position is on the extreme right of the Brigade. It is armed with the celebrated Enfield Rifle, and are now authorized to increase their number to 1200 rank and file.

☞ RECRUITING STATION, at H. D. MALLORY's Hotel, Canandaigua, N. Y. Apply at Recruiting Station or at Webster House.

Capt. HENRY FAUROT,
Commanding Co. G, 18th Regt. N. Y. S. V.
28w2 Recruiting Officer.

Canandaigua newspapers ran this recruitment advertisement for Company G. Facing competition from other regiments, recruiters enticed men with the fact that the 18th New York had just eighteen months of service left, and that new recruits would be entitled to the same benefits that three-year regiments offered (*Ontario Republican Times*, October 30, 1861).

obligation out of the country. John L. Brundage was one of these recently enlisted recruits from Middletown. Although he was only sixteen at the time, his real age was kept a secret until he made it all the way down to Camp King and was mustered into Company D on October 21. The underage Brundage was immediately discharged, but not deterred. He eventually gained success when he joined the regiment a year later.[22]

Precedence of Drill

Drill remained the top priority for McClellan's Army of the Potomac. It was a luxury that was hastened before the Bull Run fiasco. With less time devoted to the construction of Fort Ward, the 18th put more time to the instruction of drill. The practice was always a necessity, but especially with the recent additions of new recruits that seeped into the regiment. The 18th focused their time and attention to both skirmish drill and battalion movements. The new recruits transitioned smoothly into life as a soldier and picked up drill routines quickly. This ease was also largely owed to the competency of the veteran soldiers themselves.[23]

Not all of the recent recruits were of tough New York stock that the officers had hoped for. On his first day of drill during a session in October, eighteen-year-old Private Robert McCollum of Company H became so fatigued that in ten days' time he was excused from all duties. Dr. Rice had initially rejected McCollum at first inspection, but a mistake not on the doctor's part allowed him to be mustered into service. McCollum grew weaker and in order "to save his life," Dr. Rice got his way and sent the young man home before the new year.[24]

Drilling as small as squads and companies was usually conducted in the mornings. The afternoons saw battalion drill, dress parades, and even an occasional brigade drill under the instruction of General Newton. Though never asked to perform such a feat during battle, the brigade even practiced their proficiency to form squares to repel cavalry. Long marches was another item not to be overlooked, so randomly the regiment would go on treks, such as on September 29, when the right wing marched out in the morning to Mason's Hill on the Columbia Turnpike and returned to camp in the evening.[25]

Sessions of drills lasted between four to six hours, and quickly they learned and rehearsed to instantly react to an array of commands. The routine Sunday afternoon regimental inspection of arms and equipment was switched up mid–October to be performed under heavy marching orders. The standard inspection "was not much fun in it having knapsacks on," wrote Sergeant Mowatt of Company C. The extra weight needed to build up their shoulder and back strength "does not come as hard as drill with guns alone at Camp Harris," as Sergeant Blake remembered. With and without rifles, two more daily drills with knapsacks were added to the repertoire. Their aim was also tested with incessant target practice.[26]

As Fort Ward neared completion, companies of the 18th were often marched to the grounds to simply guard it. One of the last finishing touches men from the 18th helped install at Fort Ward came on October 24 when half of the regiment cut endless amounts of sharpened tree branches to finish out the abatis with all morning and half of the afternoon. As the daily ventures to the fort tapered off, a resurgence of drill and routine camp life returned to the regiment.[27]

On October 29, the brigade threw the men a twist to test their readiness and flexibility

Staff officers of the 18th New York photographed at Camp King, about September or October 1861. Pictured (L-R): unidentified guard, Dr. Nathan P. Rice, Lt. Col. William H. Young, Lt. William H. Russell, Jr., Col. William A. Jackson, Lt. John H. Russell, Maj. George R. Myers, the Rev. A. A. Farr, Dr. Alexander A. Edmeston, unidentified guard (from the collection of the Schenectady County Historical Society).

of orders. The brigade drilled together in the afternoon, followed by more done at the regimental level. Suddenly, the commanders of the different regiments yelled to their men to run to camp and don their knapsacks, haversacks, and canteens, and return at the double-quick. Men ran to grab their gear not knowing if this was all a drill or not. Soldiers seemed to overhear that they were headed to Alexandria, and Sergeant Blake added, "we did not know what it was for but the Genls did." The regiments of the fifth brigade formed quickly with their added war essentials and marched towards Alexandria. The 18th paused for three minutes to allow a few men left back at camp to sprint and join the regiment. Blake said "they wanted to be with the [regiment] if they had a brush, they suppose we were going to have a fight, & I will say I thought so too." The men trekked down King Street, and within a block of the river where steamers in the river came into view, and the men believed they would hop aboard. Just before they entered the wharf, the command to "file right" was ordered, followed by the same twice more which swung the men back to King Street. The men rounded the block and were told to "file left" back on King Street and proceeded away from the landing and marched all the way back to camp. The long march with heightened expectations was a great conditioning tool. The exercise was unlike the usual drills in camp, and Blake recalled the men were satisfied as well, despite having their hopes of a fight not come to fruition. He remarked, "I was much surprised when we got in camp not to hear any of the boys complain. I do not feel tired in the least."[28]

A Tourist Trap

Time and inactivity at Camp King prompted men to sometimes venture outside its boundaries. In one incident on October 30, Captain Gridley, First Lieutenant Daley, and Sergeant Henry "Harry" Munger, all from Company A, set off for a leisurely exploration on foot with a reporter friend from their local Schenectady newspaper. With the news of Rebel pickets having withdrawn their lines about two miles away from Mount Vernon—the former home and burial site of George Washington—the men destined to take in the sights which was nearly nine miles south of Camp King. After their noontime lunch in camp, the foursome first visited Mount Vernon and the tomb of the nation's first president. They continued their trek through the countryside and beyond Mount Vernon for more than a mile before they turned around about 2 p.m. The group decided to return via a different route. When they crested the brow of Lee Hill, they noticed a party of seven Confederate pickets down the foot of the hill. Separated from friendly pickets at the time and unnoticed by the enemy, they decided to duck and wait it out, but the Rebel contingent looked to be touring the countryside as well, and headed straight for them. In a quick decision, the foursome collectively jumped out and screamed as if they had meant for this showdown. The Rebel party was instantly stunned and quickly disappeared behind a brush heap. Neither side was certain on the strength of each other and this far from both pickets it was anyone's guess. There was a moment where both parties paused from any further action and waited for the opponent to make the first move. Enough was enough for Gridley, Daley, Munger, and their friend, so they rationalized on the side of safety and drew back to friendly pickets. When they crested a hill, the same Rebels noticed there was only four in their group and pursued with the hunt at a double-quick. The Confederates fired a couple shots in their general direction which made them dive for protection behind a nearby stone wall. The adventurists fired a few shots in return, but both parties lost interest and quit as soon as it started and before anyone got hurt. They lost sight of each other and the New Yorkers returned back to their own lines, hopefully having gained some refined wisdom for their audacious minds.[29]

New Neighbors

Around 10:30 p.m., on October 30, an exhausted regiment of Pennsylvania volunteers drifted through the 18th's camp and reported at the headquarters of General Newton. It was the arrival of the 95th Pennsylvania, there to take the place of the recently removed 15th New York. Nicknamed "Gosline's Zouaves" after their commander, Colonel John M. Gosline that organized the regiment in Philadelphia, they stood out by their button-laden French patterned Zouave petticoats and dark blue trousers. The regiment was to report into the brigade earlier in the day, but based on a confused guide that led them down wrong turns and almost into the hands of the enemy, the regiment walked the entire day for more than twenty miles without food. Thoroughly exhausted, cold, and covered in dust, the men drifted in the dark to the former campground of the 15th New York which was to be their camp, but since their regimental teams that carried their food, baggage, and tents had been diverted and mired, they had nothing. The men of the 18th took pity on them and in a great display of camaraderie they welcomed their new neighbors. Lieutenant Tilley said, "the 18th received them with an open house, packed them into our tents, and in many cases gave them up altogether for their use, and when morning came, divided their food for the day with them." The men of the 18th were actually glad of this opportunity, for the new regiment was from Philadelphia and they wanted to return the same treatment of hospitality that they received when they passed through the city on their passage. "Ever green be the love in our hearts for the extraordinary kindness of the Eighteenth New York," said one member of the 95th Pennsylvania, "and the kindly fire kindled that night to warm us burned brightly to the end."[30]

The next morning, the 18th finished their breakfast with their new neighbors and watched them establish their camp once their equipage arrived. The 18th cleaned up their own camp throughout the morning and prepared for an inspection at 10 a.m. Afterwards, they marched out with the brigade near Fort Ward—since garrisoned with soldiers—and together with the other brigade, batteries, and a regiment of cavalry that comprised their division, they were inspected by General McClellan himself.[31]

The men felt ready for war and believed it was just a matter of time before McClellan would advance his army. Tilley concluded one of his letters home that, "Every man is in fighting trim, and willing and ready to 'go marching on.'" Whenever that time came was anyone's guess.[32]

All the constant drill seemed to pay off and the men could see themselves execute commands with cohesion and move together as one. Men stayed positive and longed for the day that they could implement their training in a practical execution to defeat their enemy. Sergeant George Blake reflected at the end of October on how the regiment had fused together and looked with pride on the days ahead:

> I have not the least doubt about it that they are drilling us so that we will be all ready to march & that soon, the boys in this Regt I believe will do their duty on the field & will gain honor for the 18th. they are all ancious to to get the order to march & they long for the time to come when they will be able to meet the rebels & by the virtue of their "Endfields"[33]

The War Continues

The relative calmness around Washington and Alexandria had been reassuring to the Northerners after Bull Run, but after months of inactivity the stillness was considered hesitation and they grew impatient and demanded action. The soldiers quartered around Washington were in unison with their citizens and speculated on when the word to advance the massive army would be given. Politicians and even the president grew tired of the endless occupation and urged the necessity to kick start the wheels into motion for an offensive Army of the Potomac. McClellan felt the weight of his critics and he knew he had to do something soon, but his continued hesitation and overblown guesswork of the enemy's strength stalled him.

The Indian summer days of October were replaced by November's colder and wetter weather. On November 2, multiple companies from the 18th were sent out in a new direction for picket duty, and marched several miles from camp on the Little River Turnpike for a stint on the line that lasted for four days. It rained very hard their first morning and night, and their great distance from camp made the men yearn for the simple luxuries of tents. They had to make do with what nature provided. A few took it upon themselves to construct what Sergeant Mowatt called, "an apology for a shelter" which was nothing more than a shed built out of fence rails and covered with straw and tree branches, but it gave them the opportunity to dry out their clothes and blankets the following morning. Foraging was also an art for the soldier, and at this time and place the skill was well honed, and fat turkeys and chickens were frequently grabbed from the land.[34]

While on picket duty at the Little River Turnpike on November 4, the negligent handling of a loaded rifle claimed the life of another soldier from the 18th. From Company B, nineteen-year-old Private Richard Hennessy and sixteen-year-old Private James Rice—one of the many who lied about his age in order to enlist—were both playing with loaded rifles while on the picket line. During the course of their horseplay, Hennessy accidentally shot and killed Rice.[35]

After four days on the line, the companies detailed out were relieved at noon on November 6, having been replaced by the 26th New York. Putting the past few days behind them, Sergeant Mowatt said that when they returned to camp, they came back "hungry as bears."[36]

Vindications and Dismissals

For the five fated privates from Company F slated to be shot for their insubordination against their captain back in August, the weeks in limbo had to be solemn. During their wait, the office of General McClellan took a second look at the proceedings and outcome from the trials. They realized the offences were not worthy of the life-ending punishment and wanted to reserve this lesson for bigger crimes. McClellan ordered their exoneration, but the regiment was successful to make a demonstration of the occasion to the regiment. During the first week of November, Privates Edward Adams, Walter Allen, Alonzo Richardson, James Slattery, and Daniel Stillwell were taken out of the guardhouse after three months and presented to their regiment during one of the dress parades. The prisoners had full expectation that they were to be shot as their crime and death sentence was read allowed for all to hear. Lieutenant Tilley looked at the condemned to say, they "were overcome at the sad prospect before them." To say the least, it was a very somber scene. The chaplain offered a prayer on the behalf of the condemned. After what must have felt like an eternity for those on the line, their sentence was surprisingly reversed and as Tilley explained, "You can well imagine the joy of all." The five were released from confinement and set free to return to duty, where they all remained and served faithfully and abidingly.[37]

Another peculiar court-martial case surfaced in early November when charges of conduct unbecoming an officer and gentlemen were slapped on Captain Thomas J. Radcliff of Company I. The specifications to the charge outlined that Radcliff had a relationship "with a woman of infamous reputation" in Alexandria. Radcliff explained that "she is a woman that followed me" to camp, but that "she was a very nice girl though," despite having a reputation of being "a hips woman." Radcliff was open about his relationship with "Lizzie" and did what married couples did in her female boarding house in Alexandria numerous times in October. The problem came from the fact that Radcliff was supposedly married to someone else back home in New York. Word traveled fast around camp about Radcliff's mistress and many began to laugh at his whole charade. She had been in camp many times and Radcliff even introduced her as his wife at times, but it became clear that no one really knew his supposed wife back in New York, so he pulled it off. However, her reputation was what did him in and was considered too scandalous and ungentlemanly of a Union officer, so he still had to face a court-martial. Radcliff was given an opportunity to present witnesses, but none showed and he had to decline his defense. On November 7, the court found Radcliff guilty of unbecoming conduct and sentenced him to be dismissed from the service, which eventually took effect several weeks later on January 13, 1862.[38] But this wasn't the end for Radcliff.

Tents and Food

In preparation for the upcoming winter, the 18th was supplied with new tents in exchange for their worn ones on November 8. The tents were of the A frame style—commonly referred to as Wedge tents by the men—and was a great improvement for Camp King. The canvas tents stood about six feet in height and length and covered a seven foot square space, and three men were assigned to each tent. After their usual drills in the morning, the regiment spent all afternoon pitching their new tents throughout the camp. Around this same time, Chaplain A. A. Farr was a recipient of a large tent that could hold about 150 soldiers, in which he used for worship services. A simple white flag with the word "Bethel" was perched on a staff that welcomed the masses.[39]

The regiment was able to get a steadier supply of more wholesome foods throughout November. The regiment was even able to save surplus rations in order to sell back to the government for cash. With the extra food returned for the month of October, the 18th made over $400. The large sum of money was then divided among the companies for their own company funds, which were used to purchase luxuries needed by the men that were not supplied by the government. On November 9, six companies of the regiment swarmed the Paymaster's table and anxiously received their two months pay, with the remainder getting their allowance the next day. On the heels of the paymaster, the peddlers too returned to Camp King to entice the soldiers to buy their goods.[40]

Early November Resignations

A couple of notable resignations in early November left the 18th with a few less officers. Second Lieutenant Charles W. Heald of Company I was considered by his men as an outspoken and astonishingly frank critic of the war. His outbursts in camp somewhat distanced himself from others, and constantly professed a warped perception of generals, especially McClellan. Heald was one of the first to "call in the question the patriotism and military ability of Gen. McClellan," which appalled all those who treasured Little Mac. Heald's "controversies were frequent and very spirited" which made him constantly uncomfortable amongst his peers. No one seemed to bat an eye when he penned the colonel his resignation on November 5. Heald did so on the grounds that he was too sick and unable to procure a furlough, and his assistance was needed at home after word from family stated that one of them was gravely ill. First Sergeant James Chalmers of the company took Heald's spot.[41]

Captain Peter Hogan of Company H was a highly qualified soldier with years of experience before the war, but his service had to come to an early end after he could not shake a month long battle with bronchitis. During the last two weeks of October he was unable to tend to his duties of a company commander, so he put in for a resignation that was approved on November 6. Luckily Hogan's highly respected and skillful right-hand-man, First Lieutenant Theodore C. Rogers, took command of Company H. Rogers was a twenty-one-year-old college educated man that came from a devout Christian family from Albany. He left his promising business venture to help recruit what became a part of their company. Rogers was tall and described as "a fine specimen of physical symmetry and strength." He was well liked by his men which smoothed the transition for him to head the company.[42]

The Death of Colonel Jackson

Colonel Jackson had already been home once to recuperate from fever, but he returned unhealthy still and let his disease fester. He had always lived a healthy life, but after his brief trip home even his friends could notice Jackson's illness was getting the best of him. Despite his impairment, Jackson continued to be with the regiment and wanted to be seen doing everything he could for the men. Before his illness worsened by late October, Jackson was said to be, "hardly ever absent from the camp, and it was an extremely rare thing for him to sleep out of it." He spent every ounce of energy he could gather to employ himself in his position. Without sufficient rest and living in the unhealthy climate of an army camp, Jackson's health continued to slump. His remittent fever eventually prostrated him in his own tent for several days by the end of October, which led to his subordinate officers to plead with Jackson to relinquish his duties and seek proper medical attention. Again, Jackson was defiant at first until he finally realized the extent of his condition and consented to be removed from camp on October 30. He was put up at a private residence on 12th Street West in Washington. A civilian physician aided Jackson at his bedside and could see his condition was dire. Within days, he showed improvement and looked as if he had beaten the call of death. Dr. Rice made his way to the residence on November 5 and could tell he would not be coming back to the regiment any time soon, so he gave him two more weeks off from his duties. Two days later, Jackson's fever spiked and was compounded with a hemorrhage of the bowels. The hemorrhage quickly moved towards his brain and eradicated all optimism towards his recovery. A telegraph was immediately sent to his relatives back in New York with a request for them to come to Washington. With his last opportunity to speak before he lost the power of articulation, Jackson fought to say in a clear and deliberate voice, "I do believe in the Lord Jesus Christ, I trust in Him." Jackson lingered for a couple days, but on the morning of November 9, news came to Dr. Rice at Camp King that the colonel had hemorrhaged again and neared death. Dr. Rice, accompanied with Lieutenant Colonel Young and Major Myers, immediately traveled to Jackson's bedside in the city. Dr. Rice labored hard to stop the hemorrhage, but it was too late. The colonel's father and brother arrived from Schenectady just in time to witness Jackson's last faint breaths. On Sunday, November 11, 1861, shortly before 6 p.m., the twenty-nine-year-old colonel died from typhoid fever.[43]

The progress of Colonel Jackson's illness was closely tracked and prayed about by the men of the regiment. Until news told otherwise, the regiment continued their drills under the command of Lieutenant Colonel Young. For the regiment, November 11 was a normal day, filled with peddlers around the camp and friends from other regiments that interacted with each other between drills. In the afternoon, the regiment joined their brigade in a routine brigade drill. Shortly after Jackson's death, a telegraph traveled to the regiment that was read aloud to the men during their evening drill that broke the news of his passing. The men had held on to hope that he would recover based on the daily reports they received, so the news shocked and flattened them. "There is not a man in the Regiment who does not regret his loss," penned Commissary-Sergeant Rodney Vedder, "the Colonel always labored to please his men, and the men all loved him."[44]

The day after, Camp King saw a regiment in mourning. At 10 a.m., eight companies from the 18th fell into line for a long march into Washington in order to escort the remains of their late colonel to the Baltimore train depot. The color guard draped their flags with black crape. The band from the neighboring 95th Pennsylvania accompanied the 18th with melancholy funeral hymns, and together they marched away from Alexandria, over the Potomac River via the Long Bridge, and into the nation's capital where they collected the body of Jackson. The march continued to the train station where they paused to allow time for the body to be loaded on the train car, bound for his home and eternal rest. After the successful transfer by rail was completed, the regiment parted with their colonel and retraced the same route back to camp, a "footsore and weary" march that covered nearly eighteen miles within the day. Chaplain A. A. Farr was placed in charge of the remains of Colonel Jackson, and he was accompanied by Major George R. Myers, Adjutant John H. Russell, and Dr. Nathan Rice, for a seven-day furlough back home. Private Mark Wolff, a German-born tailor who had been pulled from Company I to be Jackson's personal attendant since July, was also asked to travel with the colonel's remains.[45]

The body of Colonel Jackson and his escorts traveled through the Hudson River Railroad and arrived into Albany about 12:30 p.m., on November 13. Flags throughout the city remained at half-mast after they were lowered the day before when the initial word of his death reached the city by telegraph. The escort party and casket were chaperoned by the Albany Zouave Cadets, who were joined by a number of other army officers from various volunteer regiments. One of these random officers who appeared was Captain John Hastings of Company B. He was in town on a medical furlough to alleviate his symptoms of a pulmonary hemorrhage he was said to have suffered in early October. The entourage guided the casket to the Capitol Building, where the coffin of the colonel lay in state for nearly three hours. Within that time, countless appreciative citizens, friends, and associates visited Jackson's coffin, which was partly covered with the United States flag, and his sword and cap placed by its side.[46]

At four o'clock that evening, the public funeral of Colonel Jackson commenced. The procession started with a detachment of police, followed by the march of music from a local band. The city's own 25th New York Militia National Guard and his former outfit of Albany Zouave Cadets were next in line and preceded the casket. The casket was placed upon a carriage hearse, drawn by four gray horses with members of Governor Morgan's staff that acted as pallbearers. The hearse was followed closely by the officers of the 18th, and just behind them walked the governor by himself. Three more regiments brought up the rear of the parade with citizens and mourners that trailed behind. The whole procession passed down State

Street to the Central Depot. Jackson's remains were again placed under the sole custody of Myers, Russell, Rice, and Farr, and were transferred onto a special train headed to Schenectady. For Albany, it was a scene played out too many times before on its streets. In all, there were more than 2,000 soldiers that marched in Jackson's funeral procession. For the representatives, friends, and family of the 18th in attendance, the scene beckoned to recall the funeral of Ellsworth back earlier in the spring.[47]

Once in Schenectady, the Jackson family received the body of their son that evening from his protective comrades. A rotating door of family, friends, and citizens passed through the Jackson home to share their common grief that night, and into the following day. Classes were cancelled on November 14 at Union College to allow the students and faculty to attend the family funeral. Even a few medically discharged men from the 18th gathered to bid farewell to their former colonel. The religious exercises were held on Union College's campus at his father's home and were administered by Chaplain Farr, assisted by a local pastor from the Schenectady Presbyterian Church and a trustee from the college. The casket was similarly dressed as when in Albany with Jackson's cap and sword placed upon the flag-draped coffin, and richly covered with wreaths of myrtle and evergreens. The funeral transitioned to nearby Vale Cemetery where the entourage gathered within the Union College plot that overlooked a slow-moving creek. At 2 p.m., Jackson was finally laid to rest amongst headstones of former faculty, staff and alumni of his alma mater. With the final scoops of dirt that covered his casket for eternity, his grave was marked by a commanding marble monument shaped like a coffin fused with a cross. Etched along the edges of the stone is a passage from Horace's Odes in Latin, "*Dulce et decorum est pro patria mori*," which roughly translates in English as "It is sweet and right to die for your country." Jackson was the first Civil War soldier to be laid to rest in Schenectady's Vale Cemetery. Soon, this sad episode at the cemetery would become routine as more dead from the war filled its grounds.[48]

This grandiose headstone forever marks the grave of Col. William A. Jackson, buried within the Union College plot at Vale Cemetery, in Schenectady (author's collection).

Back at Camp King, Lieutenant Colonel Young remained with the regiment and continued to serve as its overall commander while the rest of the staff was back in New York. The colors of the 18th flew at half-mast in camp on November 13 while Colonel Jackson's funeral played out back home. In the afternoon, General Franklin held a review of his division and took the opportunity to address the regrettable loss to the rest of his regiments. In a letter home, one young soldier penned an appropriate eulogy that both eloquently and affectionately addressed the unanimous grief felt throughout the regiment:

> We are consoled by the belief, that he has gone to the undiscovered country, where only brothers dwell together in the bonds of peace and unity, where all are members of one grand army, composed of better and purer material than any here below.[49]

November 14 was a repeat of the previous day's review, but this time the division was drawn up for General McClellan. The morning started with some housekeeping on the camp and an inspection of their streets. The three brigades and batteries of the division were drawn up in line on the parade grounds near Fort Ward by 12 p.m. An hour later, General McClellan and his entourage appeared and were instantly received with the firing of twenty cannons in unison. Brass bands throughout the division struck up with "Hail to the Chief" as the men of Franklin's division shouted in admiration for their esteemed general. McClellan, joined by the Prince De Joinville, proceeded with the routine formalities of the divisional review and everyone was promptly dismissed afterwards. Later that day, the 95th Pennsylvania celebrated the arrival of their own regimental flags which was followed by festivities full of music, food, and a gymnastics show, and they were quick to invite their neighbors of the 18th which helped lift spirits.[50]

Jackson's death opened a chain reaction of rank changes. Lieutenant Colonel Young had assumed command of the regiment during Jackson's absence, but was not officially commissioned its colonel until November 15. Next in line was former Major Myers, who stepped into Young's vacant spot of Lieutenant Colonel. Out of the ten company commanders, there were only six captains to choose from for the rank of major that had served in their capacity since the regiment's inception. Of these six, Captain John C. Meginnis of Company D was unanimously voted on to procure the rank of major. Meginnis was universally liked throughout the regiment and was an obvious choice. His inherent ability to command during the past few months quickly made a lasting impression upon Jackson who once mentioned that Meginnis stood second to none in the regiment. For the Wallkill Guards, this in turn elevated First Lieutenant George Barry to its captaincy, with Second Lieutenant Roswell M. Sayer to Barry's vacant command, and First Sergeant Robert A. Malone became a second lieutenant. As the last act to honor the passing of their commander, Lieutenant Colonel Young asked the regiment on November 18 to wear customary mourning badges for thirty days.[51]

November Number Adjustments

Jackson was the most senior soldier on the sick list in November, but fifteen others from the regiment had to either resign or were medically discharged within the month. Dr. Rice was never short of sick men to monitor, and anyone who showed little or no improvement in their health for several weeks he made sure were discharged. On November 20, he signed and approved ten privates to be discharged all on the same day, with cases ranging from relentless coughs, preexisting hernias, old age, and fevers.[52]

Though November was marred by the heavy loss of Jackson, the month still proved to be more of an influx when it came to manpower. Thirty new recruits filtered into the regiment throughout the month, and with recruiters still back home more were guaranteed. A dozen of these recruits enlisted as drummers or fifers for the regiment, ten of which were under the age of eighteen. The youngest was thirteen-year-old Joseph Napoleon Rockwell from Chicago, who proudly presented written permission from his parents that allowed him to become the drummer of Company A. At a height of four feet, six inches, Rockwell also earned the distinction to be the shortest in the regiment. Rockwell's feebleness, however, eventually got the better of him after the first campaign he participated in. Comrades took pity on the boy and constantly carried his equipage in order for him to keep pace. After many months dealing with his weakness, his company was relieved when Rockwell was given a medical discharge.[53]

As important as these latest recruits were to the vitality of the regiment, one of these new soldiers demonstrated his contribution to the 18th would be brief. By the second day of drill with the newly recruited Private Willard Price of Company G, his comrades immediately sensed something was off with him. Dr. Rice examined him and deemed Price to be insane, so he collected testimony from the men of the company and sought out citizens from the soldier's hometown in search of confirmation. The doctor's assumptions were confirmed by those who knew Price when they said he had been affected for several years with a pathological obsession that he was always being pursued by two imaginary men. He was eventually granted a medical discharge from the regiment in February.[54]

Private Dillon's Absence

On November 15, Company K's First Sergeant Freeman F. Huntington was detailed to go to the Slave Pen in Alexandria to release some prisoners from the 18th that might be contained within the common corral of absent-without-leave and disorderly soldiers. Huntington found Private John Dillon of Company E confined there, having been missing roll calls for five days straight. The Corporal of the Guard at the time was Corporal John Redman from Company K who explained to Huntington that he had found Dillon drunk and locked him up with another soldier from the regiment. Dillon explained that the other soldier was his reason for his absence and that he was not deserting the regiment. He said he had tried to help a sick comrade—Private John Scully of Company A—to help him find somewhere to lodge in Alexandria after Scully had fallen out during the regiment's recent march to the city to escort the body of Colonel Jackson. But Dillon had already been away from the regiment two days before that. The Corporal of the Guard found the two without a pass in Alexandria and locked them both up. Luckily, Dillon's compliance and record as a dutiful soldier prevented him being charged with desertion, but rather absent without leave which cost him to forfeit seven dollars a month for six months, and he had to pull police duty in the camp for two months with a ball and chain attached.[55]

A Grand Review of the Army of the Potomac

Colder weather and rain moved in more frequently which saturated the camp and fashioned mud obstacles. The 18th attempted to perform the regularities of drill and inspections throughout these variables, but with a constant cold and unshakable wet spells in mid-November, many days were spent with the men confined to their own tents during storms, wrapped up in their winter coats and blankets. A preview of winter weather appeared on the morning of November 19 when the men awoke to the first sign of frost for the season, which accumulated to about a quarter of an inch thick on the ground.[56]

The morning of November 20, the regiment awoke to a schedule unlike most days. The men were instructed to don all of their equipment, to include knapsacks, twenty rounds of ammunition, full canteens, and they were given a day's ration of food for their haversacks. All the camps around were abuzz. Some men believed the stir was just another special dress parade, but some were optimistic and hoped that perhaps a scrap with the enemy was about to unfold. Brass epaulettes for officers were instructed to be taken off their uniforms, and the neatness of the regiment's dress was highly emphasized. The regiment ignored those sick in the hospital or sentries posted on guard, and formed eight companies in line, and organized them to form up the brigade. Later that morning, the rest of the brigades in Franklin's division came together and formed an impressive sight on the Leesburg Turnpike. Everyone seemed to present themselves in grand form. The bayonets and muskets of the infantry caught the sunshine and shimmered like a sea of glass, the cavalry were erect in their saddles with their greatcoats draped over their shoulders. The artillerymen were dressed to impress with their caped overcoats buttoned back to reveal their signature red lining, and the burnish and polish emanated from their cannons and caissons. But this sudden mass formation was about to get even bigger.[57]

The order to march was called and the division set out towards Munson's Hill. After a short walk, the division reached Bailey's Crossroads, and being as familiar as they were to the area they immediately noticed that all of the fences as far as the eye could see had been removed. What once were familiar and separated fields had become a large open countryside. A Grand Review of the Army of the Potomac had begun, and soon the field became a sea of blue-clad soldiers from a never-ending supply of brigades and divisions spread out amongst plain. The men of Franklin's division stood by for almost two hours—most in ankle deep mud—and waited for the placement of the numerous organizations to fall into their designated position. It was an awe-inspiring sight to see how the formations all came together. The Army of the Potomac—70,000 strong—brought together for the first time. The ground turned blue with twinkling silver flashes from swords and bayonets, and it all stretched out for miles in all directions. Franklin's division eventually found their mark and took their designated placement and assumed the position of attention.[58]

About a quarter past noon, the thunderous roar of artillery bellowed out from the far right of the line. In the center, the similar explosive power from the throats of the artillery boomed out in succession, followed by the same from a battery on the left of the line. This was repeated seven times, but by then the men had figured the demonstration was the traditional twenty-one gun salute for the president. Then, like a gust of wind that passed through the ranks, the sound of a unified cheer struck up by the thousands started from the right down to the left of the line and was held like a chorus that made "the woods and valleys ring." As the decibels of cheers subsided, the faint sound of a brass band far away played "Hail to the Chief." For those in the front rank, it was easier to see down the line and spot a cavalcade of men on horseback that rode before the long line of blue. Sprinting out in front of the mounted procession was General McClellan, who was received again in resounding cheers as he passed by the regiments. McClellan, President Lincoln, along with Secretaries Cameron and Seward and their entourage of staff members rode passed and inspected the endless wall of blue, which in itself took almost two hours. After the lengthy inspection, the Army of the Potomac broke into column of companies and began the longest pass in review that the 18th would ever be a part of. The day was windy, muddy, and slow to unfold. Private Samuel Hodgkins of Company K recalled that they "stood at 'parade rest' until our hips seemed to be driven up into our shoulders." After they waited for nearly half of the army to pass the reviewing stand, the 18th took their turn to go by. Citizens from Washington made the eight mile journey and gathered near the stand to be closer to the president and General McClellan to watch the regiments march by. Each soldier could barely suppress an undying sense of pride to be a part of such an awesome show of military might. The president looked upon thousands of soldiers in their robust fighting trim who just seven months before were ordinary citizens. The 18th marched with their rifles nestled in their shoulders until what Hodgkins mentioned, "our right shoulder was ready to drop out." They eventually made the walk back to Camp King just before dark set in and the men were thoroughly exhausted and sore.[59]

Camp Life as Winter Comes

The Alexandria weather continued to change between warm and pleasant, to rainy and cold. November 21 was a clear day, and the regiment conducted company drill in the morning and brigade drill in the afternoon, again with full packs. The following day was just as warm, and the men were pleased to leave their coats and gloves in their tents. They perfected their skirmishing drills in the morning and brigade drill in the afternoon, where they again practiced forming squares to repel against cavalry charges. Rain set in November 23 which kept everyone confined again. The weather continued to fluctuate in this pattern for the rest of the month. Aside from the normal 7 a.m. dress parade and inspection of arms for the regiment on Sundays, the holy day was still one filled with rest.[60]

Three individuals from Company A decided to desert together on November 24. Privates Frederick Bendine, John Crowley, and Henry Hipp slipped away from Camp King. Crowley and Hipp were not to be heard from again, but Bendine was eventually arrested at his home in 1863.[61]

Thanksgiving fell on November 28, and the holiday put a halt to standard skirmish and regimental drills normally held daily. Instead, at 10 a.m., the regiment formed a hollow square around Chaplain Farr and listened to him read the Thanksgiving Day Proclamation written by Governor Morgan, which asked that the day be celebrated by people everywhere, with "praise, thanksgiving and prayer to Almighty God." Afterwards, Farr preached a sermon to the men that concluded with a prayer.[62]

After a little more than a month since their last camp inspection from the Sanitary Commission, an inspector paid Camp King another visit on November 29 and was pleased with what he saw. Camp streets and tent drains were clean and free of debris. The 720 men at present strength were in generally good health, uniformed, and presented a clean appearance. Colonel Young was very particular about order and cleanliness of an encampment, and his captains assured that their companies stayed disciplined to its upkeep. The occasions of bathing lessened, probably owed to the lower temperatures, and an officer was no longer required to supervise the men to wash themselves. Even the privy 100 paces from camp had by then received a screen for a bit of privacy. The food continued to be well handled. Men still received fresh meat and vegetables three times a week. Even the cooks who prepared the meals had by then gained experience enough to not destroy it. Fresh baked bread continued to be imported from a general bakery from Alexandria. All of the companies in the 18th had by then established company funds in which men would contribute earnings for purchases that benefited their companies. There was also a new sutler available to the men, one of whom was appointed by the Secretary of War and bargained with more appropriate prices. Other peddlers were still allowed access to the men in camp, and they dealt mostly with the sale of oysters and apples. Intoxication at this time seemed to be wholeheartedly absent, and the daily average of men confined to the guardhouse was listed as zero. Recreationally, it showed that men played ball games and even organized a debating society. The inspector did scrutinize the men's discipline and said that it looked better than usual. Salutes between officers and enlisted men were still rendered, coats were still fully buttoned when on duty, and the regiment was frequently drilled in difficult field maneuvers, about four to five hours a day. The shoulder strap for their cartridge boxes was not mandatory, and men had the option to wear it or rely on just the belt. The inspector did make a comment that the sentries were a bit too relaxed. Dr. Rice provided details about the general health of the men, and said that remittent fever was the only prevailing disease at present. Six patients were hospitalized in city hospitals, two of which had recovered and were retained as nurses. Another twenty-one men were at the time patients in the regimental hospital, and twenty-eight others were confined to their tents, but there were no serious cases that the surgeon specified.[63]

With what the government did not supply that the men felt they needed for the upcoming winter, they still had to rely on purchases from peddlers or on shipments from loved ones back home. The men still had the faithful support of benevolent societies, church groups, and donation drives from their hometowns that supplied the men as often as they could. Throughout November, the Ladies' Aid Society of Canandaigua held several donation drives and gathered several items of comfort that their men in Virginia would benefit from. Captain Henry Faurot received a large package for Company G mid-month that consisted of twenty shirts, sixteen pillowcases, sixteen pairs of socks, fifteen blankets, twelve pairs of flannel drawers, ten pairs of wool gloves, eight bed sheets, four pillows, and eight bottles of familiar native wine from Canandaigua. These items were well received by the men who put good use to them to combat the impending winter. Faurot wrote back to the Society an appreciative letter, but with one small request for an overlooked necessity of "thick mittens. We need nothing else."[64]

Snow started to fall as early as December 3, but was not the kind that stayed around for long. The regiment had spent the past few days with brigade drills, and practiced several iterations of firing blank cartridges. They practiced maneuvering and falling into line of battle, and fired sometimes as much as ten rounds off during one afternoon of instruction.[65]

On account of a crippling cold night, the men were excused from routine drills for the morning of December 4 until 1 p.m. Instead of their morning drill they were ordered to go out and cut logs and bring them into camp and begin construction on winter quarters. Warmer quarters meant a great relief for those who shivered through sleep at night, but the construction of winter camp meant the Army of the Potomac showed no sign of an offensive. Regardless, the men fanned out that morning and lugged back logs to serve as the foundation of their tents. The day still finished with a recurrent brigade drill in the afternoon.[66]

This fashion of construction in the morning and brigade drill at 1 p.m. continued the following day. The drill, however, was a very muddy one due to the ground being frozen at night and thawed out during the day in which the men trampled the field quite a bit during the exercise. The mud may have not been suitable to drill in, but it was a great sealer for their log huts. The logs they hauled and acted as their foundation before their tents were erected over the wood walls, with the gaps between timbers sealed with the plentiful Virginia mud.[67]

The weather on December 6 proved as pleasant as a spring day, and the men worked a comfortable long day where most finished their log foundations by the afternoon, and spent the evening putting up their canvas roofs. Camp King transformed into a site ready to embrace the upcoming winter. Anything left seemingly abandoned around the encampments did not go ignored when the ingenuity of a soldier got creative with their winter quarters. Sergeant Blake could not help but notice the abandoned houses near their picket line had quickly become ghostly skeletons. He remembered that many faces greeted their passing in the summer months, but no one remained and he wondered where the "happy families" could have been flushed out to. The only evidence of their existence was the partial remains of houses which were by December merely

> a heap of ashes with the chimneys partly stand for our troops take all the bricks they can to build fire places in their tent ... floors torn up windows out chimney with bricks taken out where most convenience anything & everything that a soldier want is taken without asking.[68]

December 7 started with some housekeeping, as the men prepared themselves and their camp for a grand review from Governor Morgan. Every regiment around was drawn up that afternoon in their own camp as Morgan made his rounds. The day before the governor's review, Colonel Young had submitted a request for a personal furlough to his superiors. He asked for ten days back home in order to assist in the recruitment of volunteers for his regiment, plus the time at home with family did not hurt either. The request passed through several officials before it was finally approved. Colonel Young left for home on December 9 and put the regiment in Lieutenant Colonel Myers' hands.[69]

Witness of an Execution

A heavy white frost coated the ground on the morning of December 13. The usual dress parade was conducted in the morning, which was followed by company drill that finished around noon. After lunch, the regiment was called upon to form with the rest of Franklin's division in order to bear witness to a scene that would be the first of its kind for the Army of the Potomac—a military execution.[70]

The accused was a private named William H. Johnson, from the 1st New York (Lincoln) Cavalry—the mounted contingent from Franklin's division. Originally from New Orleans, Johnson removed north to New York before the war and enlisted shortly after it was declared. During picket duty with his company in November, Johnson deserted his post and traveled to a point where he believed Confederates to be. He ran into a gray-clad detachment of soldiers, but what he did not know was that these troops were from a New Jersey outfit. Before loyalties were made known, Johnson grabbed their attention and confided with one of the scouts about a scheme he devised in order to have his company captured while on picket duty. A piqued soldier from New Jersey played along and led Johnson on with interest. Before he knew it, guns were drawn on Johnson by the New Jersey scouts. They disarmed Johnson and marched him back to his camp as a prisoner. After a prompt court-martial, McClellan showed no sympathy and intended to use this incident as a deterrent to others, so he ordered Johnson to be executed.[71]

On Friday, December 13, at 3 p.m., the entirety of Franklin's division was placed in a formation structured for the execution that was modeled off a very explicit order the day previous. The execution site was a wide plain north of the Fairfax Seminary, just off the Leesburg Turnpike nearest Camp King and Fort Ward. The three brigades of Franklin's division— under the commands of General's Henry W. Slocum, Philip Kearny, and John Newton—each formed three sides of a hollow square. Slocum's brigade stood on the Leesburg Road and faced north, and were stretched out in two lines, separated by twenty paces between them. To the right of Slocum's brigade and formed at a right angle stood Kearny's brigade in similar fashion of two ranks with a twenty pace gap between the two. Directly across from Kearny's brigade was Newton's brigade, which formed the opposite right angle off of Slocum's. As prescribed, Newton's men—to include the 18th—stretched their two lines out and faced towards Kearny's men. On Newton's left, the cavalry formed and faced the artillery that were tied in on the right of Kearny.[72]

When the division was set, the melancholy music from the Lincoln Cavalry began to play. A mounted captain from the cavalry was appointed the provost marshal for the division and led a small procession of the key players for the execution. Behind the provost marshal marched twelve men, one from each company from the Lincoln Cavalry, who acted as the firing squad. Their carbines were loaded prior in the day by a separate detail where one carbine was loaded with a blank cartridge. This gave the opportunity for each man to believe they shot the blank round in order to keep a clear conscience. Behind the firing squad was an open wagon in which the blindfolded prisoner sat atop his own coffin. Seated next to the condemned was a Catholic priest, who softly read passages from an open prayer book. Bringing up the rear of the procession was one company of mounted cavalry.[73]

The haunting chords of the band set the dismal occasion as the cortege slowly entered through the lines of the division. As they penetrated the formation at the top right of the division, the front rank did an about-face and created a gauntlet of onlookers to soak in the weight of the situation with an up-close inspection of the condemned. As the procession passed through the walls of blue, the bands played their gloomy soundtrack of dirges. Eventually, the caravan passed through the entire horseshoe of soldiers and Johnson and his coffin were placed at the open side to the north of the square. Franklin's entire division had since refaced their front rank and looked on, silent as death itself, as the chaplain gave a muffled prayer to the fated and the firing squad properly positioned themselves six paces in front of Johnson. Blindfolded and seated on his coarse pine coffin, Johnson squared himself up in front of his comrades and addressed his apologies, but from the vantage of the 18th his words would have been inaudible, but the pause before the inevitable added to the suspense. The marshal waved his signal to the firing squad, and immediately the six men in the first rank fired a crisp volley. Bullets pierced the region of Johnson's heart and sent him flying to the ground next to his coffin. With life still left in him, the second rank of the firing squad held in reserve for just this instance, was brought to line and fired a second volley which swiftly ended the life of the convicted traitor. The execution was a solemn experience for all of the participants. Private Joseph C. Jones of Company G remembered the emotional impact the event had on him and others and said, "We were new recruits at this time. You can judge the sensation that it caused," but an example had to be made to deter further desertions and traitorous crimes. Even General Franklin was moved, but his purpose for the event was to let the scene dwell in his men's thoughts, so he ordered them to march by Johnson's body in slow files on their way back to camp. The division commander made sure the event was the only military exercise conducted by his regiments for the rest of the day.[74]

7

With Winter Comes Changes
December 14, 1861–March 1, 1862

> "We hear nothing with us of a forward movement. At present
> in fact, if any one mentions such an idea, he is laughed at."
> —*Second Lieutenant Edward M. Tilley, Quartermaster, February 18, 1862*

The Days Go On

In mid–December, the 18th enjoyed a string of days wrapped in warmer weather. With improved weather came better drills. Drilling as a brigade in the afternoons led to a few new movements which were mostly done in the speedy double-quick. Skirmish drills as a brigade, to include firing, were conducted daily and sometimes lasted all day which replaced company drills usually held in the morning. When there were times of company drill, captains marched out their groups a short ways from camp and perfected their aim by firing live rounds at a target of a hundred yards distance. The days were long but beneficial, and they helped groom the new recruits and to those officers who donned new shoulder straps.[1]

Sundays still presented time for men to listen to the sermons and scripture readings of Chaplain Farr in his "Bethel" tent during morning worship services. Farr was universally respected by the men, and was attentive to their spiritual needs. His sermons were truthful, and he had a way with his audience to link their spiritual interests and wants. Farr was also keen to make his words hold true with tremendous significance, centered around their duty as soldiers for both the country and God. He was praised to be "truly the soldier's friend, and was ever ready to meet his temporal and spiritual necessities." Prayer meetings were usually held two to three times a week. During one church service, the regimental band from the 95th Pennsylvania played for the worshippers and "a bully band it was too," as one soldier from Company E remarked.[2]

Sundays were also a day of implemented rest. Soldiers cleaned up the camp, or caught up on the latest developments from newspapers that circulated around. Men who were able read books or letters from home, or took the opportunity to pen a letter to loved ones or newspaper editors did so. The illiterate ones pressed a friend to write a letter for them.[3]

With six months of experience, the men of the regiment grew a natural camaraderie amongst them. The stories, songs, and jokes told between friends never seemed to cease. Occasionally, a prank or two transcended outside the camp which amplified the joke at the victim's expense. Recently promoted Sergeant Gregoire Insse of Company G fell victim to a prank that surfaced all the way back to his hometown of Canandaigua. Someone from his company had forged his signature in a letter to the editor of their local paper and announced that he had married a woman in Alexandria. The falsity was published on December 4, and thereafter read at a later time in camp by Insse while his company looked on and laughed. After a quick request for a redaction on December 18, the newspaper publically apologized to Insse and tried to rectify their blunder after they received a note in the original handwriting with the explanation that the marriage was a hoax.[4]

Hastings Exonerated, Thompson Punished

In mid–December Franklin's division had racked up a sufficient amount of court-martial cases to warrant another round of proceedings to convene. The detail for the court consisted of nine officers from the division, and the compliment from the 18th consisted of Captain William S. Gridley, Company A, and Captain Henry Faurot, Company G. Like past court-martial trials, several men with differing charges faced their peers through the campground court room. One man to be brought up on the weighty charge of conduct unbecoming an officer and a gentleman was Captain John Hastings of Company B. He had recently returned to the regiment a month before after a thirty-day convalescent stay at home in Albany following what the regimental surgeon determined to be a pulmonary hemorrhage. In his absence, men in the regiment heard stories and passed rumors that pointed towards Hastings having faked his injury with the help of Dr. Peter Sickler so he could obtain a pass home. Dr. Rice was the one who slapped the charges on Hastings after he felt he had been deceived by the captain. After the testimonies of five men that lasted all day, Hastings jumped at a chance that would put an end to the trial. While Dr. Sickler was on the stand, Hastings boldly asked him, "Did you ever lacerate my gums?" Dr. Sickler replied that he did not. Hastings then asked the witness, "Did I ever express a desire for a furlough?" Dr. Sickler replied, "No sir, you never did ... on the contrary you were rather opposed to receiving such, and I do not think you would have taken it, unless pressed by the late Colonel Jackson." That seemed to resolve the whole matter and Hastings was cleared from all charges.[5]

A soldier that absented himself from his company on December 15 was slapped with charges of desertion when he reported back six days later. Private John Thompson of Company C had originally asked for a pass by his captain the day before a group was going to attend a distant church and he wanted to join them. Captain A. Barclay Mitchell had always regarded Thompson as one of his best soldiers, when sober that is, but Mitchell had never seen the private get drunk on duty before. Unfortunately, Thompson's impressed captain was away from the regiment on recruitment duty at the time and Thompson's pass was requested but denied for reasons unknown by his substitute, First Lieutenant John Mooney. Thompson went away without a pass from Mooney, but somehow obtained a pass from someone else. Although he reappeared within his company on his own free will, Thompson was ordered to lose half of his monthly salary for six months, placed in solitary confinement every other week for three months, and interchange those weeks with police duty with a ball and chain strapped on his left leg. An example needed to be set to others to show that they could never do as they please.[6]

The Turkey Can Affair

Still there were those that took the risk of getting caught in order to get something they wanted. On the evening of December 18, the men of Company C had been posted on guard duty and were posted all around the regimental line, and more guarded the adjacent commissary tent of the fifth brigade. One of the sentries posted at the commissary store was Private Whitley Preston who was too tempted by the tent's inventory. He left his post and snuck into the tent and filled his haversack with ten pounds of stolen tea and sugar. Preston did not act alone, as other privates posted near him likewise snagged goodies from the tent. Private Urband Conkling was one that was posted to watch over the commissary tent, but after he was relieved from one of his shifts, he walked past the next sentry who manned the line of the camp, Private John W. Jaycox, who convinced Conkling to stand at his post while he crossed the road and entered the front entrance to the commissary tent. Jaycox stole several cans of preserved turkey meat and hurriedly ran back to his original beat on the line. He gave Conkling some of his bounty and the two both acted like nothing had happened.[7]

The company officer in charge of the guard that night was Second Lieutenant Thomas M. Holden, and while he made his rounds around 11 p.m. he noticed that a few soldiers that should have been at the guardhouse resting between shifts were not there. Nothing too out of the ordinary, but he asked Sergeant William Burt to go back to the company street and see if anyone was back in their tents that should not be. Burt trekked back to their bivouac and immediately stopped at his tent to get himself some coffee. He sifted through his belongings and woke his tent mate, Sergeant Augustus Mowatt, in the process. Then the tent flap opened and sixteen-year-old Private Sylvanus L. Swimm entered. The two sergeants would have normally questioned why Swimm was in the company area when everyone was to be at the guardhouse, but on this occasion they noticed he held a desirous can of turkey in his hands. With no upfront questions, the three passed the can around and they all had a share. The tent flap flipped back open and First Sergeant William R. Green entered. To evade the inevitable questioning as to why Swimm was in the sergeant's tent, Swimm told Burt to let Green get a helping which he did. Mowatt then questioned the young boy how he got to the tent, with which the kid was blunt about and said he just walked up. Mowatt informed him that he had better get back to the guardhouse before he would report him. As Swimm ducked out of the tent, Burt mentioned that he liked the turkey and asked him where he had gotten it from. Swimm responded with, "I bought it, God damn you where do you think I got it?" For a private to address his sergeants that way was uncouth for sure, but even First Sergeant Green mentioned that the men "are not very particular" with the usage of language. Swimm was adamant that he bought the can of meat from a sutler as he scurried off back towards the guardhouse.[8]

Burt was really smitten by the can of turkey and again approached Swimm to ask if he could fetch him more. Swimm believed Burt knew that the cans were coming from the commissary tent but he overlooked that. Only when Swimm said he could not get anymore Burt threatened to report Swimm, but he would have been just as culpable having already eaten the stolen goods. Swimm felt confident that he could procure other items such as candles, tea, and sugar and Burt appreciated his sneakiness.[9]

When the captain of the commissary department walked into his store on the morning of December 19, he immediately noticed the lost inventory and wanted to question those who stood guard the night before. The captain and another commissary sergeant for the fifth brigade walked over to Company C and started to search tents of the individuals who pulled guard. Word got out fast to the regiment as to what had happened to the store overnight. Private Preston had little time to hide anything and his haversack was full of ten pounds of tea and sugar, which were found outright. He admitted to the crime. Around 8:30 a.m., Conkling and Jaycox had gotten word of the flash inspections and the two quickly began to kick some grass clumps behind their tent in an effort to hide their stolen goods. During their hasty burial they had no idea that they were being watched by a neighbor in the adjacent company street. Private Patrick Rarick of Company H had already heard the commissary had been pilfered and from what he saw of Conkling and Jaycox he thought the two suspiciously buried something close to his company to transfer the blame. Conkling and Jaycox eventually caught eyes with Rarick and knew they were busted, so they ran off. Rarick called a fellow soldier of his company, Private Sylvanus B. Downing, and the two proceeded to the kicked sods and found three cans of meat and other goods inside a haversack. They reported everything that transpired to First Lieutenant John Mooney who turned it over to the commissary officers, who by then had already discovered another can of meat hidden within a stovepipe. Mooney moved to Company C's street to arrest Conkling and Jaycox, but he found that the company had left camp at 9 a.m. for target practice about a mile and a half from camp. The company returned and broke ranks at 11:30 a.m. and the two retired to their tents to await the inevitable. Around noon, the sergeant called for the two and placed them under arrest. All of the players would eventually be gathered and confined at the Provost Guard House to await their chance at a court-martial hearing.[10]

The men waited a whole month by the time General Franklin ordered another round of court-martial cases for Newton's brigade which handled the Turkey Can Affair. The commissary thieves of Company C were swiftly convicted to multiple offenses. Preston, Jaycox, Conkling, and Burt forfeited half of their monthly pay for six months and served police duty with a ball and chain on their left legs every other week for three months. Preston, Jaycox, and Burt received an additional penalty of solitary confinement for the weeks opposite of their police duty as punishment for abandoning their posts. Burt also lost his sergeant stripes. Swimm not only broke a vow with his comrades when he implicated everyone involved, but he too had to forfeit half of his monthly earnings for six months.[11]

Filling the Gaps

Acting as ambassadors of the regiment, several members were selected and sent to their hometowns throughout the fall for recruitment drives. Advertisements popped up throughout local newspapers that asked for men between the ages of twenty-one and forty. The colonel had hoped to have 200 men signed up, but recruiting was no easy task. By December, Company C was the smallest of the regiment. Their commander—Captain A. Barclay Mitchell— spent almost the entire month recruiting in downtown Schenectady and pushed the phrase, "If you want to feel at home among your own boys, enlist with Capt Mitchell." First Lieutenant Alexander H. Wands went home to Albany and opened a recruiting office on State Street. Despite having missed the first six months, Wands professed that anyone who signed up would still be entitled to the same pay and bounty as those that enlisted in three-year regiments, and the 18th only had eighteen months left. The enticement of 160 acres of bounty land or $100 was again advertised. Sergeant George N. Goodno, Company K, opened an office on Ford Street in downtown Ogdensburg. The town was quite sapped for recruits after a full regiment of volunteers had just been formed of Ogdensburg men in October. For the advertisement that asked for "200 able bodied men," Goodno signed up one. The pockets of recruiters spread across the state still managed to add twenty-four men during the month of December. These new recruits were quickly shipped south and plugged into the gaps of the companies, except for Private John H. Houghtaling, who was rejected as soon as he got to Camp King.[12]

Dr. Rice tried to do the same when he first inspected Joshua Pangburn. Pangburn was at least forty-four years of age, if not more, when he understated his age to be forty-one when he joined Company F. One not to spoil his true age was Private William H. Hall of the same company, who happened to be Pangburn's son-in-law. Since he had already been accepted in the North the doctor could not refrain Pangburn from serving, but he did find him an assignment to work as a cook. In a similar instance but on the opposite scale of age, Thomas Minix was just sixteen when he lied and said he was two years older in order to join Company K in December. Throughout the war men both young and old continued to lie about their age in fears of disqualification, but the examinations were hardly thorough in the early stages of the war, and bodies were needed. Dr. Rice felt the impact of lackadaisical medical inspections more than anyone and spent the first few months in service filing stacks of discharge papers for soldiers with preexisting conditions that should have never been allowed in.[13]

Few and far between, the Civil War did have instances where women disguised their gender in order to sneak into the military. In December of 1861 a woman in Rochester dressed herself in male apparel and attempted to enlist as a drummer, and when the recruiting officer discovered her true gender he arrested her. The woman claimed she worked several adventurous jobs disguised as a male, one of them being a drummer in the 18th for two months under the alias of Edward D. Hamilton, but that name has never appeared on any roster or report.[14]

The added recruits in December helped patch the holes of eleven soldiers who were medically discharged. Private Morton P. Pittenger of Company G was

Having the smallest company in the regiment, Capt. A. Barclay Mitchell of Company C spent nearly a month at home in Schenectady recruiting for more men and ran several advertisement like this one in local newspapers (*Evening Star and Times*, December 19, 1861).

one to be dropped after his nervousness and chronic muscular rheumatism left him unable to walk since the Bull Run campaign. There was also the loss of Private Ephraim C. Clarke of Company B who was detached to serve with General Franklin's Headquarters.[15]

No discharge for the month of December is more peculiar than the one for Private John Bulchey of Company G. Captain Henry Faurot explained that Bulchey was "mentally incapable of doing his duty or taking care of himself." Faurot cited one incident while the company conducted target practice and Bulchey returned to camp with several charges rammed down his barrel, unsure of whether he had fired or not. The captain deemed him a danger to himself and others and Dr. Rice backed up Faurot's fears. In the doctor's official discharge request for Bulchey, Dr. Rice described:

> Mental incapacity.... This man can never be made a soldier because of utter stupidity. It is considered dangerous to trust arms in his hands, both for himself & others. His habits are so filthy that his company objects to his remaining & both for his sake & the Regt it would be a mercy to have him discharged.[16]

The highest ranking soldier to leave in December was Company E's original organizer and commander, Captain Stephen Truax. Preceding his decision to resign, the fifty-three-year-old was tackled by an unshakeable fever since July, and he felt that his age also caught up to him which restricted his ability to perform to the level that his rank required. Colonel Young's input on Truax's resignation mentioned that "although well advanced in years, [Truax] has been an efficient officer, but his health is failing him and I doubt his ability to withstand the hardships of this campaign." The captain's resignation, however, did not echo the same heralding praise by some of his men of Company E. During Truax's month-long furlough in August, men in the company heard through letters from family that the captain ran his mouth back home in Schenectady with unkind stories about several individuals. Corporal Andrew D. Barhydt heard from his sister that Truax "told the folks that the boys would not come home if they could and that there was not one in the company but what had gained over ten pounds." Barhydt took obvious offense and tried to correct the assumption back home, that "this is not so, we do not fare any better than we did before." Even his comrade and distant cousin, Private G. Dallas "Dal" Barhydt, had to correct his own sister in a letter after she was told by Truax that he "had been in the Guard House about twenty times and that he would not do any duty without being put in there." Both Barhydts were outraged by this blatant lie and the truth was that Dal had never been in the guardhouse even once, and did just as much work as the next soldier. Corporal Barhydt carefully explained his stance on the captain when he said, "you must not believe everything he says. I know how he is, he talks to hear himself talk." Truax's resignation was approved on December 27 and he left four days later. The captaincy was handed over to his successor, First Lieutenant William Horsfall. Barhydt finalized his opinion of the former captain and stated, "we are a good deal better off without him than with him."[17]

Even Colonel Young took a shot with the recruitment drive and went home on a furlough for ten days. He returned to the regiment on a chilly December 20, just in time to spend Christmas with the men. After a daylong dump of a snow and rain mix that led to a bitterly cold night, the morning of Christmas Eve remained notably chilled. The camp was also hammered by a cold blustery wind as they stood in line for dress parade. Their afternoon battalion drill was cut short due to the weather. Company E went out on picket duty for the next four days and spent their Christmas apart from the regiment. They made the best of their holiday spirit and foraged around their area near Annandale where they reined a bull. They butchered and cooked the beast for their Christmas dinner. Back at camp, the 18th refrained from drills or work details in order to observe Christmas Day. In its place, all the men were treated during the course of the day to a barrel full of hot whiskey punch located in front of the hospital tent. Sergeant Mowatt mentioned that "everyone had as much as was good for them to drink."[18]

A New Year

As the month and year drew to an end, the regiment spent December 31 with a division review. At 10 a.m., the division formed on a level ground near the 18th's camp and was reviewed by General Franklin and his staff. Each company took their turn as they marched passed him in review before they headed back to their respective camps. The following day—January 1, 1862—was the start of a hopeful new year, and the army around celebrated with the firing of cannons and songs from bands. Regiments from surrounding camps added to the ambience and fired off several celebratory volleys, to the point where citizens of Washington and Alexandria were concerned a battle was under way. The 18th ushered in the New Year with the usual morning

First Lt. William Horsfall was promoted to command Company E after Capt. Stephen Truax's resignation on December 27, 1861. Seasoned before the war with service in the militia, Horsfall quickly became a favorite of many throughout the regiment (author's collection).

dress parade, but were held off from drills on account of the holiday. Two companies, however, did not have the luxury of rest, as they were tasked out for their turn of picket duty.[19]

Daily drill practices continued, but so too did the strong winds and winter weather. In between pockets of cooperative weather, the regiment, and sometimes brigade, would try different things with each other. On January 3, Newton and Slocum's brigades staged a fake battle between the two on the drill field and fired blanks and attempted new movements they had learned. Gathered within their tents later that night, the men listened as hail fell and bounced off their canvas shelters.[20]

On January 4, the regiment changed their mode of guarding the camp with a full company at a time, and downsized the manpower to small detachments. More snow also meant less drills, but that forced the men to seek refuge in their tents during the days, which asked for more wood for fires. Company C had nothing to do on January 5 since drills were canceled, so they trudged through the mud and two-inch snow and went down the Leesburg Turnpike a couple of miles and hauled back two wagon loads of wood for the cooks. Snow continued to accumulate two more inches the following day, which impelled all of the companies of the regiment to clean away the snow from the streets between the tents, which was their only duty of the day. On January 7, they took their snow removal details out on the parade ground in order to have a brigade drill at 2 p.m. where they practiced firing more blank cartridges.[21]

The Picket Life at Benton's Tavern

Constant showers of wintry rain crept in and soaked the land for more than a week. A mixture of cold winds, mud, and more rain prevented drill for several days. Those on picket were not spared much mercy from the elements as they too took their position miles from the comforts of camp. On January 9, Companies B, C, and D went out on picket and had to march about seven miles on the Little River Turnpike through a rainy and mud-infested hike. That far from camp, the men were only able to find temporary comfort within an old abandoned dwelling called Benton's Tavern which was stripped of all furniture from the previous owner who fled months before. The tavern served as a perfect shelter to house those of the regiment that were on picket duty on the advanced line. Men kept a steady pace with wood for the fireplaces in order to keep warm and dry out.[22]

Picket duty provided the important buffer of safety that allowed moments of peace to exist in camp, but the task had grown tiresome for many. One soldier in Company G wrote in January about the months on the line:

> Our regiment has had its full share of picket duty, and be assured that standing guard on a dark, stormy night within rifle shot of the enemy's lines, is no child's play, saying nothing of keen winds and drizzling rains. We have no sluggards, and every man does his duty promptly.[23]

There had been orders in place that outlawed pickets from discharging their weapons while on the line near Benton's Tavern. Very few were aware of this order as several shots were heard to go off throughout the area at random times. Privates Edward Timmins and Edward McGuinness of Company C had heard nearly fifty shots fired during a single day and were likewise unaware of any order that forbade it. Timmins and McGuinness were stationed together about a half a mile inside the cordon of pickets. By January 12, the two had become soaked to their core from the excessive rain. Timmins followed protocol and received permission by his lieutenant for him and McGuinness to take a walk within reach of their post and fire off their rifles and ensure that the powder down their barrels had not clogged. During the early evening, the two walked out near a line of railroad tracks and fired their rifles at a fencepost. Almost instantly, they were approached and reprimanded by a group of men from the 1st New Jersey—neighbors on the picket line. The two privates exclaimed their ignorance to any such order that prevented the firing of rifles. Their act was reported to higher command who later withheld one month's pay from Timmins and McGuinness as their punishment.[24]

After about four days on the picket line, the rotation of relief moved in. Companies B, C, and D were relieved at noon on January 13 by men from the 27th New York. The companies then made the seven mile march back to Camp King shortly after two o'clock that afternoon. The regiment had been paid another stipend of two-month's pay on January 10, but for those on picket that had missed the paymaster received their dues on January 14, along with an unwanted two inches of snow. Some of the men felt swindled by their distribution of pay. One soldier wrote home to a relative that when they received their two months' pay, they could not use the money unless they paid a 10 percent discount on the U.S. Treasury notes.[25]

Return of Bull Run Prisoners

January came as a huge relief for six men of the 18th who had spent the past few months farther south than their comrades. Privates Abram Crozier, Hugh McKinley, Calvin B. Potter, John W. Browning and Sergeants Chester Shaw and Henry B. Stall, had all been captured during the Bull Run campaign in July and confined together in a tobacco factory in Richmond that was converted into a Confederate prison, which came to be known as Libby Prison. In August, Private Crozier of Company B had attempted a daring escape from the prison with another soldier from Ohio. The two jumped out of a second-story window of the factory and fled on foot. They spent several days on the run and made it as far as King William County, but they were arrested despite having given false names and returned to Richmond. Finally, at seven o'clock on the morning of January 3, these six men from the 18th and 234 other Union prisoners boarded the Confederate side-wheel steamer *Northampton* and set sail towards friendly lines. The Union steamboat *George Washington* was dispatched from the Union-occupied Fort Monroe near Hampton, Virginia, and sailed up the James River nine miles beyond Newport News to intercept the *Northampton*. Under the protection of the national flag, the two ships linked together and collected the paroled prisoners. Cheers from both boats rose as they neared and the music from a band struck up with the familiar tune of "Home, Sweet Home" which set the happy tone as the men's names were read aloud. With the soldiers once again in the custody of their fellow comrades, the *George Washington* returned to Fort Monroe in the evening where the men were given uniforms to those that needed them. The paroled prisoners were then transferred to another ship bound for Baltimore where they would eventually be reunited with their respective regiments later in the week. The liberated prisoners from the 18th made their reunion at Camp King on January 17, and were quickly granted furloughs to their homes for thirty days. For the paroled Private John W. Browning of Company G, his time with the regiment would come to an end on account of his foot wound he received during the Fairfax skirmish. Private Crozier had already demonstrated a knack for escape while imprisoned, but once freed and returned to the regiment he deserted days after his parole and was never heard from again.[26]

Weather Prevents the Chance to Advance

The lack of drill during the course of January continued due to the inclement weather. On account of the rain, snow, wind, and mud that the men had been subjected to not only halted drills, but they locked the Army of the Potomac from any expected advance. Second Lieutenant Edward M. Tilley, quartermaster of the 18th, said that "if any one mentions such an idea, he is laughed at." Private Charles W. Huston of Company K wrote on the conditions of the roads as "almost impossible, and we are waddling in the mud up to the ankles." Tilley was in a consensus with Huston when he sarcastically wrote, "our camp is nothing but mud, mud, and in traveling on horseback over the roads, it appears, as though the bottom had fallen out, in some places for it is difficult to find it." Companies still had to rotate through their picket duty out near Benton's Tavern which lasted for a few days at a time. The grounds at Camp King became a miserable quagmire. Men spent days at a time confined to their canvas homes. When it snowed, it would most always be followed by rain, which melted and continued to turn the grounds into a thick marshy mud. During some heavy rainstorms, tents would occasionally get flooded with several inches of water which sent the occupants fleeing to dryer tents of comrades'.[27]

Men did what they could in order to pass the time. They tried to stay clean and dry, they wrote, read, made repairs to their tent, or routinely collected wood to keep their fires warm which was their biggest concern, especially amidst such awfully wet weather. Their boredom amidst a winter wonderland led to many snowball fights. The regiment was still able to squeeze a lesson in when they marched to Bailey's Crossroads on January 17 for exercise and witnessed an artillery demonstration by Battery D, of the 2nd United States Artillery, who had garrisoned Fort Ward since its completion. In the afternoon of January 24, the skies had cleared that day enough to initiate a quick practice of target shooting. The entire regiment marched out about a mile from camp and had each company perfect their aim at targets of their own. Target shooting and instructions on the bayonet drills were held more often.[28]

Food at Camp King continued to be the same victuals that the government could supply. The regimental quartermaster, Tilley, was often referred to as a temperance man of strict moral character. He kept the delivery of provisions of all kinds except alcohol as plentiful as he could get. Still, there were always peddlers around if one had spare money to spend, but there was never a price for food found in the wild. On February 4, the whole regiment gathered in the morning and marched out about a mile from camp without their weapons. They fanned out and deployed as skirmishers in order to flush out rabbits from the bushes and grounds. Several were caught, killed, and feasted on by the men.[29]

The Other Enemy Is Fever

With the men of the regiment confined to their tents so often on account of the weather, this heightened the threat of disease to be spread. Dr. Rice, aided by the assistant surgeon, Dr. Alexander A. Edmeston, took great lengths with the men to prevent the spread of illness with perpetual care and preventative measures. Ventilation was paramount for the tents and their upkeep was strictly enforced by the medical staff with weekly inspections.[30]

Regardless of how much care and attention the surgeons provided, disease still found its way to pass through the ranks. A neighboring camp had an outbreak of smallpox which prompted every man in the 18th who had not been vaccinated for the disease to be done so on January 29. Throughout their time at Camp King in early 1862, different illnesses and ailments kept the hospital staff busy with patients. Roughly thirty to forty soldiers from the regiment were attended to by the staff throughout January and the first week of February. Symptoms ranged from simple headaches and colds, to harder to control fevers. All were treated first at the regimental hospital at Camp King, but the more severe cases were pushed out to hospitals in Alexandria or Washington.[31]

A month and a half into the new year, five more soldiers from the 18th were discharged for medical reasons. One of these was twenty-two-year-old Alfred LeMaire, drummer for Company C, who never mentioned at his initial enlistment that he had been a sufferer of epilepsy since the age of eight. By January, LeMaire had suffered six convulsions in four weeks' time in camp which was enough to merit a medical discharge.[32]

Disease always remained the bigger killer of men during the Civil War. Wet weather always lent for more time and opportunities for germs and diseases to spread amongst the men when they were confined to their tents. In a period of two weeks, typhoid fever claimed the lives of five young soldiers in the 18th. Starting on January 17, the first to succumb was seventeen-year-old Private John James Warfield. Affectionately called "Johnny" by his brother and comrades in Company G, he was barely given time to learn the basics of soldiering since having joined in November. When his company left camp of January 17 for four days on the picket line, Warfield was held back, prostrated by typhoid fever, and placed in the regimental hospital. He died two days later. When the news made its way to the picket line the next day it hit the company hard. As soon as they got back to camp they placed Warfield's remains in a metallic coffin, sealed it, and sent it by express to his hometown of Clifton Springs.[33]

Eighteen-year-old Private James K. Strathern was regarded by those who served with him as "one of the best men" in Company K, and was always quick and ready to do whatever he was asked to do. Being in a company full of Northern New Yorkers, Strathern was from Albany and joined the company there when the regiment was formed. He was one of the many to succumb to typhoid fever and died at Camp King on January 31. Immediately after his death, Captain Seely penned the sad news in a letter to his fifteen-year-old sister back in Albany who was the only family he had left. Strathern's parents had brought the family over from Scotland in 1848, but they both died in the 1850s and James supported his sister with his soldier salary. Seely had Strathern's body shipped north to Albany for internment in the city's cemetery.[34]

Two days after Strathern's death, Private Isaac B. Walden of Company F died from the same typhoid fever in the regimental hospital. Private David Place of Company G had been unfit from his fever for nearly seventy days by the time he received his disability discharge on January 24. He was sent home to Naples, New York, where he died four days later. With Place having received a discharge days before his death at home meant it had never been included in the regiment records.[35]

On February 4, Private George W. Culver, Company G, was another victim killed by typhoid fever at the regimental hospital at Camp King. Culver left an indelible mark with his company who best memorialized him in a write-up in his hometown paper:

> He was an ever ready volunteer in all the dangerous enterprises incident to a soldier's life, and when amidst their surrounding terrors, he endured the risks of death with an unflinching spirit. His manly worth, his moral courage and his patriotic enthusiasm and fortitude endeared him to all of his associates, and by his strict attention to duty, by his prompt obedience to orders and his ready acquiescence in the wishes of his superiors, he won the respect and esteem of all the officers of his regiment. His companions in arms will long remember

his cheerfulness and honesty that were so beautifully blended with courage as to render him a model soldier and an exemplary patriot; and while we who note that another of the defenders of our country's constitution has passed away, let us drop a tear to his honor, memory and worth.[36]

Camp Jackson

After the sudden deaths of five soldiers, something needed to be done to stop the breeding ground of disease and escape the mud pits of Camp King. The doctors had prescribed ample amounts of quinine to the men, but that could only do so much for their health. Health authorities eventually condemned Camp King and ordered the regiment to relocate to a more suitable location. Colonel Young and Dr. Rice eventually found a fresh tract of land not far from their camp. February 10 was a clear and pleasant day, which allowed three companies of the regiment to dismantle their tents and initiate the start of a new camp a little under a mile north of Camp King. The following day was a cold one, and the remainder of the regiment made the move. Everything was taken from one camp to the next, down to the log foundations of their winter quarters. They spent the next few days perfecting their homes from lessons learned in their former camp. This new encampment was set up on a slight rise of the ground which helped rain drain better to prevent excessive mud in camp. The new encampment was aptly named Camp Jackson in honor of their late colonel. It was located on the property of Alexandrian resident Edward Daingerfield, who had died a few months earlier. Camp Jackson

Photographed from atop Fort Ward, Camp Jackson was established by the 18th New York on February 10, 1862, and named in honor of their late colonel (from the collection of the Schenectady County Historical Society).

was in many respects an improvement from Camp King. Plenty of peach trees filled the front yard of the house. The tents were pitched on a gentle slope in front of the house and the trees, which were fruitless at the time, were left to randomly pop up between company streets. The streets were twenty-feet wide, and the tents spaced six-feet apart across the entire camp like city blocks. The front of Camp Jackson faced Fort Ward which dominated the landscape with its commanding position and a reminder of the hard work the regiment had put in with its construction. The backside of their camp had a very large and spacious building in which the regiment used as a hospital, and other buildings on the premises were similarly occupied as headquarters. Cobblestones were in abundance around the area, and on February 14 several companies spent the day laying down cobblestones on the company streets with four-foot wide sidewalks and still had enough to pave the front of their tents. Camp Jackson quickly emerged in grand form, and Sergeant George Blake of Company H commented that the camp looked "quite city like." Sergeant Mowatt, Company C, called it "the handsomest appearance of any we have had yet." The camp was finished just in time for a heavy day-long snowfall on February 15, which accumulated several inches.[37]

During the heavy snowfall that same day, a carriage rolled into Camp Jackson that brought one of the first guests to visit. Captain Theodore C. Rogers of Company H bounced in the carriage, bundled next to his wife. During his first and only furlough in January, Rogers spent it back in New York and married his fiancé. He returned to camp with his new wife to show her a glimpse of the life that he lived as commander of Company H. His men were interested to see the new bride, but the heavy snowfall kept them sheltered inside their new camp dwellings.[38]

The first week at Camp Jackson was showered with rain which prevented drill. The rain also melted the snow at a rapid pace and converted the ground to mud. Men fought back by collecting more cobblestones to spread throughout the streets in their camp. February 20 was the start of better weather and drills. Companies took their aim to targets in the morning, bayonet exercises in the afternoon, and the usual dress parade in the evening. The following day the regiment continued with more target shooting before they marched down to their brigade drill ground in the afternoon and rehearsed maneuvers with the rest of their battalion. On a hazy February 22, Companies B, C, and H ventured back down the Little River Turnpike for six days of picket duty at Benton's Tavern. They found that the highways were still in a condition that was far from ideal for marching purposes.[39]

On February 24, an inspection of Camp Jackson was conducted by another official from the Sanitary Commission. The regiment was still new to the land and Camp Jackson had hardly been broken in, so the inspection did not yield alarming infractions. Company streets were kept clean, and the logged tents were suitable and clean for the men. Colonel Young continued to give a careful inspection of cleaned uniforms every Sunday morning which helped maintain a good appearance for the regiment. The inspector did notice that most men relieved themselves in camp, both day and night, despite a privy at their disposal down the hill about fifty paces from camp. A well and a surface spring gave the men good drinkable water, and a nearby stream was used for washing, which was done whenever the weather was pleasant enough. Just like their last camp, the food rations remained consistent and good. Fresh vegetables lessened, and more dried ones made their appearance, mostly in soups. Peddlers no longer drifted through the camp to prey on paydays, yet for three to four days after any payment was issued men always seemed to find alcohol. With an average of about two soldiers a week placed in the guardhouse, all of these instances were owed to intoxication. Overall, the men were said by the inspector to be in good spirits, and their discipline was listed as, "excellent." One complaint by the men was that Dr. Rice ordered the men to wear the shoulder strap for the cartridges boxes which had always been a personal preference. The surgeon saw its benefits, "but the men don't like it." The 18th had increased since their last inspection, and thanks to successful hometown recruitment, the number of men at their present strength was 779. As big as the regiment was, the surgeon could also boast an even lower number of sick when compared to past inspections. Only one soldier was quartered in a city hospital. Eighteen soldiers were lodged at the regimental hospital which was within a house, and Dr. Rice said most cases were typhoid fever or pneumonia. Another sixteen soldiers were confined to their tents with lesser sickness or pains. The inspector concluded his inspection of the 18th with a note, "This regiment claims a remarkable exemption from disease, and shows with pride its small number of dead."[40]

While the sanitation inspector conducted his assessment, Camp Jackson was subjected to a heavy windstorm. Several tents were blown down and a number of recently felled trees were lifted from the ground and sent in various directions. Luckily, no one was hurt. After the windstorm had passed, weather proved better in which the regiment resumed drilling again and focused heavily on target shooting. With less rain and a chilled breeze, the conditions of the roads improved quickly.[41]

After weeks of mud-ridden roads, the consensus of an impending advance on the enemy was still non-existent and laughable. "We hear nothing with us of a forward movement," Tilley explained. The mood changed on February 26 when General Franklin received orders that asked them to prepare to march at a moment's notice. Officers in the 18th were given four wagons for storage of their personal luggage. Everything else was to be immediately packed and ready to be sent by express. The enlisted men were restricted to bring one change of regulation clothing, and anything extra was at the expense of what they were willing to carry. The heightened buzz in camp hung around a few days which also kept everyone interested not to desert. On February 28, the High School near the Seminary that was used by the division for such events like court-martials, accidently burned down in an impressive show of flames, but was greatly regretted by the division, especially Franklin. Companies B, C, and H returned to camp on March 1 after six days on the picket line.[42]

Soldiers Come, Soldiers Go

During the early part of the year the government had started to draw manpower from the infantry regiments nearby and transfer men to the army's freshly unveiled Western Gunboat Flotilla. Several gunboats had been built and the crew to man the vessels was almost desperate. The government stepped in and "recruited" men to be transferred out of their regiments in order to man these gunboats. Three privates were selected from the 18th and would forever see a different perspective of the war. Private Alvah Golden of Company F was sent to Gunboat *Benton*, and Privates Charles "Charlie" W. Cochrane of Company K and James Lamson of Company A both ended up on the Gunboat *Pittsburgh* together. A comrade of Cochrane had spoke of him as "a brick" and would "give a good account of himself" within his new role.[43]

Four more soldiers deserted from the camp during the first two months of the year, two of which were caught and brought back. One to get away was Private Michael Daniels of Company F, who had made a habit to absent himself without authority. On January 12, Daniels had left camp without permission and remained missing for nearly a month. Sightings of him in Alexandria surfaced several times, and Sergeant Hiram L. Fisher of his company scoured the city on three different occasions without finding him. After twenty-six days on his own, Daniels was caught by guards in Alexandria and delivered back to the regiment in February. Daniels confessed that he had never intended to desert and had a story ready to tell. He said that he "went down to Alexandria—met some friends, got drinking, and finally into the slave pen." Daniels said he had tried to return to the regiment but the guard kept him confined. He was eventually sent to the public works and ordered to work at hard labor for six months.[44]

Private Henry Horace Faurot of Company G was also listed as a deserter after he failed to return to the regiment after having been sent home on a recruiting endeavor on January 20. Sharing the name of his captain, who was also his father's cousin, Faurot differentiated himself and always went by his middle name. His reason for not returning was on account of being overpowered by sickness and confined to his home in Manchester, New York. When February 1 came and Faurot was not back in camp, he was listed as a deserter despite having received a surgeon's note. Eventually he was medically discharged without ever returning to the regiment, but the desertion charge was never scrubbed, despite having served out the rest of the war with another regiment.[45]

What always kept the regiment functional was the continuous influx of recruits. Since the inauguration of 1862, the 18th received twenty more recruits who had to adapt and learn quickly before the anticipated move which by then was anyone's guess. Fifty-four-year-old Henry Nugent shaved off twelve years of his age when he enlisted in mid–February into Company H, which made him the oldest in the regiment. Lewis and William McCoy, brothers from Goshen, enlisted together in Middletown and served side-by-side in Company D. Amongst this latest batch of recruits, one was very important in the eyes of the regiment's commander. On March 1, eighteen-year-old David W. Young became a private in Company K. He was the colonel's son.[46]

8

Making Moves
March 2, 1862–April 1, 1862

> "All are anxious to do their duty, and wait with patience
> for the time when the word shall be given to move forward."
> —*Private Charles W. Huston, Company K, February 5, 1862*

Preparing for the Long Awaited March

As the weather changed and the grounds began to dry, the men knew they would be advanced soon after months of a wintry wait. The days were cool but pleasant the first few days of March. On March 5, the 18th perfected more bayonet drills in the afternoon and the men were issued forty rounds of ammunition. At 10 a.m. the following day, everyone was placed under heavy marching orders and were issued their first shelter tents, just in time for the upcoming campaign. They unloaded five volleys at targets at 150 yards distance and as Sergeant Augustus Mowatt of Company C mentioned, "the target was well riddled with balls." All signs pointed to be ready at a moment's notice to abandon their present camp. Writing on the anticipation of the expected move, Private Charles W. Huston of Company K spoke for everyone when he wrote:

> All are anxious to do their duty, and wait with patience for the time when the word shall be given to move forward. It is admirable to see how the men behave under these trying circumstances. Not a word, not a murmur; all are confident that those delays, which in the eyes of frivolous politicians are worthless, are for the best, and that when the move forward begins, then such a blow shall be struck that will shake the very soil of old Virginia.[1]

On March 7, the regiment spent their morning with tent rehearsals to test their ability to have them pitched and struck. In the afternoon, the battalion formed and practiced firing blank cartridges together, but did it in a way to simulate street fighting. The next day's battalion drill was done with everything the men would carry on a long march to get accustomed to heavy marching orders. In the afternoon, the companies inspected the men's clothes to ensure everyone had what they needed.[2]

With plans of a spring offensive, the president reorganized the Army of the Potomac on March 8 into four full-strength corps, and a provisional corps. Major General McDowell was given command of the I Corps, of which Franklin's division was placed under McDowell as the first of three divisions. Regiments as they were organized in divisions remained the same, so there was very little ripple effect from the organization into the corps structure.[3]

The reorganization of the army and the recent drills with full gear made the consensus in the camp that they would march soon and would not return to Camp Jackson for some time, if ever. Company commanders ordered that their men pack up all that they could not bring with them and have the gear stored in Alexandria. The men made bundles or combined with comrades to fill boxes with private property such as extra blankets, clothing, and books. These boxes were then marked with their names, company, and regiment and were left behind inside their tents.[4]

March to Fairfax

Army headquarters started to receive a flood of dispatches and messages that the Confederates west of Alexandria had started to vacate their entrenched positions at Manassas and Centreville. There were no signs that they were on an offensive march towards Washington, but rather that they were on the move south. From the Union line, one could look west and see large columns of smoke which confirmed the fleeing Rebels had put their supply depots to torch. Once word got to McClellan of the development, he telegraphed Washington and stated that he would make a move west to see how far he could push back the Rebels.[5]

At nine o'clock in the morning of March 9, companies lined their streets for general inspection. An hour later, they performed the standard dress parade, but it was greatly altered by the exciting arrival of letters from loved ones, and an order that was read aloud to them. The moment had finally come to again advance towards the enemy. After the dress parade and orders read, the regiment bowed their heads and listened to a prayer by Chaplain Farr.[6]

The following morning of March 10 started as a rainy one. Colonel Young instructed Dr. Rice to gather the sick and convalescent soldiers under his care and leave them behind to guard the camp. The most senior to stay behind was First Lieutenant William E. Carmichael of Company H who received a verbal order from the colonel to take charge of the camp and its guards. Carmichael was still recovering from an injury to his side after having been thrown from his horse after it was frightened by a sentry while on picket duty a few weeks before.[7]

Later that morning, the regiment fell in formation under heavy marching orders and tightened their packs and blankets. The 18th formed in front as the vanguard for Newton's brigade and were in position by 10 a.m. Franklin's entire division assembled behind them and together finally stepped off for a long and wet, yet highly anticipated march.[8]

Rain hovered above the division throughout the early afternoon march. The division traveled west down the Little River Turnpike for about thirteen miles until they reached their destination of the Fairfax Court House in Fairfax, Virginia, which had been recently vacated of Confederate occupation. With heavy knapsacks and the distance traveled, the march was a sobering reminder of what the infantry was all about. The regiment set up their new shelter halves and wrapped themselves in their blankets and encamped for the night.[9]

March 11 came with agreeable weather, or as Sergeant Mowatt described it, "a clear pleasant spring day as the heart could wish for." The regiment picked up their encampment at Fairfax Court House and shifted down a short distance from the town and settled within a lot of woods. The tents were pitched immediately to the rear of an emptied Rebel rifle pit.[10]

The officers of the regiment were surprised to see a familiar, yet unexpected face enter their camp. Daniel Leary, a trusted civilian that peddled stoves to the regiment met up with them at Fairfax. He was full of questions regarding the responsibility of the personal property that was left back at Camp Jackson. The talk in camp was that Mr. Leary should be given all that was left behind and have it stored in Alexandria, and if the men returned and wanted what was theirs then they would pay for the storage of said items and receive them back. Anything that was neglected would be appropriated by Mr. Leary for his personal use. With reasonable profit at stake, Mr. Leary made the journey to Fairfax to get the permission in writing. He met with all of the company commanders and received penciled permission from all ten. No one really knew at the time if they would ever return to Camp Jackson. Captain Donovan of Company F urged patience for Mr. Leary, and mentioned that all the property left at Camp Jackson was safe and under the watch of Second Lieutenant Thomas M. Holden of Company C. Holden had remained in camp after he complained to Dr. Rice of being sick before the march. The surgeon did not notice any noticeable symptoms to prevent him, but he took his word as an officer and did not press the matter. The day after the regiment marched off, those left behind were checked on by a doctor from the High School Hospital who pushed out a small handful to rejoin the regiment, and the dire were sent to his hospital. Lieutenant Carmichael was one to proceed back to the regiment so he put the lone officer Holden in charge to look after all the property in camp.[11]

On March 12, the supply train caught up with the men at Fairfax that brought rations of crackers, pork, tea, and sugar which were soon after served to them. For the next few days the men drilled with the battalion in the afternoons, held dress parades, and conducted picket duty at the company level. Men started to get creative with their new tents like good seasoned soldiers in the field would often do. They connected tent halves, sometimes three at a time like a long tarp, and spread the insides with dry leaves which were plentiful. Some of these canvas creations comfortably housed up to six men.[12]

Word got to Colonel Young that the direction of the army would change and that he should make final plans to close-out Camp Jackson in Alexandria. Second Lieutenant Edward M. Tilley—regimental quartermaster—received orders from General Newton to relinquish all of the government property back to federal supply and proceed back to Alexandria at once. The colonel also sent his son, Private David Young, to join Tilley and ensure that his personal and some regimental property left in his tent could be stored somewhere in the city.[13]

Tilley and Young made it back to Camp Jackson on March 14 and found the guards left behind had had a relaxing detail. Lieutenant Holden and a couple others who remained behind had enjoyed watching escaped slaves dance and even held a rifle shooting contest between each other in camp. Tilley meant business and knew that things needed to happen fast. Tilley had all government property inventoried, and he could not wait for the representative from the quartermaster department in Alexandria to meet up with him before he proceeded back to the regiment. Tilley instructed Holden that he be the one to turn the government property, not private, back to the representative whenever he should show. Holden asked Young what he was going to do with his father's items, and he said he would just as well connect it with Tilley's order, but Holden said he could take it all and have it stored by his brother who happened to own a place in Alexandria. Everyone seemed to get on the same page and parted ways, but there was a clear mix-up of what was private and public property.[14]

The regiments encamped around Fairfax Court House packed up everything but their tents during the morning of March 14, and were told to expect a review of the troops later that evening. A change of plan occurred during the afternoon when the regiments held a battalion drill and orders were suddenly received that told them all to proceed immediately back to Alexandria. To be countermanded meant something had changed, and excitement of what that was triggered many a man's speculations. Everyone quickly packed up their tents and left Fairfax at 4 p.m. Rain again returned to escort the men during their travel back towards Alexandria. Before they reached Annandale, the regiment halted and encamped for the night after having marched about five miles. The morning of March 15, the 18th finished their breakfast, struck their tents, and resumed their rainy trek back to Alexandria. After nearly eight miles, the soaked regiment arrived to their familiar home of Camp Jackson around one in the afternoon. The men were tired and eager to escape the continuous downpour and dry themselves off in their winter quarters.[15]

Of obvious notice was the fact that most of the company bundles and boxes of soldiers' private property were either picked over or missing. Lieutenant Holden had in the meantime misinterpreted what should be done with the camp equipment and he had three wagonloads of property loaded up and stored down at his brother's residence in Alexandria. He even had Company E's stove for their cook taken off, which were all promised back to the peddler, Mr. Leary, who showed up the same day to collect what he was promised. Holden's error had irked everyone as soon as they got back, but the man of the hour was not in camp to answer the questions that everyone had for him. They seemed to be asking where Holden was at all hours. The men were tired, wet, and footsore, and seeing their private bundles and boxes either missing or broken open and ransacked only increased their irritability.[16]

Prelude of the Peninsula Campaign

McClellan's unrewarding march towards Manassas yielded nothing more than vacated campgrounds and more embarrassing Quaker guns, which disappointed Lincoln and fueled critic's ongoing disappointment in the general. A new plan several weeks in the making was settled upon in Washington, which was of course not McClellan's first intended idea, though the plan had similarities. The Army of the Potomac, still under McClellan's leadership, was now asked to launch a large-scale invasion upon Virginia's Peninsula by way of the Chesapeake Bay, and move overland seventy-five miles west and triumphantly take Richmond.[17]

Being the great communicator to his troops, a reenergized McClellan used his portable printing press within his headquarters baggage and pumped out an address on March 14 to tell his men of their next great adventure:

HEADQUARTERS OF THE ARMY OF THE POTOMAC,
FAIRFAX COURT-HOUSE, Va., March 14, 1862.

Soldiers of the Army of the Potomac:

For a long time I have kept you inactive; but not without a purpose. You were to be disciplined, armed and instructed. The formidable artillery you now have had to be created. Other armies were to move and accomplish certain results. I have held you back, that you might give the death-blow to the rebellion that has distracted our once happy country. The patience you have shown, and your confidence in your General, are worth a dozen victories.

These preliminary results are now accomplished I feel that the patient labors of many months have produced their fruit. The Army of the Potomac is now a real army, magnificent in material, admirable in discipline and construction, and excellently equipped and armed. Your commanders are all that I could wish.

The moment for action has arrived, and I know that I can trust in you to save our country. As I ride through your ranks, I see in your faces the sure prestige of victory. I feel that you will do whatever I ask of you.

The period of inaction has passed. I will bring you now face to face with the rebels, and only pray that God may defend the right. In whatever direction you may move, however strange my actions may appear to you, ever bear in mind that my fate is linked with yours, and that all I do is to bring you where I know you wish to be—on the decisive battle-field. It is my business to place you there. I am to watch over you as a parent over his children, and you know that your General loves you from the depths of his heart. It shall be my care—it has ever been—to gain success with the least possible loss. But I know that if it is necessary you will willingly follow me to our graves for our righteous cause.

God smiles upon us—victory attends us. Yet I would not have you think that our aim is to be obtained without a manly struggle. I will not disguise it from you, that you have brave foes to encounter—foemen well worthy of the steel that you will use so well. I shall demand of you great, heroic exertions, rapid and long marches, desperate combats, privations, perhaps. We will share all these together, and when this sad war is over, we will all return to our homes, and feel that we can ask no higher honor than the proud consciousness that we belonged to the Army of the Potomac.

GEO. B. MCCLELLAN,
Major-General Commanding.[18]

Alexandria was chosen as the obvious launch for the Army of the Potomac to board transports. Soldiers around the little city shuffled about for the massive orchestration, and rumors traveled faster than anyone could move, which also spread confusion in the camps. Orders came down on March 16 for the 18th to plan for another immediate march. Cooks scrambled to prepare five days rations of meat for the men, but the entire order was later countermanded. Instead, the brigade sat tight and awaited their turn. They conducted a couple days of battalion and skirmish drills during their wait. Soldiers from other brigades and divisions marched by Camp Jackson daily in preparation to board transports, and made those on standby anxious for their turn. McCall's division—one of the three divisions of the I Corps under which the 18th belonged in—marched passed Camp Jackson on March 16. A brigade of Wisconsin and Indiana soldiers from King's division set up an encampment for the night near Camp Jackson, but vanished by morning. More would come and go near the camp as regiments waited for their turn to embark onboard the transports to sail south. With all these troops coming and going around the 18th's camp, guards about the camp were doubled as a precaution to 100 per shift.[19]

Colonel Young had heard enough in camp about the grumblings of the whereabouts of many of the men's private property after their recent march. Young tackled the issue and directed Adjutant John H. Russell to write out an order that forced Holden to turn all the 18th's property he had over to Mr. Leary free of charge. Holden was tied up at his brother's residence on Prince Street as several waves of men from the regiment came by asking for their property. Company G seemed to be the only company that found all that they were looking for, but other companies could not seem to find what was theirs. Property ranged from extra blankets, quilts, clothing, books, cooking utensils, harnesses, stoves, and other articles that were estimated to be valued at $500 to $1,000. The colonel's property was luckily untouched as his son had not finished packing it all by the time the regiment came back to camp. On March 18, Mr. Leary took the order to Holden at his brother's residence in Alexandria and demanded all the property. Holden at first denied the possibility, but he had papers with the colonel's endorsement and he had to let it all go, but there was much that was missing and their whereabouts were never explained by Holden. The next day, Holden was back in camp and inside the colonel's tent to air his grievance at the unfairness to not let his brother store the property. Holden asked to at least be compensated for the cost of hauling, but was denied on the grounds that he was never asked or instructed to take anything from camp. In the presence of Dr. Rice and Captain Gridley, Young told Holden that he was under arrest and relegated to his tent until a court-martial investigation could resolve the matter. The formality of Holden to turn his sword over to Young did not take place since he was not wearing one, but the procedure was taken for granted by the colonel when he found out that Holden left camp again. He returned two days later and this time had a guard placed outside Holden's tent to ensure he did not go anywhere.[20]

Reviews, skirmish and battalion drills, and rain became the pattern for the days that pressed on while they waited in camp. In the afternoon of March 19, amidst the movement of the army, McClellan reviewed Franklin's division once more next to Fort Ward. Men were issued rations of hardtack on March 21, and with its issuance meant the coming of a hard march, but weather delayed plans when rain swept in. The roads bogged down to mud and confined them to their tents for a few more days.[21]

During their wait, a hasty court-martial was assembled by the brigade to put an end to the Holden ordeal. The familiar judges of regimental representatives met at 6 p.m. on March 22 at the camp of the 18th. The trial was quite a drawn out affair and had twenty-four men testify their oaths to decide whether Holden was guilty of being absent without leave, neglect of duty, and breach of arrest. The court eventually concluded on March 25 with a conclusive guilty sentence that asked for him to be cashiered, and that his "nefarious offence proven against him ... be published in the newspapers in and about the camp and in those of the State of New York." Holden was ruined, and on March 27 he ran away. Four months later, the Secretary of War penned on order that put the matter to rest and dismissed Holden.[22]

As the grounds dried out and the passing of boots beat down the roads, the 18th lost count of the regiments that daily marched towards the wharfs of Alexandria to be sailed south. Soldiers naturally grew curious to where exactly they were headed, but when they tossed questions to passing troops on where they were headed they were responded with equal speculations and questions.[23]

March 25 was a more pleasant day, and began with company drill in the morning. At 1:30 p.m., the regiment marched up to the back of Fort Ward where a level field was used as a drill ground for the brigade. Afterwards, the entire I Corps—of which Franklin's division fell under—were formed, inspected, and reviewed by their corps commander, General McDowell.[24]

The following day, the regiment and the rest of Newton's brigade, took part in a drill with four other brigades on the same review field behind Fort Ward. McClellan was on hand for the Grand Review and looked over McDowell's corps. On March 27, yet another review at the same location was held, this time for a Championship Review which matched two divisions against each other to show who conducted themselves better during a review format. On the familiar parade ground behind the fort, Franklin and King's divisions performed against each other as McDowell and McClellan looked on. Based on the lack of bragging from anyone in the 18th, the competition did not go in their favor.[25]

Snow returned near the end of the month, but that could not stop the regiment from drill. The snow was a light one and melted fast, so the men remained out in the field where they conducted afternoon brigade drills. On March 29, the regiment took part in a morning sham battle which included artillery that fired blank cartridges. Rain in the afternoon ended the day's training. Rain hung around but cleared by month's end. Despite the excessive mud, some officers in the regiment made an attempt to get a game of ball started. The skies cleared up on April 1, and the regiment fired off more blank cartridges as they perfected their skirmish drill for a few hours.[26]

The sixth and last inspection of the 18th's encampment from the Sanitary Commission occurred on April 1. The camp had a sense of disarray and cleanliness was almost ignored, but the inspector was told the regiment expected to move and slackened on its upkeep. The men themselves looked good, and their weekly adherence to wash uniforms was apparent, and the men looked most prideful during dress parades. Still, the men did not bathe frequently, and were only forced to wash their faces and hands regularly, but even this practice was apparently neglected in the eyes of the inspector. The regularly issued fresh meat and vegetables lessened, as would be expected as the army prepared for a movement. The strength of the 18th that day was 778, and their health was still pretty good. The regimental hospital had been closed up by the time of the inspection. Two sick soldiers were quartered in Alexandria, and one in Washington, but their cases were not serious. Twenty-nine others in the 18th had slight cases but remained with the regiment. Overall, the inspection was much as it was when one was conducted back in February, and their moral was said to be good, and discipline was still rated as "excellent."[27]

9

A New Campaign
April 2, 1862–May 3, 1862

"We are waiting just like a flock of sheep before the slaughter house,
but the 18th Regt is composed of bully boys that will fight."
—Sergeant Gregoire Insse, Company G, April 27, 1862

Another Push to Manassas

After a few more days of skirmishing drills, marching orders finally came down on a warm April 4 for the regiment to again prepare to advance. No drills were held during the day, but rather the companies were ordered to wash all of their clothes and to prepare themselves for a long march. Some took the opportunity to write to family back home and reminded them that they should not fear from the lack of correspondence that would occur and that they would write as early as situations would allow. Rumors instantly grew amongst the men that they were headed to Gordonsville, Virginia, where the Confederate forces at Manassas Junction were said to be encamped. They expected to step off the next morning, but rain swept in that lasted all day and kept everyone motionless. The impending march came with great disappointment to the men, as they had witnessed the Army of the Potomac leave Alexandria in the other direction aboard transports. McDowell's entire corps was detached from McClellan and held back from the Peninsula expedition by order of the president and secretary of war as added protection for Washington. This sudden decision greatly fumed McClellan who believed the withholding of McDowell's vital corps was a political move intended to foil his whole operation. Franklin, being the trusty friend and ally of McClellan, had similar viewpoints and took the blame for the corps being held back as punishment for his division's open fondness of the general. Though McClellan's conspiracy was greatly unfounded, he began a series of dispatches to change the opinions of Lincoln and Stanton to take the risk of lessening the rear guard of Washington if Richmond was ever to be captured.[1]

The weather cleared up on April 6 and the regiment formed up fully equipped and stepped off at 8 a.m. in the opposite direction of where they all thought the war was. Franklin's division was asked to push out west towards Manassas Junction to help relieve the position of another corps that was pulled for the embarkation of the Army of the Potomac. The 18th marched close to two miles down to the Orange and Alexandria Railroad at Springfield Station and waited for a couple of hours on behalf of an unexpected train delay. At 11 a.m., the 18th and the rest of their brigade embarked on the freight cars and proceeded towards Manassas. One of the cars broke down near Union Mills Station and needed repairs. A separate train from Manassas was dispatched and came down the opposite way to assist in their malfunction, but somehow the train managed to slam into the train carrying the brigade. Five soldiers from the 18th received bumps and bruises, but Corporal Andrew Barhydt of Company E took the brunt of the aches and received a cut above his eye, but nothing to warrant an evacuation. The same could not be said for the 95th Pennsylvania who had one of their soldiers killed and six others slightly injured. For those who saw the railcar, they "considered it a wonder that half the men in the car were not killed." While the train went under repairs, the entire brigade spent the night aboard their cars.[2]

The next morning of April 7, the train started up again and continued the short route to Manassas Junction and reached it by 8 a.m. The brigade disembarked and cooked up a quick breakfast. Going by foot instead of cars, the men finished their journey and marched down the railroad line for a couple miles until they reached their destination of Bristoe Station by about noon. Bristoe Station, also referred to as Bristoe [present-day Bristow], was a remote village about five miles from the town of Manassas. By the time the 18th arrived, nearly half of the buildings that made up the town were burnt down by Confederates during their most recent retreat.[3]

The regiment only intended to remain at Bristoe Station for a few hours, but Mother Nature swept in and altered plans. Rain started to fall, but just as the men began to pitch their tents the rain turned to snow. The flakes continued throughout the night and gradually warmed back to become rain. The regiment remained at their makeshift encampment under the inclement weather, short of fuel and supplies. There was little the men could do to escape the discomforts of nature. Some of the lucky ones found shelter in some nearby houses. This temporary and unhappy camp saw the return of a despised moniker to call this place "Camp Misery."[4]

While on picket duty on or about April 8, the regiment lost yet another soldier to an accidentally discharged rifle. Corporal Wesley Cooper of Company F handled his own rifle that fired when his left hand was over the muzzle. The bullet took off his index finger of that hand. He was eventually sent back to be hospitalized at Alexandria, and was discharged from the service within a month's time.[5]

Campfires for their morning breakfast on April 9 were complicated by a light rain, cold but manageable. Lieutenant Colonel Myers had become very ill through the night, and by morning he was noticed by his friend, First Lieutenant Horatio Goodno, Company K, to have great difficulty mounting his horse, but there was nowhere to go for any sick soldier that far out on the march. The regiment's afternoon fires were extinguished by a heavy snowstorm that set in and continued well into the night. The weather cleared the following morning but the regiment was blanketed in snow. Sergeant Nathaniel G. Whittemore of Company I believed "there was more snow fall than we have had all winter." Luckily the sun proved its worth and quickly melted the snow, but a carpet of mud was created. Company E woke up with one less man when Private Michael Melany decided enough was enough and deserted the regiment. Before he left, Melany stole two watches, a pair of boots, and an overcoat and was never heard from again.[6] Hardtack, sugar, and coffee were supplied to the weather-worn men who were more than eager to resume their march now that the skies cleared. One Company A soldier penned:

The hardest five days we have seen since we come into the army, having only our small shelter tents to keep the storm off. Here we lay on the cold wet ground, not able to get straw to lay on, for two days, and the men began to think they were soldiers in earnest; you could here them talk of home, and wish they were where they could lay on a feather bed once more, and every now and then you would hear one of them sing out 'Johnny, what made you go for a soldier?' Quite a number went in search of better quarters, and every house within three miles of the camp was filled with soldiers.[7]

The welcoming sun on April 10 melted the remaining snow so fast that the increased amount of mud delayed the march yet another day. While everyone waited for the muck to subside, First Lieutenant Daley went to forage with another soldier around the outer area of their encampment. They proceeded almost three miles away from camp before they returned, only to find the creek they had crossed earlier in the day had risen about four feet. They walked along the bank for nearly a mile to find a better place to cross without having to forge the stream. They could not find a suitable crossing, so they were left with no option. The two stepped in and water rushed up close to their necks. Luckily there was nothing important on the days' agenda, and the two built a hearty fire and dried themselves off the rest of the evening, and most assuredly laughed about their excursion.[8]

McClellan Gets Franklin

Meanwhile, the distanced Army of the Potomac was under fire down in the Peninsula as the siege of Yorktown raged. Union forces utilized heavy artillery, siege guns, and boats to pound out the Rebel stronghold before the Army of the Potomac could even think of moving up the river closer to Richmond. Talkative Rebel captives divulged false information of enemy strength which was enough to fool the timid McClellan to slow his pace.[9]

McClellan had his head wrapped around Yorktown, and getting McDowell's I Corps down there. In a dispatch to Lincoln on April 5, McClellan begged the president that "If you cannot leave me the whole of the First Corps, I urgently ask that I may not lose Franklin and his division." Secretary of War Stanton fought back and explained that reports of enemy strength near McDowell's force necessitated their placement from the rest of the army to protect Washington, but McClellan saw his operation was the bigger bait to lure the enemy south and he needed all the troops he could get. Aside from his undying loyalty to McClellan, Franklin's division also offered an engineer brigade that was attached and trained for amphibious landings which worked into his Peninsula plan and was urgently desired. The next day, McClellan sent the president another "urgent request that General Franklin and his division may be restored to my command." The administration eventually conceded to McClellan and told him on April 11 that Franklin's division would be brought back to Alexandria and forwarded to his command.[10]

Earlier that morning, the 18th broke camp at 8 a.m. and started a march down the railroad tracks towards Catlett's Station. After a march of five miles that put them nearly two miles away from their original destination, several dispatches from Washington met up with Franklin that detailed an urgent order to return his division to Alexandria and embark on transports.[11]

"With three cheers and a tiger," Franklin reversed his division and marched them back the way they had come. Everyone gladly retraced their previous five mile march for they knew they were to be placed on transports and sent to where the war was happening. They pushed about a mile out passed Broad Run and their previous and forgettable "Misery" encampment they had left that morning. When they arrived near Bristoe Station a rest was granted, so they dropped their packs, set up their tents, and passed another night alongside the railroad tracks.[12]

Familiar Territory

It was an early wake-up for the regiment on April 12, on this the first anniversary of the start of the war. The men placed their knapsacks on the cars of a train and continued their lightened march at 8 a.m. towards Fairfax Court House. The division shifted to march to the left of Manassas Junction and passed through familiar territory of the battlefields of Bull Run and Blackburn's Ford from the previous July. Around noon, the regiment arrived to the Stone Bridge which crossed the stream that the battle had earned its name. The regiment rested a bit at the bridge before they resumed the eastwardly march. Along the way, dead horses and soldier graves from the distant battle could still be seen by the passing men. Patches of familiar woods had since disappeared and were replaced by abandoned log huts that were the winter quarters for Confederate soldiers. The location brought images and tales to surface for the veterans that were present from that earlier campaign and to remember the regiment's own actions. One soldier in Company A took pen in hand as they marched through memory lane and wrote:

> The old barn where our battery stood, still remains unharmed, and as soon as we saw it we all remembered how we were moved about from place to place when the sun was hot enough to roast us alive. The ruin has greatly changed since that day; the woods have all been cut down, and had it not been for the old house and barn we would hardly have known the place. A large number of log huts have been built here, and are still standing. As we marched along, every one saw something that reminded him of that hard day's work. Now we come to an old tree standing by the road, about the only one left; this is where our late Col. Jackson told Capt. Green, when he came off the field, without any support, that his regiment would stand by him and his battery as long as there was any fighting to be done. Up the road, and to the right a little further, is the hill where the battery stood when they sent the cavalry back that attempted to follow us; and here the last gun was fired on that disastrous day.[13]

The 18th eventually arrived to Centreville Heights which gave the men a splendid and familiar view of the landscape. Veterans of that first battle saw more changes. Acreages of woods in all directions had been cut down and replaced by log huts, and earthworks were thoroughly spread across the land. The regiment pressed on and finished the day's march of more than fifteen miles when they finally arrived at Fairfax Court House around 6:30 p.m. They rested at the same encampment grounds of where they were back in March when they first left Camp Jackson.[14]

The pause was brief and the march continued the next morning at 7 a.m. on April 13. Without their knapsacks the march was still arduous and they were able to knock out fourteen hard miles in nearly four hours and arrived back at Camp Jackson in Alexandria around 11:30 a.m. The 18th made their march from Fairfax a friendly race with the 95th Pennsylvania, and beat them back by half an hour. Despite the lightened weight, Private Samuel Hodgkins of Company K would forever remember this march and recalled it decades later:

> This proved to be the hardest march of my entire army life. The roads were wet and soft from frequent rains, and made walking extremely difficult, especially as we were facing a terrific storm of rain and sleet.[15]

Leaving Camp Jackson, Transports to the Peninsula

The regiment returned to their camp but found that it had been pilfered through. Almost all of the stoves from their tents were removed, but they were found at a neighboring camp that had since been vacated also. Those who sought out a stove went and reacquired one and brought it back to Camp Jackson.[16]

The regiment recovered from their hard marching and remained in their camp for the next three days with occasional drills. They prepped themselves to move at a moment's notice to embark on transports whenever called upon. Much needed uniform replacements were supplied to restore the tattered and torn. The regimental hospital had to clear out the patients too ill to bring along, and pushed them out to hospitals in Alexandria or Washington. Three other soldiers saw their service ended when they were medically discharged while the regiment was out on their recent travels during March and April, but four more new volunteers were brought into the regiment.[17]

Encampments around Alexandria had quickly turned to ghost camps, and on April 17, Camp Jackson was added to the growing list. Camp Jackson was emptied for the last time and the regiment fell into marching formation and stepped off at 7 a.m., bound for Alexandria's wharf. Before they boarded transports, Privates Matthew Cassidy, Company A, and Edward Maguire, Company B, managed to slip the guards and deserted from the regiment.[18]

The regiment had to wait several hours before they could load on the transports. The fleet to carry the division consisted of the flag-ship *Mystic*, with steamers *Nantasket, Louisiana, Kent, Columbia, Daniel Webster, Gipsey*, and *Ocean Queen*. Five companies of the 18th that formed the right wing under Colonel Young's command loaded on the *Nantasket*. The remainder of the regiment made up the left wing and was commanded by Lieutenant Colonel Myers, and crammed onto the *Louisiana* with the 31st New York. At four o'clock that evening, the fleet departed Alexandria and sailed together down the Potomac River. Private Hodgkins mentioned that the men were "mighty glad to get away from Alexandria and to get at something that would show that we were doing something for our Uncle Sam." The fleet sailed more than five miles before they anchored just opposite of Fort Washington for the night. Nearly fifty sloops, schooners, tugboats, and steamers were in accompaniment with the fleet, and as nighttime fell, the red and green signal lights on each of the vessels produced a beautiful effect that illuminated the dark night and expressed by a soldier in Company E as "grand beyond description."[19]

The weather continued to remain warm as the fleet remained anchored the morning of April 18. They waited for the remainder of their division to reach the fleet before finally settling back down the river by mid-morning. As the fleet passed Fort Washington, the men on the boats received several cheers and salutes from the garrison. They would spend all day aboard their transports which traveled south down the Potomac River. The colors flew atop the ships while bands bellowed out patriotic anthems. Everything looked so alive and grand for the men. In regards to the passing scenery, one unimpressed soldier from the 18th described the banks of the Potomac, "entirely devoid of beautiful scenery, and, with the exception of Mount Vernon, there is nothing worthy of note. The gigantic yarns told by travelers in regard to Virginia and the Potomac, are, to use a vulgar expression, 'all in my eye.'" The fleet sailed through the night and finally arrived to Ship Point near the southern mouth of the York River about nine o'clock in the morning of April 19. More vessels and steamers filled the waters as the *Nantasket* and *Louisiana* dropped anchors and waited nearly three hours for the rest of their fleet to catch up. The half of the 18th that was on the overcrowded *Louisiana* changed onto the *Long Branch*, which came with great relief, especially to Company I, who were relegated on the uncomfortable and chilly open upper deck of the *Louisiana* without any shelter. On the roomier *Long Branch*, the companies were given quarters to pass their time in.[20]

While General Franklin awaited his instructions for his impending landing, the men were not allowed to disembark. The divided 18th remained aboard their anchored vessels in the Poquoson River for nearly two weeks. Word had it that they would land soon, but only after some Rebel batteries between them and their expected landing zone had been thoroughly pounded with shells. The regiment was first told that they would be landed at Gloucester Point, opposite Yorktown, but the enemy was entrenched there and had a superior number of batteries. Colonel Young was frank with the men and told them that they would have to land amidst an iron rain of heavy shells from the Rebel batteries that would undoubtedly cause heavy casualties.[21]

The men were eager to initiate the impending fight, and could not wait to get off the cramped ships. Officers vied for their attention and managed to squeeze in drill sessions onboard their vessels. Rain and cold temperatures fell occasionally, but the days were mostly pleasant. Only the small things broke their boredom, such as when a school of porpoises were spotted playing about a half a mile off of their starboard side on April 19. Occasionally, Franklin's troops took turns to get off their ships and embark on the shore while their steamers could be cleaned. Men quickly went to task collecting oysters and other bivalves where the water was low. Some men satisfied their curiosity and explored empty Rebel fortifications in small groups at Ship Point. What brought joy to the entire regiment was when the paymaster came around and gave the men their pay while aboard their transports on April 20 and 21. The men were "in high glee," as Sergeant Frank Seymour of Company E put it, "as a soldier with money in his pocket is the happiest of mortals."[22]

The artillery pounded away at Yorktown in late April and the men listened along aboard their steamers. "Heavy firing is heard at Yorktown, at long intervals," wrote Sergeant Seymour, "but the battle has not yet commenced in earnest. Little Mac [McClellan] is only giving them a salute occasionally, to keep them alive to a consciousness of their sins." The men had long to think about the impending campaign ahead while they remained stuck on the steamers. On April 27, Sergeant Gregoire Insse of Company G wrote a letter to his brother from aboard the *Long Branch* steamer and boastfully mentioned, "we are waiting just like a flock of sheep before the slaughter house, but the 18th Regt is composed of bully boys that will fight as long as there is a drop of blood left we can stand anything as long as McClellen is with us." Finally on April 29, the 18th finally disembarked back on Virginian soil at Ship Point, near Cheeseman's Creek after twelve days aboard.[23]

A Visit from Groot

A civilian to accompany the regiment during their ferried adventure was a familiar face to those from Schenectady. Twenty-year-old Edward W. Groot was a former lieutenant from Company A that had been medically discharged back in December after being one of the first from the regiment to be wounded on the march to Bull Run. His wound to his left hand healed and he rebounded from his attack of typhoid fever which put the thought of returning to the regiment forefront in Groot's mind. He met the regiment in Alexandria just before they boarded transports and spoke with Colonel Young and Lieutenant Colonel Myers about his want of a commission as a second lieutenant in the officer-starved Company C. Groot even accompanied the regiment aboard the *Louisiana* and sailed south, and remained onboard until they disembarked at Ship Point.[24]

During the morning of May 1, Second Lieutenant E. Nott Schermerhorn of Company E, First Lieutenant Alexander H. Wands, Company B, and Captain George Barry of Company D decided to go on a little outing on the water and invited Groot to tag along. The four first asked Colonel Young for permission to have a foraging expedition in hopes of collecting oysters and possibly shoot some ducks. Young did not see the harm and allowed them to leave that morning. Wands acquired a canoe from the provost marshal and affixed a tent fly to act as a sail, and the four set forth down to the mouth of the river. They successfully floated into a cove and fired several shots at some ducks, but their efforts produced no bounty. They parked their canoe on the shore and approached a house near the cove and were pleasantly surprised to be invited to eat with the owner where the four dined on oysters. After an hour, the four decided to head back to camp but the wind was too strongly against them. Barry admitted that he could not swim and convinced the men to row back ashore where he and Wands decided that they would walk back to Ship Point.[25]

Groot and Schermerhorn were much more daring and tried several times more, but their efforts were just as futile and further complicated by a dense fog that settled over the water. The two kept trying and eventually the fog lifted, but they had realized that they had drifted a mile or so downstream. They had actually drifted down to the mouth of the river near the Gloucester shore, and were right in the middle of the cordon of the blockading fleet and gunboats. Their adventure had now gotten serious and they began to row towards one of the Union vessels. One ship lowered a small boat that soon met them and took Groot and Schermerhorn aboard. The two were held in detention all night and interrogated to make sure they were who they said they were.[26]

Schermerhorn was very detailed with his explanation and could speak with exactness regarding the history of the regiment in order to prove himself. When the interrogation reached back to places he had lived at before the war, the twenty-three-year-old Schenectady native divulged a story about his family that resonated with the dramatic brother-against-brother concept of the Civil War. Families with sons in both the Union and Confederate armies were not uncommon amongst border states, but for families in New York, especially the Schermerhorn family who had been in Schenectady for generations, the concept was all the more rare. Hardly ever using his first name Eliphalet, E. Nott Schermerhorn was born on December 22, 1838, the last of nine children. Before he attended Union College to become a lawyer before the war, E. Nott's older brother, Jonathan Crane Schermerhorn left Schenectady in 1852 to work as an engineer on the railroads in Savannah, Georgia, and eventually throughout Alabama. Another brother ventured south for the same reason which was enough to entice E. Nott to follow. He lived with his brothers for two years in Alabama and worked as a conductor on the Alabama and Tennessee Railroad. E. Nott eventually had to return home by himself after the events of the John Brown raid in 1859 made things "too hot for him" and his life was threatened. E. Nott was "accused of reading Abolition newspapers to the negroes on the train," which brought threats that he would be tied to the rails and run over by a train. With almost a decade down south, his brothers were never threatened and had time in Alabama to fit in. When war came in 1861, Jonathan was a resident of Salem and "his interest at that time being wholly in the South." He served as an officer in the local militia that naturally rolled into the Confederate army which secured himself a position as a first lieutenant in the 8th Alabama. With a year into his own service in the Union army, E. Nott had not heard from his two brothers since before the war and was often skeptic if one or both had decided to join the Rebel army or not. Although the 8th Alabama shared a few battlefields with the 18th New York, Jonathan only served the first eight months and resigned in January 1862 before the two regiments were ever pitted against each other.[27]

The next morning, Schermerhorn was kept under the arrest of the Provost Marshal guards and brought to army headquarters near Yorktown until his rightful commanding officers came to claim him later that day. For Groot, his hopes to return to the 18th ended with this embarrassing escapade and he was not granted a commission back into the regiment. Military authorities viewed Groot as just another unemployed civilian that had no use to be where he was, so they had him removed to the extreme rear of the army, and eventually was given passage back home. In July, Groot got his wish in a roundabout way when he received a commission as a lieutenant in a new regiment formed in Schenectady.[28]

A Prayer for Things to Come

The first few days of May, the regiment conducted drills at company, regiment, and even battalion level. The men knew they were in preparation for a scrap with the enemy very soon. Corporal Thomas Alexander, Company D—an English immigrant and brewer by trade— proved to be quite the eloquent correspondent with frequent letters to friends back home in Middletown. As Alexander searched within to find the strength for the impending battle that was expected, he did what many men believed and trusted faith to dictate the fate of the regiment:

> We are all anxious for the time, and shall be glad to smell powder. I suppose we shall have a very hard fight here, but we trust our cause to Almighty God, and feel sure of success, and hope for a speedy settlement of this cruel Rebellion.... I feel better than ever I did, and far better prepared for action. My life is in the hands of the Almighty, and my trust is in him, and God grant that if it should be my lot to fall, I may be gloriously fighting in the ranks of the brave and true, supporting those Colors of Liberty and Freedom which I have sworn to defend with my heart's best blood, and which must be carried safely through the war.[29]

10

Like Devils Incarnate
May 4, 1862–June 26, 1862

> "They then pretended to make a charge, that is their officers gave the order charge and they began to yell and jump about in the bushes, thinking by that to make us rise and draw our fire, but they could not succeed."
> —*Corporal Thomas Alexander, Company D, May 9, 1862*

Up the York River

The camps were all astir the morning of May 4 after a night of heavy gunfire exchanges between Union gunboats and entrenched Confederates within their fortifications at Yorktown. As things quieted during the morning, rumors quickly sped through that the fortified Rebels had slipped out and abandoned their works. The speculation was later confirmed and the news raced through the Union lines, which dawned the proverbial battle cry, "On to Richmond" which seemed to become an attainable reality. Later that night and into the morning of May 5, Franklin's division again boarded transports at Ship Point and left Cheeseman's Creek [present-day Chisman Creek] via the Poquoson River. The division was to make an amphibious landing up the York River and become a pivotal flanking element that would eventually be met with the rest of McClellan's army who moved overland. The 18th shuffled aboard the steamers *Emperor* and *Pioneer* and set sail up the York River towards Yorktown. The division sailed en masse with the infantry and most of its cavalry on the same transports that brought them south from Alexandria. The division's artillery rode in canal boats that were fastened together in pairs. Five gunboats and a few barges and schooners accompanied the division. The entire flotilla reached Yorktown before the end of the day.[1]

The ships dropped their anchors between the dominating banks of Yorktown and Gloucester Point, near enough for the men to obtain a fine view of the abandoned earthworks of their enemy. Their camp equipage, baggage, and siege guns left behind told of their hasty retreat. The regiment remained onboard and passed the night through a heavy rain that forced men to find respite any way they could.[2]

They were not to stay at Yorktown long, for they were quick to continue their journey on the heels of the enemy. The following morning, May 6, dawned with perfect sailing weather, complete with clear skies and a high wind. The fleet of gunboats sailed up the York

River and headed towards West Point, Virginia, followed closely by the armada of troops. West Point was a peninsula that split the York River into its two tributaries; the Mattaponi and Pamunkey Rivers. Strategically, it was also the tail end of the Richmond and York River Railroad line which offered McClellan a vital avenue for his final coordinated march into the Southern capital. The fleet sailed for the rest of the day with one momentary pause when some pontoons pulled by steamers accidently broke loose. Houses along the shore flew flags of white in hopes of protecting themselves and their property.[3]

Brick House Landing

An area known as Eltham, derived from a large plantation that still dominated the elbow curve where the Pamunkey meets the York River, became the division's landing destination. Pressed along the shallow waters just south of this river junction was an area known locally as Brick House Point which became the ideal spot for an amphibious landing, for the ground was a semi-circle of meadowland that stretched from the Pamunkey to the York River. A grand brick colonial mansion had once stood at this point during the seventeenth and eighteenth century but had long since vanished by the time of the Civil War, but its reference still carried in name, nestled within the greater hundreds of acres of Eltham's plantation. The ideal point of entry to disembark was the ferry landing at Brick House Point, which was edged by a thick and entangling line of woods that ran in the same direction of the meadowland. Under the cover of the five gunboats, a wave of pontoon boats on reconnaissance neared the shore around 2 p.m. on May 6. Three Confederate pickets spotted on the beach were quickly dispersed by an artillery shell from one of the gunboats, which sent the trio into a sprint back towards the curtain of pine woods. Corporal Thomas Alexander of Company D saw their comical dash, "double quick, tumbling over the fences like sheep." Union pontoons then flooded the shore and emptied their troops just after 5 p.m. Wave after wave of boats ferried men and supplies from the fleet to the shore at a steady pace, without any harassment from the enemy. Canal boats and pontoons floated an abundant supply of planks which were then assembled into a floating wharf, 400 feet in length, which helped man and beast get a foothold on the beach. The landing intensified and lasted for several hours throughout the night. Most of the men of the 18th made landfall sometime between 7 and 10 p.m. The rest of the division continued their landing by torchlight well into the following morning.[4]

As soon as they reached the shore that night, the 18th moved off the beach and into a perfect semi-circle field of wheat. The grounds at Brick House Point started swampy at the water's edge, but leveled out and opened up before it became surrounded by a semi-circle wall of thick pine woods farther inland. Farm fields just beyond the water's edge were cultivated with wheat which was at that time nearly eighteen inches high and close to harvest, and despite the farmer's protest, the crop became ideal padding for soldiers to lie on. Corporal Alexander made a joke with seriousness when he said the wheat made "an excellent couch" for him and his comrades. The owner of the meadowland came out and verbally condemned the landing forces that swarmed his property. His rant proved to be a waste of his breath as everyone blatantly ignored him.[5]

General Franklin sided with caution and did not intend to seek out a hurried fight, but rather defend what he had and wait for the other three divisions who were still at Yorktown.

Confederate General Joseph E. Johnston's entire Rebel army was at or near Barhamsville, six miles southwest from Franklin, but they too demonstrated patience. They merely wanted to keep Franklin's forces in check to buy time to consolidate and move their army and trains westward closer to Richmond.[6]

The night of May 6 was surprisingly quiet, aside from the occasional exchanges between pickets that rang out at random. Talks of the enemy being in large numbers nearby put the expectation of battle on the forefront of everyone's thoughts. Union pickets operated with doubled numbers. Major John C. Meginnis took Companies A, D, F, and K under his command and posted them in the tangles of the thick woods on the extreme left of the brigade's line. Confederate soldiers were occasionally spotted as they peeked out of the woods that skirted the landing plain. Sometime around midnight, a soldier from the 27th New York was shot and killed by an enemy picket, but a reactive comrade quickly felled the Rebel shooter a few feet away. Union pickets also brought in two Confederate soldiers from Brigadier General John B. Hood's Texas brigade. These Texans divulged information to Franklin that their force was large in strength and massed in front of them. The talkative Texans also hinted that they had recently tried to return to the area a few days before, but the intimidating Union gunboats near the shore had forced them to abandon the plan. They also forewarned to their captors that the landing division would be attacked in the early morning. To foil such an attack, General Franklin implemented "extraordinary precautions" for his pickets, and ordered more trees to be felled to block avenues of approach.[7]

Battle of Brick House Landing (West Point)

Shortly before 4 a.m. on May 7, Major Meginnis ordered his four companies on picket to form a straight line with each other. His intention was to have the picket line creep forward and flush the woods out by the break of day. The news of the slain picket from the 27th New York had reached their lines an hour before, so they knew the enemy was close. The rest of the 18th back at Brick House Point was rallied from their bivouac and formed in picket formation near a road to their front that led into the woods. As the morning sun broke over the Eltham area, the regiment reached the edge of the woods and stumbled across the cause of everyone's concern. They came across the body of the slain Confederate picket that had killed a member of their brigade. Stretched out on his back, the gray-clad combatant was a sergeant from the 4th Alabama. One of the 18th soldiers described him to be, "laid out as cool as if he had been made of iron." Only ten feet of separation was between the bodies of the Rebel and the dead 27th New Yorker. As the 18th went about their way to form the line near the edge of the woods, several men from the 18th uttered, "one Rebel less" when they passed the body.[8]

The regiment remained on the road close to an hour before the realization that the enemy was not as near as suspicion and rumors had led them to believe. General Franklin conducted an early morning reconnaissance on foot with Newton and inspected his brigade's placement and surveyed the advantages and disadvantages that the land gave them. Stretched out and facing west, they found that the left and right flanks of the brigade were protected by creeks, but one dangerous point was found at the right of the left flank. The cautioned area was a space of about 200 yards wide and had a well used road that led into their plain

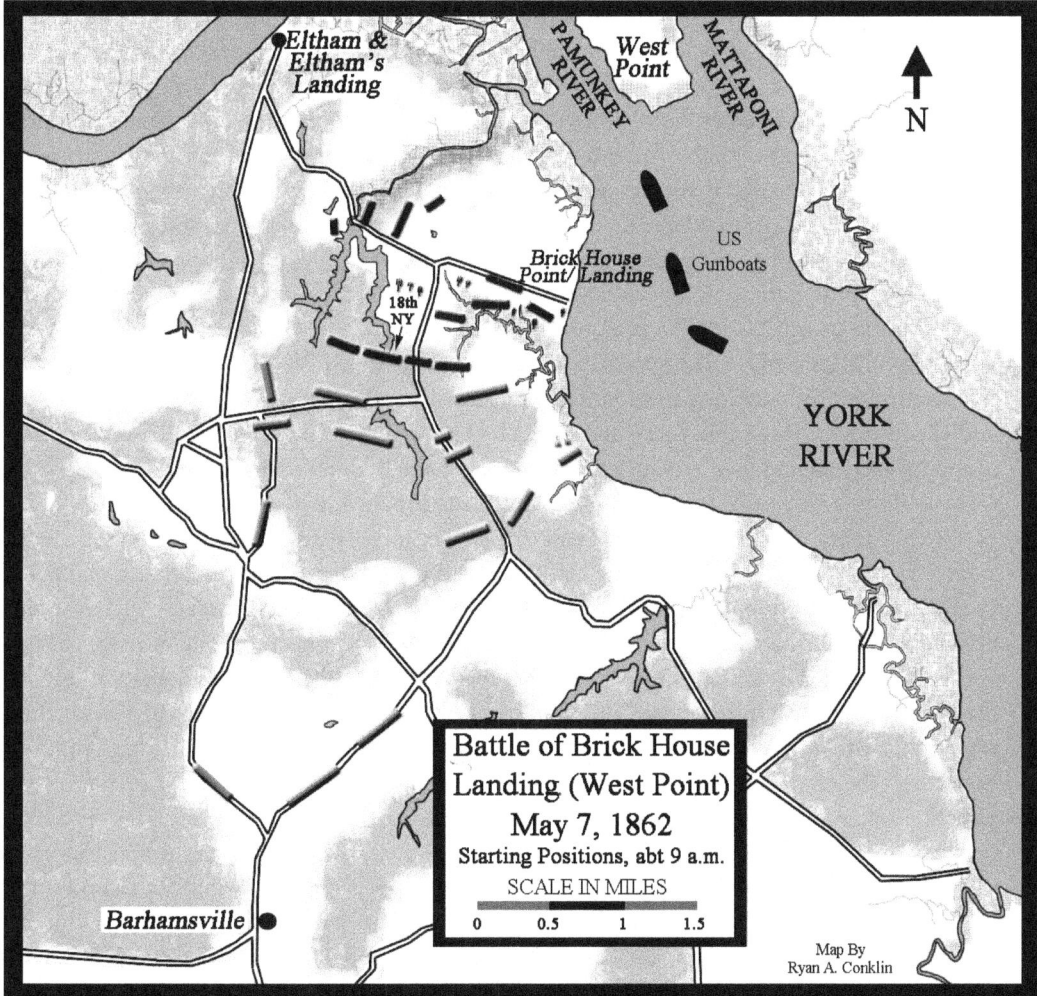

Map of the starting positions of the 18th New York before the battle of Brick House Landing, Virginia, or what most Union soldiers called West Point (author's collection).

that was bordered on both sides with thick woods. The generals were curious to know more about the land around them and where the enemy could be, so skirmishers were again asked to push out farther in all directions. Still on the left of the line, Meginnis kept control of his skirmishing elements and pushed Companies D, F, and K to the edge of what their original orders limited them to advance to. They stopped around seven in the morning and were reinforced by Company A. The rest of the regiment returned to camp and cooked up breakfast. The skirmishing New Yorkers patrolled through the woods with instructions that should they get overrun by a large force, they were to fall back onto the division which would be drawn up in formation to bounce back any attack.[9]

After an hour and a half of the skirmishers slow flush through the woods, a soldier in Company A spotted a dismounted enemy picket and his horse near a barricade in the road. Captain Gridley was notified and immediately halted their undiscovered advance in order to assess the situation. Without any evidence that this soldier had companions nearby, Gridley sought to capture this lone picket. He pointed out eight men from his company to go after him. Gridley took four men and advanced them up the left of the road, and the other four of the party went up the right of the road. Gridley's stealthy reconnoitering party continued to advance closer to the sentry, but they were quickly spotted before they could round him up. The enemy combatant quickly mounted his horse and rode out of sight up the road.[10]

Gridley became dissatisfied in how "he had lost his game," and was hell-bent to pursue the enemy lookout now that he had been discovered. He pushed his men farther up the road until they came to an open space of land, which was about a mile beyond their friendly line of pickets behind them. Gridley halted his group after he deemed it unsafe to pursue any farther from the skirmish line. He took out his field glass and surveyed what was in front of them, but saw no signs of the enemy. The party changed locations and skirted the edge of the woods until they came across a house. The home looked abandoned so they bypassed it and shortly thereafter came upon another. They approached the second small house and found it was occupied by a servant girl and a couple small "contrabands." Gridley asked her for water for his men, and also pried for more information on enemy activity. On the question of whether there were any Rebels around the area in the present or the day previous, she informed him that there was quite the collection gathered recently. She also mentioned that twenty-three cavalrymen had stayed on her property the previous night and left just as soon as Gridley' skirmishers advanced. When questioned if she had heard of one of these cavalrymen being killed overnight she said she had, and then mentioned that his horse was left in the barn. As soon as Gridley heard this, he ordered his men to proceed to the barn and take the horse. Suddenly, a volley of musketry erupted about 100 yards away from the right of the house near the road, shortly after 7 a.m. The men instinctively ducked for cover as the volley took them all by surprise. First Sergeant Joseph Strunk jumped into a shed nearby as the balls flew all around. Two more volleys rang out before Gridley realized they had no business to stay where they were any longer. He quickly ordered for everyone to dash for the wood line they were just in and to seek cover.[11]

As soon as the fleeing New Yorkers got back into the safety of the woods, Captain Gridley consolidated his party and inspected everyone. He was amazed to find no one was hurt. He pushed his element farther back towards the rest of their Company A left on the skirmish line. Gridley surprised them when his party returned with everyone intact. The skirmish line had since been stirred up after the sound of musketry and his men assumed the worst for Gridley and his team.[12]

Firing exchanges across the picket line began to crescendo and was heard far behind the line back to Newton and his staff a little before 9 a.m. The sound of the firing came from the direction of the road that led to their open plain that Franklin and Newton stressed the importance of earlier that morning. Pickets signaled the spotting of a large force of enemy infantry, cavalry, and artillery, which advanced toward Newton's brigade. Union pickets from the regiments put up a light resistance to the overwhelming force they were up against but they fell back out of the woods to the safety of the awaiting regiments in the clearing.[13]

The left of the 18th's picket line were fired upon by Confederate cavalrymen at the opening of hostilities. "We immediately heard considerable noise amongst the Rebels and blowing of bugles," wrote Corporal Alexander. He was quickly dispatched by Major Meginnis to inform Colonel Young in the rear with the remaining six companies of the regiment that the enemy was upon them. By the time Alexander reached Young, the companies were quite aware of the situation based on the intensity of the sound of musketry that had increased. He found the camp "all in commotion, prepared for action."[14]

While the Rebels continued their retiring march from Yorktown, Confederate Brigadier General William H. C. Whiting was directed from his higher command to use his division and prevent Franklin's division from advancing into Barhamsville from their landing point. General Johnston still needed time for supply trains to pass through unmolested. Whiting's division needed to buy that time, so they were ordered to drive back Franklin's skirmishers to a point where they could gain the open ground between the woods and the river and establish their artillery to take aim on Union troops and transports at the landing. General Johnston still asked that Whiting's advance be more of a probe, and if events escalated he was instructed to fall back.[15]

When the front line pickets were driven back more than a mile, the 32nd New York and a portion of the 95th Pennsylvania pushed forward through the dense woods and supported them as they withdrew. These two regiments of Newton's brigade then put up a stubborn stance in the woods choked full of pine trees and underbrush, but by 11 a.m. the enemy became more than they could handle. The two regiments were pushed back to the edge of the woods by the Confederates, and Newton read this as a sign that the enemy intended to push their whole force into the clearing in front of them and allow their artillery and cavalry to be utilized in strength. Newton needed to hold the woods in front of the right of the line in order to prevent this and control the only viable road that led to their landing zone.[16]

By 1 p.m., Newton ordered forward several regiments up to bolster the two advanced regiments at the edge of the woods. Issuing this information simultaneously to the regiments was done through several aides on Newton's staff. One of these was a recent transfer from the 18th—First Lieutenant William H. Russell, Jr.—the former quartermaster who shifted to serve as Newton's aide-de-camp. The 31st New York was ordered to move forward into the right of the field, and when they did they charged into the woods towards the enemy. They quickly earned some new ground as the Rebels buckled back, but at a hefty price. On their left, the 5th Maine similarly pushed forward to support the left flank of the 31st. The remaining six companies from the 18th not already deployed elsewhere as skirmishers—B, C, E, G, H, and I, under Colonel Young—had spent the morning supporting batteries on the right of the line. Under this renewed push, Young and his companies similarly moved ahead into the dense woods with the 5th Maine and 31st New York. Three companies each from the 16th and 27th New York were also sent forward. The 95th Pennsylvania had since pulled out of the woods and rested on the road and acted as a support to the regiments that were forwarded. "The fight now grew hot and fierce," as one witness pointed out, "and the volley's of musketry sharp and incessant." A stalemate ensued as the two opposing forces pushed back and forth through the same overgrown terrain, and neither left the comforts of the woods. The thick undergrowth offered loads of protection but the visibility was impossible, unable to see deeper than thirty or forty yards ahead. Newton would later bolster the line with more companies from two nearby New Jersey regiments.[17]

The last of Franklin's artillery brigade had finished landing shortly after the sound of musket fire intensified by mid-morning. Batteries were rushed forward in the clearing near the landing and posted throughout the line to cement the feet of the division as the enemy tried to flush the Union infantrymen out of the woods. Predominantly a musket affair, Franklin's artillery had a small strategic role during the battle. The woods obscured enemy positions completely, so the Union batteries based their aim on smoke from enemy musketry and sent shells right over the heads of their own men. A portion of Confederates from Hampton's Legion briefly appeared on the edge of the woods but were rerouted and pushed back when Union artillery spotted them. Confederate artillery only had time to fire seven quick shells, but most had too much elevation and landed in the river. Their time on the line was cut short by the Union batteries and large-caliber naval gunboats on the York River who spotted them and lobbed shells their way. The chief of artillery remarked the men of Franklin's division acted "worthy of veteran troops … in this their first engagement."[18]

The standoff in the woods lasted for several hours. Teases of bayonet charges occurred throughout the line, but none of which came to fruition. The 18th kept their rifles quiet and held their ground behind the 5th Maine. Accounts from the soldiers of the regiment tell of the Confederates before them were well positioned behind protection and how they used intimidation as a tactic to reroute their opponent. The following is from Corporal Alexander's perspective:

> We could not see them, though they could see us, and were heard to say "Fire low, boys, the damned Yankees have come the drop game on us." They then pretended to make a charge, that is their officers gave the order charge and they began to yell and jump about in the bushes, thinking by that to make us rise and draw our fire, but they could not succeed; but the 5th Maine, which were just in advance of us, were panic stricken: they jumped up and ran all over our men, still our men laid firm—prepared to meet the enemy with a volley and charge as soon as they became visible; but they did not come, so after a short time we charged were they were and routed them.[19]

Unlike the buckled Mainers, the 18th advanced for three-quarters of a mile. Their push was "like devils incarnate," as Second Lieutenant E. Nott Schermerhorn of Company E put it. This was the last they saw of the enemy. The 18th remained cool under the pressure of having both the enemy before them, and the 5th Maine retreat through their position. George W. Bicknell, adjutant of the 5th Maine, went on to publish a postwar history of his regiment but never mentioned a breakdown of their position, and that his unit stood as, "masters of the situation…. Our regiment received great praise for its conduct during the day." The 18th's contribution to the fight earned positive remarks and was later complimented by General Newton. Corporal Alexander went on to write:

> Not one regiment in a hundred would lay and allow another to retreat over them. Had we been like the other regiment, probably we should all have been cut off, for the whole brigade of Rebels would have charged on us.[20]

Before the fight blossomed to something bigger, Confederate high command ordered General Whiting to withdraw between 1 and 2 p.m., and reposition closer to Barhamsville. The extra time needed to pass their trains and equipment beyond the town was successfully attained. Before they left, Confederate troops were able to capture forty-six Yankees, most of which were helpless wounded. By 3 p.m., the Confederates were clear from the Eltham area and on their way to New Kent Courthouse. The naming of this battle adopted a few inaccurate titles by both sides. Northerners would come to call the clash as the battle of West Point, despite the fact that there was no fighting on the soil of that town, which was located on the opposite shore. Union troops could be given the excuse based on their unfamiliarity with the geography, but Southerners were just as guilty of having lent an inaccurate name to the battle. Confederates recognized the day's skirmish as the battle of Eltham's Landing, despite the fact that neither side was on that site either, located north of the battlefield on the Pamunkey. To be precise and encourage a future of correctness, the most accurate name would be the battle of Brick House Landing.[21]

Newton's men had advanced far beyond their morning positions and the important road and woods was theirs to control. The gunboats still fell under their protective umbrella. Franklin was actually displeased with how Newton's troops were so recklessly shoved deep into woods that had such bad visibility. Newton reported that his brigade was hit with 200 killed, wounded, or captured, most of which came from the 31st and 32nd New York. Several volleys at fairly close range had been fired at the six companies of the 18th under Colonel Young's control, but because of the crowded thicket in the woods and the colonel's order to lie on the ground, the regiment miraculously survived the day without a single soldier killed, wounded or captured. They were the only regiment in the brigade that could say that. Their feat was also done without ever firing a volley in return which greatly impressed Newton. Confederate losses also benefited from the safety of thick woods while fired upon by a sustained musketry, which they reported was aimed too high. Whiting's loss paled in comparison when he reported only eight killed, forty wounded, and none missing.[22]

If accidents are brought up into the picture, then the regiment tallied with one. In the early morning before the companies from the regiment were drawn for picket duty, Private James Brown, Company D, accidentally shot a ball from his musket through his left hand while in camp when he pulled his rifle out of a stacked set. His wound was severe enough to draw him out of the company and later forwarded to a New York hospital. Brown was a well-liked Wallkill Guard, and his company held him in high regards as a trusted soldier, and they were saddened by his accident. "He was one of the finest young men in our company," wrote Corporal Thomas Alexander, "and his accident caused quite a depression of spirits amongst us; for he was universally loved by all his companions in arms." Brown recovered quickly and returned to the regiment before they left the peninsula, and ascended to the rank of acting sergeant-major of the 18th in August.[23]

Though the battle of Brick House Landing (West Point) would be characterized as a sizable skirmish that ended in a stalemate, the Yankees there would chalk it up as a victory. As men excitedly wrote home to their family and friends to boast of their achievement, a common thread of the telling of atrocities from the recent fight was repetitive. Where Slocum's brigade was, the stripped body of a private in the 16th New York was found in a pool of water with his throat cut. The Yankees knew Rebels pilfered valuables off the bodies of the slain, but to whoever slit the throat of a mortally wounded soldier went against the last bits of dignity that this so-called gentleman's war had left. Newton himself heard the story and severely condemned the incident in his official report on the battle. This story ran its course through the ranks like rumors so often did, and the lone atrocity—which did occur—morphed into exaggerations of having occurred many times over, which was untrue. Needless to say, the men of the 18th were vehemently appalled by what they heard, and when Lieutenant Schermerhorn wrote home about it he avowed, "They will meet no mercy should any of them fall into our hands." Said with such bravado, the incident never incited the 18th to retaliate in violent ways. In fact they complimented the troops from Tennessee to say they took great care of the wounded at Brick House Landing by being attentive to their needs with food and care and having the wounded placed in relative safety during the fight. "The barbarities," as Corporal Alexander was led to believe, "were committed by the Alabamians, Texans and Niggers, of whom they have plenty bearing arms." Without being validated in any official reports on either side, Alexander mentioned "we captured one whole company of niggers. We shall for the future show niggers no quarters when found under arms."[24]

From Eltham, to Cumberland, to White House

The day after the battle of Brick House Landing (West Point), the 18th moved about a mile to the front and supported Battery A of the 1st New Jersey Light Artillery, just in case the enemy attempted another attack. But one never came, and Franklin's division quietly held their ground around Eltham for the next couple of days. The men resumed their place on the picket lines and provided the forward eyes and ears of the division.[25]

On May 9, the wounded and severely sick soldiers—180 in all—were gathered up from around the landing and sent off on steamboats run by the Sanitary Commission. Even the wife of the colonel of the 16th New York was aboard and helped care for the wounded as a nurse. Those able to be transported were eventually hospitalized in Northern hospitals closer to their homes.[26]

Franklin's men quickly reorganized and refitted themselves to prepare to relocate on May 9, but their march was delayed when all of a sudden Little Mac rode up to the 18th for an impromptu pep talk. The regiment formed a square around the mounted general and his staff. McClellan's compliments to the regiment's conduct during the recent fight were documented by Corporal Thomas Alexander:

> Officers and Soldiers of the 18th. I wish to compliment you on your gallant conduct in your late action. I consider you the best skirmishers in the United States Army. You were in the heaviest of the firing, yet kept yourselves so well covered as not to lose a man, and best of all not to allow the enemy to draw your fire; but reserving it for sure work, it needed. When I order you to the front as skirmishers or to charge bayonets, I only ask you to do as you did then, and victory is sure to be yours; and I am sure you will.[27]

With a hearty response of the customary "cheer of three times three and a tiger" from the men, the general puffed his chest and rode off with his staff. The rejuvenated regiment picked up a light march of just under three miles to Brick House Point. Despite not having achieved the desired flanking movement that McClellan wanted from Franklin, the generals breathed easier on May 10 when the advance guard of McClellan's army beyond Williamsburg reached Franklin. The men of the 18th relieved the 5th Maine and went on picket duty and stumbled through the "almost impregnable" woods in search of the enemy. The only Confederates they saw were deserters that willingly surrendered. With the entire regiment stretched out on picket duty, on May 10 the men also acted as human telegraph poles, and relayed a few messages back and forth between friendly forces.[28]

On May 11, the regiment resumed another short march of three miles inland and encamped on the grounds of an impressive southern mansion called Eltham's plantation, which had an interchangeable name that reflected its wartime owner, Lacy. The following day, McClellan and the rest of the main body of the army finished their march from Yorktown and linked up with Franklin's division, reuniting the entire Army of the Potomac. Naturally, the 18th spun themselves into a cheering frenzy when McClellan rode through.[29]

The 18th got back in the marching mode early on May 13, and took up a long march west that spanned twelve hot miles and ended at Cumberland. Cumberland Landing was quickly established as another supply base for the Federals, and the Pamunkey River that

10. Like Devils Incarnate   195

Unidentified Union troops look out over Cumberland Landing, which quickly boomed as another supply base for the Federal army along the Pamunkey River during their march towards Richmond, May 1862 (Library of Congress).

snaked around the landing with its many bends allowed Navy gunboats to chaperone the army. Upon arrival to Cumberland, the 18th immediately formed a line of battle in expectation of an enemy attack, but one never came. The regiment was then ordered to encamp where they were, which was in a plowed field near the river. Their rest was brief and they resumed a march at four o'clock on the morning of May 15. Companies A and C acted as the advance guard for the entire division as they trekked westward through a relentless rainstorm. After a muddy and wet nine mile march, the division reached White House and encamped.[30]

White House became the army's vital supply port to shuttle supplies up the river. White House was also significant in more ways than one, and the men were quick to learn its history. Strategically, it was a point where the Richmond and York River Railroad crossed over the Pamunkey River which gave them access to both rail and water to use for shipments. McClellan designated White House Landing as his base of operations that would help him wage his war towards Richmond. The naming of White House came from the large estate that dominated the land, which happened to be owned by General Robert E. Lee's son, William H. F. "Rooney" Lee, who like his father was an officer for the Confederacy. Historically, the men learned the connection of White House had to the nation's most revered founding father, which was better explained by Private George J. Green of Company C:

> [White House] is the place where Washington first became acquainted with his wife, in days of yore. The old house was burned down a few years since, but the new one stands upon the same foundation.[31]

General Lee's wife had occupied the house since leaving Alexandria, but her connection with the general and fear for her safety prompted her to leave the house just days before the Union army rolled in. One of the first Yankees in the advance guard that arrived to the house

On May 15, 1862, four days before the creation of the VI Corps, officers from Franklin's division posed for a photograph while at White House, Virginia. Front row (L-R): Col. Joseph J. Bartlett, Brig. Gen. Henry W. Slocum, Brig. Gen. William B. Franklin, Brig. Gen. William F. Barry, and Brig. Gen. John Newton. Back row: unidentified staff officers (Library of Congress).

found a note pinned on the door. Signed by "a grand-daughter of Mrs. Washington," Mrs. Lee begged to have the property respected, and hoped the connection to Washington would prevent the home from being ransacked. The plea worked and McClellan ordered guards posted on the house and refrained from its use to the army.[32]

The 18th remained at White House for four days, while they waited for docks to be constructed to allow crucial supplies to reach them at the nearby landing. The large-scale depot popped up almost overnight, with extensive docks, boats of various sizes with hefty cargo loads, and numerous boxcars from the rail line.[33]

Sickness Prevails

After a month had lapsed since the regiment left Alexandria, and although spared from death in battle, the ranks of the 18th continued to be chiseled. Four men deserted the regiment soon after they set sail. Private Corydon A. Dawley of Company I was taken sick and hospitalized at Fort Monroe on May 8, but records of him stop there and the military chalked him up as a deserter. Somehow he made it back to his hometown of Lanesborough, Massachusetts, and told anyone who asked about his service that he was discharged based on sickness.[34]

Three other soldiers were discharged back in Alexandria after doctors lost hope that they would recover and be returned to the line. Before the chance for a medical discharge, twenty-two-year-old Irish-native Private John H. Shaughnessy of Company I died in a hospital in Alexandria from tuberculosis on April 19. Private George W. Dunkle, the youngest of the three Dunkle brothers of Company G, died ten days after Shaughnessy in the same city after pneumonia flooded his lungs.[35]

Disease on the front lines continued to attack the vulnerable men during their expedition, which prompted several soldiers the necessity to be released and sent back down river for proper medical attention. Most often, the worst were shipped north aboard steamers and hospitalized. Four days after the battle of Brick House Landing, sixteen men from the 18th had been shipped away. It can be suggested that the healthy soldiers were not exactly healthy or immune to the wanton sickness, but were simply not dire enough to be removed in order to have their lives saved. Sometimes this judgment call by doctors came too late, or situations prevented such action. Such as the case of Company H's Private William Speenburgh's bout with typhoid fever. He was evacuated on May 11 and placed on the transport *Ocean Queen*, but died later that day onboard before the transport reached the destined hospital in New York City. May 11 was also his twenty-fourth birthday.[36]

With a shared sickness that knew no rank or privilege, not even Colonel Young was immune. Rendering himself unfit for duty, he placed Lieutenant Colonel Myers in charge of the regiment on May 14, and had himself shipped off from White House Landing about a week later. Major Meginnis stood in as second-in-command of the regiment, which elevated Company A's Captain Gridley to act as major until Young returned. When Young landed back in New York on May 26, a separate steamer from the Virginian peninsula had arrived to New York the day before that carried a handful of sick soldiers from the 18th—one of which was the colonel's son, Private David W. Young of Company K. With less than three months of active service with the regiment, the eighteen-year-old was done with the front and was eventually discharged in New York for his sickness on August 1.[37]

McClellan Reorganizes, Franklin Gets VI Corps, Slocum Commands Division

For the regiment encamped around White House, May 17 came as an almost forgotten anniversary. After having been in service for a year, they had hopes that less than a year was all that was left. By then, it was rare to not have acquaintances in the numerous surrounding regiments. Dozens of other regiments from their native state occupied the land around White House. Private George J. Green commented, "I can hardly go into a regiment from York State but what I find some familiar face."[38]

With most of the Army of the Potomac at or near White House, McClellan enacted his final building block to modify his corps organization. Displeased with his pockets of uncontrollability of incompetent corps commanders at Williamsburg, McClellan demanded from Washington "full & complete authority" to restructure the Army of the Potomac. On May 18, his demands were met and the creation of two more corps was put into effect. The newly added V Corps was given to Brigadier Generals Fitz John Porter, and McClellan's friend

William B. Franklin was given command of the VI Corps. The VI Corps consisted of a small cavalry and artillery contingent, with six brigades of infantry. The infantry brigades were then divided into two divisions, the first under the command of Brigadier General Henry W. Slocum, and the second going to Brigadier General William F. Smith. Within Slocum's First Division, there were three brigades of infantry, each composed of four infantry regiments. The 18th New York fell under the third brigade of the First Division, along with the 31st and 32nd New York, and the 95th Pennsylvania. Their brigade continued to be commanded by Brigadier General John Newton.[39]

General Slocum was a familiar face to the men. A New York native, Slocum was a West Point graduate and served in the antebellum years as a field artillery officer in the regular army. He resigned a few years before the war and settled in Syracuse as a lawyer and politician. Slocum started the war at the helm of the 27th New York as their first colonel. At Bull Run, he was wounded in his hip, but his recovery was quick. As the Army of the Potomac was restructured, Slocum was inched up the command ladder with promotions. Slocum had commanded one of Franklin's brigades, but with this most recent restructure, he ascended to command one of the divisions under Franklin. With each command he oversaw, he quickly won the confidence and respect of his men.[40]

One of two division commanders in Franklin's newly formed VI Corps, Brig. Gen. Henry Warner Slocum (pictured as a major general) commanded the First Division, of which the 18th New York was part of the third brigade. Having started the war as the first colonel of the 27th New York, Slocum quickly won more than just promotions—the confidence and respect of his men (Library of Congress).

Nearing Richmond

The men would barely notice a difference that day, as May 18 passed as yet another hot one at White House Landing. They had company inspections at 9 a.m. and spent the day with camp duties to clean clothes and bathe. An abundance of overpriced sutlers also showed themselves amongst the camps and preyed upon those with money.[41]

Dark clouds rolled in the morning of May 19, but rain failed to fall when the regiment started a march in the direction of Richmond. At 6 a.m. they stepped off and tramped six miles in four hours to reach Tunstall's Station. They pulled off the road and into a large open field and commenced to pitch their tents. The rain that was held at bay finally let loose as soon as the first tent pegs struck the ground. Men always moved quicker to erect tents if wetness could be avoided.[42]

At 3 p.m. the following afternoon, orders came to fall in, and everyone picked up the march to inch closer to Richmond. Little Mac passed the men along their journey and was "heartily cheered by the boys." The sound of heavy firing was heard off in the distance to their left, but the men could not tell who or how far it was coming from. The men arrived to Cold Harbor

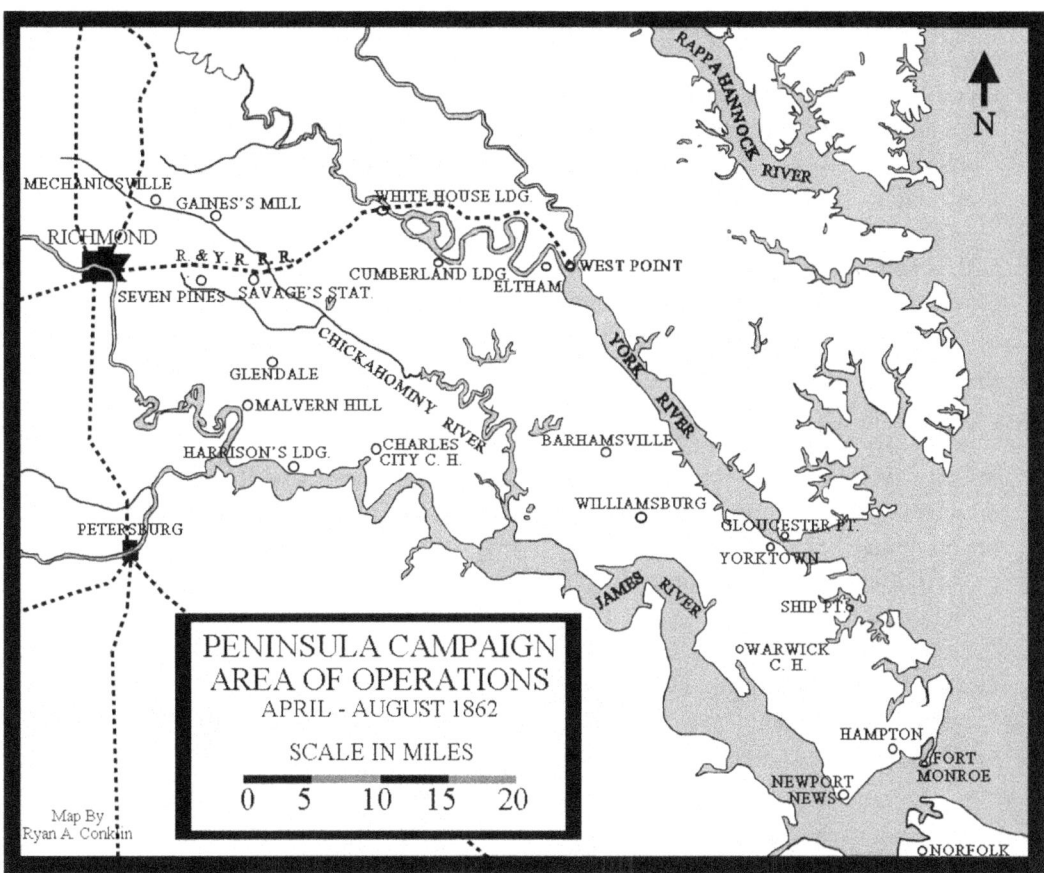

Map of the area of operations during the "On to Richmond" Peninsula Campaign of April–August 1862 (author's collection).

at 6 p.m., having marched five miles within the day. They peeled off the road and encamped for the night in a large cornfield near the edge of a small patch of woods.[43]

The endless marches had been conducted in the most unfavorable mixture of muddy roads and temperate days. These daily advances would only continue as Richmond slowly became within their reach. The 18th regained their march on May 21 and left Cold Harbor at 7 a.m. The heat had only started to climb by the time they pulled off the dusty road by noon, but the men had by then marched nine miles. The temperature and arduous march was strong enough to have a few men fall out of formation and onto the wayside, but the regiment pushed on. They set up their camp in the early afternoon on the property of Dr. William G. Gaines. He was the largest landowner in the area and was also recognized for his dedicated support of the Rebellion. Some Federal troops who recently died from disease had to be quickly buried, and much to the chagrin of Gaines, many of these soldiers were interred on his property. Gaines made his anger known to all and proclaimed to the invading troops that once the Yankees were quickly routed from his property that he was going to exhume the bodies and let his hogs feast on them. His rebellious allegiance led to an utter disregard to his property from the Union army. The 18th took advantage of the abundance of sweet potatoes prevalent about his land and filled up their water supply from a nearby spring that was suitable to drink.[44]

The regiment remained encamped on Gaines's property for several days which gave them time to recoup and refresh. The surgeons were the busiest of all and tried to curtail the increasing sick list. Richmond stood nearly eleven miles away from the men, but between them and the city was a strong army of Confederates about four miles away. Crossing the Chickahominy River at New Bridge would have granted an easy access road straight to Richmond and was only three miles away, but it had since been destroyed by the Rebels.[45]

Over the next few days, rain, thunder, and lightning seemed to hover above their heads as they waited in camp. During a break in the weather on May 22, the men witnessed another ascent of the balloon corps near their camp, similar to the ones they witnessed six months prior in Camp King. Professor Lowe continued to impress generals with his aeronautic capability but rarely wielded Union generals with superior impressions of enemy intentions. More cannonading was heard a few miles off to the right of the 18th's camp which proved to be small clashes of the Yankee advance guard and Rebel rear guard that touched on account of their proximity to each other. The sound of cannons was quickly replaced by the sound of thunder as storms poured in over those in camp who waited for the remnants of other units to consolidate.[46]

On May 25, the regiment struck their camp at 10 a.m., and picked up a short march to New Bridge. It was a warm dry day with which they walked two miles with the advance of the army. They pitched their tents in a large grassy field near the edge of some woods, within three-fourths of a mile from the banks of the Chickahominy River. It was a beautiful spot for a makeshift encampment, near the local landmark called Gaines's Mill. Many curious soldiers

Unidentified soldiers surround Professor Thaddeus Lowe's "Balloon Camp" before a launch in May 1862 at Gaines's Mill, Virginia. On May 22, 1862, soldiers from the 18th New York watched an ascent of Lowe's balloon at this location and could very well be the soldiers photographed (Library of Congress).

from the regiment stepped through the nearby woods and looked towards the direction of Richmond and could clearly see off in the distance their first church spire that stuck out above the tree line of the Southern capital. Their target city was roughly six and a half miles away from this encampment. They had their eye on their prize, but as Private Hodgkins of Company K put it, the vision of the steeples in Richmond seemed, "so near and yet so far." Men naively saw the war's end in sight.[47]

Corduroy Roads, Picket Duty, Icklin Wounded

At 9 p.m. on May 26, fifty soldiers from each regiment in the 18th's division were tasked out to build a bridge over the Chickahominy River, about two miles to the left of their line. They reached the point and initiated construction, but were quickly drenched in an unrelenting rainstorm. Private George J. Green wrote that it "rained as hard as it could pour all the while we were at work." Tree trunks were cut and sunk in the ground as piers over the river, connected by logs in corduroyed fashion and covered with mud to smooth over a walkway. The wet and dirty labor continued for hours in the dark until construction was called off and the fatigued men returned to their soggy camp around 4 a.m. For the next few weeks

Union troops are photographed on May 27–28, 1862, engaged in the backbreaking task of building corduroy roads and trestle bridges to get the army through the swampy lands along the Chickahominy River (Library of Congress).

the regiment was occupied with picket and fatigue duty, and tried their best to repel a contagious fever that ripped through the army. Roads and bridges were needed to be constructed in order to cross the Chickahominy. McClellan also needed a secure connection between his army north of the Chickahominy and his left wing that had made a successful foothold on the south side. Roads were also needed to be built which connected the railroad at Dispatch and Savage's Stations to the camps. The engineering brigade went to task to build a series of bridges and roads, and the infantrymen were always available for the added labor.[48]

In the early hours of May 27, the men awoke to the sounds of war. A couple miles away, General Porter's V Corps moved north upon Hanover Court House after McClellan received tips that his right flank was to be threatened. A force was met there around noon, but Porter's element had far superior numbers than their adversaries they met there. When darkness ended the one-sided fight, Confederate losses far outweighed Porter's, most of which were the nearly 800 Georgian and North Carolinian soldiers that were captured. The battle was handled by Porter without the need to spin up another corps, so the others continued their important fatigue duty of bridge-building. Despite the sounds of fighting a ways off, company inspections for the 18th were still held in the morning. Each man was handed an extra issuance of ammunition as a precaution. Another launch of one of Lowe's balloons was sent up nearby which drew the fire of five rounds from the enemy. During the 18th's evening dress parade, rules to observe for the impending battle were read to them.[49]

The land had been bogged down everywhere from the soaking rains, roads were choked with mud, and the water levels rose which flooded the shores. On May 28, the regiment put down their rifles and picked up axes to combat this traversing problem. All morning and late afternoon, the men chopped down acres of trees and collected timber in order to build more corduroy roads and trestle bridges to pass through the swampy lands along the Chickahominy River. Usually under the supervision of engineers, the infantry continued to provide the back-breaking task of chopping, hauling, and aligning the wood in successive side-by-side patterns to carpet the ground with a long wooden trail.[50]

After his guard shift at the camp later that same day, Sergeant Augustus Mowatt decided to stretch his legs on a brief walk towards the neighboring V Corps on their right. He got as far as General Porter's headquarters and saw more than 300 Rebel prisoners that were captured at the V Corps' battle at Hanover Court House the day before. Dressed in their gray and coffee-colored cotton uniforms with slouched hats, Mowatt ascertained most of these men were from North Carolina, and were what he called "a hard looking set."[51]

For these North Carolinians, the war would have to wait, but back in their own Southern state, hundreds of previously captured Union soldiers finally obtained their release. Two of these paroled prisoners, Privates Henry Hayden and George House—both of Company D— had already seen the Southern capital up close during their time in captivity. Both were captured back on August 29, 1861, while skirmishing at Bailey's Crossroads when the 18th was encamped outside Alexandria. They were both briefly confined in Richmond before they were relocated to New Orleans, and finished their last few months of captivity in Salisbury, North Carolina. It would still take several months before they returned to their company.[52]

On May 30, an inspection by the Inspector General of the Corps was to take place. The 18th had spent a significant amount of time cleaning the camp the previous day, but the inspection never came through. What did happen was the unexpected appearance of a bold Confederate battery atop a range of hills on the opposite side of the river that fired towards the skirmishers of Newton's brigade on the northern bank right when pickets were being relieved. Several shells and solid shot were thrown at the pickets, but luckily most were off target or did not burst and no injuries were reported from the harassment.[53]

About four o'clock that evening, a very heavy thunderstorm rolled in with such violence, that men from both armies would comment that it was one of the worst they had ever witnessed. Rain fell is torrents which prompted Private George J. Green to say that "it rained so hard that most of us were floated out of our tents, which are no better protection in a hard storm than a linen coat." The sky flashed like relentless artillery from the heavens. The storm was a menace and continued at intervals throughout the night.[54]

Trusting that the storm had flooded the river to a point that would make it troublesome for McClellan's troops to pass, Confederate General Johnston initiated an attack on May 31 upon Keyes's IV Corps who were south of the Chickahominy. The Confederates had not yet learned that Heintzelman's III Corps was also south of the river. Both armies marched towards each other and converged at a crossroads marked by seven large pine trees, and started what became known as the battle of Seven Pines, also known as Fair Oaks, which commenced at 1 p.m.[55]

Throughout the afternoon, the camp of the 18th could plainly hear the battle that raged opposite of the river, about two miles away. They could look out in the southern distance and plainly see the smoke of the fight that lingered above the treetops. The men instinctually prepped themselves to be called upon to join the battle as reserves, and they were jubilant at the prospect, but the request never came.[56]

The fighting around Seven Pines ended on account of nightfall, and in its wake was an inconclusive victor and hundreds of casualties. The Union loss stood at 468, but after a late offensive start and several miscommunications, the Confederate's loss fared steeper with 1,270. The biggest shakeup of the day was the wounding of the Confederate's top army commander. General Johnston was both shot in the shoulder and then knocked off his horse by a piece of shrapnel to his chest. He was rushed to Richmond where his wounds were declared not life-threatening, but Johnston would never serve again with the Army of Northern Virginia. Jefferson Davis found his successor the following day, and gave the reigns of the Confederate army to General Robert E. Lee.[57]

In the early balmy morning of June 1, soldiers in the 18th were jolted awake by the returning booms of heavy cannons and unison musket volleys south of the river. The battle of Seven Pines (Fair Oaks) had resumed over the same ground. Once again, the fight was inconclusive and losses were almost identical, with 1,203 Union, and 1,132 Confederate. Fighting tapered off around 11:30 a.m. without the need for reinforcements from the VI Corps. As soon as the fighting ended, news of a Union victory swept through the camps and was received with hearty cheers. Three batteries from Slocum's division fired several rounds over the river in the direction of the enemy, but nothing was ever received in return.[58]

The next morning, the regiment formed up at 8 a.m. for picket duty along the northern banks of the Chickahominy River. They marched about one-fourth of a mile from camp and relieved the 2nd New Jersey. While eight companies settled themselves to serve as a reserve to the pickets if needed, Companies A and C were sent a mile farther to the river's edge. Divided into small squads, these two companies established outposts on hills within rye fields. From their vantage, they could see Confederate movement off in the distance, but no warnings of an offensive move by them was made. Rain from a heavy thunderstorm swept in overnight, and for the men on the forwarded outposts who were without shelter tents or blankets, trees did little to keep the men dry.[59]

The drenched soldiers were relieved the following morning of June 3 by a different New Jersey regiment, but the rain hung around. Once they got back to their camp, everyone was ordered to turn in their Enfield rifles that they had carried since the start of the war in exchange for Springfield rifles. Rumors of the trade had circulated for about a week. With more than a year of service, the 18th's Enfield's were in a rough condition, which prompted them to be condemned. The new muskets had subtle differences. Both fired a .58-caliber *Minié* ball. With Springfield rifles, the entire brigade was now outfitted with the same rifles, though there were those in the 18th who grudgingly accepted the new weapons. For an infantryman, one's rifle was the most cherished and important tool to have, often regarded as an extension of themselves. Private George J. Green put it best when he had to turn in his trusty steel comrade and challenged its condemned status and stated, "I would rather have them yet. I had carried mine so long that it seamed like parting with an old friend." No other changes were made to the arms of the 18th again.[60]

Over the next couple of days, the men continued to be rained on as storms cycled in and out which halted the movements of the right wing of the army. During the occasional breaks in the sky, a few sporadic Confederate shells were lobbed around them, none of which caused any harm. As Private Green said, it was enough "to let us know that [the enemy] were there." One of the only temporary reliefs from the constant soaks was that the men in the regiment received a ration of whiskey, twice a day. A quarter-pint in size, the whiskey ration was the medical experts answer to help ward off the effects of exposure. When the rain held off, the men did their best to dry their clothes and ammunition, but with leaky shelter tents it was a recurrent lost cause.[61]

During a break of a heavy storm on June 7, Privates Sam Collard and George J. Green, both of Company C, went for a walk to visit some friends in a neighboring regiment in the V Corps. Along their way they came across the body of a soldier who was killed in the fight at Hanover Court House. The soldier was being unceremoniously packed up in a barrel of whiskey in order to be sent home. The gruesome scene was not only played out before these two soldiers, but the poor father of the slain soldier stood nearby and watched his lifeless son packed away like cargo. To say the least, the father "was much affected," as Green noticed, "but such are the horrors of war."[62]

On June 8, four companies from the regiment were detailed at 7 a.m. for fatigue detail. The day's task was to continue the construction of a corduroy road that would pass over a 100-foot wide stream and swamp that ran diagonally to the Chickahominy River. The job had been started by other regiments from the brigade, and their work had drawn the attraction of Confederate artillery that harassed their efforts with shells. The Rebel harassment was soon quieted by Federal cannons, but the peace was short-lived. The four companies from the 18th tasked out on June 8 joined twelve others from the remaining three regiments within the brigade. Together, they all marched about three miles to their left and continued the construction of what became Woodbury's Bridge.[63]

The early morning work was performed in relative peace and absent of enemy harassment. Unbeknownst to them, a squad of Confederate marksmen sneakily stalked close to the working parties. Two hills loomed before the bridge on the side of the enemy, linked by a patch of pine and cedar bushes. Six or seven Rebel sharpshooters crawled throughout the late afternoon undetected and positioned themselves amongst bushes, nearly 400 yards from the bridge under construction. Close to 4 p.m., the boys in blue were hard at work when they were startled by a crisp enemy volley. The surprised soldiers threw their axes and shovels down and jumped towards the nearest cover they could find. Only one well-aimed Confederate rifle found its mark and wounded Private John J. Icklin of Company C, with a bullet that penetrated his right breast, half-an-inch above his nipple. The bullet tore through his right lung and scratched his liver, and exited through the bottom of the shoulder blade near his spine. His wound was severe but the tough Irishman fought through the pain. Icklin was carried off just as two of Franklin's cannons were wheeled up near the work site which lobbed several shells across the river. For five minutes, the Rebel sharpshooters were unchallenged and fired several, until these Federal cannons arrived and ran them off when they snapped their lanyards. Icklin was rushed by comrades to a nearby barn that served as a temporary hospital. The barn was almost entirely shelled out which did not protect those within to be protected from the outside elements. Icklin dealt with his wound for four days in that hollowed barn, and when mixed with the openness of the weather he developed a severe cold and quickly lost vision in his left eye, and nearly all in his right. Somehow, Icklin survived his wounds.[64]

Photographed in June 1862, unidentified Union soldiers stand atop the newly constructed Woodbury's Bridge. On June 8, 1862, four companies of the 18th New York were detailed to work on this bridge until Rebel sharpshooters harassed their efforts and wounded Pvt. John J. Icklin of Company C (Library of Congress).

The construction of the bridge was slower than most anticipated. Companies worked for more than a week with endless hours of wood chopping and placement, a taxing work that was also performed under the occasional harassment of Rebel sharpshooters. The brigade orchestrated sharpshooters of their own to counteract with their bullies from the other side of the river.[65]

A few scattered showers appeared throughout the construction period. Some guys in Company H had one of their boxes of hardtack so thoroughly soaked by rain, First Sergeant George Blake said "that it will take 3 weeks of sun shine to dry it." Sunday, June 8, still came as a day of rest in the camp. For those not on the details of bridge building or picket duty, company drills were conducted instead. If one was not present for company drill, then they lost their ration of whiskey for the day which came as a great disappointment to the individual. When Monday came, Companies D and K went on fatigue duty to work on the bridge.[66]

On June 14, Company C managed to find special amusement while out on guard. The entire regiment had been posted out on the picket line like usual, but on this particular evening Company C was held as a reserve near the home of a local resident named Sydnor. To pass the time, the soldiers gathered Sydnor's slaves from the property and corralled them by a barn where they were made to sing and dance for their enjoyment. With ages that ranged from three and up, these slaves performed steps and actions that amazed and delighted the soldiers. Private George J. Green captured the rest of the evening in writing and turned his attention to other actors within their theater:

> They performed for us until about 12 o'clock, when we spread down our blankets and turned in; not to sleep, for that would be impossible on the edges of that swamp. I never saw anything that deserved the name of mosquitoes until I came here. They are the size of a common horse fly, with bills of cast steel. Our blankets afforded us no protection, and I was forced to set up and smoke till daybreak ridded us of our tormentors.[67]

Crossing the Chickahominy

The corduroy bridge was finally completed by June 16 after the regiment's last finishing touches were completed by nightfall. The regiment remained in place and conducted some last minute drills during the heat of the day before they were ordered to move again. The II and VI corps had both received orders to cross the Chickahominy and dig in on the southern side with the rest of the army. At 8 a.m. on June 18, the regiment packed up their camp in preparation for movement. They were on the road by 10 a.m., and their camp was turned over to reserve soldiers from Pennsylvania. The 18th were marched down passed a division from General Porter's command and farther on to New Bridge where they halted for about twenty minutes in order to allow the stragglers to rejoin the regiment after their lag from the march. They crossed over Woodbury's Bridge and finally entered the southern bank of the Chickahominy River. They continued until they passed General McClellan's Headquarters at the Trent House, where they took a short halt and rested for five minutes. They continued their journey by winding around a series of woods and hills in order to conceal themselves from enemy observation. Within the day the regiment covered nearly ten miles until they reached the line of Smith's division, about two miles north of where the Seven Pines/Fair Oaks battle had been fought. At this location, the men halted and pitched their tents. At one point, the 18th was formed into a battle line and waited for orders to join a nearby skirmish, but reserves were not requested and whatever fight that happened quickly fizzled out. The 18th advanced a little farther to reach Golding's farm, where they established a new camp. Throughout the evening the regiment was called to arms more than once, but none of the alarms coincided with any serious threat.[68]

The regiment remained at this position in order to again be detailed to construct more passageways for artillery over a swamp to their front. They spent all afternoon chopping down trees for the continued construction of corduroy bridges and roads which by then had become second-nature. On account of the prevalent swamps that plagued the land, this was a vital job in order to ensure the movement of artillery and other wagons to inch closer to the Rebel capital.[69]

Chickahominy Fever

Sickness and desertions created a vacuum to the fighting prowess of the entire Army of the Potomac. Most of these holes came from men so sick that they were pulled from the line and shipped out aboard steamers and transferred to hospitals up north. From the lowest private to the highest colonel, the 18th was no exception. Even General McClellan was stricken with a debilitating bout of malaria. By June 20, the Army of the Potomac listed 11,000 men sick or unfit for duty which was nearly one-tenth of its manpower. The 18th alone had lost thirty-four men from discharges, desertions, and death since the start of the campaign. One soldier that was bested by disease was Sergeant John Callan of Company H. A married man and father of six, Callan lost his life from consumption of the lungs and heart disease on May 26, at a hospital back in Annapolis, Maryland. Both armies felt the effects of unpredictable weather, mosquitoes, heat, and the unforgiving murky waters that seeped from the Chickahominy. Dysentery, diarrhea, and fevers wreaked havoc. The worst and most prevalent was malaria, typhoid, typhus, or other similar forms of fever that were lumped together and called by a common name that would forever usher shivers to the men—Chickahominy fever.[70]

Throughout the Peninsula campaign, the 18th did what every other regiment did during these trying times and they plugged their vacancies and persevered. Lieutenant Colonel Myers continued to guide the regiment in Colonel Young's absence. Young battled his bout with malarial fever back at home but showed little sign of favorable improvement. His leave of absence since late May was extended into July. Myers, a man who had turned twenty-five years old a month previous, continued to maintain his control of the regiment, albeit sick himself. Myers' commanding ability was similarly hampered by the common sufferings along the Chickahominy, and by mid–June, Myers had developed a low grade remittent fever that worsened to typhoid and overpowered him, and yet he tried his best to carry on.[71]

With the lack of men, especially commissioned officers, this factor could have been the reason Captain Thomas J. Radcliff was reinstated to his command of Company I on June 13. After having been dismissed back in January by reason of a court-martial over an inappropriate relationship with a woman in Alexandria, Radcliff penned a letter to General McClellan and asked for reinstatement. His efforts paid off and when approval was granted, Radcliff sped off from his home in Albany and rejoined his company.[72]

Armies Collide, the Start of the Seven Days' Battles

Near the end of June, the two armies were more consolidated and closer to each other than they had been that far into the campaign. Daily checks between pickets continued to probe and test each other's lines which heightened the assurance of an impending large-scale attack. On June 20, the men were still afforded the luxury to receive their hard earned two-month's pay while deployed. Union pickets were briefly driven in by Confederates on June 21 not far from the 18th's line, and at 3 p.m. they were drawn up to form in battle line, but the Rebels there were repulsed before other units like the 18th were needed in support.[73]

On June 22, company inspections did a thorough check of the men's equipment and ammunition. Life on-the-go during these times exposed the men to a lot of mud and rain and their equipment required constant attention and inspection. Weather had some improvement with several sunny and temperate days, but more storms again moved in just as soon as the Confederate capital was in the Army of the Potomac's grasp. On the night of June 23, Private George J. Green was detailed to guard the general's headquarters tent when a severe thunderstorm rolled in near midnight. "It seemed to me as if all the artillery in our army and all the waters of the Chickahominy were playing on me at the same time." Green got the scare of his life when a bolt of lightning stuck so close to him that his reaction forced him to drop his rifle from the impact of the bolt. Two horses a short distance from where he stood, fell dead from the lightning shaft's strike.[74]

The 18th were ordered to turn out before daylight on June 24 for a fight that was expected, but which never came. Dark clouds lingered and dripped rain throughout the day which prolonged the expected fight. On June 25, the weather cleared off and the armies took their chance upon each other, igniting a chain reaction of daily battles that would last for a week, forever remembered as the Seven Days' Battles of the Peninsula campaign.[75]

Over the same contested battleground of Seven Pines, Heintzelman's III Corps pushed west towards the Williamsburg Road and met the enemy at 8:30 a.m., and started the battle of Oak Grove. What started as an intense skirmish between pickets, the fighting escalated to a pitched battle with charges and countercharges, and at one point McClellan took it upon himself to join the front and ensure his lines were held. General Lee did the same, but more for assurance that McClellan's move was not an effort to spoil his own plan of attack for the day to follow. Once again darkness ended yet another stalemate, but the 600 yards of ground lost after the Seven Pines battle was now part of the stiff Union line. The costly price for the Army of the Potomac was the loss of 68 dead, 503 wounded, and 55 missing. Slightly under, the Confederates ended the day with 66 killed, 362 wounded, and 13 missing.[76]

A couple miles north of the fight, the 18th eagerly listened, but like always the noise was impossible to gauge the battle's actual progress. The regiment busied themselves by shifting their camp in order to consolidate with the rest of Slocum's division in reserve, and be closer to Smith's division and Sumner's II Corps. They settled a camped about a mile northeast of Fair Oaks Station on the Courtney Clearing. They were called up twice in the night, but their services as reserves were never needed.[77]

Disease claimed the life of another young soldier from the regiment on June 26. Private Percival Smith, Company G, was a fairly new acquisition to the 18th, having been with them for just six months. Smith succumbed to the common camp sufferings of typhoid fever and diarrhea, which proved vicious enough to kill him that morning at the regimental hospital before he ever had a chance for an evacuation.[78]

Sounds of cannons and musketry resumed in the late afternoon of June 26—Day Two—this time on the Union army's right wing. General Lee had taken a gamble to open an avenue to Richmond for his opponent after he moved most of his army north to Mechanicsville. His purpose was for a surprise counteroffensive flank attack on Porter's V Corps, which was the only portion of McClellan's army still north of the Chickahominy. They were in a favorable entrenched position, however, and thwarted the mismanaged Confederate attack. Had Lee's plan gone as it should have and Stonewall Jackson's Valley army arrived on time, McClellan's army would have been in peril. McClellan still did not take the bait of the opening of Richmond, and instead remained in place on the defense, which ultimately gave Lee time to try his plan again the next day. Overall, the battle of Mechanicsville (Beaver Dam Creek) was Lee's first failure, but his wounds scarred quickly. Confederate loss stood at 1,475, against Porter's 361.[79]

Slocum's division, and the rest of the VI Corps, remained planted in their encampment. The cannonading sounded more intense that the one heard during the battle of Seven Pines (Fair Oaks). Similar to that fight being played out in the distance, the 18th were again held off but remained under arms if and when reinforcements were needed. They weren't, and the firing eventually died down after 9 p.m. The first hints of a Union victory quickly made its run through the camp. A soldier from Company E viewed the report of their opponents skedaddle as, "a big joke," but the men had hardly ascertained honest and accurate details. The enemy was actually more poised for a victory than anyone in blue saw coming.[80]

Promoted at the start of the month, Sergeant Thomas Alexander of Company D wrote about what he knew and what effect Porter's victory had on his fellow soldiers:

> We were kept under arms all day, and expected to be called out, for the artillery firing was terrific, and did not cease until 9 p. m., when we received a despatch that we had routed the enemy and were driving them, they throwing away their guns and equipments. Of course there was great cheering, and for the first time in a month, bands playing, for previous to that we had not been allowed to sound a bugle or a drum. There was very little sleep that night.[81]

Troops all around their neighborhood heard what they wanted to hear. They understood that the enemy had been driven off by Porter and scattered in all directions, and that was cause for excitement. Men broke out in cheers and regimental bands struck up songs of victory, and the enthusiastic celebrations continued after midnight. McClellan and the Army of the Potomac did not know they were on borrowed time. While the men were amidst their premature celebration, their enemy finalized a coordinated plan of attack for the following morning.[82]

11

Battle of Gaines's Mill
June 27, 1862

> "The most terrific storm of bullets we
> received at all, and many a brave man fell."
> —*Sergeant Thomas Alexander, Company D, July 6, 1862*

Early Morning Wakeup

As the night hours ticked over to start June 27—Day Three—McClellan had joined Porter at his headquarters north of the Chickahominy. McClellan hardly had time to be joyous of the day's earlier outcome as a new thought gripped his strategy that entailed changing his army's overall position. Porter argued that with his high ground and fortified position he could withstand another attack. Cautious to a fault, McClellan needed time to think of where or how to move the army, but one thing the two generals agreed upon was that it was too late in the night to push Porter's V Corps to the southern side of the river. Until McClellan's new plan could begin, he emphasized to Porter the importance of holding the bridge crossings, even if it meant his total destruction.[1]

McClellan's sudden change of heart was due to the realization that Stonewall Jackson's added military might was not thwarted by Porter in the day's previous battle. In fact, Jackson's whereabouts were unknown, possibly off to Porter's right, or worse—his unprotected rear. So plans were disseminated from McClellan that called for Porter to shrink his line to the high ground next to the four bridge crossings and prevent Confederates from crossing, all in an effort to buy the precise time McClellan needed to move baggage trains, heavy guns, and supplies. With their backs to the bridges, the V Corps stretched out a line along the heightened plateau that bent like a bow, facing west and north, just under two-miles in length.[2]

Lieutenant Colonel Myers' fever continued to sap his strength and felt bested by his illness. Feeling that his abilities as the commander were hampered, he placed Major John C. Meginnis in command of the 18th just before orders of the day were issued. This also prompted senior Captain William S. Gridley to step away from his Company A and serve in a role that was two ranks above his. In the regiment's most trying day, they would be commanded by a major and a captain, but capable they were. Myers still did his best to be present and refused to pass the day in a hospital bed but rather rode as a spectator with Meginnis and Gridley.[3]

Private Samuel Hodgkins of Company K stood in line with his company with hopes that the bandage wrapped around his leg would not garnish attention. One of the doctors had wrapped Hodgkins' left leg the night before after he complained of a muscle rupture in the back of his left calf as a result of hauling timber during their bridge building work earlier that month. With the regiment's expected placement in battle, Hodgkins did not want word to pass back home to his father that he was not present, and being that proving his bravery to his father was his motive to enlist, Hodgkins left no room for anyone to accuse him of being a coward.[4]

There was little rest for Slocum's division after an early morning wakeup at 3 a.m. As Porter's troops north of the river altered their positions and built up their defenses in the dark, Slocum's division were ordered under arms to cross and assist with their efforts. The three batteries and twelve regiments within Slocum's three brigades fell in line in light marching order

Brig. Gen. Fitz John Porter (pictured as a major general) headed the V Corps and commanded the defensive fight at Gaines's Mill. His lines were bolstered by elements from other corps, including Slocum's division from the VI Corps (Library of Congress).

with two days rations in their haversacks, and pushed out together at 5 a.m. towards the river.[5]

Only a portion of the division actually crossed the Chickahominy via the Woodbury's Bridge. The 18th trekked for about a mile and halted beneath a hill that shielded them from the enemy's vantage. The ground before them had a significant incline which fanned out to the favorably elevated oval-shaped plateau where Porter's men had consolidated themselves. With a couple scattered dwellings, the elevated hill was known locally as Turkey Hill. Despite the fact that the fighting would take place atop this tract of land, the battle would never reflect this name. A gristmill owned by the area's largest landowner, Dr. Gaines, that was nearly a mile from the fighting would lend its name for what became known as the battle of Gaines's Mill. As the troops waited below the hill, officers crept to the higher elevation and were surprised to look out and see hints of the distanced enemy in force out and encamped where Porter's men had just vacated. As the pack of officers came down the hill, a telling reminder of the enemy's intent came when an artillery shell struck the top and sent a shower of dirt high into the air, and luckily no one was hurt. After an hour's wait, Slocum's elements received orders contrary to expectations and were countermanded back to their morning camp. Begrudgingly, the units turned around and marched back over to the southern side of the river. The 18th pulled off into an open field by the bridge and anxiously waited for orders to change. Impatience was contagious and men yearned for the simple luxury of shade as the day's temperature crept in. "The sun," Sergeant John S. Bantham of Company F characterized, was "burning our very eyes out." After having sweated for nearly two hours in the open field without new news, the 18th moved back to their morning camp as earlier ordered, having tacked four miles in vain.[6]

As the senior line officer in the regiment, Capt. William S. Gridley stepped away from his Company A to stand in as the regiment's second-in-command during the battle of Gaines's Mill after disease incapacitated the top field officers. Although he was small in stature, Gridley was described as "large in the face of the enemy" (courtesy Clark Hotaling).

Battle Begins, Camp Gets Shelled

With a battle expected, men quickly fumbled through their tents and bags in search for some last minute items, most of which was something to eat. As soon as they got to their tents, the regiment was recalled near the midday hour after a nearby Confederate battery presented themselves and shelled the neighboring camp next to Smith's Division. The 18th scrambled back into battle line formation in front of their camp like they had done earlier in the day. A few of the Rebel shells intended for Smith's camp actually overshot and landed close to the 18th's camp, yet they held their ranks and awaited further orders as casually as dress parade. The first close one whizzed over their heads and undoubtedly raised a few eyebrows when the shell crashed behind them. The second would be much closer and deadlier.[7]

Captain Donovan of Company F had his mind in a calmer place as he poured over the words of a letter from home during the barrage. Seated on a tree stump a few feet in front of Company I, who stood to the right of his own company, Donovan got the shock of his life when an enemy shell ripped into the base of his stump and tore clean through with wood splintering effects. The shell exploded on the other side of the mangled stump which launched hot shrapnel into the line of Company I. Nineteen-year-old Private Edward Nugent took the brunt of the blast and was killed immediately, and three others from his company lingered with wounds. With a look of amazement painted on his face, Donovan walked away from his shattered stump wide-eyed but without injury.[8]

"We thought that rather tough work, as we could do nothing in return," said Sergeant Thomas Alexander of Company D, "A great many shells burst over our camp and around it … still we stood firm until we received orders to move out of range." Wise to the situation, the men were ordered to drop on their rifles and level themselves with the earth. As soon as they did, Meginnis got additional orders to shift the 18th to safer grounds behind a hill near their encampment. When they shuffled to the other side and into some woods, Meginnis still instructed them to lie on their rifles, which they did in relative safety for nearly two hours. The sick men in the regimental hospital in camp were also gathered and carried to the safety of the base of the hill. General Franklin had strict orders that blocked him from doing much, lest he bring on an engagement, so little was done other than a few random answers from Union batteries. As the Rebel shells eventually tapered off, their own batteries slackened their shots, and eventually calmness returned around the VI Corps. The men were dismissed back to their tents when the all clear was given.[9]

Porter's men had been probed with skirmishers throughout the early afternoon and the general kept a close watch from his hilltop headquarters at the Watt House. Situations changed by 1 p.m., when the general noticed a considerable build-up of Confederates at his center. Lee had mounted six divisions, totaling 54,300 men who stalked closer to the Boatswain's Swamp that slithered along in front of the Union entrenchments. Porter had started the day with 27,160 men, but he had nearly 100 cannons on elevation which helped split the difference. Porter noticed dust clouds in the distance which indicated more enemy forces were on their way. He needed help.[10]

Newton's Brigade Called Forward

At 2 p.m., Porter sent an immediate request to McClellan for reinforcements to bolster his line. Just like earlier that morning, the answer came with Slocum's division. Newton's brigade was the first to be called up. The 18th had only just ventured back into their tents after their hideout from behind the hill when orders to form came. Lieutenant Colonel Myers, still struck with his fever and body aches, struggled just to mount his horse, but Meginnis had the 18th formed and ready to march with the other three regiments that formed Newton's brigade. With time lost due to telegraphs and couriers, the march was started close to 2:30 p.m. The brigade moved fast for a long and tiresome march, and the route was on a different path than the morning's futile foray. They proceeded in an eastwardly direction and passed General McClellan's headquarters at the Trent House.[11]

The brigade pressed on and again crossed the Chickahominy River over Alexander's Bridge, and finished their three mile march from their camp and arrived near the Adams House hospital atop the elevated Turkey Hill. From its vantage, the men could look out a mile distant and see the battle played out in a level plain flanked on both sides by woods, with Union troops in various formations holding their lines as shells exploded indiscriminately around them. The same time the 18th had been called up to march, so too did the enemy make their timely attack. General Newton took a moment to pause his brigade and had his men stack their rifles and fill their canteens from a stream near the hospital before their expected placement on the front lines. It was a searing day and the temperature was poised to get hotter. Minutes into their water break, they were quickly reunited with the rest of their division and formed together into columns.[12]

"Nearer, clearer, deadlier than before!" Corporal Edmund B. Hawley of Company E surmised from the sounds. His thoughts were confirmed as they neared closer to the field of contest when packed ambulances and walking wounded from other regiments in retreat streamed passed the 18th. The wounded cried out to the advancing reinforcements with foreboding warnings of what they should be prepared to face. Various accounts were rattled off to the new arrivals which left many puzzled on the overall situation of the battle. Nerves were certainly not calmed by what they shared. From what Hawley pieced together, the one thing that seemed to be corroborated from what they said was "that there was hot work over the hill yonder."[13]

The men had a clear view of the battle from atop the Turkey Hill knoll, and watched the progress of the panoramic battle from less than a mile behind. They itched for the orders to join. Newton aligned the brigade in column by division and waited on the hill near the hospital at the Adams House for nearly a half hour atop the hill until the rest of Slocum's division had reassembled. A member of Porter's staff came with orders to Slocum on how the division would have to be divided to plug necessary gaps in the line. Upsetting the cohesion of a division by splitting their brigades far from the reach of their commanders was not commonplace, a bit risky, but at this juncture Porter was desperate. Slocum's brigades would be the bandages to his battered line. Orders asked for Newton to detach from Slocum and place his four regiments and Upton's Battery to the center line of battle. There was a sizable gap to the left of the center owed to a dip in the terrain and diminishing troop strength. Slocum's other two brigades would be sent to opposite ends of the line. Newton formed his brigade in two lines, with the first line made of two deployed regiments, followed by the second made up of two regiments in double column. The 18th were deployed in the first line and Meginnis moved them up through woods that were on the right of the hill. They skirted the edge of the woods for nearly half a mile until Upton's Battery could set up a position. The 18th to the right of the battery acted as their support only momentarily, because orders quickly changed and Meginnis was asked to file left out of the woods and cross the field to take a position on the front line. Meginnis formed the regiment into column by division, and soon

Newton reappeared and took the reins and re-formed the brigade and led them to the crest of a hill where the battle raged. Porter met with Newton and pointed out a patch of woods on the front line that jutted out towards them with a wooden ravine, and he ordered Newton to divide his brigade to occupy the line on either side of the woods. This would complicate Newton's span of control even more, but orders were orders. Newton split his brigade in half and personally took the 31st New York and 95th Pennsylvania under his command to attack on the left of the woods. The 18th and the 32nd New York went under the command of Colonel Roderick Matheson, commander of the 32nd, and were to enter the woods from the right. Both halves were to approach at right angles to each other until a link between them was made. The brigade split and pushed to their ordered position. The 18th and 32nd moved by the right flank and crossed a road and entered an adjoining field where they deployed in line of battle with the 32nd on the left of the 18th.[14]

Colonel Roderick Matheson, circa 1861–1862, from Healdsburg, California, commanded the 32nd New York Infantry. After Gen. Newton separated himself and split the brigade to plug the Union center at Gaines's Mill, Matheson took command of the 18th and 32nd New York. He was mortally wounded at Crampton's Gap, Maryland, September 14, 1862 (Healdsburg Museum and Historical Society).

It was near four o'clock in the afternoon and Porter's line seemed to hold after Slocum's division patched the gaps. Porter telegraphed headquarters that told of a successful repulse of an assault from Confederate General A. P. Hill's division. Matheson moved the 18th and 32nd New York regiments at the double-quick to relieve two from Porter's who occupied a fortified line on a slight rise of ground that overlooked a large patch of woods in which the enemy were within. The 18th moved forward in line of battle, as did the 32nd on their left, and both were quickly touched with a rain of rifle balls and shells. Sergeant Thomas Alexander expressed their advance was done, "with a hearty good will." Together, the two regiments took a position behind others that were engaged and nestled behind entrenchments that ran along the ridge and extended across the field. Their arrival came to the delight of those on the line that had already been thinned of men and ammunition. Porter's hard pressed troops had struggled to maintain their ground on the hill and several lines of dead soldiers on the field marked the various lines held. Alexander observed, "We could see heaps of killed and wounded before us, but we had no time to look at them." More and more wounded soldiers from Porter's front line defense were carried off to the rear and passed the 18th on their way to the front. Most of them were regulars and "Red Devils" of the extravagantly uniformed 5th New York (Duryea's Zouaves), all of whom had reached a dangerously low level of ammunition and a high rate of casualties.[15]

The companies on the right wing of the 18th received a terrific fire of grape and canister from the enemy artillery that sent the men instinctively to the ground, similar to their survival during the recent engagement at Brick House Landing (West Point). One soldier in Company

G was killed on the onset and the same shell injured another in Company C. Meginnis complimented the men for taking the punch "with great coolness."[16]

In the meantime, Matheson ordered the 32nd forward through the ravine and their battle line was formed under the cover of a hill. They bolstered the weakened Union line which had already commenced to fall back just as they reached the brow of the hill. One regiment wholly used up in the fight broke through the 18th as they were marched into a swamp. Answering the famed Rebel yell that poured out of the woods in front of them, the 32nd unleashed their first volley. Matheson then sent orders to Meginnis to move the 18th to the left, and for another line of battle behind the 32nd, near the ravine.[17]

The 18th remained behind the 32nd only momentarily. Matheson looked back to Meginnis and asked him to cross the ravine and relieve the 32nd. Meginnis moved the 18th up under a terrific fire of musketry and shell, but most of the shells sailed over their line. Private David D. Sheldon of Company F said that "the enemy met us with grape and canister. We had to hug the ground as we advanced."[18]

The day neared 5 p.m. and the 18th had finally taken their place in front of the enemy and finally ordered to open fire. The regiment fought by wings at first, alternating turns at the front. After the 18th tested their own mettle with their first vigorous volley, "no one thought of danger," as Corporal Hawley stated. Meginnis, Gridley, and even the ill-struck Myers could look on the regiment with pride. Private George J. Green of Company C described the mood of the men as they took their place on the front, "We went in with a hearty cheer and immediately commenced firing, and it was then nothing but the roar of musketry and cannon ... except when we stopped to cheer." The 18th had pieces of timber and fences for their protection, but the Rebels too had a shield of thick woods from where they launched their numerous pushes. With a creek between them filled with greenbriers and underbrush, the 18th's position at times placed them as close as 200 yards from the enemy, and near enough for Confederate artillery to wreak havoc. Hawley explained that "the wood echoed and reechoed with volley after volley and the cannon planted in the rear of us threw grape and canister over our heads into the enemys ranks."[19]

The definition of the term veteran was redefined for Private Anthony Cole Bullent of Company F when the regiment took their position out front. He reflected back to how he felt the first time he marched into battle, and was "trembling in my boots, and jaw bones working one hundred chatterings per minute," but this day was different. "We walk up to the scene of slaughter with a determined, steady tramp and serious pace," Bullent confided in a letter to his parents, "knowing there is no backing out."[20]

Just as soon as the regiment took their place on the front, Adjutant John H. Russell was knocked out of the fight. Like so many soldiers throughout the campaign, the regiment's adjutant was a sufferer of an unshakeable sickness. Chaplain Farr, his tent mate, could attest that Russell was "unwilling to give up and be called a sick man" and continued to work his role, albeit with much struggle. The soft-spoken adjutant ignored his illness and performed his role in a way that exemplified what people respected about him. Shortly after the double-quick brought the regiment to their position, Russell was wounded in his left ankle by what was most likely a spent ball as it did not break any bones. He was ordered to go to the rear and hobbled to the nearest surgeon.[21]

For the next ninety minutes the battle raged without intermission and the 18th feverishly held their line. Men throughout the 18th's line began to fall, but the rate would have been

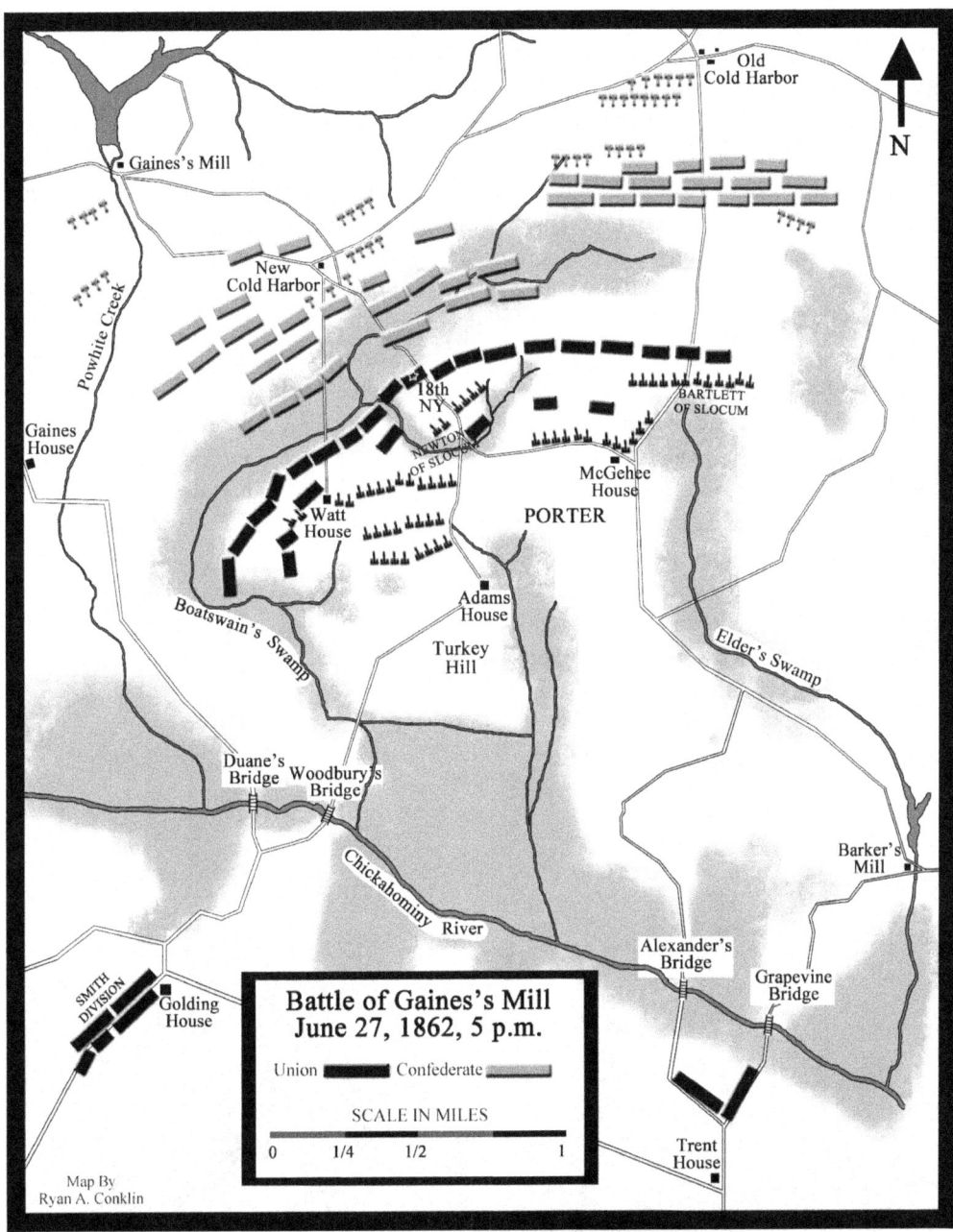

Map of the battle of Gaines's Mill, Virginia, June 27, 1862, near 5 p.m., showing the position of the 18th New York shoring the center of the Union line (author's collection).

higher had they not occupied a position behind a ridge. Wounded men fell out of the ranks at random and screamed in painful agony as lead balls tore flesh and broke bones. Private John B. LaQue of Company A would forever remember his narrow escape when a comrade in front of him was shot down by a bullet to his breast from a Rebel sharpshooter. Private John Hagerman of Company B had a bullet that bored clean through his body after it entered the right side of his groin. While in the rear rank of Company K, Private Jehiel J. Stevens was knocked off balance when a shell exploded next to him and lodged a fragment into the side of his left leg below his knee. Stevens fought the pain and limped terribly just to stay amongst his company. A ball penetrated the left arm of Sergeant Robert Wiseman, Company B, and fractured the Irish lumberman's right clavicle. A ball ripped into the left elbow joint of Private Michael Weymer of Company D which had enough force to break his arm. The ball passed through his arm but the shattered bits of bone were what caused him pain, gangrene, and surgeries for nearly a year. Private John A. Putman of Company A had his pinky, ring, and middle fingers of his left hand ripped off by a shell. Corporal John J. Southard of Company H had a similar wound when a bullet tore off his index and middle fingers of his left hand. Private John Blackwell, Company C, received almost the same injury when a bullet blasted through his middle finger of his left hand and exited out of the back of his palm. A *Minié* ball also ripped into the left hand of Private James Flynn, Company C, which broke his metacarpal bones and forever paralyzed three fingers. First Sergeant Freeman F. Huntington of Company K was injured not by an enemy bullet, but the rifle of one of his comrades. The soldier in front of him was wounded, and his rifle flew up and fell upon Huntington's shoulder. Painful as it was, Huntington continued his duties.[22]

For others, death came quick. Soldiers like Privates Joseph Snyder of Company F and Henry W. Taylor of Company G, rested in motionless blue heaps on the sanguinary field where they last stood their ground and took their final breaths. When Private Gardiner King

Left: Pvt. Jehiel J. Stevens, Jr., of Company K received a slight wound in his left leg from a shell at Gaines's Mill, Virginia, June 27, 1862. His wound was not life-threatening, but an illness kept Stevens confined to a series of Philadelphia hospitals for the remainder of his enlistment (author's collection). *Right:* Twenty-year-old Pvt. George Edgar Homan of Company H was killed in action at Gaines's Mill, Virginia, June 27, 1862. Because his enemy won the day and took ownership of the battlefield, Homan was never given a marked grave (courtesy New York State Military Museum).

of Company G was killed, so too ended the main source of income for his destitute and feeble parent's back home in New York who still had three small children to raise. To sustain the impoverished family, the parents would have to enlist their next eldest son to enter the war. Similarly, the death of Private George E. Homan of Company H who was killed outright during the fight, inspired his brother two months later to join a regiment from Middletown, only to be killed later at Gettysburg.[23]

With almost every regiment at his disposal committed to battle, Porter's optimism of victory fleeted fast. The men throughout their defenses had fought back assaults that ebbed and flowed, but Porter knew he would still need more reinforcements if he were to hold his ground. At the same time the 18th had taken their line on the front around 5 p.m., Porter telegraphed McClellan and asked for more available units. With time lost to confer with other generals, McClellan eventually ordered General Edwin Sumner to send Porter two brigades, but being as the ones chosen were on the southern side of the river, they would not reach the battlefield for nearly three hours later. During that wait, the Confederate strength swelled with the addition of Stonewall Jackson's Valley army.[24]

Sergeant Thomas Alexander found the fierce fighting hard to describe and said that "it was one continued roar of musketry, with artillery in front and rear." Major Meginnis rode up and down the line and screamed directions, cheers, and encouragement to the men. As a perpetual target on horseback, Meginnis escaped injury, but his horse took a bullet through its hind leg. Meginnis had a lot to prove to the men amidst his new role and he did not disappoint. He had some help from Colonel Matheson who assisted Meginnis periodically throughout the fight. Though Lieutenant Colonel Myers struggled just to be present, he was too sick to be of any use and could not even utter an order, and was eventually asked by Dr. Rice and General Newton to leave the battlefield and head to the rear.[25]

Captain Henry Faurot, Company G, was likewise sick with fever and diarrhea that he endured for several weeks, and he refused to sit out from leading his company into battle. His fragile strength weakened by disease hardly allowed him to stand for more than a few minutes yet he demanded to be present with the company. The acting company commander should have fallen to Faurot's second-in-line, Lieutenant Isaac S. Green, but he too was sick and absent from the battle. Therefore, Second Lieutenant William H. Ellis, Jr., took command of Company G while Faurot fought just to be near the company. Ellis dropped a blanket on the ground near the company in which Faurot laid himself upon during the battle. Ellis was aided by the most senior non-commissioned officer in the company, which happened to be his younger brother, First Sergeant George W. Ellis. But even the younger Ellis was debilitated by diarrhea and fever and before the battle was ordered by the doctors not to enter the fight, but rather a hospital. George tried to compose himself and shrugged off the doctor's order. William said his brother made mention to him that "the boys might think he was playing off if he went to the hospital just before a fight." On this day, Lieutenant Ellis needed every man that could be spared, so he supported his brother's decision, but tendered special care for him during the battle with frequent swigs of whiskey.[26]

Ears deafened and lips streaked black from gunpowder. The men had been subjected to blood and smoke to the likes of which they had never seen, but naively most had hoped for. They stayed resilient and continued their fire while exposed to highly concentrated enemy bullets and shells. Like veterans, the 18th again checked the Rebel advance and kept up a continuous fire for nearly an hour, but their right flank had withered away. Bodies of dead and wounded comrades continued to pile up and when possible were carried to the rear. Private James Garvey of Company C was struck down from a bullet that smacked into his right leg. Friends quickly grabbed him and brought him away from the carnage and delivered him to a triage. Private Theodore Langdon of Company B, a native of Germany who worked before the war as a farm laborer in Watervliet, New York, fell lifelessly out of the ranks when he was killed defending the adopted country he chose to protect. Private William H. Thompson of Company D could not escape his fate when his life was cut short on that bloodied field. He left behind a wife and five-year-old son.[27]

The color guard was more exposed than anyone and stood in a forward position out in front of the regiment. The squad of honor consisted of corporals and sergeants selected from the different companies. Regimental flags were both prized and protected and bore a majority of rifle aims. Twenty-year-old Corporal Sinclair L. Stevenson of Company C was the object of many aimed enemy bullets while he served as a corporal of the color guard. The Fishkill native was eventually hit by a bullet to his neck, but lucky for him his wound was not mortal. Second Lieutenant Mortier L. Norton of Company B was eventually ordered to bring men forward and bolster the thinned color guard.[28]

The smoke from the firearm exchanges from the day's battle lingered like a thick fog and created a universal menace for several regiments at different spots on the battlefield. The 31st New York moved toward the front slightly behind the 18th and delivered a dangerous volley from behind, some of which clipped men on the right wing of the 18th. One soldier was killed and another two wounded fell from the friendly fire. The 31st was about to fire again but was halted after a major from the neighboring 32nd raced back on his horse and prevented them. It was also reported by members of the 18th that behind them—Battery A, 1st New Jersey Artillery—dropped a couple shells short that fell within their line and caused some unintentional injuries. What seemingly felt like a whirlwind of projectiles from every direction caused panic in the 18th. This actually buckled the right wing of the regiment back a few paces before they were quickly rallied and returned to the front line.[29]

Command and control throughout Porter's line was scrambled once the general started to plug up gaps with Slocum's division, and regiments from McCall. Officers had to figure out who to take orders from, and who to give them to. If the troops held their ground where they were, there was no real threat of confusion as to who to report to, but if the line was to break down, so too would the haphazard chain of command.[30]

A cease-fire was eventually yelled across the lines around 6:30 p.m., after the rate of fire had lessened. The necessity of Union troops to ascertain the position and intent of the enemy

Pvt. William H. Thompson of Company D was killed in action at Gaines's Mill, Virginia, June 27, 1862, and left behind a wife and five-year-old son (courtesy New York State Military Museum).

led to the abrupt cease-fire. The temporary pause also gave a moment for their muskets to cool. The rapid firing heated up their rifle barrels "so hot that the cartridge would explode while loading," Sergeant Alexander recalled.[31]

During the lull, Company D's commander, Captain George Barry, stepped forward of the line to peer over the top of the hill to see what the enemy's next move was. What came into his view was a resurgence of a massed Confederate advance greater in numbers than ever before. Barry turned around and alerted that the enemy was coming. He waved his sword to point the direction for his men to aim but a Rebel bullet stopped him in the act. A musket ball pierced his heart. Private Charles E. Norris stood just behind his captain when Barry received his fatal blow, and instinctively reached out and caught him as he fell. The captain's fading life shocked and numbed the company. The pain had to have been further troubling for Sergeant Samuel Barry, the captain's younger brother who stood nearby.[32]

Promoted to command the company in the wake of Colonel Jackson's death and Meginnis' promotion to major, the Irish-born captain boasted years of military experience before the Civil War. Barry's father died when he was eight which forced him to help support his mother and siblings. Amidst the Great Famine that choked Ireland, his mother and siblings left the Emerald Isle in 1849 and settled in New York, but Barry stayed behind and served in the English army during the Crimean War. A few years before the start of the American Civil War, Barry's family pulled together funds and paid for Barry's release from the English army and was reunited with his family in Wallkill. As a captain of a new army, of a different war, for a foreign country, Barry's only wish was to mold citizens-to-soldiers and prove himself worthy of their leadership. Day's after the scuffle at Brick House Landing (West Point), Barry came to the realization that his company's "behavior on the field of action was that of old veterans, instead of young soldiers." Writing to a friend a month before the battle of Gaines's Mill, Barry mentioned, "In my military career, I never saw a firmer, more determined set of men, and I only hope I shall prove myself worthy of the command of such brave men, when our turn comes for the next battle." Living up to his words, Barry gave everything to his men and country on June 27.[33]

As soon as the ranks of butternut and gray surged forward, the New Yorkers challenged their advance and opened fired. The Rebels were momentarily halted, fired an equally devastating fire back in return, but retired as quickly as they had appeared. The command of Company D suddenly fell into the hands of First Lieutenant Roswell M. Sayer, as did Barry's literal sword. Sayer immediately detailed Second Lieutenant Robert Malone and three other Wallkill Guards to help Norris carry the body of their revered captain off the battlefield. They wrapped the captain in a blanket and hauled him to the rear. Barry lived but a few minutes before he died without a groan. The squad dropped Barry's body off at a nearby house and hastened back to rejoin the regiment.[34]

After the Rebel's most recent halt, Colonel Matheson sent orders to Major Meginnis to have his regiment hold their fire. Matheson ordered the cease fire after he got word that the New Jersey brigade had somehow shifted and formed in front of them. After a few moments the smoke lifted enough for Meginnis to see a line of troops that he was led to believe were the New Jersey men to their front across the field near the woods. Through the continuous haze of smoke, Meginnis watched the line of soldiers as they moved towards the regiment. Men of the 18th exchanged confused looks at each other as they held their fire. The men became unnerved and unsure that this line of troops before them might not be friendly. Officers had to dissuade many who tried to encourage their peers to open fire. Meginnis quickly changed his thought process and became convinced a mistake was made and hurriedly reported his findings to Matheson. Meginnis was certain when he stated that New Jersey soldiers would not be approaching his front in line of battle, and that only Confederates were the troops before him. There were plenty of incidents of confusion to draw upon during the day, so Matheson again cautiously ordered Meginnis to hold the 18th's fire until he was absolutely certain on their identity. Meginnis quickly returned to the regiment's front to peer ahead and noticed they had begun to trot steadily at the double-quick straight for them. The regiment backpedaled nearly a hundred yards beyond the ditch they were in which gave them all more time to decide who approached.[35]

As soon as they moved back, a saddled officer on a white horse popped out of a blanket of smoke and rode up to the 18th. With an unidentified flag tightly clasped in his hand, the officer shouted orders for the men to hold their fire. His appearance was an uncanny likeness to a field officer associated with the regiment, and several soldiers immediately interpreted him as such. As he rode closer to within fifty yards of the regiment, others grew weary as something about him made him look more like a Rebel officer. Some men heard him cry out to hold their fire as they were friends, while others were certain he demanded they surrender, or demanded to know who his brigade was up against. Sergeant John S. Bantham of Company F was convinced the flag in the officer's hand was a Rebel banner, so he took aim but a comrade quickly shoved his rifle skyward and cried out, "what in hell are you doing going to shoot one of our own officers?" A true example of the fog of war, men were torn on what to do during this fast-moving moment, and others like Bantham still drew a bead on the unknown officer with demands that "he must come down."[36]

Corporal Thomas Kearns, a talkative Irishman who never shirked duty, stood with the 18th's color guard as their acting sergeant after some vacancies from injuries occurred. At a height of six-foot-one-inch, he literally stood over the regiment as one of their tallest. From his position he saw the mounted Rebel closest and quickly drew down his rifle and shot the officer dead. As the Confederate officer slumped down his saddle, his foot got caught in his stirrup and his frightened horse whipped around and dragged the lifeless body back into the enemy lines. Many believed the soldier was Stonewall Jackson, but that proved to be only wishful thinking. Immediately after the officer was dragged back to his own lines, Meginnis gained the certainty he needed. With just 150 yards of separation, the Confederates made their loyalties be known and erupted in what Sergeant Alexander remembered to be "the most terrific storm of bullets we received at all, and many a brave man fell," and Alexander was one of them. The former brewer-turned-soldier was shot in his left thumb from the volley, and another bullet passed through his wool pants near his groin. Meginnis screamed his order to return fire to answer the match between the two lines.[37]

Kearns' feat of killing the brazen Rebel officer was quickly followed by his own wounding. Every enemy muzzle seemed fixed on him when he was struck by numerous wounds simultaneously. His first injury came from an enemy bullet that hit the right side of his scalp. As blood poured from his head, shrapnel struck his left leg that broke his tibia. His right leg had also been punctured with three small entrances around his calf and thigh from buckshot, and his right heel of his foot was hit. The force of the cannon shrapnel that peppered his legs practically launched Kearns facedown onto the ground, but such was the price of those gallant few who willingly took the added risk to protect the flag. Men recalled Kearns held the flag at the time he was knocked out of the fight, and it's hard to argue that the banner and his height did not make him an ideal target for the enemy. With the color guard pushed out in front of the regiment, everyone witnessed Kearns fall. Lieutenant Horatio G. Goodno of Company K related the moment:

> I saw the colors struck and shivered. I saw [Kearns] standing there way out in front and saw the colors sway over. He had 2 corp[oral]s with him and when the colors fell I remember every one cried out, "*Kearns is killed.*" It was greatly lamented by the whole Rgt when it was known that he had been hit.[38]

Private Daniel D. Stillwell from Company F quickly helped Kearns up to his feet. He leaned on Stillwell and together they limped to the rear. Luckily for Kearns, he was strong as he was tall, and he survived his wounds.[39]

Private William A. Shaw proved himself worthy as a soldier to his peers of Company H. Shaw was one of their newest recruits and had just joined the regiment the previous April when they advanced up the York River. More surprising than that was the fact that he had lied about his true age of fifty and enlisted as a forty-two-year old private. Nothing could keep him out of the fight, not even after a bullet nicked his head. Second Lieutenant Thomas S. Lane took notice of Shaw's actions and "complimented him on the field in the heat of battle for his coolness and courage." Although many wounded men were sent to the rear with wounds just as slight as Shaw's, "he still persisted in blazing away at the enemy."[40]

With what ammunition they had left, the 18th continued their fire an hour after their last cease-fire. The holes created by those who fell were quickly closed up by the men left standing and the officers nearby made sure of it. The sun had nearly set and tinted the sky with an orange glow. The enemy's troop level surged yet again around 7:30 p.m., and their renewed effort and fire was too much for the battered 18th. Throughout the entire two mile Confederate front, they nudged forward not in one perfect wall of grey and brown, but a concerted push nonetheless. The regiment to the left of the 18th eventually collapsed which drew the aim of enemy bullets upon them. As Meginnis watched their own right flank crumble in, he rallied the regiment as best he could and yelled for them not to run, but it was clear the game was up.[41]

Twenty-two-year-old Captain Theodore C. Rogers of Company H looked at his men that remained together and begged them for one last rally. They were outnumbered by fresh Confederates, yet when the enemy was just about 150 yards away Rogers ran out in front of his company and made an earnest plea for them to make a stand. He waved his unsheathed sword wildly and pointed directions of where his men should shoot, and for a moment they began to reassemble on him. The

Twenty-two-year-old Capt. Theodore C. Rogers, Company H, made a brave attempt to rally his men before they were overrun at Gaines's Mill, June 27, 1862, but was killed for his effort. He left behind a wife who was six months pregnant with their first child (courtesy Daniel Rogers Carpenter).

Confederates before them also took notice of Rogers' courageous act and were tempted to make him a target. Company H adhered to Rogers' words and reformed just fifteen paces behind their captain, which put him in between the two sides and thus all eyes fixed on him. Rogers offered himself as an act of bravery to reinvigorate his men, and due to the heavy firing that befell them he must have known his heroic deed would be sacrificial. The fire was concentrated and Rogers was struck down just as his company rallied. A bullet pierced Rogers' groin which dropped him, yet he still cheered his men from the ground. He lived for a few moments, but death set in quickly as blood rushed out of his body. Just like when Captain Barry fell earlier, Rogers' body was gathered by his men and carried a short distance closer to their receding line and propped against a tree. The enemy that pressed upon them forced the men to regrettably leave Rogers' body and be passed over by the advancing Rebels in order to outrun their own inevitable capture. One considerate member of the company grabbed his captain's unsheathed sword from his death-clenched hand and eventually forwarded it to Rogers' father.[42]

Rogers left behind a grief-stricken family that included his newlywed wife, six months pregnant with their first child. Luckily for them, a sense of comfort and closure about his death came not so much from his own men, but from the enemy. In the ensuing months that followed the battle, Rogers' family heard little particulars regarding how he died, and they never received his body that was so desperately wanted. In the most unusual crossings of two strangers on vacation at the island of Nassau (Bahamas) during the winter of 1863, a female friend of Rogers became acquainted with a Confederate colonel there. She struck up a conversation with the officer that naturally turned to the war, and their topic narrowed to the battle of Gaines's Mill and by strange coincidence Rogers' death was brought up in a roundabout way. The Confederate turned out to be Colonel Duncan McRae—commander of the 5th North Carolina—who commanded a portion of Confederate General Samuel Garland's brigade. He told her many things about a particular Yankee captain that captivated his attention on the battlefield, one that he later learned the identity to be Captain Rogers. Shocked as she was, the family friend was adamant that the Rebel officer should relate his account to Rogers' father who searched for closure on his son's death. Addresses were exchanged and eventually in May of 1863, a letter from Rogers' father reached McRae, who by then was in London. McRae made mention that despite Rogers being a player "in that invasion which has brought desolation to our homes and affliction to all our families," his heart tugged at a mourning family and a newborn daughter that would never know her father. McRae detailed the battle for Rogers' father from when their "advance was rapid and impetuous," and he became personally awestruck by the sight of a brave young officer as he swung his sword to rally his company. McRae said he was mesmerized by his fearlessness and poise in the face of an overwhelming force. Several other Confederate officers took notice of the Yankee captain and similarly admired his conduct. Some Rebels even yelled to each other to spare his life and attempt to capture the captain in order to save him. A volley from McRae's men was fired and their smoke obscured his vision of the captain. As the Union army fled from the field and the Confederates pressed forward, McRae noticed in the corner of his eye the young officer was propped against a tree by himself. After the battle concluded, McRae tasked out one of his own officers to track down the young captain that had grabbed his attention. McRae was told that the officer was dead. McRae was so moved that he ordered one of his officers to personally examine the body and search for any articles that would lead to his name. A watch and three letters were found on his body, one addressed from Rogers' father, mother, and pregnant wife. Later that night after the battle had been decided, McRae shared the story with General Garland and the two read the letters of Captain Rogers and were deeply moved. At dawn the next morning, McRae paid his respects to his enemy and personally supervised the burial of Rogers in a single grave, "in the same manner in which our own officers were interred." The Confederate officer that searched the captain's body after the battle eventually forwarded the watch to Rogers' father, but only after the war.[43]

Captain Rogers became the second captain from the regiment to be killed within the day. Second Lieutenant Thomas S. Lane was the next highest in rank present for the company and assumed command after Rogers' death. Next in line to the captaincy would have been Rogers' tent mate, First Lieutenant William E. Carmichael, but he was back in the rear because he was not fit to take the field due to sickness and a previous injury from being thrown from his horse in February.[44]

Confederates Break the Union Line

The battle of Gaines's Mill near sundown had quickly spun out of control for the Union army and Porter's entire line was in hell-bent retreat. Matheson and Meginnis could plainly see their right flank was rolled in. He quickly sent Meginnis orders to fall back and form a line of battle in the road to their left. Meginnis screamed to march by the left flank, but as the regiment maneuvered, the enemy began to turn their left flank just as they had done on their right. The 18th was practically out of ammunition. The enemy had them nearly surrounded, being almost thirty yards to their front and enclosed on their sides. Meginnis strained to pull back the 18th but could not safely comply with the orders given. The friendly troops now to their left had since retreated in disorder, and the 18th quickly found that they were in an unfavorable bind. Hostile fire of balls and shells funneled upon them from three sides, but their back-stepping distanced the rivals to nearly eighty yards. The fight was lost. Meginnis quickly sent them running to the cover of the woods behind them along the ravine to the rear of the batteries, running for their lives like the rest of the army.[45]

The regiment sprinted like it was a time trial, "in not very good order" as Corporal Hawley recalled. Several of the men taught themselves how to shoot on the run. Private George J. Green wrote that "it was then every man for himself until he got out of the reach of that murderous fire." Corporal Isaac DeBaum of Company C and Private John O'Hara of Company K both received wounds in the region most soldiers feared to be struck—their backs. O'Hara's wound was merely scratches across his back that came from a buck shot. Captain Henry Faurot was lucky to get off the field as he was too sick to run, but two privates from his company picked him up during the retreat. Lieutenant William H. Ellis, who commanded Faurot's company with the help of his first sergeant brother, George, lost sight of each other during the run and George was captured. Hawley became separated from the regiment amidst the confusion. He stopped at a spring in the woods to get a drink of water and lucky for him he was screened by the trees and underbrush because the Rebels passed him by a matter of a few feet and never saw him. Hawley had avoided an inevitable capture, but tempting fate was the name of the game for him that day. Of the three privates he shared a tent with, he saw two of them killed and the other wounded.[46]

As one of the eldest in the regiment, fifty-one-year-old 1st Lt. Horatio G. Goodno of Company K was not defined by his age, but his mettle. At Gaines's Mill, he was shot through the right side of his neck which broke his jaw, shattered teeth, and tore off a chunk of his tongue as it exited his mouth. He was captured after the battle but escaped under the cover of darkness, and eventually returned to the regiment (courtesy Jeff Sauter).

During this chaotic retreat, the 18th ultimately received the most concentrated and accurate crossfire of the day which amounted to their heaviest loss of the day. The drum of Company D rolled no more as the twenty-seven-year old farmer-turned-drummer, William H. Murphy was shot and killed. Another nearby Wallkill Guard fell silent when former railroad employee and Irish-native Private James Dailey was gunned down.[47]

Hell was present for soldiers like fifteen-year-old drummer George W. R. Goodno who witnessed what looked to be the death of his own father. First Lieutenant Horatio G. Goodno of Company K was shot in the right side of his neck just below his jaw line. The *Minié* ball broke his jaw, shattered several teeth, ripped through the base of his tongue and exited out of his mouth. Blood and teeth spewed out of Goodno's mouth and his bushy light gray beard was tinged bright red. His son ran to his aid and helped him walk towards the hospital, and somehow Goodno would survive this ghastly wound. As one of the eldest of the regiment at the age of fifty-one, he strived to be tougher than men half his age. Goodno was a firm man that most of his company admired, but there were those who held their disdain. Private Thomas Trabilcox from Company F remembered having overheard some men of Company K say in certain circles, "it was a pity [Goodno] was not shot through the neck & have had his jugular cut." In the scheme of things, it was Goodno's stubbornness and matter-of-fact words that snubbed his company from being a part of the Northern New York regiment which seemed to have worked out that day in Company K's favor. At the end of the day's fight, Company K of the 16th New York—which would have been their placement—suffered thirty-one casualties.[48]

Cannons, caissons, and men were being scooped up in droves by the Rebels. The breakdown of command and control for the Union reinforcements came during the Federal collapse. Slocum's 4th New Jersey and McCall's 11th Pennsylvania did not stand a chance when they were quickly surrounded during the confusion. They had no choice but to surrender.[49]

"We were pretty much scattered," Sergeant John S. Bantham of Company F described the retreat, "no order appearing to be possible although each company kept together pretty well considering the manner in which we were pressed at last." Men were dropped all around him in rapid succession and he felt his time was just moments away. As he ran to keep pace with those in his company during the run, the rifle he carried had its butt plate shot off. His rifle was useless so he dropped it and picked up the first one he passed over lying on the ground and continued to sprint. Bantham struggled to find the strength to run faster, and soon found his energy was depleted:

> I became too tired to keep up and could scarcely walk. The way the bullets whizzed was astonishing two men came running along side of me, one said run, the Rebs are just behind us. I shoot my head for I was too tired even to talk, so they went on, and I suppose did not get ten rods when a shell exploded and struck them both down, and so it went men fell on all sides of me and never rose, while I did not receive a scratch which is still a matter of astonishment to me.[50]

The rapid speed of the Confederate attack and the confusion from battle and overwhelming fatigue led to several captures of men from the 18th. Nineteen uninjured soldiers from the regiment were overpowered, surrendered, or collected as stragglers by the rolling Rebel horde. During the "every man for himself" sprint, Private John H. Pollard of Company E veered away from the regiment to escape the concentration of "bullets flying so thick" and took a different road in his retreat. He escaped injury and corrected his direction that should have led him back near where the regiment was headed. Pollard spotted what he thought was the 18th, so he walked straight into the regiment that turned out to be the 13th North Carolina. He was actually greeted with a cheer from the Southerners. His capture was sealed and Pollard was escorted to the rear of the regiment. Several Rebels began to ask Pollard if he carried a dirk knife or a revolver, since souvenirs from the enemy were always of someone's interest. A few guards turned Pollard over to a lieutenant who walked him and other collected prisoners for awhile until they were turned over to a prisoner collection point at a church far behind the enemy lines. From thence, the prisoners were forwarded to Richmond later in the evening and imprisoned in a tobacco house.[51]

Before the war, Sgt. John S. Bantham of Company F was a pattern maker in Troy, New York. The rifle he carried in the battle of Gaines's Mill was rendered useless after its butt plate was shot off (courtesy Joan Bantham Byer and Dave Byer).

Many of the badly wounded had to be unfortunately abandoned on the field which invited an easy capture by the conquerors of the battlefield. After Private William H. Linkletter of Company G was wounded and captured, he developed a sickness that got so bad that his captors freed him in July, only to die days later from disease on August 1. Private Reinold Ritzenthaler of Company G was taken out of the fight by a bullet wound in his right arm which would later be amputated, and he had to rely on the care given to him by the enemy after he was captured. When Private John Schwantner of Company A was captured, the gunshot wound that fractured his left shoulder did more than cost him the eventual loss of the arm. His psyche was so jolted that when Northern doctors assessed Schwantner's injury months after the battle, they said his nerves were "so shattered as to wholly unfit him for service," which brought an end to his time in uniform.[52]

Major Meginnis pushed what was left of the routed and bruised regiment about three quarters of a mile through the woods and to the hillside in rear of the main Union hospital at the Adams House. Captain Gridley, and the next senior Captain Michael H. Donovan of Company F, tried their hardest to keep the regiment in some form of semblance. They quickly began to rally the men there after they had become pretty much disordered during the retreat.[53]

As the setting sun provided its last allowable light, the two fresh brigades from Sumner's II Corps south of the Chickahominy finally arrived to Turkey Hill. These two brigades fought through waves of skedaddled and wounded soldiers and advanced to the hospital and formed themselves in battle line in front of what was left of the rallied and exhausted regiments from the fight. They stood poised to halt the Confederate surge and shield what could have been the complete annihilation of Union troops north of the river. Private Samuel Hodgkins of Company K saw these reinforcements as godsends, and their arrival "saved our bacon for us." Their arrival was enough to halt the enemy. As nightfall set in, the new line held firm without much fighting which afforded the battered troops time to withdraw across the Chickahominy. The 18th was largely broken and scattered in the confusion, and whether in groups or on their own, men retreated towards the bridge. They had had enough fighting and they were not going to stand with the fresh brigades. As Dr. Rice put it, "We had been pretty well pounded out during the afternoon."[54]

During the hours they waited, Meginnis did what other regimental commanders tried desperately to do and consolidated who was left standing from the companies. Looking at them in the darkness, it was evident that the regiment was a shell of what it was when they awoke early that morning. The dead and wounded was one thing, but there were many more unaccounted for. Men lost in the melee trickled back into the regiment throughout the night and lowered the number of missing, yet several others remained lost or presumed captured. It would take days and a lot of cross-references from witnesses to ascertain accurate figures.[55]

The men went into the fray with sixty rounds of ammunition, and a few took more than prescribed. "I don't think a man left the field with half a dozen in his box," recalled the injured Sergeant Alexander. The sound of battle diminished as night settled over the land, but the audible cries of the wounded from the fields filled the air. At 9 p.m., a Provost Guard was thrown out to prevent the stragglers from walking off on their own. Only the wounded were allowed to pass to the rear. The bridges over the river were clogged with units that scrambled for the safe passage to the other side of the river. Meginnis waited for further orders but none ever came, so he led the 18th back over the Chickahominy River at 10 p.m., and slowly marched them for two hours until they reached their camp from which they left that morning. This time, they had returned noticeably different; bloodied, tired, and significantly smaller.[56]

Heavy Casualties

The battle of Gaines's Mill was a devastating loss to the Army of the Potomac that essentially botched McClellan's plan to take Richmond. The country had not yet seen a single day get as bloody and be as costly as this battle had been. Porter's command, to include all of his reinforcements, totaled a casualty loss of 6,837; with 894 killed, 3,114 wounded, and 2,829 captured. Confederates that had attacked fortified positions came with a steeper price. Their casualties totaled 7,993; with 1,483 killed, 6,402 wounded, and 108 men missing. Lee had won his first victory with the Army of Northern Virginia and changed the tide of the war. Richmond was now off the table for McClellan as he dealt with the damage control.[57]

The battle was a frustrating and unforgettable day for the men. Private Hodgkins would forever remember the day and said in later years, "I never was so discouraged in all my life." General Slocum tallied his division with an estimated loss of at least one-fourth of his force that he crossed the river with earlier in the day. The outcome of the fight severely affected the regiment and every company incurred losses. With the compounding sick list that increased daily along the Chickahominy preceding the fight, the regiment was thrust into battle significantly lessened and ill. By losing the field where soldiers fell and fled, the task to accurately ascertain the regiment's total loss would only be made possible in hindsight. To specify the outcome of all the men astray from the regiment after the retreat was very vague, and the list of missing was made with its highest figure. Their assumed loss immediately after the battle stood around 150 killed, wounded, or missing from the regiment, but the number lessened slightly as a few lost men found their way back to the regiment.[58]

What was true was that by the end of hostilities of June 27, the casualty list of killed, wounded, and captured for the regiment was 121. Twenty soldiers from the regiment were killed outright, and another two mortally wounded were soon to succumb. The body of Canadian-born laborer Private Myron Burton of Company G was nowhere to be found and his death would not be confirmed for more than a month. The blood-soaked body of Sergeant Isaac F. Hall of Company F was left abandoned somewhere near where he fell in line of battle. Somewhere scattered about the darkened fields or woods was the body of a twenty-year-old farmer from Ticonderoga, New York, named Private Samuel Lilly of Company A. These men and many others were left where they last stood or crawled to, never to be seen again by someone that knew them. Private Washington Irving Sawyer of Company H had always been regarded as a hero in the eyes of his native Westport, New York. He dropped out of school when war broke out in order to join the 18th, and his quick enlistment made him not only the first man from Westport, but the first from the entire Essex County, but their admiration for him turned to mourning when word of his death reached them. Private Henry Stalker was the youngest to be killed. He was one of many who lied about his age when he enlisted in Company B, and his death came just two weeks after he turned eighteen. Private Levi Swartout of the same company was twice as old as Stalker and was the oldest from the regiment to perish that day.[59]

Private Thompson "Tom" H. Snyder of Company F was killed during the fight by grape or canister shot from enemy artillery. He was the only mulatto soldier to serve in the regiment at a time when segregation was the law. Back home in Schoharie, Snyder was known as "Dean's Tom" and was described as a "three quarter white boy, handy at doing chores." Private Lewis Spawn of the same company watched Snyder get hit just as he had fired an aimed shot that knocked down a Rebel officer. Comrades in his company last saw Snyder wounded on the field and held on to hope that he pulled through, but his death was confirmed a few weeks after the battle. His hometown recognized his service after the war in a book about Schoharie veterans that remembered him to be more than just someone handy at doing chores, for they mentioned Snyder, "was of African and American descent and very nearly white, and accounted a brave soldier."⁶⁰

Captain William S. Gridley had his hands full during the battle as he assumed the lieutenant colonel position for the regiment. Although he was small in stature, he was characterized to be "large in the face of the enemy." First Lieutenant Daniel H. Daley handled Company A in Gridley's absence. William's younger brother Private Nathan Gridley fought with the company until he was shot through the neck and killed during the day. "Little Nate" was even shorter than his brother at five-foot-one. He was a twenty-year-old clerk by trade before the war and was the youngest of the orphaned Gridley family. Nathan idolized his older brother and was one of the first names to enlist when William formed the company. He was far advanced with his preparatory studies and was described as "a youth of fine promise, energetic, ambitious," and had a suitable self-education with the aspiration to use his military earnings to study the law after the war. He had served a great deal of time in uniform as General Newton's private secretary, but Nathan complained that the general was "harassed and overborne with business cares" and oftentimes "very testy." Gridley was "independent in nature and could not put up with ill-humor" so he put down the pen and rejoined the firing line shortly before the Peninsula campaign commenced, a decision that ultimately led to his demise. As if the day was not hard enough for Captain Gridley, his seventeen-year-old cousin in Company A, Corporal Joseph W. Gridley, was captured.⁶¹

Musician William H. Daniels of Company D was wounded slightly in the leg at Gaines's Mill, Virginia, June 27, 1862. The Wallkill Guard was eventually shipped off the peninsula and sent to a hospital in Washington where he spent the remainder of his enlistment as a nurse (courtesy Jeff Sauter).

The Van Kuren brothers—Isaac, Simon, and William—from Phelps, New York, enlisted together in Company G, at age twenty-eight, twenty-one, and nineteen, respectively. They served side-by-side since the 18th's inception, but middle brother Simon had since been discharged with an ankle injury in September of 1861. At

Gaines's Mill, the remaining Van Kuren brothers were both struck down. William, the youngest, was shot and for a time was believed by his comrades to have died that day after he was last seen abandoned on the field, wounded. William managed to survive the fight and eventually recovered from his wound. Private Spencer Wood, Company G, was the last to see the eldest brother Isaac, after they crossed the ditch towards their own battery. Wood told Isaac to veer to the right, as the battery was on the left and began to send shells through towards the enemy. Isaac still moved left into the path of friendly artillery and was never seen by anyone again. Wood would later confide to the Van Kuren's mother that he had no doubt that Isaac "was killed by our own battery."[62]

It seemed almost a rare feat to be unscathed at the end of the day. Far exceeding initial totals hastily constructed after the battle, a thorough sift through the compiled service records at the National Archives and pension records showed a total of eighty-two men from the 18th were wounded at Gaines's Mill. Five of these men were commissioned officers from the regiment, three of which were previously mentioned—Faurot, Goodno and Russell. The recently reinstated Captain Thomas J. Radcliff and Second Lieutenant Jim Chalmers were two out of the three commissioned officers in Company I that both received wounds to their legs from artillery shells. Both recovered quickly thereafter and stayed with their company. Two first sergeants fell with wounds during the day. First Sergeant Alfred M. Chesmore of Fitchburg, Massachusetts, received a slight bullet wound to his left elbow while he directed his men of Company I, and First Sergeant George Blake of Company H fell when a ball struck into his right arm.[63]

First Lieutenant John M. Dempsey of Company F thought it was miraculous for anyone to have gone through unscathed. Dempsey had a bullet graze his shoulder strap on his right shoulder. After the battle he had a moment to recall how lucky he and others were and mentioned, "how wonderful that so many of us escaped the terrific fire."[64]

Every company is represented under the wounded category from the regiment. Company G and I suffered the highest with each having eleven men wounded. Nearly all of the injured were from the result of gunshot wounds, as shot and shell from the artillery made up only a small portion. The span of injuries received in battle ranged from the slightest of scratches to the most horrific and unimaginable severing of limbs. Of those wounded and identified with which part of the body was struck, a majority were hit on their left sides, through their legs, knees, hands, elbows, and shoulders. During an infantry faceoff, it was commonplace to have one's left shoulder facing

After a bullet grazed his shoulder strap at the battle of Gaines's Mill, 1st Lt. John M. Dempsey of Company F recalled "how wonderful that so many of us escaped the terrific fire" (courtesy New York State Military Museum).

towards the enemy. It was a rifleman's natural stance during rapid reloading and it also lowered the body's profile for the enemy which made themselves a smaller target.[65]

Private Samuel Hodgkins had all but forgotten the pain from his bandaged left leg from his pre-battle strain. Seeing so many men get wounded around him he considered himself lucky and kept his mouth shut about his pain. The adrenaline of the day made his ache vanish early in the battle.[66]

Friends helped run wounded comrades to the rear to receive medical attention whenever the opportunity surfaced, but the extraction was not a guarantee of survival. Private Joseph Payne of Company A received a contused wound to his left arm from a shell, most likely a ricochet, but other than his severe bruise he recovered quickly. In addition to Goodno and Shaw, eleven other soldiers survived with head and neck wounds that ranged from slight to life-threatening. Private Edwin Martin, Company G, a man who raced to get married just before he left home, received a terrible wound to his head from an artillery shell. His mortal wound was not an instant killer having lived seven agonizing days until his death finally set in.[67]

The youngest to be wounded was sixteen-year-old Private James M. Larkin of Company H who was hit by a bullet that went straight through his right leg, centimeters above his knee. Seventeen-year-old Private Robert Courtney of Company A took a bullet in his left wrist. Private Charles A. Getty of Company K, also seventeen years old, received a grievous chest wound. The ball entered his right breast, tore through his right lung, and exited out of his back. Miraculously, Getty was a resilient young man and recovered in time to return to the regiment ten months later.[68]

The wounded Yankees that escaped the battlefield and an inevitable capture now faced a grim situation on their southern side of the Chickahominy that compounded the discomforts and pain of their injuries. The wounded could no longer be shipped off the peninsula on transports through the established White House base after it was abandoned. This prevented the possibility of advanced care in Northern hospitals for the wounded. In its place, a large yet overcrowded field hospital was established on the York River Railroad at Savage's Station, and the wounded poured in steadily.[69]

The Confederates began their own consolidation after the day's fight and regrouped for their continual push. Winning the day also coincided with the responsibility to treat the thousands of wounded that filled the night air with screams. Surgeons were stretched thin and worked nonstop to treat patients from both sides. Every home and barn in the area converted to makeshift hospitals that overflowed with wounded, staffed by exhausted surgeons and local women.

More than 2,000 bodies were strewn throughout the bloodied fields of which the sharp-tongued Dr. Gaines never in his wildest dreams could have ever envisioned would be buried throughout his property. Burial parties fanned out and undertook the daunting task to bury the dead throughout the evening and into the night. They had to work fast because the expected continuation of the bloody campaign would undoubtedly create more dead, which often led to unpleasant shortcuts. Several mass graves were hastily dug and bodies were insolently thrown in unceremoniously. One Virginian Confederate divulged to his wife that they conveniently discarded a large, yet unspecified, number of Yankee dead into the nearby rivers and creeks. A great many more remained unburied and bubbled under the sun as they decomposed. The men in the 18th tried their best to rescue the bodies of their slain comrades to prevent the inevitable. Even their attempt to place Captain Barry's body far behind their line before it broke proved futile, and his body was left on the field. Of the twenty soldiers from the 18th killed outright during the day, only one received a properly marked grave for family to say their final prayers to. Private Washington Irving Sawyer's tall six-foot-one frame was the only body that remained in safe hands and subsequently shipped up North to be buried in his family's plot at Hillside Cemetery in Westport. For all the others, their final resting place remains hidden underneath the field over which they perished, or within a shared grave marked under the mutual name—*Unknown*.[70]

12

A Change of Front Is a Retreat
June 28, 1862–August 24, 1862

"Hundreds of strong healthy men are now
either dead or as good as dead from disease."
—*Corporal Edmund Burke Hawley, Company A, July 14, 1862*

Retreat to Savage's Station and White Oak Swamp

The two fresh brigades from Sumner's II Corps protected the retreating forces while everyone else crossed towards safety over the Chickahominy River. The retreat continued through the night and into the early hours of June 28. The bridges became choked with troops and wagons, with the last remnant setting the bridge ablaze behind them after they crossed in the early morning. To say the least, everyone was exhausted both physically and mentally, but the retreat was a necessity to escape the range of trailing Confederate artillery. For the soldiers on both sides, there would be little rest. After returning to camp shortly after midnight, the 18th received orders to return back to the battlefield by 3 a.m. Luckily, these orders were changed and they were instructed to pack everything up. Havoc took form and men purposely destroyed mess chests and anything of quantity that could be of benefit to the enemy. Acting as the regimental quartermaster, First Lieutenant Alexander H. Wands threw away all of the company books and clothing records to lighten his load.[1]

Some of the injured had made it back to camp and were consolidated back into the regiment. Adjutant John H. Russell was carried back to his tent that he shared with the chaplain just as the regiment returned at midnight. Despite his illness and ankle wound, Russell seemed pretty jovial and certain that he would have a quick recovery. Chaplain Farr cared for his friend until the morning of June 28 when he and others from the regiment too sick or wounded to stay were sent off to a nearby field hospital at Savage's Station.[2]

After the 18th gathered all they had and sent their wagons away, they walked down in the woods behind their former camp at 5 a.m. and waited in rear of the pickets to act as the rear guard for the army. For the rest of the day they watched over the road until all of the wagons and troops passed by on the massive retreat. Confederates tight on their heels commenced to shell the woods near the 18th, but none fell close enough to cause any harm. At 8 p.m., part of the 18th was sent down into a large tract of woods close to the Chickahominy River and detailed to chop down trees as obstacles for the Confederates and to increase the gap between the two armies. Private Bronson Mills, Company D, tried to find the rationalization behind the "possible object our commanders could have had in setting us to work in the middle of the night, in a dense woods, felling trees, more than I can comprehend." Men were also ordered to destroy camp and garrison equipment, extra baggage, and commissary stores. With the task completed by the evening of June 28, more orders flowed to General Slocum who was instructed to push his division three miles south towards Savage's Station on the York River Railroad to await further orders. The division tried to step off at 11 p.m., but the roads were so congested with other units near McClellan's headquarters at the Trent House, which made Slocum division's march delayed until 2 a.m., on June 29. Three hours later, they arrived to Savage's Station in the dark during a rainstorm and were quick to set up a camp.[3]

Thousands of Yankee sick and wounded that made it over the Chickahominy had been consolidated at a large make-shift field hospital at Savage's Station. Bloodied and maimed troops from the Gaines's Mill battle filled the triage area, and overworked surgeons labored feverishly to attend to them. More wounded kept rolling in every second and the work load never lessened for the doctors.[4]

One station at the hospital had four separate tables that performed rapid and continuous

After the battle of Gaines's Mill, Virginia, makeshift field hospitals like this one pictured at Savage's Station on June 28, 1862, became flooded with Union soldiers. Soldiers from the 16th New York can be recognized by the signature white straw hats that were issued to the regiment. An untold number of 18th New York men are also scattered among the injured (Library of Congress).

amputations all day. Nineteen-year-old Private John Nicholas Bovee of Company E, a compositor for Schenectady's *Evening Star and Times* before the war, had been shot in his right leg and waited for his turn to be stretched upon these streamlined amputation tables. The wounded Private James Garvey of Company C was a butcher by trade, but he could never have imagined his right leg would be treated in similar fashion when doctors sawed off his limb at Savage's Station. The right arm of forty-four-year-old Private Michael Looney of Company B was amputated after his gunshot wound became inflamed and warranted its removal and was added to the growing pile of severed limbs callously tossed aside.[5]

With the division's brief pause at Savage's Station, the hospital was also crammed with many more uninjured soldiers who tried their best to track down wounded comrades. Captain Michael Donovan of Company F was surprised to stumble across Corporal Thomas Kearns as he limped around the hospital. Donovan did not witness Kearns receive his multiple injuries, but believed by word of mouth that he had been killed. Someone had carried Kearns to the hospital in a litter earlier that day. Donovan was thrilled to see him, for in his words, "Kearns was as willing and good a soldier as far as duty is concerned as there was in the Regiment." However, his multiple injuries were severe enough that he would never return to the line.[6]

Unbeknownst to many of the wounded, McClellan had already made plans to abandon Savage's Station. Lee's Confederates were closing in on McClellan and his only option was to shield what was left of the Army of the Potomac and get them to the James River. His only viable path to get there meant they had to cross over the White Oak Swamp to the southeast. McClellan shuffled his commands to press on and left half of his force to make a stand around Savage's Station as a rear guard to build time until its inevitable sacking. McClellan had issued a circular the day before that asked the wagons to be used exclusively for the shipment of ammunition and subsistence for the ongoing movement. The young general could feel the breath of the enemy and looked for shortcuts anywhere he could. He ordered "all tents and all articles not indispensable to the safety or maintenance of the troops must be abandoned and destroyed." Before the 18th arrived to Savage's Station, McClellan's short-lived headquarters there had already packed up and moved south towards the crossing. In compliance to the general's order, Union troops slashed baggage and clothing and destroyed extra camp equipage with knives, bayonets, axes, and anything else with a sharp edge. Mass burnings were at first refrained from so the enemy could not surmise their actions, but the bonfires happened inevitably.[7]

With a renewed sense of direction, McClellan met with Slocum in person and ordered him to detach from the VI Corps and take his division across the White Oak Swamp. McClellan knew of the hard fighting Slocum's division had endured two days before and felt they had yet to recover from its exhaustion, so he wanted them to cross immediately. They traversed through the swamp on June 29 at 2 p.m. and were further ordered three hours later to proceed one-and-a-half miles beyond White Oak Swamp to a point on the Long Bridge Road in order to relieve Couch and Peck's divisions. The nearest village there was Glendale, which was located about two miles south of White Oak Swamp. Glendale was also the intersection of four main roads commonly referred to as the Charles City Crossroads. Slocum's men reached their designation around seven that evening and established a position that was nearly a mile northwest of Glendale on the Charles City Road, and about an equal distance from Brackett's Ford from where they just came. Slocum anticipated an immediate attack from approaching Confederates headed their way so the men immediately destroyed the bridge near Brackett's

Ford and felled trees and clogged the approach down Charles City Road late into the night. Slocum's division had to hold this passage on the Charles City Road in order to protect the retreat of the forces to the south of him. They were only aided by some cavalry scouts and a couple batteries of artillery. Slocum also tasked out half of his division to act as pickets the night of June 29 to both stall the enemy and increase the obstructions.[8]

The helpless wounded back at Savage's Station field hospital could sense the army was in panic mode and presumed by all indications that they would be left behind during the retreat. The extra food and medical supplies were the only items not destroyed. No official announcement was made by headquarters of the exodus, yet enough was said when the surgeons started to be pulled away and reattached to their regiments. Empty ambulance wagons left without patients, which meant they were prepped to have them filled after the next expected fight. Dozens of men from the 18th remained helpless at the hospital and wondered about their fate. Dr. Rice needed to be with the regiment and was forced to leave the hospital. He joined the march towards Glendale when the 18th left midday. The 18th's assistant surgeon, Dr. Alexander A. Edmeston, nobly stayed behind with the injured and continued his care for the sick and wounded knowing full well that they would soon be overrun by the enemy. Private Mark Wolff, Company I, and Private Elias P. Knapp, Company G, also opted to continue their services as nurses with Edmeston. Private William H. Lamson of Company A also worked as a nurse, except his service was self-appointed when he left his company a month earlier. Lamson was considered a deserter and would eventually forfeit his pay while he was gone from the regiment. For those that could, some patients took it upon themselves to prevent the inevitable capture and gambled their odds and walked off in the direction the army was headed. Supported by rifles or friends, an exodus of walking and limping men disappeared from the hospital and into the woods. Adjutant Russell benefited by his younger brother William being detailed on General Newton's staff as aide-de-camp. William placed his wounded brother in the general's staff ambulance and brought him away from the collapsing hospital.[9]

There were still 3,000 or so soldiers too ill or injured to walk. When the Confederates rolled into Savage's Station later that afternoon, they inherited all the helpless wounded abandoned by their army. Richmond papers blasted McClellan, and as one editor put it, "in McClellan's headlong flight he left nearly 3,000 of his deluded followers, helpless and in a starving condition, on the wayside." Luckily, the work that was being done by the captured doctors at Savage's Station was allowed to carry on and were joined by Rebel surgeons that helped save an untold number of lives. Private John Bovee's right leg was amputated later that evening by a Confederate surgeon. Edmeston, Wolff, Knapp and twenty-two sick and wounded soldiers from the 18th were captured at the hospital. Nine of these were severely ill, one of which was Private Harmon Griepe of Company A, who died from disease the day after their capture. Private Edwin Martin of Company G had nowhere to go and remained in the hospital, being wholly insensible from his dangerous shell wound to his head. He died there on July 4. The other ten wounded prisoners all had injuries to their lower extremities which prevented them from walking, which makes the number that fled hard to judge. With his face wrapped in bloody bandages, a speechless First Lieutenant Goodno and his young son waited until darkness to slip away and escape after being captured since the battle. They swam the river and completed over twenty miles until they reached the retreating Union troops by morning. As the Confederates pushed farther south they continued to collect many more stragglers to their bounty. The 18th lost seven more men who were plucked out of the woods by Rebels in the days that followed and were forwarded to Richmond.[10]

Battle of Charles City Crossroads (Glendale)

Down near Glendale, Confederate Brigadier General William Mahone's brigade of Virginians, part of Major General Benjamin Huger's division, had driven Slocum's pickets in by 11 a.m. on June 30, along the Charles City Road. Luckily the mass amounts of obstructions that seemed to stretch for more than a mile crippled their advance into a halt. Several Union

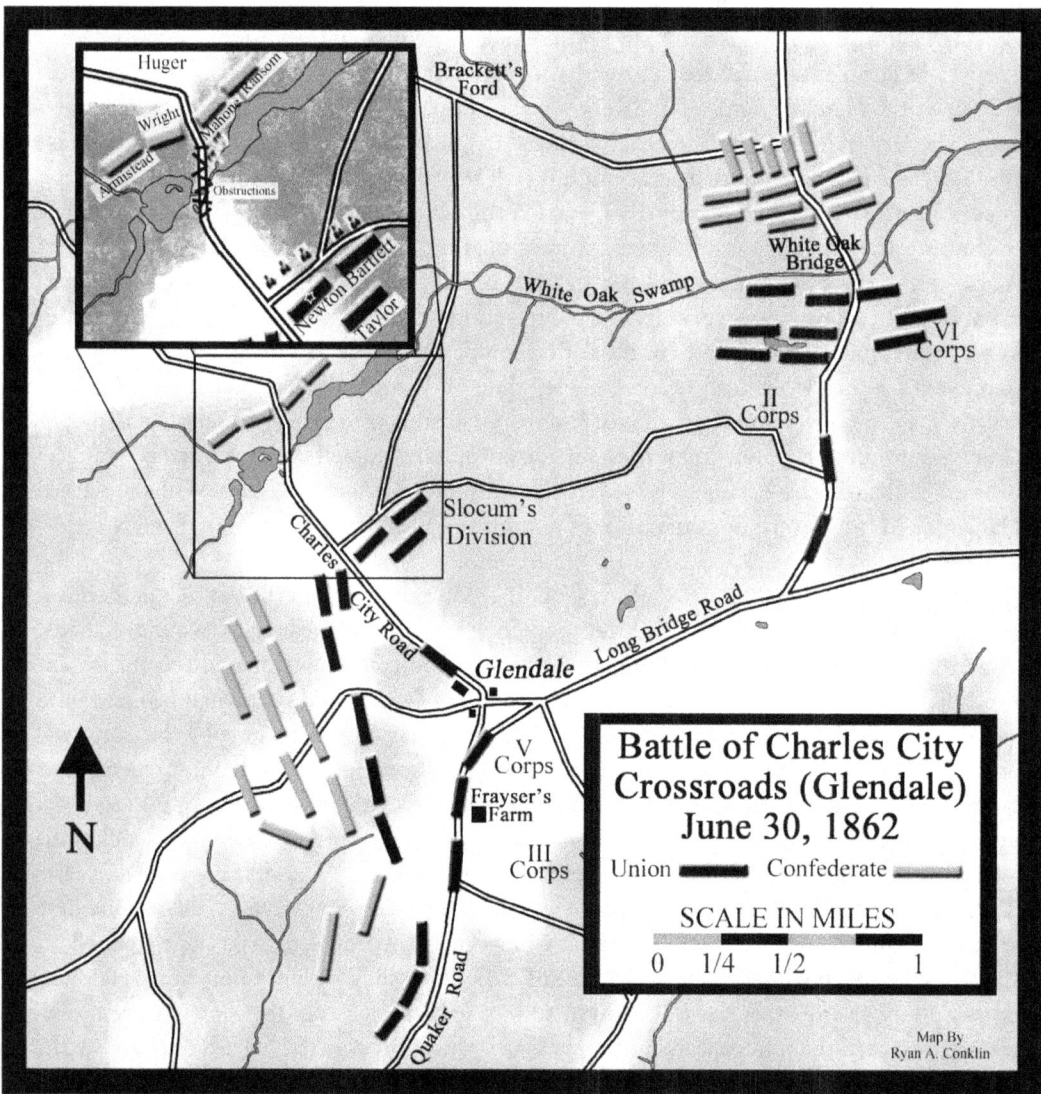

The three brigades of Slocum's division broke from the rest of the VI Corps in order to bolster the right of the Army of the Potomac's line near Glendale, Virginia, and successfully held the Confederates at their front with an abundance of obstructions and incessant artillery (author's collection).

batteries were drawn up and positioned in front of the division and quickly fired upon two Rebel batteries when they appeared. The artillery elements inaugurated a dual that would last for the rest of the day, but the blocked roads had successfully held the Rebels at bay. The 18th laid low in a cornfield near the crossroads and were blocked by ground from the enemy's perspective. They laid in safety behind Battery D, of the 2nd United States Artillery, and acted as their infantry support if needed. The batteries had a terrific field of sloped ground in their favor, with a clear opening of land that Mahone was too apprehensive about to shove his forces through a field of superior fire.[11]

The obstructions over the road were so extensive that Mahone forced his men to cut a road around the obstructions, but their lack of tools prolonged the stall. From the 18th's vantage, all they could do was patiently look on as shells were liberally exchanged back-and-forth between the lines all day. Sergeant Thomas Alexander of Company D was still with his company after his left thumb had been shot three days before and he was on hand with his comrades when he recalled that, "The shells were falling thick and fast around in all directions, as we lay all day in the broiling sun in an open field, not daring to speak above a whisper." The division saw themselves surrounded and "expected every moment to be annihilated or taken prisoner." The enemy infantrymen to their front were partially screened by a narrow strip of woods but never seemed to pierce through the obstacles and into their division's front. Slocum's division was not surrounded, but they were exposed. Their position marked them as the extreme right flank of the Federal forces around Glendale, but with the sounds that carried and the order to be quiet made it easy to presume one was surrounded. Alexander mentioned that they "could hear the enemy at work, and talking, but our orders were to let them come within 30 yards of us, then up and fire and charge."[12]

Throughout the day, the men of the 18th felt very much terrified and were convinced their position was bound to be encircled by the enemy and cut off, and their thoughts were not far from reality. Private Bronson Mills best described the regiment's action at Charles City Crossroads:

> We had scarcely got fixed in our position before the Rebels began shelling us. We were in a cornfield, the ground was very dry and soft. We had to lie right down in the dirt and dust, and were not even allowed to raise our heads up for six hours, or till dark, while all this time, our three batteries were pouring in the shell,

Artist correspondent John R. Chapin sketched this scene of Slocum's division on the Charles City Road (Glendale) on June 30, 1862. The prone 16th New York is drawn, acting as infantry support behind Slocum's artillery, just as the 18th New York did throughout the day (Library of Congress).

grape and canister faster then ever I heard it before. It was one continual thunder all the time. At the same time the battle was waging with other divisions on our right and left, and at dark we were completely surrounded.[13]

The Union line stretched almost two miles from Slocum's left, and reached near to Malvern Hill. Several other Union brigades were hotly engaged with Confederate Generals Longstreet and A. P. Hill's troops throughout the day. Without Slocum, the rest of Franklin's corps was posted along the swamp near the White Oak Bridge and helped hold off General Jackson's forces. The 18th tended to refer to the battle of Glendale as Charles City Crossroads. For them, the day was filled with relentless artillery bombardment between the dueling batteries before them and the constant fear of being captured that all lasted until dark. The brigade was never called up to "fire and charge" which Alexander said they would have "done it with a will." Nor was the brigade transitioned towards the front line to reinforce their counterparts that were engaged. Slocum fought through the fear of being surrounded and held their favorable ground and basked in the power of their obstructions. Casualties remained at a minimum for Slocum, with nearly twenty-five men killed or wounded, mostly confined to the artillery. The 18th came through with only one slightly wounded soldier—the bugler—who was at the extreme left of the regiment. The bugler was twenty-two-year-old Julius Becking of Company D. Becking was a tile-maker and naturalized immigrant from Hesse-Kassel, Germany. He received the sole injury of the day from a shell wound that pierced his left toe, and punctured two holes in his upper left thigh. Comrades carried him off the field in a hurry and Dr. Rice was able to assess his non-life-threatening wounds before he was sent off to a hospital. Two days later Becking was transported north to be treated and returned two months later. The actions of the Union batteries at Charles City Crossroads produced a carnage that took a higher toll on their targets. Mahone's brigade had tried to work through the timber obstacles and sustained serious casualties in the process. His single Rebel battery responded to the relentless Federal shells the best they could, but the three Virginian infantry regiments took the brunt of the shelling. Slocum's batteries killed 24 men and wounded 52 others from Mahone's brigade. Overall, the losses for both sides at Glendale were nearly equal. Confederates suffered 638 killed, 2,814 wounded, and 221 missing. For the Union, their loss equaled 297 killed, 1,696 wounded, and 1,804 missing.[14]

Pvt. William Bronson Mills of Company D felt certain the regiment and division was surrounded and destined to be captured at Charles City Crossroads on June 30, 1862, but all they could do was "lie right down in the dirt and dust, and were not even allowed to raise our heads up for six hours, or till dark" (courtesy New York State Military Museum).

Though the overall battle of Glendale was a tactical draw, the Confederates managed to bully the Union troops farther south towards their destination of the James River, but the Rebels did not capitalize on a swift victory that they had hoped for. The Confederates were poised to either obliterate or slice the Union army in half, had their plan gone flawlessly. Mahone's troops were to signal the Confederate attack, but the sea of trees that blocked their advance essentially dissolved their operation. After the war, Franklin called out his late adversary, General "Stonewall" Jackson, to say how easily his Rebel troops could have crossed at Brackett's Ford, and essentially annihilated Slocum's division, and turned the whole Union line, but now they stand as missed opportunities that feed historians.[15]

Fighting dwindled on both sides before they transitioned to attend to the nighttime evacuation of their wounded. Reinforcements around the Union line were shifted throughout the night to bolster the areas left unsteady after the day's fighting. The 18th held their unchallenged ground in the cornfield until 11 p.m. Slocum silently withdrew the division under the cover of darkness away from their position and rejoined the main army by midnight. Private Samuel Hodgkins of Company K remembered seeing the batteries wrap their caissons and cannons in blankets to deafen their rattling sounds. Slocum pushed south for nearly three miles. Their hurried march safely brought them first to Turkey Bend near the James River, where they took a short halt. They did not rest long knowing the enemy was on their heels, so they continued their movement towards Malvern Hill and arrived there on July 1 by early daylight.[16]

Malvern Hill

As the sight of Malvern Hill came into view on their march, the gently sloped ground was a heavenly one when compared to the swampy lowlands they had trudged through. Located a mile north of the James River, the mile-wide plateau that dominated the surrounding terrain was practically treeless, but crowned with a heavy presence of Union troops and artillery prepped for its defense. Consolidated with the bulk of the Union army, the 18th finally saw their chance for some shuteye. The pace of the past week had caught up with them, as the days felt like one continuous battle, with little sleep, half rations, and unremitting marches that were enough to wear the ablest infantryman down. Their anticipated rest, however, was short-lived. "After pitching tents and getting things in readiness for a good snooze," as Private Bronson Mills explained, "orders came to *Fall in!*" The men scrambled to pack up. At 9 a.m., Slocum moved the division to the right of the Union line. The entire army was still destined for the James River, but now a majority of the army was behind the 18th's brigade, division, and corps. Closing in on them was Lee's army that continued their hot pursuit which sped the Union's retreat farther and faster towards the river. Just as soon as Malvern Hill was cleared of Slocum's division and positioned south of the slope, the rear divisions of McClellan's forces came in contact with the Rebels for the seventh straight day in a row.[17]

For the first time during the Seven Days campaign, both sides had finally turned out their entire force on the same field. An elevated plateau and bordered by streams, the hills offered a breeze and was a respite out of the fetid swamps they had so often trudged through. The Union line built up at Malvern Hill was a prime defensive position that was much better than Gaines's Mill. Porter's battered V Corps and the IV Corps made up the main line that hoped to bounce off the Rebel assault. With the help of Federal gunboats, a heavy artillery duel started the fight in which the Union batteries greatly outnumbered their opponents. By 3 p.m., General Lee tried an infantry assault that fizzled quickly. The day favored the Yankees, who put up a successful defense that made the Confederates practically forget their victory at Gaines's Mill. Rebel casualties amounted to 5,650, whereas the Union lost 3,007. The sobering and failed assault by the Confederates helped stop their aggressive attacks and put an end to a bloody weeklong string of battles.[18]

The 18th, with the rest of Franklin's VI Corps, were posted more than a mile south from the fighting and in such a lowly elevated ground that the progress of the battle was impossible to monitor. When they arrived to their position, the men hastily constructed abatis out of wood and strengthened their position, but an attack upon them never transpired. They were not needed as reinforcements and stopped their abatis-building as the sound of the clashing armies over the hill faded off.[19]

Harrison's Landing

The 18th again fell in line around 1 a.m., on July 2, and proceeded ahead of the majority of the army and continued the overall retreat under a heavy rain for another seven tiring miles towards the James River. Slocum would pen his praise for the endless movements of the past week made by his weary division by saying, "the troops were allowed scarcely an hour of undisturbed rest either by night or day, yet the division marched into its present camp in good order."[20]

Around 8 a.m. that rainy morning, the 18th arrived to McClellan's choice spot of Harrison's Landing to reconsolidate the army. When the landing came in view for the 18th, the sight came with both grace and beauty. One vast plain stretched before them of about forty to fifty acres of superb golden chest-high wheat. Within a half hour, the feeding frenzy of 1,000 heads of cattle and horses, wagon trains, artillery, a day-long rain, and a trampling army all culminated to instantly demolish its splendor. The unfriendly rainstorm lasted all day in torrents, but was better than another brutal fight with the enemy. With the encampment of the Army of the Potomac huddled en masse and the combination of the merciless rain, Private Bronson Mills mentioned, "not a spear of grain was left standing" in the ankle deep mud that was Harrison's Landing by mid-afternoon. The excessive rain bogged the roads into a river of mud and made the movement of both armies impossible. Wagons and ambulances by the hundreds were lost, and straggling was rampant. The 18th lost several wagons, and men fought for their release from the thick Virginia mud. Baggage of the officers and even knapsacks of soldiers from the regiment were mercilessly tossed out, which left many men without a change of clothing. Enough was enough for Corporal John H. Murray, Company F, and Private George Bulson, Company A, as both deserted the regiment as soon as they got to Harrison's Landing.[21]

Rain cleared off the following morning which allowed two Confederate cannons to be rolled up on the high ground that faced the Union encampments. The bold Rebel battery launched a couple worthless shells towards the sea of tents. Their harassment was brief and fruitless, for they were quickly silenced and routed by the overpowering Union artillery. The 18th and other troops relocated their camp to a position two miles from the spot that the gutsy Rebel battery had occupied. Their encampment became one of the last lines of defenses for the Army of the Potomac pressed against the James River. It was a short muddy walk, a little more than a mile from the river, to where they set their tent stakes.[22]

General McClellan's offensive Peninsula campaign came as an aggravating defeat for everyone who believed and desired a victory to quell the Southern revolution. The week of hard fighting did not deter the celebrated holiday of July 4 from being anything less to the beleaguered Army of the Potomac. The day was spent with marginal relaxation and stillness which was a welcoming change. McClellan took the opportunity to appear before his troops in an afternoon review and despite the recent routs, Little Mac was still received with the same vociferous cheers. Bands around the camps struck up the sounds of popular marches all evening and the batteries of artillery fired off salutes.[23]

Shortly past midnight on July 6, the regiment again moved their camp, a half a mile closer to the front, near the rest of the entrenchments that the army busied themselves to build. The 18th immediately began the same task and worked until 2 a.m., and finished a line of rifle pits for added protection. Details on the entrenchments continued at all hours. Work during their first full day there was briefly suspended when news of an attack was falsely reported. Reports like these were bottomless. Two days later another location was chosen and the regiment shifted to a site on the bank of a creek. For the next several days the men continued their task to build entrenchments around Harrison's Landing. Some worked through the day while others worked through the night in order to construct quick and efficient defenses in case the enemy actually approached their encampment.[24]

With the relative peace between the two armies, the men regained a sense of normalcy in their camp. Rarely was there a day when the men did not take measures to fortify their protection. The entrenchment building and picket duty was a refreshing alternative to being constantly on the go like they had been. Like their days in Alexandria, the regiment was surprised to see President Lincoln ride through the streets of the camp as he personally inspected the troops.[25]

Calculating the Loss

The grounded time also allowed the opportunity for the officers to pen their official reports of recent battles so higher leaders could grasp the bigger picture on their strengths and weaknesses. Overall, Meginnis was pleased with the conduct of the regiment at Gaines's Mill, and when he formulated his account he praised the men, specifically company commanders and subordinates who stepped up after deaths created vacancies. Meginnis said that the men "who were in the battle behaved with the greatest coolness and bravery." He also submitted his casualties from the fight, dated July 5, which was still at that time grossly understated. Even a week had passed since the battle and his count of 110 casualties was less than reality. He counted twelve dead on that date which by then should have reflected twenty-one, but within days this number would again increase. His wounded list was understated by eighteen, and the thirty-five missing was his best guess after he lumped his number with the regrettable loss of Savage's Station hospital into his figures. Had the hospital not been seized by the enemy, those doctors and patients could have cleared up a lot of uncertainty regarding the fate of many. A few scattered soldiers who were adrift around the regiments of the Army of the Potomac had still not found the 18th by the time they arrived to Harrison's Landing, and were considered missing until they reunited. By losing the battle space from the previous days it was hard to ascertain which of their wounded succumbed and died on the field and the figures were really based on varied witness accounts. The hard reality of their loss would take time to come to light and only aggravated the grieving process.[26]

Second Lieutenant Thomas S. Lane, who was propelled to command Company H after Captain Rogers' death and First Lieutenant Carmichael's sickness, wrote about his company's mentality days after the battles and it easily reflected upon the entire regiment on how they dealt with their grim situation:

> The rest of the boys are well and ready for another fight, with the exception of four or five that have given away under the hardships we have endured the last ten days, but even these will be in the fight we expect tomorrow or the next day, as the enemy is still in front, and we are expecting an attack at any moment.[27]

Families back home scrounged for news after every engagement that their relatives were said to have been present for. Ambiguous wires traveled fast but detailed letters shipped slowly and newspapers seemingly printed any rumor they heard from the front without caution. Newspapers most often broke the unsettling heartbreak of casualties to relatives in public print. Reports from the Gaines's Mill fight made their way north faster than transports and filled the columns of the *New York Times*. Until letters from survivors reached their hometowns, the families of the 18th referenced the larger syndicated *Times* and speculated what role their boys had and how bad they fared. Names of sick and wounded soldiers from the peninsula started to appear in the *Times* on June 30. *The Whig Press* in Middletown put a notice in their July 2 publication that confirmed the 18th had participated in the recent fights but still had not received what was most desired; a concise list of casualties. On July 3, the *New York Times* submitted a laundry list of named casualties that were broken down by regiments, and the 18th was sizable. Most of the names were collected at Savage's Station just after the battle and were riddled with inaccuracies. The partial list mentioned twenty names of killed and wounded, but three did not even belong to the 18th. To further complicate matters, all but one were grossly misspelled or designated with the wrong company. The family of Private Samuel Lilly might not have speculated that "S. Silec" was their kin. "Jas. Flynn, Co. C" may have been a different soldier with the same name in the eyes of the family of James Flynn, Company G. It is doubtful that the family of Corporal Isaac DeBaum would connect to the name listed as "J. Duhoum." *The Atlas & Argus* in Albany saw the name of "Capt. Ryers, Co. H" to be their Captain Rogers. They could not confirm his death until July 8. "Capt. Foote, Co. G" in the wounded column was supposed to be Captain Henry Faurot, Company G. When his brother Jacob back home in New York received a private dispatch that confirmed Henry was wounded and possibly captured, an anxious Jacob traveled to the offices of the *Tribune* in New York in hopes to obtain more concrete details before he set south in search of his brother. Editors from the *Evening Star and Times* in Schenectady read the name listed as "N. Griley, Co. A" to connect with Private Nathan Gridley, but were optimistic for a mistake. The loss of "little Nate Gridley" was eventually confirmed by a letter from his brother William on July 9. Middletown was gripped with fear when the *New York Times* listed the death of "Capt. Beng, Co. D" under the 18th's losses. A Middletown paper reported Barry's death on July 9. While at Harrison's Landing, First Lieutenant Roswell M. Sayer penned a solemn and sympathetic letter on July 5 to Barry's mother regarding how he died in battle. With the travel time of mail and the allowance of Barry's family to publish the letter, Barry's death was known to his community by July 16. Flags were drawn to half-mast and a memorial service was held the following afternoon at his hometown church in Middletown. As more letters from men at Harrison's Landing poured into their family homes, their recounts of the battle and casualties were made public and published in their hometowns so the news would circulate.[28]

Rumors were unreliable and oftentimes panicked a family for no reason. The *Fishkill Journal* ran a story the day before the Gaines's Mill fight that told of the death of Private John W. Jaycox of Company C, who was said to have been killed in battle earlier that week. Unbeknownst to his family, Jaycox was alive. Furthermore, he was not even present at the Gaines's Mill fight, probably due to illness. News of his false death was not squashed until July 9 when comrade Private John Gracey arrived in town and spread the news of Jaycox's existence. In another instance, Second Lieutenant William H. Ellis wrote a letter to his father on July 4 that included a list of casualties from his Company G. As an eyewitness in the battle, Ellis' list carried a sense of legitimacy and was quickly published in Canandaigua's newspaper. Ellis listed twenty-one names from his company, most of which he categorized as being missing, one of which was his brother George, captured at Savage's Station. Unfortunately, Ellis got one wrong and listed the severely wounded and captured Private Reinold Ritzenthaler as having been killed. His accepted death stood as confirmed until July 19, when to the surprise of many, Ritzenthaler was paroled and sent home. He happily showed off "the loss of an arm instead of his life."[29]

Myers Worsens, Meginnis Continues, Young Returns

Evacuating the wounded and gradually declining sick was a priority at Harrison's Landing. A few of the slightly wounded who could nurse their wounds without leaving the regiment did so, but the majority required special care that could only be found in Northern hospitals. Private Jehiel J. Stevens of Company K surprised some faces when he was spotted in a doctor's tent at Harrison's Landing. He had tried his best to stay with the regiment after he received a wound to his left leg at Gaines's Mill. Using his rifle as a crutch, Stevens hobbled with his company for two days that followed the battle, but was compelled to fall behind because of his wound and typhoid fever. With tough grit, Stevens found his way to a hospital at Harrison's Landing on July 2.[30]

Wounded and sick soldiers from the peninsula poured into Union hospitals as quickly as the ferry transports could allow. Several transports operated as floating hospitals that ferried men to different ports such as Fort Monroe, Washington, Philadelphia, and New York, where the sick and wounded would then be properly treated in a hospital suitable to care for their needs. Dr. Rice had time at Harrison's Landing to assess the wounded and sick, and he was inundated with patients. Dr. Rice orchestrated the removal of the most precarious as soon as transports were available on July 2. Dozens of wounded and sick men of all ranks from the regiment were sent off over the course of the week aboard steamers and headed North, and what was left of the 18th was further reduced.[31]

As soon as the regiment arrived to Harrison's Landing, one of the first patients Dr. Rice inspected was Lieutenant Colonel Myers. His struggle with a debilitating malarial fever had only worsened since he relinquished his duties to Major Meginnis days before. With the army on a constant move, Myers was deprived of medical attention, rest, and necessary foods that could have done him good. When Dr. Rice examined Myers as soon as they got to Harrison's Landing, he found him "much debilitated and very sick." The conditions and location of the army did not favor a recovery for him. The rest of the medical staff at the hospital agreed with Dr. Rice's request and Myers was immediately placed on a transport and sent home to recover. Myers was given a fifteen-day furlough, but was eventually granted an extension on his convalescence to improve his health. It would take more than a month before Myers was healthy enough to return.[32]

Major Meginnis was the only staff officer left and he continued to run the regiment in Myers' absence. His men could see he was under duress, which was clearly understood by them given the past few days they had endured. Still, the men found faith in his efforts. Private Henry Clay of Company D said of his former captain, "a braver officer never lived." Sergeant Thomas Alexander spoke expressively about Meginnis' capabilities:

> The Major has had hard times lately … but nobly and gallantly has he done his duty, and gained the love and esteem of all the men. They praise him highly, and have the greatest confidence in him. Long may he live to lead us bravely on the foe; and as long as there are any of the Wallkill Guards left, they will stand by him with their colors flying.[33]

Colonel Young finally returned back to the regiment on July 15 after nearly two months of battling typhoid fever back home. However, after having spent several weeks of recuperation in New York, Young still returned without a full recovery to a regiment that wallowed with the Chickahominy fever. He had missed the opportunity to command the regiment during its most trying time and returned to the same unfavorable conditions with which debilitated him. Recognizing that a perfect recovery would be unobtainable and his fever inclined to relapse, Young had to make a tough decision. His absence caused subordinate officers to take on the responsibilities of the rank above them without the pay scale honoring their efforts, and their skill of the challenge was matched. Dr. Rice gave a thorough checkup with Young three days after his return, but his findings concurred with Young that he was "by no means perfect as yet" and considered him unfit for duty. His speculation on a recovery was inconclusive and doubtful due to the present location that fostered improper nourishment, exposure, and a disagreeable climate. He encouraged Young that a permanent restoration of health was more likely upon his return to the North for an unspecified time. Therefore, with the best interest of the regiment on his mind, Young penned his indisputable and immediate resignation on July 18. His paper was then shopped around for approving signatures to set his action into effect. With "great regret" General Newton approved his resignation. As the commander of the VI Corps, General Franklin was dire for good soldiers like Colonel Young. Franklin regarded Young as "being too valuable an officer to be lost," and instead recommended that the colonel take a leave of absence for twenty more days and spend the furlough at Old Point Comfort in hopes to reestablish his health. Young accepted his orders with hesitance, thinking he was only prolonging the inevitable.[34]

Prisoner Exchanges

The Confederates dealt with thousands of Union prisoners after the peninsula, and nearly fifty of them were from the 18th. The imprisoned life in Richmond was described by many to be surprisingly tolerable. First, the location took them away from the disease-infested camps along the Chickahominy that derailed everyone's health. Inactivity was commonplace for the prisoners which had to be a welcomed respite after the constant movements that correlated to the Seven Days' battles. Each day the men were given a ration of half a loaf of bread, but sometimes it was scaled to a quarter. Coffee was only offered for the costly price of two dollars a pound. Tea and other luxuries could not "be had at any price," as Private John H. Pollard of Company E said, but "sometimes we would have soup and the cooks would skim the fat off and sell it to the boys for 25 cents a cup." Meat was seldom provided, and when it was it was most often spoiled. Still, soldiers like Pollard wrote home and assured his family that he "was treated very well while at Richmond."[35]

An open dialogue of prisoner exchanges had already begun, and the Confederates wanted to rid themselves of the responsibility of the critically sick and wounded before they died. Private John D. Phillips, Company I, was a wounded prisoner for just a few days after his capture at Savage's Station and was paroled on July 3. The health of Private Lucius W. H. Ball of Company C was so dire that he could not be moved to Richmond and died from typhoid fever at Savage's Station on July 11.[36]

By the end of July, both armies forwarded several waves of released prisoners to be ex-

Shown here in a family photograph taken less than a year after his resignation, Col. William H. Young left for health reasons caused by the reviled "Chickahominy fever." Pvt. David W. Young, standing behind his father, of Company K was also taken sick and discharged thirteen days before the colonel, after having served only five months (courtesy Bob Haarde).

changed. First Sergeant George W. Ellis, Company G, was paroled at Haxall's Landing with a group on July 17, followed two days later by Privates Reinold Ritzenthaler, Company G and John Schwantner of Company A, both of whom had arms removed. The 18th's assistant surgeon, Dr. Alexander A. Edmeston, was paroled on July 25, along with five others from the regiment that were quickly hospitalized. Dr. Edmeston had been paroled a few days prior, but he and a few other surgeons elected to remain a few days more to tend to the excessive wounded at Libby Prison. Seven more prisoners were paroled July 27. Private William H. Linkletter, Company G, spent nearly a month in a Richmond prison after he was wounded and captured at Gaines's Mill. His wound healed, but it was his health that plummeted from typhoid fever. Linkletter was paroled on July 27 and sent to the Episcopal Hospital in Philadelphia, but died from his disease there on August 1.[37]

The Richmond prisoners were eventually relocated to Belle Isle just before their parole and transfer. One of the last major exchanges occurred on August 5, but their freedom culminated with a demanding march. Confederates marched their Yankee prisoners for twenty miles until they reached City Point, a Rebel port on the southern banks of the James River. Many men were unhealthy to begin with or just could not garnish the strength to make the march and had to be left behind. Private William H. Harris of Company E attempted the march, but the nineteen-year-old had been wrecked from typhoid fever and during the march he suffered from sunstroke that nearly claimed his life. Harris finished the trek in the back of a wagon. Twenty-one soldiers from the 18th completed the August 5 march and boarded the transports at City Point. Finally, 300 or so prisoners returned "fairly tired and sleepy" to the familiar faces of their regiments at Harrison's Landing the following day. Eventually, the paroled prisoners would have to be hospitalized or sent home on furloughs as part of the parole requirements. Harris was shipped to New York to be hospitalized, but his father had other plans, and without authorization, brought his son home where he undoubtedly received better attention, despite earning the label as a deserter.[38]

The recently returned prisoners were good for the regiment that had little to get excited about, but their return did little to bolster the dwindling manpower. So many of the men were sick and spread out in Northern hospitals that on paper the regiment looked sufficient, but the camp was pretty skeletal.

Sickness Prevails at Harrison's Landing

Life in camp went on with dress parades, regimental inspections, and picket duty while the regiment awaited the next move of the army. Harrison's Landing offered suitably high and dry ground to camp on. It also provided the men with a large stream nearby for baths, an abundance of blackberries were close at hand, and several springs offered incredibly cool water to drink. Provisions were adequate, and of course there was an unending supply of hardtack available daily. In addition, each soldier was given a two-inch square piece of salt beef or pork every day, as fresh meat came but once a week. Coffee was offered in the morning and at night, and occasionally molasses to go with it. On July 23, the regiment slightly shifted their camp for a more sterile environment after their immobile occupation drained its sanitary state. Towards the end of the month, Companies A, E, and F spent a day constructing a bridge.[39]

Company F was taken by surprise when the face of a deserter nonchalantly strolled into their camp on August 4. Private John H. Rediker strolled into camp in uniform as calmly as if he had never left, anxious to tell his story of his absence. Nothing had been heard from him after he deserted on May 2 while posted as a guard of the quartermaster store aboard one of the floating vessels off Ship Point. Rediker left and made his way to Philadelphia, where he eventually enlisted into the 17th United States Infantry on June 7. He traveled with his new regiment to Maine, and eventually to Harrison's Landing in August which was where he decided to say hello to his old comrades. Having joined another regiment did not deter the fact that Rediker was still considered a fugitive from the 18th, so he was arrested as soon as he arrived into the camp. The regular army quickly scratched him off of their books the next day as a deserter, and Rediker served out his time with the 18th, although punished financially by the forfeiture of his owed allowances.[40]

The stiff summer heat exacerbated the near-epidemic levels of fever that snaked through the ranks and forced countless soldiers to be transported off the peninsula and checked into Northern hospitals. Only the most dangerously ill patients were hospitalized and logged into record books, but there was an untold number more whose health was similarly hampered but remained where they were in camp. Corporal Edmund B. Hawley of Company A spoke on the health of the regiment at Harrison's Landing and said, "hundreds of strong healthy men are now either dead or as good as dead from disease." Forty-five-year-old Private Charles T. Cordell of Company K had served less than six months by the time he contracted the disease that afflicted so many during the Peninsula campaign. He was sent to David's Island General Hospital in the New York Harbor and died there on July 11. When Port Jervis resident Private Griffin Sheldon of Company D was struck with typhoid fever, he first was hospitalized at Harrison's Landing on July 9. His case worsened, however, and Sheldon died there while onboard the transport *Vanderbilt* on July 19. Major Meginnis' little brother, Private Samuel G. Meginnis, Company D, was hospitalized in New York the same day as Griffin with the same disease. When the brothers parted ways at Harrison's Landing, Major Meginnis could not foresee it would be the last he would see of his brother. Days after his hospitalization at the Brooklyn City Hospital, Samuel Meginnis died from typhoid fever on July 22.[41]

Despite being slightly wounded in his ankle at Gaines's Mill, Adjutant John H. Russell suffered more from disease that he acquired along the Chickahominy. He suffered great fatigue from the days after the battle and was moved around by an ambulance. He thought that he could shake his illness if he could get home and be tendered proper attention in a hospital. From Harrison's Landing, Russell was placed on a transport that eventually brought him to Philadelphia on July 7. By the time he arrived, however, he had become totally exhausted from his disease and was brought to the home of a friend in the city where he passed away on July 28. As soon as word of Russell's death reached the regiment, Second Lieutenant E. Nott Schermerhorn of Company E continued his perpetual rise in rank and duties and was promoted to adjutant.[42]

One of the most peculiar soldier deaths to occur at Harrison's Landing for the regiment was that of the newest recruit. Having joined the regiment at the start of the Peninsula campaign, Private William A. Shaw of Company H was a young soldier, but not so much in age. At fifty years old, he was one of the oldest in the regiment. He was quick to prove his bravery when he refused to leave the front line after he received a slight gunshot wound to his head at Gaines's Mill. After the battles subsided, Shaw was bothered with heavy symptoms of diarrhea and fever which consumed him and was cared for in the regimental hospital for a week. By the beginning of August he seemed to rebound. All was normal after the afternoon supper was served on August 4 and Shaw emerged from his tent and went to go rinse his cup out. As calm as can be, midway through Shaw's rinse of his cup he fell lifelessly to the ground without any moans or signs of struggle and died. He was buried near the camp the following dawn. Second Lieutenant Lane eventually penned a letter to break the news to Shaw's brother back home, and eulogized his time within the company:

> Although his stay with us was so short, he had made himself beloved and esteemed by his officers and comrades, and in his loss I feel that we have lost one of our best men, and the country one of her best and tried soldiers and patriots.[43]

The health of the regiment was at an all time low while at Harrison's Landing, and August failed to change the pattern. In just four days' time between August 7 and 11, twenty-two men from the regiment had to be transported north. Private Robert Huson of Company F left Harrison's Landing with a group of sick soldiers on August 7. Huson battled typhoid fever and made the journey to Philadelphia where he was hospitalized on August 10, but died two days later. Private William Snell of Company H was shipped off the landing the day after Huson and was similarly checked into the same hospital in Philadelphia. Snell was struck with hepatitis from which he struggled with for several weeks, but died from its effects on September 5. Private William L. Christian of Company E was another to be ravaged by the despised Chickahominy fever. He was shipped off to Philadelphia and died two days after Snell.[44]

Private Charles H. Reed of Company D was sent off on August 7 and similarly hospitalized in Philadelphia. Diarrhea and pneumonia had consumed Reed for over two months until death set him free on October 15. An autopsy performed later that day showed that his lungs had suffered harshly from the penalty of the Chickahominy.[45]

Aboard one of the first shipments of sick troops sent north was twenty-year-old Private George C. Furniss of Company K. He started a long-term hospitalization where doctors tried to rid his body of typhoid fever and diarrhea. Furniss suffered long without signs of improvement and was eventually discharged in October, but he still wrestled the illness at home. After the regimental books were closed, Furniss became a late casualty of the Chickahominy when he died from his sickness at his home in Parishville, New York, on August 20, 1863.[46]

Another to leave during the Harrison's Landing occupation happened to be the most sanctified member of the 18th. Chaplain Farr had shared a tent with Adjutant Russell and closely monitored the young lieutenant's failing health until he was sent off, but in his duty the chaplain may have acquired the disease from him. Farr quickly became emaciated from fever that also spurred a dormant hernia to flare up and worsened his condition. Dr. Rice urged the chaplain to seek rest at home, "in order to save his life." Wise to the doctor's orders, Farr penned his resignation to Major Meginnis on July 28 and was approved three days later. The loss of the regiment's chaplain hit the men with a heavy sense of regret and sadness and his void would be felt every Sunday. Farr returned home to Albany where he focused his energy on his health and remained hopeful to someday rejoin the regiment.[47]

Company H had been under the care of Second Lieutenant Thomas S. Lane after Captain Rogers was killed and second-in-command First Lieutenant William E. Carmichael was injured in February from being thrown from his horse and compounded by a debilitating sickness that came just before the battle. Carmichael showed little improvement to his health so he made it official and resigned on July 16. Four days later, Carmichael arrived home to Middletown and returned the swords of the two fallen captains to the families of Barry and Rogers.[48]

While at Harrison's Landing, Captain Henry Faurot of Company G could barely get out of his tent after sickness sapped his strength. As soon as he resigned on July 21, Faurot was offered a position on the staff of General Wadsworth in Washington, but his health was too impaired for the task and was compelled to decline the offer.[49]

Company G fell into the command of Faurot's subordinate, First Lieutenant Isaac S. Green, despite the fact that Second Lieutenant William H. Ellis had commanded the company after Faurot and Green were both sidelined throughout the Peninsula campaign. Green eventually was forced to resign at Major Meginnis' behest since he cited Green as unable "by any means" to meet his expectations and allowed the company to suffer "for want of an efficient officer." When Green penned his resignation on August 8, he first explained his reason was to return home and care for his ailing father, but he quickly changed his tone and made clear that he did not have "the heart or ambition" to be a soldier and that he was "sick and tired of the service." Green's fed up attitude was clear to Meginnis who was more than happy to see him leave. Green was not entirely drained of military service, but rather more exhausted by those he worked with, because a year later he donned another officer's uniform when he became a captain in a different regiment and finished the war as a battle-scarred veteran.[50]

Hoping to quell the declining health of the 18th, a young physician from Albany was added to the regiment. Twenty-eight-year-old Dr. Frank J. Mattimore enlisted his skills on August 11 in Albany and signed on to become another assistant surgeon for the regiment. Indebted to his brother that paid for his education, Dr. Mattimore studied at the Jesuits' College in Montreal, St. John's College in Fordham, New York [present-day Fordham University], and graduated from the Albany Medical College in 1860. Dr. Mattimore began his work as a resident physician at the Alms House Hospital in Albany on May 4, 1860, which lasted until April 7, 1862, when he left and started an office of his own in the city. Born near Troy, New York, his parents came to America from Ireland, and his Irish roots and blossoming experience as a city physician at the start of the war quickly led to a proposal from an Irish regiment to make him their surgeon in September 1861, but the opportunity never took form. Almost a year later, Dr. Mattimore's opportunity came when he joined the 18th as their assistant surgeon.[51]

The End of the Peninsula Campaign

Just as soon as a dispatch from the War Department reached McClellan on August 4 that asked him to abandon his efforts and backpedal to Washington, the proud general showed he still had some fight left in him. The Army of the Potomac caught wind of McClellan's intention to seize Malvern Hill that had since been occupied by the enemy. On August 4, the 18th was ordered to cook two days rations and await further instructions. They spent the next two days on picket duty without any added orders. When elements from the III Corps pushed towards the hill on August 5 and reported the enemy in large force, McClellan got cold feet with fear of losing all that he gained with the safety of Harrison's Landing. The campaign was over and McClellan complied with Washington and started plans to remove the army from the peninsula.[52]

On August 11, the men made preparations for what they understood to be a retreat. They shipped their knapsacks and extra baggage as their first preparation. A paymaster also made his appearance for the regiment to issue their pay. The following day, the regiment cleaned up their camp and prepared for the long awaited movement of the entire Army of the Potomac. The first to leave was actually a squad of recruiters from the 18th who left on August 13 with hopes to cash in on men back home needed to plus-up the companies, especially after Lincoln's call for another round of 600,000 more volunteers.[53]

Of all the recent exits from the regiment, none was more significant than the final approval of Colonel Young's resignation. His recent protracted furlough at Old Point Comfort did little to improve his condition and break his severe attack of typhoid fever. Young's resignation was finally accepted and approved by the office of Major General McClellan and he was honorably discharged on August 14. The interim positions that officers had filled during Young's absence were officially approved but it would take almost two months before the paperwork was finalized and their new titles were changed. Twenty-four-year-old Lieutenant Colonel Myers took command as the colonel of the 18th on August 14. Myers had just returned to the regiment after a couple weeks' stay on convalescence at home. Major Meginnis took the rank of lieutenant-colonel, which allowed Captain Gridley to officially depart from the company that he initially raised and became the regiment's next major. Company A was kept in the trusted hands of Gridley's right hand man, First Lieutenant Daniel H. Daley. Colonel Young promised the men of the 18th that he would continue his loyalty to them, and when he returned home he helped recruit men in Schenectady to join the regiment.[54]

The same day that brought news of Young's resignation, the 18th received their long awaited orders to evacuate Harrison's Landing. Their destination became the embarkation points at Newport News where river transports awaited their arrival. The distance was long and would take several days of hard marching over terrain that men despised. Still, they knew it was their ticket off of the dreaded peninsula. The 18th prepared for the familiar march and struck their tents on August 15, only to await their turn to begin at any given hour. The camps around them began to disappear as wagon trains of supplies, extra baggage, horses, artillery, and regiments began to move out that night at 9 p.m. One man from the regiment heard estimations that they had seen more than 10,000 wagons filed past the regiment all day and into the next early morning until 2 a.m. Shortly thereafter, the 18th started their march and trekked more than six miles until they passed Charles City Court House and paused there at 6 p.m. and set up an encampment. The spot chosen was a fenced field of luscious green corn, of which both rails and corn were stripped in a matter of moments, and the men dined on several helpings of roasted corn.[55]

At 7 a.m. on August 17, the 18th resumed the march and once again crossed the Chickahominy near its mouth at Barrett's Ferry. They passed over the river on an engineering masterpiece of a pontoon bridge crossing about 2,000 feet in length, made by the 50th New York Engineers. Two ranks of infantry could pass on either side, while artillery or wagons rolled through the center, all under the safety net of nearby gunboats. This march spanned at least sixteen dusty miles under intolerable heat that lent this march to become one of the most fatiguing ones ever covered by the men. Exquisite mansions and wide-ranging plantations were passed on the way that brought a glimmer of pleasure along an otherwise miserable march. The annoyance of constant delays from trains obstructing the roadways prolonged the daytime march and sapped motivation, but they eventually settled a camp at 6 p.m. Private Charles Sullivan, Company E, somehow became separated from the regiment and was captured by Confederates the following day back at Charles City Court House. His 'On to Richmond' journey would come true when five days later he entered the city, but as a prisoner of war.[56]

The men had conquered many hard marches, but this one was different. Their quickened speed over dusty roads was grueling and made worse by the sun that blistered them. One cannot stress how greatly fatigued the men were from the hardships of such taxing marches from which many fell out. Many of the cases of those who fell out were caused from sunstroke. Corporal Francis W. Howard and Private Timothy Donohoe, both from Company F, fell out of the ranks and ended their military service on their own accord by desertion. Private Anthony Cole Bullent of Company F felt the shared ache that the men experienced. He tried to relate the pace of the tough march in a letter to his parents, and Bullent took special notice of the sacrifices of the animals that helped move the army:

> I can't tell you the distressing sights to be witnessed on a long march under a burning sun. Our distresses mostly arise from want of water, blistered feet and other casualties. Our poor beasts—team horses and mules—drop by hundreds, drawing heavy artillery wagons. They are mostly splendid animals, but when they drop are doomed to be shot.[57]

The daily trend of rushed marches continued early the next morning of August 18, when they started at 4:30 a.m. and walked several more miles and eventually passed through Williamsburg. This march was much more agreeable than the day previous, although still arduous. Upon their arrival to the moss-covered town, the regiment pushed nearly three miles beyond Williamsburg's limits and established another temporary camp. The 18th stepped off the following morning of August 19 for yet another forced march at 6 a.m. They tramped nearly fifteen miles until they arrived and encamped at the entrenchments at Yorktown at two o'clock in the afternoon. The journey was exhausting, but was worthwhile when every man in the 18th indulged in a refreshing salt water bath.[58]

The days remained hot, but the nights brought chilly dew to settle atop the men. Sometimes their simple survival through the conditions still surprised veterans like Private Bullent:

> 'Tis wonderful how it is endured—nothing to cover us up. Thus when marching, we throw ourselves down on the ground and snore away to dream of home and loved ones, or of sitting at the domestic board feasting on some imagined dainty, and waking at early dawn, cold and shivering, to find it's all a vision! Such is the romantic happiness of a soldier's life.[59]

On August 20, they started another tiring march before dawn, trekking about twelve miles beyond Yorktown, and passed through the deserted Warwick Court House. One 18th soldier repugnantly described the town to be inhabited by "a few old negroes, and some of the largest rats ever seen." The continued march passed through Little Bethel, and went on for another six warm miles beyond the town until they finally reached their objective of Newport News at half past midnight on August 21. The 18th passed the night in the area of the Denbigh Baptist Church and its century-old cemetery. Finally, after a week of continuous hard marching that covered roughly eighty miles, their journey came to an end when they reached the fleet of transports along Newport News. Upon their arrival, the regiment was reunited with Lieutenant Colonel Myers who had been at home on convalescent leave since July 2. Whole regiments of soldiers, including horses and mules, splashed through the water for a last-minute bath before boarding. First Lieutenant John Vedder had commandeered a mule for himself that he insisted to keep. He did so but the officers above him forbade him to ride it during marches. Vedder accepted the rule and made the mule carry his blankets and other small items instead.[60]

The same ships that brought the enthusiastic soldiers down to the peninsula at the start of the campaign had run continuous voyages back and forth. First to bring the army down, then to evacuate the sick and wounded, and lastly they withdrew the Army of the Potomac back closer to Washington. The men from the 18th and the 32nd New York crammed onto the transport steamer *Daniel Webster* around 6 p.m. on August 22 and dropped down the James River and into the Chesapeake Bay, where they anchored until midnight. Transports came as a relief despite their overcrowded conditions. Spirits on the backtracking steamers were quieted when compared to the boisterous days when "On to Richmond" was the exuberant battle cry. Several shades of bobbing colorful signal lights affixed to vessels bounced off the dark waters as they traveled up the Potomac River. Through heavy swells, the fleet arrived to Aquia Creek on August 23 for a brief pause. Their short break was followed by another anchor drop off the coast of Mount Vernon, but eventually their steamer finished its last leg of travel and churned into the wharfs of Alexandria. Four months had elapsed since their initial departure from Alexandria back in April. The regiment touched land at Dock Number Two of the familiar city at 9 a.m. on August 24, which effectively concluded their participation in the Peninsula campaign.[61]

13

From One Campaign to the Next
August 24, 1862–September 13, 1862

"You will hear of a Big Battle being fought in Maryland
within ten days or sooner."—*First Lieutenant Horatio G. Goodno,
Company K, September 10, 1862*

Losses and Gains of a Changed Regiment

Upon their arrival in Alexandria on the morning of August 24, the 18th marched up the Little River Turnpike and encamped just off the road, about a mile-and-a-half from the city, near Fort Ellsworth. General Franklin had orders to camp his VI Corps on Alexandria's outskirts, along the rail lines of the Orange and Alexandria Railroad. It was familiar territory for the regiment, but they understood their stay would be brief. Orders from the War Department were quickly drawn on August 26 for a next day's march for the VI Corps, but they were countermanded less than an hour later.[1]

The men barely had time to reflect or mourn on what and who was lost during their last campaign before the next one began. The regiment had shrunk greatly from numerous deaths, discharges, and hospitalizations which also forged new leadership roles throughout the Peninsula campaign. When the 18th returned to Alexandria, they had 178 fewer men than when they left the city on April 17. Private Anthony Cole Bullent of Company B wrote home to his parents on August 27 during a moment when he seemed to realize this sad reality:

> I felt a solemn feeling creep over me this morning, while looking around, aware how many brave fellows that went out with us in anticipation of victory or returning conquerors, are now laying in their lonely swamp graves on the Chickahominy and Harrison's Landing. Many of the citizens of Alexandria, who knew us from our long encampment, grasped us by the hand and expressed all the joy that old acquaintances could have done, but looked for many in vain.[2]

Between the retreat from Harrison's Landing and the end of August, there were nine desertions, three of which happened as soon as the regiment returned to Alexandria. Others slipped through the cracks of the lightly guarded hospitals when they were admitted as patients and were never to be heard from again.[3]

What helped bolster the regiment was the return of a couple of previously sick or wounded soldiers, and the lot of paroled prisoners. What helped the most was the recruiting drive that was enacted in mid–August which sent a dozen men from the 18th to scour their hometowns for volunteers. From August 12 to September 2, hometown recruiting gained the names of an additional twenty-two volunteers, one of which was rejected and three others that deserted before they reached the regiment. First Lieutenant John Mooney, Company C, was in charge of the squad of eleven recruiters that he spread out in Albany, Schenectady, and Middletown, where they all found stiff competition from other regimental recruiters. Second Lieutenant Robert A. Malone and Corporal Amasa "Amzy" Fuller, both of Company D, headed to their home territory in Middletown, and were joined by Sergeant Michael Hulligan, Company K, and Private Aurelius Webster of Company I. Malone also put an advertisement in the local Middletown paper that explained all of the benefits that would befall on anyone who enlisted, and the enticements were tempting:

> All who wish to join this veteran Regiment can now have an opportunity, and by so doing be at once mustered into active service. All who join old regiments are less liable to sickness, for the reason that those used to camp life know best how to care for the new volunteer. Besides this, all who join the 18th will have only to serve until the 17th of May next, and will also be entitled to share the honor of belonging to a Regiment that has inscribed on its flag the memorable Battles of "West Point," "Gaines' Mills," "Charles City X Roads," "Malvern Hills"—contests that will be "a recompense of glory" to the soldiers of the veteran "18th" for all future time. Sons of Orange and Sullivan! Once more you are called upon to fill up the ranks of your favorite regiment. It is to be hoped that the fortunes of war may be such that it will be the last. Come forward, then, with alacrity, and go with us where "glory waits you." Those who enlist in the "Eighteenth" can join any Company in the Regiment they may prefer.[4]

To top it off, each recruit received a bounty of $92 in advance, and a $75 bounty and land warrant granted at war's end. Everything sounded almost too good to be true, but the actuality of the advertisement carried the inaccuracy regarding the length of service a recruit would have to serve, which would only come to light when the regiment reached their expiration of service. Malone's efforts encouraged two more men to enlist for Company D on September 8 and 9, but they would not join the ranks until several weeks later.[5]

Malone's first recruit was a man looking for a fresh new start to his life. Twenty-six-year-old Oliver P. Fortner of Windsor, New York joined on September 8, but just two months before he did not have his citizenship rights due to the fact that he was a felon. Convicted for burglary in 1858, Fortner spent two years behind bars at the Auburn State Prison, but in July 1862, Governor Morgan restored Fortner's rights, which led him to enlist two months later.[6]

Sergeant Charles C. Walley of Company E and Sergeant Byron Geywits of Company A were detailed to Cleary's Saloon in Schenectady during the August and September recruitment drive. They expressed similar conditions to anyone who joined; that they could choose the company they wanted, and a hefty bounty of $304. If all of these incentives were not appealing enough, then the hint of fear was used like when Walley stated "delays are dangerous" and that "in a few days you may be drafted."[7]

The recruitment drive in Fishkill that August was enough to entice seventeen-year-old Henry D. Wilbur to lie about his age and enlist. Wilbur intentionally avoided the 18th recruiters and signed up with the 128th New York. This was because Wilbur had already signed up with the 18th at the start of the war. As a founding member of Company C, Wilbur had barely associated himself with them by the time he deserted just before the regiment left Albany in June of 1861. Either his youthful lapse of judgment got the better of him or he betted that the government would not make the connection to his prior desertion, Wilbur got caught. On September 3, 1862, a U.S. Marshal met up and arrested him at Hudson, New York. Wilbur was eventually returned to the rolls of the 18th, but was kept distant from the men and spent his time in uniform as a cook for the Lincoln General Hospital in Washington.⁸

Union Failures at Second Manassas and Chantilly

Elements of the Army of the Potomac did not stay idle in Alexandria for long, for they were requested several miles west to reinforce the Union's Army of Virginia under the command of Major General John Pope, as his troops stretched out in battle lines for another fight near Manassas on August 28. Not exactly a team player with Pope's army, McClellan conceded to send elements of his Army of the Potomac in piecemeal towards Manassas to help. Fighting broke out in the evening before reinforcements could have altered the battle, and casualties dumped more than 1,000 from Pope's command.⁹

In the early hours of August 29, the 18th packed up their camp near Fort Ellsworth. Franklin's VI Corps was up and put in motion for a march that left at about 6 a.m. The 18th marched six miles to Annandale and arrived at 4 p.m. They bivouacked for the night and established their standard picket procedures on the road that connected the Little River Turnpike and old Braddock Road.¹⁰

McClellan had halted the corps at Annandale after he feared they might run into the enemy unprepared. At most, each man had roughly forty rounds of ammunition, and they had no wagons to bring up more when needed. McClellan had chronic qualms to commit the VI Corps, having felt they were not in a condition to wage serious battle yet. Moreover, McClellan felt that by committing the VI Corps to General Pope's engagement at Manassas would lower Washington's defenses. McClellan held out as long as he could, but his wait was regrettable and angered officials in Washington.¹¹

Late summer recruiting brought Pvt. Oliver Fortner of Windsor, New York, into Company D on September 8, 1862. He was convicted and incarcerated for burglary in 1858, but Governor Morgan restored Fortner's rights, which allowed him to enlist. When the 18th New York mustered out, Fortner was transferred to the 121st New York, at which time this photograph was taken (United States Army Heritage and Education Center, Carlisle, Pennsylvania).

Before the VI Corps could be of any use on August 29, General Pope's command put up another valiant effort in the evening and fought over the same killing fields of Manassas. Squabbling between Union commanders who fought more for ego and pride allowed a concerted effort from the Confederates to plow down their ranks as they hashed out orders and plans. Reinforcements from Porter's V Corps helped temporarily shove the Rebels away and gave a sense of victory to favor the Yankees. In words that are hard to stomach, General Pope telegraphed Washington that his casualties were "not less than 8,000 men killed and wounded," and yet he continued to solicit as to where Franklin and his resupplies were at.[12]

The 18th left Annandale August 30 at 6 a.m. for a march that brought them to Centreville by 4 p.m. Orders quickly arrived for the regiment to proceed a couple miles westward, closer to the Bull Run battlefield. They pushed out and reached the Stone Bridge just before dark. General Franklin ordered his troops to form a line of battle across the fields on each side of the road so that they funneled and protected the battered Union regiments from General Pope's command as they limped back towards Centreville. The 18th helped cover the defeated and hungry troops back within the relative safety of the village. Later that night, they fell back to the refuge of Centreville and made another last stand in the event of an attack. The regiment eventually passed the night within the fortifications of Centreville. The heights at Centreville were massed with heavy cannons outside the works that could sweep multiple angles of approach. A sea of cabins stretched through the town that were built and previously occupied by the Confederates from the prior winter.[13]

Somehow during the shuffling of marches and retreating troop movements of the day, Privates William H. Post, Company H, and Lewis Spawn, Company F, became separated and were captured by the nearby enemy. Nothing proves or disproves the notion that they were both attempting to desert, but the charge was slapped on them, and they both demonstrated desertions in different units later in the war. However, their capture was short-lived and they were paroled within days, and returned to the regiment several weeks later to answer the accusations.[14]

Confederates were within a close proximity of the rallied VI Corps near Centreville. On August 31, the 32nd New York took over the fortifications that the 18th had held overnight. Just outside of them, the 18th made another stand and formed in line of battle in preparation to repel the enemy had they come as expected. Upton's Battery was with the 32nd within the fortifications and sent out a few shells in the enemy's direction as feelers, but they never received anything in response. Only heavy remittent rains showered down on them as they occupied the defenses at Centreville.[15]

On the cusp of major victories that demoralized the North, General Lee saw his prospects looked golden if he could get his Southern army north of the Potomac into Maryland, and possibly even Pennsylvania. Seizing the moment of the Northern people's feeling of dissention and low morale, topped with a win in the North might encourage strong-armed England to support the Southern cause. Confederates pulled back their presence on Washington and instead pushed to the northern banks of the Potomac River and into Maryland. The sphere of operations now widened and Union commanders were quick to stifle their opportunity and prepared for a showdown in Maryland.[16]

Divisions from the III and IX corps on reconnaissance just west of Germantown, Virginia became engulfed by an overpowering number of Confederates during the evening of September 1. The troops in Centreville could hear the battle played out off in the distance, but was soon masked by heavy thunder, rain, and lightning storms that dumped at 5 p.m. The heavy storm also played a part in the battle which confused both opponents, and led to another demoralizing Union defeat, called Chantilly, also known as Ox Hill. The casualties from the fight ushered the call for any available surgeons within the area to descend upon the wounded. A hasty field hospital and several aid stations popped up in the path of retreat that tended to the wounded and dying. Doctors from the 18th were dispatched and helped treat countless injuries. The newly appointed assistant surgeon for the regiment—Dr. Frank J. Mattimore—quickly settled himself into his new and demanding role with the rest of the medical staff. Just five days after he arrived in camp with the 18th, Dr. Mattimore quickly got his hands bloodied and saw firsthand the awful and gory consequences of an unromantic war up close.[17]

Many of the Union wounded and dead had to be left behind as orders provoked all to abandon their former positions and retreat back to Alexandria. At 10 p.m. on September 1, the 18th left the defenses at Centreville and trekked a cold wet march in the dark east on the Warrenton Turnpike towards Fairfax Court House. They arrived to within a mile from the Fairfax Court Livery the following morning's daybreak at 5 a.m. The regiment established a brief encampment for rest on the hills until about 2 p.m. and stepped off an hour later. At one point, the regiment was randomly drawn up in battle line when a rumor of the proximity of the enemy was feared nearby. No opposition surfaced and they regrouped on the road and continued their beleaguered journey the rest of the way to Alexandria by 9 p.m. In the late night darkness, the men settled upon familiar grounds by the toll gate near the Fairfax Seminary that was once Camp King.[18]

Start of the Maryland Campaign

After just one brief night on the former Camp King grounds, the 18th shifted their camp on September 3 at 7 a.m. The move was short, as they literally crossed the road and set up their bivouac in the space that was formerly held the preceding winter by the 31st New York. The following day the men were reunited with their knapsacks that were shipped since the start of their recent hasty marches west. On September 5, large-sized tents reached the camp and the regiment arranged details to clean up and organize the campground. The tents were pitched the following day, but as soon as the finishing touches on a comfortable camp were worked out, the arrival of urgent orders came in that asked the men to immediately pack up and prepare to move with haste. General Lee's push into Maryland was no longer a possibility, but a reality. There would be no respite from hard marches for the time being. At 10 p.m., on September 6, the 18th—along with the rest of their division and corps—poured onto the road and marched toward Washington. They marched a few miles and crossed over the Potomac via the Long Bridge and passed through Washington. The night march was arduous but made pleasant by a constant and impressive glow from a bright moon and stars. The steady cadence of marching boots on pavement had drawn out Washington residents who crowded the sidewalks to get a glimpse by moonlight and cheer the veterans. A rest was called for at the village of Tenleytown, three miles beyond Georgetown. The entire VI Corps was stretched throughout the northwestern portion of the District of Columbia—from Georgetown to Tenleytown.[19]

John Van Santvoord—a citizen of Washington—was moved with compassion when he witnessed the wretched condition of the marching army pass through the city. From his residence, Van Santvoord quickly saw the city clogged with thousands of sick and wounded soldiers from the recent campaigns throughout Virginia and was moved to act. He knew that the army was on a new campaign which would quickly create more sick and wounded that would boomerang back to the capital. During the night march through the city on September 6, Van Santvoord set out with a friend and grabbed a collection of random personal effects that he dispensed to the most haggard-looking men from the VI Corps. He gifted shirts, supplies, pickles, tomatoes, and even small doses of wine to men. Van Santvoord had nearly depleted his own family's supplies, but he always managed to find other items. Van Santvoord happened to be a former resident of Schenectady but had relocated his family to Washington during the war, and knowing the 18th had men from his former home and were in the area, he ventured to find them the next day. He walked the path of the troops from Georgetown to Tenleytown and found the 18th around 2 p.m. Van Santvoord eventually spotted some familiar faces from Schenectady, but by then he was cleaned out of gifts. He spoke with fellow Schenectady natives Captain William Horsfall and First Lieutenant E. Nott Schermerhorn, both of Company E, and found them to be "hearty and well" despite not having eaten since the evening before. If the officers had fasted by lack of supplies, you can guarantee their men shared the same discomforts. The want of food was never far from anyone's thoughts. Horsfall admitted to Van Santvoord that the "best thing to sustain life and strength is dried and smoked beef." Unfortunately, Horsfall left what little piece he had back in his camp chest and personally could not stop thinking about it during the march. Back out on the search for more supplies, Van Santvoord later crossed paths with Sergeant Frank Graves of Company A, not far from where the regiment was at near Fort Pennsylvania in Tenleytown. By then, Van Santvoord had collected some dried fruit in which he gave to Graves under the directive that he share with Horsfall, who was probably still gripped in thought about his piece of abandoned beef. Like so many in the regiment, Graves had mutual respect for Horsfall and gladly received the gift, despite being loaded down with his own weight of war essentials.[20]

Recovering in Washington from his Gaines's Mill wound, First Lieutenant Horatio G. Goodno of Company K took a brief excursion from his hospital when he caught wind that the 18th had passed through the city. When Goodno located the regiment near Tenleytown, he found them in what he described as, "in a mournful state nearly all sick or worn out." Wearing the faces of exhaustion from the recent march, Goodno knew these men would have to find it deep within themselves for what everyone knew would be a new campaign that would usher more carnage. In a letter to his wife a few days later, Goodno wrote to inform her that "you will hear of a Big Battle being fought in Maryland within ten days or sooner."[21]

Pleasantly surprised to have a longer wait before the next march, the 18th did not get back on the road until 5 p.m. on September 7. They blew through Tenleytown and traversed another ten miles and rested a few miles shy of Rockville, Maryland, at a place called Rabbit's farm. They picked back up the next morning and pushed out at 7 a.m. for a couple more miles until they reached the village. McClellan and his staff had made temporary headquarters at Rockville, and when the 18th got there they lessened their load in the village when they dropped their knapsacks and every other article of camp equipage they could possibly part with. The men were basically left with nothing more than their shelter-tents, blankets, arms, and ammunition. Everything they dropped was sent back to Washington with each individual hoping they would see their things again in the future. By sending off their extra equipment the men understood a fight with the Rebels was imminent. With less weight, the 18th passed through the town center and stopped for the night at a location called Muddy Run. At 9:30 a.m. September 9, the 18th started a nine mile march that put them at Seneca Run, just beyond

Darnestown by the evening. At one point in the day the regiment was formed up in line of battle after rumors of the enemy's close proximity warranted its exercise, but the enemy never appeared. They set up a brief encampment where they stopped and passed the night undisturbed.[22]

The transient life of the infantrymen and hard marches under the summer sun had sculpted the men's resilience. Occasionally, one or two soldiers straggled from the formation, unable to keep pace, and there were a few more brazen ones who still chose desertion. Privates Warren Warden and Peter Van Hoesen, both of Company B, dashed from Alexandria on September 6 before the regiment began their series of marches. Privates Frank Boyle and John F. Krug, both of Company F, deserted on September 7. Musician Robert T. Ardill of Company K left the regiment on the march at Rockville on September 8.[23]

Private Alonzo Richardson of Company F had walked a mile with his company on September 6 before he realized he had left his canteen back at camp. Whether his mistake was valid is up for contention, for he never made it back to the regiment. Richardson later stated that after he relocated his canteen, he tried to gain ground towards the company, but while crossing the Long Bridge his arm was broken by a runaway team and was hospitalized. During a later attempt to rejoin the regiment Richardson was incarcerated for being accused of stealing sheep. Richardson would not reunite back with his company for several months, but they had already chalked him up to be another common deserter.[24]

The morning of September 10, the regiment marched three-and-a-half miles and passed through the village of Dawsonville, but they pushed on for another nine rainy miles and reached Barnesville where they again set up another encampment about 4 p.m. Three miles north of Barnesville loomed the commanding position of Sugar Loaf Mountain. Its natural physical shape granted its name, and stood 750 feet above the surrounding land. A forward Union cavalry force with two guns attempted to dislodge the hill from a small Confederate cavalry occupation to no avail. Its importance was later emphasized to Franklin to help rid the enemy from its strategic heights, but his hesitation postponed any attempt until the following day. The 18th remained encamped at their position in Barnesville for over thirty-six hours. As the other divisions and corps nearby shifted their position the following day of September 11, Franklin finally sent Hancock's brigade and a brigade of cavalry and dislodged the cluster of enemy cavalry from atop Sugar Loaf Mountain. The remaining brigades under Franklin passed the rainy day quietly in their same camp.[25]

At 8 a.m. on September 12, the regiment picked up the march and passed through Barnesville and on towards the Monocacy River, via Urbana. For several hours the men trekked a "tedius and disagreeable march" until their arrival to the last named place by 4 p.m. They established another hasty camp on the east side of the friendly occupied Sugar Loaf Mountain.[26]

While the 18th pushed through Maryland, two more ailing soldiers were shipped out by the surgeon's recommendation to join the increasing roster of hospitalized soldiers stretched throughout Northern cities. Most often those who were hospitalized rarely recovered enough to return to duty, but nothing could deter Private Bronson Mills of Company D from missing the inevitable action with his company. He had recently been hospitalized for sickness in Alexandria when the regiment left the city. Three days behind the regiment, Mills decided to take his ailing self out of the hospital and track down the regiment before they got too far away. He tramped nearly seventy miles, a march that was said in his words, "enough to kill or cure a sick person, and it cured me."[27]

Captain John Hastings, commander and original organizer of Company B, accepted a promotion outside of the regiment and became a lieutenant colonel in the newly formed 113th New York. He left the 18th for his new position on September 8, and began a new path of service with the 113th—which later became the 7th New York Heavy Artillery. With Hastings out, the company was without officers on account of one lieutenant's resignation and the other housed long term in a hospital with a disease. The company fell in the hands of the company's senior non-commissioned officer, First Sergeant William B. Purdy. The captaincy was eventually filled by the transfer of Second Lieutenant Robert A. Malone from Company D. The fact that Malone skipped the rank of first lieutenant entirely proved he was reliable and capable, but he would not join his new company until his recruitment drive in Middletown finished in October, which made him miss the regiment's most memorable battle.[28]

On a positive note for the regiment, more captive soldiers from the 18th were paroled and released from Richmond. Nine privates and one sergeant who were all captured during the Seven Days campaign, were paroled at City Point, Virginia, on September 13. The joyous news would have to take time to travel before it reached the ears of their comrades who were more than 160 miles away. These released prisoners would have been a helpful boost for the regiment, but their distance prevented them from joining the regiment in time for the next fight.[29]

The 18th now stood at roughly 300 strong when they entered Maryland. This startlingly low number for a regiment was commonplace for the veteran regiments in the Army of the Potomac of late 1862. Their experience was still better than a raw regiment, such as the newly formed 121st New York, of which their division received just days before.[30]

The cat-and-mouse game of army occupied villages continued on September 13 when the 18th passed through Buckeystown, just hours after the Rebels had packed up and left. The 18th started their eight mile march early that morning and reached within three miles of the village of Jefferson. Heavy firing was heard to the left of the Union army. The regiment remained in their forward position and retired in an open field at the foot of South Mountain, about three miles east of Jefferson. Constant sightings of the enemy throughout the past few days—occasionally in battle array—made everyone wonder when the next great battle would unfold. Those fated few who would fall in the coming battle had no idea that the night of September 13 would be their last, and an exceptionally chilly one at that.[31]

From his latest headquarters in a camp near Frederick, Maryland, General McClellan finalized his plans of attack on the enemy in Maryland, and he had specific orders for Franklin's VI Corps. Dividing his army into three wings—the center being held in reserve—each were given an attack point at specific gaps, or passes, along the South Mountain range in order to wedge themselves between Lee's divided force on the eastern side. Franklin, commanding the left wing which comprised of the VI Corps and eventually a division from the IV Corps, was given the pivotal role to break through the mountain near Burkittsville, at a place called Crampton's Gap, also known as Crampton's Pass. The added division, under General Couch, had not yet linked up with the VI Corps by September 13, and McClellan stressed that Franklin should move upon the gap at daybreak, even if Couch had not arrived. About seven miles north of Crampton's Gap, was another pass known as Turner's Gap, site of where the I Corps was ordered to punch through the mountain. A mile south of Turner's Gap was Fox's Gap, assigned to the IX Corps to pass over the range. Union reconnaissance still could not verify if Crampton's Gap was occupied by the enemy or not, but if they were found to be in force, McClellan ordered Franklin to attack and take the gap a half hour after fighting is heard from Turner's Gap. Franklin's added task was to "cut off, destroy, or capture McLaw's command" who were reported to be their opposition. Upon that success, Franklin had additional orders to travel through Pleasant Valley and move upon Harpers Ferry and relieve Colonel Dixon S. Miles, whose small force of garrisoned troops were threatened by either total annihilation, or mass capture by the Rebel army that surrounded the heights. The task at hand was a tall order for the VI Corps, and they did not want to disappoint.[32]

14

Battle of Crampton's Gap
September 14, 1862

"On we move with set determination to do or die."
—First Sergeant John Smith King, Company D, October 1, 1862

Setting the Stage

Major General William B. Franklin complied with orders from McClellan to make his move upon his appointed thoroughfare over South Mountain. From a point three miles east of Jefferson, the VI Corps advanced towards the mountain range at daylight on September 14. When the regiment entered the little town of Jefferson they were pleasantly surprised to find a strong Union sentiment among its inhabitants. Maryland was a divided state of allegiances and town influences varied, but in Jefferson nearly every house they passed flew the Stars and Stripes banner. Little children brandished small national flags in their hands and waved them as the soldiers marched through their streets. The allegiance was a welcoming change of pace to the men who were so accustomed to the abject hospitality of Virginians during their unwelcomed stay. A late morning halt was ordered when they passed through Jefferson which allowed the men to stack their rifles and get a brief rest. The broader purpose of the stop was Franklin's attempt to allow an element of the IV Corps to link up with the VI Corps.[1]

The delay of the IV Corps' appearance proved the distance between them and the VI Corps was far greater than initially expected. Instead of extending their halt, Franklin made the men grab their stacked rifles and pushed his corps into the vicinity of neighboring Burkittsville, a small village closest to the mountain range. They arrived at Burkittsville at noon and found the village had just been evacuated of enemy skirmishers. As usual with any halt, the men again stacked their rifles but as soon as they did so they were fired upon by two Rebel batteries. The cannonade ushered the day's fight and were directed upon skirmishers from the first brigade, which was the leading brigade of Slocum's division.[2]

Sergeant Frank Seymour of Company E recalled that "the shells whizzing over our heads proclaimed the close proximity of the Rebels." A few miles off to the north, on their right, the fighting of the I and IX corps at their appointed gaps had been launched, and the 18th could see the smoke from the guns slowly rise up in the distance. In respect to his orders,

14. Battle of Crampton's Gap   265

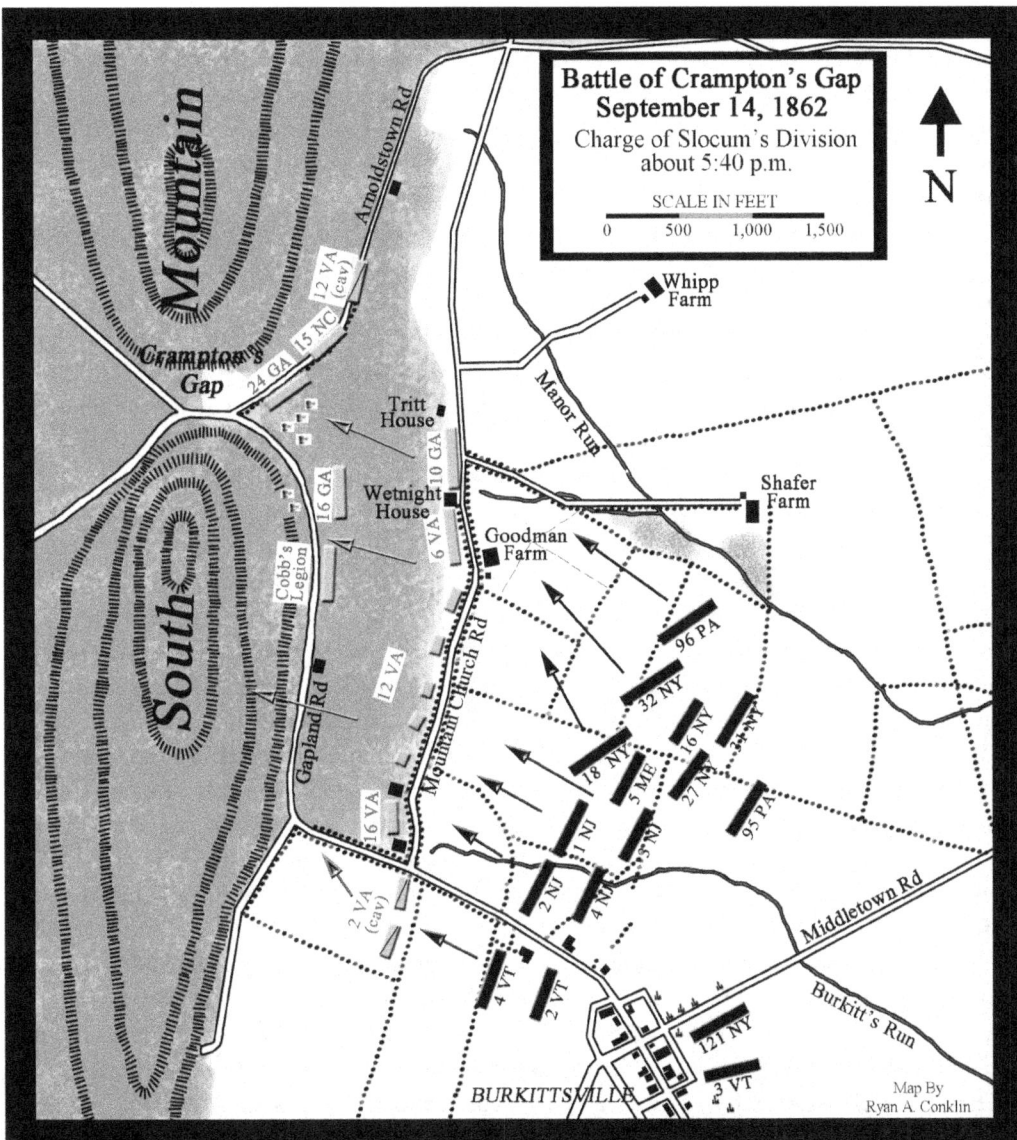

Map of the battle of Crampton's Gap, September 14, 1862, just before the charge of Slocum's division. The 18th New York rushed at an angle, on a path right through the Goodman farm, and farther on to the gap (author's collection).

Franklin had to initiate his attack now that the fight to the north of them was under way, and this meant he would do it without the added element from the IV Corps. At the base of the Confederate-protected ridgeline that Franklin's men faced, the land leveled out, groomed from generations of farmers that cultivated the fertile farmland. A dip in the ridgeline that carved the mountain range before them was their avenue of Crampton's Gap. It was now clear that embedded Confederate forces filled the pass and were poised to defend it. The curvy road that led through the gap was occupied on both sides by an unknown strength, and the Mountain Church Road that ran perpendicular to the pass gave the enemy a long stone wall that was angled perfectly to protect themselves from a frontal assault. The land steeped greatly behind the stone divider and was heavily wooded, which made the pass the only viable avenue over the mountain range. Confederate artillery at Crampton's Gap were staged at six different points that commanded this avenue of approach. From their vantage, they had clear open fields and a couple of farms from which the Yankees would have to traverse through to get to them. The gap was definitely in the Rebel's favor.[3]

With nearly 12,300 men on hand that was the VI Corps, Franklin did not know he was stronger than his foe. Despite Franklin's overestimation of the enemy within the gap, their opposition was actually low in numbers and stretched dangerously thin. Three slimmed infantry regiments from Virginia—6th, 12th, and 16th—under the command of Colonel William Parham, was joined by two dismounted cavalry regiments—2nd and 12th Virginia Cavalry—under Colonel Thomas Munford. Detached from Brigadier General Paul Semmes's brigade, the 10th Georgia joined Parham and Munford's stand. One battery and a section of the short-ranged boat howitzers were posted about halfway up the mountain.[4]

Franklin and his generals gathered for a last minute consultation and reconnaissance of their objective and it was plain to see that the task before his men would not be easy. Franklin and his division and brigade commanders sat casually on the grass and puffed their cigars and conversed on how the day should be played out. Colonel Joseph J. Bartlett showed up to the group mid-conversation after being requested by Slocum to join. Slocum looked at him and asked nonchalantly as to what side of the road that led through the pass he would attack. Bartlett quickly replied, "On the right." Franklin immediately chimed in and said, "Well, gentlemen, that settles it." Bartlett missed the earlier conversations and was confused on what had just been agreed upon. When Bartlett asked Franklin to clarify, he responded with, "the point of attack." Bartlett was perplexed as he felt the generals before him had the better judgment to dictate such a decision, but Slocum related to him that the group had reached a split decision, and it was Bartlett's call that tipped the scale to decide the point of attack.[5]

Franklin chose Slocum's First Division to be the assaulting element that would slip into the gap and attack upon the right, and the 18th belonged to his third brigade under Newton. A field officer with the neighboring 32nd New York was within earshot of the conference of generals and overheard Newton offer and get acceptance for his brigade to lead the assault. The Second Division of the VI Corps under the command of Major General William F. Smith was held in reserve on the east side of Burkittsville. Union artillery posted themselves to the left of their division on commanding ground and joined in the uninterrupted artillery barrage upon the enemy's batteries.[6]

The Starting Line

About 1 p.m., the regiment moved forward with the rest of their division towards the direction of Crampton's Gap. The division had marched nearly ten miles that day and reached a position that put them within a mile of the mountain by about 2 p.m. Utilizing the land to their advantage, the division entered a small ravine along Burkitt's Run that proved convenient for its deep cut under the sloping hills concealed their own numbers and movements from the enemy's perspective.[7]

Eight pieces of enemy artillery had been stationed on the road along the Rebel wall, and also to the left of the pass on its sides and summit. Occasionally, Confederate batteries sent aimless shells in the direction of the division's haven. First Sergeant John S. King, Company D, regarded the meek Confederate shells thrown towards their protected position as a task reserved for an artillerists' "pastime." Union artillery were positioned away from the infantry on their left, and planted themselves behind Burkittsville. They began a steady shelling towards the Confederate lines in the early afternoon.[8]

The weight of the fight fell squarely on the golden shoulders of Slocum, and the assault was arranged in the following order: Slocum chose Bartlett's brigade to shift to the right and begin their direction of attack. His former regiment, the 27th New York, was chosen to spearhead the attack as skirmishers, and the 5th Maine and 16th New York followed in line of battle 200 yards behind the 27th. The regiments of Newton's brigade followed the fashion of Bartlett where two regiments were formed in battle line with 200 yards separation between the follow-on troops. Lieutenant Colonel Myers received his orders from Newton at 3 p.m. and advanced the 18th to their requested position behind Bartlett's brigade. The 31st New York and 95th Pennsylvania formed behind them as support to the 18th and 32nd. General Alfred T. A. Torbert's brigade became the third wave and formed the same formation and distance behind Newton's line. The 96th Pennsylvania of Bartlett's brigade briefly remained behind in the village but would later be called upon to join the assaulting column. The 121st New York, being as it was the newest to the corps just days before, kept their untested recruits held in reserve in Burkittsville behind all of the assaulting elements, blind to the battle.[9]

At nearly 4 p.m., skirmishers of the 27th New York were the first to be pushed out towards the enemy line and went untouched for a short while. When the interval behind the skirmishers was reached, Bartlett pushed out the 5th Maine and 16th New York at the double-quick. The 18th watched from 300 yards behind the rushing wave and waited for the inevitable. Suddenly, a large puff of smoke rose from the middle of the mountain near the gap, followed by the delayed echo from the cannon blast. Bartlett's entire line got hotly engaged under a concentrated artillery fire from the heights above but held firm their line as if they were performing a drill. The Union skirmishers quickly drew rifle fire the closer they approached the Rebels who were nestled safely behind their high stone wall. The rifle fire increased for the main assaulting lines of Bartlett's men behind the skirmishers. A rough visual estimation of the enemy's strength was hard to establish because the woods concealed their numbers, so they had to go in blind with hopes for the best. Skirmishers withdrew and melted into the battle line of their brigade. Under the heavy fire and exposure over open terrain, Bartlett's two regiments reached a wooden rail-fence less than 300 yards from the enemy's heavier protected line and held their position nestled behind its wooden fixtures. The front line commenced in a lopsided shoot-out that greatly favored the defensive Confederates.[10]

Confederate soldiers remained snug behind their stone shields with their artillery in the mountain pass to help. The stone wall along the Mountain Church Road that the enemy occupied was at places piled low and topped with a wooden zigzag fence, and men hugged the ground wherever the stones seemed highest. Slocum quickly shifted his view in support of the necessity of Union artillery support. He feared that "the stone wall behind which the enemy had taken cover would prove an insurmountable obstacle" to his infantry advance. He expended every effort to have the artillery brought forward, but they would not arrive in time to help the infantry who were about to prove they did not need the support. The commanding generals all agreed that the reliance of infantry alone would swiftly cleanse the desired ground.[11]

18th Takes the Front Line

Newton had been consumed with sickness during the days that led to the battle. He actually traveled in an ambulance, but on this day he mustered up strength and saddled up. When Bartlett looked back for the rest of the attacking column of Newton's brigade who were supposed to be on his heels, he noticed that their distance somehow stretched back to about 1,000 yards. Newton focused on the Rebel battery before him that appeared in the mountain pass which fired upon the forward skirmishers. He looked upon the 18th and 32nd New York regiments to silence them and bolster Bartlett's line on his right. The 18th and 32nd broke off from Newton's control and fell under the temporary command of Bartlett. Newton's two other remaining regiments were then attached to Bartlett's left. First Sergeant King recalled a more vivid account of Newton's decision to advance the regiment after the split of the brigade:

> As this moment Gen. Newton came riding up, and, with his usual sang froid says: '18th, that battery is becoming very annoying. I wish you to silence it. You have good eyes, good hearts and good arms, and if you cannot do it I give you all up. *Shoulder Arms*! *Forward March*!' and on we move with set determination to do or die.[12]

First Sgt. John Smith King of Company D served in the role of first lieutenant for the Wallkill Guards during the battle of Crampton's Gap, Maryland. When the regiment advanced towards the gap, King said, "On we move with set determination to do or die" (archive of the Historical Society of the Town of Warwick, gift of Joan and Tom Frangos).

Over the open terrain, the 18th and 32nd moved towards Bartlett's men. Artillery fire seemed to shadow their advance. One shell knocked the rifle out of the hands of Private Vinson H. Clark of Company D and wounded his hands slightly. Though he was miraculously saved from any life threatening injury, the close call derailed the nerves of the thirty-five-year-old farmer from Milford, New York, who would from then on refuse to enter another battle.[13]

One shell almost took out the leadership of Company K, who were already under the transferred command of First Lieutenant John Vedder of Company E. With no officers left in the company, Vedder was temporarily transferred to lead the company. He was almost killed when a shell struck so close to him and Corporal John M. Fay that they were both knocked over and showered with dirt. Both with wide-eyes and a self check for any wounds, Vedder and Fay brushed the soil off and considered themselves quite fortunate.[14]

Company K was hit with a shell while on the advance which exploded next to Private James Garrity, originally from Summerhill, Ireland. The cannon shell struck so near to him that a large portion of both of his buttocks were ripped off. He fell in painful agony and was quickly carried off to the rear, away from what would be his last battle. Garrity survived his wound but would be discharged on account of the disability incurred.[15]

First Sergeant King still wore the diamond and chevrons of his rank, but served as second-in-command for Company D as a lieutenant before rank was properly bestowed upon him. As he encouraged his men to stay steady during the advance the actions that surrounded him were notable:

> the battery, as if aware of our intentions, sent their defiance in the shape of shells. They had calculated the range with great exactness. They strike at the left of Co. D, prostrating some half a dozen from the effects of the explosion, and wounding pretty severely some of the adjoining company. On we go, those who are able jumping quickly to their feet, and clutching gun and cap rapidly regain their places in line. As we move on I glance back. Two still lay there, seemingly without life or motion, but we have no time to attend to them, and they are left.[16]

First Lt. John Vedder of Company E became the interim commander of Company K at the battle of Crampton's Gap, Maryland. The company was depleted of officers before the fight. Vedder himself escaped a certain death early on when an enemy shell struck so close that he was knocked over and showered with dirt (courtesy New York State Military Museum).

Mourning the dead would have to wait, and the bodies were left where they fell. The 18th eventually reached to within fifty yards behind Bartlett's men who were still lodged behind a rail fence less than 300 yards from the Mountain Church Road where the enemy held firm. Myers brought the 18th to a halt there behind Bartlett's men who continued their unending fire upon the enemy to their front. The 18th itched to enter the battle, but Myers waited for the order which soon came when one of the general's aides rode up to him with additional instructions. He pointed out the placement to Myers which would be on the right of Bartlett's line. Myers complied and shifted the 18th by the right flank and settled them behind a stone wall where they finally began to fire upon the enemy. They wedged themselves between the 16th New York who were on their left, and the 32nd New York on their right. The 18th continued to fire towards their foe to the front, but their distance was too great to be accurate. They wasted their ammunition in the process. The only precise killings inflicted upon their enemy were from those who peered over the stone-piled line to take aim but be exposed enough to take a bullet in their head.[17]

Bartlett eventually pulled back the 16th New York and 5th Maine twenty paces behind the 18th and 32nd, as almost all of their ammunition had been depleted by then. The 18th stepped over the 16th who crawled behind them and allowed the 18th to nestle themselves behind the fence. "We covered ourselves as well as possible behind a rail fence and spent a couple of hours popping away at each other without any definite result," wrote Sergeant Seymour. Rebel artillery on the mountain zeroed in on the Yankee line and walked their shrieking shells closer to the 18th's position. The Confederates embedded behind their stones and fences along the Mountain Church Road were stretched thin, and only massed about 800 defenders, and had Bartlett known this figure he would not have waited as long as he did to push a frontal attack. Until he did, the time allowed Confederates to choose their shots with careful aim. The screams of the wounded throughout the 18th's line only multiplied unless death hushed their agony. Private Nelson McDonald of Company E became impaired from firing a musket when a bullet smacked into his right hand and essentially tore off two of his fingers. Captain Michael H. Donovan, commander of Company F, watched one of his soldiers get shot just a few paces from him. Private Francis Noonan of Donovan's company took a bullet to his right shin, just above his ankle. Donovan immediately had Noonan removed a short distance and aligned him behind the protection of a slight cover on the ground to avoid any further injury. Donovan could tell the regiment would not remain where they were and personally promised Noonan the company would return for him when the battle was decided.[18]

Torbert brought up his brigade of four New Jersey regiments behind Newton and they secured the same fence rail and established the left of Bartlett's line. The front force similarly began to open fire as soon as they got in place. Bartlett was also returned with the appearance of his 96th Pennsylvania, in which he pushed out to connect to the far right of the line on the right of the 32nd New York.[19]

The Charge of Slocum's Division

Bartlett could tell that only a swift and united sweep of the infantry would quickly dislodge the enemy. With the line set as best as planned, Bartlett had a brief council with Torbert and issued the words for a charge. As the word trickled down the lines, Bartlett also called for a cease-fire. The orders of the cease-fire reached Myers first, and he knew a charge was in order. Everyone seemed to feel it. The rifle fire tapered off all along the stretched line of Slocum's division. A strange silence settled through the Union line, but Confederate artillery continued to perfect their range upon the burrowed infantrymen. The point of no return had arrived to the men of blue during the standoff. They were granted just a few moments to survey the terrain ahead of them and to mentally prepare themselves and motivate each other for what was next. Cheers for "Little Mac" rose up and down the line in rapid succession. Slocum's division had been exposed to an hour and a half of perpetual fire and they understood that their casualties had mounted higher than that of their entrenched enemy. Now the tide was about to turn. Orders to fix bayonets was hollered and obeyed by Slocum's entire line, which affirmed that a charge was indeed expected. The slaps of steel to their musket tips echoed across the land, and the dark blue line acquired an intimidating silver glow.[20]

About 5:30 p.m., Bartlett gave the signal to charge, but somehow the universal command did not liftoff a unison charge. Torbert's New Jersey men to the left of the 18th may have been a bit premature, but they jumped first and eventually their howls were enough to spread the signal to the rest of the division.[21]

"Forward, Eighteenth!" was screamed by Lieutenant Colonel Myers and the regiment sprung to their feet and slipped over the fence rail. At the double-quick, Myers pushed the 18th forward through a cornfield and obliterated the stalks as they busted through. The stretched line of New Yorkers formed an impressive front of blue across the landscape as they sprinted towards the Rebel wall behind the Mountain Church Road. Company officers out front pointed forward their swords with shouts to follow to the men behind them, but were mostly drowned out by the sound of battle and screams of the charging troops that could have rivaled the famed Rebel Yell. Myers, Meginnis, and Gridley encouraged the men excessively. Their coolness and courage was infectious to those they led. Random soldiers tumbled to the ground as bullets picked them off and knocked them out of the rushing horde. Animate soldiers instantly turned to lifeless corpses that at random crashed to the dirt with total disregard. Private Maurice E. Haythorne of Company C was a nineteen-year-old cigar-maker by trade, but his death on the field marked him as the youngest from the regiment to die. Forward they continued and the habitual elbow rubbing within the ranks opened as holes grew. Men screamed. Eyes were determined. With quick feet, the regiment dashed through an orchard next to the Jacob Goodman farm and neared the Mountain Church Road at the base of the hill.[22]

All Lt. Col. George R. Myers had to yell was, "Forward, Eighteenth!" and the regiment successfully stormed the Rebel line at Crampton's Gap, Maryland, September 14, 1862 (Roger D. Hunt collection, United States Army Heritage and Education Center, Carlisle, Pennsylvania).

The regiment quickly retook its shape. By then, the charge by Torbert's New Jersey men signaled Myers to do the same. The 32nd on their right started just before the 18th, and they moved obliquely to the right after the 96th Pennsylvania likewise unleashed their charge. "The example is contagious," said First Sergeant King, "from right to left the whole front are madly rushing on." The mad rush of the regiment "had become somewhat broken" after the right half of the regiment veered to the right and closer to the 32nd. Myers immediately halted them and snapped out commands to reform. The 16th had moved up on some pockets in the middle and to the left of the 18th. Myers ordered the end-all command to charge. "With the bound of race horses and the yell of demons, our men sprang at the hill," wrote First Lieutenant E. Nott Schermerhorn. His vantage of the regiment was supreme, as he controlled and led the left wing as the adjutant. When their wave began to crest the hill of the road that ran along the side of the mountain, they received a punishing volley from the enemy behind the wall at close range. The 18th took the punch near Mountain Church Road like a sudden gust of wind had hit them and staggered for a moment, but as the smoke cleared they regained their objective and were unleashed into a frenzied charge against what was left of the depleted 6th and 12th Virginia. "Hurrah! They're running!" First Sergeant King yelled when he realized the enemy had abandoned their stand after their volley, "At them boys!" They broke the enemy, but at a price. Bullets from this "well directed and fatal" volley at the crest of the hill felled more soldiers from the regiment than any other portion of the day's fight. Dozens of 18th men coated the ground, and several twisted in painful agony while others remained motionless at peace. Twenty-year-old Private William J. Storms of Company C was killed almost immediately after a ball penetrated right through his forehead. Storms, an unwed man, supported his widowed mother with the money he earned as a soldier. Also among the dead was Corporal Edward M. Fogerty, Company I, who was an Irish native that worked at the same moulding foundry in Albany that Colonel Young had served as his supervisor. Private Abraham Blaisdell of Company K and Private George

Modern view from the Confederate line on Mountain Church Road, looking towards the open field where the 18th New York charged, starting from the right of the photograph, and on an angled path to the bottom left. The dip in the terrain where the 18th New York took their last brutal volley at close range can still be seen (author's collection).

Martin of Company B were both Canadian-born citizens that fell dead and would never see the success that came from their sacrificial charge. Martin was killed outright when he was shot in two places, one of which entered his left side near his heart, and the other in his shoulder. He left a wife and child back home in Albany to mourn. Blaisdell, a single father whose own wife passed away a month before the start of the war, orphaned his two-year-old daughter.[23]

In blood covered pants, Private Anthony Cole Bullent of Company F grimaced in pain from a bullet that crashed into his left thigh. A silversmith born in Yarmouth, England, Bullent could tell from his wound that there would be little that could be done to save his leg, but one wonders if his thoughts were also with his little brother—a corporal in the neighboring 32nd New York—who went through the same hellish charge.[24]

One of the most beloved soldiers in the regiment was Captain William Horsfall, who was out in front of his Company E when he was felled by this final Rebel volley. With his sword pointed towards their objective, Horsfall encouraged his men to follow him, but was stopped by a musket ball from the volley that pierced his chest just above his heart and passed through his body. First Lieutenant Schermerhorn was close at hand and rushed to his friend "Billy" as he fell and heard him utter what became his last words, "I am gone up." Schermer-

Left: Born in Yarmouth, England, twenty-six-year-old Pvt. Anthony Cole Bullent of Company F was wounded in his left thigh at Crampton's Gap, Maryland, September 14, 1862, and had the leg amputated the day after the battle (courtesy New York State Military Museum). *Right:* One of the most beloved soldiers in the regiment was Capt. William Horsfall of Company E. "Billy" was killed while out in front of his company during the charge at Crampton's Gap, Maryland, September 14, 1862 (author's collection)

horn looked around and yelled for help at the nearest privates and had them place Horsfall in a blanket and carried to the rear, but death settled quickly for the captain. Being a close friend and the last to see him alive, Schermerhorn would take the solemn duty to pen a letter to Horsfall's brother two days after the battle with an explanation on how he died, and render a tribute to say, "Billy was a favorite with the entire regiment, his noble qualities won the respect of all, while his social and generous disposition won their affections. He was in truth a charming gentleman and his place cannot be filled." Horsfall had served more than twenty years as a member of his city's militia, the Schenectady Washington Continentals, and had been a long acquainted associate of Captain Gridley during the antebellum years. Gridley and Horsfall's friendship carried over to their time together in the 18th, and after his death Gridley attempted to publically eulogize Horsfall in a Schenectady newspaper:

I have always found him at home a gentleman and a good citizen; in the field he was a brave and true patriot, and has done all that man ever did for his country. I wish I were able to do justice to his memory, but I am not and must leave that task to an abler pen.[25]

One of Horsfall's non-commissioned officers, Sergeant Frank Seymour, penned a similar offering of lament about his captain to friends back home:

In him our country loses one of its bravest defenders and this regiment one of its brightest ornaments. Great military proficiency, added to kind, genial, nature, made him one of the best of officers, such a one in fact as it is hard to find, and his loss cannot easily be replaced. Another name is added to the long list of 'Our Country's Martyrs'—another brave, true heart now lies pulse-less a victim of this unholy rebellion, and another 'stark, stiff seal of condemnation,' is laid upon the arch traitors who inaugurated this fratricidal war. Peace to his ashes.[26]

As 1st Lt. Daniel H. Daley led Company A during the regiment's charge at Crampton's Gap, Maryland, September 14, 1862, he was shot in his right shoulder and his arm was rendered useless but was saved from amputation. He received an overdue promotion to captain but had to resign on account of his injury. Pictured as a captain, Daley seems to hide his injury that eventually worsened and killed him in 1866 (courtesy Clark Hotaling).

The other Schenectady company narrowly escaped the same fate as Company E. Twenty-one-year-old First Lieutenant Daniel H. Daley was out in front of Company A and led them in the charge. He did so until two musket balls from the same final volley found their mark with Daley, which both penetrated into his right shoulder blade and lodged into his chest. Daley was a natural leader and had the full confidence of his company, proven first in battle during the Peninsula campaign. When the time came for his official report of the battle, Lieutenant Colonel Myers could not say enough about Daley and extended his praise to include Captain A. Barclay Mitchell of Company C to say, they were "courageous to a fault, rallying and encouraging their men under the heaviest fire." Daley's grievous double wound rendered the whole limb from the shoulder down almost entirely useless, but the arm was saved from amputation. After a lengthy hospitalization Daley penned his resignation in February. Before he was discharged, Gridley made sure his friend received the rank he had earned and pinned captain bars on Daley's shoulders two months after the battle. Daley's wound led to life-long health complications such as swelling, abscesses, and hemorrhaging of the lungs. Three-and-a-half years after the battle, doctors removed one of the musket balls, but it came as little relief to his emaciated body. Consumption of the lungs after the surgery got the better of him, and Daley died in Schenectady on October 16, 1866, at the age of twenty-five.[27]

Following Daley's example, Private John Van Bueren of Company A ran behind him with his comrades in the charge until a bullet crashed into his skull and killed him almost instantly. The twenty-nine-year-old had the taste for adventure and unlike many of his comrades he had the experience of a worldly traveler. Van Bueren and his family immigrated to America from their home in Dordrecht, Holland, in 1848. When Van Bueren turned twenty, he left the household and began a seafaring life and traveled to several countries during a three-year course. When he returned to Albany, Van Bueren began an intense study of the Bible at the Holland Dutch Reformed Church in the city. He would have become a member of the church had he not been spun up in the war and enlisted, but "his heart was with his adopted country," friends said, "and he was willing to offer up his life, if necessary, to sustain it." His mother had begged him not to go, but the good son reassured her, "Mother, you will be proud of me when I return home." But he never did. Van Bueren did not utter a word when the fatal bullet took him down.[28]

Second Lieutenant William H. Ellis, Jr., had commanded Company G through the battles on the peninsula, but on this day he had the help from newly promoted First Lieutenant Alfred M. Chesmore from Company I who was transferred to Company G shortly before the fight. Disregarding the fact that aggressive company commanders made enticing targets for Rebels, Chesmore and Ellis exemplified leadership and kept themselves out in front of their men until the same volley that felled Horsfall and Daley struck them too. Ellis received a rifle ball that penetrated straight through the inside of his left thigh four inches above his knee and created an even worse exit wound. Ellis instantly dropped to the ground and tried to control his own bleeding. Miraculously, Ellis' wound missed his femoral artery which would have ushered a quick death. The wound peeled back and exposed a large portion of his skin and muscle and was excruciatingly painful. He was hauled from the battlefield and dropped off at a nearby house where Dr. Rice applied the first bandages that helped save Ellis' life. He made a brief return to the regiment in November, but had to resign on account of his wound in February. Chesmore's wound was minor in comparison to Ellis. Chesmore was considered lucky to have had the skin knocked off one of his thumbs by a musket ball. At the end of the fight he inspected himself and found two bullets

Transferred to Company I from Company F a month before the Maryland Campaign, 1st Lt. Alfred Milton Chesmore found two bullets had passed through his cap, two through his jacket, and one through his canteen after the battle of Crampton's Gap, Maryland. He also received his second wound in a battle after a bullet scraped skin off his thumb (United States Army Heritage and Education Center, Carlisle, Pennsylvania).

had passed through his cap, two through his jacket, and another pair bored through his canteen. Previously wounded at Gaines's Mill, Chesmore was one of the few men in the regiment to be wounded in more than one engagement.[29]

Enemy troops saw nothing was going to stop the Union assault. Before the smoke lifted from their final volley at close range, their line behind the wall dissolved. They broke for their rear in haphazard disorder as the wave of blue chewed into their line. Some Rebels stood their ground and were either sliced down by the bayonet or captured. Southerners that chose to fight another day had to hike up a steep and treacherous mountaintop behind them that was chock-full of protruding rocks, ledges, underbrush, and timber.[30]

Enemy reinforcements in the form of two new infantry regiments under the command of General Howell Cobb entered the gap from their side of Pleasant Valley. They arrived under a double-quick, but their entrance was just in time to witness the overthrow of their compatriot's position and ensuing melee. Cobb had been delayed in getting to the mountain earlier in the day which without could have greatly altered their measly defense. Munford was outranked by Cobb and turned the withering defenses over to the general. Cobb asked Munford to place his two regiments where they were needed most, and Munford tried but he spoke of these regiments to say, "they behaved badly and did not get in position before the wildest confusion commenced." The reinforcements only worsened their own rout and erased the opportunity for another rally. Their fresh troops were instantly pelted with demoralized and scattered Rebels, injured and non-injured, who broke through their lines at hell-bent speeds in order to save themselves. Munford added, "General Cobb attempted to rally the men, but without the least effect, and it would have been as useless to attempt to rally a flock of frightened sheep." The scene was a welcomed reversal of past conflicts for the men in blue. The 18th hurdled over the enemy stone wall and raced into the darkened woods with an almost perpendicular incline that gradually grew steeper and rougher.[31]

The second line of Confederate reinforcements was still able to fire a volley from the crest of the mountain that managed to be semi-effective. Colonel Roderick Matheson, commander of the 32nd New York, received a mortal wound from this effort. As he was rushed to the rear by his men and passed by the 18th, Matheson was heard to have yelled, "Forward, Eighteenth, the Thirty-Second is with you." There was little more than Matheson's injury that could further fuel the 32nd, but the 18th felt the sting too. Matheson helped see the 18th through their last major engagement and shadowed them when Major Meginnis led the regiment. Matheson died from his wounds in less than a month.[32]

The 18th and the 32nd pushed out the Rebels and had since greatly depleted their ammunition. Major Meginnis sought out Colonel Bartlett and yelled to him, "Colonel, my men are out of cartridges." Bartlett replied, "Never mind, Major. Push on, we have got 'em on the run. The regiments each side of you have got ammunition and are using it." Meginnis smiled and turned back to the regiment and encouraged them as they pushed onward.[33]

The vain Confederate reinforcements that appeared were quickly dispersed and pushed out of the gap and over the other side of the mountain, "scattering them like sheep." The mishmash of unrelenting Yankees flushed the woods and remained tight upon their heels. One Company D soldier joked in a letter home to relatives that "you must not think the rebels were any better on the run than our own men." The pursuant New Yorkers came face-to-face with pockets of freely surrendering foe who threw down their rifles, but their focus was beyond them. The will to fight had noticeably left their enemy as they walked defenselessly

"Rebels flying like frightened hares before us," was how Sgt. Frank Seymour, Company E, described the Confederate retreat at Crampton's Gap, Maryland, September 14, 1862. He was wounded in his left arm during the battle, but eventually returned to the regiment. He later served with the 1st New York Veteran Cavalry, but died in 1864 as a prisoner at Andersonville (courtesy New York State Military Museum).

down the mountain toward the Union rear in scores without guards. The advancing Yankee line barely stopped to corral and escort them, as they had "no time to take prisoners," and instead they climbed higher into the forest and continued their hunt.[34]

When most of the men had reached the crest of the hill nearly out of breath, Myers attempted to halt what was left of his regiment and reform the companies. Regimental identity had become an intermeshed mob of New Yorkers and Pennsylvanians. The singular charge of the division was short-lived but proved incredibly effective. The adrenaline-infused Yankees seemed unwilling to stop their pursuit. Formerly of Company K, Captain Edward M. Tilley viewed the battle with Newton's staff where he served as the brigade quartermaster. From his vantage, Tilley stated that "the boys went up the hill with a will and did not stop until everything in sight in the shape of a rebel, was cleaned out." A soldier in Company D noted that the climb was so steep in areas that their chase of the enemy was done so at times on hands and knees, all the while under sporadic potshots from Confederates who hunkered behind trees and rock ledges. Sergeant Seymour stated that, "our bodies seemed endowed with supernatural strength, and forward up the mountains we pushed, the Rebels flying like frightened hares before us." Seymour's feeling of immortality changed when he was awakened by the reality of a ball that entered his left arm about two inches below his elbow. Lucky for him, the ball lodged against the bone instead of breaking it, which would have meant a certain amputation.[35]

The Gap Is Won

Officers scrambled to reorganize and reform their intertwined regiments who surpassed the stone wall. In near darkness, Major Meginnis bumped into Colonel Henry L. Cake, commander of the 96th Pennsylvania, and promised to form what was left of the 18th on Cake's left and jointly push up the mountain with the 16th and 32nd. Cake wanted to maintain a line of defense in the event a stand was made by the enemy at the crest. Despite their best efforts, men continued to stay outside of a formation and ran at their own fervent pace. Those who made it to the top had to stop their pursuit to both catch their breath and wait for more men. A winded First Lieutenant John M. Dempsey of Company F who made it to the top ahead of the bulk of the regiment took notice that he was one of three officers of the 18th that trekked to the top. One Wallkill Guard who crested the ridge recalled that only ten others from his Company D kept the tiresome pace and rallied around their company and regimental colors. The Wallkill Guards' flag had since been allowed to be carried in battle and had amassed only four bullet holes from battles previous before the day. At the commencement of hostilities at Crampton's Gap, Corporal Thomas Curry stood at the mountain's crest with the company flag in his clutches which he then counted twenty-two holes had riddled through its silk. "Through and through its silken folds," as First Sergeant King characterized, "go the leaden messengers of death." Those first few that sprinted ahead of the regiment eventually backtracked down the crest when things quieted down and rejoined the rest of the regiment. Myers sent off his adjutant to ascertain further orders while he helped his company commanders regroup the regiment. Instructions came back quickly with the adjutant with orders from a staff member of General Slocum that dictated Myers needed to immediately reorganize the 18th, and have them rest in place on the ground that had just become hallowed. The sun slipped away and formally brought a close to the bloodshed.[36]

The welcomed breather lasted for merely an hour, but was enough to usher in the harsh realization of their loss to come to light. Men looked around and searched for close friends and felt the absence of many. The bodies of their pale friends and foe remained strewn behind them. Being on the reverse side of the Confederate wall, the men surveyed piles of dead and saw the effect of their fire when they noticed numerous bodies with horrific head wounds. Rebel knapsacks were still piled in heaps as they were before the escalation of the battle. Shouts of requested help from the wounded stirred up the morbid atmosphere. Circles of friends gathered together and recounted the actions of the day to each other. Personal prayers and halleluiahs were undoubtedly spoken by the survivors of the thinned regiment as reality began to settle in.[37]

Calculating the Casualties

Private Richard Hennessy of Company B was a twenty-year-old Irish immigrant who worked as a laborer before the war, but he was one of many who paid the ultimate sacrifice during the day. Most in the regiment knew of his name for a sad incident that took place back in November 1861, when he was the soldier that accidentally killed sixteen-year-old Private James Rice of his company after having mishandled a rifle. Now, as if in an effort to repay the debt of Rice's lost life, Hennessy gave his during the regiment's finest hour.[38]

The strength of the regiment stood at roughly 300 men before the day. By the end of the day, ten soldiers were dead, and another forty-seven were wounded, according to the compiled service records and pension records housed at the National Archives. Two days after the battle, the regimental adjutant, First Lieutenant Schermerhorn, tallied a nearly identical total loss of fifty-eight killed and wounded. With the exception of Horsfall, all of the soldiers that died on the day of the battle from the 18th were enlisted men. Additionally, seven of the seriously wounded eventually died at later dates from their injuries. Companies D, G, and H ended the day without the death of a man, but they had their wounded. E, F, I and K all lost one man by the end of the fight, and A, B, and C each lost two. Once all the mortally wounded men died in time, every company had a loss of life except Company D.[39]

Three commissioned officers and forty-four enlisted soldiers from the regiment were wounded by gunshots or shells. Whereas all companies averaged about four men wounded in the day, Company F stood alone with the most, having eleven. Three soldiers from the 18th were also shortly

Pvt. John Webley Jaycox of Company C was wounded in his left leg at Crampton's Gap, Maryland, September 14, 1862 (courtesy New York State Military Museum).

declared missing immediately after the battle by Gridley, but within a day or two they were accounted for. Once rumored by Fishkill newspapers to have died the previous spring, Private John W. Jaycox of Company C almost fulfilled the previous error when he received a ball that pierced into his left leg, just above his knee, but he lived to tell his friends back home about it. Private William Henry White of Company C was one of the many adolescents who lied about their age in order to join a man's army. White was a laborer from the same hometown as Jaycox and had turned eighteen just two months before the battle. He was wounded twice at Crampton's Gap, shot in the left leg and hand. Another comrade from Company C to fall with two wounds was Private Leonard Raymond, shot in both legs, but he was back on his feet after a few months of recovery and returned to the regiment. Private Joseph Taylor of Company H suffered a skull fracture from the fight, but he too would recover in time to return to the line. An unfortunate accident occurred to Private John Burns of Company G during the battle. He was shot in the shoulder from behind by one of his comrades, which could be explained either by a musket being dropped, or during the melee of the charge he could have stepped in front of someone's aim. Luckily, he recovered and later returned to the ranks. A few soldiers had such minor wounds that they were never tallied to the total number of wounded until now. Soldiers like Private Thomas J. Ketcham of Company D took a small wound to his face, but as he explained, "it was just a flesh wound on the cheek" which healed quickly without a scar, but he was never noted on the original list of wounded. Private Peter Bird of Company F was wounded in his left heel, and not far from him was an enemy combatant from the 2nd Virginia Cavalry that shared his exact name, except he was dead.[40]

About an hour after the battle subsided, Privates Thomas McCormick and William H. McKinney of Company E scoured the field in search of their longtime friend, Private Alexander Abercrombie. McCormick had seen Abercrombie fall during the charge, but McCormick stayed with the advance. Retracing their path, the two eventually came across Abercrombie who was alive but a victim of dual wounds. Abercrombie was knocked out of the ranks when a *Minié* ball pierced through the top of his right ankle. It edged around his tibia, fractured his fibula, and popped out near his Achilles heel. Almost immediately after he fell to the ground, another bullet ripped through Abercrombie's upper left thigh that entered near his buttocks and traveled out his front thigh which left a gash of about six inches in length. McCormick and McKinney secured an ambulance for Abercrombie and had him taken to the regimental surgeons where his wounds were patched and his life saved.[41]

Records for casualties on both sides varied widely as their strengths and losses were inaccurately estimated, never filed, or lumped with casualties from the subsequent battle of Antietam. Author Timothy J. Reese compiled a postwar study of casualty statistics at Crampton's Gap from a cross-reference of sources from which numbers can serve as the nearest reflection of authenticity. Confederate losses trumped Union casualties with 179 killed or mortally wounded, most of which came from Georgia. The Union loss, though great when compared to how many were engaged, tallied to around 152 killed or mortally wounded. The injured on both sides were hefty, but given the fact that the Union advance was exposed longer over open terrain and subjected to artillery, their number still stood less than their adversaries: Union, 289; Confederate, 317. Capturing the enemy was the game of the day, and the bounty of prisoners was great for the Federals that captured over 400 Confederates. This massive collection of Rebel prisoners made their casualty list far exceed the boys in blue. Captured Rebels swarmed all around the men from the 18th who must have felt like they were amidst a sea of butternut and brown. Visual estimates from the excited troops wanted to believe they had captured nearly 1,000 Rebel prisoners.[42]

Leading up to the South Mountain victory, the Army of the Potomac had been greatly reduced in numbers since their stay on the peninsula. General Slocum concluded his official orders of the Crampton's Gap fight and gave full praise to the men of his division who never gave up on themselves or each other after months of hardship between two campaigns:

> Although fatigued by long marches and constant service since the opening of the spring campaign, each regiment—indeed, every man—did his whole duty, not reluctantly, but with that eagerness and enthusiasm which rendered success certain.[43]

Caring for Wounded

The ambulance corps followed closely behind the firing line and had brought out the wounded on litters as the waves of fallen men increased as the troops pushed up the mountain. The surgeons and medical staff stretched throughout the regiments were consumed with patients, but luckily they had adopted a new procedure to handle wounded that was changed after the Peninsula campaign. Before, regimental surgeons were restricted to treat the men of their specific regiment, but now surgeons within the same brigade equally distributed the workload and treated men within the same brigade. The VI Corps tried its trial run at Crampton's Gap and immediately took a liking to the restructure.[44]

All of the 18th's wounded were transported and treated by the doctors and townspeople in the hospitals that filled quickly. Confederate wounded were similarly hauled to the surgeons until the runs were stopped at midnight after the staff were overcome by exhaustion. Agents from the Sanitary Commission entered the bivouac on the mountainside shortly before midnight on September 14 and dispensed supplies to help treat the sick and wounded from both sides hours before the sun illuminated the macabre landscape.[45]

Corporal Peter M. Fullerton, Company D, was slightly wounded from a spent ball that fractured his collarbone without entering his skin, but it left a sizable bruise on his left shoulder. Fullerton stayed at a Burkittsville church that quickly transformed into a field hospital and remained there for several days and helped as a nurse. He cared for two wounded privates from his company; Private David L. Rude, shot through his left side, and Private Andrew G. Knox, shot in his right thigh. More help for the hospitals came from loyal Union citizens that inhabited the nearby towns. Sergeant Seymour spent a few weeks in a hospital near Burkittsville and saw firsthand of the kind treatment he received from the people of the area. He called them "Angels in earthly apparel" who were seen traveling "house to house dispensing the necessaries of life to helpless cripples. God bless them all!"[46]

The medical treatment the patients received after the battle was as adequate as things were when churches and homes were so quickly converted to makeshift triages and hospitals. As a patient in one of these makeshift hospitals, Sergeant Seymour wrote that "Hospital accommodations here are very poor, and food very scarce. I trust, however, that in a few days these deficiencies will be remedied, and that the wounded will be, to say the least, comfortable." Bullent's grizzly wound to his left thigh prompted the doctors to remove his leg at the femur the following day in order to save his life. Two days after being shot in his lower leg, Private Samuel B. Cole of Company H had his lower limb amputated in a field hospital in

Burkittsville. Eighteen-year-old Private Andrew G. Knox had the bone of his right thigh broken by a bullet, which eventually required two separate amputations. Dr. Frank Mattimore had only been with the regiment for less than a month, but he was quick to be thrown to the horrors of war. Like many doctors and nurses that remained behind in the wake of clashing armies, Mattimore stayed in Burkittsville for several weeks and attended to the masses of wounded. The greatness of Sunday was still penetrated by hellish sights and sounds a week after the battle when Mattimore penned in his diary that "nothing can be heard except the moans of a few wounded."[47]

Seven wounded soldiers from the 18th died in nearby field hospitals in the days and weeks that followed the battle which pushed the final number of killed at Crampton's Gap to stand at seventeen. At six feet three-and-a-half inches, Private John Litchult, Jr., of Company G was the tallest in the regiment present in the battle which made him an enticing target for the Rebels. He took a grievous wound to his breast, one that he would not recover from and died eight days after the battle. Private Cole lasted a few weeks after his leg was amputated, but too much damage was done and he died completely exhausted from his fight on October 21. From Company F, Private Allen Goodrich's gunshot wound in his right shoulder was only part of his troubles after he came down with an infection while a patient at General Hospital A in Frederick, Maryland, and died there on December 11. Goodrich left behind a wife and four children under the age of six back in Albany. Corporal Isaac DeBaum, Company C, and Private John Miller, Company F, were two of the other mortally wounded, but they both had the distinction of being previous survivors of wounds at the battle of Gaines's Mill. DeBaum's wound in June healed quickly which put him back on the line, but his second at Crampton's Gap was much worse and his death came on September 25 after his wounded leg was amputated. Miller likewise recovered from his June gunshot wound to his right leg, but a bullet to his right chest at Crampton's Gap led to an agonizing couple of weeks before his inevitable death on November 16. Private George Reed was also wounded for his second time, but unlike DeBaum and Miller, his wound was merely a contusion to his right side and he was lucky enough to bounce back to the regiment.[48] The last wounded 18th soldier from Crampton's Gap to die was thirty-four-year-old Private Francis Noonan, of the hard hit Company F. Struck down by a gunshot to his right leg, Noonan had a lengthy hospitalization in Frederick where his injury developed an ulcer which caused his leg to be amputated. Noonan was further troubled by tuberculosis which ultimately killed him on August 8, 1863, making him the last casualty attributed to the 18th.[49]

Nightfall

Their actions to seize Crampton's Gap became the 18th's first decisive victory that could not be misinterpreted. From his hospital bed, Sergeant Seymour stressed in a letter home that "The importance of this victory cannot be under rated," yet much of history has overlooked the success of Crampton's Gap, dwarfed by the catastrophic casualities that Antietam created three days after.[50]

As nightfall fell upon the wooded mountain, Myers and Meginnis formed a rough council of neighboring field officers from differing regiments on the heights to the right of the pass. Colonel Cake remained the most senior officer within the vicinity and issued orders for

Myers' regiment. As prescribed, Myers pushed the 18th down the hill to the foot of the mountain towards the gap where the division began to reform. The VI Corps huddled in masses and occupied both east and west sides of the pass. Myers marched the 18th to their specified point and established a camp on the left of the road that cut through the gap on the western side. Resting on the fields of Thomas H. Crampton's property, the 18th were posted just below a friendly battery to act as their support.[51]

Heaps of abandoned enemy rifles, ammunition, knapsacks, canteens, haversacks, and blankets lay strewn throughout the roadside, but their true trophy was the land they so rightly earned. Smith's division reached the gap later that night and relieved Slocum's men. As the 18th descended down the mountainside and into the gap, their adrenaline had since subsided and their utter exhaustion settled in. They sluggishly stacked their arms and collapsed into a deep sleep, despite being surrounded by hundreds of dead and dying men.[52]

15

The Worst Bloodshed Imaginable
September 15, 1862–October 31, 1862

> "I thought I knew something about a battle field from what
> I saw on the Peninsula, but there was nothing there like this."
> —*Captain William Seward Gridley, Acting Major, September 23, 1862*

Burials of Friend and Foe

The campfires on the morning of September 15 continued to crack as the 18th awoke in their mountainside camping spot as close to habit would allow, but the environment was tainted. The sounds of distant cannons roared in the distance all afternoon on their right and Union cavalry continued to turn in squads of captured Confederates throughout the day that they rounded up on the other side of the mountain. Skepticism on the army's intended move consumed their curious minds, which was better than dwelling on the horrific images that surrounded them. The previous day's dead were still spread about the fields and hillside. Sergeant Nathaniel G. Whittemore of Company I was astonished by the grizzly scene before him and commented "the dead lay thicker on the field than I ever dreamed of on a battlefield." In forty-eight hours, Whittemore would see one far worse. The task at hand was immense for burial parties as they fanned out and organized hundreds of corpses from both sides that still littered the ground, and yet more seemed to appear as the light of day set in.[1]

To the victors came the responsibility of the dead, which gave the Yankees an opportunity to properly bury their friends with honor and respect, which was a virtue they were denied at Gaines's Mill. Clusters of Union soldiers scoured the land and retraced their charge in search of the bodies of comrades. First Sergeant William B. Purdy commanded Company B on account of the lack of officers present in the company, and under his leadership he lost two men in the fight. He personally ensured that they were buried and marked in hopes that friends could find them if they ever visited the battlefield.[2]

Comrades of the slain Private John Van Bueren of Company A had similarly backtracked their route, found his body and carried it a short distance to the Jacob Goodman farm and buried him there near where the regiment had punched through the Mountain Church Road. When the news of his death reached home, Van Bueren's father traveled to Burkittsville from New York but was unable to locate the grave. A brother of Van Bueren's that served in a separate New York organization came near the area at a later date and was pleased to find that someone had marked his grave with a wooden plank scratched with his brother's name, unit, date of death, and a kind tribute that simply read, "A Brave Soldier."[3]

As the last gesture of true friendship, survivors collected valuables or letters that may have been left in pockets or haversacks of the dead, in which they would then reluctantly forward to the families. Private Edmund Burke Hawley of Company A was killed instantly in the fight by a bullet that pierced his breast, and inside his coat was a lengthy letter penned to his brother that became soaked in his blood. Hawley had left his apprenticeship of a shoemaker's trade and was one of the first to respond to Captain Gridley's recruitment when war broke out. He had a close friendship and was tent mates with Gridley's late brother, Nate, who was killed at Gaines's Mill. With half of his soldier wages Hawley supported his two young half-siblings and his step-mother back home in Schenectady, after both of his parents died when he was a teenager. Hawley's haunting last sentence in his final letter, "Hoping this letter will find you well," was smeared by his blood. Captain Gridley got a hold of this soldier's last message, but before he mailed it to Hawley's grieving family, Gridley offered his own tribute in the space available at the end to give a sense of closure for them. Gridley described how bravely Hawley died, which he ensured was peaceful. With the same respect given to Van Bueren, Hawley was similarly buried by his comrades on the Goodman farm beneath an apple tree.[4]

The day after the battle, First Lieutenant E. Nott Schermerhorn placed Captain Horsfall's body in "a respectable coffin" and buried him in a churchyard cemetery in Burkittsville, with full respects tendered by many of his friends in the regiment. When feasible and with expenses paid, select bodies of slain soldiers were shipped back to their respective hometowns and buried within family or veteran plots. After Crampton's Gap, Schenectady prepared for the lamented shipment of another beloved and respected son's body to return for final interment. Horsfall's remains were dug up a day after his makeshift funeral and shipped north, where they eventually reached Schenectady on September 25. The following day, the city wore its emotions publicly for Horsfall's funeral in a display similar to when the late Colonel Jackson

Tucked back in a wooded corner of Vale Cemetery in Schenectady, Capt. William Horsfall's grand Italian marble monument was cut and set in May 1863, and forever marks the grave of one of the most beloved soldiers of the regiment (author's collection).

was laid to rest. With flags at half-mast and black mourning shrouds everywhere, family, friends, and formerly discharged veterans of the 18th once again gathered graveside at Vale Cemetery, a short walk from Colonel Jackson's plot. The Schenectady Washington Continentals were in attendance, led by founder and former captain of Company E, Captain Stephen Truax, whose resignation for bad health nine months before put Horsfall in charge of the company. The Rev. A. A. Farr, the former chaplain of the 18th, presided over the funeral and provided a handsome tribute that reflected how the boys viewed Horsfall with reverence, his love of country, the hardships faced in the field, and of his ultimate sacrifice. One local newspaper editor commented that the Reverend Farr's words "were worthy the memory of so brave a soldier, and a fitting testimonial to his characteristic heroism and loyalty."[5]

The bodies of the enemy were hardly granted the same care and respect. Burial details, most of which were Confederate prisoners, cut long trenches in the side of the mountain and filled the hole with Rebel dead, shoulder-to-shoulder, and then stacked another row on top before dirt was thrown over to hide them. First Sergeant John S. King of Company D seemed to lose count after he saw what seemed to surpass 300 burials by the men. Given the rocky terrain and wooded thickets, many bodies remained unfound and undisturbed, and suffered a deplorable fate of being devoured by wild hogs.[6]

Franklin Fails Harpers Ferry

Franklin's seizure of the gap was a success, but his orders were not finished. McClellan was adamant that Franklin push his troops farther down into Pleasant Valley and drive through any enemy they come across in an effort to relieve Colonel Dixon S. Miles' occupation at Harpers Ferry. Having delayed the fight the day before, Franklin showed his feet were still cold and was too cautious to advance on the enemy, which could be seen two miles in front of him near Rorhersville, despite being only a brigade of Rebels drawn in battle line. Franklin even had his added force from the IV Corps who had arrived the night before, but still he was hesitant to attack. At 8:50 a.m., Franklin sent a dispatch to McClellan about his worries and his agenda, but mentioned that he feared Harpers Ferry was already a lost cause, having heard the cessation of artillery shortly before he wrote. Franklin's speculation was correct, as Miles had surrendered his garrison at Harpers Ferry at 8 a.m. that morning. Always a man of caution, McClellan accepted Franklin's report and ordered him to watch and hold the enemy, and protect the Union army's left and rear. Historians tend to agree that had Franklin not waited for the stalled IV Corps element and made a quicker attack on September 14, and followed up with a pursuit on the enemy into Pleasant Valley, Union troops at Harpers Ferry could have been saved.[7]

Stonewall Jackson's troops had encircled the heights around the mountain town of Harpers Ferry. Earlier that morning, Jackson unleashed a punishing bombardment upon the garrisoned troops under Colonel Miles, who was left with no alternative than to send out a white flag of surrender. After having almost been cashiered for accusations of drunkenness at the first battle of Bull Run, the cantankerous Miles had been barred from rapid promotions like his adversaries had experienced, and he was relegated to a smaller command of newer garrisoned troops. After the surrender, a few sporadic shells still descended upon Harpers Ferry before word had spread of the cease-fire. One of the last Rebel shells to fall after the surrender exploded right next to Miles and tore into his leg. He died of his wound the next day.[8]

Union prisoners at Harpers Ferry amounted to 11,500. One man amidst the sea of captured Yankees was a former 18th soldier. Fifty-one-year-old Private Hiram R. Richmond had lied about his age when he joined Company G when it was formed, but after four months of service he received a medical discharge for his age and bronchitis. The Livonia native did it again when he was fifty-two and joined the 126th New York in July 1862. His entire regiment was captured when Harpers Ferry fell, but they were paroled soon after. The aged Richmond eventually came down with consumption while in the service which killed him on May 4, 1863.[9]

Battle of Antietam (Sharpsburg)

During the afternoon of September 16, the 18th received orders to be prepared to march at any given moment. The sound of heavy cannonading continued to be heard over Pleasant Valley, this time from the direction of Sharpsburg, Maryland, which carried into the darkened hours. Franklin's VI Corps was called to join the rest of the Army of the Potomac that was headed for a showdown ten miles away at Sharpsburg. Franklin received their orders to join the main body at Keedysville, Maryland later that night, but they did not step off until the next morning.[10]

In the early hours of September 17, the rumbling roar of war echoed once again over Pleasant Valley from the west. This time the men knew that the sound was where they were headed. Franklin's men started their march from Crampton's Gap near daybreak, with Smith's Second Division going first at 5:30 a.m., followed by Slocum's First Division. The 18th stepped off around 7 a.m. and beat feet eight miles to Keedysville.[11]

The sounds of war that the 18th had awoke to was the start of what became America's single-most bloodiest day on American soil. Off the northern edge of the town of Sharpsburg, the two armies once again clashed over farm fields in fierce mortal combat that made all previous fights pale in comparison to its brutality. With the Potomac River to the backs of the Confederates, the Union traversed over a much smaller and winding tributary known as Antietam Creek, from which the day would forever be remembered by.

During the 18th's hastened march, the carnage heard over the land ushered fantasies in the minds of men who wondered what the situation would be by the time they arrived. What they didn't know at the time was probably for the best, for the battlefield's progress was costly. The I Corps from the Army of the Potomac started the fight at 6 a.m. on the Miller farm, and slowly pushed through a head-high cornfield cloaked by morning fog, which put rifle barrels at close range to the Rebels. As they blazed away at each other, men fell just as hapless as the stalks, and advances from both sides passed back-and-forth over the cornfield like two teams gridlocked in a football match.[12]

Artillery played a heavy role that increased the bloodshed. The XII Corps aided the I Corps, but they likewise got decimated by a Confederate counterattack. With hardly a change of ground, a division from General Sumner's II Corps entered the field and pushed into a patch of woods but their foothold was quickly routed by another Rebel surge. Casualties mounted in the thousands, and it was then only nearing noon.

The 18th, along with the rest of Slocum's division, blew through Keedysville and peeled off to the right of the Boonsboro Turnpike. They passed over the Antietam Creek across the small Upper Bridge near the Pry mill and tromped the last two miles through farm fields as the sound of battle intensified.[13]

Smith's division from the VI Corps arrived to the field ahead of Slocum's, and was ordered to shore up the right of the line where Sumner's troops had taken their most recent beating. McClellan answered Sumner's desperate requests for reinforcements and committed Slocum's division to the mix and sent them to follow Smith's division and also replenish the right of the line. Sumner borrowed Bartlett's brigade and broke them away from Slocum's other two brigades.[14]

It was shortly after noon when the 18th and their division reached the tip of the slaughter fields of Antietam. They arrived behind the Union line and moved to add themselves to the right edge. One could not simply ignore the gruesome scenes that played out over their left shoulders. Piles of dead men and horses were scattered everywhere. Union artillery deafened the air and blazed away as if their positions were bound to be overrun. Columns of infantry shuffled about in various directions as if there were several fronts. A steady flow of bloody and tearful wounded drifted passed the 18th on desperate runs to makeshift hospitals.[15]

Slocum maneuvered his division to the left of Smith's, who had just pushed the enemy out of the East Woods and cornfield. The 18th, along with their brigade, took their requested position on the battlefield just before 1 p.m. amidst shattered regiments from the XII Corps who had fallen back in confusion.[16]

They took up a spot in front of a small whitewashed church built by the German Baptist Brethren that came to be called the Dunker Church. Both armies would dance their lines around the single-room church, and its façade fell victim to crossfire and was chipped, scraped, and bored by multiple bullets and shells. The church sat back from the Hagerstown Pike that ran north-to-south, and was snuggled up against a patch of woods referred to as the West Woods, and it was there where the Rebels found refuge and launched several horrific counterattacks upon the I, II, and XII corps throughout the morning. Another but separate long-stretched patch of woods in front of the Dunker Church to the east from with the 18th took their position was fittingly called the East Woods. Between the woods was the cornfield that had seen the bloody start of the day, and although there were many cornfields surrounding Sharpsburg, it was this patch of flattened rows and piles of dead that forever solidified its title as *the* Cornfield.[17]

General Sumner's II Corps retired from the fight just before the arrival of Franklin's men, who were told to hold their position "at all hazards." Bodies of the dead and dying surrounded them and explained without words how contested the battle space was. Just as the 18th took their arranged position, Rebel infantry retreated behind a stone wall near the West Woods that Union troops from Sumner had twice tried vainly to secure. The gray and brown herd gathered amidst the haven of the woods behind the stone wall, and their artillery tucked behind the trees fired grapeshot, solid shot, and canister towards Slocum's division in an attempt to confuse and drive Franklin's fresh corps away.[18]

Quite the opposite of effect occurred to Franklin. He actually demonstrated a sense of aggressiveness that pervaded him days before and planned to commit the VI Corps to charge the Dunker Church and cleanse the West Woods of Stonewall Jackson's men. Slocum's only two brigades were then formed in a column of attack and prepped to make a push to carry the woods. Before Franklin gave the order to advance, General Sumner returned to him the one brigade he had earlier detached from Slocum, but he personally accompanied the brigade and protested Franklin's foolhardy desire. Franklin felt his corps was primed for success, but Sumner had seen the devastating effects it had on Sedgwick's men when they were earlier chewed up and spit out of the West Woods. Sumner looked at Franklin's 10,500 fresh troops and said they were, "the only troops left on the right that had any life in them," and if they were defeated it would usher the total collapse of the right line. The two argued, but Franklin would not win his case. Franklin sent a messenger to McClellan which reached the general shortly after 2 p.m., and asked for a resolve to the matter. When McClellan met up with the two argumentative generals, McClellan accepted that Sumner's command was demoralized and used up, and Franklin had the only organized command left. With successes elsewhere on the battlefield that shifted his attention, McClellan preserved the day's progress on the right and squashed Franklin's offensive desire. Franklin bitterly swallowed the order and the VI Corps did not make a wanted charge on the West Woods against the Confederate left.[19]

With the church and West Woods in their view, Slocum's men formed a line of battle along the East Woods and ordered them to lie down. The men of the 18th sprawled atop their rifles and got as flat as they could and braced for the metal rain. Private Bronson Mills, Company D, recalled the shelling to be, "the severest that our boys ever received, shell and solid shot were everywhere visible." Mills witnessed a white oak tree to the rear of the 18th—about two-and-a-half feet in diameter—slammed by a cannon shell that passed clean through the center of the trunk. He mentioned that had he not witnessed the phenomena occur with his own eyes he would not have believed what happened.[20]

To combat the vulnerability of the exposed infantry to enemy artillery that came at random intervals, batteries from Slocum's division took up a position near the infantrymen and answered back with shells of their own. The Confederate artillery were twice driven back, but not before the brigade was subjected to blasts that lasted nearly six hours. All afternoon and evening Newton's brigade hugged close to the hot earth, but together they came out with extremely minimal casualties; one killed and twenty wounded. After the cannons were silenced, enemy sharpshooters attempted to inch forward and pick off the gunners of Slocum's batteries, but they were quickly dispersed by well aimed grape and canister, which effectively ended any further interactions between the lines on the right.[21]

Private Walter W. Weatherwax of Company E had both of his eardrums ruptured from the constant concussion of artillery blasts. Left with a constant roar that hummed in his head, Weatherwax incurred a severe hearing loss that never improved for the duration of his life. In the weeks that followed Antietam, his inability to hear made him miss commands from his company officers who grew irritable towards him for it. Weatherwax refused a disability discharge when he was offered, so instead he was moved off the firing line and detailed as a teamster with the wagon train for the rest of his time in service.[22]

Miraculously, only two soldiers from the 18th were slightly wounded, as reported by Captain Gridley—the 18th's most senior captain and acting major—but the official records indicated four were injured from the regiment. For Privates James Cunnihine and Patrick McLane, both of Company F, both felt that they had seen enough death and destruction and used a field hospital as a launching pad to desert from the regiment.[23]

Dusk ushered the end of the battle of Antietam yet the regiment remained where they were, close to their artillery. The men remained grounded atop their rifles in battle line amidst

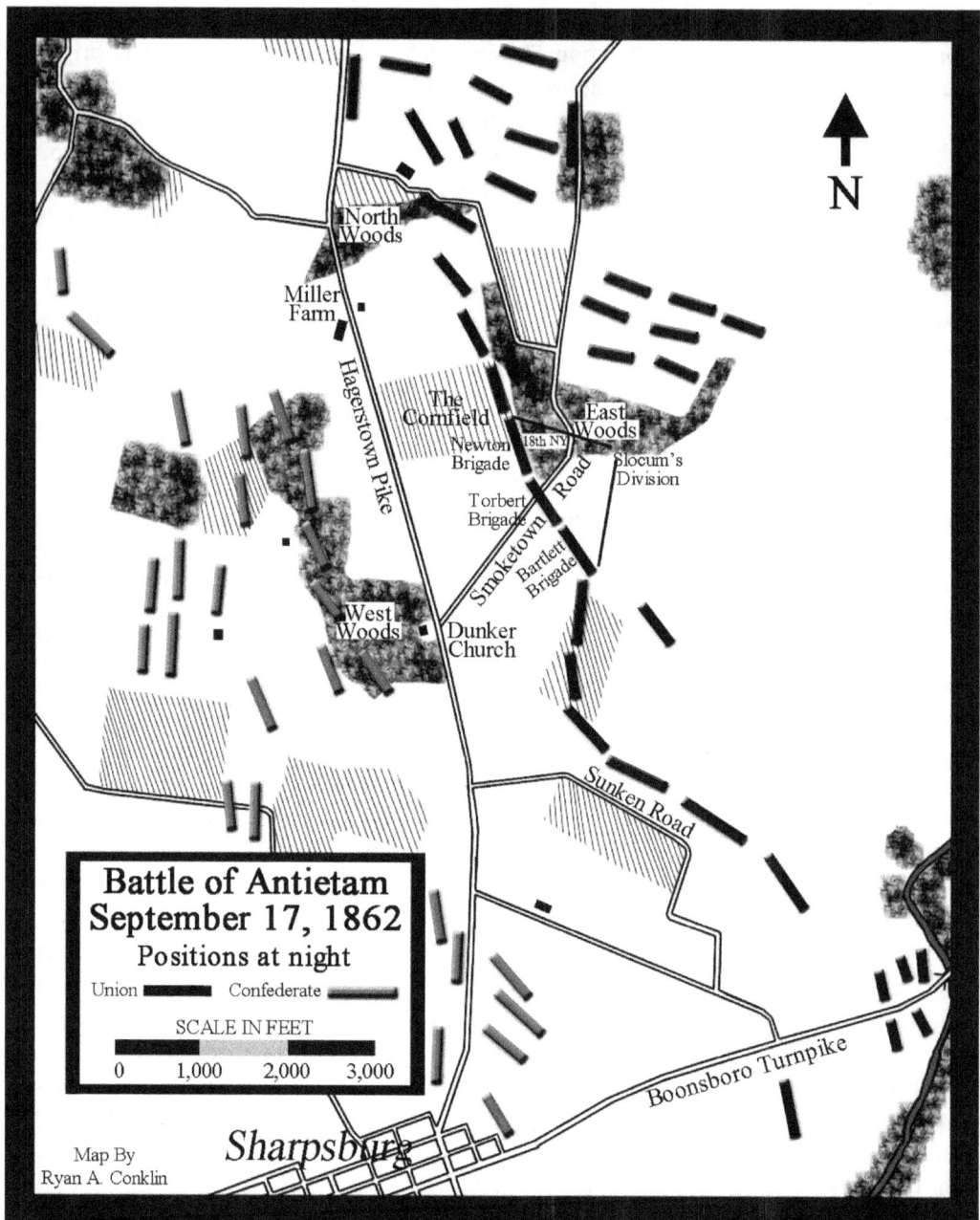

Map of the positions at night after the battle of Antietam, near Sharpsburg, Maryland, September 17, 1862. The 18th New York was near the East Woods (author's collection).

the dead and dying, which in some places were piled two or three deep from different advances and retreats. Even the darkness of night could not erase fears that the Confederates might opt for a nighttime or dawn attack, so they stayed frozen in their position. Nighttime did provide some relief to allow men to turn over and go fill their empty canteens to quench their thirst and scratchy throats. Occasional rifle cracks were exchanged throughout the night that confirmed to both sides that no one planned to leave. Captain Gridley dictated that if they were challenged on the ground they were told to hold, Gridley puffed his chest and confirmed that, "we had a little of the same medicine left that we gave them at Crampton Gap." Gridley's pride of the regiment's South Mountain charge was further confirmed by some of the captured Confederates from the battle of Antietam who had earlier escaped the gap. Gridley mentioned that "some of the rebel prisoners told our men that they all would like to know what division that was at Crampton Gap; they don't want to run against them again. They say such a charge as was made there is not made every day."[24]

The battle of Antietam was a different and shocking bloodbath for both sides to deal with. During the day, the carnage around the Cornfield and Dunker Church was only what transpired on the Union army's right, but the center and left entered sanguinary sites into American history's lexicon such as the Bloody Lane and Burnside Bridge. After twelve hours of combat, McClellan was able to push back and hold Lee's army to where he had started earlier in the day. The Army of the Potomac alone shed 12,410 casualties, the death toll immediately being 2,108. The Confederate record mixed their reporting with those from the South Mountain battles, but historian Stephen W. Sears pulled apart their lists and estimated them to be 10,318. Overall, nearly 23,000 Americans were killed, wounded, or captured in America's bloodiest day that has withheld its mark through all previous and subsequent battles of different wars.[25]

With no clear winner of the day, the Union army commanded the field afterwards and Washington was relieved of its present threat. Lee's hope for a campaign in the North was ended for the time being. Lincoln used the battle as a catalyst to implement a death knell upon the Confederacy's slavery system and put forth his Emancipation Proclamation that freed all slaves.

Like so many of the men that night, Private Perrie "Peter" Soule of Company B dreaded the next morning that he was certain would bring another fearful slaughter. Soule had just turned eighteen years old the day before the battle, but there was little to celebrate. While sprawled atop his rifle on the ground that night, Soule fell into what he called "a peaceful slumber," but even in his dreams he could not escape the visions of war. As clear as reality, Soule had visions of the Rebel army making a move behind the stone wall which scared him awake, only to be reminded that he was surrounded by the real nightmare of being "among the groaning and dying comrades." He looked for the comfort of conversation and quickly reached his arm out in the dark and grabbed the closest friend near him, sixteen-year-old Private Cornelius Houghtaling. "What in hell do you want?" Houghtaling said in a low short-tempered voice after being shaken awake. Soule tried to explain that the Confederates

Shown here years after the war, Perrie "Peter" Soule was a private in Company B who lied about his age when he enlisted, and had just turned eighteen the day before the battle of Antietam (Department of Rare Books, Special Collections and Preservation, University of Rochester River Campus Libraries).

were about to make a retreat, but when the sleepy-eyed teenager listened and questioned where he ascertained his information from, Soule calmly explained to his friend that he had dreamed it. Houghtaling immediately snapped back, "O, hell, you damn fool. If you disturb me again tonight I will stick my bayonet in you. Good Lord, you had better think of something else than silly dreams. You will find out by daylight how nicely they have retreated." Houghtaling rolled over and went back to sleep, but Soule simply could not erase the vision in his head which kept him up all night.[26]

As the sun rose above the land the next morning, light illuminated the ghastly horrors that surfaced from the fields, but at least there was no attack. "All was now silent," recalled Private Soule, "save the pitiful groans of the wounded and dying heroes." Previous accounts of Civil War combat were almost washed away in comparison when America's single bloodiest day came into view. Captain Gridley tried his best to recount the wanton carnage in a letter to his brother-in-law back home:

The acting-major, Capt. William S. Gridley, gained a new perspective of what true carnage looked like after the battle of Antietam. In a letter written to family back home, Gridley described the battlefield "was the most horrible scene that ever a man put his eyes on" (United States Army Heritage and Education Center, Carlisle, Pennsylvania).

> You had ought to have been at Sharpsburg, and gone over the battlefield: it was the most horrible scene that ever a man put his eyes on. I thought I knew something about a battle field from what I saw on the Peninsula, but there was nothing there like this. The rebels lay in many places as thick as if they had been standing up in line of battle, and the order had been given to lie down. In some places they lay by whole brigades, some with one arm, some one leg, some with one half a head, some no head, some all torn to pieces, dead horses, cannon balls, exploded shell, and many that had not exploded. Everything thus belongs to our army all over the field. No pen can tell you all, you must see these things with your own eyes to know anything about the terrible carnage that takes place at a great battle.[27]

Another account from First Sergeant John S. King, Company D, further explained the grizzly horrors of the morning that followed the battle. The portrait of carnage that surrounded the 18th was insurmountable and became forever etched in the memory banks of the eyewitnesses:

> Never shall I forget the horrors of that field. Before us, behind us, amongst us, on our right and left lay the ghastly remains of those who had fallen the day before, blackening and festering under the scorching rays of the sun. In some places the rebel dead lay in rows as they had fallen in line of battle; in others they were piled up in heaps, while the whole ground around was covered with them, laying in every imaginal attitude, many of them clutching their muskets with a death grasp. All day long the ambulances were carrying off the wounded, while parties of soldiers with the remains of one of their comrades in a blanket were constantly passing to the rear.[28]

A flag of truce was brought in during the day that followed the battle from the Rebel's side with a request to bury their dead and gather their wounded. Both sides reached an agreement and went at the shared task to deal with their dead and dying. Though the truce sounded like a gentleman's offer to enact with the enemy, the cease-fire allowed Lee's army to slip away

Top: The battle-damaged Dunker Church and West Woods pictured in the background shortly after the battle of Antietam, with Confederate dead awaiting burial in the foreground (Library of Congress). *Bottom:* Unidentified Union soldiers handle the grim task of burying the dead on the Miller Farm near Sharpsburg, Maryland, September 19, 1862 (Library of Congress).

during the day with a suitable head start. The Rebel burial party seemed peculiar when it was noticed that there was no surge of enemy ambulances on the field. As Gridley recalled after the fact, "they only sent a few men who pretended to be about the business they were sent about." No one in the 18th could have known Lee's exit from Sharpsburg took place, as they were certain that they would make another attack that day, especially after Rebel pickets continued harassment on their lines throughout the night of September 18.[29]

Even after a day of burial details that shuffled around the dead, King hardly noticed a difference in the scattered quantity of bodies. By then, the sun had hastened decomposition which tainted the air with an unforgiving pungent odor. King added, "the aspect of the field had not changed," and the next morning light still seemed to illuminate a valley coated with the same number of death's relics.[30]

Rebels Retreat, Williamsport, and Bakersville

The regiment passed another night on the bloodstained field of Antietam. September 19 started with a welcoming calm and quietness that felt odd, as the sound of thundering artillery somewhere had become the usual harbinger of morning. The Rebel pickets who did not leave with their army freely gave themselves up that morning just as the 18th began to make a push toward the wall. Private Soule recalled, "we were ordered to advance with pallid cheeks the wavering lines of blue sweep forward. We had nearly reached the stone wall, not a shot had been fired by the rebel pickets in front of it, till within a rod or two of them when they dropped their guns and threw up their hands. The Rebel line of battle that we so feared back of the wall had vanished."[31]

The Rebel army had slipped off over the Potomac River without chase and outwitted the Federals with the clever use of the ambulance corps. When the Union army realized where the Rebels actually were, they set themselves off to follow their tracks. The 18th finally left their position next to the Dunker Church that morning at 10 a.m. They performed a three mile march southwest of Sharpsburg to the Potomac River, near a ford just above Shepherdstown, Virginia [present-day West Virginia], and eventually the division came in contact with the Confederate rear guard. Union artillery echoed over the land as they shelled the Rebels from across the river, and a regiment of Rebel cavalry was actually captured near there by Union forces. One brigade from the division—not the 18th's—pushed across the river and captured a battery. The hunt was called off and a rest was enacted at the river where everyone hunkered down and passed the night along the slow-moving Potomac.[32]

The regiment remained in this camp near the river for nearly twenty-four hours and filled their stomachs on the bounty of corn that was close at hand. They waited in place until the entirety of Franklin's corps picked back up during the night of September 20, and started a march on the turnpike shortly before midnight. They walked towards Williamsport to support General Couch who was there with rumors that the Rebels planned to turn the Union right flank. The 18th marched in the dark on roads that retraced their most recent march back through Sharpsburg and over the bloodied battlefield of Antietam. Luckily, the darkness of night shielded most of the horrors from view of the passing troops, but the odor of death was a prevalent reminder of what was out there. Their route of travel utilized Sharpsburg's turnpike north to within a mile or two of Williamsport, and after six hours of walking they reached their destination at 6 a.m., September 21. What they found was that the purported Rebels had already left.[33]

On September 23, the men left Williamsport that morning and tacked on a little more than six miles on the Hagerstown Pike in the direction back south, and settled a camp on the outskirts of Bakersville, Maryland. The regiment established a rotation of picket duty and operated as normal as circumstance would allow. They remained at Bakersville for nearly three weeks which was a good break from constant movements. The broader army began to shift its focus less on hunting their enemy and more on resupply and assessment of losses from the recent campaign.[34]

While they awaited guidance from army headquarters, the 18th passed a succession of warm and pleasant days at their Bakersville encampment, filled with the returned formality of recurrent dress parades and drills. Their welcoming pause from rapid relocation was in partial result to McClellan's decision to halt and reorganize, but President Lincoln thought otherwise and demanded swift movement. Lincoln personally met up with McClellan in early October and urged the general to press forward, a stalemate of ideas reminiscent of McClellan's failed Peninsula campaign.[35]

Lincoln also mixed his time with the troops and toured nearby battlefields, greeted patients at hospitals, and oversaw a few grand reviews. The 18th buffed their brass and looked their best for one such review by Lincoln and McClellan on October 3. General Franklin formed the entire VI Corps on a level plain and had the familiar formalities of cannons to signal the approach of their guest. With an understanding of what the VI Corps had recently endured, the president declined to have the troops march in column past him. Instead, Lincoln rode on horseback with the other generals and their entourage became the moving pieces that rode past the divisions drawn up in line. The men responded to the president's gesture with resounding cheers.[36]

As the Army of the Potomac worked out its kinks to reorganize and prepare for an autumn campaign, a shake-up to the 18th's command structure came when their divisional commander, General Slocum, was taken from his office. Owed to the vacancy of a general killed at Antietam, Slocum was promoted and assigned to command the XII Corps on October 15. He left in quick fashion five days later and joined his new corps stationed in and around Harpers Ferry, which was by then back in the custody of Federal troops.[37]

New Additions and Resignations

The final swing of hometown recruiting in the early fall was able to gather nineteen men during the last two weeks of September. One bounty collector took the money and bolted two days after he signed papers. Fifty-seven-year-old Roswell J. Laraby lied about his age to join Company K in September, but his elder age was not conducive to the rigors of the infantry and disease quickly broke him down and was discharged before the end of the year. Albert and John Brundage were brothers that enlisted together in Albany and joined Company D. This was John's second attempt after having enlisted in the 18th a year previous, only to be discharged on account that he was found to be sixteen years old. Still underage, his second attempt was successful. October was the last month of recruiting which brought in the addition of four more recruits. Private Isaac Hoyt of Company D saw his seventeen-year-old

Photographed on October 3, 1862, President Lincoln visited McClellan at his headquarters tent, shortly before the VI Corps was drawn up for a grand review (Library of Congress).

brother, Hezekiah W. Hoyt, enter the ranks after having bumped up his age when he enlisted into the company on October 14, but nothing was said because he turned eighteen a month later.[38]

The structure of the regiment still suffered from the lingering effects of the Peninsula campaign, as the sick list continued to chip away names from the rosters. Captain Albert

Seely of Company K returned to the regiment shortly after Antietam after having been home for a month while he dealt with diarrhea and fever contracted at Harrison's Landing. Seely's health was still fragile when he returned and he understood that he could no longer "withstand the fatigue & privations incident to a campaign," and resigned on October 1. He was well liked by his company, and was considered a strict disciplinarian, which actually won him the praise from men above and below his rank. Colonel Myers had known Seely for many years and grew up in Ogdensburg together. As a company commander, Myers considered Seely "one of my best officers" and his resignation came as "a great loss to the regiment." His replacement stood as First Lieutenant Horatio Goodno, who returned to the regiment on October 26 after his second hospitalization owed to his nasty wound to his mouth during Gaines's Mill that he still had not fully recovered from.[39]

More shakeups came in October. On October 7, the regiment's assistant surgeon, Dr. Alexander A. Edmeston, resigned after he accepted a promotion to become a full surgeon for the 92nd New York. Another officer to tender his resignation in October was Second Lieutenant Mortier LaFayette Norton of Company B. Similar to Seely, Norton was sent off sick from Harrison's Landing in August, and spent three months away from the regiment while he battled symptoms of fever and diarrhea. When he returned in mid–October, Norton knew he was in no condition to perform to the standard of an officer amidst a rigorous campaign. He was concerned with the fact that he occupied "a position that should be filled by a man capable of doing the active duties of an officer and soldier, which I am not." Norton resigned on October 24, and his position was replaced by the transfer of Sergeant George N. Goodno from Company K. Goodno was transferred without having been present, as he was hospitalized in Philadelphia after sickness from the Peninsula campaign got the better of him. It would be another two months until Goodno returned to the line and fulfilled Norton's vacancy.[40]

Second Lt. Mortier LaFayette Norton of Company B resigned after a three-month hospitalization for sickness in October 1862, having felt his position "should be filled by a man capable of doing the active duties of an officer and soldier, which I am not" (courtesy Ronald S. Codding-

Temperatures and Troops Move South

Only a couple of weeks had passed since the Civil War achieved its bloodiest day with Antietam. Regardless of the faint fault lines between skirmishers that usually harassed each other when the opportunity rose, the picket line remained unusually quiet in October. Companies ran through a rotation that put everybody on the line throughout their present encampment near Bakersville. Call it complacency or human nature, there were still some individuals who never lost sight that Americans still manned both sides of the picket line. Interactions of Union and Confederate pickets, although rare, did occur. On October 4, a member of Company E noted in his diary that several soldiers from the regiment on picket duty near Dam Number 4 had cordially interacted with Rebel pickets. These curious soldiers of the 18th did not stop with small talk, but actually put down their rifles and met halfway between their lines for a handshake. Their conversation was warm enough to earn some New Yorkers an invitation for dinner within the Confederate picket line, of which some jumped at the chance and crossed over to dine. Upon their unmolested return, their stories were undoubtedly the continual topic of inquisitive banter over the evening campfires from those who did not cross.[41]

The 18th was relieved after two days of picket duty on October 6 by the 121st New York. Coming off the line the men were finally allowed to receive new tents, and soon enough, the assembly of camp was in full swing. The task also coincided with a much needed cleansing of the company streets. A sense of winter garrison life returned to the regiment as the army remained idle and performed daily drills, inspections, and dress parades.[42]

Occasionally, the regiment was put under arms when rumors flew that Confederate Cavalry under General J. E. B. Stuart were nearby. Stuart's cavalry was in fact behind the Union line, as far as Pennsylvania, which prompted the VI Corps to be ordered to Hagerstown on October 11. Throughout a heavy rainfall, they reached the city the next morning. They never found the cause of alarm, and the 18th was never infiltrated. Heavy firing was heard in the direction of the Potomac River closest to Williamsport during the night of October 15, but they did not rush to these sounds.[43]

Temperatures began to decline by mid–October. On October 18, the brigade eventually received orders to move closer to Williamsport on behalf of more rumors of an expected attack. The news was welcomed on account of such an uncomfortably cold night. Tents were struck at night and the 18th stepped off at 10 p.m. for a five mile journey. The pace was enough to temporarily warm the men up, but when the call to halt came their sweat became a bitter enemy during another awfully cold night. No attack ever came, so the men occupied the usual picket detail in an area referred to as Shaffer's Mills, roughly two miles south of Downsville, Maryland. The regiment would later come off the picket shift on October 20 and they settled an encampment in Downsville. Their stay was brief and was mostly marred by strong winds and rainstorms. Still without a commander for their division, the regiment was reviewed with its sister regiments on a rare and clear day on October 25 by Brigadier General William T. H. Brooks of the second brigade of the Second Division of the VI Corps. The date of the review was a wise choice, because the following day a heavy storm of cold rain soaked the men. A chilled soldier from Company E shakily penned in his diary that day that they were "laying in our tents almost frozen." On October 27, the regiment manned the skirmish line east of Downsville, between Dam Number 4 and Williamsport. They remained on the frosty picket line until some companies were pulled in on October 29, and the remainder the following day. Their brigade began to relocate its camp back to the river near Bakersville starting on October 29. Just as the regiment was entirely pulled from the picket line they followed the brigade and marched back to their former camp near Bakersville and picked up the familiar duty of guarding the banks of the Potomac.[44]

The Army of the Potomac was once again on the move down south into Virginia and the VI Corps received orders to follow on October 31. The 18th broke down their camp in the morning and started an eleven mile hike over familiar roads and towns toward South Mountain. The march was a pleasant stroll through the open country, and the closer they got to the foothills of Pleasant Valley the more the roads weaved. By the afternoon, they approached the backside of the ridge, where memories of their famed charge through the gap over a month before came to their minds. The painted leaves of autumn had started to emerge, but as they passed through the mountain via Crampton's Gap, they noticed how everything was still marked by the touch of war, just as they had left it. Trees all around the gap were still bored by bullet scars, and some looked practically peppered with holes. They had plenty of time to reminisce and peruse the battlefield, because they halted their march in the shadow of the mountain pass close to Burkittsville. Of utmost importance, the men of the 18th were mustered in to receive their pay that covered the past two months. With a pocket full of money and as north as they were going to get, twenty-three-year-old Private Walter Horton of Company C felt the time was right to pack up and go on his own. He slipped out of camp that night and was never heard from again.[45]

16

No End in Sight

November 1, 1862–December 31, 1862

"The sun refused to appear to cheer us up."
—Dr. Frank J. Mattimore, Assistant Surgeon, November 21, 1862

Back to Virginia

With orders for the corps to move to Berlin where they would pass over the river, they continued their march the morning of November 1. As the troops began to pass through Burkittsville that morning, they were greeted and cheered by former comrades that were still hospitalized in the village since the September battle. The 18th slipped through Burkittsville at 9 a.m. and marched closer to their designated river crossing.[1]

McClellan's objective with his foray back into Virginia was to unite the Army of the Potomac, whose several corps had become scattered, and push his unified force south into the Shenandoah Valley. McClellan still held on to the possibility to separate his foe and destroy them in detail. If he could not totally annihilate them, he had a plan to push the enemy as far back as Gordonsville, seize Fredericksburg and use the city as a launching pad towards Richmond. He even entertained the idea of returning to the Peninsula, knowing that he could safely maintain a route of supplies.[2]

After a seven mile march, the 18th passed the night near the village of Berlin, [present-day Brunswick], which was a settlement along the banks of the Potomac River that separated Maryland and Virginia. As the sun rose on November 2, men polished off whatever measly breakfast they could gather before another leg of their journey began. At 6 a.m., orders were yelled, bugles sounded, and the men fell into line and reset their eyes on the Old Dominion State. Parallel to the stone piers of where the original covered bridge once stood before being burned by Confederates the previous year, they crossed the Potomac River from Berlin over two long-stretched pontoon bridges built by engineers. The engineering marvel was only a few days old but had already been crossed by the I, V and IX corps, which made the VI Corps one of the last to cross. The II and V corps crossed at Harpers Ferry days before. Dr. Frank Mattimore penned their return to the Virginia side of the Potomac, was a "cold and cheerless" one. The 18th pushed farther south down the Berlin Pike another three miles and settled for the night in Lovettsville, Virginia.[3]

The trend of fatiguing marches over hills and through valleys continued for several days

View of Berlin (present-day Brunswick), Maryland, looking towards Virginia. On November 2, 1862, the 18th New York and the rest of the VI Corps crossed on these two pontoon bridges over the Potomac River and returned to Virginia, officially ending their Maryland campaign (Library of Congress).

and registered close to thirty miles. On November 3, the regiment marched at 7 a.m. and covered twelve more miles, from Lovettsville to Purcellville. During their march, the sound of heavy firing from advanced Union cavalry was audible out ahead of them as they drove the enemy out of Upperville. On November 4, the 18th and the rest of the VI Corps journeyed a nine-and-a-half mile march to Union [present-day Unison], near Moore's Mills. On November 5, the march was resumed from Union and continued another seven-and-a-half miles to the Aldie Pike, east of Upperville.[4]

During the course of their march toward Upperville, a mighty pen in Washington struck paper that created a chain reaction of astonishment amongst the marching men that same day. The Army of the Potomac was shocked to learn that McClellan—their beloved leader and founder—was relieved of his command by President Lincoln. The men had given Little Mac so much respect and admiration, even through his shortfalls as commanding general.[5]

New Leaders, New Directions

The war still went on and the deeper trek into Virginia continued its fashion the next morning at 8 a.m., November 6, with a twelve mile march. There was plenty of time for men to speculate and debate the impact of McClellan's release while they walked. By 6 p.m., the men finished their daylong march and reached White Plains, a town that was skirted by the Manassas Gap Railroad, and initiated the familiar encampment on the go.[6]

The regiment stayed put at White Plains on November 7 and watched the first snowfall of the season fall upon them in the morning. Many of the wooden rails from the nearby Manassas line kept the troops warm overnight. Temperatures dropped the following day, and the sun failed to break through the storm clouds during the day.[7]

The 18th left White Plains on November 9 and marched another six miles on a hilly highway until they arrived to New Baltimore, the designated point of consolidation of the VI Corps. McClellan had ordered for a final review of his troops to take place the following morning. Bright and early on November 10, the Army of the Potomac spread around Warrenton formed up for their last review under Little Mac "with heavy hearts." Their revered general appeared with his staff at 7:30 a.m. and was also joined by his replacement, Major General Ambrose Burnside. The official review started closer to 8 a.m., and one observer from the corps recalled the event as being both "solemn and impressive." McClellan rode by the men who stood "as still as death" as they presented their rifles and officers held their salutes. McClellan and his mounted staff rode down to pass through the gauntlet of the II and V corps who lined the street and instantly broke out into a wild cheer at his appearance. With his hat held high in adulation, McClellan first passed through the two corps and trotted back towards Warrenton by way of the I and VI corps. As McClellan turned to ride back on his return, everyone erupted in a long and drawn out cheer. Hats were tossed, men cried, and the rigid lines of formed regiments swayed as each man struggled to gain a last glimpse of their gallant leader. McClellan looked on with pride during the cheers and the band struck up with "Hail to the Chief." Just as quick as the review had started, McClellan turned and "rode mournfully away." The next tactical order would come from their new commander who began a long journey to earn the trust of the Army of the Potomac.[8]

Burnside quickly went to task with a new plan to seize Richmond, by way of Fredericksburg. By his design, he would cross over the Rappahannock alongside the city and seize the heights of Fredericksburg before the enemy could reinforce, which would hopefully open an avenue to Richmond. While Burnside awaited the approval of his plans by Lincoln, he further took initiative to restructure the Army of the Potomac. On November 16, Burnside took the six corps of his army and grouped them in pairs called "Grand Divisions." What became the Right, Left, and Center Grand Divisions were each supplemented with cavalry and artillery elements that allowed each division to operate independently as a smaller and sustainable army. The VI Corps was matched with the I Corps to form the Left Grand Division, and at its helm was their own elevated commander, Major General William B. Franklin.[9]

An officer from within was named the newest commander of the VI Corps. Major General William F. Smith, the former commander of the Second Division, took the reins of the corps. Nicknamed "Baldy" by his circle of friends that spanned as far back to his days at West Point, Smith graduated a few years behind Franklin. The two were both assigned in their early military careers as topographical engineers, and they forged a close and lasting friendship that proved vital many times over with their appointments during the Civil War.[10]

After Slocum's earlier exit, Smith's promotion, and the addition of a third division, the VI Corps took on a larger look, but the 18th felt the change very subtly. Still falling under the First Division, the 18th remained a part of the third brigade, with no changes to their

partners; the 31st and 32nd New York, and 95th Pennsylvania. They did lose their brigade commander, Brigadier General John Newton, who shifted over to command the newly created Third Division of the VI Corps.[11]

General Smith appointed one of his West Point classmates, Brigadier General David A. Russell, to command the third brigade that the 18th was aligned with. Russell proved his courage fighting guerrillas in the Mexican War which earned him a brevet for gallantry and meritorious service. He entered the Civil War as a colonel for the 7th Massachusetts and eventually left the volunteer side for an assignment in the regular army where he was quickly elevated with rank and responsibilities. With the other two brigades in their division commanded by colonels, Russell's rank gave him the seniority within the brigade.[12]

Left: **Maj. Gen. William F. Smith was promoted to command the VI Corps after Burnside's creation of grand division elevated Franklin to a higher office on November 16, 1862 (Library of Congress).** *Right:* **Brig. Gen. David Allen Russell was appointed to command the third brigade, First Division, VI Corps. A West Point graduate and veteran of the Mexican War, Russell had originally started the war as a colonel of a volunteer regiment from Massachusetts (Library of Congress).**

The First Division was finally given a permanent leader that was found within the VI Corps. Brigadier General William T. H. Brooks was promoted from his command of the second brigade of Vermont men from the Second Division, and took charge as commander of the First Division of the VI Corps. Mild mannered at times, "Bully" as he was called by friends, was an energetic commander whose bravery was never questioned. While commanding troops in battle, Brooks survived two wounds from both the Peninsula campaign and Antietam. He would have to learn a lot of new men below his rank, but at least they too were battletested. Brooks would still answer to General Smith, just as he had done when they were both in the Second Division.[13]

On the cusp of a successful recruitment campaign back home in Middletown, Second Lieutenant Robert A. Malone of Company D returned to the regiment and was surprised to learn he had been transferred to a new company as its commander. Malone was summoned to Colonel Myers' tent where he was told he would skip a rank and become the captain of Company B, after the vacancy made by Captain Hastings' exit. It was a move that highlighted the skill and respect that Malone had attained. Without a captain for months, the company had been under the command of First Sergeant William B. Purdy, who similarly received a promotion as Malone's second-in-command as first lieutenant.[14]

Brig. Gen. William T. H. Brooks took charge of the First Division, VI Corps, while the 18th New York belonged to his third brigade. Nicknamed "Bully" by his friends, Brooks was mild mannered at times, but his bravery in battle was never questioned (Library of Congress).

To break up the monotony of an idling army that covered the land around the heights of New Baltimore during their regrouping, men took the opportunity to meet up with former acquaintances from the conglomerate of newer regiments that encamped within a few miles of each other. Several three-year regiments had made their entrance into the army throughout the summer and fall. A few of the fresher organizations from New York contained familiar faces of men from their hometowns, and these reunions between friends, family, and acquaintances became a pleasurable conduit to life back home. For Companies A and E, a welcomed reunion of friends was found with the recently formed 134th New York, a regiment predominantly organized in Schenectady and encamped within three miles of the 18th. The 134th's adjutant was none other than First Lieutenant Edward W. Groot, a former officer of Company A and one of the 18th's first casualties in the skirmish before Bull Run. The gleeful reunion took place on November 13 and made the homesick men feel a sense of escapism, like a trip back home to Schenectady. They especially loved to share the story about First Lieutenant John Vedder and his mule companion that he employed ever since the Peninsula campaign. He was still not allowed to ride the mule on a march and it was only used to haul his blankets and other small items.[15]

Stafford Court House

On the same day of Burnside's alteration to the army, the men ended their six-day stay at New Baltimore and continued their chilly journey south. Burnside's Grand Divisions started their move to converge on Fredericksburg. After a night of hearing heavy cannonading out towards the army's front, the 18th broke camp at 7 a.m. on November 16 and left their cold encampment for a fifteen mile hike that passed through Greenwich, turned south through

Weaverville, and arrived to the railroad junction town of Catlett's Station [present-day Catlett], next to Cedar Run. They continued the following morning at 7 a.m. for another day-long march of ten miles. November 18 was their third day of their pursuit and was started in the morning. Another day-long march of fifteen tough miles put them and their Left Grand Division at Stafford Court House. The latter leg of the day-long hike was marred by a hard cold rain that bogged and rutted the highways. Once they arrived to Stafford Court House, the regiment fanned out and maintained the picket line for the night and stayed soaked by frigid rain. The Army of the Potomac had traversed a brutal pace of hard marches for three consecutive days. Scores of horses died along the journey and littered their path like trail markers. Stragglers were few as they maintained a motivation that the capture of Richmond was again a possibility.[16]

The unyielding cold rain hung around for the duration of the 18th's brief stay at the heights around Stafford Court House. For more than a week the men stood firm, cold and wet, hostage to their canvas shields on the soggy ground. The persistent rain bogged the roads and rendered additional movement south through Virginia impossible. Thick heavy clouds lingered above for days that denied any possibility of temporary natural warmth from the sun. Dr. Mattimore wrote of the unfavorable condition when he stated, "the sun refused to appear to cheer us up." The rain faintly tapered off a bit on November

After a successful recruiting drive back home, 2nd Lt. Robert A. Malone of Company D returned to the regiment on or about October 31, 1862, and found that Col. Myers had promoted him to captain, and transferred to command Company B (archive of the Historical Society of the Town of Warwick, gift of Joan and Tom Frangos).

22 which was enough to momentarily lift their dampened spirits, and even sparked a few to look ahead and dust off the former battle cry, "On the Richmond." General Newton and his staff joined the men in their regularly scheduled mass in camp on November 23, which impressed Dr. Mattimore to say their appearance at church was "a really imposing scene." Exemplifying their true grit, their diet for the past two weeks remained the trusted and bland staple of army hardtack. General Brooks assured himself that the men were still primed to fight and conducted a personal inspection of the division on November 24.[17]

A New Doctor, Return of the Chaplain

After Dr. Edmeston left for a promotion outside of the 18th on October 7, his position was eventually filled by the appointment of Dr. John H. Bartholf. An 1854 graduate of medicine from the college of Physicians and Surgeons at Columbia University, Bartholf had left additional schooling in Paris when the war broke out. Before his appointment to the 18th, Dr. Bartholf had already seen military service as an assistant surgeon, stationed in Frederick, Maryland at General Hospital Number 1. Days before the South Mountain campaign, Confederates had occupied Frederick and Bartholf and the rest of the medical staff had to burn most of their medical supplies and ship out patients to Pennsylvania. Once the Union army took back the city, Dr. Bartholf went to work as surgeon for many of the wounded from the Maryland campaign, and a few 18th soldiers were treated at his hospital. An order from the Army of the Potomac relieved him of those duties on November 15, and what felt merely like a transfer, Dr. Bartholf took his place with the 18th as their assistant surgeon, and met up with the regiment at Stafford Court House on November 26.[18]

Company D was surprised to be returned with Privates Henry Hayden and George House on November 7, who had quite the tale to share with comrades. Both were captured back on August 29, 1861, while they were picketing at Bailey's Crossroads in Alexandria. They had since been shifted around to several Southern prisons in Richmond, New Orleans, and Salisbury. No return to the regiment was of greater benefit than when they regained their Christian pillar of strength. The Rev. A. A. Farr made another go as the regiment's chaplain and returned in late November. He had resigned during the ill-infested Peninsula campaign in July, and had recuperated enough to his own standards and returned to his uniformed congregation. To the delight of the regiment, Farr was reappointed on November 27.[19]

Photographed in 1862, thirty-two-year-old Dr. John Henry Bartholf was brought into the 18th New York in the fall of 1862 to fill the assistant surgeon vacancy made by Dr. Edmeston's exit. Bartholf spent a lengthy career in uniform and retired in 1894 (courtesy Anne C. Clark).

Deaths from Disease

November was a rough month for six ailing soldiers from the 18th who perished from disease. Private James Frasier of Company K had been hospitalized in Washington for nearly two months until he died from anemia on November 1. In a Hagerstown hospital that same day, Corporal Samuel Green of Company C died from typhoid fever. After Private William A. Ellison of Company D was gripped by disease and fell out of the march before Second Manassas, he was hospitalized in Alexandria and died there on November 5. Private Charles Van Steinberg of Company B had been hospitalized in Philadelphia for more than two months from chronic diarrhea that eventually killed him on November 14. On November 22, Private Aaron Chapman of Company G died from a losing battle with typhus in a Hagerstown hospital.[20]

The sixth death in November was the unexpected passing of Private George W. Royce of Company G. He was one of the first volunteers from his community to join the company, and he frequently sent letters of his military adventures to his father, a printer for the local newspaper in Canandaigua. His father often shared his son's correspondence from the front and printed them in the paper to be shared with the community so families could gain a better grasp of what their sons were going through. Royce had been wounded in the left arm at Gaines's Mill of which he rebounded just fine, but it was diarrhea that he contracted near the end of October that hospitalized him in Hagerstown. He spent more than three weeks prostrated in a crowded and understaffed hospital and watched his own health deteriorate. When the news of his condition reached his parents in Canandaigua, his mother immediately traveled to be by his side. The condition of her failing son was heartbreaking and she begged authorities for a furlough to get her son home in hopes that the cleaner environment and motherly care could rebound her son. Her appearance at his bedside had immediate effect on his condition which, "for a time to give him strength and inspire the hope of his ultimate recovery." His furlough was granted and they both arrived to Canandaigua in the evening of November 28. Two days later was a Sunday morning and Royce showed good recovery, even in the eyes of his friends and physician, but by the afternoon his health plummeted and "it became evident that he had not many hours to live." The twenty-one-year-old Christian patriot died, "just as the church bells commenced ringing for evening service."[21]

The Fredericksburg Campaign

Near the end of a cold and rainy November, the threat of a Confederate raid in the direction of Warrenton prompted elements under Franklin's command to be pushed west to prevent the action. On November 28, the 18th, along with the rest of their brigade, pushed out beyond the picket line about six or seven miles closer to Warrenton at a place called Spotted Tavern. The 18th took up a position at Wood Cutting Cross Roads with Hexamer's battery in expectation of the rumored raid. They waited for two cold days with little excitement. Occasionally the regiment was drawn up in battle line owed to more bad rumors, but nothing came about and the western line remained quiet. On November 30, they pulled back their line three miles back closer to the Stafford Court House area.[22]

The 18th would only remain back at Stafford Court House for three frigid days. Orders to move reached the officers after a chilly battalion drill on December 3. In the early morning hours of December 4, Burnside's shifting pieces broke down their encampments and formed into their line of march on the road. The 18th started their morning at 5 a.m. and marched off an hour later. They headed south and walked all day and logged roughly seventeen miles through hilly countryside to a point three miles beyond Belle Plain Landing, near Fletcher's Chapel. Franklin's Left Grand Division was now in and around White Oak, just shy of seven miles east of Fredericksburg.[23]

Their first full day in their new spot was saturated with a continuous freezing rain that stirred the ground to mud, and by evening the downfall turned to snow. Luckily, rest and respite from the weather was their agenda and nothing more. The men were at the mercy of the elements and tried their best to stay warm, but thin tents and blankets could only do so much. The following day of December 6 continued with more of the same wintry mix. Roads turned to a muddy slush and the simple walk about camp became a cold tricky mess. Winter weather was there to stay and with a campaigning army nights under tents became unbearable and were no way near as warm and cozy as men dared to remember from the previous winter. Belle Plain certainly did not become a place remembered fondly.[24]

When days proved favorable, standard company and regimental drills consumed their days and mass was still held on Sunday mornings. As soon as the wintry weather cleared, Burnside focused on a plan to spring his army on the enemy. The 18th prepared for the eventual move on December 8 when officers reissued ammunition and rations to last four days.[25]

The regiment's sick continued to act like a revolving door where sizable handfuls were sent off sick but only a few healthy men returned. A regimental hospital was established at a nearby rustic chapel in King George's County simply called White Oak Church. The whitewashed building was modest in character, and its dilapidated appearance looked more suited as a barn for animals than a sanctuary. Private Gleason C. Bell of Company A was not a patient for long after he quickly contracted typhoid fever. The disease came suddenly and fast, and Chaplain Farr posted himself at his side. Farr attended the young man and recited verses of scripture and prayer. Just before life slipped from him around 5 p.m. on December 8, Bell uttered what stood as his last words in response to a question from Farr, to say that he "trusted in the Savior." The following morning, Bell was buried near the church and members from his company marked his grave with a wooden board. Chaplain Farr took up the solemn duty to pen a letter to Bell's father in Schenectady and broke the news. Bell's father had Farr's letter printed in the *Evening Star and Times* newspaper in Schenectady, which was a fitting tribute for his son who was the firm's compositor before he enlisted.[26]

The projected march did not take place the following day like the regiment had expected,

White Oak Church in Falmouth, Virginia, was utilized as a hospital for the regiment's sick, before being taken over by the U.S. Christian Commission (Library of Congress).

so the men remained poised to pass another cold night in a lull. The time to advance seemed likely to fall on December 10 when orders floated down to prepare for a midnight march, but that too was countermanded. The time of departure was eventually extended to the following morning and stuck.[27]

Battle of Fredericksburg

After all of the arrangements were settled, supplies readied, and engineers anxious for the word to build, General Burnside gave his nod to let his plan unfold. In hopes to surprise the enemy by his choice of river crossings into Fredericksburg, each Grand Division was designated a point of crossing that correlated with their alignment in the army. General Sumner's Right Grand Division was directed to build pontoon crossings at the upper and middle approaches of the city. In rear of them was General Hooker's Center Grand Division that was to follow. A mile south from the middle crossing was the lower pontoon crossings where Franklin's Left Grand Division was directed to build two to pass over.[28]

During the night of December 10, engineers moved up near their points at the river with their materials. Shortly after 3 a.m. on December 11, the engineers ripped into their supplies and started their bridges. Before the engineers finished the lower pontoon construction, the 18th was put into motion towards the crossing two hours after the engineers began their work. During the short walk, Private John Baker of Company B began to complain of sore feet and fell out of the formation. He stopped at a house along the way and decided to opt out of any battle that loomed and was chalked up as another deserter. After less than a mile, the regiment finished their short march to where both corps converged at 7:30 a.m. by the bank of the Rappahannock, the designated crossing point. None of the bridges for the VI Corps were completed that early, so General Smith ensured that they were sheltered out of view of the enemy as much as possible. Both bridges before Franklin's Left Grand Division were the first of the three Grand Division crossings to be completed and were ready by 11 a.m. Burnside had specified that Franklin not cross before the other divisions had done so at the middle and upper crossings, in order to prevent the likelihood of the Left Grand Division from being stuck between the Deep Run and Hazel Run streams and unable to be reinforced. Franklin even made it known that he wanted the risk in order to outflank the Confederate defenders in Fredericksburg, but Burnside shrugged off the idea. The massed troops of the Left Grand Division would have to yield near the crossing in relative quiet and wait.[29]

Thousands of Franklin's troops swarmed the lower crossing and grew stir-crazy to cross. The middle and upper crossings had come under significant resistance which aptly slowed the progress of the engineers which kept Franklin's wing dormant to the south. Once the upper crossings gained a foothold, Franklin eventually received the word to cross, and Smith sent his first brigade across at 4 p.m. Union artillery poured scattered shells towards the plateau on the other side to clear out any networks of Rebel sharpshooters that had gathered around the Bernard house and other small structures. Devens' brigade from Newton's Third Division of the VI Corps were the first to cross. Devens' men cleared the crossing and climbed the opposite embankment and scared off the few sharpshooting Rebels from around the houses. They successfully took up a semi-circle position on the south bank and protected the bridgehead just before dark. Following Devens' example, troops from Brooks' First Division, second brigade (27th and 121st New York) were ordered to cross next on the lower of the two bridges, but modified orders from Burnside reversed their advance. The hesitation to cross came from the loss of light that Burnside feared would cause confusion and stall his force if they attempted to cross at night. Leaving Devens' brigade where they were to protect the bridgehead on the opposite bank, Burnside ordered Franklin to stop his crossing and similarly withdrew the elements from Brooks' division back and wait to cross at sunrise. A division of troops nearer Burnside at the upper crossings managed to get across and occupied the city overnight.[30]

With the dawn of light, Burnside's crossing began in earnest the morning of December 12. Unlike the lag from the day previous, General Smith was pleased to start the day's operation with as much daylight as possible. The first to cross at the lower pontoon crossing was Brooks' division, and the first regiment to go was the 18th at sunrise. Brooks wanted them to cross first and relieve the forwarded skirmishers of Devens' brigade who passed the night skirmishing alone on the southern bank. Feeling the slight bobs and sways characteristic to pontoon bridges, the entire regiment walked unimpeded over the crossing and deployed as skirmishers. They were supported from behind by the rest of the regiments within their

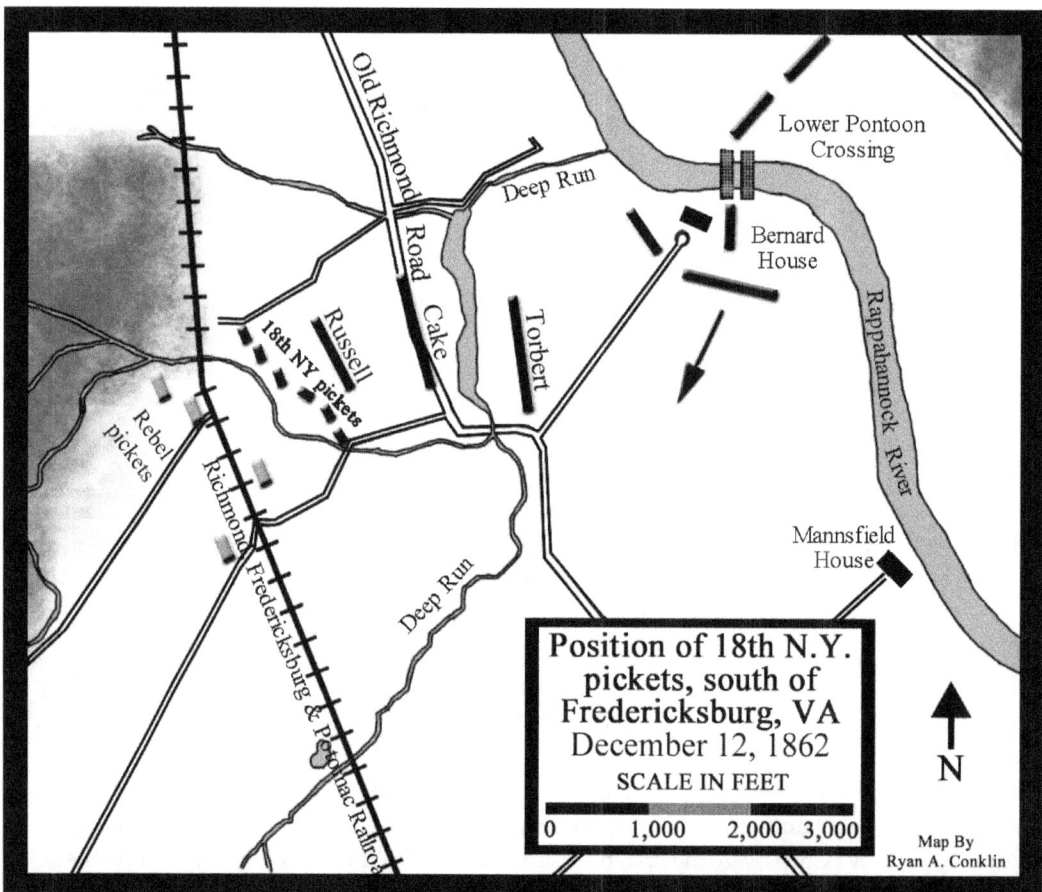

Map of the Lower Pontoon Crossing on December 12, 1862, that shows where the 18th New York occupied the picket line south of the city of Fredericksburg, Virginia (author's collection).

brigade. From left to right their line was set; 95th Pennsylvania, 31st and 32nd New York, and Battery D of the 2nd United States Artillery. Like feelers for the division, the 18th pushed beyond Devens' established line and ventured across the Old Richmond Road and occupied a line 500 yards beyond Deep Run, and they anchored their right line near the railroad. The 18th's brigade under Russell became the advanced line on the southern side of the river at the lower crossing. Behind their brigade was the second line held by Cake's brigade in the Old Richmond Road, and in rear of them was a third line held by Torbert's brigade in the valley of Deep Run. Anything could happen and this is what they trained for.[31]

Things remained relatively quiet on the advanced picket line owed to the shroud of excessive fog. As the vapors began to dissipate and visibility cleared in the later morning hours, Rebel pickets before them came into view. In front of Company K, a couple soldiers noticed two enemy horses equipped with saddles, one dead and the other wounded. Their appetite was whet for potential booty and Captain Horatio G. Goodno made moves for it. He probed his company for willing volunteers to rush the horses in view of enemy pickets. Private Ashbel Dings and First Sergeant William H. Mayette felt spirited and jumped at the dare. Goodno described Dings and Mayette sprinted forward, "amidst a shower of bullets from the rebel pickets," and were able to strip the horses and miraculously brought back their loot to the company uninjured.[32]

The rest of the moving pieces of the VI Corps completed their movements just as the fog that protected them lifted. The enemy nestled in the hills before them quickly began to calculate, strategize, and harass the VI Corps. From a commanding elevation, the Confederate batteries of heavy artillery that encircled their lines erupted upon them and lasted throughout the day. The shelled soldiers were protected to a degree as best as the topography allowed, but General Smith knew the task was taxing on the men. Smith spoke on behalf of the forwarded skirmishers with the 18th and said, "there was nothing to be done but maintain our skirmish line, which was engaged nearly all the time, and to submit quietly to the feeble and spasmodic artillery fire of the enemy." Just like at Antietam, the men would have to endure.[33]

The shelling increased through the day and eventually became too much for one man. The artillery was so close and constant for Private Malcolm E. Colby of Company E that he became incensed. He turned to two of his tent mates—Private John Jenner and Private Henry Schermerhorn—and yelled, "Great God my head will burst!" Afterwards, Colby complained of hearing a constant "rumbling noise" in his head which coincided with his unyielding maniacal passion to "go and surround the Rebels over on the other side." Almost a century before this level of combat stress was ever recognized or properly treated, there was little the doctors or his tent mates knew to do other than keep an eye on him. Colby's stress never lessened, but worsened throughout the coming weeks while he remained on the line.[34]

The regiment's proximity to the enemy deemed it unwise to make camp fires that night. Vigilance was imperative for those forward skirmishing regiments posted on the front like the 18th were. The day had been frosty but temperatures during the night sank terribly low. Their bodies shook as they felt the suffering cold effects that night brought. Officers felt the pressures of their rank and made sure their men adhered to the order that prohibited fires.[35]

By nightfall, the Army of the Potomac had finished their crossings and worked on the arrangement to attack by sunrise. The I Corps crossed with the VI Corps at the lower crossings and tied into their left, almost at right angles, with the left of the I Corps connected to the river. The VI Corps stretched out basically parallel to the river, and their right was connected at Deep Run close the left of the IX Corps, who were practically parallel with the Old Richmond Road.[36]

Brooks' three brigades alternated the lines on picket the next morning of December 13, and the 18th was happy to be relieved early by the 15th New Jersey. The 18th moved back to a safer position where the third line was held overnight by Torbert's brigade in the valley of Deep Run. The men stacked their arms and settled down on the ground in the ravine.[37]

Unwilling to press their luck, three privates from Company A—William H. McIntosh, John Shultz, and John McNeal—wanted no part in the coming battle and slipped away when their officers were not looking. When the regiment crossed to the safer side of the river three days after the battle, the trio stopped hiding and returned to the regiment as if nothing happened, but their commanders were quick to draw up charges of desertion for them. They were all found guilty in a court martial two months later and had their pay and allowances revoked and sentenced to hard labor at the Rip Raps in Florida and all three were dishonorably discharged in March.[38]

December 13 was filled with the sounds of war for the 18th, and from their reserve position all they could do was speculate its progress. Burnside's plan called for Franklin's Grand Division to puncture the Rebel line on Prospect Hill, which he would then launch the attacks of the other Grand Divisions on the heights to the west of the city. He specified that these attacks were not to be simultaneous, but triggered from Franklin's success, and as history would have it these plans got scrambled. For the assault of the Left Grand Division, Franklin committed one of his smallest divisions from the I Corps at 9 a.m. The artillery shook the earth in the early afternoon, and shortly after 1 p.m., three divisions were pressed forward and matched by enemy infantry and artillery as they approached the heights. They were driven back with disastrous results an hour later, and by 4:30 p.m., Franklin gave up hope on any more advances and held the foothold his side of the lower crossing. Burnside lost it with Franklin. The commanding general was vehemently angered that the VI Corps was not thrown into the mix. Burnside considered the VI Corps, "the strongest and one of the most reliable in the army," but Franklin held back his former corps. Not only did Franklin have two corps at his disposal, but he was also given an extra division from the IX Corps in which he likewise did not commit. Both generals would both go down for these blunders, amidst their own finger pointing directed at the War Department.[39]

As the battle played out to their right and left, Brooks took a look at the line held by his division in the middle of the Union army. Things were quiet in the center and relatively distant from the enemy line. Brooks was satisfied with his right that rested on the road, but he wanted to extend the left of the picket line beyond the railroad. He looked to Torbert's brigade to advance the line, and he grabbed two regiments from Russell's to aid in the effort. The 18th was not one of the two pulled for the assignment. Torbert's brigade and his added help extended the line as expected and drove off the enemy beyond the road. Once the ground was gained, the added support from Russell was returned to their earlier position with their brigade. Soon after they left, the enemy reinforced their own lines and eventually recovered what was lost which came with a severe and futile beating to Torbert's brigade. Again, the 18th in the rear could only wonder what the bigger picture was based on what they heard.[40]

Although not actively engaged in the day's heavy fighting, a consistent shelling from enemy artillery from the heights that surrounded them reached the other two brigades of Brooks' division. The 18th ended the day with three wounded soldiers—Private William R.

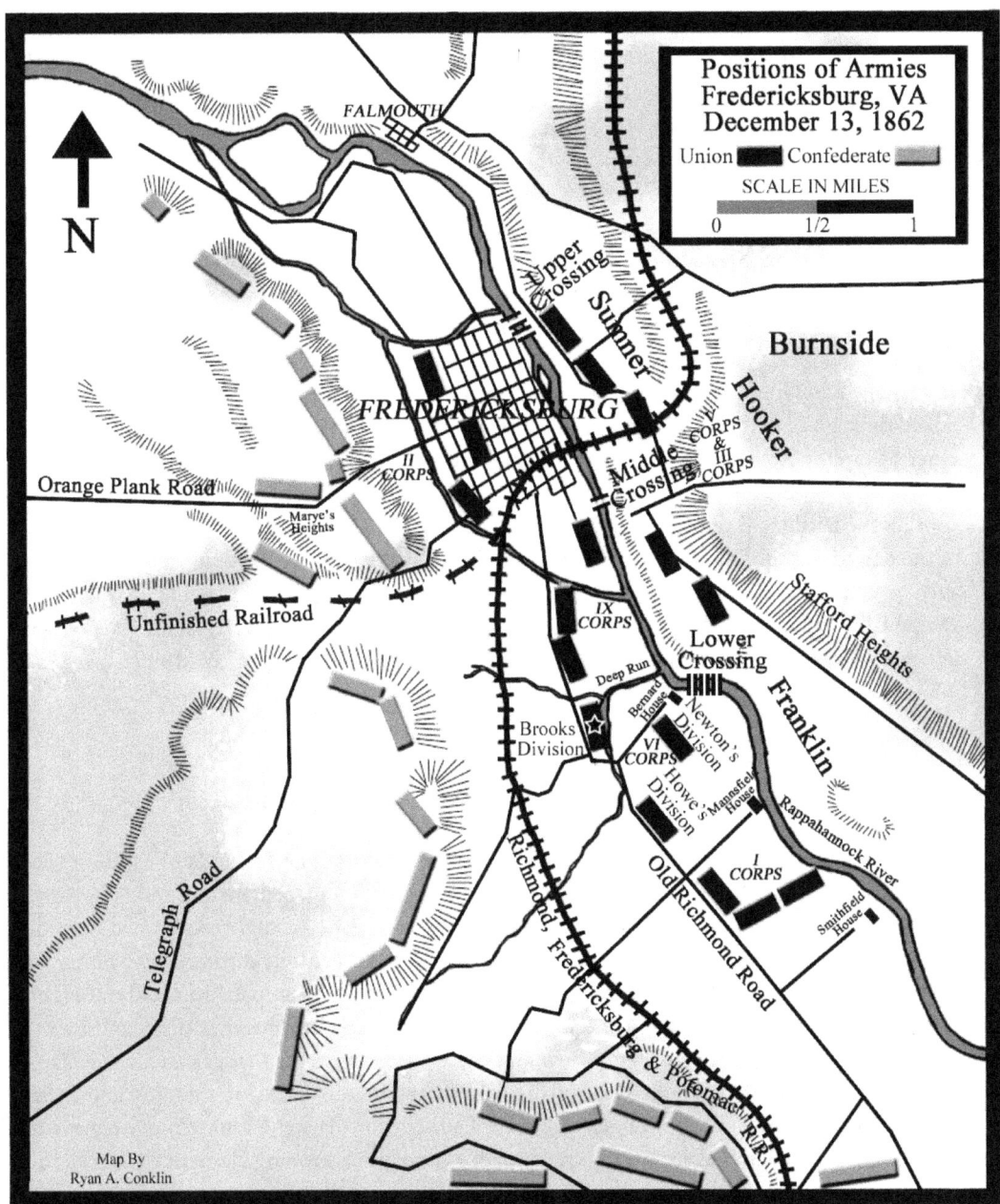

Marked with a star, Brig. Gen. Brooks' Division (First Division, VI Corps, Left Grand Division) consisted of three brigades and an artillery contingent. The Third Brigade (Russell) consisted of the 18th New York, 31st New York, 32nd New York, and 95th Pennsylvania (author's collection).

Armstrong and Private John Hunter, both of Company B, suffered minor wounds. Hunter was struck in his left shoulder blade by a spent ball that he described left a lump "as big as a hen egg." Private Jacob Sheil of Company H was also slightly wounded while on the skirmish line with a ball that penetrated through the inside of his left palm. He was taken off the firing line and sent to a hospital in Philadelphia where his middle finger was removed.[41]

In front of the enemy on December 13, Private Ernest Groffman left Company E and skedaddled, only to be immediately captured by Rebels. Groffman was not held in high regard to the majority of the company. Captain John Vedder said he was seldom found at his post, so his exit came with little surprise. Groffman's time as a prisoner was short, as he was paroled four days later, but he did not return to the regiment and was never heard from again.[42]

Franklin's problems at his front pales in comparison to the grim situation the other two Grand Divisions faced. With superior numbers, the Union attack on Marye's Heights was not a concerted charge. Instead, wave after wave of brigades were sent forward through open fields but could not break the impregnable stone wall that concealed the enemy. Burnside grew furious after countless herculean attempts failed to puncture the line, and he felt the weight of the thousands of casualties that the Rebels inflicted without much loss to themselves. The Left Grand Division had the most promise, as troops from the I Corps temporarily poked through a line, but they were similarly wrecked by a counterattack and lost their pocket. Once again, the Army of the Potomac was punched by defeat.

With thousands of dead and dying troops lying in fields like forgotten crops, the 18th's spot on the battlefield rendered them lucky to be alive. Without knowing the broader scope of the day, they could not fully comprehend just how lucky they were. With the insight of an aged veteran long after the war, Joseph C. Jones reminisced about his days when he was a private in Company G and thought back to the battle at Fredericksburg, and stated, "We, of the left, were very fortunate compared to the right and center as to the loss in killed and wounded. We were badly beaten…. I do not like to talk about it."[43]

Retreat from Fredericksburg

Minor skirmishing occurred throughout the battered lines and sounds of artillery resonated again during Sunday, December 14, but no general engagement ensued. The 18th received a resupply of ammunition and other important items at night. After two days of being held in reserve in the Deep Run valley, the 18th moved out during the evening of December 15. The Left Grand Division limped back across the Rappahannock about eight that evening, and the 18th was once again held back as pickets. Between midnight and 1 a.m. of December 16, the 18th took their turn and backtracked over the bridges above the Rappahannock at the lower pontoons and pushed on towards familiar and safer territory, and the entire division crossed without confrontation. During their darkened march, the regiment was split into two wings in order to protect itself as two quick-moving elements. With about a half a mile distance between the wings, they set up separate encampments on the hills around 6 a.m. The men of the regiment were still close enough to observe their previous night's camp on the other side of the river on the plains that had quickly been overtaken by their enemy.[44]

The left wing eventually moved the half mile distance to reunite themselves with the rest of the regiment in their encampment on December 17 where the brigade was near White Oak Church. Company C was surprised by the sudden death of forty-three-year-old Private Martin Fritz, who died in camp from heart disease that same day. Food was scarce and prompted some men of the regiment to slaughter a beef cow close to their camp for the rare feast of fresh meat. On December 19, the regiment marched back towards the vicinity of

White Oak Church and consolidated themselves and set up a more permanent encampment in the woods in preparation for winter.[45]

The Army of the Potomac had settled in for a long winter encampment a few miles from Fredericksburg, amidst farm fields and tracts of woods from Falmouth to White Oak. Just under a mile east of the White Oak Church, the 18th, along with the rest of Russell's brigade, hunkered down within a large virgin forest of pine that quickly fell to the mercy of hundreds of army ax blades. The 18th lent differing names to this encampment such as Camp Russell, White Oak Church, and despite being four miles away from Falmouth Station, their camp sometimes reflected that name.

Burnside needed time to regroup after his butchering, and the weather was hardly ideal for another attack. The men passed the remainder of the cold fleeting days of 1862 in relative peace, ensconced in close proximity with the other regiments of the Army of the Potomac. The cold snaps of weather came and went, but life in camp was generally simple. General Russell inspected the brigade at 10 a.m., on December 21. That same day, the adolescent drummer, William J. True, was returned to Company D after having deserted back in August. Christmas came with the gift of unseasonable warmth, but aside from a special mass held for the occasion, the holiday was quite dull.[46]

From December 28 to 31, the 18th was posted on outposts around their White Oak Church camp on picket duty. Before the men retired back to their camp, word had arrived that the army was to be placed under marching orders, and several men on the picket line took the opportunity to butcher another cow and boost their weakened bodies for travel. Upon their return to camp on December 31, they found out that the movement was false, but instead were pleasantly surprised to be issued another two-month payment from the government, all the while on a full stomach.[47]

Earning money did little to lift spirits as the dawning of another year was upon them. Morale was at an all time low and there is no doubt some tried and true veterans contemplated if they would make it a few more months to the end of their contract, which by all likelihood seemed more viable to come before the war's end.

17

A Bleak Winter
January 1, 1863–April 26, 1863

"Time yearns to drag with some of the boys
they are in a hurry for may to come around."
—Sergeant Gregoire Insse, Jr., Company G, March 5, 1863

Another New Year

A new year paved the way for hopeful speculation that 1863 would be the last year of the war. Very little change came about during the 18th's extended stay near the White Oak Church. The biggest news of the year was the proverbial birth of freedom to slaves still in bondage that went into effect, freed by the controversial Emancipation Proclamation. As with any landmark decision that ever came out of Washington, there were mixed emotions and heated debates over the campfires of both armies.

Winter camp life remained the same tedious routine of inspections and dress parades. On January 3, the men started construction of comfortable log quarters to help ward off the winter weather. Individual creativity and ingenuity perfected these cabins the best they saw fit for the second winter of the war. Green pine was in great abundance and steadily burnt, which took some getting used to as men's eyes became irritated from the constant haze of smoke that hung in camp. The food was just as dull as their days and consisted mostly of wheat pancakes or hardtack fried in pork fat. Someone took it upon themselves to slash open a sutlers tent one night and stole $150 worth of food, but with the absurdly overpriced goods they charged, a thief was never found, and no one pitied the peddler.[1]

Chapman Resigns

First Lieutenant George Chapman of Company I stumbled into camp footsore the night of January 3, after a solo walk of four miles from Falmouth. Chapman returned to the regiment from his home in Amsterdam, New York after a lengthy recovery from sickness since November 24. He meandered unnoticed in the dim-lit camp, cloaked by heavy smoke from fires. He proceeded directly to the tent of his best friend, Second Lieutenant James "Jim" Chalmers. Chalmers was amidst a game of cribbage with Captain Thomas J. Radcliff when Chapman suddenly barged in and surprised them both. There was much to share between the officers that transpired during his absence and they excitedly swapped stories. "It seemed very much like getting home again to get back into camp again," wrote Chapman. He spent the next morning doing "a great deal of shaking hands ... and a good many how'dy' do's to answer." Chapman was shocked to see Private David Hennessy of his company, who he was led to believe was dead based on what he was told from another comrade while at home. When Chapman met with Captain Goodno of Company K, they talked about Private Peter Santaus of Goodno's command, who had chaperoned Chapman home on his furlough but failed to return. Santaus had even written to Chapman and arranged when and where they would meet, but when he failed to appear at the train station Chapman accepted him as a deserter, "and he can go thunder now for all I care." Goodno was "in an awful stew" about Santaus' actions, but Chapman expressed that "if a man deserts the consequences are on his own head no one elses."[2]

A furlough at home was not enough to rebound the health of 1st Lt. George Chapman, Company I. He resigned from the regiment on January 15, 1863 (courtesy New York State Military Museum).

Aside from the happy reintegration of friends amongst camp, Chapman's return to the rigors of military duty proved too challenging to endure. Chapman's appetite had rebounded at home, and his stomach was not ready to return to the scraps served in camp. Chapman stated that if he had more money he would "board in Co. K's mess and get three meals a day of [Private Gabriel] Willets' cooking." The foul weather during the regiment's winter encampment compounded his already fragile health, and during a daylong rainstorm on January 6, Chapman sat under his tent and came to the conclusion that his health had taken enough abuse. He made the decision to resign from the regiment.[3]

Although weather and health played a role with his decision, there was a bigger issue that encouraged Chapman to leave the regiment. Like any social or political organization at the time, politics had a tendency to burn bridges, and no one felt more slighted than Chapman when it came to the recent promotions that occurred while he was away. After Daniel Daley was promoted to captain, Chapman was the senior first lieutenant in the regiment and had once served as captain of Company I after Captain Radcliff's court-martial, yet Chapman was overlooked for a promotion to captaincy when other open slots were made available. Other officers had received promotions while away from the regiment, so Chapman took this overlook personally. Lieutenants Roswell M. Sayer of Company D and John Vedder of Company E were both made captains in their companies, despite Chapman's seniority on them. Another opportunity surfaced when Captain Goodno of Company K penned his resignation while Chapman awaited his own resignation papers, but he did not second-guess his decision and the position went unfulfilled. When Chapman handed his papers to Colonel Myers, the commander told Chapman that he was sorry to see him go, but Chapman internally disregarded his sympathy.[4]

After eight anxious days of waiting for confirmation, Chapman finally received his discharge papers on January 15 and joyously packed for his permanent return home. After numerous personal farewells with comrades, Chapman's pockets were stuffed full of letters and messages from comrades that he promised to deliver during his journey home. His joyous parting was bittersweet, and when Chapman crept into his tent that night for the last time, he penned a note of regret to himself:

> They are all very much surprised to think that I got my papers through. Everybody thinks I am very lucky but for my part I would not turn my hand over whether I go or stay though at the time I sent in my resignation the prospect of my health improving seemed rather poor. I do not care about quitting the service but would like to be where there was a fair shake in appointments.[5]

Burnside's Mud March

Whether the men were ready for it or not, another campaign for the Army of the Potomac was on the verge on January 16 after rumors that Rebel forces had removed themselves from Fredericksburg. Burnside quickly penned out marching orders for his army. The men were ordered to cook three days' rations and pack sixty rounds of ammunition, and they readied themselves for instant travel. Orders came for the sick to be sent off to the First Division hospital for the VI Corps at Windmill Point, Virginia on January 17. Like many forward movements before, the launch was delayed and the men saw a couple cold days come and go while they waited.[6]

All of the signs of another advance could be seen, and it was true that Burnside wanted another crack at Fredericksburg. Conceding that his attempt in December failed on account of lost time, especially with the prolonged wait for pontoons, Burnside was still hopeful that he could secure the south bank of the Rappahannock and strike the Rebels by surprise out of their entrenchments. After reports surfaced that Lee had shed some 75,000 troops to aid in a problematic attack in North Carolina, timing became opportune. Burnside's plan was similar to his previous attempt, only he would not divide his army and would cross the Rappahannock River at a more northern locale. Banks's Ford became the decided point of crossing the river, located about four miles to the west of Fredericksburg, and General Smith's VI Corps was chosen to lead the expedition. Burnside's proposal was opposed by almost all of his constituents, but the pressure from Lincoln had seized his better judgment, and he stated he had no other plans for that winter. Burnside settled on January 20 to launch his plan and with his credit on the line, he claimed full responsibility and offered to resign if the venture failed.[7]

Apprehension to Burnside's fickle attack was not limited to the higher echelon officers, but could be felt all the way down to the lowest private. Dissension in the ranks amongst the two Schenectady companies surfaced just as everyone prepared for the ordered march on January 20. No one seemed too excited to make their latest push, but the officers of Companies A and E were not willing to give their men any opportunities to sit it out. Company officers denied their men the chance to be placed on the sick list if they were not already committed before the marching orders had arrived. Private Joseph Payne's eyes were swollen from an infection yet Dr. Bartholf did not grant him an absence. He did not even have a musket and other equipage as it had been handed off to someone else before the movement. Private Frank Underhill, Company E, looked emaciated and would eventually be treated, but he was ignored that morning. Private Patrick Conway of Company E similarly complained that Dr. Bartholf would not excuse him or anyone from his company who complained that morning of being sick. Private William A. Cooley, Company E, was legitimately marked as being sick that morning, but Dr. Bartholf stepped in and said that he was not sick enough to be taken to the hospital. Cooley had to disobey Captain John Vedder's order to fall in and reiterated, "I am not well and will not go." Private John Scully of Company A had gotten in an intoxicated scuffle with Private Thomas E. Atkinson the night before the march and had three cuts on his head made from a bayonet, a swollen hand, and the nauseous effects that surfaced from a binge. Atkinson too was slightly inebriated the night previous, but said the fight was not his fault and said he "was attacked in his tent without provocation." Soldiers like Corporal Frank Mooney and Privates Andrew Myers, Samuel C. LaRue, William H. Stanton, and Wilhelmus L. Bink, all of Company A, blatantly defied to form when their first sergeant formed the company prior to the march. Men spoke of legitimate injuries or illnesses yet were still refused to stay behind, and were threatened with charges of desertion if they did not fall in line. Whatever excuse was given, no one was put on the sick list from the two companies, so they were unwilling to march.[8]

The ordered appearance of neat cabins looked abandoned as canvas roofs were dismantled and stowed. Their move towards the river began after a late start when the 18th left their encampment near White Oak Church about noon on January 20. Having started a march midday meant the mileage would not be excessive. The regiment walked an easy trek with their corps on dirt paths in a northwesterly direction towards Berea Church.[9]

Tensions remained hot in Company E during the march which prompted more privates to snap. Private Dennis McKinney did not make it far before he decided to fall out of formation and head back to camp. Private Jerry Maher made the march as far as White Oak Church before he "hurt my side with a stick coming across a ditch," and he too started a backwards journey towards camp. To the surprise of no one in the company was when Private Alphonso Green absented himself during the march and went back to camp. Captain Vedder could not stand Green and viewed him as "a noted coward never having been in a battle with his Co. or Regt, availing himself of every opportunity to escape when there was a prospect of a battle, [for example] at Crampton Pass … and Antietam," and this time felt no different. The most errant display of disrespect came from the captain's own distant cousin, Private Barney M. Vedder. As the men traveled, Private Vedder made himself heard when he repeatedly stated such phrases that, "he did not care a damn for the Captain or Lieutenant. They might go to Hell … he would desert," and that he "would never cross the Rappahannock again for them." The embittered private eventually snapped, stepped out of the line, and walked back to camp alone.[10]

The regiment pushed on for several miles to a point located about three miles above Falmouth. The men settled a bivouac in a dense pine grove and sought the natural canopies of tree branches and needles to protect them from a rain that started just as they arrived near 8 p.m. Tents were out of the question as the pegs hardly sank into the frozen ground, and those that tried saw their canvas shelters blown away by a stiff wind that swept through the

Artist correspondent Alfred Waud sketched this scene of the Army of the Potomac's struggle to advance to the Rappahannock River near Falmouth, Virginia, on January 21, 1863. The worst weather conditions imaginable seemed to come all at once, which brought the army literally to their knees in mud (Library of Congress).

camp. Soaked from rain through the night, the men tried to make fires to stay warm, but the abundant green pine wood would not take a flame. Meaner the storm grew, and with it came strong gale force winds that violently rocked the trees and blew loose debris.[11]

The storm intensified the following day, and churned the hardened ground to a slick pool of mud. Hardly did anyone find time to sleep overnight, and by morning men found themselves soaked in puddles of freezing rain. In later years, when men ever got cold, all they had to do was think back to this moment to know nothing else compared. Weighted down by the rains, the 18th started to walk at 7 a.m. but only trudged two miles before they stopped and formed an encampment near Banks's Ford. The rain again prevailed through the night and completely prevented the saving graces of campfires. The rain was cold enough to literally freeze the Union army in their tracks. Boots, wheels, and hoofs became cemented under the muddy quagmires of previously suitable dirt roads, and yet Burnside was still certain his men could cross the river and catch the Rebels off guard. The river level rose as more rain fell, and the rocky crossing of Banks's Ford rushed with rapid currents. Burnside's plan unfolded before his eyes and he eventually receded after he knew he had lost the element of surprise upon the enemy. His premature offensive trek that ignored the power of nature led to an embarrassing event that would forever be remembered by its participants as the doomed "Mud March."[12]

For the next three days, the soaked and mud-covered men of the 18th spent every ounce of their strength and willpower to free themselves from the muck. The entire regiment was detailed on January 22 to help pry out mud-jammed wagon wheels and artillery pieces out of the turnpike. The work seemed endless, and the entire division was put to task to free the pontoons and artillery out of the mud. The colossal effort to free Union forces from the clutches of the Virginian mud was never fully achieved, and their hopeful crossing of the river never panned out. Men ached in new ways even from those with nearly two years of service. Dr. Rice took pity on Private William Elliott of Company I who was wholly used up and excused him from duty. Dr. Rice made Elliott carry his box of medical instruments instead.[13]

All of the rain had beaten through the dirt surface and liquefied the loam and clay to slush unlike anything the men had ever encountered. Wagons and artillery pieces sank to their axles. Thousands of horses, mules, and cattle struggled to the point of exhaustion, many drowned, and others had to be killed in the name of mercy. Soldiers from Brooks' division tried in vain to save wagons by chopping wood and building corduroy roads, but they too sank under the earth and took the wheels down like quicksand. The added weight from rain made men heavier and more susceptible for their boots to sink deeper, losing lots of footwear during their struggles. It was no laughing matter when one stumbled and sought help from others. The journey was treacherous for everyone.[14]

By January 22, General Smith somehow was able to near his corps close to Banks's Ford, but they were stretched thin and stuck in places throughout their path. Brooks' division was closest to the river crossing, but by nightfall they discovered an added menace. Enemy campfires were spotted on the other side of the river, which meant the Rebels had figured out their plan, and the fear of being attacked when at their most vulnerable became a dangerous reality.[15]

Captain Donovan of Company F had to take a double-take when a former deserter returned amidst their mud-filled journey on January 22. Private Alonzo Richardson made the difficult trek in an effort to prove to his captain that he was not a deserter, despite having drifted from the regiment days before the Crampton's Gap battle. Richardson handed his captain a paper signed by a police magistrate in Washington that said he had been confined in the Washington Penitentiary with a charge of stealing sheep, of which he was later found not guilty. Donovan had heard of Richardson being in Alexandria after Major Meginnis received a letter that explained his situation. The captain was impressed to see the young private return on the eve of an expected battle. Donovan had always held Richardson in high regard as a good soldier, but "for the good of the service," as Donovan proclaimed, "and particularly my own company," the captain still drew up charges of desertion upon Richardson. He was later found not guilty, but his absence without permission still caused his pay to be docked.[16]

After nearly thirty hours and several inches of rain, precipitation tapered to a drizzle during the morning of January 23, but it was too late. The new campaign had quickly come and gone before it truly got under way. The Army of the Potomac was forced to retreat to the safety of their previous camps back near Falmouth. After having led the advance, Brooks' division about-faced and became the rear guard of the army and obtained a full view of the abysmal atrocities that the Mud March created. The 18th started their retreat on January 24 about 7 a.m., but the entire division was stalled with the time-consuming and arduous task to pull their artillery out of the mud. After having helped free Battery D of the 2nd United States Artillery, the 18th arrived back to their former quarters near White Oak Church around

7 p.m. Browned by mud and soaked to the core, the men felt a different but still demoralizing sting of defeat, this time one that came without a bludgeoning from their enemy.[17]

When Companies A and E stumbled back in camp, the men they lost when they fell out or quit during the miserable jaunt were already in camp awaiting their return. But Captain Vedder and Second Lieutenant Joseph Strunk had something waiting for them too. They slapped these protesters with charges of absence without authority and disobedience.[18]

Burnside Out, Hooker In

The changing seasons grappled for dominance which usually brought the worst weather forward. The wintry mix continued to bog the roads to the same discouraging mire that pervaded the aborted Mud March. The army recoiled from that disaster by staying put and settled for the long haul of winter. Back pay for the past four months came to the men on January 25 which always helped spirits. The 18th finished the last three days of the month posted out on picket duty which started out with a downfall of eight inches of snow their first night.[19]

Burnside's futile Mud March wrecked more than morale and supplies, it ended his reign as commander of the Army of the Potomac. When the 18th shuffled in line to receive their pay, fifty miles away in Washington, Burnside made good on his promise of resignation. In a meeting with the president, the dejected general tendered his own termination, along with an infamous order that called for many generals to be cashiered, those he felt undermined his efforts. The domino effect in the Army of the Potomac was large. President Lincoln directed General Orders No. 20 that relieved Burnside, and in his place, the Army of the Potomac was placed under the leadership of Major General Joseph Hooker. For the other two grand division commanders, Major General Edwin Sumner was relieved of duty and sent home, and Major General William B. Franklin was relieved and would never again serve with the Army of the Potomac. The change was immediate, and by January 26, Franklin was gone. General Smith took temporary command of the Left Grand Division.[20]

Having held his own with a division in force that changed the tide of the battle of Williamsburg, General Hooker had since cemented for himself the nickname of "Fighting Joe." The career soldier had only known triumphs and promotions since his graduation from West Point, service in Mexico, and his successes against Confederates. Appointed by Lincoln to command the Army of the Potomac, the zealous general was similar to McClellan in regards to his efforts to restructure the army, improve moral, and unearth the *esprit de corps* that had faded since Little Mac's removal.[21]

Assessing the damage control left from Burnside's tenure, Hooker's first executive decision was the cessation of the grand division structure. Without Sumner and Franklin, no replacements were needed, and instead Hooker reverted back to how McClellan operated his commands and left the corps commanders stand as the highest field commanders that acted on his word.[22]

As a late casualty of General Burnside's scathing order to relieve army generals by the wholesale, General William F. Smith was relieved of his command of the VI Corps on February 4, but his removal was done so under the assumption that he would head the IX Corps. As luck would have it, Burnside requested and was granted that position to command his old corps, which left Smith without an equivalent position. Smith's exit from the VI Corps was immediately given to Major General John Sedgwick. A Connecticut native, Sedgwick was another product of West Point with undisputed skill and dependability on the battlefield. While a division commander in the II Corps at Antietam, Sedgwick was thrice wounded and carried off the field. Sedgwick recovered and returned with gusto to command the VI Corps. With an overt knack to tender great care for the men he commanded, the nickname of "Uncle John" always followed him.[23]

Part of Hooker's overhaul of the Army of the Potomac affected the VI Corps not just with a new corps commander, but brigades and divisions were rearranged. There was even a creation of separate light division that was more like an extra but separate brigade. The 18th was still part of the third brigade under Brigadier General David A. Russell, and were still a part of the First Division under Brigadier General William T. H. "Bully" Brooks. The 18th and 32nd New York and the 95th Pennsylvania remained where they were, but the brigade lost the 31st New York who were assigned to the new fast-moving light division within the corps. To fill their vacancy was the addition of two battletested regiments—the 49th and 119th Pennsylvania—that had come from the Second Division of the VI Corps, scrambled out as part of the realignment of the corps. Organized in Harrisburg of men from the counties of central Pennsylvania, the 49th first saw battle at Yorktown at the start of the Peninsula campaign. Their rosters had thinned so much that when they were transferred to Russell's brigade, the ten companies of the regiment were consolidated and formed into four companies. By April, new recruits, substitutes, and drafted men were piped into the 49th to bring the regiment up to strength, but the veterans of the regiment were then outnumbered by raw, green, and untested men. The 119th hailed from Philadelphia, and they first joined the Army of the Potomac shortly after Antietam. Nicknamed "The Gray Reserves," their battle experience was very limited, owed to what little involvement the VI Corps had during the Fredericksburg campaign.[24]

To better manage his span of control on the battlefield, Hooker implemented a unique system of corps badges that would help distinguish units from a distance. With such shapes as diamonds, crescents and circles, the VI Corps was given the badge of the Greek cross. Color variances of these badges helped distinguish between divisions, the first being red, second as white, and the third being blue. Red crosses cut from flannel cloth soon flooded in and around the 18th's camp and were adorned to their kepis and hats. The adoption of badges had the added effect to instill pride between divisions and other corps, and ushered a harder will to prevent anything shameful on the battlefield that the enemy would surely correlate with their distinct symbols.[25]

One of the biggest morale boosters that Hooker put into action was the return of fresh soft bread that was dispensed four times a week. Brigade bakeries soon popped up and company cooks saw an increase of other eatables that brought smiles to the troops. Private Joseph C. Jones of Company G was surprised to see these bakeries pump out fresh bread that he confirmed lasted all winter.[26]

Hooker revamped the efficiency of the cavalry and restructured them to be utilized more like their Confederate brethren who had proven their use better than Union troops had. Hooker made the cavalry more of a fighting asset instead of glorified guards of Rebel property. This lessened the overused comment that Private Joseph Jones related was often shared between infantrymen—"Who ever saw a dead Cavalryman?"[27]

The winter of 1863 was a bitter one. Only a few pleasant days peaked through the

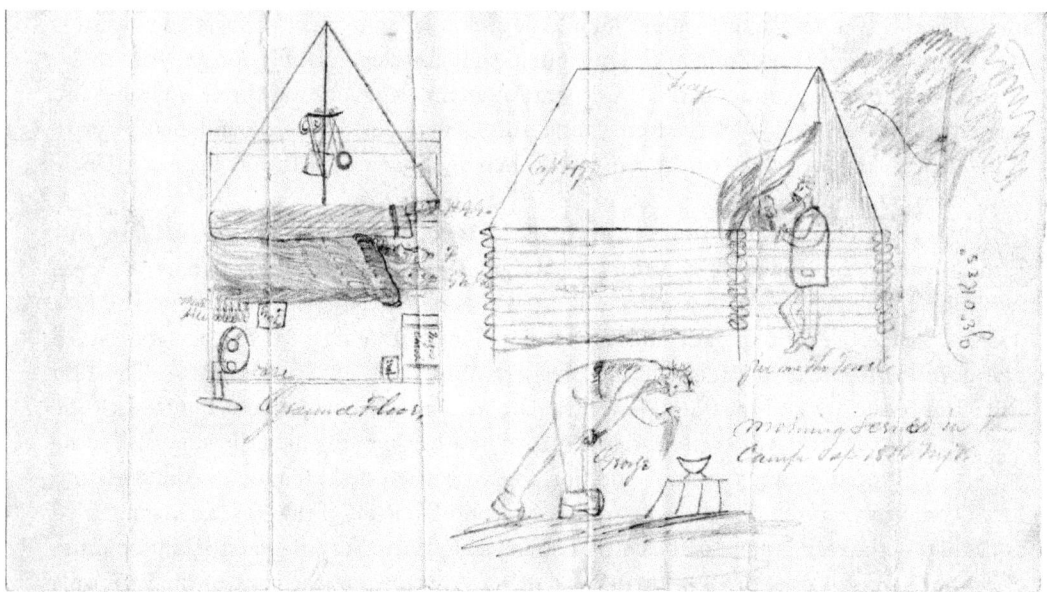

Drummer for Company K George W. R. Goodno drew this lead pencil sketch of his company commander's winter quarters, occupied by his father, Capt. Horatio G. Goodno. He drew his father flipping a tent flap and demanding him to "give me the towel" (courtesy Jeff Sauter).

continual dumps of snow as February began. The 18th idly waited in their winter encampment and took the brunt of winter's worst. Road conditions were "utterly impossible for man or beast to travel," as Dr. Frank J. Mattimore explained. The quagmire roads were so bad, Mattimore added, "the horses can go not over twenty feet when they are buried, 'stuck in the mud' as the old saying is." Sometimes, the poor mules would become so stuck in the roads that the men had to pry them out with boards and poles, which was all too reminiscent of the Mud March. Days of inactivity turned into weeks while they waited the arrival of the new season to dry out the roads and set the stage for a new campaign under their newest leader.[28]

The slower pace of winter quarters filled the men with unyielding boredom, but still faithful to their cause. Mail came the first of the month which helped raise spirits. In early February, a reporter from the upstate *St. Lawrence Republican* paid Colonel Myers and the regiment a visit on a Sunday and attended church with the men. He also watched them parade for inspection, and marveled at the tattered and soiled flag from battles past. When he looked upon the men, the reporter noted that they appeared every bit like they had suffered since leaving home, "but I did not see the man who desired to recall the past twenty months." Despite the heavy press reports that the Union army wallowed in despair, this reporter was proud to tell that this sentiment was not overbearing with those from the regiment that he interacted with. The two-year men counted down the days to their release, and as Sergeant Gregoire Insse of Company G put it, "every day makes quite a lump off of our time." Insse also mentioned that "time yearns to drag with some of the boys they are in a hurry for May to come around."[29]

Lessons learned from previous encampments of prolonged stays prompted the regiment to slightly shift their camp half of a mile to new grounds on February 11, at 8 a.m. The New Yorkers again perfected and customized their quarters and frequently manned their turn on the picket line when the cycled duty fell upon them. Daily drills and inspections were performed when weather permitted, which helped groom new line officers within their new posts. Men caught up on correspondence from home, and those who could read consumed whatever literature that was within reach.[30]

Snow in the latter part of the month accumulated to nearly fifteen inches by George Washington's revered birthday on February 22, which was enough to remind men of winters back home. Finding fun in the snow allowed the men to gleefully release the toils of boredom. Dr. Mattimore mentioned, the snow gave "the boys a splendid snow balling season." Massive impromptu snowball fights amongst the 18th took place on February 23 and 25, and as Dr. Mattimore added, "many and many a battle has been fought over and over again by the boys, with snow shells, and they enter the contest with as much ardor and enthusiasm as if they were engaged with the Rebs."[31]

On February 27, the 18th participated in another review by their commanding general, but this one by Hooker was markedly different than ones performed for others. The event "was more like a funeral than a Review," as Sergeant Insse so matter-of-factly stated. He mentioned that "it was no such Review as we had when under McClellen. We did not cheer him nor did not present arms to him." The Army of the Potomac had seen a lot of commanders come and go, but none held more affection in the eyes of the soldiers as McClellan, but Hooker was untiring to win their trust.[32]

One of the persistent problems that plagued the Army of the Potomac that Hooker vowed to end was the gross rate of desertions. As soon as Hooker took command he attacked the problem with revamped protocols to first calculate the rates, and secondly, to put an end to those that opted to slip away. Desertions during this demoralized period ranged around several hundred a day from the army. Four privates deserted the regiment in January, which added to the 138 others that did the same since the regiment began. On January 30, Hooker had asked every regiment to furnish a detailed list of each absentee, to include possible whereabouts and physical descriptions. The total list soared to show more than 85,000 soldiers from the Army of the Potomac were listed as absent or detached.[33]

Hooker also enacted a renewed priority placed on the picket line, and the cessation of free roaming between the camps without proper authorization. Sentries were told to shoot anyone who failed to respond to their summons. Packages to soldiers from home were rerouted through the provost marshal's office and inspected in an effort to seize any civilian clothes that were sent to the front. Lastly, local authorities in the North were tasked by the War Department to round up deserters, and their captors would be repaid by cash bounties.[34]

Before many of Hooker's measures on desertions took effect, the army was returned with 467 deserters by the new commander's first week. On February 6, Hooker declared that the desertion problem was "at an end, or nearly so," and in relation to the 18th, no man fled during the month. The regiment was actually returned a former deserter when Private John Allen of Company B was escorted by guards and brought to camp on February 18, after having been gone for nearly twenty-one months. Allen was listed on the company rolls as having deserted a week before the regiment left Albany. Having left before he learned any serious drill or earned a dime from the government, there was no need for a person like him in the regiment. He was tried under a court-martial and dishonorably discharged "as a worthless soldier, and a burden to the government."[35]

With the idle time and lack of talks about a movement, the VI Corps requested the brigade to sift through some of their court-martial cases left on standby. The fifteen Schenectady soldiers from Companies A and E who refused to venture on with the Mud March were quickly sentenced without contest with charges of unexcused absences and disobedience. The men had to forfeit anywhere from two-to-four months pay based on their case, which was essentially all that they had coming to them with the length of their service that remained. There were only a few exceptions with this band of fallouts. Private Frank Underhill's obvious state of feebleness was enough for the judges to recommend his sentence be remitted. Stricter punishment was dealt to Private Barney Vedder for his blatant contempt and verbal disrespect towards his superior officers. He lost all his future dues and was sent to the Rip Raps at Fort Jefferson—located in the Dry Tortugas of Florida where he would be kept at hard labor until his term of enlistment expired in July and released under dishonorable conditions. Captain Vedder's added charge of cowardice for Private Alphonso Green landed him with the same penalty and joined Barney Vedder down in Florida.[36]

The strictest of punishments was reserved for a man who deserted the regiment just before the battle unfolded, and showed no effort to return. Private John Baker of Company B complained of sore feet when he decided to fall out of formation just as the regiment traversed the crossing that kicked off the battle of Fredericksburg. Baker claimed that he received good advice from friends that the enemy was all around him and that was his reason for not getting back to the regiment sooner. He was eventually returned not by his own will but by the escort of guards on January 29, after an absence of fifty days. If he had returned quicker and on his own will like the three from Company A did, his sentence may have been altered. His alibi did not hold up for the panel of judges who by majority sentenced him at his March 2 court-martial to be shot by musketry.[37]

Luckily for the sake of Baker, his life and countless others would be spared by the forgiveness of the new commanding general and president. Lincoln enticed deserters to return by a proclamation on March 10 that gave amnesty to any absent Union soldier to return without penalty—except loss of pay—if they returned by April 1. Hooker took the measure further and extended it to those that had already been apprehended for the crime. Hooker penned a pardon for Baker on March 31 and had it accepted by Lincoln. Private William R. Green was once the first sergeant of Company C until Colonel Myers ordered his demotion. He spent several months in hospitals in Brooklyn and Washington detailed as a nurse, and in March of 1863 he fled from an army hospital in Brooklyn. Green was quickly arrested and forwarded to the regiment. After seven months away, Private Samuel Jordan of Company H was arrested and returned on March 27. Not only was his pay forfeited as punishment, but he was responsible to repay the government $36.87 for the reimbursement of clothing, transportation, musket, and equipage that he lost, which was a hefty fine for someone on a private's salary. The 18th's former drum major, John F. Giffen, turned himself in to authorities at Fort Columbus the day before the end of Lincoln's mandate after his absence of more than seven months. Veterans of Company H were also surprised to see the face of Private Edward Schufeldt when he was returned on April 3. He had been listed a deserter ever since the depressing retreat from the first Bull Run rout on July 22, 1861.[38]

In another effort to curb the demoralization of the troops, Hooker rewarded his faithful men with an increase of furloughs. Hooker hoped a taste of home would recharge his men. To prevent furloughs from turning into desertions, stipulations to the policy were created.

Factoring the time it took to get to New York, furloughs could not last longer than ten days. No more than two line officers were allowed to be given leave at the same time. For the enlisted men, only two for every 100 men present for duty earned furloughs, but these were selective for those with "the most excellent record for attention to all duties." Only a select few from the 18th—mostly officers—enjoyed this brief vacation home, but the impact it had on maintaining the overall troop levels was enough to at least delay the inevitable draft.[39]

Camp life during the tail end of winter was slow-moving, and was noticed more for its changing weather than by major events. The entire regiment started a four-day cycle of picket duty on March 2, which was marred by rain, heavy winds, and a constant cold snap. Gaps between storms allowed the snow to melt which cleared the grounds to allow the camp craze game of baseball to start up on March 11. Teams were most often formed under the banner of their regiment and challenged rival regiments within the area. Several games were played and watched throughout the month whenever the weather cooperated. For one game, nine officers from the 18th formed a team and challenged nine other officers from the neighboring 32nd. Men from both regiments were spectators and cheered their officers, but the victors of that game went to the 32nd. Still, plenty of rain and occasional snowstorms kept the roads murky enough to keep the men grounded in their place, daring not to again ignore Mother Nature's unpredictability. A good reminder came on March 15, which started with a gorgeous blue sky, but dark clouds rolled in at noon, and two hours later the heavens opened with

Artist Greg Trax's rendering of an actual wartime photograph of Company I in a camp setting. The size of the company and lack of their State of New York shell jackets dates this image to late in their service, most likely winter 1863 (courtesy Greg Trax).

heavy lightning, thunder, and hail. The hail carried into the night and switched to snow by the next morning. Five days later, another twenty-four hour snowfall painted the camp white at White Oak Church.[40]

Better days came near the end of the month and paved the way for more frequent drill sessions and dress parades on the company and regimental level. The month finished off with yet another snowstorm on the morning of March 31, which cancelled drill for the day. On April 3, the regiment, along with the brigades of their division, gathered on the chilly parade field near White Oak Church at 11 a.m. for an inspection by General Hooker. A snowstorm that started the night of April 4 and continued into the following morning was the last of the year to fall on the men, and it melted quickly. The familiar smell of gunpowder returned on April 6 and 7 when the 18th picked up the practice of shooting at targets.[41]

All eyes were on Hooker as April came with hopes of his inevitable push to finish the war with a new spring campaign. Hooker got his men moving with a series of reviews for the Army of the Potomac which started in early April. President Lincoln even ventured from Washington to pay Hooker and the army a visit, and he brought along the First Lady and youngest son. The entire cavalry force that was consolidated on Hooker's implementation was reviewed in a cavalcade of nearly 17,000 men on horseback for the president on April 6. The 18th spent the day elsewhere perfecting their aim at targets. After a thorough buff and polish crusade the following day, the 18th took part in the infantry review for Lincoln that took place on April 8. At 8 a.m., on that cold and windy morning, the VI Corps marched en masse with the II, III, and V corps, and assembled more than 75,000 men for the display at Falmouth. Each corps marched to their designated area marked with various signs in the shape of their new corps badges. Uniformed herds painted the fields blue and flags fluttered against a stiff and constant wind. Bands and drum corps filled the air with beats and songs on a scale not seen since McClellan's final review in November. Large-scale reviews always came with a lot of idle stand-by time to allow the proper placement of regiments. The men waited for their turn to march, albeit impatiently due to a brisk wind that swept across the flattened ground and chilled their core. Men could only stomp their feet in place or rub their fingers vigorously to prevent the numbness to find temporary relief of warmth. When the event finally got under way shortly before noon, each corps formed into columns of divisions and were reviewed separately. By 2 p.m., the 18th was back in their camp. Noah Brooks—a journalist who accompanied Lincoln and his entourage—wrote of the spectacle of the day from the president's vantage:

> It was a splendid sight to witness their grand martial array as they wound over hills and rolling ground, coming from miles away, their arms shining in the distance, and their bayonets bristling like a forest on the horizon as they marched away. The President expressed himself as delighted with the appearance of the soldiery.... It was noticeable that the President merely touched his hat in return salute to the officers, but uncovered to the men in the ranks.[42]

Two days later, the Army of the Potomac asked of its regiments to create a "Grand Muster" in an effort to ascertain its total troop strength. The event was to find the number of recruits each regiment would need to bring the personnel level back to a minimum standard and match each state's quota. It was also a chance for the Union army to brace for the impending loss of many two-year regiments from New York and Maine that inched closer to their expiration dates. April would be the end of five of the two-year regiments, but May had thirteen, and June would have seventeen. The 18th was one of the thirty-eight regiments from

New York that formed to serve two years whose numbers were tallied separately, as they were about a month away from their long expected muster-out. Conventional wisdom made higher officials question the integrity of how committed these men would be this late in their contracts if they were to be thrown into another campaign.[43]

General Sedgwick had many of these two-year regiments in his VI Corps, and with his old soldiering ways even he had doubts about them. Written with blunt honesty, Sedgwick wrote a letter to his sister soon after the Grand Muster and explained, "No troops with but a few days to leave are going to risk much in a fight."[44]

Many had quickly grown accustomed to the administration creating loopholes to keep up the number of troops and some speculated that something would be spun that would refrain them to be mustered out. Draft threats were real and Sergeant Insse speculated that possibly New York State, "are waiting to draft us when we get back." Others kept faith and pondered what they would do after the war. The war, in fact, had no endgame in sight which made postwar plans a premature idea. Insse even tossed ideas to his brother in a letter with what he would be best suited for, but he too wanted to see the war come to an end more than anything. As the Union army moved towards another foray into Fredericksburg, Insse wanted the war settled where it began:

> I want to go down to Charleston South Carolina. I would like to see that place Bombarded if they would only take us down to Charleston to help take that place I would enlist for six months more. I would like no better fun than to Ransack the city and then help burn it, but I suppose we will have to make another attempt on Fredricksburg before we get out of the servis well let it come.[45]

Even up to this time the men still had no definite date on when they would muster-out. They were hopeful that their promise would be met and released at the appropriate time in May, yet no one could write that home for certain. On April 9, Sergeant George Blake of Company H wrote home to his cousin and explained his prospects of coming home on time:

> I think that within the next week I can tell how soon I will be home, it will not be over 6 weeks more any way they can fix it, this idea of keeping troops 30 days after their term of enlistment expires I think is eronious & will not be done it looks more likely that we will be home so many days before than after.[46]

Times were quiet in camp, but the return to a sense of normalcy was uplifting. Men could plainly see improvements with the army under Hooker's command who quickly won their confidence. Sergeant Blake made a mention of their esteemed general on April 10:

> Hooker is liked more & more every day they think that he will show them bloody work when the time comes, some think that we will not move before the 1st of May if then. I think that it cannot be said of the Army of the Potomac all quiet along the lines" 20 days will show.[47]

The 18th showed every sign of a veteran unit and would be going in with its lowest troop strength they had ever dealt with. During the winter months, fourteen previously wounded soldiers returned to the regiment, which was always better than a raw recruit. Still, there was always more that left the regiment than returned. During their White Oak Church encampment, the 18th medically discharged thirty-six men during the first four months of 1863; January yielded sixteen; eleven in February; six in March; and three in April.[48]

Most of these disability discharges at White Oak Church were from men previously wounded in battle. They had since been separated from the regiment and dispersed in hospitals since their wounding so their names being struck from the rosters was not a shock to the cohesion of the ranks, but it was regrettable.[49]

Of these thirty-six medical discharges, fifteen were unrecoverable wounded from battles past. Three of the wounded were officers who vainly attempted to endure their injury and maintain their jobs. Hospitalized twice for his grizzly wound from Gaines's Mill, Captain Horatio Goodno of Company K ignored Dr. Rice's recommendation to remain longer under a physician's care. The rifle ball that pierced through his neck exited out of his mouth and took with it a portion of his tongue, teeth, and jaw. His second return to the regiment on October 26 lacked improvement to his health and Goodno struggled with speech that affected his abilities and duties of a company commander. After several weeks of feeling the magnitude of his injury he accepted the realities of his wound and the fifty-two-year-old resigned his position on January 19. His sixteen-year-old son George W. R. Goodno—the company drummer—dropped his drumsticks six days later and deserted.[51]

Dating back to the time the regiment occupied a skirmish line at Fredericksburg under a day-long harassment of artillery in December 1862, Private Malcolm E. Colby of Company E was said to have snapped under the stress. With no known treatment for combat stress, Colby's complaints of a constant "rumbling noise" in his head fell on deaf ears. In the weeks that followed Fredericksburg, he seemed to only dwell on his crazed notion to cross the river and fight the Rebels. Colby was considered "a very bad man" by his comrades because of how combative he turned, and that he tried to fight with every person that stumbled into camp, which earned him the apropos nickname, "Wild Man." On January 27, Colby exploded into such a hysteric that he was pulled from the regiment that morning and hospitalized for insanity. Just as soon as the acting surgeon Dr. John H. Bartholf wrote his request that day for Colby to be institutionalized in Washington, he escaped and fled the camp at White Oak Church. Colby was caught a week later, and "for his safety and that of his comrades," he was held in the regimental guardhouse. On February 13, Colby was escorted out of the regiment and taken to Washington, where he was institutionalized at the St. Elizabeth's Hospital for the insane.[50]

Disease continued to be the frontrunner of reasons why names were shaved off the roster from January to April. No less than twenty of these discharged men were sent home because of diseases. Diarrhea, tuberculosis, and even scurvy made its way to seize a hold of susceptible men. Fever continued to be the main agitator of men's health, in which most cases still originated from the disease-rampant Peninsula campaign.[52]

Even Dr. Frank J. Mattimore came down with a serious bout of malarial fever at the end of February which confined him to his bed. With no hope to improve his health amidst unfavorable camp conditions, the assistant surgeon was sent home in March and ended his duties with the regiment. Mattimore never shook free from fever and eventually died from the disease at his Albany home on October 11, 1863.[53]

There were still the instances that disease set in so quickly that time did not allow for recovery or discharge papers to save a soldier. Private Mathew Dee of Company F was hospitalized with typhoid fever at the VI Corps hospital at Windmill Point, Virginia on January 20. The thirty-seven-year-old Irish moulder could not last twenty-four hours under a doctor's care and died the following day. In a hospital in Hagerstown, Maryland, Private William H. Fox of Company G died from diarrhea on January 22.[54]

Even with a discharge in hand, some could not escape the death sentence that some illnesses had on soldiers. Private Daniel H. Aldrich, Company F, and Private Stephen Hardick, Company B, shared a parallel journey towards their deaths. They were both eighteen years old when they enlisted and eventually came under debilitating bouts of typho-malarial fever that lingered for several months. In March, the health of both privates sank low which prompted Dr. Rice to quicken the paperwork to get them out of the service. Dr. Rice finalized Aldrich's medical discharge at the regimental hospital on March 14, but he was too late. Just hours after the ink dried on his discharge paper, Aldrich succumbed to the disease and passed away. Just two days before Aldrich's death, Dr. Rice had finished Hardick's papers and was discharged, but he died from his fever on March 20 before he had the chance to make the journey home.[55]

In a similar instance, Private Frank K. Underhill of Company E was an underage youth that collected the Chickahominy fever during the Peninsula campaign, and he was still too feeble to make the Mud March of which he was later forgiven when he refused to march. He wrestled with his disease for months and often ignored great pains just so he could stay in the ranks with his brother and comrades. By February, his fever turned into chronic diarrhea that rendered him unable to perform his duties and Colonel Myers authorized Underhill's discharge from the regiment on March 28. His health outside of the regiment failed to improve and Underhill died five weeks after his discharge at his home in Charlton, New York.[56]

In April, Company H was finally given a captain to head their company after almost ten months without one. Captain John Mooney was granted the promotion and was transferred to his third company he would serve in within the regiment. This was a bit of a slap in the face to First Lieutenant Thomas S. Lane who had commanded the company since Gaines's Mill and every episode afterwards. Just as the men prepared to return home in what was believed to come in three weeks, Lane did not warm up to the idea, and the men of Company H felt the same.[57]

An Offensive Once Again

The second anniversary of the war's inauguration was spent with the men doing the routine evening dress parade at the brigade-level. That same day, the 18th received orders for their turn to man the picket line for another four-day stint to begin the next day. This time, only seven companies from the regiment marched out on April 13 to the picket line for the regiment's rotation. New marching orders from the army headquarters at Falmouth arrived on April 14 while the men were out on the line. Preparations for the long awaited march upon their enemy finally fell into place. Rations for an eight day march were handed out to the men not on the picket line. Large tents also had to be struck and turned in to the quartermaster's department. After the dreary winter, the warm spring weather helped reinvigorate motivation for what they believed to be the last campaign push to end the war, hopefully before the 18th was to muster-out in a month. With the exception of a rain-filled day on April 15, weather during their time on the line was relatively pleasant. When the seven companies came off the picket line on April 16, the regiment received their sixty rounds of ammunition, a hefty nine day's worth of rations, and their baggage was sent off.[58]

The planned march became delayed as soon as they got ready, and the veterans were hardly surprised. April showers snuck in and bogged roads that conjured up memories of the Mud March. While the regiment stood by and waited for the weather to improve and official orders to trickle down from higher, the routine of camp life prevailed. Company drills and brigade dress parades continued to occupy most of their time during the wait. On April 18, the division was once again formed up for an inspection at 11 a.m., this time to show off to a Swiss General named Augusto Fogliardi. The next week prevailed with a series of rainy days that cancelled the usual daily dress parades and drills. On one of the finer days, the 18th's brigade was formed up near White Oak Church and inspected by their commander Brigadier General David A. Russell on April 22, which they completed just before rain roared in.[59]

After two more days of solid rain without drills, the sunshine poked through the clouds and hung around long enough to put the army in motion. The paymaster swept through the camp and paid the 18th their overdue owed sum on April 25. That same day, the recently pardoned deserter Private John Baker of Company B abandoned the regiment a second time, never to be heard from again. Attention shifted away from Baker when the troops received orders on April 27 to march upon the enemy. Their expected homecoming seemed to fall out of reach, committed to a campaign that no one could predict the outcome so close to the end of their contracted time.[60]

18

Committed to the End
April 27, 1863–June 4, 1863

> "How many of those who then went with you in the pride
> of their manhood and strength now fill a soldier's grave!"
> —*Charles C. McQuoid, Middletown lawyer, June 3, 1863*

The Chancellorsville Campaign

At 6 p.m. on April 27, official orders arrived for the second time to the different corps commanders that finally asked for an early morning push the following day. The men packed their gear and the non-commissioned officers paced through the ranks and ensured everyone had their essentials to wage war. A general inspection was held during the evening where a circular address from General Hooker was read aloud to the men that told his expectations for the new campaign. Each man was again loaded down with eight days rations of pork and crackers, three rations of which were put in their haversacks and five in their knapsacks. They were also issued no less than sixty rounds of cartridges. Haversacks were stuffed with extra ammunition packets and clothing was removed from knapsacks to allow more room for their food. Feeling they were the true essence of "human trucks," a few soldiers from the brigade were curious enough to weigh themselves. They walked to the quartermaster's headquarters and stepped on his scales. With all of their equipment donned as they would be for the next day's march, each man weighed roughly eighty pounds heavier than their body weight.[1]

Finally, after a lengthy winter of isolation that left less than a month on their contract, the 18th was once again committed to another campaign with the Army of the Potomac. After months of changes, Hooker's army was his, and he was going to use them the best way he saw fit. With an offensive plan seemingly half-hatched from Burnside's tactical playbook, Hooker organized the movements and roles of different corps based on their layout of winter encampments established by his predecessor. However, he would use all of his assets of engineers and his revitalized cavalry in ways that would help surprise and stall the enemy. The first Fredericksburg offensive could be said to be the dress rehearsal for Hooker's renewed attempt. By moving the bulk of his troops towards Chancellorsville, and others flanking south of Fredericksburg, Hooker saw an opportunity to cross the Rappahannock and split Lee's troops and destroy them, or at least open a path to Richmond.

The Army of the Potomac was about to embark on a ten-day campaign referred to as the Chancellorsville campaign, under new leadership, and the VI Corps went forth with a new corps commander. The I and VI corps comprised Hooker's left wing south of Falmouth, and his planned diversionary demonstration called for them to construct bridgehead crossings two miles below Fredericksburg. The VI Corps was given the familiar north bank of the Rappahannock area known to them as Franklin's Crossing, which was memorable territory for them during the first attempt in December. With lessons learned from that failed exploit, they were intended to throw up three pontoon bridges simultaneously at the same site, but only after a midnight crossing of infantry secured the opposite shore. The I Corps was given the identical task less than two miles south from Franklin's Crossing, at a point designated as Fitzhugh's Crossing.[2]

Commanding what was very similar to Burnside's short-lived Grand Divisions, Sedgwick was put in charge of the I and VI corps, and for a time had the III Corps at his disposal as reserves. As events played out during the campaign and positions were rearranged, Sedgwick was eventually thinned to the command of just his corps.

Franklin's Crossing

"Reveille" was beaten in camp at 5 a.m. on a cloudy April 28. The camp of the 18th came alive as the men woke up and donned their uniforms and equipment. Rain made its unwelcomed return in the late morning and the order to break down the camp was delayed.[3]

Being committed to yet another battle when the regiment had just less than a month left of service, some men decided not to test fate and got spooked. Privates Vincent H. Clark and Sanford S. Clauson, both of Company D, understood when a battle neared. Clark had once been wounded when his rifle was ripped out from his hands from an artillery shell at Crampton's Gap and he vowed to himself that he would not enter another battle again. Clauson was said to be "a good fellow, but constitutionally timid and could never be induced to go into battle with the company." Both boldly refused to enter the Fredericksburg fight and were summarily brought up on charges for cowardice. Clark and Clauson deserted just moments before the order to march forward was given.[4]

The rain eventually tapered off in the late afternoon and the order to pull down the shelter halves above their cabins was finally given. The log huts which served as the men's "home away from home" were stripped of their canvas roofs and were tucked away amongst the men's already weighty haversacks. What was left was a sea of bare boned cabins organized into timber villages, with logged roadways and gangplank sidewalks that spanned the landscape for as far as the eye could see. What was once a vast spread of thick forests of pine, cedar, and oak back in December, one could hardly find a tree left standing. The men bid farewell to their winter encampment and became energized as the regiment formed up and took its place in line with their brigade.[5]

On General Sedgwick's call, the VI Corps started after the I Corps, and began their march toward Franklin's Crossing at 3 p.m. Accompanied by a light rain, General Russell's brigade traversed over soggy and muddy paths, which also compounded the weight on their backs. They had a lot of ground to gain to get to the Rappahannock on behalf of the late afternoon start, but a halt was called for about a mile from the river just before nightfall. They were placed in line of battle upon the crest of a hill that hugged the north bank of the river and watched what available light was left fade away. The night would have to be spent where they were, but to continue the cloak of surprise of their movement the men were forbidden to make fires of any kind during the night. Warm food for dinner would have to wait, but this was nothing new for them.[6]

After whatever meal they scrounged from the depths of their haversacks, most tried to shut their eyes. The respite was brief as all were roused around 10 p.m. with some important information that needed to be disseminated. Colonel Myers and the other four regimental commanders within the brigade reported to General Russell's tent. The brigade commander explained the particulars of the VI Corps' planned demonstration for the next day and of what role he wished for each of his colonels. Russell stressed that silence and surprise was of utmost importance. The VI Corps' vanguard for the demonstration fell squarely upon Brooks' division, specifically Russell's brigade, which meant many eyes would rely on their success. The meeting was kept short so the regimental commanders could prepare their men to move. Colonel Myers sped off to the regiment and gathered his staff and company officers and reiterated the plan he had just learned.[7]

The plan called for an armada of pontoons to cross the Rappahannock—a width of about four hundred feet—under the cover of darkness for a surprise seizure of the northern bank. They would then have to rid the grounds from the enemy pickets posted there and keep them in check to allow the engineers to construct a pontoon crossing behind them. Forty pontoon boats were called for that fit nearly fifty men each. Four men from the 15th New York Engineers were assigned to each boat as coxswains, and when one wave was ferried they would return the empty boat back across the river and bring across the remainder of the brigade. For the past two weeks before the crossing, men had routinely launched boats around the river as a feint to their enemy.[8]

From the vantage of the heights, the VI Corps overlooked the river and land to the southwest of Fredericksburg, about one-and-a-half miles away from the city. Several slopes dotted the land and most contained narrow ravines along their base, and some had roads. These roads made it possible for the artillery and pontoon trains to easily traverse over moderately level ground closest to the river bank. Being as Franklin's Crossing was familiar territory, they already knew how best to take advantage of its natural protections and prepare for obstacles. Their foothold on the southern bank leveled to a degree around the water's edge, protected by a range of eroded walls of earth that crested at spots fifteen to twenty feet tall above the water's edge. Beyond these was a series of steeper bluffs with more protection that ranged from forty to fifty feet high, cut at random by more ravines. This natural protection would be used to its fullest to corral and conceal their numbers. Finally, behind the bluffs the land leveled out into an open plain homestead locally known as Mannsfield.[9]

To put the plan to action, the regiments of the brigade were quickly spun up. Russell emphasized silence and moved his entire brigade closer to the embankment and huddled down on a road that ran parallel with the river. They gingerly traversed down the slick muddy hillside in the dark while a light misty rain sprinkled from above. The men cautiously felt their way through the darkness until the column was halted when they reached the engineers near the embankment who had already begun unloading the pontoons off of their trucks. The 95th, 119th, and 49th Pennsylvania, along with a portion of the 32nd New York were to be the first wave sent across at 11 p.m. and the 18th was to await their turn while formed in line of battle near the bank with what was left from the 32nd.[10]

Darkness worked against them more than it shielded their actions, which created a combination of delays that postponed the first launch. Russell did not even receive Brooks' crossing plan of an eleven o'clock launch until midnight. Subordinates of Russell immediately drew blame for the delay on his cautionary hesitation. These delays were also credited to the time that was wasted figuring out troop arrangements and how to properly divide officers aboard pontoons. Tempers were short due to lack of sleep, and officers got frantic as the hours of dawn drew near. The biggest setback came from the engineer in charge of the pontoons, Brigadier General Henry W. Benham, who threw a sherry-infused tantrum towards several VI Corps officers who challenged his instructions and delayed the timetable. Despite orders to remain quiet, Benham bickered loudly with several officers of Brooks' division, specifically Russell, who was demanded by the engineer to be arrested after Russell scoffed at his instructions. Usually a reliable officer, Benham's choice to fight fatigue with alcohol got the better of him. Being the professional soldier he was, "Bully" Brooks intervened and settled the squabble between the two. As the third brigadier general in the mix, Brooks backed Russell, meaning Benham had to realize his powers did not put him in Russell's chain of command. Brooks turned a blind eye to Benham's lack of sobriety, who wisely returned the favor to forget his want of Russell's arrest.[11]

The generals ratcheted their focus back on the crossing. A solution emerged which put all matters to rest that assigned one company (or forty-five men per boat), plus four engineers to row. Once the assignments were hashed out and the boat parties were ready, they waited in silence for the word to push off. By Russell's watch, the crossing force was not even ready

As sketched by artist Alfred Waud, Russell's brigade of the First Division, VI Corps, are shown at Franklin's Crossing on their early morning amphibious assault over the Rappahannock River on April 29, 1863 (Library of Congress).

until 4:20 a.m. on April 29. Daybreak was moments away just as Russell gave the signal to shove the boats. Engineers down the line jammed their oars on the bank and pushed off into the dark water. Twenty-three pontoons, with Russell aboard one with the 49th, sliced into the river just as the light of dawn seeped through.[12]

A thick patch of fog lingered above the Rappahannock River which added to the armada's concealment as morning light increased. The boats crept into the fog and disappeared before the eyes of those spectators waiting on the shore for their turn to cross, including the 18th. Drawn up in battle line, all the 18th could do was wait in silence and prepare for the battle they knew was coming. The quiet sound of oars splashing the water was all but silenced by the slight patter of rain, which gave those on the shore nothing to track the status of the first fleet that disappeared into the fog.[13]

For those drifting across, the fog was fortunate but likewise concealed the northern bank. Everything was quiet. Tension helped silence the men as they rocked in their boats and neared the shore, with no speculation of what kind of reception awaited them. Soon, the blackened silhouettes of trees took form through the darkness and fog, and the ground of the shore seemed to crawl towards them. About midway over the river, the crack of a lone Confederate rifle broke the silence and alerted all of the players that the new campaign had begun. Oarsmen crouched and lowered their profile and hastened their strokes until the crunch of the wooden boat bottoms scraped along the rocks of the opposite shore. With the achievement of surprise, the first wave of infantrymen scrambled out of the boats and slipped in their attempts up its slick bank. The bits of rain that fell made the landing even more slippery and most men lost their initial footing. They helped each other stagger up the minor climb and refocused on the enemy before them. From their rifle pits atop the bluffs, a scattered collection of Confederate pickets opened fire upon the beached New Yorkers and Pennsylvanians. Rifle shots were exchanged, but due to the limited light, fog, and rain both sides threw ineffective bullets at each other. They could only rely on the flashes of fire from their rifles to concentrate an aim.[14]

The 18th and other landing forces on the opposite shore waited for the boats to return, eager to smell gunpowder like those sent before. General Benham's engineers quickly went to task to build their three pontoon bridges. The 18th, along with those from the 32nd yet to have crossed, aimed their elevated muskets towards the faint muzzle flashes of enemy rifle pits across the river and fired an intimidating volley, thrown over the heads of their own beached comrades. Some troops in the 49th Pennsylvania yelled back over the river to have them raise their aim higher. One soldier in the 95th Pennsylvania who recalled this volley from behind him as a "leaden hurricane" and "startling as it was to us, had a most practical effect upon the rebels in the rifle-pits, who ceased firing, thereby giving us an opportunity to form line." The effect was profound and basically rid the rifle pits of enemy pickets, who fled on foot. The Pennsylvanians stretched out as skirmishers and pushed forward under the welcomed light of day. They pushed forward away from the river where the fog shrunk to hover just above the grass. As the natural shroud dissipated, the Pennsylvanians came upon the sight of massed enemy infantry that crouched amongst the fading fog and were separated by only a hundred yards. The Rebels quickly delivered a volley into the skirmishers that somehow did no harm. Instead of returning fire, the Pennsylvanians charged at them with bayonets fixed and reignited the Rebel retreat away from the crossing. They kept running toward the shelter of the Deep Run ravine, which had once been their own refuge during the first battle of Fredericksburg.[15]

With the Confederates pushed away about a half mile from the river and under the watchful eye of skirmishers of Russell's brigade, the successful seizure of the crossing was complete and the engineers began construction of the bridges. The prize came with minimal casualties. The first wave of Pennsylvanians yielded the loss of one man killed and ten wounded, which included the colonel of the 49th Pennsylvania. Three soldiers from the 18th were mentioned to have received wounds, but they must have been so slight that they were overlooked and not tallied into the official report. The amphibious forces became the first casualties of the campaign. The brigade also captured one enemy officer and private, along with several discarded rifles that were dropped when their owners fled.[16]

The engineers that operated the pontoons paddled back to the opposite shore to load up with the second wave, which included the 18th. Private Carson S. Middaugh of Company D always seemed to find a way to slip away from the ranks in the moments before a battle. This time his comrades made a special effort to retain Middaugh in line, but as the boats were loaded the pretentious private made his unseen exit. The 18th was divided throughout the boats just as the first wave had done. Colonel Myers and the color guard floated together in the center of the 18th's drifting line of boats.[17]

Once the 18th beached, they climbed out of the boats and immediately took a position on the picket line which continually stretched left in order to intersect with pickets south of them from the I Corps. The engineers labored with the bridges, while others oared countless trips to ferry troops to the opposite shore. After an hour of steady boat crossings, Brooks' division had made it to the other side without incident. By 7 a.m., the first of three pontoon bridges was completed.[18]

A handful of 18th men were pulled from the picket line in the evening and detailed to help change the front of the captured enemy entrenchments. After some vigorous shoveling, the pits were flipped for the defense against an enemy attack if one came. The only artillery on their side of the shore that day was Battery D, 2nd United States Artillery, which consisted of six Napoleon cannons that were wheeled into these converted breastworks. The 18th continued their picket duty until their brigade was relieved at 5:30 p.m. by soldiers from the first brigade of Brooks' division.[19]

The vigilant eyes of Union pickets tried to figure out the maneuver and intent of the enemy that was not far from their front. The 18th waited behind the stretched line of pickets in reserve near the bridges and braced for a possible attack. As daylight faded out the men dropped themselves in place and spent the night where they were. No further movements were made that night.[20]

Rain welcomed a new day on April 30, as the 18th remained in waiting near the river crossing. Heavy cannonading was heard off to the left of their line, and soon the same was heard off on their right. To the front of the 18th, the men sat tight in relative peace aside from the rolling thunder of war heard off in the distance. The enemy could still be seen out along the road to their front, within rifle range between pickets, but no one encroached on the grounds each other held. Orders came again later that evening for the men to sleep with their equipment on in the event of a hurried assembly in the dark, but the nighttime hours passed as calmly as it did the night before.[21]

While Sedgwick waited for orders from Hooker, little occurred on a cloudy and warm May 1, aside from the continuous rumble of cannons that boomed off out on the right of the line, signaling action somewhere on Hooker's end. The VI Corps again remained relatively

18. Committed to the End   339

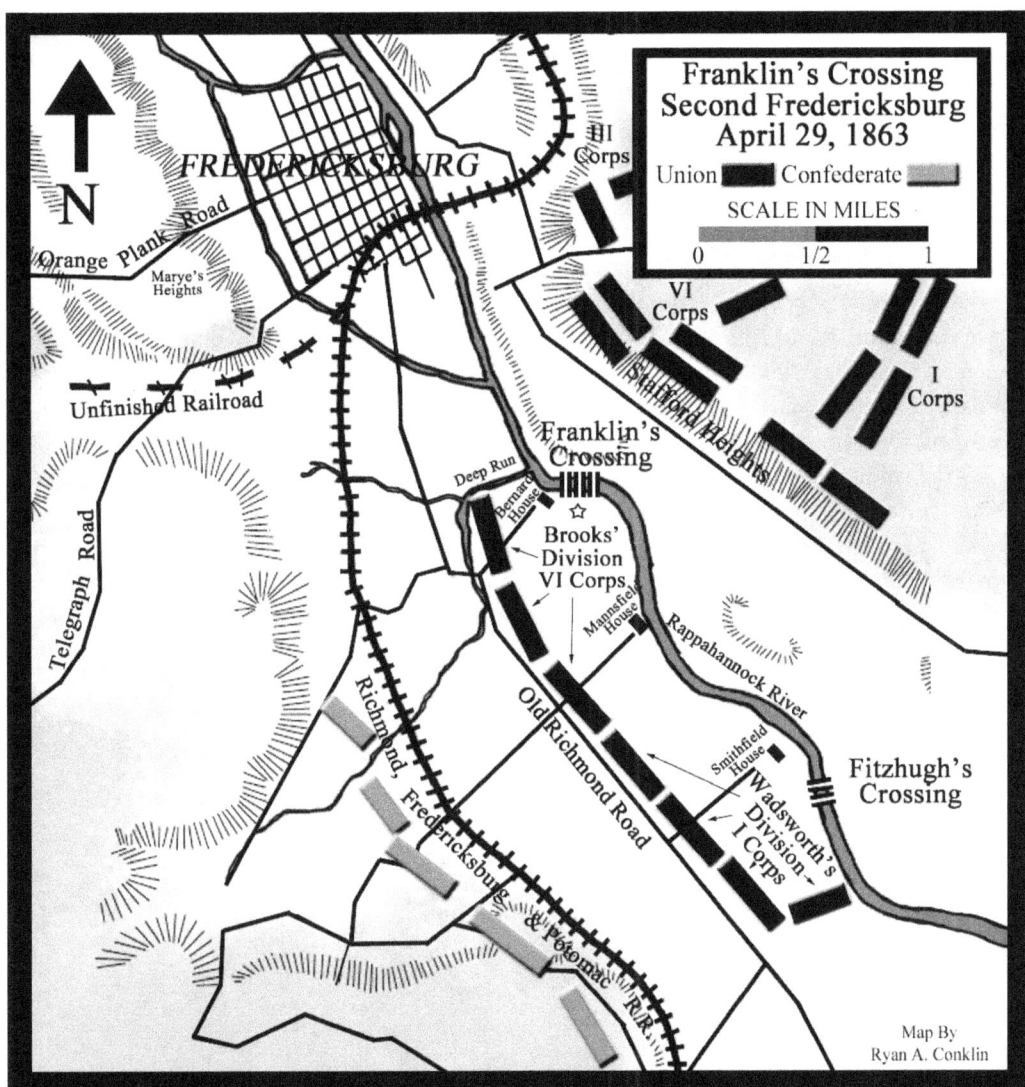

With an early morning amphibious assault, Russell's brigade was the first to cross the Rappahannock River, followed by the rest of Brooks' division, becoming the only elements from the VI Corps to pass over Franklin's Crossing on April 29, 1863 (author's collection).

idle protecting their static crossing, with the rival pickets quieted enough to make it seem like there was an unofficial truce. The men stacked arms at daybreak and passed the day with little to do. Aside from the sporadic sounds of skirmishers keeping the enemy in check, the sounds of bands and cheering Rebels made some wonder if they were not spread before the very jaws of the enemy. In the early evening, the light division from the corps crossed the river and relieved Russell's line.[22]

The 18th received a new man on May 1 who was appointed to become their latest quartermaster. As a newly commissioned first lieutenant, twenty-five-year-old Solomon W. Russell, Jr., had already served a six-month stint as a captain in the 7th New York Cavalry at the start of the war. Russell was from Washington County, New York, and had recently finished up his studies at Union College with the Class of 1863, and was former classmates with First Lieutenant Henry E. Munger of Company A. More notably, he was a cousin of Brigadier General David A. Russell. When the expiration of the regiment came later that month, Russell was transferred to the brigade staff of his cousin. As an added bonus for manpower, Privates Amos Groom, Company G, George M. Hoyt, Company I, and Jacob Sheil, Company H, returned to the regiment after lengthy hospitalizations.[23]

Around 7 a.m., May 2, Rebel artillery opened up and sent several shells towards their positions, but the men huddled together and nestled under the crest of the slight rise in the ground near the river bank. Under this protective lip of earth, the men gathered on the leveled ground behind it, and relished in the relative safety between the bank and bluffs. Most of the men seemed to ignore the very presence of falling shells, callous to their dangers. Shells were mostly overshoots and either slammed into the opposite bank with a thud or fell vertically into the river which sent an entertaining plume of water twenty or thirty feet in the air. Unfazed soldiers lounged in close proximity to each other amidst clusters of stacked rifles. Many curled up in piles and napped while others chose to stir up lively discussions. They all retained an alertness to react and move at a moment's notice if they were needed to support the skirmish lines that remained active throughout the day.[24]

Some circles of friends even broke out into varied games of chance, chiefly card games.

On May 2, 1863, photographer Andrew J. Russell took this image from Stafford Heights, looking over Franklin's Crossing, in the direction of Mannsfield. Around 7 a.m., the 18th New York and their neighbors grouped behind the crest of the hill during an enemy shelling, and their line of troops can be seen at the top right of the image (Library of Congress).

They wagered the money that had recently been paid to the corps before they had an opportunity to mail it home. One witness from the brigade described how the groups of gamblers nonchalantly conducted their games under a sporadic rain of artillery:

> [They were] seated around a gum blanket spread upon the ground, with their stakes piled in front of them, while they anxiously watched the dealer as he shuffled the cards; suddenly the whiz and shriek of a shell would be heard approaching, as it would draw uncomfortably near; now their hands stretched out instinctively towards their money, while their eyes were turned aloft, like ducks looking for a squall. As the unwelcome intruder passed beyond their immediate vicinity, their hands would be withdrawn, and the game go on serenely.[25]

During the afternoon of May 2, the 18th and the rest of their brigade moved up a half a mile to support the skirmishers of the 31st New York, part of the light division that replaced them the day before. Throughout the day, the skirmishers had pushed forward beyond the road that the enemy held earlier that morning. Around 5:15 p.m., a menacing roar of battle bellowed from the direction of Chancellorsville. Stonewall Jackson had made his historic flank attack that rolled the XI Corps on Hooker's right which resolutely changed his battle plans. Completely surprised

With previous service in a cavalry regiment, 1st Lt. Solomon Wright Russell, Jr., was late to join the 18th New York when he was enrolled as a quartermaster on May 1, 1863. He also happened to be the cousin of the brigade commander, Brig. Gen. David A. Russell (author's collection).

and stampeded, Hooker's only saving grace was the night that allowed time for both armies to regroup. The campaign now swung in the Confederate's favor. Hooker's knee-jerk reaction was to reel in the separated I and III Corps. The VI Corps would also be beckoned to join Hooker, but they would have to fight through the enemy-held heights to reach him. Several miles south on the Union's left, Sedgwick sifted through dispatches from Hooker that were easily misinterpreted and written before the rout of the XI Corps. Sedgwick knew he could no longer stay idle where he was but he did not want to venture too far from the river, so he decided to advance a few of his brigades forward. Newton and Howe's divisions of the VI Corps crossed on the two bridges that were left at Franklin's Crossing at 7 p.m. and bolstered the swarming levels of blue troops on the south bank. The second brigade of Brooks' division shoved off Confederate pickets and gained a foothold of the Bowling Green Road by 8 p.m. Continuous cannonading still echoed off on the distant right that made many men of the VI Corps wonder what events the rest of the army experienced. Making matters worse on the VI Corps' front, the heights before them that had massacred the Union army in December was occupied that night by brigades from Confederate General Jubal Early. Their arrival was heralded by the ominous yelp of a thousand Rebel throats, which only spurred men from the VI Corps to scream their own cheers to drown them out.[26]

Marye's Heights (Second Fredericksburg)

Action and activity spun back up overnight when General Russell received new orders to have his brigade ready for movement by 1:30 a.m. on May 3. The 18th had little to prepare for, as they had remained in an elevated state of preparedness since their crossing days before. A representative from Hooker's staff met up with Sedgwick to tell of Stonewall Jackson's route on their right. He was also there to clarify earlier orders for the VI Corps to strike a blow on Lee's rear at first light. Being twelve miles south of Chancellorsville, Sedgwick knew he could not make the strike by daylight, especially after Early's troops occupied the heights behind Fredericksburg. Under the spotlight of the moon, Russell's regiments maneuvered in the darkness and were formed around 4 a.m. The brigade's responsibility was to be the extreme left of Sedgwick's long stretched line and protect the pontoon bridges after legitimate fears that the Rebels might try to attack on their left and seize the crossing. Russell wedged his brigade on the plain between the Bowling Green Road and the Rappahannock. Aside from a battery, their brigade was the only one left behind to protect the crossing. By daybreak their positions were set, just as the rest of the corps made their advance towards the Fredericksburg heights. The 18th and the 32nd New York shared a position near the ruins of the Mannsfield mansion, one of two nearby homes owned by the Bernard family. This traditional Georgian-style stone mansion sat upon a plain, about a half mile distance from the Rebel line stretched on higher ground. Back in December, the lavish home was used as a hospital during the first battle of Fredericksburg, but was accidently burned down by Rebel pickets from North Carolina. On its walls, the New Yorkers found a snarky inscription written in chalk: "This ruin is a monument of the hatred of North Carolina troops to Virginia."[27]

By 5 a.m., the assaulting VI Corps chased out a small faction of Rebel protectors from Fredericksburg and controlled the city. The II Corps linked up with Sedgwick who worked them into a plan to probe the enemy near the northern edge of the city, while he set his eyes on the elusive position of Marye's Heights. Prelude to an attack, Union artillery softened the infantry's target with a thorough pounding. With no time to waste if he were ever to get his men to Chancellorsville, Sedgwick had to attack the enemy on the heights, concluding to himself, "Nothing remained but to carry the works by direct assault." The VI Corps would have to attack the same point that waves of multiple corps could not take in December, but the heights this time were thinly defended.[28]

As soon as the attack on Marye's Heights became general, situations back at Franklin's Crossing raised the eyebrows of the reserve troops. General Russell took notice of a Rebel mass grouped in the woods to the left of his reserve line, as if poised to make a flanking probe to seize the crossing. Russell sent word to Brooks of his situation and assumptions, and was quickly given support from Battery D, 2nd United States Artillery, who took a position at the crossing with the brigade. Almost immediately after Russell posted the battery and strengthened his line of skirmishers, the enemy before him disappeared.[29]

Opposite top: **With the 18th New York mixed somewhere among this huddled mass of Brooks' Division, this photograph taken on May 2, 1863, depicts how nonchalantly the men passed the day under a sporadic harassment of Confederate artillery while nestled behind the protective bluff on the southern side of Franklin's Crossing (Western Reserve Historical Society, Cleveland, Ohio).** *Bottom:* **Another shot of unidentified regiments from Brooks' Division taken on May 2, 1863, as they passed the day in waiting on the flats between the bluff and river bank on the southern side of Franklin's Crossing (NARA).**

At the VI Corps' center, a successful charge upon Marye's Heights was swiftly won, and they celebrated loudly from within the captured earthworks. The once impregnable Rebel wall was worth its weight in gold to the Army of the Potomac, but it came with a hefty price of life lost from the VI Corps to around 1,500 killed and wounded. Russell's brigade was far removed from the fight, and Brooks' division did not have an active role in the attack, as they were tucked safely under Deep Run's banks, but neither were void of the harassment of enemy artillery.[30]

As the fighting at the VI Corps' center was under way, General Brooks looked to strengthen his position with an increase in numbers, so at around 10 a.m. he pulled the 95th and 119th Pennsylvania regiments from Russell's brigade on the reserve line. The two regiments sped off from the river crossing and reinforced the left of Sedgwick's battered center. The 18th saw an opportunity to join the fight come and go and remained where they were near the ruins of Mannsfield with the other two regiments and battery. Although being on the relatively safe reserve line, the duty was short of heroics, especially when the rest of their Greek Cross brothers could be seen and heard grappling with the enemy, etching the corps into the lore of history.[31]

Despite being away from the main action and largely ignored by Rebel infantry, the 49th Pennsylvania, 18th and 32nd New York, and Battery D were still subjected to nearly four hours of sporadic enemy shelling throughout the morning. Casualties were minimal due to the fact of how naturally sheltered they were by terrain, but still one artilleryman was killed and four soldiers from the 18th were reported to have sustained injuries.[32]

By noon, the VI Corps accomplished what was proven impossible in December and took possession of the heights behind the city. General Brooks sent word to Russell to have his reserve force move up and protect the corps as they withdrew troops to occupy Fredericksburg. At 1 p.m., Russell's half-brigade left the crossing and marched north byway of the Bowling Green Road into the city and occupied a temporary bivouac in the streets. Captain Roswell M. Sayer and his Company D was detailed away from the 18th and took over as guard of a division hospital in the city.[33]

Salem Church

As the Rebels reworked their positions after being stunned by the loss of Marye's Heights, Sedgwick regrouped and pushed for another offensive up the Orange Plank Road in his quest to link with Hooker at Chancellorsville. Being as they were not an active participant for the earlier storming of Marye's Heights, Brooks' division was tapped to spearhead Sedgwick's next frontal push and were in position shortly after 2 p.m. Brooks was still short three regiments from Russell's brigade, who were still mid-march somewhere between the city and Deep Run.[34]

As Brooks pushed his division west down the Orange Plank Road, Confederates closed in east on the same road towards a battle space that awaited them both. A small schoolhouse and simple two-story brick church called Salem Church sat in the middle of a clearing bordered by thick woods which set the stage for the next pitched battle of the VI Corps during the late afternoon of May 3. Regiments from all three of Brooks' brigades formed a front on both sides of the road and charged the church that was defended by Alabamians and Georgians under Confederate Brigadier General Cadmus Wilcox. Brooks' men became tangled within the thicket and undergrowth which practically held them up as immovable targets, of which the Rebels took advantage. The 95th and 119th Pennsylvania that were detached from Russell's brigade formed the right of Brooks' assault, and at one point suffered terribly from an enfilading fire that devastated their lines. The 16th New York jumped into the line to help bolster the Pennsylvanians and were similarly chopped up. Swirling around the little house of God, the fight at times got close enough for the bayonet to kill. The short-lived battle was over as quickly as it began, and Brooks' division pulled away from Salem Church in pieces, unable to punch through the Rebel line.[35]

From the sound of the gunfire from their reserve position in the city, Russell knew his reserve troops would be needed and acted preemptively before Brooks' expected order. The 18th dropped Company D and left them in charge of their detail to guard the hospital in the city. Russell's partial brigade of three regiments packed up their bivouac in the city streets and left Fredericksburg at 5 p.m. Russell was already in motion with his troops by the time an aide from Brooks' staff met him with those very orders to join the rest of the division. During their four mile push west down the Plank Road towards Salem Church, the battle had concluded without them. Just as darkness crept in, Russell and his fresh troops entered the battlefield and could see and feel the aftermath of an awful defeat. Russell quickly learned of the repulse of the division and became incensed with General Brooks' hurried decision to

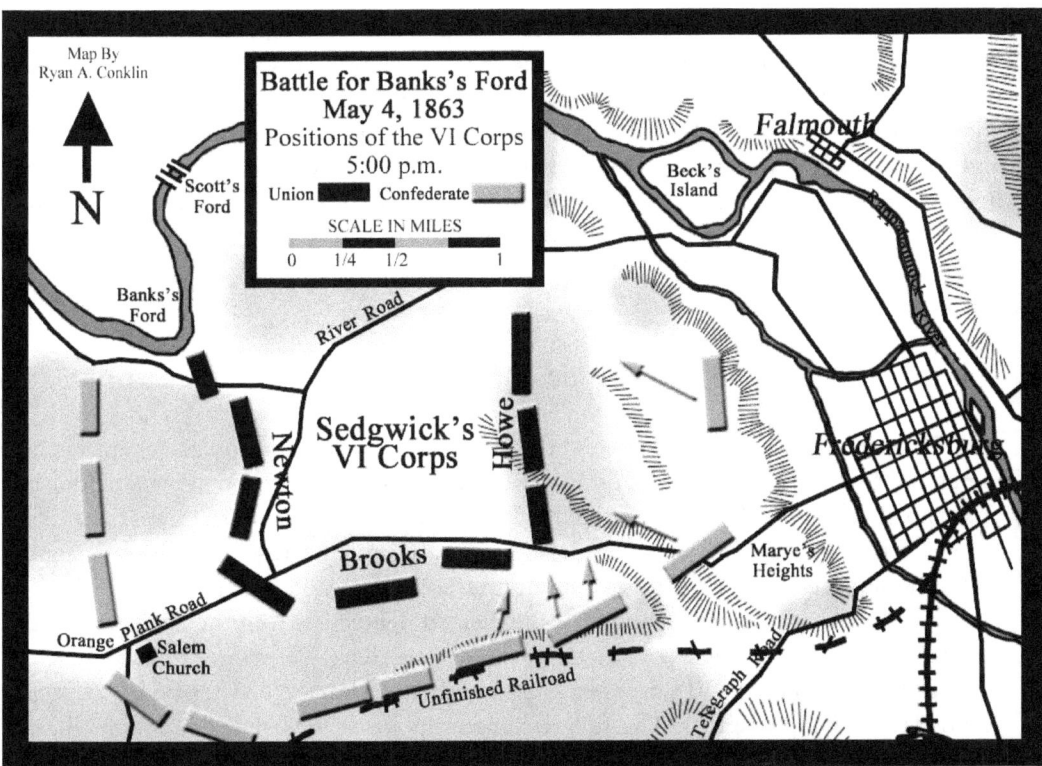

Just before their ultimate retreat at Banks's (Scott's) Ford, Sedgwick curled his corps to defend its space by the time the 5 p.m. attack occurred on Howe's front, which was to the left of where the 18th New York held their line under Brooks' control in the woods (author's collection).

commit his force before they were regrouped at full strength. He showed no restraint in front of Brooks' aide and candidly stated that had his division commander waited for him to bring up the remainder of his brigade before the fight, "it would have made all the difference in the world." The aide agreed.[36]

Russell was returned with his two bloodied Pennsylvania regiments before their rifle barrels had cooled. When the brigade was reformed there was an obvious price paid from what was left standing of the 95th and 119th Pennsylvania. Only then could men from the 18th and 32nd New York—both two-year regiments soon to expire—comprehend how lucky they were not to have been pulled from the line like the Pennsylvanians were. At Salem Church, the VI Corps shed 1,523 casualties from its ranks. The 95th Pennsylvania lost their whole command staff when their colonel, lieutenant colonel, and adjutant were shot and killed, and their major was felled with a wound. A soldier of the regiment that survived the fight mentioned, "Almost 200 of the Ninety-fifth were left weltering in their gore upon the bloody plain." When troops from the 49th Pennsylvania moved in and saw their first glimpse of their comrades of the 119th Pennsylvania, 49th men called out to Colonel Peter C. Ellmaker of the 119th and asked him where his regiment was. Ellmaker's voice was hardly cordial when he snapped back, "All gobbled up." Out of the 432 present in battle from the 119th, 12 were killed and 112 others were wounded. No one was hit harder than the 121st New York in what was their first battle where they formed the front line. Out of 453 men at the start of the battle, 276 became casualties.[37]

Russell took charge of the front line with his brigade and some regiments from the Third Division, and established a rotation on the picket line. The 18th took their turn at nighttime on May 3 and relieved the 49th Pennsylvania. The scenery that surrounded them was hellish and was brushed by the bloody wake that followed a sharp contest. Throughout the evening and night, men from the regiment pulled in wounded men that were scattered around their line, located by their screams and calls for help. Luckily the Confederates conducted similar mercy missions of their own and there was but little exchanges of rifle fire between each others' pickets.[38]

The Escape of the VI Corps

Throughout the night, men of the VI Corps also listened as enemy troops dug entrenchments and shuttled regiments around to mass two fronts. General Lee knew that Hooker posed no threat on his left flank, so he committed several thousands of fresh troops to handle the VI Corps that had given them more problems than any other corps during the campaign. By the morning of May 4, the VI Corps felt the pressure of being totally annihilated. The precious heights behind Fredericksburg that the men so righteously won the day before had easily relinquished its ownership when it fell behind enemy lines. Threatened by a semi-circle of possible approaches, the VI Corps remained stretched in a horseshoed position, with each end tied to the Rappahannock. The 18th remained in place on the bended middle and held their picket line for the bulk of the day.[39]

The 18th was probed repeatedly throughout the day by enemy skirmishers. Around four o'clock that afternoon, the Confederates renewed a concerted attack on the left of the VI Corps' hooked line. From where the 18th was located on the bowed middle of the hook,

Rebel skirmishers tested their lines and were matched, none of which caused any casualties. The enemy harassment there was merely a test, intended to keep them where they were so as not to reinforce the main effort where the enemy centralized their attack on the rear of VI Corps.[40]

A viable path for Sedgwick to get his corps closer to Hooker would not happen on the enemy's side of the river, but he could not sit still any longer and give Lee a chance to strike with a fresh day. Uncle John Sedgwick was not willing to surrender, nor would he let the corps be destroyed for the sake of glory. Late into the evening the entire VI Corps retreated under orders. His parenting care of his men certainly upheld his nickname. As the sun began to tuck behind the horizon, so too did the pickets recede from the line. Russell's brigade was tasked to protect the Second Division as they withdrew over pontoons at the nearest crossing at Banks's Ford. Just as soon as the troop movements spurred into action, shells from Union batteries were lobbed over the corps in the direction of the enemy in an effort to build the buffer zone between them and the Confederates. Enemy artillery fired blindly through the darkness, keyed on the path of the retreating corps, but with little effect. No injuries were inflicted on anyone from the 18th, but Colonel Myers did have the horse he rode on mortally wounded from underneath him.[41]

As the VI Corps retreated across Banks's Ford on May 4, 1863, the last casualty of the 18th New York could be given as the horse that Col. George R. Myers rode on, mortally wounded from underneath him. Myers turned twenty-five-years-old just four days before he returned the regiment to Albany (courtesy Jeff Sauter).

The Confederate vanguard pressed tight on their heels of the corps during the nighttime push to the crossing. The night was cloudy which darkened their path and a thick fog seemed literally trapped within the thickets that worsened the closer they neared the crossing. Union soldiers struggled to keep pace, many of which fell out and became lost during the retreat.

Nearly 1,500 men from the VI Corps would be reported as missing from this campaign, and close to two-thirds came from this nighttime dash to the river. Sergeant John Delaney of Company H was one of the unlucky few to be plucked up by the enemy, as was Private John D. Phillips of Company I, who was captured for his second time in the war. Luckily for them, their time in uniform neared an end and they only spent a little more than a week imprisoned in Richmond before they were both paroled and discharged with the regiment.[42]

Near 9 p.m., Russell's brigade had traversed nearly five miles and reached the heights that overlooked Banks's Ford and protected the crossing of the Second Division. The brigade got their chance and crossed to the northern shore of the river by two o'clock in the morning of May 5. Two hours later, the rest of the corps' infantry and artillery assets made it across to the northern bank and retracted the bridge and cut themselves off from enemy. The hastened pace of the retreat slowed as the men stopped to set up a camp in the woods above Falmouth. The regiment established a bivouac in the woods near Berea Church. A strong picket line was left on their side of the shore to act as a warning signal if the Rebels attempted to cross, but no side seemed aggressive after the bridges were cut.[43]

Captain Sayer and his Company D somehow found the regiment amongst an entangled sea of camps at night. When news of the retreat was initially heard of in the city, Sayer broke his company's guard detail of the division hospital and fled with the wounded. Captain Sayer successfully returned his company to the regiment with all of his soldiers accounted for and unharmed.[44]

Leaving the Warfront, Transfers of the Late Recruits

The 18th, along with the rest of the corps, rested in their temporary camps around Falmouth for a few days, harassed by rain instead of artillery. After the engineers finished the task to recover their pontoons, the men were put back in motion at 8:30 a.m. on May 8. The 18th were marched all the way back to where they had initially started the campaign from—their former camp near White Oak Church—which looked just as it did when they left.[45]

Whether it was luck or divine intervention, the soldiers of the 18th with two years of service under their belts dodged many literal bullets with the recent campaign. With just days until their expected discharge, these short-timed regiments were committed to one last battle and paid a heavy price with high casualties. The 18th's fortune to be where they were left the regiment virtually intact after another grueling campaign for the Army of the Potomac. The same could not be said for neighbors like the 16th New York, who were similarly days away from being discharged, but at Salem Church they lost 24 killed, 12 mortally wounded, 101 wounded, and another 17 captured.[46]

Taking into consideration the time it would take for the men to be shipped from the front and make it back to Albany on time meant their exit from the war had finally come. This also gave rise to a problem with those in the regiment that had enlisted during the recruitment drives of 1862. There was a great deal of grumbling that erupted from those soldiers that were told and believed that they would be discharged at the expiration of the regiment with the rest of the men who enlisted at the outset of war, only to find out now that their enlistment would be carried into another regiment for the remainder of a three-year term. As the logistics for the regiment's return to the North were hashed out, these confused men who joined midway were told that they still owed a contractual commitment to Uncle Sam and would be transferred, despite what they were told by recruiters when they joined. Colonel Myers received orders to have them transferred to the 121st New York on May 9. The recruits had felt that their enlistment into a veteran regiment was what was best for the army at the time instead of joining a brand new organization, and their promises went ignored. Their protest was presented to a Board of Investigation, but the Secretary of War caught wind of it and struck it down. Whatever assumption the recruiters had used to entice the volunteers at their enlistment was not his doing.[47]

As the newest addition to the division and a regiment slated to serve three years, the 121st New York became the obvious choice to consolidate these men to, especially after their ranks were greatly thinned at Salem Church. On May 10, 275 disgruntled three-year men from the 16th, 18th, 27th, 31st and 32nd New York were transferred to the 121st. The 18th sent thirty-five over; two from Company A, twelve from Company C, eleven from Company D, five from Company E, one from Company H, one from Company I, and three from Company K. Together, these VI Corps transferees actually outnumbered the strength of what was left in the 121st, so their addition more than doubled the regiment to bring them up to strength, but they went begrudgingly.[48]

The 16th New York was the first two-year regiment around them to exit the winter camp, having marched out the morning of May 11. Seeing them leave was the confirmation the men of the 18th needed to know that going home would be a reality. Later that day the 18th was ordered to return all of their government property over to the brigade quartermaster, with the exception of their firearms. For the next twenty-four hours the men continued to shake hands and bid their adieus to comrades in the regiments throughout the VI Corps.[49]

On the evening of May 12, all of the 18th officers gathered at General Russell's quarters and formally gave their handshakes, salutes, and goodbyes to their brigade commander. After the loss of the two-year regiments the strength of the VI Corps was drastically reduced which enacted another overhaul and reorganization to take place. With the loss of the 18th and 32nd New York, and the transfer of the 95th Pennsylvania, Russell's command was cut in half. He eventually received the 5th Wisconsin and 6th Maine to form the new third brigade of the First Division and went on with the war.[50]

Headed for Home

Finally, on May 13, the 18th awoke to the last drum rolls of "Reveille." They bid their final farewell and departed from their White Oak Church encampment at 8 a.m. and officially left the VI Corps. They marched to Falmouth Station where the loaded up into railcars. The train ride was short which took them to Aquia Creek at 1 p.m., where the men changed their mode of transportation and boarded a steamer. The regiment shuffled onto the decks of the *Metamora* and ferried north up the Potomac River to Washington. They arrived back to the nation's capital at 6 p.m. and took up temporary quarters at the Soldiers' Rest for the night.[51]

Retracing the route of which brought them to war in 1861, the regiment then mounted back onto another line of railcars in Washington at noon on May 14 and departed the nation's capital. The regiment slipped into Baltimore at 5 p.m., switched trains, and took a different rail line up towards Pennsylvania. As night darkened their journey, their train arrived back

Artist Edwin Forbes drew this scene that depicted the exit of two-year regiments as they left the Army of the Potomac near Falmouth, Virginia, in May 1863 (Library of Congress).

in Philadelphia on May 15, around 5 a.m. Since the start of the war, the City of Brotherly Love had continued to warmly receive regiments as they passed through, and the 18th was again entertained at the Union Volunteer Refreshment Saloon near the depot just as they had two years before. The saloon was tipped off earlier that morning to prepare 550 meals for the regiment which was the expected troop strength of the 18th. For the benevolent volunteers that ran the refreshment saloon, it was all in a day's work, but the soldiers were just as grateful as they were when they first passed through its halls. As a token of their appreciation the 18th cut a small piece of their already shredded flag and presented a one-inch square to the staff as a keepsake. The saloon still had enough food on hand and successfully catered 400 more paroled prisoners later that day. The 18th shuffled back on a new train that left Philadelphia at 10 a.m. and continued their journey with more pit stops in Jersey City and New York City. In the latter city, the regiment was given temporary quarters at the Park barracks and treated to a dinner. After their meal, the regiment made a short march to the Hudson River Railroad and left New York City at 9 p.m. They then heard the jubilant words that their next stop was their final one—Albany.[52]

Soldiers on the trains increased with each stop as detached and convalescent men from the 18th left their respective hospitals and rejoined the regiment for their official muster-out. These little reunions with comrades were joyous, but some of the returned still needed time to recover. One simply did not want to miss this longed for event. Private John J. Icklin of

Company C, who was wounded in the chest by a sharpshooter just before Gaines's Mill, had subsequently lost his vision and was so blind that he had to be led through the streets by his comrades, but at least he was finally back with the regiment.[53]

There were still plenty of others from the regiment that were too unhealthy to be forwarded to Albany in time for the pageantry. Private Joseph Lang of Company G never made the trip back to his home state. He had been hospitalized in Frederick, Maryland after chronic diarrhea diminished his health. He died there on May 5 and was buried in the hospital's cemetery. Private John O'Hara of Company K was too sick to travel and was left in the VI Corps hospital when the regiment left Virginia. O'Hara's lengthy struggle with diarrhea ended when he passed away on June 2.[54]

Albany's Homecoming

At 5 a.m. on May 16, the screech of brakes brought the train that carried the jubilant 18th to a halt in Albany. Emotions peaked for those who had longed to set their eyes on familiar buildings and streets. Finally, boots stepped off the cars and men took their first deep breaths of familiar air. Tired from their journey home, the men became reenergized as soon as they disembarked the train. The regiment was treated to "a sumptuous breakfast" at the Delavan House, courtesy of the select committee of the Common Council of Albany. To sit at a table with a magnificent spread before them was a forgotten luxury to those who had gone two years of taking meals on the ground, tree stumps, or cracker boxes. After breakfast, the men walked off their meal by being marched to the city arsenal at 8 a.m. where they stacked their arms and waited to be formed up for a procession through the city's principal streets. A firemen escort from ten Albany fire departments took a considerable time to form while they donned their uniforms, but at eleven o'clock in the morning the firemen, along with a police escort and a brass band that joined the regiment and stepped off from Eagle to State Street on their way to the Capitol Building for their formal reception.[55]

This was not Albany's first homecoming reception, but the energy never got stale, especially to people with connections to regiments from the city. Citizens in great numbers clamored along the parade route, "all anxious to see the brave fellows." From first glance to those who remembered their sendoff in 1861, the 18th looked every bit a tried and true regiment of veterans. One had to remember the sight of just over 800 untested volunteers clad in suits of blue that marched behind the 18th's pristine silk banners on the city streets just two years before. A fiery Colonel William A. Jackson then led the uniformed mass of New York's patriots who embodied boundless confidence that they would soon return after they restored the Union. Now, along the same city streets and watched by many witnesses from two years before, nearly 500 bronze-faced men dressed in dusty, torn, and faded uniforms, "bearing the marks of exposure and fatigue." Hardly a uniformed appearance, few New York State shell jackets remained as most had been replaced by federal-issued sack or frock coats. Colonel George R. Myers, who had just passed his twenty-fifth birthday four days before, marched what was left of this prideful band of veterans. Sergeant Elijah L. Chadderdon, Company H, served as the color-bearer and held the regiment's bullet ridden and torn flag high for all to see, which fluttered more like a staff full of ribbons. Private Jehiel J. Stevens, Jr., of Company K mentioned that "little of [the flag] was left except the fringe, and the staff had some six or seven bullet marks."[56]

As the cadence from the drum corps behind the companies of riflemen kept their steps in unison, their neat lines were broken by friends and family members that jumped in from the street sides. The regiment shrunk together after their pace in the front lessened after hundreds of these friendly infiltrators pressed into their lines in order to set their eyes on their heroes and shake their hands. Many more spectators remained stretched along the street sides and waved their customary white handkerchiefs. As the jubilant troops marched on State Street and down North Pearl Street, the men were unexpectedly attacked with oranges when they passed the Albany Female Academy. The young ladies had boxes of the fruit on hand and playfully tossed them at the regiment, "pelting them without much mercy, judging from the precision of their aim." It was all in good fun and the men replied with an enthusiastic cheer. Colonel Myers smiled at the spectacle and halted the regiment and rendered a sweet and witty speech to the girls.[57]

The parade passed through Pearl Street, to Lydius, then up Broadway, back to State, Pearl, Van Woert, Broadway, Columbia, Pearl, back up State and eventually arrived to the Capitol. The 18th and its followers were joined by another recently returned two-year regiment, the 28th New York. The 28th had arrived the previous night and similarly dined a supper at the Delevan House. Now both regiments formed alongside each other for the midday welcome reception by their governor. The cheers subsided when the mayor grabbed everyone's attention and introduced the main speaker. As his words concluded and a second round of applause subsided, Governor Horatio Seymour took center stage and addressed both regiments with the following:

Sgt. Elijah L. Chadderdon of Company H had a brief hospital stay that made him miss the Maryland campaign. Once his health improved, he returned and served as color bearer for when the regiment returned home from the war (author's collection).

> Soldiers of the Eighteenth and Twenty-Eighth Regiments, I welcome you to the State of New York, as I have welcomed your gallant comrades in arms who have returned to their homes within the past few days. But with this welcome are mingled emotions of sadness; for all who went forth with you have not returned.

> We mourn the noble Jackson, who was stricken down in the prime of life, and the brave Donnelly [28th], who fell while fighting the battles of his country. Some of you have struggled for the cause of the Union along the sluggish Chickahominy, others on the banks of the Potomac, almost within sight of the Nation's Capital, others still in the valley of the Rappahannock, and along the skirts of the Blue Mountains.
> Wherever your services were required, there have you achieved renown for yourselves, done honor to the State of your residence and conferred lasting benefits on your country. Whether you shall decide to return to the peaceful pursuits of life, or to re-enlist for the defense of your country, I shall pray Almighty God to bless and protect you, for your zeal, your valor, and your devotion to the cause of the Union.
> And now, soldiers, let me give you a kindly word of advice. You will soon be paid the bounty which you have earned by risking your lives for our common country, and unprincipled men will follow you to persuade from you the result of your toils. Let me beseech of you not to do yourselves such injustice; but to treasure it up for the benefit of yourselves and those who are dear to you.
> Once more, soldiers of the Eighteenth and Twenty-Eighth, as Governor of the State of New York, and Commander of its Military, I welcome you back to its midst.[58]

The colonel of the 28th spoke on his regiment's behalf and thanked Seymour for Albany's welcome and his helpful advice. Colonel Myers followed and spoke words of similar appreciation to the governor, along with a presentation of their national flag that the 18th soldiers guarded so dearly. Being a principally Albany-organized regiment, it was only fitting that their highest trophy should remain with the city forever. Myers presented "the tattered banner of the Eighteenth, which they had all loved and protected," to the governor. Seymour graciously received the "memento of their fidelity to the Nation" and stated that his administration had already preserved a place for these irreplaceable banners within the archives of the Capitol.[59]

After the eloquent address by the governor was complete, the 18th shouted "nine hearty cheers" and marched their way to the familiar Industrial School Barracks where they had first received their indoctrination as soldiers. The barracks and streets of Albany were once again filled back up with soldiers just like the early days of the war. Some of the recently returned regiments that arrived before the 18th had since vacated the barracks and sent to their respective hometowns. The 18th, although a conglomerate of companies from differing counties, was predominantly an Albany regiment and had to wait in the capital city until they could be mustered out by the proper authorities. Officers of the companies scrambled to finish filling out their muster rolls in preparation for the paymaster, but after one day in the city only one roll was completed but was bounced back as being defective. Training and drill was irrelevant which allowed time for men to frequent the city liberally to take in the sights and sounds. Some men mingled with family and friends if they were from the area or had rendezvoused to be there. Coincidentally, saloon owners in Albany found themselves working overtime.[60]

With the train depots between Albany and Schenectady distanced less than twenty miles apart—and undoubtedly with Major Gridley's influence—Companies A and E were allowed a leave of absence to head to Schenectady later that afternoon of May 16. The two companies climbed aboard a special train and left Albany at 3 p.m. Word was spread rapidly through Schenectady that their men were coming home. City bells chimed, flags were run up every staff, firemen scrambled to don their uniforms, and people gathered at the depot to await their arrival. Schenectady's depot at State Street which crossed the tracks filled up quickly with citizens—mostly women—to await the signal of the train's arrival. Around 4:15 p.m., the train was spotted from a signal gun positioned on a hill that marked their arrival with their cannon. Their salute instantly triggered church bells to commence and cheers to rise. Groups of impatient citizens elbowed around others to get their first glimpses of their returning heroes. Some advanced into the train cars and freely mingled with soldiers before they had the chance to disembark. Spectators and families continued to struggle to gain a vantage of the men who looked "begrimed with dust and jaded with their long journey, but in excellent spirits and overjoyed to get home again." A row of firemen in their best uniforms stood in formation to receive the companies, while the horns of the Albany Brigade Band fought over the cheers and applause. Handshakes, kisses, and tears of joy were plentiful. Major Gridley and First Lieutenant Schermerhorn managed to form the two companies amidst the ecstatic crowd. A procession was formed and led by the chosen Marshal, a local resident J. A. Barhydt, father of Corporal Andrew D. Barhydt of Company E. The procession stepped off and went up State Street and through Barrett Street, and then down Union Street where they were stopped by another hub of people at the Court House. Companies A and E formed in double columns and were surrounded by firemen and citizens. Once the crowd was hushed and order restored, the companies were addressed with speeches from two local judges, Potter and Paige, who both harped on patriotism and lifted the names of the deceased Jackson and Horsfall to be remembered as martyrs from the regiment. After reciting the names of battles fought with congratulatory praise of the pride they should feel, Judge Paige concluded his speech with hope, "that as a reward for your priceless services for your country, your future lives will be as prosperous and happy as your two years service in the army of the Union has been honorable and heroic."[61]

After the judges wrapped their delivered speeches, Major Gridley accepted their remarks and gave a few short words of praise to the council and citizens for their reception, but he joked that he was "but a soldier and not an orator." The procession then formed again and marched back near the depot where the companies were treated to a dinner at the Givens Hotel, next to Cleary's Saloon where Gridley had first started a group of volunteers in what had to have felt like a lifetime ago. After the dinner, the men were dismissed and allowed to spend two nights in their own homes to find "feather beds and happiness" with their families.[62]

The regiment's two-year anniversary on May 17 was a joyous occasion for the men, but the day ended with an unfortunate accident that claimed the life of one of these returning heroes. Private Ernest J. Crist of Company D took a nighttime walk alone on the wooden planks at the foot of Albany's Division Street when all of a sudden he fell overboard and into the Hudson River. His cry for help amidst his splashing was heard by a policeman who was close at hand and rushed to the proximity of Crist's distress. By the time the policeman arrived to the origin of the screams, they had since ceased. The patrol officer came upon a young boy on a canal boat in the basin nearby who explained he witnessed at a distance a soldier fall into the water and pointed wildly to where it occurred. They both peered out into the darkened waters, but heard nothing. In fact, five days passed before Crist's body, still clad in his uniform, was discovered floating on the basin's surface near the point where he fell. His body was recovered which showed a hurried state of decomposition, but the coroner still concluded that his death was from an obvious accidental drowning. The twenty-six-year-old native of Germany had been with the regiment since the beginning and had survived numerous battlefields and diseases, only to lose his life in an untimely and unfortunate accident. Crist's death added a tinge of melancholy to what was supposed to be a great celebration. His body was placed in a coffin and sent to his shocked family in New Jersey who had prepared for an entirely different homecoming.[63]

Companies A and E gathered back at the Schenectady depot the morning of May 18 and trekked back to Albany and rejoined the regiment for their time of waiting at the Albany

Barracks. Collectively, the 18th turned in their arms and equipment at the city arsenal on May 19. Social parties in honor of the regiment were thrown on several occasions throughout Albany and Schenectady during their wait, one of the biggest being the social hop at Fuller's Hotel on May 21.[64]

Local newspapers outside of the Albany and Schenectady region from which the other companies of the regiment belonged to intensified the chatter that surrounded their speculations on their return. They would absorb and reprint any entry that related to the regiment in order to pacify their anxious families who subscribed. The news also acted as a call to prepare the towns for their expected reception of the men upon their final return home. For the men of the 18th not from the Albany or Schenectady area, the wait had to have been just as restless as what their families experienced.[65]

Albany residents felt the same anxiousness to have the men quickly discharged and returned to their homes. Albany at one point had some 3,000 recently returned troops who suddenly cut ties from a strict disciplined army life and flooded the city. With all of the temptations that the city life offered, Albany was not deprived of occasional misconduct from soldiers, but the prevalence seemed subdued when compared to people's expectations. The city newspaper downplayed the occurrences and tried to debunk "the generally accepted theory that camp life unfits men for the quiet walks of private life."[66]

On May 18, Privates Aurelius Webster and Daniel McClinch, Jr., both of Company I, were implicated in a fight that broke out on River Street. The two assaulted and tried to rob an army captain from a different organization. McClinch got away but Webster was arrested and made bail, but he failed to appear in accordance to his bond two days later and was rearrested. When McClinch came as a visitor for Webster later that afternoon, he too was locked up. They were both sentenced a week later to pay a fine of forty dollars or serve four months in the penitentiary.[67]

Groups of close-knit comrades spent many dollars and coins in the local saloons of the city. Unsurprisingly, copious amounts of libations paved the path for clashes between friends, civilians, and the police. On May 24, a couple of highly intoxicated 18th soldiers were approached by a policeman on State Street after their intoxicated antics demanded his intervention. The group acted "very noisy, and frightened women off the sidewalk." The patrolman tried to quell the boisterous group by rationalizing with them, but one drunken soldier blatantly ignored his warnings. Private Edmond Riley, an Irishman of Company B "was perfectly wild and would not obey the officer," which resulted in his instant arrest. The rest of the group was given a warning and ordered to disperse, but Riley was jailed. Private Jeremiah Ryan of the same company was similarly committed a short time later for "making a great noise in the street."[68]

Private Thomas Austin of Company H came down with symptoms of diarrhea and was hospitalized in Albany just three days before the regiment was to be mustered out. Doctors diagnosed him with delirium tremens, a severe form of alcohol withdrawal that wrecked his health slowly and painfully killed him on May 29.[69]

Mustering Out, the Companies Go Home

Final arrangements were eventually coordinated and relayed to the regiment to prepare for their official muster-out at the Albany Arsenal on May 28. As the officers looked upon their men in their fleeting moments of their duties, the companies had taken on a larger presence since their battle-trim readiness just two weeks before. More sick and wounded soldiers that spent months away from the line in hospitals in Frederick, Annapolis, Baltimore, Alexandria, Washington, York, Philadelphia, and New York City, that were not collected by the passing regiment in their cities took up independent journeys to Albany. During May, the 18th was returned twenty-seven familiar faces from hospitals. Almost all had been patients that battled diseases, a few were detached as hospital stewards, and eight were recovered wounded from battles.[70]

To be present at the arsenal on May 28, the occasion was a special one for the veterans after two trying years at war. They had learned new jobs and tactics through hundreds of hours of drills, faced contagious breakouts of diseases, and marched hundreds of miles throughout Washington, Maryland, and Virginia. They adapted to living under changing seasons and dealt with arduous weather patterns. After being planted at the front of numerous skirmishes and battles, veterans felt more like survivors at the end of it all.

In the regiment's two-year existence, 1,069 men attached their name and became a part of the 18th. The largest the regiment ever stood was when they were first mustered in, with 834 strong. After two years at war the strength of the regiment reflected hard service, having lost nearly 500 men from resignations, transfers, deaths, discharges, and desertions. Eighteen months of recruiting helped sustain the regiment's fluctuating roster with the addition of over 200 recruits. Only 578 men were present to answer their name before the paymaster on their final day together as a regiment. A quarter of those present were men that had just reunited days before after long hospital stays.[71]

No one can argue that the 18th did not sacrifice itself for the cause. The regiment lost 42 men that were slain in battles and skirmishes, and 119 others escaped this fate and lived beyond their wounds, many of which were at the cost of amputated limbs. Four soldiers had the unfortunate demise to perish as a result of accidents. Disease remained the predominant killer of troops during the war, and 44 men from the 18th died from sickness.[72]

With a careful survey or existing records for the 18th, 145 soldiers deserted the regiment. Startling as the number may seem, the percentage is quite average for a volunteer regiment, if not below. Regardless of their individual motives, when one deserted they became a marked man wanted by the government. Fugitive hunting became a lucrative business to those back home, and anyone who successfully captured a deserter was handsomely rewarded by the government with cash. Most deserters won out and were never seen or heard from again. Out of the 145 that left the regiment, only 40 were brought back before the war ended either by arrest or on their own free will. Most returned while the 18th was still in existence and faced varied punishments, but fifteen were arrested after the regiment mustered-out and served their time in confinement.[73]

First Lieutenants Henry E. Munger of Company A, Alfred M. Chesmore of Company G, and Freeman F. Huntington of Company K all entered the war as sergeants, but returned as company commanders. Only Companies F and I returned back with their original captains they left home with. The regiment cycled through three colonels, with fever having killed the first and nearly sealed the same fate of the other two. Faces came and went, but for the few veterans that were there since the beginning, the romance of war that had lured them into the uniformed service was certainly by then a distant sentiment.[74]

The history books for the 18th were closed when they were officially mustered out at the arsenal on May 28. Their last formation was overseen by an appointed officer from the regular army who went through the formalities and filed paperwork to have the 18th mustered out. The final order to break ranks was commanded by the officers to the men for the last time. Companies withered away as individuals parted in different directions, thusly ending the record of the 18th.[75]

Apparently an issue with their pay surfaced that prevented the companies to immediately flee from Albany, so they stayed a few more days until the problem was rectified. A couple of soldiers that had joined less than a month after the 18th was mustered in learned they were just shy of their promised two-year service by mere days, so they were retained to their anniversary date and acted as guards at the barracks.[76]

Company G was the first to return their muster rolls a day before the rest of the regiment and received their final payment in full and $100 bounty on May 30. They quickly boarded a train and took the rail ride that reached their hometown of Canandaigua on May 31.

Having left home as a sergeant, 1st Lt. Henry Elias Munger of Company A returned home after two years of war with the 18th New York as a company commander, and acting adjutant (courtesy Elodie Pritchartt).

The company that numbered a mere fifty-one members was embraced by their townspeople and were said to have "appeared remarkably well and behaved as well as they looked." Company G reconvened in their hometown ten days later for the last time. They did so in order to receive another company of Canandaigua men from a different regiment, and with the help of the community they gave them a welcome full of patriotic speeches, songs, and cheers.[77]

The rest of the 18th finished their paperwork and submitted them to the proper finance authorities on June 1, and received their payment at the arsenal on June 2 at 9 a.m. The companies from Albany and Schenectady dissolved that day without specific fanfares for their individual companies, but they had already experienced the hometown welcome on account of their initial return. After they received their final payment they too broke down their order and returned to their homes. A lot of men used their money to buy civilian attire before they boarded the evening trains for their homes.[78]

Those from Company H who were from Middletown tagged along with Company D for the reception of the Wallkill Guards. As soon as a committee of citizens had finalized plans for a welcome party on June 3, a notice arrived that same afternoon that told of the Guards' immediate arrival. The late notice derailed the welcome agenda, so they had to rely on improvisation. Acting fast, the people gathered a crowd and scrambled together the fire department and a cornet band. The blast of an artillery piece fired later that evening announced the coming of the Guards. The crowd that gathered at the train station became wild and the Middletown Band struck up a tune. When the train rolled to a stop the men jumped out and searched for the faces of friends and family that they had waited long to see. After this brief delay of warm hugs and handshakes, the assemblage took order and formed up. The Middletown Band proceeded out of the depot, followed by several companies of the fire department, and lastly the guests of honor marched together one last time through the

The national flag presented in 1861 to the Wallkill Guards served for a time as the regiment's banner near the end of their service. This flag was brought back to Middletown in 1863 and displayed for several decades in a shop window and library. In 1941, the flag and encasement seen above were donated to the Historical Society of Middletown & Wallkill Precinct in Middletown, New York, where it remains today (author's collection).

main streets of Middletown. Eventually, the parade halted at Franklin Square where the men practically recreated their exact send-off in reverse from when they left in 1861. At Franklin Square, the men were addressed by the same prominent Middletowner, Charles C. McQuoid, that had presented them with their company flag. McQuoid remembered when they first left home, "Your ranks were then full. But oh," he took notice, "how fearfully have they been thinned! How many of those who then went with you in the pride of their manhood and strength now fill a soldier's grave!" McQuoid's lengthy but eloquent speech highlighted their battles, touched on those they lost, and ended with the reminder as to why they did all that they did—trying to restore the Union.[79]

As McQuoid's last word echoed in their ears, the brass band struck up a hearty rendition of "Hail Columbia." Corporal Thomas Curry—the 18th's color-bearer in every engagement—stepped out of formation during the song and drew the crowd's attention. There was little more to say than the sight of the soiled and tattered flag could say itself. The Guards' banner, first having been put aside for a time after the regiment was presented with a separate national flag was carried, eventually became the one carried for the regiment after Lieutenant Colonel John C. Meginnis was in charge and swapped the original soiled and worn one. A young girl in the crowd emerged and met Curry and placed a decorative wreath of flowers around the flag. Meginnis—who had been the original captain of the Wallkill Guards when the war began—stepped forward and "addressed the ladies in a felicitous and feeling manner." Meginnis retraced the journey of the regiment, having recalled with pride the presentation of the flag and the love they received from the crowd throughout their two-year journey. As Meginnis wrapped up his impromptu speech, Curry finally relinquished the flag that he never broke from, "with evident emotion," to the Ladies of Middletown that had originally furnished the banner. On behalf of the Ladies of Middletown, the last to speak was another prominent citizen who was never short for words, Moses D. Stivers. His speech was protracted but continued the same patriotic rhetoric and reverence for their sacrifice. As Stivers neared the end he could sense the men's understandable impatience to break free. "But, soldiers, I will not detain you," he said, "You are impatient, I know—and these anxious, waiting, expectant friends are likewise impatient, and eager to grasp again, each of you war-worn veterans by the hand, to give you a warmer welcome than any poor words of ours."[80]

Waiting no longer, the final speech concluded and the troops were given their last order of dismissal. The conglomerate of soldiers and citizens fused together in long informal greetings. Despite the lack of planning, the day was as close to the city's original plan and the Guards were grateful with their welcome. Many gathered later that evening at Hoyt's Union House, owned by the father of Company D's Isaac and Hezekiah, where a large supper had awaited the men. Still, there were others who decided to enjoy their first meal out of the military at their own tables within their homes, surrounded by the families they missed.[81]

The town of Fishkill felt the same sense of panic that Middletowners felt and thought they would have more time to prepare a gala before their honored guests arrived. A committee formed and convened a meeting downtown the day before the arrival of Company C, Fishkill's first company sent to war. Before the train that brought the company home arrived, the town fused together in the afternoon of June 4 and prepped their festivities. Early that morning fire departments from Fishkill, Mattaewan, and Fishkill Landing came together and formed up in the yard of the Reformed Dutch Church. The local Denning Guards militia was there, and fitting it was that a couple veterans had former ties to them. Two brass bands and a drum corps were also in attendance, along with what seemed like every local citizen from the surrounding area. Around three o'clock, the fifty-two soldiers of Company C returned by rail to Fishkill Landing and were treated with a worthy and enthusiastic fanfare. Captain A. Barclay Mitchell formed the company amongst the cheers and applause and positioned the company in front of the church. Once the line of march was in order the procession paraded through the principal streets of the town. The Newburgh Brass Band stepped off first and belted out jubilant songs that bounced off the storefronts and homes. Behind the band strolled the committee that hastily organized the day's event, followed by the Denning Guards. The militia preceded Captain Mitchell and the veterans of Company C who marched in step and were kept in sync by the cadence of the drum corps that followed them. To close up the parade's order was the cavalcade of three fire engine crews, the Fishkill Cornet Band, and the large concourse of citizens that desired to be present. The procession marched through Fishkill, Fishkill Landing, and lastly Matteawan's main streets before they all returned and entered the grounds that surrounded Mackin Hall. The units in the parade broke ranks and gathered around a temporary platform that was erected and taken by two ministers, who delivered speeches of praise and prayer before the audience. At their conclusion the company was reformed and entered the hall where they were treated to two long tables full of food, flowers, and refreshments, "and the portion of the hall near the doors, were filled with ladies, who had turned out in large numbers to greet the gallant soldiers." After all the entertainment and dining had concluded, Mitchell formed his company one last time outside the hall and officially dismissed everyone to return to their "respective places of rendezvous."[82]

Thus concludes the history of the 18th New York Infantry, finished with citizens who wished they could have celebrated the same finality of a war that lingered without end. The men returned as heroes with laurels bestowed upon them by their communities, having proudly represented their hometowns in far off fronts. They left at a time when the reality of combat's brutal toll was still unknown, before the threat of drafts and enticements of bounties swayed decisions to enlist, these early volunteers rose from the ashes of Fort Sumter and clambered to fight for love of country.

Epilogue
The Boys in Blue Fade to Gray

"So fall the brave. Exit soldier, officer and gentleman."
—*Calvin B. Potter, Company B, August 18, 1902*

The 18th found its finale, amidst a war that still had no foregone winner. The summer warfare of 1863 actually ratcheted up and changed directions when the two armies waged fierce combat on northern soil in Pennsylvania. The first to fight men of '61 saw their share of the war, but there was unfinished business that they were determined to see through. The veterans of the 18th had put their lives on the line and shared the burden of crippling campaigns during their contribution to preserve the United States. The hometowns they left behind took up the slack in their absence and bore their own scars of sacrifice in the sense of lost sons, brothers, and fathers after two years of war. Soldiers from the front returned with experiences that would live with them for the rest of their lives. Some bore visible scars from wounds or amputations from battles, yet others stored injuries deep within their minds which replayed in vivid detail, often unprovoked. Their service meant a lot to them on a personal level, and was uniquely understood by others that served. Most of them felt their welcome home was tainted with unfinished business as the war continued in its third summer. The fight continued on several fronts throughout Dixie and the New Yorkers who proudly raised their right hands at the war's inception would most assuredly do so again until the southern insurrectionists declared their unconditional surrender.

Transferees of the 121st New York

For the thirty-five men from the 18th who were retained in service and unexpectedly transferred to the 121st New York, their transition was anything but smooth. The men who enlisted into two-year regiments in 1862 did so under false pretences, and instead of a discharge at the expiration of their regiment, these men in the VI Corps were lumped into the 121st. The number of transferees actually outnumbered the strength of the regiment. One clerk from the 121st observed these transferees as "a fine body of men, thoroughly inured to army life in all its phases," but they felt cheated and duped, and their anger towards their detention went unrestrained. Colonel Emory Upton, the commander of the 121st who had lobbied for these VI Corps men in order to rebuild his regiment, gathered the transferees and smartly addressed their discontent. He praised their patriotism and reminded the men of the reasons why the war was still worth fighting for. Upton's reasoning helped win them over, and they banded together and returned to duty with a renewed passion.[1]

With a mix of experienced officers, eager recruits, and hardened veterans, the 121st became a potent muscle for the VI Corps. The rebirth of the regiment happened just in time for the Army of the Potomac's next epic showdown in Pennsylvania. They held a relatively inactive position atop Little Round Top without a single death. When the Union army started their delayed chase on the enemy after the battle was concluded, a handful of men from the 121st checked themselves out before they crossed back into Virginia, and five deserters were recent transferees from the 18th. Four evaded authorities and remained hidden, but one returned on his own accord.[2]

In November 1863, the 121st clashed with the enemy at Rappahannock Station and the Mine Run campaign, and came out with relatively low casualties. One to be captured on November 27 was Private Henry Stevens (Co. K). He was eventually returned to the regiment in January 1865.[3]

On May 10, 1864, the 121st was pushed to the front for a dangerous assault on heavily fortified enemy entrenchments at Spotsylvania. After a charge through an open field under a concentrated fire from multiple fronts, the 121st jumped atop the Rebel ramparts and started a desperate hand-to-hand fight. The charge was a success and the Confederate line broke momentarily, but their gained ground was lost when enemy reinforcements arrived. Only the onset of nightfall ended the fighting, and both sides returned to their original positions.[4]

Thirty-three men from the 121st were killed outright on May 10, with an even larger number of wounded, with several mortally. Privates Stephen Walker and Simeon H. Mann had served together in Company C of the 18th, but were both killed during the attack. Walker, a Scottish immigrant who worked in the iron foundries around Albany, left behind a wife and three children. Private Simeon Mann, serving in what was his third regiment in three years, was shot dead atop the works, but his comrades noticed he had a dead Rebel impaled at the end of his bayonet.[5]

The death of Corporal Robert Bradshaw (Co. E) developed a record of confusion. He was listed by the 121st as having been killed May 5 during the Wilderness campaign, but his family was told his death came on May 10, neither of which happened. Bradshaw was wounded, captured, and imprisoned at the infamous Andersonville Prison. Bradshaw's story still did not give way for a happy ending, for he died from diarrhea at the prison on August 24, 1864.[6]

After the bloody charge of May 10, the 121st stayed in contact with the enemy and their strength dwindled because of it. Just like the rest of the Army of the Potomac, the 121st continued to lessen as they settled themselves with the stalemate and costly occupation around Petersburg in the summer of 1864. By June, the regiment had shrunk to nearly 100 healthy men. Another clash around Winchester occurred on September 19, and the 121st were again engaged at the battle of Opequon. Private Henry Mathise (Co. A) was wounded and bounced back, but the bigger loss was from the death of their division commander, Brigadier General David. A. Russell.[7]

A month after Opequon, Union forces were taken off guard by a surprise attack from

Confederate General Early in the early morning hours of October 19, 1864. The Army of the Shenandoah at Cedar Creek had little time to prepare before an all out melee broke apart division unity. As the 121st and others scrambled together a hasty resistance, a fog and smoke covered battle unfolded that swept over the encampments twice, and the Union troops eventually reclaimed their ground which had then been littered with bodies. Private James Turnbull (Co. E) was among the wounded, but his injuries were not life threatening.[8]

Private Charles R. Arnold (Co. D) was on detached service from the 121st that fateful morning and had just arrived to the camp with wagons loaded with stretchers, but was quickly overwhelmed by a squad of Rebel cavalry that made Arnold their prisoner. In January 1865, while imprisoned at Salisbury Prison in North Carolina, Arnold attempted an escape with several others but they unexpectedly ran into a Confederate regiment that opened fire on the escapees. Arnold received gunshot wounds to his left hip and left side of his neck and had to be his own doctor, for in his words the Rebels treated his band of fugitives "like a pack of dum brutes," and denied them hospital treatment. He was eventually paroled before the end of the war.[9]

After the battle of Cedar Creek, the 121st had a string of relatively quiet months. In that time they tried to gain healthy men to replenish their regiment still deficient in strength, but both sides were plagued then in their fourth year of the war. On April 2, 1865, the 121st captured war-ravaged Petersburg, and were tight on the heels of a desperate and tired Rebel army. They clashed the same day at Fort Fisher and had more than two-dozen of their men dropped with wounds, with Private Charles Van Housen (Co. E) being one.[10]

On April 6, 1865, the Confederate army could not retreat fast enough before the Union forces there pounced on them. Entrenched Confederates at Sailor's Creek forced the 121st to again charge over an open field and overtake their position, but their resistance was meager compared to previous ones. The 121st captured nearly 500 Rebels, but at a severe price to an already thinned regiment. The youthful Corporal James "Jimmie" Norris (Co. C) was among the dead, less than seventy-two hours before General Lee's surrender.[11]

Disease in the 121st claimed the lives of three soldiers that once belonged to the 18th. Private William Harrigan (Co. C) was sent home sick just after Gettysburg, and died from disease at his home on October 16, 1863. Prussian-born Private Jacob Heintz (Co. C), wounded in the ankle at Spotsylvania, died not from his injury but from bronchitis on June 2, 1864. Six months later, Private Reuben Miller (Co. D) also died from bronchitis at a Winchester hospital on December 3, 1864.[12]

Pvt. Reuben Miller of Company D was one of the thirty-five men transferred to the 121st New York. He died from bronchitis on December 3, 1864, at the Sheridan Field Hospital, in Winchester, Virginia (courtesy Donald LaMunion, Jr.).

Of the thirty-five transferees from the 18th that were placed into the 121st, only twelve were left standing in line when the regiment was mustered out near Hall's Hill, Virginia on June 25, 1865.[13]

Back in Uniform

A vast number of men from the 18th still in good health reenlisted in other organizations. Most tried a new angle on the war and joined cavalry or artillery regiments, but there were plenty who felt the infantry was where they fit best. Augustus Rexman (Co. A) was one of the quickest to reenlist after having returned with the 18th. When Company A went their separate ways on June 2, 1863, Rexman spent six days as a civilian before he went to New York City and enlisted into the 13th New York Cavalry. He would not see war's end, because he died from disease as a prisoner on February 27, 1865.[14]

For some, the question to continue their service was an easy one. James A. McFetrish (Co. I), frankly stated, "I hadn't had enough yet." In January 1864, McFetrish had met up with two of his old comrades from the 18th and found they shared the same sentiment. The three went to Albany and passed their medical examinations and joined the 7th New York Heavy Artillery. A total of thirty-one veterans from the 18th joined the 7th Heavy who were churned through some of the war's most brutal frontal assaults at Cold Harbor and Petersburg, and suffered eye-opening numbers of casualties. Through attrition, the regiment for a time fell to the command of the former organizer and captain of Company B of the 18th, John Hastings, who left the regiment just before Crampton's Gap to accept his elevated promotion of lieutenant colonel of the 7th Heavy.[15]

Just before John M. Dempsey (Co. F) mustered out with the 18th, his sister grew weary that he would end up back in uniform. Dempsey searched for a comforting answer for her, but could only say, "I make no promises. A man cannot tell in these times what he will do. One thing is certain. If God spares my life and blesses all with health, I shall have a pleasant long furlough at home, when my time expires." Dempsey demonstrated natural leadership within his role as a first lieutenant and won the esteem of his men. Soon after their return home, many of his former soldiers offered him money as a token of their appreciation, but each time Dempsey refused. Unable to yield feelings of a "higher spirit" that called him to duty, Dempsey was back in uniform in less than a year as a lieutenant in the 43rd New York Infantry. He quickly found himself back at the front but was wounded and captured while he led his company at the Wilderness. He was eventually paroled and returned to his post, only to be wounded again near Petersburg on March 25, 1865. A bullet shattered Dempsey's femur which slowly and painfully ended his life in a Union hospital on May 6, 1865.[16]

Out of the 1,069 men that ever belonged to the 18th, it can be determined that at least 452 men joined subsequent units. They were spread out amongst no less than 160 other organizations, to include regular army and volunteer regiments from sixteen different states. Undoubtedly, more would have served again if they were healthy enough after their first stint of service. As members of other organizations, thirteen former 18th veterans paid the ultimate sacrifice and were killed in battle or died from injuries on different fronts during the remainder of the war. Another forty-two dealt with wounds that ranged from slight to severe, but they still escaped the war with their lives. Twenty-two others from the 18th died during the war from sicknesses or accidents.[17]

With prospects set to enlist again, Christopher G. Burn (Co. F) returned home and mustered out with the 18th, but he did so with an unshakable typhoid fever. Another opportunity to serve was not in the cards for him after his weakened health quickly became ravaged by consumption soon after he got home to Albany. He died from the disease on November

29, 1863, at the age of twenty-four. Since his death occurred after the regimental books were closed, he was never included in the summary of regimental casualties, despite his disease being connected to his service. It should be mentioned that Christopher was one of five brothers that served in Albany regiments during the war. His older brother, Richard A. Burn, served alongside him as a sergeant in the 18th. Shortly after Christopher's death, Richard again left home for the warfront when he joined the 93rd New York. Richard had missed the birth of his first son who was born while he was deployed with the 18th in 1861. While in service with the 93rd in Virginia, Burn missed the birth of his second son in June 1864. To honor his dead brother, he had this second son named Christopher, but the two would never meet. Two months after the child's birth, Richard was killed in action on August 16, 1864, at Deep Bottom, Virginia.[18]

Two former members of the 18th who departed the regiment early went on to serve elsewhere in the war and were both given the nation's highest medal for bravery. The most unassuming patriot to win this honor was Peter Van Hoesen (Co. B), who had deserted the 18th days before Crampton's Gap. He was eventually arrested in New Scotland, New York on July 3, 1863. Van Hoesen was sent to the Albany Barracks outside of the city, but his familiarity there led to his escape two days later. While hiding amidst the bustling metropolis of New York City, Van Hoesen found a rare opportunity to join the military which was too lucrative to ignore. He met a man from Connecticut who had recently been drafted, but wanted nothing to do with the war. This man propositioned Van Hoesen to act as his substitute for an extra $300. This worked out for Van Hoesen who knew he could not enlist under his true name. There was also the fact that he was married at the time and did not want his wife to draw his pay, so he decided to assume the identity of the man and became "James Sullivan." Under Van Hoesen's new alias, he went to Bridgeport, Connecticut and joined the 7th Connecticut on October 24, 1863. His regiment fought along the southern coast and as deep as Florida, but in April 1864 he was transferred to the Navy and placed aboard the USS *Agawam*, still under his alias. He volunteered for a dangerous mission on December 2, 1864, where he was a part of a small crew that piloted a powder boat which was detonated in fiery fashion on the beach near Fort Fisher and was awarded the Congressional Medal of Honor for his actions. After the war, Van Hoesen dropped his alias and returned to New York, but he revisited the name when the time came for his pension. Despite his demonstrated courage which earned the nation's highest honor, his pension was revoked once Washington connected his identities and uncovered his desertion from the 18th. Van Hoesen vainly pled his case with explanations for several years, but he died without his pension at the age of eighty-six on May 9, 1918, and was buried in Coeymans Hollow, New York.[19]

The second recipient that once belonged to the 18th was Christopher C. Bruton (Company G), who left the regiment prematurely on account of ill health during the Peninsula campaign. After his health rebounded, the Irish-native returned to his hometown of Riga, New York, but was back in uniform in January 1864. He recruited his own company and was commissioned a captain in the 22nd New York Cavalry. At Petersburg, Bruton had an enemy bullet enter above his right knee that stayed with him the rest of his life. He was injured a second time at Winchester when his left index finger was shot off, but still he stayed in service. On March 2, 1865, Bruton captured a Rebel flag at Waynesboro, Virginia—one that happened to be the headquarters flag for Confederate General Jubal Early. The daring stunt was recognized by Congress, which approved and awarded Bruton with the Congressional Medal of

Honor. Bruton continued to serve in the military beyond the war and at times served on the staff of General's Custer and Sheridan. He eventually contracted a disease while on the Rio Grande River in Texas which killed him on June 14, 1867, at the age of twenty-seven. The Medal of Honor Historical Society—a preservation group that tracks the burials of recipients—had marked Bruton "lost to history" after the whereabouts of his burial was never known. In 2014, the author discovered his headstone in Caledonia, Michigan, a town that the Bruton family settled to after the Civil War. After 150 years passed since his wartime action that earned him the honorable medal, his grave was restored by the town and given a plaque to indicate his decoration in 2015.[20]

While in his second enlistment with the 22nd New York Cavalry, Capt. Christopher C. Bruton, formerly of Company G, 18th New York, captured Confederate General Jubal Early's headquarters flag on March 2, 1865, at Waynesboro, Virginia. His stunt earned him the Congressional Medal of Honor (Steve Rogers collection, United States Army Heritage and Education Center, Carlisle, Pennsylvania).

War's End

Six days after the war ended, the jubilation of peace was cut short when President Lincoln was assassinated. To help a grieving country, Lincoln's body was embalmed and placed on a special train that made nearly a hundred stops in communities across several northern states. The procession lasted thirteen days before it reached its final resting place in Illinois. Just before midnight on April 25, 1865, Lincoln's funeral train reached Albany. The casket was brought to the Capitol and displayed on a platform in the Assembly Chamber, and a special overnight squad of Albany soldiers was detailed to guard the president's body. Starting at midnight, a rotation of six military officers manned shifts that rotated every three hours. On the first watch was the 18th's second commander, Colonel William H. Young. Colonel John Hastings, the former captain of Company B of the 18th and lieutenant colonel in the 7th New York Heavy Artillery, stood watch after Young. Crowds were ushered in at 6 a.m. and the sounds of tears, prayers, and feet shuffling were the only sounds that resonated in the chamber. At 9 a.m., the fourth watch started which had Captain Mortier LaFayette Norton, a former second lieutenant in Company B of the 18th and captain in the Veteran Reserve Corps. Thousands of citizens, to include several veterans from the 18th, made the pilgrimage to the Capitol and paid their final respects before the casket was eventually transferred out of the city later that afternoon and on to the next community.[21]

To help change the mood of a mournful nation after Lincoln's assassination, President Andrew Johnson called for a celebratory formal review of Union troops in Washington. None of the two-year regiments from New York were reformed, but there were still hundreds of former members in other organizations that took part in the large-scale parade. On May 23, 1865, over 100,000 Union troops converged on the capital for the Grand Review of the Armies and were triumphantly paraded through its streets over a span of two days. Union troops from all fronts marched in what became the final appearance of the army that reunited the nation. Samuel Hodgkins (Co. K) neared the end of his second enlistment as a sergeant with the 14th New York Heavy Artillery, and as he marched with his regiment he described the review as "the grandest sights of a lifetime." Hodgkins was moved to remember in later years, "those old bullet ridden flags, and we all tanned with a hundred hard marches! It cannot be described … where brother fought against brother and father against son. Each for liberty as he saw it … we were all Americans fighting for a cause that each considered just and right. There will never be another such a war."[22]

Customarily celebrated as a festive holiday, the first Fourth of July commemoration that followed the end of the war was nothing short of extravagant, especially in Albany. As soon as the clock struck into the first minute of July 4, 1865, adolescents across the city began their reckless detonations of powders and fireworks. People crammed the streets by mid-morning and gazed upon seas of National Guardsmen paraded about. The governor's honored guests were a dozen Union generals and staff officers with connections to the state, to include General U.S. Grant, whose mere presence awestruck the spectators. After an afternoon parade, nearly 6,000 people gathered on the lawn of the Washington Parade Ground to listen to a handful of speeches from the governor and his dignitaries. After all of the addresses were concluded, the last scheduled event of the ceremony was the presentation of the flags carried by New York regiments, which were formally given to the Chief of the Bureau of Military Record for the state. One-by-one, colors from more than 100 regiments, some in shreds, were turned over to the state. A newspaper editor in attendance wrote, "all hearts were touched as the tattered emblems of the great struggle, borne in some instances by representatives of the regiments to which they belonged, were passed before the audience and deposited on the state." As the names of regiments were announced in numerical order, people in the audience cheered wildly for those in which they held a connection, a fondness, or were former members of. When the colors of the 18th were called forward, amidst shouts and applause, the silk national flag still inscribed with their motto, "Rally around it" was forever returned to the state. Many of the 18th veterans in attendance could reflect back when they were first presented the flag four years before, when they were given strict orders to return the flag, "only when your country is one and united forever." Their duty was finally complete.[23]

Fighting on the Frontier

Although the country braced arms with their former enemy during the reconstruction years, the Federal military put a renewed effort to shift fighting prowess towards their other adversaries on the frontier plains out West. The military life was a suitable career for a few 18th veterans who continued their service for many years in the postwar army. First Lieutenant William H. Russell transferred to the regular army after the war and served out West as a second lieutenant in the 4th United States Cavalry. On May 14, 1870, Russell and his outfit conducted an afternoon patrol at Mount Adam, near Lampasas, Texas, when they were suddenly attacked by Native Americans. Russell was shot in his liver by a pistol ball which caused major internal hemorrhaging. Russell and his men tried to gallop to their post twenty miles away from the encounter, but after five miles the lieutenant looked grim, so they stopped at a ranch and extracted the bullet. His excessive bleeding was irreparable and by midnight Russell was dead. He was thirty-one.[24]

After First Lieutenant Alexander H. Wands (Co. B) resigned from the 18th near the end of the Peninsula campaign, he took some time off before he returned to service in the Veterans Reserve Corps. In 1866, Wands transferred to the regular army as a second lieutenant in the 18th United States Infantry. His unit was nearly overrun by Native Americans in July 1866 at Crazy Woman Creek in Wyoming, and he almost gave the command to mercifully kill the two women in his party, one of which was his own wife, but they were rescued in the nick of

Left: First Lt. William H. Russell, Jr., transferred to the regular army after the war and served out west as a second lieutenant in the 4th U.S. Cavalry. While on patrol on May 14, 1870, Russell was shot and killed by a Native American ambush near Lampasas, Texas (courtesy New York State Military Museum). *Right:* A veteran of Company B, Alexander H. Wands served until 1870 in the postwar army out west and survived several attacks from Native Americans. He spent the rest of his life in San Francisco, at which place this undated photograph was taken (courtesy Jeff Sauter).

time by an unexpected detachment of their regiment. Ambushes on the prairie became the norm for Wands throughout his years on different assignments throughout the Wyoming Territory, but at his own request he was honorably discharged in 1870. He stayed out West and died in San Francisco on August 25, 1887, at the age of forty-seven.[25]

Walter Allen (Co. F) ended a long military career with Custer's 7th Cavalry in the Dakota territories. Preferring the name William instead of Walter, Allen and another soldier were detailed in November 1874 to erect a mail station outside of their fort. During their expedition, the two soldiers got drunk and tussled in a brawl that left Allen with a broken jaw, missing teeth, minor hearing loss, and bruises. He took up a lengthy hospitalization at Fort Totten until Custer had him discharged and sent home in July 1875. His shameful end to over a decade of service cost him his pension, but it also saved his life on account of the 7th Cavalry having been outright massacred at the battle of Little Bighorn eleven months later.[26]

Field and Staff Officers After the War

While in service as a military surgeon and acting medical inspector at Fort Monroe, Dr. Nathan P. Rice suffered a stroke in January 1864. The attack caused minor speech problems and debility with his left side, and a lengthy hospitalization. After doctors felt his attack lessened his motors skills and left him with emotional nervous disturbances, Dr. Rice was honorably discharged on July 27, 1865. As a civilian doctor, he continued his medical practice and was for a long time employed at the Custom House in New York. Periodically, Dr. Rice received requests from former 18th soldiers regarding their medical history during their service, but by 1890 he had lost his records from the regiment, which greatly hampered several men seeking pensions. Dr. Rice learned to live with cerebral degeneration which continued to have affects on his coordination and balance. As his health declined and spastic paraplegia increased, Dr. Rice died from his condition at his home in downtown New York City on November 10, 1900, at the age of seventy-one.[27]

Dr. Alexander A. Edmeston waged a losing battle with a war born disease that followed him home. Shortly after Antietam, Dr. Edmeston left the 18th for a promotion as full surgeon for the 92nd New York, but was later forced to resign in 1864 on account of chronic diarrhea. He returned to his home in Albany and busied himself with his medical practice. Fellow colleagues of Dr. Edmeston spoke highly of him and said he "was a man of great energy of character, which sometime caused him to overtask his physical strength." His chronic diarrhea ulcerated and inflamed his bowels, with continual hemorrhages that often confined him to his home for several weeks at a time. Each time he would battle through until the next hemorrhage set him back, but they gradually worsened. He had a caring wife and many friends in the medical field that tried all they could to help him rehab. With a sense of clairvoyance that his death was near, Dr. Edmeston asked to be shaved which was not a typical request from him. When asked why, he simply said, "I have a purpose." The next day, April 5, 1871, his final and most prolonged attack consumed him and died within a few hours. He was forty-one years old.[28]

When the 18th was mustered out of service, the fifty-two-year-old Rev. A. A. Farr returned to the pulpit in Albany. He had an untiring zeal to preach and convert sinners, and much like he did before the war, he cycled with different churches and organizations throughout the city. His first appointment back from service was at the Ash Grove Church in Albany in 1864. Two years later he became the director of the Young Men's Christian Association. In 1867, he tended to soldiers again when he became the chaplain of the Albany Soldiers' Home. He added to his workload a year later when he became a city missionary of the Albany Methodist Sunday School Union. On October 25, 1874, the Reverend Farr preached his last sermon at a church in Fort Plain, New York. At the time, he was sick with congested lungs and he seemed to know his speech from the pulpit would be his last. His audience remembered him to say, "I have felt that my time on earth is short, but I thank God I am ready to go home. I have tried to be ready for a long time for two things, namely, to preach and to die." Farr went back home to Albany where his wife and son were by his side when he passed away on November 4, 1874, at the age of sixty-four. In a display of outpouring appreciation for both him and his work, Christians from multiple denominations filled the First Methodist Episcopal Church for Farr's funeral, and scattered amongst the crowd were many former soldiers.[29]

Colonel William H. Young returned to the peaceful duties of a private life at home after his early resignation from ill health in August 1862. He continued to grow his family, and in 1863 another son was born but, like two others before him, this boy died before his third birthday. His last two children, both daughters, were born in 1866 and 1869, respectively. Upon his return to the civilian sector, Young went back to work as superintendent of the moulding department of Rathbone, Sard & Company stove foundry in Albany. His respectable

Left: An oil painting of the Rev. A. A. Farr that still hangs in the home of his descendants. The former chaplain returned to the pulpit of several churches and organizations around Albany, perpetually training for two things, "namely, to preach and to die." Farr passed away on November 4, 1874, at the age of sixty-four (courtesy Sarah Roach). *Right:* Appearing as the honored marshal of a nighttime parade in Albany on October 31, 1876, fifty-two-year-old Col. William H. Young rode a horse that became spooked by a firework and reared and threw him off. Young's head forcibly impacted the curb and he died within minutes (courtesy New York State Military Museum).

title of colonel followed him and he continually held himself to the standards of an officer. For a man who converted to Christianity so late in his life just before the start of the war, Young became very active in church when he returned home. For the Broadway Mission where he had first accepted the faith under the guidance of the Rev. A. A. Farr, Young financially aided the construction of a new edifice. Young helped organize the Grace Methodist Episcopal Church in Albany and served as the president of their Board of Trustees from its inception until his death. He also served the church as a steward and Bible class instructor.[30]

When the 18th came home in May 1863, Young was undoubtedly on hand, and at some point he was given the supreme honor of taking custody of one of the 18th's most prized possessions. Old Bull, the wounded dog found during the battle of Bull Run who the men rehabilitated and crowned their mascot, was handed over to Colonel Young which he took with open arms. For the next several years, whenever a former soldier from the 18th paid a visit to Colonel Young, Old Bull was said to have always remembered and recognized each man. In 1870, Jehiel J. Stevens, Jr. (Co. K), visited Young at his office in Albany, and Old Bull "recognized me at once by every demonstration a dog could give of joy at meeting an old comrade." It is unclear to when the dog died, but for a mention of him in 1870, the dog was by then at least eleven years old.[31]

With just a week before the nation's presidential election, Republican enthusiasts in Albany organized a torchlight parade as a show of force before the vote on October 31, 1876. Young was delighted to have been invited to appear as their honored marshal. After nightfall, crowds drew in overwhelming numbers along the principle streets that were illuminated by handheld torches. Fireworks sporadically flashed over the black sky as drums, bands, and horses passed through the gauntlet of fire. Thousands of marchers from differing social clubs converged together, along with nearly 700 men on horseback, and the spectacle was reminiscent of a military parade. Being as most voters were former soldiers, those who marched were divided into six divisions with the first headed by Colonel Young on horseback. When the procession was still on Lark Street, just as they passed Washington Avenue, Young observed a huddle of young boys igniting roman candles. Young had just made a comment to another rider that the horse he was given to ride was "a very vicious horse," and Young "was afraid he would kill somebody before the parade would end." He maneuvered his jittery horse toward the boys but one of them had already thrown a pack of firecrackers towards Young that detonated just in front of his horse. The feisty sorrel was instantly spooked and reared up, then slammed forward and launched Young right out of the saddle and over his horse. He was thrown with great force, as Young was said to have weighed over 200 pounds. His body crashed onto the curb, with the base of his skull having impacted first with the curbstone. Young had severe head trauma from a partially crushed skull that immediately gushed blood from his nose, ears, and mouth, and his breathing became labored. Young never uttered a word as onlookers rushed to his aid and whisked him away to the adjacent corner drugstore, but within ten minutes the colonel slipped out of consciousness and died. He was fifty-two years old. A man who lived by strict Christian morals, survived battles without scars, died in a peaceful parade a few blocks from his home. The parade continued, but as news of his death raced through the crowd the atmosphere softened.[32]

Four days later, thousands of saddened citizens from Albany, Schenectady, and other surrounding villages, converged upon the city for what local newspapers expressed to be one of the largest funerals Albany had ever witnessed. People gathered by the thousands in mourning to pay their respects and filled the path from the Young family residence at 928 Broadway to the Grace M. E. Church that the colonel had helped form. Dozens of veterans from the 18th descended upon the Young house to grieve and march together, which made Colonel Young's funeral become an unofficial reunion of the regiment since mustering-out thirteen years before. Although the reunion was impromptu and entirely unexpected, it was shrouded in melancholy with little to celebrate. Colonel George R. Myers became the last living commander of the 18th, and took a part in the funeral as one of the pallbearers. A firing detail of thirty-two veterans comprised from three local Grand Army of the Republic posts were under the command of Captain Michael H. Donovan (Co. F). After a small private funeral at the family residence, the pallbearers passed the flag-draped coffin out of the house and onto an awaiting hearse while an audience of thousands looked on. Friends, coworkers, and comrades lined the streets all the way to Young's church where people massed in unexpected numbers. The congregation was filled to overcapacity, and still others waited outside to hear the echo of the service. The attendance spoke volumes on how Young was respected by so many, and the minister mentioned that "never since the death of the lamented Lincoln have I seen a whole community so deeply moved as has been this great city by the sad event." When the minister touched on Young's service during the war, he said the colonel "never forgot the men with whom he had thus served, for while family and church were *first* in his affections, he gave his comrades the next place." One former 18th veteran in the audience who felt the loss a bit heavier was the colonel's son, David W. Young (Co. K), who put a brave face on as he comforted his grieving mother during the service. After many prayers and hymns were read and sung, the last act of his funeral was where the lid of his coffin was removed to allow the people one last chance to see their revered resident. This in itself took more than an hour-and-a-half as an estimated 4,000 people said their last goodbyes. The funeral eventually relocated by rail to Schenectady where a short Masonic graveside service took place at Vale Cemetery, not far from Colonel Jackson's grave. As the pallbearers lowered the casket into the earth, Donovan's detail fired three volleys to conclude a funeral worthy of a soldier.[33]

The three field officers from the 18th that came home with the regiment never again led troops in battle, but they still found ways to aid the war effort. On November 6, 1864, a Home Guard was formed in Ogdensburg that consisted of many former soldiers and officers that fused a local militia force in case the bridge from Canada was ever attacked. Colonel George R. Myers was elected captain of one company on the east side of the bridge, and was aided by former comrade J. C. O. Redington (Co. K). The company on the west side of the bridge was commanded by Horatio G. Goodno (Co. K). The Home Guard drilled in tactics nightly, but were never tested. Myers was later offered a commission in the regular army, but his uncertain health that flared at random prompted him to decline the promotion. Before the war ended, Myers received gratitude from the government in the form of a brevetted rank of brigadier general of United States Volunteers for meritorious service.[34]

After the war, Myers returned to his prewar occupation as a lawyer in Ogdensburg. Aside from his practice, Myers also held a position in Albany as a superintendent for a stove factory, and as a clerk for the New York State Canal Department, and was even in charge of the Money Order Department at the Chicago Post Office for a time. He married and had two children, but his daughter died less than a year old in 1877, and his son died at the age of thirteen in February 1881. In December of that same year, Myers' father and sister died just days apart, and a month later his own wife died after a short-term disease. Myers' mother died two years after his wife, so after the loss of his family he fashioned some big changes and left the state in 1886. He took the job as the superintendent for the National Military Home in Dayton, Ohio, where veterans were cared for. A few former 18th men ironically found themselves under the orders of their former colonel. Myers died in Dayton at the age of sixty-seven on June 3, 1905, and his body was shipped to Ogdensburg and interred amongst his family within the city cemetery.³⁵

Lieutenant Colonel John C. Meginnis returned to his prewar occupation and went back to work on the railroads while the war was still under way. For a man of his talent and experience, it was only natural that Meginnis went to work on the rails that stretched through battle lines. On November 1, 1864, Meginnis was employed as the civilian General Engine Dispatcher for the U.S. Military railroads in Nashville, and a month later the Confederate army set to attack that very city. With the necessity to defend the Union army stationed around the city, everyone on hand feverishly prepared for its defense, which included the entire force of civilian railroad employees. Meginnis once again found himself in command, albeit a force of railroaders instead of troops. Under his temporary command, the railroaders built earthworks for the defense of Nashville. One of Meginnis' "soldiers" was a former member of the 18th, eighteen-year-old George W. R. Goodno, who still stood as a Union deserter after he left Company K when his father Horatio resigned. When Meginnis wrote a letter to the elder Goodno to let him know his son was unhurt during the battle of Nashville, Meginnis shared a bit of what he witnessed during the campaign which "vividly brought to mind the days we spent together in the old 'Eighteenth.'" Meginnis watched the two-day battle play before him, and the enthusiasm of the troops, "who rushed forward, singing 'Rally round the flag boys,'" greatly moved him. "As I watched our boys," Meginnis wrote, "driving the demoralized and disheartened foe, steadily before them, the thought of where I was forsook me for the time being, and I longed to be among them, as they became, perfectly frantic with joy at their achievements." Nashville was saved and served as a major Union victory, and a lot can be attributed to the many civilians that took up an effort to protect the city. Meginnis continued to earn his $200 a month as the General Engine Dispatcher for the military until January 31, 1865.³⁶

This postwar image of Col. George R. Myers was taken at the time he served as superintendent for the National Military Home in Dayton, Ohio. He died there at the age of sixty-seven on June 3, 1905 (MOLLUS-MASS collection, United States Army Heritage and Education Center, Carlisle, Pennsylvania).

As a lifelong locomotive engineer, Meginnis continued his career after the war. He served on a number of lines that sent him all across the country, and for several years he was the traveling engineer on the Kansas Pacific Road. Still referred to as "Colonel," Meginnis eventually fell out of employment when jobs dried up and went to Denver, Colorado in search of opportunities. He lived in the city for a couple of years, having found employment in a saloon, but he never settled for a home of any permanence and instead chose to lodge in hotels. On the night of September 8, 1878, Meginnis checked himself into the Colorado House for a night's stay. Without any bags, Meginnis paid for his room and went to bed in a room that was shared by two other men. Sometime during the night, one of these men heard what he thought was someone vomiting, followed by the sound of the same person falling out of bed. The next morning, one of these men woke up and found Meginnis face-up on the floor next to his bed, in a large pool of blood. His hands were stiffly clenched and the blood had obviously poured steadily from his mouth that still hung open. A coroner was called and deemed Meginnis' lonely and painful death was from the result of strangulation caused from an internal hemorrhage.[37]

In September 1863, Major William Seward Gridley helped organize a battalion of volunteers in Schenectady for the 16th New York Heavy Artillery. First Lieutenant Alfred Truax, formerly of Company E, also helped recruit troops with Gridley. The local newspaper relied heavily on the names of Gridley and Truax to entice volunteers, yet the two never officially joined the regiment, even when Gridley was at a time appointed as their major. He had his sights aimed at higher office outside of the volunteer realm, and tried to encourage his namesake, William Henry Seward, to confer him a commission as a captain in the regular army. Gridley actually specified his preference of branches he wanted to be commissioned into, with cavalry being first, and infantry his last. He may have asked for too much when he propositioned the Secretary of State to backdate his commission to when he mustered out of the 18th on May 28, 1863. Gridley's plan never came to fruition and the war ended with him on the sidelines. In October 1866, Gridley was bestowed a brevet rank of colonel from New York Governor Fenton for meritorious services while in the 18th. Gridley returned to study law and was readmitted to the bar in 1867. Gridley married that same year. One of the first tasks his new wife took up without her husband's knowledge was that she too reached out to the secretary and tried to leverage an appeal to have Gridley appointed a high position in the regular army, but her try proved just as empty. His wife shared the Gridley surname before marriage, but he knew best where and how separated they were because Gridley spent a great deal of his free time in search of and documenting family genealogy, and descendents to this day benefit from the work he compiled. In 1868, Gridley moved to his wife's hometown in Jackson, Michigan and continued his practice of the law. He spent a year away from Michigan in 1869 when he engaged his practice in Nebraska and served as the Deputy Clerk of the District Court and commissioner for the U.S. Judicial Circuit for the state. He eventually held similar positions in Michigan and served as clerk and secretary of the Judicial Committee of the Michigan State Senate. The family eventually moved to Chicago, but Gridley died soon after on June 17, 1889, at the age of fifty. His wife, Eleanor Gridley, lived five decades beyond her husband and found fame as an ardent researcher of Abraham Lincoln and became a preeminent biographer of the late president.[38]

Reunions of the 18th

Twenty-five years had passed since the regiment was mustered out of service before some veterans started conversations that hinted at hosting a reunion. In April 1888, a small group of Albany veterans from the regiment met and formed a committee that organized an official reunion. They settled on a date that was a nod to their finest achievement, so on the twenty-six anniversary of the battle of Crampton's Gap, veterans of the 18th gathered in

Albany on September 14, 1888. In the years that passed since they last touched elbows in formation, many of those still alive had spread themselves out across the entire country, and they were either unable to afford the journey or were simply unaware of the reunion. Only twenty-six veterans of the 18th met on the designated day, and with the exception of three, the men who gathered were from the Schenectady and Albany companies. The only surviving colonel of the regiment, George R. Myers, was unable to attend with obligations in Ohio. As if time had not diminished the long ago prestige of being a commissioned officer, the former captain of Company F, Michael H. Donovan, found himself as the senior man of the veterans gathered and gladly took charge and presided as president of the reunion committee. Donovan organized the men that evening like soldiers and paraded them through city streets on their way to the Lark Street rink at the Academy of Music where a banquet awaited them. A fife and drum contingent helped provide cadence for the men to keep their step, and their march quickly gained onlookers who acknowledged them with applause. One observer made notice that, "the passing years have left their weight on the boys of '61," who showed obvious age. Their hair had grayed, their gait had slowed, and their ability to keep pace with the march was a new challenging oddity. The newspaper reporter singled out Donovan, who at sixty-five-years of age, "was compelled to acknowledge this and drop out of line in order to take his own time in reaching the rink." Seating for seventy-five was prepared inside the rink, and with a scattering of spouses nearly a quarter of the seats remained vacant. Even if everyone left alive had attended, the reporter made mention that "it would have been but a skeleton of the vigorous and enthusiastic phalanx which so early responded to the call of patriotism and duty." After a hearty meal was consumed that was deafened by lively conversations, Donovan hushed

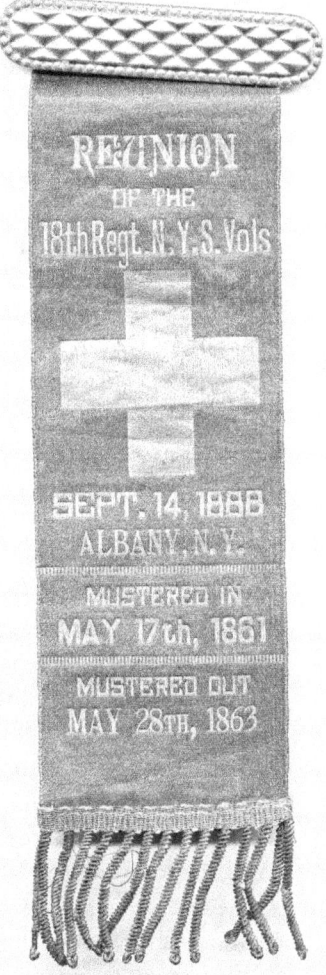

Ribbon worn by a veteran of the 18th New York at their first reunion on September 14, 1888, in Albany (author's collection).

the chatter and brought the room to order. He made a special acknowledgement to David W. Young (Co. K) who prepared the banquet at the rink. Young had also brought along his mother, the widow of the late Colonel William H. Young, who was quickly swarmed by the men who treated her as their honored guest. After official matters were handled, the men loosened their ties, pulled out their pipes and cigars, and rekindled old friendships with stories, jokes, and anecdotes from their service days. The night spiraled into an unending swap of tales that stretched beyond midnight. Men parted with handshakes and ended the first successful reunion of the 18th.[39]

Exactly one year later, the men who called themselves "survivors of the 18th," reunited again, this time in Schenectady. This second regimental reunion had a higher attendance, with thirty-seven veterans that gathered at the city armory, but once again the representation lacked men from Ogdensburg, Middletown, Fishkill, and Canandaigua. Like the year before, the veterans under Donovan's command were paraded around the city, joined by a conglomerate of national guardsmen, brass bands, and interested civilians. They were all treated to a massive feast in the armory, which had every wall within its spacious room bedecked in flowers and flags. George R. Myers was once again unable to attend and sent a letter of regret that was read to the crowd. Myers enclosed a copy of his original report of the regiment's action at Crampton's Gap, which was also read aloud and cheered at its conclusion. A handful of orators rendered poignant speeches, but the night was won by a band that was twice asked to play drum and bugle calls that captivated the old men, and was said to have "stirred the souls of every veteran present, and carried his thoughts back twenty odd years to the time when he was on duty." The reunion was deemed another success, and after a brief but lively debate their next host city chosen for the following year was settled on Albany.[40]

Being as September 14 fell on a Sunday in 1890, they met the following Monday with nearly the same number of survivors that attended a year before for the third reunion in Albany. Just as they had done for the first reunion, the survivors gathered downtown and were marched to the Lark Street rink and indulged on another sumptuous feast. As the perpetual president of the reunion committee, Donovan left a sick bed to be with those he still affectionately called "the boys," despite its youngest member being just shy of fifty. More speeches and stories were shared that went late into the evening, so late that a news reporter that covered the reunion had to leave before its conclusion just to get the story to print.[41]

Canandaigua was chosen as the host city for the fourth annual reunion on September 14, 1891. Unfortunately, the change of location did not yield the numbers hoped for and attendance was very small. During the course of their gathering, the committee decided to hold the fifth annual reunion back in Albany. What the men did not consider or foresee, was that the Grand Army of the Republic (GAR) held their massive national convention of 1892 in Washington during mid–September. This invitation welcomed all Union veterans and was a supreme event that many 18th survivors chose to attend instead of their annual regimental reunions. Albany newspapers did not run any recap of the fifth reunion, if it even happened, and there would be no more attempts at regimental reunions. The reunion committee faded away just as silently as many of the survivors did as they neared the turn of the century. Donovan, the committee's invariable president, died in Albany on August 17, 1899, less than a month before what would have been his seventy-seventh birthday.[42]

The GAR, Soldiers' Homes, and Pensions

Reunions rekindled old friendships and promoted healing and remembrance, but once Union veterans as a whole realized the political sway they could wield when they unified, there was nothing that stopped them. When the GAR was born, they quickly came to be the preeminent organization for Union veterans with chapters throughout the country and boasted their highest memberships during the latter half of the nineteenth century. They organized like modern labor unions and were exclusive to only honorably discharged veterans that fought for the Union. Almost every county in every state had at least one post that met monthly for the purpose to promote remembrance of their service and to fight for pension

Top: Chartered in 1875, Schenectady's GAR Post 90 was named in honor of Capt. William Horsfall, and many veterans of the regiment were members. This undated photograph shows members of Horsfall Post 90 marching down State Street in a Schenectady parade (from the collection of the Schenectady County Historical Society). *Bottom:* Ribbon worn by a member of GAR Post 644 in Albany, named in honor of Col. William A. Jackson and chartered in 1889. Many former veterans of the 18th New York belonged to this post (author's collection).

reform for veterans. Local organizations usually bestowed a name for their post after an honorable resident of the community who had most likely died during the war. Albany honored the first colonel of the 18th when they designated one of four GAR chapters as the William A. Jackson Post 644. Schenectady did the same and named their Post 90 as the William Horsfall Post, of which several veterans from the 18th were members.[43]

Extending their debt of gratitude to the defenders of the nation, the government opened several branches of National Soldiers' Homes throughout the country that cared for aging Union veterans. The assisted living cared for men in a paramilitary manner and dozens of former 18th soldiers surrendered their pensions to cover the expenses. In later years, Francis J. Conaty (Co. F) was a resident of the Mountain Branch home at Johnson City, Tennessee. On September 17, 1904,

Conaty ventured off the campus and traveled up to Bristol, a city shared on the border of Virginia and Tennessee. Unfortunately, the sixty-two-year-old died there that day, and his death gave rise to a matter of complications. The jurisdiction of the soldiers' home could not take charge of Conaty's body because he died off their premises. Conaty would have been placed into a pauper's forgotten grave somewhere in Bristol had it not been for the most unlikely strangers to step in. A group of ex–Confederate veterans in Bristol banded together and purchased a casket for Conaty's remains, and had them shipped to Johnson City where the old soldier was given a proper military funeral at the national cemetery. This act of solidarity speaks volumes to how far former enemies had healed four decades after the end of the war.[44]

John W. Farr (Co. F) finished the war as a captain in a cavalry unit and was mustered out in Texas, and spent the rest of his life in the Lone Star State. He took up residence in the town of Palestine and found work in the railroad business. As an ardent Republican and former Union officer, Farr had to put up with a great deal of ridicule and hatred from the town that had deep ties to the Confederacy. Farr worked as long as he was able, but by 1922 he had no income. When he tried to enter the County Poor House, he was turned away because the staff never forgot he was once a Union soldier. Luckily, a local charity stepped up and opened their doors, and they even helped him earn a federal pension. He still died penniless on October 10, 1926, less than a year before he would have turned ninety. With no family to take ownership of his remains, Farr's body was destined for a potter's field until a local undertaker took pity on the forgotten Yankee and provided an honorable funeral.[45]

A veteran of Company F, John W. Farr lived the rest of his days after the war in Palestine, Texas, and their deep ties to the failed Confederacy refused him at every chance. He died alone and penniless in 1926, and had it not been for the compassion of an undertaker, Farr would have been buried unmarked in a potter's field (MOLLUS-MASS collection, United States Army Heritage and Education Center, Carlisle, Pennsylvania).

The Federal Government began to issue pensions to qualified veterans, widows, and children since before the war ended. Pensions originally started as monthly stipend for medically discharged soldiers, or their family in the event of their death. Requirements for a pension eventually broadened to cover more men as they aged and attributed an array of injuries and ailments to their days in uniform.

The benefits of the financial assistance helped thousands, but in a few rare incidents a pensioner became a vulnerable target for corrupted minds to take advantage of. Targeted for his most recent pension payment, eighty-six-year-old Jacob A. Moore (Co. D) and his ninety-year-old housemate were viciously murdered in their home in Bushville, New York, on February 21, 1894. Both elderly occupants were bludgeoned with an iron shovel, shot multiple times, and had their throats slashed. The house was ransacked but the attacker never checked Moore's breast pocket which was where he kept his check. The double murder put a lot of media attention on Bushville, but without hard evidence the crime was never solved.[46]

A similar mysterious outcome befell another former Wallkill Guard. On January 25, 1902, two fox hunters in the woods of Millmay, New Jersey stumbled upon the skeletal remains of sixty-two-year-old Julius Becking (Co. D). He had been a reported missing person since February 15, 1901, and was last seen by his wife at their home, located about a mile from where the body was discovered. When authorities heard he had his pension money on his person, they immediately feared "that he was waylaid and robbed and his body was hid." Becking's wife reported her husband left home incensed after a "spell" that he often experienced when he slept. Suspicions rose when detectives were notified by a local physician that Becking needed assistance to walk because of his partial paralysis on his left side, but his cane was found at home. Millmay residents revealed that the aged veteran had a turbulent relationship with a neighbor who was said to have been associated with Becking's wife. She did not deny her husband's jealousy but discredited all other rumors concerning the neighbor. She eventually skipped town and moved to Rhode Island where she applied for a widow's pension just three months after her husband's disappearance. Investigators never found the silver dollars and pension papers on Becking's body that his wife said should have been with him. When Becking's skull was examined and showed indications of a fracture, homicide was suspected but a coroner's jury somehow reasoned his death came from natural causes.[47]

While a resident at the Soldiers' Home in Milwaukee in 1895, Edward Corbally (Co. B) was excited to hear news that an old comrade from his company had entered his institution. Corbally tracked down the man who claimed to be Edmond Riley from Company B of the 18th, but when they met the meeting was the first either had ever seen of each other. The man who claimed to be Riley was not who he said he was, and Corbally knew immediately. It had then been nearly thirty-two years since Corbally had last seen the actual Riley, but one tends not to forget with whom they served alongside. The stranger had all the opposite qualities in appearance to the actual Riley, and instead of the Irish accent he should have had, this man spoke with a southern drawl. After having his own fun with questions about the regiment that the man never answered correctly, Corbally reported the incident to the staff, and the fraud soon fled to Macon, Georgia, which left everyone to believe the imposter was an ex–Confederate.[48]

From a jail cell in Frankfort, Kentucky, Robert Farrell (Co. K) applied for a pension in 1891, but was quickly denied from a lack of actual debility. Farrell had been a horse jockey in Maysville, Kentucky, and had been jailed since 1884 after a guilty charge of murder put him away with a life sentence. Farrell had gotten into an argument with his landlord and claimed he did not draw his pistol first, but acted in self-defense when he fired a fatal shot into his landlord's head. After his jailhouse pleas for a pension fell through, Farrell gained national attention in 1896 when he claimed to be a participant of the infamous Lincoln assassination. Farrell stated he was in Washington in 1865 and was supposed to locate the president's carriage in order to murder Lincoln on the day before the actual assassination took place. A few months after the story ran, he died in his Frankfort jail on November 6, 1896. It was reported that the governor had approved and signed a pardon for Farrell just before he died, but the fated never knew.⁴⁹

Alcoholism, Despondency, and Suicides

A serious health concern that many Civil War veterans battled alone in the postwar years was alcoholism. Former members of the 18th were no exception as there were many that bore this struggle which often led to a life of loneliness, wretchedness, injury, and death. Men drank away savings and used their pension payments as stipends at saloons. This habit usually led to other social and moral taboos such as homelessness, divorce, and abandonment of children.

By 1885, Shubael Durkee (Co. I) liquidated his funds to support his addiction to alcohol and had to be admitted to the poorhouse in Wayne County, New York, where he died two years later at the age of fifty-two. Henry Ebel (Co. K) was no different and was regarded by the residents of Ogdensburg as the city drunkard. He was in-and-out of prisons for petty thefts and drunkenness and was constantly berated by the local newspaper who exploited his problems. Ogdensburg seemed liberated when the Soldiers' Home in Bath, New York gave Ebel shelter in 1886, where he died alone at the institution nine years late. Robert Myers (Co. E) left Schenectady in 1877 and headed west to work for the Washington Iron Works in Seattle. Myers also indulged in lengthy binges, and after one night of heavy drinking on June 2, 1899, friends put him to bed at his home. When they came back the next day to check on him, they found fifty-eight-year-old Myers dead in his bed with two bottles of whisky at his side.⁵⁰

As the last acting adjutant for the 18th, Henry "Harry" E. Munger (Co. A) came home from the war a different man. He went to work for the commissary department in Illinois, got married, and fathered three children, but depression and a dependency to alcohol weaved its way into all facets of his life. After relocating his family numerous times in pursuit of railroad jobs that he quickly lost from routine binges, his wife took the children and left him in 1871. He tried to reconcile with her two years later, but did so amidst another angry intoxicated state. It would be the last the family ever saw of him. Munger fled to Texas and became a vagabond who moved throughout the state in search of work. He was a building contractor in Houston, a lumberjack at a Beaumont saw mill, and constructed railroads in Orange and Kirbyville. Munger kept to himself but continued to drink to excess and was said by saloon regulars in Texas to be "ugly and quarrelsome" when he binged. He nearly lost the use of both of his hands in two separate work accidents which eventually earned him a pension. Munger's last whereabouts was Beaumont in 1901 when the village morphed into a city during its oil boom, and when he failed to pick up his last pension payment there it was suspected he died, but where, when, and how were questions the family never had answered. Working with information provided from Munger's descendents, the author discovered information in 2014 that sheds some light on his demise. Seventy-five miles northwest of Kirbyville, Texas, where Munger was believed to have died, there is a grassy one-acre field in Lufkin that at the turn of the century was used for burials of local African-Americans in unmarked graves. Originally known as Frost Cemetery, burial records of interments did not begin until the graveyard opened for paupers in 1901, and the overwhelming numbers of drifters buried there prompted a name change to Stranger's Rest Cemetery. A small stone plaque placed in the cemetery in 1997 displays the names of known burials from early records, and in alphabetical order one can find the name of Harry E. Munger.[51]

Joseph S. Raines (Co. G) cut ties and literally distanced himself from his prominent family in Canandaigua by a couple thousand miles. He was a loner who drifted west with little money and fashioned a precarious livelihood at a poorhouse in Phoenix, Arizona. His only income was what little came from his pension, and each quarter he got paid he blew his government allowance at the saloons. The cycle continued until the seventy-year-old dropped dead in a Phoenix casino saloon on March 15, 1906. When no family of his came forward, Raines was prepped for a pauper's grave, that is until one of his saloon chums stopped by and had a conversation with the funeral director. A side comment from this friend mentioned that "if the relatives of Raines knew of his death they would give him a princely funeral." The man referred to was Senator John Raines of New York, a cousin who championed the "Raines Law" which regulated and taxed the sale of alcohol on businesses. The funeral home sent a telegram to the senator that seemed to fall on deaf ears, but the message eventually found its way to the departed's sister who sent the proper funds to cover burial expenses.[52]

Having finished the war as an officer of a Colored Troops regiment, Calvin B. Potter (Co. B) returned to his prewar studies of the law and passed the state bar in Michigan in 1866. In 1874, Potter was elected to the Michigan House of Representatives. Throughout his life, Potter would be prostrated by pains in his head and limbs, stiffness throughout his whole body, diarrhea, and exhaustion that he complained originated from the war. Many soldiers during the war had an aversion to hospitals unless their health was legitimately dire, and Potter was so rooted in this stigma that he continued to avoid doctors later in life. "Unless a soldier was wounded," Potter explained, "he was scrutinized closely if he returned from a hospital." This headstrong notion created a lack of medical records which hurt Potter's appeal for a pension in later years when his health continued to be

Calvin Brittain Potter, a veteran of Company B, is photographed with his youngest son, Rupert, circa 1902. This was the last photograph taken of Potter who committed suicide on August 18, 1902. It was found among his effects (courtesy William F. Potter).

weakened by war born sicknesses. His health eventually led to his early retirement from law and legislature in 1882. Even without medical paperwork, Potter was able to secure a minimal pension after a lengthy wait, but it was one that he felt barely aided his debility. Under the advice that a climate change could be beneficial to his health, Potter left his wife and children in Michigan in 1900 and moved to Salt Lake City, Utah. Potter continued to plead with the pension board to increase his allotment, but his requests were continually rejected which greatly distressed him. He became depressed and self-medicated heavily with an addiction to morphine and alcohol that his own wife said "was his own worst enemy." From inside his little rented attic apartment above a church, a dejected Potter penned a letter to his son on the night of August 18, 1902, that lambasted the Pension Commissioner, having felt his pleas for help fell on deaf ears. Potter concluded this final letter and said, "I guess there was insufficient evidence of physical incapacity. So fall the brave. Exit soldier, officer and gentleman." Potter then swallowed enough morphine pills to kill several men and calmly stretched himself out on his couch until his life slipped away. He was sixty-five.[53]

The Last Survivor

As the boys in blue faded to gray amidst their golden years, the nation rapidly lost the witnesses of the war. By 1916, Samuel Hodgkins (Co. K) had not heard from any comrades for such a long period that he believed himself to be the last survivor of his company. In reality he was not, but he was far removed from New York after he left the state in 1870 to settle an unbroken prairie that became known as Freedom, Minnesota. He farmed a couple hundred acres over a few decades until his slowed pace with age led him to parcel his land to his children. After having outlived his wife and been able to witness the birth of a couple great-grandchildren, Hodgkins lived to the age of eighty-five, and died in Waldorf, Minnesota on October 8, 1924.[54]

By 1930, the surviving veterans of the 18th had diminished drastically to less than half a dozen. The final chapter of the regiment ended with the passing of its last survivor—John B. LaQue (Co. A). Born on August 12, 1840, in the French-Canadian province of Quebec, LaQue moved to America with his family to

Photographed in 1929, John B. LaQue, a veteran of Company A, was a lifelong member of the Horsfall Post 90. Born on August 12, 1840, in Quebec, Canada, LaQue was the last survivor of the 18th New York and died on May 1, 1938, at the age of ninety-seven (from the collection of the Schenectady County Historical Society).

Albany when he was a young child. After Lincoln called for troops after the war broke out, the twenty-year-old ax maker jumped at the chance and joined Captain Gridley's company in Schenectady on May 1, 1861. Two months after the regiment mustered-out, LaQue married and eventually had ten children, six of whom lived to adulthood. A son that shared his name served in the Spanish-American War. Always passionate about military matters, LaQue followed intently the progress of his son's war and the brutal fighting of the First World War. LaQue had been a machinist by trade and worked for many years at the American Locomotive Works, and retired from there in 1922. He was active with the GAR and a member of Schenectady's Horsfall Post, and was often sent to faraway conferences as a delegate. Throughout the 1930s, LaQue drove himself in his Model T Ford around the northeastern states and attended many conferences and conventions almost monthly. LaQue and his automobile became a novelty together, and by 1936 his odometer had clocked over 141,000 miles. That same year, LaQue became the oldest resident of Schenectady and was one of two Civil War veterans left in the city. With the advent of radio, LaQue found fame when he made an appearance on the *Major Bowes Amateur Hour* on February 16, 1936. Listeners around the country heard Bowes describe LaQue's appearance, and called on the aged veteran to stand up from the audience and be recognized. Amidst a studio of applause, the spry ninety-five-year-old stood from his seat and waved a little silk American flag. On May 1, 1938—the seventy-seventh anniversary of the day he enlisted into the 18th—LaQue died peacefully at his home in Schenectady at the age of ninety-seven. With his passing, the last witness to know the hardships, the voices, the horror, and the joys of the 18th New York Infantry died with him, and finally closed the history of the regiment.[55]

Roster

The following roster for the 18th New York Infantry was originally based from the *Annual Report of the Adjutant-General for the State of New York for the Year 1899*, No. 19 (Albany, N.Y.: J.B. Lyon, 1900), pp. 959–1083. After finding perpetual misspellings, errors, missing dates, and insufficient data, I constructed a corrected and accurate roster for the regiment by incorporating information found from compiled service records, pension records, and discharge papers at the National Archives, as well as other primary sources such as Federal Census data, family genealogy, and cemetery records.

ABERCROMBIE, ALEXANDER—Age 27 years. Enlisted May 2, 1861, at Schenectady. Mustered in as private, Co. E, May 17, 1861, to serve two years. Wounded in right ankle and left thigh, September 14, 1862, at Crampton's Gap, Md. Hospitalized. Transferred to Camp B General Hospital, October 24, 1862, in Frederick, Md. Transferred out of Camp A, March 10, 1863, and entered McKim's Mansion General Hospital, March 11, 1863, in Baltimore, Md. Transferred to West's Buildings General Hospital, May 8, 1863, in Baltimore, Md. Transferred to Albany, N.Y., May 9, 1863. Entered Post Hospital, May 12, 1863, at Albany, N.Y. Mustered out with company, May 28, 1863, at Albany, N.Y. Subsequent service in Co. B, 2nd New York Veteran Cavalry.

ABERS, CORNELIUS D.—Age 19 years. Enlisted May 17, 1862, at Port Jervis. Mustered in as private, Co. B, same date, to serve unexpired term of two years. Mustered out with company, May 28, 1863, at Albany, N.Y. Subsequent service in Co. A, 16th New York Cavalry.

ACKER, JUSTUS H.—Age 27 years. Enlisted May 2, 1861, at Schenectady. Mustered in as private, Co. E, May 17, 1861, to serve two years. Wounded in left shoulder, September 14, 1862, at Crampton's Gap, Md. Hospitalized. Transferred to Camp B General Hospital, October 24, 1862, in Frederick, Md. Transferred out of Camp A, March 10, 1863, and entered McKim's Mansion General Hospital, March 11, 1863, in Baltimore, Md. Mustered out with company, May 28, 1863, at Albany, N.Y. Brother of Munson S. Acker & Brother-in-law of William A. Cooley.

ACKER, MUNSON SHULTS—Age 21 years. Enlisted May 2, 1861, at Schenectady. Mustered in as private, Co. E, May 17, 1861, to serve two years. Sent off from Harrison's Landing, Va., August 14, 1862, to be hospitalized in Satterlee General Hospital, in West Philadelphia, Pa. Discharged from hospital and regiment, December 7, 1862, in Philadelphia, Pa., by enlistment in the Regular Army under Provisions of General Order No. 154. Assigned to Battery C & G, 3rd United States Light Artillery. Brother of Justus H. Acker & Brother-in-law of William A. Cooley.

ACKERMAN, SEWARD (Leonard)—Age 22 years. Enlisted May 12, 1861, at Ogdensburg. Mustered in as private, Co. K, May 17, 1861, to serve two years. Promoted sergeant, November 1, 1862. Mustered out with company, May 28, 1863, at Albany, N.Y. Subsequent service in Co. B, 14th New York Heavy Artillery.

ADAMS, EDWARD J.—Age 18 years. Enlisted April 17, 1861, at Albany. Mustered in as private, Co. F, May 17, 1861, to serve two years. Promoted corporal, December 8, 1862. Mustered out with company, May 28, 1863, at Albany, N.Y. Subsequent service in Co. I, 13th New York Heavy Artillery.

ADAMS, GEORGE C.—Age 34 years. Enlisted April 24, 1861, at Albany. Mustered in as private, Co. B, May 17, 1861, to serve two years. Deserted, June 11, 1861, at Albany, N.Y.

AHREET, MARQUIS W.—Age 19 years. Enlisted May 2, 1861, at Schenectady. Mustered in as private, Co. E, May 17, 1861, to serve two years. Promoted corporal, October 11, 1861. Promoted sergeant, September 20, 1862. Mustered out with company, May 28, 1863, at Albany, N.Y.

AINSWORTH, JAMES WILLIAM—Age 23 years. Enlisted May 2, 1861, at Schenectady. Mustered in as private, Co. E, May 17, 1861, to serve two years. Mustered out with company, May 28, 1863, at Albany, N.Y.

ALDRICH, DANIEL H.—Age 18 years. Enlisted April 19, 1861, at Albany. Mustered in as private, Co. F, May 17, 1861, to serve two years. Discharged for disability, March 14, 1863, at White Oak Church, Falmouth, Va. Died of disease, March 14, 1863, at White Oak Church, Falmouth, Va.

ALEXANDER, ROBERT—Age 18 years. Enlisted September 27, 1861, at Ogdensburg. Mustered in as private, Co. K, October 30, 1861, at Camp Williams, Va., to serve unexpired term of two years. Detached as teamster for Brigade Headquarters, January or February 1863. Mustered out with company, May 28, 1863, at Albany, N.Y. Subsequent service in Co. C, 18th New York Cavalry.

ALEXANDER, THOMAS—Age 26 years. Enlisted April 30, 1861, at Middletown. Mustered in as corporal, Co. D, May 17, 1861, to serve two years. Promoted sergeant, June 1, 1862. Wounded in hand, June 27, 1862, at Gaines's Mill, Va. Hospitalized at General Hospital, July 1862, at Craney Island, Va. Detailed as a clerk for Distributing Camp, in Alexandria, Va. and for 3rd and 6th Army Corps for March and April 1863. Mustered out with company, May 28, 1863, at Albany, N.Y.

ALLEN, CHARLES T.—Age 19 years. Enlisted April 29, 1861, at Albany. Mustered in as private, Co. I, May 17, 1861, to serve two years. Detailed on recruiting service, January 21, 1862. Returned to regiment, April 25, 1862. Mustered out with company, May 28, 1863, at Albany, N.Y.

ALLEN, JOHN—Age 35 years. Enlisted May 1, 1861, at Albany. Mustered in as private, Co. B, May 17, 1861, to serve two years. Deserted, June 11, 1861, at Albany, N.Y. Arrested, February 1863. Returned to regiment, February 18, 1863. Court-martialed for desertion, March 3, 1863. Dishonorably discharged, March 20, 1863, by sentence of general court martial.

ALLEN, JOHN SEYMOUR—Age 26 years. Enlisted May 12, 1861, at Ogdensburg. Mustered in as sergeant, Co. K, May 17, 1861, to serve two years. Wounded in left arm and left side, July 17, 1861, near Fairfax Court House, Va. Died of such wounds, August 9, 1861, at hospital, Washington, D.C.

ALLEN, LEVI LEWIS—Age 27 years. Enlisted May 7, 1861, at Canandaigua. Mustered in as corporal, Co. G, May 17, 1861, to serve two years. Reduced to private, date not stated. Mustered out with company, May 28, 1863, at Albany, N.Y.

ALLEN, WALTER—Age 19 years. Enlisted April 19, 1861, at Albany. Mustered in as private, Co. F, May 17, 1861, to serve two years. Mustered out with company, May 28, 1863, at Albany, N.Y. Subsequent service in Co. C, 18th New York Cavalry, Battery F, 2nd United States Artillery (post war) & Co. D, 7th United States Cavalry (post war).

ALLEN, WILLIAM HOWARD—Age 22 years. Enlisted May 17, 1861, at Albany. Mustered in as private, Co. I, same date, to serve two years. Mustered out with company, May 28, 1863, at Albany, N.Y. Subsequent service in Co. A, 2nd Massachusetts Infantry.

AMES, JOHN T.—Age 21 years. Enlisted April 22, 1861, at Schenectady. Mustered in as private, Co. A, May 17, 1861, to serve two years. Mustered out with company, May 28, 1863, at Albany, N.Y. Subsequent service in Co. G, 91st New York Infantry.

AMMANN (Amman), JOHN—Age 32 years. Enlisted April 19, 1861, at Albany. Mustered in as musician, Co. F, May 17, 1861, to serve two years. Reduced to private, date not stated. Mustered out with company, May 28, 1863, at Albany, N.Y. Subsequent service in Co. K, 13th New York Heavy Artillery.

ANDERSON, GEORGE HAMILTON, Jr.—Age 17 years, but gave age as 18 years. Enlisted September 1, 1861, at Albany. Mustered in as private, Co. H, same date, to serve unexpired term of two years. Mustered out with company, May 28, 1863, at Albany, N.Y. Subsequent service in Co. B, 7th New York Heavy Artillery.

ANDERSON, JOHN—Age 37 years. Enlisted May 9, 1861, at Albany. Mustered in as private, Co. B, May 17, 1861, to serve two years. Deserted, July 1, 1861, at Washington, D.C.

ANTHONY, WILLIAM JOHN—Age 22 years. Enlisted May 2, 1861, at Schenectady. Mustered in as private, Co. E, May 17, 1861, to serve two years. Mustered out with company, May 28, 1863, at Albany, N.Y.

ARCHIBALD, JOHN—Age 44 years. Enlisted April 19, 1861, at Albany. Mustered in as private, Co. F, May 17, 1861, to serve two years. Discharged for disability, July 25, 1861, at Alexandria, Va.

ARDILL, ROBERT T.—Age 18 years. Enlisted May 12, 1861, at Ogdensburg. Mustered in as musician, Co. K, May 17, 1861, to serve two years. Deserted, September 8, 1862, at Rockville, Md.

ARMSTRONG, WILLIAM R.—Age 26 years. Enlisted April 24, 1861, at Albany. Mustered in as private, Co. B, May 17, 1861, to serve two years. Wounded, December 13, 1862, at Fredericksburg, Va. Sent to General Hospital in Washington, D.C. Returned to regiment, March 3, 1863. Mustered out with company, May 28, 1863, at Albany, N.Y.

ARNOLD, CHARLES R.—Age 20 years. Enlisted September 18, 1862, at Albany. Mustered in as private, Co. D, same date, to serve three years. Transferred May 10, 1863, to Co. C, 121st New York Infantry.

ASTON, WILLIAM HENRY—Age 28 years. Enlisted April 23, 1861, at Fishkill. Mustered in as corporal, Co. C, May 17, 1861, to serve two years. Mustered out with company, May 28, 1863, at Albany, N.Y. Subsequent service in Co. H, 83rd New York Infantry.

ATKINSON, THOMAS E.—Age 21 years. Enlisted November 20, 1861, at Albany. Mustered in as private, Co. A, same date, to serve unexpired term of two years. Absent-without-leave, January 20, 1863, from Camp Russell, White Oak Church, Falmouth, Va. Returned to regiment, January 24, 1863, same place. Court-martialed for absence and disobedience, February 24, 1863, at same place. Mustered out with company, May 28, 1863, at Albany, N.Y.

AUER, MICHAEL—Age 38 years. Enlisted April 26, 1861, at Schenectady. Mustered in as private, Co. A, May 17, 1861, to serve two years. Discharged for disability, May 4, 1862, at Alexandria, Va. Subsequent service in Co. K, 177th New York Infantry & 1st Regiment, Veteran Reserve Corps.

AUSTIN, THOMAS—Age 35 years. Enlisted May 7, 1861, at Albany. Mustered in as musician, Co. H, May 17, 1861, to serve two years. Hospitalized, May 25, 1863, at Albany, N.Y. Died of disease, May 29, 1863, at hospital, Albany, N.Y.

BABCOCK, SAMUEL—Age 19 years. Enlisted April 30, 1861, at Middletown. Mustered in as private, Co. H, May 17, 1861, to serve two years. Mustered out with company, May 28, 1863, at Albany, N.Y. Subsequent service in the United States Navy on Gunboat *Metacomet*, *North Carolina* & *Savannah*.

BABCOCK, WILLIAM H.—Age 23 years. Enlisted April 30, 1861, at Middletown. Mustered in as private, Co. H, May 17, 1861, to serve two years. Wounded slightly in hand, September 14, 1862, at Crampton's Gap, Md. Mustered out with company, May 28, 1863, at Albany, N.Y.

BAILEY, WILLIAM—Age 31 years. Enlisted September 1, 1861, at Albany. Mustered in as private, Co. H, same date, to serve unexpired term of two years. Mustered out with company, May 28, 1863, at Albany, N.Y.

BAKER, JOHN—Age 23 years. Enlisted April 24, 1861, at Albany. Mustered in as private, Co. B, May 17, 1861, to serve two years. Deserted, December 11, 1862, near Fredericksburg, Va. Returned to regiment, January 29, 1863, at Stafford County, Va. Court-martialed for desertion, March 2, 1863. Deserted, April 25, 1863, from White Oak Church, Falmouth, Va.

BAKER, JOSEPH—Age 24 years. Enlisted May 12, 1861, at Ogdensburg. Mustered in as private, Co. K, May 17, 1861, to serve two years. Mustered out with company, May 28, 1863, at Albany, N.Y.

BALL, FELIX—Age 19 years. Enlisted April 19, 1861, at Albany. Mustered in as private, Co. F, May 17, 1861, to serve two years. Mustered out with company, May 28, 1863, at Albany, N.Y. Subsequent service in the United States Navy on the USS *North Carolina*, *Brandywine*, *Minnesota*, *Gunboat Ceres* & *Savannah*.

BALL, JAMES "Jim" M.—Age 23 years. Enlisted May 2, 1861, at Schenectady. Mustered in as sergeant, Co. E, May 17, 1861, to serve two years. Detailed on recruiting service, August 14, 1861. Returned to regiment, October 12, 1861. Detached for engineer service, November 7, 1861, and December 1861, by Brigadier General Newton. Mustered out with company, May 28, 1863, at Albany, N.Y.

BALL, LUCIUS W. H.—Age 21 years. Enlisted April 23, 1861, at Albany. Mustered in as private, Co. C, May 17, 1861, to serve two years. Captured, June 29, 1862, while sick at Savage's Station, Va. Died of disease, July 11, 1862, at hospital, Savage's Station, Va.

BANTHAM, JOHN S.—Age 26 years. Enlisted September 1, 1861, at Albany. Mustered in as private, Co. F, same date, to serve two years. Promoted sergeant, September 19, 1861. Detailed on recruiting service, November and December 1861, at Albany, N.Y. Reduced to private, September 1, 1862. Hospitalized, September 10, 1862, at Harewood General Hospital, in Washington, D.C. Discharged, May 14, 1863, at Alexandria Hospital, in Washington, D.C. Mustered out with company, May 28, 1863, at Albany, N.Y.

BARBER, HENRY—Age 21 years. Enlisted September 18, 1862, at Albany. Mustered in as private, Co. D, same date, to serve three years. Transferred May 10, 1863, to Co. H, 121st New York Infantry.

BARHYDT, ANDREW D.—Age 19 years. Enlisted May 2, 1861, at Schenectady. Mustered in as corporal, Co. E, May 17, 1861, to serve two years. Reduced to private, October 11, 1861. On ten day furlough, March 1, 1863, in Schenectady, N.Y. Returned to regiment, March 10, 1863. Mustered out with company, May 28, 1863, at Albany, N.Y.

BARHYDT, GEORGE DALLAS "Dal"—Age 17 years, but gave age as 18 years. Enlisted May 2, 1861, at Schenectady. Detailed as captain's cook. Mustered in as private, Co. E, May 17, 1861, to serve two years. Sick in hospital at time of muster out. Mustered out, June 30, 1863.

BARNHART, JOSEPH CULVER—Age 16 years, but gave age as 18 years. Enlisted June 12, 1861, at Albany, as private, Co. G. Refused to be sworn in and left the regiment. Never mustered. Subsequent service in Co. K, 148th New York Infantry.

BARRINGER, ALVIN—Age 19 years. Enlisted, April 30, 1861, at Middletown. Mustered in as private, Co. D, May 17, 1861, to serve two years. Deserted, July 23, 1861, from Camp Myers, Alexandria, Va.

BARRINGER, GEORGE C.—Age—years. Enlisted May 2, 1861, at Schenectady. Mustered in as private, Co. E, May 17, 1861, to serve two years. No further record after May 17, 1861.

BARRON, JAMES—Age 39 years. Enlisted April 24, 1861, at Albany. Mustered in as first sergeant, Co. B, May 17, 1861, to serve two years. Reduced to private, date not stated. Deserted, August 10, 1861, from Camp Myers, Alexandria, Va.

BARRY, GEORGE—Age 25 years. Enrolled April 30, 1861, at Middletown. Mustered in as first lieutenant, Co. D, May 17, 1861, to serve two years. Promoted captain, November 11, 1861. Killed, June 27, 1862, at Gaines's Mill, Va. Commissioned first lieutenant, July 4, 1861, with rank from April 30, 1861, original. Captain, December 2, 1861, with rank from November 11, 1861, after Meginnis was promoted. Brother of Samuel Barry.

BARRY, SAMUEL—Age 22 years. Enlisted April 30, 1861, at Middletown. Mustered in as corporal, Co. D, May 17, 1861, to serve two years. Promoted sergeant, December 1, 1861. Mustered out with company, May 28, 1863, at Albany, N.Y. Brother of George Barry.

BARTHOLF, JOHN HENRY—Age 32 years. Enrolled October 21, 1862, at Alexandria, Va. Mustered in as assistant surgeon, November 5, 1862, to serve two years. Arrived to regiment, November 26, 1862, at Stafford Court House, Va. Mustered out with regiment, May

28, 1863, at Albany, N.Y. Commissioned assistant surgeon, October 27, 1862, with rank from October 21, 1862, after Edmeston resigned. Subsequent service in United States Volunteers as Assistant Surgeon on January 12, 1865. Brevet captain on October 6, 1865, for faithfully and meritorious service. Honorably mustered out October 9, 1865.

BARTLETT, DAVID LEONARD—Age 50 years. Enrolled May 12, 1861, at Ogdensburg. Mustered in as captain, Co. K, May 17, 1861, to serve two years. Resigned, August 4, 1861. Commissioned captain, July 4, 1861, with rank from April 30, 1861, original.

BEARUP, ANDREW "Andy" C.—Age 22 years. Enlisted May 2, 1861, at Schenectady. Mustered in as sergeant, Co. E, May 17, 1861, to serve two years. Reduced to private, October 1, 1861. Promoted to ordnance sergeant, October 6, 1861. Transferred to Co. C, July 2, 1862. Mustered in as second lieutenant, December 9, 1862. Mustered out with company, May 28, 1863, at Albany, N.Y. Commissioned second lieutenant, November 10, 1862, with rank from July 22, 1862, after Holden was dismissed.

BECKING, JULIUS CONRAD—Age 21 years. Enlisted, April 27, 1861, at Middletown. Mustered in as bugler, Co. D, May 17, 1861, to serve two years. Wounded in left toe and left thigh, June 30, 1862, at Charles City Crossroads, Va. Hospitalized, July 2, 1862, to Fort Monroe, Va. Sent north, July 3, 1862, onboard Steamer *State of Maine*. Hospitalized, July 7, 1862, at Bellevue Hospital, in New York City, N.Y. Reduced to private, date not stated. Discharged from Bellevue Hospital, August 12, 1862, and transferred to Fort Hamilton, N.Y. On brief furlough, August 1862, at Middletown, N.Y. Returned to regiment, August 28, 1862. Mustered out with company, May 28, 1863, at Albany, N.Y.

BELL, GLEASON C.—Age 20 years. Enlisted April 22, 1861, at Schenectady. Mustered in as private, Co. A, May 17, 1861, to serve two years. Deserted, September 25, 1861, from Camp King, Alexandria, Va. Died of disease, December 8, 1862, in regimental hospital, in White Oak Church, Falmouth, Va.

BELL, ISAAC NEWTON—Age 16 years, but gave age as 18 years. Enlisted April 23, 1861, at Fishkill. Mustered in as private, Co. C, May 17, 1861, to serve two years. Promoted sergeant, September 14, 1862. Mustered out with company, May 28, 1863, at Albany, N.Y.

BENDINE (Bendean), FREDERICK (John Smith)—Age 33 years. Enlisted April 25, 1861, at Schenectady. Mustered in as private, Co. A, May 17, 1861, to serve two years. Deserted, November 24, 1861, from Camp King, Alexandria, Va. Arrested, July 22, 1863, at Glenville. Confined at Fort Columbus, in New York Harbor, N.Y. Forwarded, August 14, 1863, to Washington, D.C. Transferred to Co. D & B, 49th New York Infantry, for remainder of term of service.

BENJAMIN, EUGENE—Age 19 years. Enlisted April 19, 1861, at Albany. Mustered in as private, Co. F, May 17, 1861, to serve two years. No further record.

BENJAMIN, JAMES LEWIS—Age 22 years. Enlisted April 30, 1861, at Middletown. Mustered in as private, Co. D, May 17, 1861, to serve two years. Mustered out with company, May 28, 1863, at Albany, N.Y. Subsequent service in Co. L, 15th New York Cavalry.

BENNETT, FENNIMORE GARRETT—Age 20 years. Enlisted, April 19, 1861, at Albany. Mustered in as private, Co. F, May 17, 1861, to serve two years. Wounded, September 14, 1862, at Crampton's Gap, Md. Hospitalized, at Burkittsville, Md., and remained in hospital as a nurse. Returned to regiment, March 31, 1863. Mustered out with company, May 28, 1863, at Albany, N.Y.

BENNETT, WILLIAM—Age 29 years. Enlisted December 26, 1861, at Albany. Mustered in as private, Co. B, same date, to serve unexpired term of two years. Mustered out with company, May 28, 1863, at Albany, N.Y. Subsequent service in Co. K & B, 7th New York Heavy Artillery.

BERMINGHAM, CHARLES—Age 19 years. Enlisted May 12, 1861, at Ogdensburg. Mustered in as musician, Co. K, May 17, 1861, to serve two years. Captured, June 27, 1862, at Gaines's Mill, Va. Confined at Richmond, Va. Paroled, August 5, 1862, at City Point, Va. Never returned to regiment. No further record.

BIBBINS, NATHANIEL EDWARD—Age 17 years, but gave age as 18 years. Enlisted May 17, 1861, at Albany. Mustered in as private, Co. H, same date, to serve two years. Captured, June 27, 1862, at Gaines's Mill, Va. Confined at Richmond, Va. Paroled, August 5, 1862, at City Point, Va. Hospitalized, August 8, 1862, at Satterlee General Hospital, in West Philadelphia, Pa. Discharged for disability, February 16, 1863, at Convalescent Camp, Alexandria, Va. Subsequent service in Co. "U" 13th New York Heavy Artillery.

BILLINGS (Pillings), CHARLES H.—Age—years. Enlisted May 2, 1861, at Schenectady. Mustered in as musician, Co. E, May 17, 1861, to serve two years. Deserted on or about May 20, 1861, at Albany, N.Y.

BINCK (Bink), WILHELMUS L.—Age 18 years. Enlisted April 25, 1861, at Schenectady. Mustered in as private, Co. A, May 17, 1861, to serve two years. Absent-without-leave, January 20, 1863, from Camp Russell, White Oak Church, Falmouth, Va. Returned to regiment, January 24, 1863, same place. Court-martialed for absence and disobedience, February 24, 1863, at same place. Mustered out with company, May 28, 1863, at Albany, N.Y. Subsequent service in Co. B, 2nd New York Veteran Cavalry.

BINK, PHILIP—Age 20 years. Enlisted, April 25, 1861, at Schenectady. Mustered in as private, Co. A, May 17, 1861, to serve two years. Mustered out with company, May 28, 1863, at Albany, N.Y.

BIRD, PETER—Age 30 years. Enlisted November 20, 1861, at Albany. Mustered in as private, Co. F, same date to serve unexpired term of two years. Wounded in left heel, September 14, 1862, at Crampton's Gap, Md. Transferred from Camp A hospital and hospitalized, October 24, 1862, at Camp B General Hospital in Frederick, Md. Returned to regiment, February 26, 1863. Discharged on account of wound, April 10, 1863, at hospital in Baltimore, Md.

BIRDSELL, PETER—Age 21 years. Enlisted May 2,

1861, at Schenectady. Mustered in as private, Co. E, May 17, 1861, to serve two years. Discharged for disability, July 12, 1861, at Washington, D.C.

BIRMINGHAM, JOHN W.—Age about 49 years, but gave age as 43 years. Enrolled, April 25, 1861, at Fishkill. Mustered in as first lieutenant, Co. C, May 17, 1861, to serve two years. Resigned, June 16, 1861, at Albany, N.Y. Commissioned first lieutenant, with rank from April 25, 1861, original.

BLACKWELL, JOHN—Age 22 years. Enlisted April 23, 1861, at Fishkill. Mustered in as private, Co. C, May 17, 1861, to serve two years. Wounded in left hand, June 27, 1862, at Gaines's Mill, Va. Hospitalized, August 31, 1862, at Steuart's Mansion Hospital in Baltimore, Md. Transferred to West's Buildings General Hospital, September 19, 1862, in Baltimore, Md. Returned to duty, December 20, 1862. Mustered out with company, May 28, 1863, at Albany, N.Y. Subsequent service in Co. I, 4th New York Heavy Artillery, Co. M, K, 11th Kentucky Cavalry & Co. K, 12th Kentucky Cavalry, under alias Leonard Raymond.

BLAIR, JASPER WITT—Age 19 years. Enlisted May 7, 1861, at Canandaigua. Mustered in as private, Co. G, May 17, 1861, to serve two years. Mustered out with company, May 28, 1863, at Albany, N.Y.

BLAISDELL, ABRAHAM (Abram)—Age 24 years. Enlisted October 17, 1861, at Ogdensburg. Mustered in as private, Co. K, same date, to serve unexpired term of two years. Killed, September 14, 1862, at Crampton's Gap, Md.

BLAKE, GEORGE—Age 21 years. Enlisted May 7, 1861, at Albany. Mustered in as sergeant, Co. H, May 17, 1861, to serve two years. Promoted first sergeant, November 6, 1861. Wounded in right shoulder, June 27, 1862, at Gaines's Mill, Va. Hospitalized, July 1862, in General Hospital in York, Pa. Returned to regiment, date not stated. Mustered out with company, May 28, 1863, at Albany, N.Y.

BLONDON, WILLIAM H.—Age 19 years. Enlisted May 17, 1861, at Albany. Mustered in as private, Co. I, same date, to serve two years. Deserted June 3, 1861, at Albany, N.Y.

BODINE, CHARLES H.—Age 25 years. Enlisted September 23, 1861, at Middletown. Mustered in as private, Co. D, same date, to serve unexpired term of two years. Detailed, March and April 1862, as ambulance driver. Detailed, May 1862, as teamster. Detailed, June 30, 1862, as regimental teamster. Mustered out with company as regimental teamster, May 28, 1863, at Albany, N.Y. Subsequent service in Co. K, 15th New York Cavalry & Co. K, 2nd New York Provisional Cavalry.

BOGARDUS, JOSEPH E.—Age 24 years. Enlisted May 2, 1861, at Schenectady. Mustered in as private, Co. E, May 17, 1861, to serve two years. Mustered out with company, May 28, 1863, at Albany, N.Y.

BONNER, JAMES—Age 19 years. Enlisted April 19, 1861, at Albany. Mustered in as private, Co. F, May 17, 1861, to serve two years. Mustered out with company, May 28, 1863, at Albany, N.Y.

BOOTH, WASHINGTON IRVING—Age 16 years, but gave age as 19 years. Enlisted May 7, 1861, at Albany. Mustered in as private, Co. G, May 17, 1861, to serve two years. Discharged for disability, January 3, 1863, at hospital, Portsmouth Grove, R.I. Subsequent service in Co. H, 4th New York Heavy Artillery.

BOUTWELL, HIRAM—Age 29 years. Enlisted April 19, 1861, at Albany. Mustered in as private, Co. I, May 17, 1861, to serve two years. Mustered out with company, May 28, 1863, at Albany, N.Y. Subsequent service in Co. A, 169th New York Infantry.

BOVEE, JOHN NICHOLAS—Age 18 years. Enlisted May 2, 1861, at Schenectady. Mustered in as private, Co. E, May 17, 1861, to serve two years. Wounded in right leg, June 27, 1862, at Gaines's Mill, Va. Right leg amputated, June 29, 1862. Captured, June 29, 1862, at Savage's Station, Va. Paroled, July 27, 1862, at City Point, Va. Discharged on account of such wound, September 15, 1862, hospital in Philadelphia, Pa.

BOWER, HARVEY L.—Age 52 years, but gave age as 42 years. Enlisted April 23, 1861, at Albany. Mustered in as private, Co. C, May 17, 1861, to serve two years. Discharged for disability, November 20, 1861, at Camp King, Alexandria, Va. Subsequent service in Co. K, 56th New York Infantry.

BOYLE, FRANCIS (Frank)—Age 21 years. Enlisted April 19, 1861, at Albany. Mustered in as private, Co. F, May 17, 1861, to serve two years. Deserted, September 7, 1862, at Alexandria, Va. Arrested on June 13, 1864, at Rochester, N.Y. Assigned to 5th New York Veteran Infantry by Special Order 225.

BRADSHAW, ROBERT—Age 27 years. Enlisted September 24, 1862, at Rotterdam. Mustered in as private, Co. E, same date, to serve three years. Transferred, May 10, 1863, to Co. E, 121st New York Infantry.

BRANDOW, CHARLES H.—Age 21 years. Enlisted May 7, 1861, at Albany. Mustered in as private, Co. G, May 17, 1861, to serve two years. Hospitalized, on or about September 10, 1861, at regimental hospital at Camp King, Alexandria, Va. Transferred, September 25, 1861, to general hospital, in Alexandria, Va. Discharged for disability, December 21, 1861, at Camp King, Alexandria, Va. Brother-in-law of Jesse Parshall.

BRANDT, HENRY W.—Age 34 years. Enlisted May 7, 1861, at Albany. Mustered in as private, Co. H, May 17, 1861, to serve two years. Discharged for disability, September 23, 1861, at Alexandria, Va.

BREWSTER, JOHN EVERETT—Age 19 years. Enlisted April 30, 1861, at Middletown. Mustered in as private, Co. H, May 17, 1861, to serve two years. Mustered out with company, May 28, 1863, at Albany, N.Y.

BRIGGS, SANFORD H.—Age 22 years. Enlisted April 24, 1861, at Albany. Mustered in as private, Co. B, May 17, 1861, to serve two years. Mustered out with company, May 28, 1863, at Albany, N.Y.

BROADWELL, THEODORE—Age 17 years, but gave age as 21 years. Enlisted May 12, 1861, at Ogdensburg. Mustered in as private, Co. K, May 17, 1861, to serve two years. Wounded slightly in hand, June 27, 1862, at Gaines's Mill, Va. Sent off, July 2, 1862, from Harrison's Landing, Va. Hospitalized, July 4, 1862, at

Washington, D.C. Mustered out with company, May 28, 1863, at Albany, N.Y. Subsequent service in Co. L, 83rd New York Infantry & Co. H, 97th New York Infantry.

BROOKS, GILBERT CASPER—Age 21 years. Enlisted April 29, 1861, at Albany. Mustered in as private, Co. I, May 17, 1861, to serve two years. Discharged for disability, September 24, 1861, at Alexandria, Va. Subsequent service in Co. M, 6th New York Cavalry & Co. M, 2nd New York Provisional Cavalry.

BROTHERS, JAMES H.—Age 22 years. Enlisted April 22, 1861, at Schenectady. Mustered in as private, Co. A, May 17, 1861, to serve two years. Mustered out with company, May 28, 1863, at Albany, N.Y.

BROWN, DANIEL A.—Age 30 years. Enlisted April 30, 1861, at Middletown. Mustered in as private, Co. D, May 17, 1861, to serve two years. Detailed as teamster, November 25, 1861, and remained in that capacity until expiration of term. Mustered out with company, May 28, 1863, at Albany, N.Y. Subsequent service in Co. K, 15th New York Cavalry & Co. K, 2nd New York Provisional Cavalry.

BROWN, DAVID—Age 22 years. Enlisted October 8, 1861, at Ogdensburg. Mustered in as private, Co. K, same date, to serve two years. Hospitalized, November or December 1862, in Sixth Corps hospital at Hagerstown, Md. Deserted March 5, 1863, at Smoketown, Md.

BROWN, GEORGE—Age 18 years. Enlisted May 1, 1861, at Albany. Mustered in as private, Co. B, May 17, 1861, to serve two years. Mustered out with company, May 28, 1863, at Albany, N.Y. Subsequent service in Co. G, 18th New York Cavalry.

BROWN, JAMES—Age 22 years. Enlisted April 30, 1861, at Middletown. Mustered in as private, Co. D, May 17, 1861, to serve two years. Accidentally wounded by self, May 7, 1862, at Brick House Landing (West Point), Va. Sent to New York Hospital. Returned to regiment, July 15, 1862. Promoted acting sergeant-major, August 10, 1862, after Stall's hospitalization. Mustered out with company, May 28, 1863, at Albany, N.Y. Subsequent service in Co. D, 9th New York Veteran Infantry & Co. H, 17th New York Veteran Infantry.

BROWN, JOHN—Age 19 years. Enlisted April 30, 1861, at Middletown. Mustered in as private, Co. H, May 17, 1861, to serve two years. Mustered out with company, May 28, 1863, at Albany, N.Y. Subsequent service in Co. A, 25th New York Cavalry.

BROWN, STEPHEN M.—Age 32 years. Enlisted April 30, 1861, at Middletown. Mustered in as private, Co. D, May 17, 1861, to serve two years. Sent sick, August 7, 1862, onboard Steamer *State of Maine* at Harrison's Landing, Va. Hospitalized, August 1862, at Satterlee General Hospital, in West Philadelphia, Pa. Discharged for disability, September 12, 1862, at Philadelphia, Pa. Subsequent service in Co. G, 176th New York Infantry & Co. H, 159th New York Infantry.

BROWNING, JOHN WILLIS—Age 18 years. Enlisted May 7, 1861, at Albany. Mustered in as private, Co. G, May 17, 1861, to serve two years. Wounded in right foot and captured, July 17, 1861, near Fairfax Court House, Va. Confined, July 23, 1861, at Richmond, Va. Paroled, January 17, 1862, at James River, near Richmond, Va. Discharged on account of wound and as a paroled prisoner of war, February 1, 1862, at Washington, D.C. Subsequent service in Co. I, 3rd New York Infantry.

BRUNDAGE, ALBERT LEWIS—Age 23 years. Enlisted September 18, 1862, at Albany. Mustered in as private, Co. D, same date, to serve three years. Transferred, May 10, 1863, to 121st New York Infantry. Brother of John L. Brundage.

BRUNDAGE, ALTON—Age 55 years, but gave age as 42 years. Enlisted April 23, 1861, at Fishkill. Mustered in as sergeant, Co. C, May 17, 1861, to serve two years. Reduced to private, date not stated. Discharged for disability, September 24, 1861, at Camp King, Alexandria, Va. Subsequent service in Co. B, 168th New York Infantry & Co. F, 5th New York Heavy Artillery.

BRUNDAGE, JOHN L.—Age 16 years, but gave age as 18 years. Enlisted September 5, 1861, at Middletown. Mustered in as private, Co. D, October 21, 1861, to serve two years. Discharged as a minor, October 21, 1861, at Camp King, Alexandria, Va. Again enlisted, September 18, 1862, at Albany, for three years, and mustered in Co. D, September 18, 1862. Deserted, January 27, 1863, at White Oak Church, Falmouth, Va. Subsequent service in Co. G, 15th Ohio Infantry. Brother of Albert L. Brundage.

BRUTON, CHRISTOPHER C.—Age 20 years. Enlisted May 7, 1861, at Canandaigua. Mustered in as private, Co. G, May 17, 1861, to serve two years. Promoted corporal, July 1861. Hospitalized for sickness, July 2, 1862, at Fort Monroe, Va. Transferred aboard Steamer *Daniel Webster* and hospitalized, July 7, 1862, at Philadelphia, Pa. Discharged for disability, August 23, 1862, at Philadelphia, Pa. Subsequent service in Co. C, 22nd New York Cavalry.

BRYAN (Bryant), NATHAN—Age 16 years, but gave age as 19 years. Enlisted April 30, 1861, at Middletown. Mustered in as private, Co. D, May 17, 1861, to serve two years. Mustered out with company, May 28, 1863, at Albany, N.Y. Subsequent service in Co. L, 15th New York Cavalry.

BRYANT, CHARLES L.—Age 22 years. Enlisted May 7, 1861, at Albany. Mustered in as private, Co. G, May 17, 1861, to serve two years. Mustered out with company, May 28, 1863, at Albany, N.Y.

BRYNE, JAMES—Age 18 years. Enlisted May 17, 1861, at Albany. Mustered in as private, Co. E, same date, to serve two years. Discharged for disability, September 12, 1861.

BUCKLEY, EDWARD—Age 24 years. Enlisted December 17, 1861, at Albany. Mustered in as private, Co. C, December 30, 1861, to serve unexpired term of two years. Hospitalized, May or June 1862, at Fort Monroe, Va. Transferred, July 9, 1862, to David's Island General Hospital, in New York Harbor, N.Y. Retained as a nurse, September 2, 1862. Discharged to rejoin regiment, May 26, 1863. Mustered out with company, May 28, 1863, at Albany, N.Y.

BUCKLEY, THOMAS H.—Age 36 years. Enlisted May 12, 1861, at Ogdensburg. Mustered in as private,

Co. K, May 17, 1861, to serve two years. Discharged, July 2, 1861, at Washington, D. C, by Special Order No. 166.

BULCHEY (Bulshp), JOHN—Age 25 years. Enlisted May 20, 1861, at Albany. Mustered in as private, Co. G, same date, to serve two years. Discharged for disability, December 21, 1861, at Camp King, Alexandria, Va. Subsequent service in Co. F, 46th New York Infantry.

BULLENT, ANTHONY COLE—Age 25 years. Enlisted December 7, 1861, at Albany. Mustered in as private, Co. F, same date, to serve unexpired term of two years. Wounded in left thigh, September 14, 1862, at Crampton's Gap, Md. Left thigh amputated, September 15, 1862. Hospitalized, November 4, 1862, at General Hospital Number 5, in Frederick, Md. Discharged on account of wounds, November 21, 1862, at Frederick, Md.

BULSON, GEORGE—Age 21 years. Enlisted May 18, 1861, at Albany. Mustered in as private, Co. A, same date, to serve two years. Deserted, July 2, 1862, at Harrison's Landing, Va.

BUNNELL, FRANCIS H.—Age 19 years. Enlisted May 17, 1861, at Albany. Mustered in as private, Co. G, same date, to serve two years. Discharged for disability, September 24, 1861, at Alexandria, Va. Subsequent service in Co. H, 16th New York Heavy Artillery.

BUNTON, EDWARD—Age 20 years. Enlisted April 22, 1861, at Schenectady. Mustered in as private, Co. A, May 17, 1861, to serve two years. Promoted corporal, November 1, 1861. Mustered out with company, May 28, 1863, at Albany, N.Y. Subsequent service in Co. F, 2nd New York Heavy Artillery.

BURKE, PATRICK—Age 15 years. Enlisted November 24, 1861, at Albany. Mustered in as drummer, Co. E, December 7, 1861, at Albany, to serve unexpired term of two years. Mustered out with company, May 28, 1863, at Albany, N.Y.

BURKE, THOMAS A.—Age 26 years. Enlisted May 17, 1861, at Albany. Mustered in as private, Co. C, same date, to serve two years. Mustered out with company, May 28, 1863, at Albany, N.Y.

BURN, CHRISTOPHER GRIMWOOD—Age 21 years. Enlisted June 4, 1861, at Albany. Mustered in as private, Co. F, same date, to serve two years. Mustered out with company, May 28, 1863, at Albany, N.Y. Discharged, June 4, 1863. Died of disease, November 29, 1863, in Albany, N.Y. Brother of Richard A. Burn.

BURN, JOHN—Age 18 years. Enlisted May 17, 1861, at Albany. Mustered in as private, Co. B, same date, to serve two years. No further record since the regiment left Albany, N.Y., June 18, 1861. Also born as John Burner.

BURN, RICHARD A.—Age 26 years. Enlisted April 19, 1861, at Albany. Mustered in as sergeant, Co. F, May 17, 1861, to serve two years. Reduced to private, May or June of 1861. Promoted corporal, July 1, 1862. Promoted sergeant, December 8, 1862. Mustered out with company, May 28, 1863, at Albany, N.Y. Subsequent service in Co. C, 93rd New York Infantry. Brother of Christopher G. Burn.

BURNETT, WALTER H.—Age 22 years. Enlisted May 7, 1861, at Canandaigua. Mustered in as musician, Co. G, May 17, 1861, to serve two years. Reduced to private, June 1861. Promoted corporal, November 30, 1861. Wounded in right arm, June 27, 1862, at Gaines's Mill, Va. Detailed as teamster with ammunition train after wounding. Mustered out with company, May 28, 1863, at Albany, N.Y.

BURNS, JOHN—Age 32 years. Enlisted February 4, 1862, at Wallkill. Mustered in as private, Co. G, same date, to serve unexpired term of two years. Accidently wounded in shoulder by comrade during battle, September 14, 1862, at Crampton's Gap, Md. Hospitalized, October 1862, at Camp A General Hospital at Frederick, Md. Hospitalized, date not stated, in Hagerstown, Md. Mustered out with company, May 28, 1863, at Albany, N.Y. Subsequent service in Co. D, 15th New York Cavalry & Co. D, 2nd New York Provisional Cavalry.

BURT, WILLIAM G.—Age 23 years. Enlisted April 23, 1861, at Fishkill. Mustered in as private, Co. C, May 17, 1861, to serve two years. Promoted sergeant, May 17, 1861. Court-martialed for neglect of duty and conduct prejudicial to military discipline, January 25, 1862, at Alexandria, Va. Reduced to private, February 1862. Promoted sergeant, January 1, 1863. Mustered out with company, May 28, 1863, at Albany, N.Y.

BURTON, MYRON—Age 19 years. Enlisted May 7, 1861, at Canandaigua. Mustered in as private, Co. G, May 17, 1861, to serve two years. Killed, June 27, 1862, at Gaines's Mill, Va.

CAIN, THOMAS H.—Age 21 years. Enlisted May 6, 1861, at Albany. Mustered in as private, Co. I, May 17, 1861, to serve two years. Discharged for disability, September 24, 1861, at Alexandria, Va. Subsequent service in Co. B, 25th New York Militia National Guard & the United States Navy aboard *Commodore Read* & *North Carolina*.

CALDER, ROBERT C.—Age 20 years. Enlisted April 24, 1861, at Albany. Mustered in as private, Co. B, May 17, 1861, to serve two years. Promoted corporal, July 1, 1861. Promoted sergeant, September 20, 1861. Wounded in left arm, June 27, 1862, at Gaines's Mill, Va. Hospitalized in York, Pa. Transferred, date not stated, to hospital in Hagerstown, Md. Transferred, January 17, 1863, to regimental hospital. Returned to regiment, April 2, 1863. Mustered out with company, May 28, 1863, at Albany, N.Y. Subsequent service in Co. G, 18th New York Cavalry.

CALHOUN, BENJAMIN—Age 40 years. Enlisted April 23, 1861, at Albany. Mustered in as private, Co. I, May 17, 1861, to serve two years. Absent-without-leave, November 28, 1861, from Camp King, Alexandria, Va. Returned to regiment, November 29, 1861. Court-martialed for absence, December 3, 1861, at Alexandria, Va. Mustered out with company, May 28, 1863, at Albany, N.Y. Subsequent service in Co. E, 97th New York Infantry.

CALLAGHAN, PETER—Age 23 years. Enlisted October 23, 1861, at Ogdensburg. Mustered in as private, Co. K, same date, to serve unexpired term of two years. Mustered out with company, May 28, 1863, at Albany, N.Y. Subsequent service in Co. C, 24th New York Cavalry.

CALLAN, JOHN—Age 36 years. Enlisted May 7, 1861, at Albany. Mustered in as private, Co. H, May 17, 1861, to serve two years. Promoted sergeant, date not stated. Died of disease, May 26, 1862, in hospital at Annapolis, Md.

CAMBRIDGE, WILLIAM A.—Age 35 years. Enlisted May 12, 1861, at Ogdensburg. Mustered in as private, Co. K, May 17, 1861, to serve two years. Discharged for disability, August 29, 1861, at Washington, D.C.

CAMPBELL, JOHN—Age 43 years. Enlisted May 1, 1861, at Albany. Mustered in as private, Co. B, May 17, 1861, to serve two years. Discharged for disability, July 6, 1861, at Washington, D.C. Subsequent service in Co. I, 97th New York Infantry.

CARBINO (Carbineau), HENRY—Age 14 years, but gave age as 19 years. Enlisted May 12, 1861, at Ogdensburg. Mustered in as private, Co. K, May 17, 1861, to serve two years. Hospitalized for tonsillitis, May 31, 1861, at Albany, N.Y. Returned to duty, June 2, 1861, at Albany, N.Y. Hospitalized for typhoid fever, July 24, 1861, at Alexandria, Va. Returned to duty, September 4, 1861, at Alexandria, Va. Discharged for disability, September 20, 1861, at Alexandria, Va. Subsequent service in Co. C, 92nd New York Infantry & Co. I, 14th New York Heavy Artillery.

CAREY, EDWARD—Age 21 years. Enlisted April 22, 1861, at Schenectady. Mustered in as private, Co. A, May 17, 1861, to serve two years. Mustered out with company, May 28, 1863, at Albany, N.Y.

CAREY, JOHN F.—Age 22 years. Enlisted May 17, 1861, at Albany. Mustered in as private, Co. I, same date, to serve two years. Promoted sergeant, January 1, 1863. Mustered out with company, May 28, 1863, at Albany, N.Y.

CAREY, MICHAEL—Age 27 years. Enlisted April 19, 1861, at Albany. Mustered in as private, Co. I, May 17, 1861, to serve two years. Wounded in left arm, June 27, 1862, at Gaines's Mill, Va. Hospitalized, July 1, 1862, at Fort Monroe, Va. Sent to General Hospital in Annapolis, Md. on July 4, 1862. Promoted corporal, March or April 1863. Mustered out with company, May 28, 1863, at Albany, N.Y.

CARMICHAEL, DECATOR—Age 16 years, but gave age as 18 years. Enlisted September 18, 1862, at Albany. Mustered in as private, Co. D, same date, to serve three years. Transferred, May 10, 1863, to Co. C, 121st New York Infantry.

CARMICHAEL, WILLIAM ELLICOTT—Age 23 years. Enrolled April 30, 1861, at Middletown. Mustered in as second lieutenant, Co. H, May 17, 1861, to serve two years. Promoted first lieutenant, November 6, 1861. Resigned, July 16, 1862, Special Order No. 47. Commissioned second lieutenant, July 4, 1861, with rank from May 7, 1861, original. First lieutenant, December 2, 1861, with rank from November 6, 1861, after Rogers was promoted.

CARR, JOSEPH—Age 21 years. Enlisted May 17, 1861, at Albany. Mustered in as private, Co. A, same date, to serve two years. Promoted corporal, December 1, 1861. Sent sick, July 2, 1862, to Fort Monroe, Va. Mustered out with company, May 28, 1863, at Albany, N.Y. Subsequent service in Co. "U" 13th New York Heavy Artillery & Co. B, 2nd New York Veteran Cavalry.

CARROLL, HENRY—Age 18 years. Enlisted April 24, 1861, at Albany. Mustered in as private, Co. B, May 17, 1861, to serve two years. Wounded, September 14, 1862, at Crampton's Gap, Md. Died of such wounds, September 27, 1862, at Burkittsville, Md.

CARROLL, JOHN—Age 36 years. Enlisted December 13, 1861, at Albany. Mustered in as private, Co. F, same date, to serve unexpired term of two years. Deserted, August 26, 1862, from hospital at Alexandria, Va.

CARROLL, JOHN—Age 46 years, but gave age as 41 years. Enlisted April 19, 1861, at Albany. Mustered in as private, Co. I, May 17, 1861, to serve two years. Wounded in left elbow, June 27, 1862, at Gaines's Mill, Va. Hospitalized, July 2, 1862, to Fort Monroe, Va. Transferred aboard Steamer *Daniel Webster* and hospitalized, July 7, 1862, at 16th & Filbert Streets General Hospital in Philadelphia, Pa. Sent to 65th & Vine Streets General Hospital in Philadelphia, Pa, on November 29, 1862. Discharged on account of such wound, February 4, 1863, at 65th & Vine Streets General Hospital in Philadelphia, Pa. Subsequent service in Co. "U" Veteran Reserve Corps, Co. D, 7th Veteran Reserve Corps & 129th Co. 2nd Battalion, Veteran Reserve Corps.

CARROLL, THOMAS—Age 21 years. Enlisted April 19, 1861, at Albany. Mustered in as private, Co. I, May 17, 1861, to serve two years. Wounded slightly in left shoulder, June 27, 1862, at Gaines's Mill, Va. Mustered out with company, May 28, 1863, at Albany, N.Y.

CARTER, THOMAS A.—Age 22 years. Enlisted April 19, 1861, at Albany. Mustered in as private, Co. F, May 17, 1861, to serve two years. Promoted musician, September or October 1861. Detailed, October 1862, as guard at convalescent camp, near Alexandria, Va. Hospitalized, November 1862, at Columbian College Hospital, in Washington, D.C. Discharged for disability, February 26, 1863, at Washington, D.C.

CASEY, DANIEL—Age 22 years. Enlisted April 29, 1861, at Albany. Mustered in as private, Co. I, May 17, 1861, to serve two years. Mustered out with company, May 28, 1863, at Albany, N.Y. Subsequent service In Co. A, 192nd New York Infantry.

CASSIDY, MATTHEW—Age 29 years. Enlisted April 28, 1861, at Schenectady. Mustered in as private, Co. A, May 17, 1861, to serve two years. Deserted, April 17, 1862, near Alexandria, Va.

CAVANAUGH, STEPHEN—Age 16 or 17 years, but gave age as 19 years. Enlisted May 12, 1861, at Ogdensburg. Mustered in as private, Co. K, May 17, 1861, to serve two years. Mustered out with company, May 28, 1863, at Albany, N.Y.

CHADDERDON, ELIJAH L.—Age 23 years. Enlisted May 7, 1861, at Albany. Mustered in as corporal, Co. H, May 17, 1861, to serve two years. Promoted sergeant, August 15, 1861. Hospitalized, September 9, 1862, while on the march near Washington, D.C. Hospitalized, September–November 1862, at Harewood General Hospital, in Washington, D.C. Returned to regiment, date not stated. Mustered out with company, May 28, 1863, at Albany, N.Y.

CHALMERS, JAMES "Jim"—Age 22 years. Enlisted April 19, 1861, at Albany. Mustered in as sergeant, Co. I, May 17, 1861, to serve two years. Promoted first sergeant, July 8, 1861, after Morgan deserted, with rank from June 30, 1861. Mustered in as second lieutenant, November 6, 1861. Wounded slightly in leg, June 27, 1862, at Gaines's Mill, Va. Mustered out with company, May 28, 1863, at Albany, N.Y. Commissioned second lieutenant, December 2, 1861, with rank from November 6, 1861, original. First lieutenant, May 31, 1863, with rank from January 15, 1863, after Chapman resigned. Not mustered.

CHAMBERLAIN, SMITH—Age 17 years. Enlisted April 23, 1861, at Albany. Mustered in as fifer, Co. I, May 17, 1861, to serve two years. Straggled from regiment, date not stated. In camp for stragglers, August 1862, in Alexandria, Va. Joined regiment, March 12, 1863. Mustered out with company, May 28, 1863, at Albany, N.Y. Subsequent service in 7th New York Heavy Artillery.

CHAPMAN, AARON—Age 22 years. Enlisted May 7, 1861, at Albany. Mustered in as private, Co. G, May 17, 1861, to serve two years. Hospitalized, date not stated, at Sixth Corps hospital at Hagerstown, Md. Died of disease, November 22, 1862, in Sixth Corps hospital at Hagerstown, Md.

CHAPMAN, GEORGE—Age 22 years. Enrolled May 10, 1861, at Albany. Mustered in as first lieutenant, Co. I, May 17, 1861, to serve two years. Absent-without-leave, December 27, 1861, from Camp King, Alexandria, Va. Returned to regiment, same date. Court-martialed for absence, January 20, 1862, at Alexandria, Va. Hospitalized sick, November 13, 1862, at Grace Church Hospital, 2nd Division General Hospital, in Alexandria, Va. Furlough to New York, November 24, 1862, from Stafford Court House, Va. Returned to regiment, January 3, 1863. Resigned, January 15, 1863. Commissioned first lieutenant, July 4, 1861, with rank from May 10, 1861, original.

CHAPMAN, WILLIAM H.—Age 20 years. Enlisted April 30, 1861, at Middletown. Mustered in as private, Co. H, May 17, 1861, to serve two years. Hospitalized in June 1862. Returned to regiment, August 21, 1862. Mustered out with company, May 28, 1863, at Albany, N.Y. Subsequent service in Co. A, 13th New York Heavy Artillery.

CHASE, JOHN FREEMAN—Age 30 years. Enlisted May 2, 1861, in Co. E, at Schenectady. Mustered in as private, Co. B, May 17, 1861, to serve two years. Discharged for disability, July 12, 1861, at Washington, D.C.

CHERRY, WILLIAM R.—Age 29 years. Enlisted April 23, 1861, at Albany. Mustered in as private, Co. C, May 17, 1861, to serve two years. Mustered out with company, May 28, 1863, at Albany, N.Y. Subsequent service in Co. H, 128th New York Infantry.

CHESMORE, ALFRED MILTON—Age 22 years. Enlisted April 19, 1861, at Albany. Mustered in as sergeant, Co. I, May 17, 1861, to serve two years. Promoted first sergeant, November 5, 1861. Wounded slightly in left elbow, June 27, 1862, at Gaines's Mill, Va. Mustered in as first lieutenant, Co. G, August 8, 1862. Wounded slightly in thumb, September 14, 1862, at Crampton's Gap, Md. Mustered out with company, May 28, 1863, at Albany, N.Y. Commissioned first lieutenant, January 1, 1863, with rank from August 8, 1862, after Green, resigned. Subsequent service in Co. C, 43rd Missouri Infantry. First Cousin of Nathaniel G. Whittemore.

CHRISTIAN, WILLIAM L.—Age 22 years. Enlisted May 17, 1861, at Albany. Mustered in as private, Co. E, same date, to serve two years. Sent off from Harrison's Landing, Va., August 14, 1862, to be hospitalized in General Hospital, in West Philadelphia, Pa. Died of disease, September 7, 1862, in General Hospital, in West Philadelphia, Pa.

CHRISTIANCE, FRANCIS—Age 27 years. Enlisted May 2, 1861, at Schenectady. Mustered in as corporal, Co. E, May 17, 1861, to serve two years. Reduced to private, May 19, 1861, for disobedience. Court-martialed at regimental level, September or October 1861, at Camp King, Alexandria, Va. Mustered out with company, May 28, 1863, at Albany, N.Y.

CLARK, EDWARD—Age 21 years. Enlisted May 11, 1861, at Albany. Mustered in as private, Co. I, May 17, 1861, to serve two years. Promoted corporal, May 1, 1862. Deserted, August 29, 1862, at Alexandria, Va.

CLARK, GEORGE W.—Age 27 years. Enlisted August 26, 1862, at Albany. Mustered in as private, unassigned, same date, to serve three years. No further record.

CLARK, VINCENT (Vinson) H.—Age 34 years. Enlisted April 30, 1861, at Middletown. Mustered in as private, Co. D, May 17, 1861, to serve two years. Wounded, September 14, 1862, at Crampton's Gap, Md. Refused to fight at Fredericksburg, Va. Deserted, April 28, 1863, at White Oak Church, Falmouth, Va. Subsequent service in Co. M, 2nd Connecticut Heavy Artillery.

CLARKE, EPHRAIM C.—Age 36 years. Enlisted May 1, 1861, at Albany. Mustered in as private, Co. B, May 17, 1861, to serve two years. Detached to General Franklin's Headquarters, December 15, 1861. Returned to regiment, April 11, 1863. Mustered out with company, May 28, 1863, at Albany, N.Y.

CLAUSON (Clawson), SANFORD S.—Age 20 years. Enlisted April 30, 1861, at Middletown. Mustered in as private, Co. D, May 17, 1861, to serve two years. Promoted corporal, June 1, 1862. Never participated in any engagement. Refused to fight at Fredericksburg, Va. Reduced to ranks for cowardice. Deserted, April 28, 1863, at White Oak Church, Falmouth, Va.

CLAY, HENRY—Age 20 years. Enlisted April 30, 1861, at Middletown. Mustered in as private, Co. D, May 17, 1861, to serve two years. Mustered out with company, May 28, 1863, at Albany, N.Y.

CLEMONS, OLIVER—Age 33 years. Enlisted May 12, 1861, at Ogdensburg. Mustered in as private, Co. K, May 17, 1861, to serve two years. Mustered out with company, May 28, 1863, at Albany, N.Y. Subsequent service in Co. F, 16th New York Cavalry.

CLOFLIN, EPHRAIM, Jr.—Age 30 years. Enlisted September 1, 1862, at Albany. Mustered in as private, Co. C, same date, to serve three years. Transferred, May 10, 1863, to the 121st New York Infantry, Co. "U" 16th New York Light Artillery & the Veteran Reserve Corps.

COCHRANE, CHARLES W.—Age 21 years. Enlisted May 12, 1861, at Ogdensburg. Mustered in as corporal, Co. K, May 17, 1861, to serve two years. Promoted sergeant, August 12, 1861. Reduced to private, November 13, 1861. Detached on western gunboat service in the United States Navy aboard Gunboat *Pittsburgh*, January 1, 1862. Served in Navy beyond regimental muster-out.

CODDINGTON, ABRAHAM (Abram) D.—Age 22 years. Enlisted April 23, 1861, at Albany. Mustered in as private, Co. C, May 17, 1861, to serve two years. Detailed as regimental hospital nurse, July 31, 1862. Discharged for disability while detailed as regimental hospital nurse, January 5, 1863, at White Oak Church, Falmouth, Va.

COFFEY, THEODORE M.—Age 23 years. Enlisted April 30, 1861, at Middletown. Mustered in as private, Co. D, May 17, 1861, to serve two years. Mustered out with company, May 28, 1863, at Albany, N.Y.

COLBY, MALCOLM EDWARD, Sr.—Age 25 years. Enlisted May 2, 1861, at Schenectady. Mustered in as private, Co. E, May 17, 1861, to serve two years. Hospitalized for insanity, January 27, 1863, at White Oak Church, Falmouth, Va., but escaped the same day. Returned to regiment, February 3, 1863. Sent to St. Elizabeth's Hospital insane asylum, February 13, 1863, at Washington, D.C. Discharged from insane asylum, July 3, 1863. Discharged from military, July 30, 1863. Subsequent service in Co. H, 2nd New York Veteran Cavalry.

COLE, JOHN HENRY—Age 30 years. Transferred as hospital steward to this regiment, from Co. F, 1st New York Lincoln Cavalry by order of Adjutant General of U.S.A, November 1, 1861, at Camp King, Alexandria, Va. Mustered out with regiment, May 28, 1863, at Albany, N.Y.

COLE, SAMUEL B.—Age 19 years. Enlisted April 30, 1861, at Middletown. Mustered in as private, Co. H, May 17, 1861, to serve two years. Wounded in leg, September 14, 1862, at Crampton's Gap, Md. Leg amputated, September 16, 1862, in field hospital, at Burkittsville, Md. Died of such wounds, October 21, 1862, in field hospital, at Burkittsville, Md.

COLEY (Cooley), SAMUEL B.—Age 29 years. Enlisted April 23, 1861, at Albany. Mustered in as private, Co. C, May 17, 1861, to serve two years. Discharged for disability, September 24, 1861, at Camp King, Alexandria, Va.

COLLARD, SAMUEL "Sam"—Age 19 years. Enlisted April 23, 1861, at Albany. Mustered in as private, Co. C, May 17, 1861, to serve two years. Hospitalized, September or October 1862, at Harewood General Hospital, in Washington, D.C. Transferred and hospitalized, November 20, 1862, at Continental Hotel Hospital, in Baltimore, Md. Mustered out with company, May 28, 1863, at Albany, N.Y. Subsequent service in Co. D, 2nd New Hampshire Infantry & Co. F, 20th Veteran Reserve Corps Regiment.

COLLIGAN, THOMAS—Age 19 years. Enlisted April 19, 1861, at Albany. Mustered in as private, Co. F, May 17, 1861, to serve two years. No further record.

COLLINS, MICHAEL—Age 20 years. Enlisted April 22, 1861, at Schenectady. Mustered in as corporal, Co. A, May 17, 1861, to serve two years. Left sick, June 18, 1861, at Albany hospital when regiment left state. Joined regiment, September, October, or November 1861. Discharged for disability, November 23, 1861, at Camp King, Alexandria, Va.

COMBS (Coombs), JOHN—Age 21 years. Enlisted April 24, 1861, at Albany. Mustered in as corporal, Co. B, May 17, 1861, to serve two years. Reduced to private, date not stated. Deserted, May 7, 1862, at Brick House Landing (West Point), Va.

CONANT, GIDEON—Age 28 years. Enlisted May 2, 1861, at Schenectady. Mustered in as private, Co. E, May 17, 1861, to serve two years. Detailed as company cook. Mustered out with company, May 28, 1863, at Albany, N.Y.

CONATY, FRANCIS J.—Age 26 years. Enlisted December 16, 1861, at Albany. Mustered in as private, Co. F, same date, to serve unexpired term of two years. Mustered out with company, May 28, 1863, at Albany, N.Y. Subsequent service in Co. "U" 7th New York Heavy Artillery.

CONKLIN, ROBERT—Age 23 years. Enlisted April 27, 1861, at Middletown. Mustered in as private, Co. D,

Shown here in a family portrait circa 1891, Robert Conklin, Company D, never missed a day with the regiment. He died at the Michigan Soldiers Home in Grand Rapids on August 31, 1913. Conklin is the author's great-great-great-grandfather (author's collection).

May 17, 1861, to serve two years. Mustered out with company, May 28, 1863, at Albany, N.Y.

CONKLING (Conklin), URBAND (Freedland)—Age 18 years. Enlisted April 23, 1861, at Albany. Mustered in as private, Co. C, May 17, 1861, to serve two years. Court-martialed for neglect of duty and conduct prejudicial to military discipline, January 24, 1862, at Alexandria, Va. Hospitalized, date not stated, Broad & Cherry Streets General Hospital, at Philadelphia, Pa. Hospitalized, January or February 1863, at Washington, D.C. Mustered out with company, May 28, 1863, at Albany, N.Y. Subsequent service in Co. F, 18th New York Cavalry.

CONNORS, JAMES—Age 50 years, but gave age as 44 years. Enlisted May 15, 1861, at Albany. Mustered in as private, Co. I, May 17, 1861, to serve two years. Discharged for disability, September 24, 1861, at Alexandria, Va. Subsequent service in 132nd Veteran Reserve Corps.

CONNORS, JOHN—Age 30 years. Enlisted May 9, 1861, at Albany. Mustered in as private, Co. B, May 17, 1861, to serve two years. Drummed out of camp, June 10, 1861, at Albany, N.Y., for stealing clothing.

CONWAY, MICHAEL—Age 18 years. Enlisted October 21, 1861, at Ogdensburg. Mustered in as private, Co. K, same date, to serve unexpired term of two years. Hospitalized, May 11, 1862, at Seminary Hospital, at Hampton, Va. Returned to regiment, date not stated. Mustered out with company, May 28, 1863, at Albany, N.Y.

CONWAY, PATRICK—Age 18 years. Enlisted May 2, 1861, at Schenectady. Mustered in as private, Co. E, May 17, 1861, to serve two years. Absent-without-leave, January 20, 1863, from Camp Russell, White Oak Church, Falmouth, Va. Returned to regiment, January 24, 1863, same place. Court-martialed for absence, February 21, 1863, at same place. Mustered out with company, May 28, 1863, at Albany, N.Y. Subsequent service in Co. D, 16th New York Heavy Artillery, Co. F, 17th United States Infantry & Co. D, 12th United States Infantry.

COOLEY, WILLIAM A.—Age 22 years. Enlisted May 2, 1861, at Schenectady. Mustered in as private, Co. E, May 17, 1861, to serve two years. Court-martialed for disobedience, February 19, 1863, at Camp Russell, White Oak Church, Falmouth, Va. Mustered out with company, May 28, 1863, at Albany, N.Y. Brother-in-law of Justus H. Acker & Munson S. Acker.

COOPER, JAMES—Age 18 years. Enlisted April 19, 1861, at Albany. Mustered in as private, Co. F, May 17, 1861, to serve two years. Mustered out with company, May 28, 1863, at Albany, N.Y. Subsequent service in Co. H, 14th New York Heavy Artillery.

COOPER, LEONARD—Age 21 years. Enlisted April 19, 1861, at Albany. Mustered in as private, Co. F, May 17, 1861, to serve two years. Promoted corporal, date not stated. Mustered out with company, May 28, 1863, at Albany, N.Y. Brother of Wesley Cooper.

COOPER, WESLEY—Age 20 years. Enlisted April 19, 1861, at Albany. Mustered in as private, Co. F, May 17, 1861, to serve two years. Promoted corporal, date not stated. Accidentally wounded in left hand by self, on or about April 8, 1862, while on picket near Manassas, Va. resulted in loss of left index finger. Discharged on account of wound, May 4, 1862, at General Hospital, in Alexandria, Va. Subsequent service in Co. G, 16th New York Heavy Artillery. Brother of Leonard Cooper.

CORBALLY, EDWARD—Age 31 years. Enlisted May 1, 1861, at Albany. Mustered in as private, Co. B, May 17, 1861, to serve two years. Wounded, September 14, 1862, at Crampton's Gap, Md. Promoted corporal, March 1, 1863. Mustered out with company, May 28, 1863, at Albany, N.Y.

CORDELL, CHARLES T.—Age 44 years. Enlisted February 22, 1862, at Wallkill. Mustered in as private, Co. K, same date, to serve unexpired term of two years. Died of disease, July 11, 1862, at David's Island General Hospital, in New York Harbor, N.Y.

CORNWELL, THEODORE D.—Age 19 years. Enlisted March 20, 1862, at Alexandria, Va. Mustered in as private, Co. A, same date, to serve unexpired term of two years. Mustered out with company, May 28, 1863, at Albany, N.Y. Prior service in Co. A, 53rd New York Infantry.

CORRINE, DENNIS—Age 33 years. Enlisted May 2, 1861, at Schenectady. Mustered in as private, Co. E, no date, to serve two years. No further record.

COUCHMAN, JAMES—Age 18 years. Enlisted October 13, 1862, at Oswegatchie. Mustered in as private, Co. D, same date, to serve three years. Transferred May 10, 1863, to Co. E, 121st New York Infantry.

COURTNEY, JAMES S.—Age 18 years. Enlisted September 1, 1861, at Albany. Mustered in as private, Co. B, same date, to serve unexpired term of two years. Promoted corporal, October 1, 1861. Promoted sergeant, March 1, 1863. Mustered out with company, May 28, 1863, at Albany, N.Y. Subsequent service in Co. K, 91st New York Infantry.

COURTNEY, ROBERT—Age 17 years, but gave age as 18 years. Enlisted May 17, 1861, at Schenectady. Mustered in as private, Co. A, same date, to serve two years. Detailed as regimental clerk, November 1861 to January 1862. Wounded in left hand, June 27, 1862, at Gaines's Mill, Va. Sent off, July 2, 1862, from Harrison's Landing, Va. Hospitalized, July 4, 1862, at Carver General Hospital, in Washington, D.C. Transferred, September 3, 1862, to 5th and Buttonwood Streets General Hospital, in Philadelphia, Pa. Discharged on account of such wounds, October 9, 1862, from 5th and Buttonwood Streets General Hospital, in Philadelphia, Pa.

COYLE, WILLIAM C.—Age 19 years. Enlisted May 17, 1861, at Albany. Mustered in as private, Co. B, same date, to serve two years. Promoted corporal, September 1, 1861. Mustered out with company, May 28, 1863, at Albany, N.Y.

CRAFT, PETER BROCK—Age 20 years. Enlisted April 30, 1861, at Middletown. Mustered in as private, Co. H, May 17, 1861, to serve two years. Mustered out with company, May 28, 1863, at Albany, N.Y. Subsequent service in 8th Independent Battery New York Light Artillery.

CRAIG, GEORGE—Age 24 years. Enlisted April 19, 1861, at Albany. Mustered in as sergeant, Co. F, May 17, 1861, to serve two years. Deserted, August 10, 1861, from hospital at Alexandria, Va.

CRAIG, JOHN R.—Age 18 years. Enlisted April 24, 1861, at Albany. Mustered in as private, Co. B, May 17, 1861, to serve two years. Deserted, September 10, 1861, from Camp King, Alexandria, Va.

CRAWFORD, JOHN—Age 26 years. Enlisted April 19, 1861, at Albany. Mustered in as private, Co. F, May 17, 1861, to serve two years. Wounded in arm, September 14, 1862, at Crampton's Gap, Md. Hospitalized, October 6, 1862, at Camp A General Hospital in Frederick, Md. Returned to regiment, December 26, 1862. Mustered out with company, May 28, 1863, at Albany, N.Y.

CRIST, ERNEST J.—Age 24 years. Enlisted April 30, 1861, at Middletown. Mustered in as private, Co. D, May 17, 1861, to serve two years. Drowned, May 17, 1863, in the Hudson River at Albany, N.Y.

CROWLEY, JOHN—Age 20 years. Enlisted May 17, 1861, at Albany. Mustered in as private, Co. A, same date, to serve two years. Left sick, June 18, 1861, in New York City hospital when regiment left state. Returned to regiment, September 22, 1861. Deserted, November 24, 1861, from Camp King, Alexandria, Va.

CROZIER, ABRAM—Age 36 years. Enlisted June 4, 1861, at Albany. Mustered in as private, Co. B, same date, to serve two years. Captured, July 17, 1861, near Fairfax Court House, Va. Confined, July 23, 1861, at Richmond, Va. Paroled, January 3, 1862, at Fort Monroe, Va. Deserted, January 27, 1862, from Camp King, Alexandria, Va.

CULLEN, JAMES W.—Age—years. Enlisted May 17, 1861, at Albany. Mustered in as private, Co. C, same date, to serve two years. Deserted, August 10, 1861, from camp near Alexandria, Va.

CULLEN, PHILIP—Age 28 years. Enlisted April 19, 1861, at Albany. Mustered in as private, Co. I, May 17, 1861, to serve two years. Court-martialed for drunkenness, December 13, 1861. Mustered out with company, May 28, 1863, at Albany, N.Y. Subsequent service in Co. F, 9th Iowa Cavalry.

CULVER, CHARLES S.—Age—years. Enlisted May 7, 1861, at Albany. Mustered in as private, Co. G, May 17, 1861, to serve two years. No further record.

CULVER, GEORGE W.—Age 23 years. Enlisted May 17, 1861, at Albany. Mustered in as private, Co. G, same date, to serve two years. Died of disease, February 4, 1862, at Camp King, Alexandria, Va.

CUMMINGS, JOHN—Age 19 years. Enlisted May 7, 1861, at Albany. Mustered in as private, Co. H, May 17, 1861, to serve two years. Hospitalized, July 9, 1862. Sent sick, July 9, 1862, onboard Steamer *Daniel Webster* at Harrison's Landing, Va. Hospitalized, July 17, 1862, at Brooklyn City Hospital, Brooklyn, N.Y. Transferred, November 27, 1862, to Battery G, 5th United States Light Artillery.

CUNNIHINE, JAMES—Age 18 years. Enlisted April 19, 1861, at Albany. Mustered in as private, Co. F, May 17, 1861, to serve two years. Deserted, September 17, 1862, from hospital at Sharpsburg, Md. Hospitalized, date not stated, at Summit House General Hospital, in Philadelphia, Pa. Joined regiment, May 11, 1863, at Albany, N.Y. Discharged, May 22, 1863.

CUNNINGHAM, JOHN C.—Age 20 years. Enlisted May 17, 1861, at Albany. Mustered in as private, Co. B, same date, to serve two years. Mustered out with company, May 28, 1863, at Albany, N.Y.

CURRY, THOMAS—Age 20 years. Enlisted April 30, 1861, at Middletown. Mustered in as corporal, Co. D, May 17, 1861, to serve two years. Served as flag bearer in every engagement. Promoted sergeant, December 9, 1862. Mustered out with company, May 28, 1863, at Albany, N.Y.

CURTIS, ELI—Age 31 years. Enlisted April 27, 1861, at Albany. Mustered in as private, Co. I, May 17, 1861, to serve two years. Discharged for disability, October 2, 1861, at Alexandria, Va. Subsequent service in Co. F, 1st New Jersey Cavalry.

DAILEY, JAMES—Age 20 years. Enlisted April 27, 1861, at Middletown. Mustered in as private, Co. D, same date, to serve two years. Killed, June 27, 1862, at Gaines's Mill, Va.

DAILEY (Daley), ROBERT—Age 16 years. Enlisted November 24, 1861, at Albany. Mustered in as drummer, Co. F, same date, to serve two years. Reduced to private, date not stated. Discharged for disability, July 6, 1862, at Berkeley's Landing, Va. Subsequent service in Co. D, 177th New York Infantry.

DALEY, DANIEL HENNISON—Age 21 years. Enrolled April 22, 1861, at Schenectady. Mustered in as first lieutenant, Co. A, May 17, 1861, to serve two years. Wounded in right shoulder, September 14, 1862, at Crampton's Gap, Md. Hospitalized, date not stated, at U.S. Hotel, in Washington, D.C. On furlough for wound, October 1862, at Schenectady, N.Y. Promoted captain, December 9, 1862. Resigned, February 26, 1863, on account of wounds. Commissioned first lieutenant, July 4, 1861, with rank from April 22, 1861, original. Captain, November 10, 1862, with rank from August 14, 1862, after Gridley was promoted.

DALEY, JOHN—Age 19 years. Enlisted April 22, 1861, at Schenectady. Mustered in as private, Co. A, May 17, 1861, to serve two years. Wounded, September 14, 1862, at Crampton's Gap, Md. Mustered out with company, May 28, 1863, at Albany, N.Y.

DANIELS, MICHAEL—Age 24 years. Enlisted April 19, 1861, at Albany. Mustered in as sergeant, Co. F, May 17, 1861, to serve two years. Reduced to private, date not stated. Deserted, January 12, 1862, from Camp King, Alexandria, Va. Returned to regiment, on or about February 7, 1862, at Camp King, Alexandria, Va. Court-martialed for absence, February 24, 1862, at Alexandria, Va. Hospitalized, July or August 1862 at Judiciary Square General Hospital, at Washington, D.C. Discharged for disability, September 30, 1862, at Philadelphia, Pa.

DANIELS, WILLIAM H.—Age 23 years. Enlisted April 30, 1861, at Middletown. Mustered in as musician, Co. D, May 17, 1861, to serve two years. Wounded slightly in leg, June 27, 1862, at Gaines's Mill, Va. Sent off, July 2, 1862, from Harrison's Landing, Va. Hospitalized, July 4, 1862, and later remained as a nurse, in Trinity General Hospital, at Washington, D.C., up to March 1863. Reduced to private, date not stated. Mustered out with company, May 28, 1863, at Albany, N.Y.

DARRAH, JAMES H.—Age 25 years. Enlisted May 15, 1861, at Schenectady. Mustered in as corporal, Co. A, May 17, 1861, to serve two years. Reduced to private, date not stated. Deserted, May 7, 1862, at Brick House Landing (West Point), Va., as James Darran.

DAVIS, JOSEPH—Age 20 years. Enlisted April 30, 1861, at Middletown. Mustered in as private, Co. D, May 17, 1861, to serve two years. Mustered out with company, May 28, 1863, at Albany, N.Y.

DAWLEY, CORYDON (Coradon) A.—Age 24 years. Enlisted April 29, 1861, at Albany. Mustered in as private, Co. I, May 17, 1861, to serve two years. Hospitalized, May 8, 1862, at Fort Monroe, Va. Deserted, May 1862, at Ship Point, Va.

DEANSTATT (Denstedt), JOHN—Age 30 years. Enlisted May 7, 1861, at Albany. Mustered in as private, Co. G, May 17, 1861, to serve two years. Discharged for disability, July 31, 1862, near Harrison's Landing, Va. Subsequent service in Co. B, 140th New York Infantry.

DEBAUM, ISAAC—Age 24 years. Enlisted April 23, 1861, at Fishkill. Mustered in as corporal, Co. C, May 17, 1861, to serve two years. Wounded in back, June 27, 1862, at Gaines's Mill, Va. Wounded in leg, September 14, 1862, at Crampton's Gap, Md. Leg amputated. Died of such wounds, September 25, 1862, in hospital at Burkittsville, Md.

DECKER, ALFRED—Age 24 years. Enlisted April 30, 1861, at Middletown. Mustered in as private, Co. D, May 17, 1861, to serve two years. Promoted corporal, June 1, 1862. Mustered out with company, May 28, 1863, at Albany, N.Y.

DECKER, SAMUEL—Age 17 years, but gave age as 19 years. Enlisted May 17, 1861, at Albany. Mustered in as private, Co. C, same date, to serve two years. Mustered out with company, May 28, 1863, at Albany, N.Y. Subsequent service in 7th Independent Battery New York Light Artillery.

DEE, MATHEW—Age 36 years. Enlisted December 6, 1861, at Albany. Mustered in as private, Co. F, same date, to serve unexpired term of two years. Hospitalized, January 20, 1863, to 1st Division Sixth Corps Hospital, at Windmill Point, Va. Died of disease, January 21, 1863, at 1st Division Sixth Corps Hospital, at Windmill Point, Va.

DEGROAT, ADDRIANUS—Age 42 years. Enlisted April 24, 1861, at Albany. Mustered in as private, Co. B, May 17, 1861, to serve two years. Deserted, June 18, 1861, at Albany, N.Y.

DELANEY, JOHN—Age 20 years. Enlisted April 23, 1861, at Albany. Mustered in as private, Co. C, May 17, 1861, to serve two years. Hospitalized, September, October, or November 1862, at Harewood General Hospital, in Washington, D.C. Discharged for disability, April 18, 1863, at Summit House General Hospital, in Philadelphia, Pa.

DELANEY, JOHN—Age 28 years. Enlisted April 30, 1861, at Middletown. Mustered in as corporal, Co. H, May 17, 1861, to serve two years. Promoted sergeant, date not stated. Captured, May 5, 1863, near Fredericksburg, Va. Confined, May 9, 1863, at Richmond, Va. Paroled, May 15, 1863, at City Point, Va. Reported at Camp Parole, Md., May 18, 1863. Mustered out with company, May 28, 1863, at Albany, N.Y. Subsequent service in Co. L, 15th New York Cavalry & Co. L, 2nd New York Provisional Cavalry.

DEMPSEY, JOHN—Age 26 years. Enlisted November 4, 1861, at Canandaigua. Mustered in as private, Co. G, same date, to serve unexpired term of two years. Hospitalized, May 11, 1862, at Seminary Hospital, at Hampton, Va. Returned to regiment, date not stated. Detailed as teamster, date not stated, for Division Headquarters. Mustered out with company, May 28, 1863, at Albany, N.Y. Subsequent service in Co. H, 16th New York Heavy Artillery.

DEMPSEY, JOHN M.—Age 26 years. Enlisted April 17, 1861, at Albany. Mustered in as first sergeant, Co. F, May 17, 1861, to serve two years. Promoted second lieutenant, October 19, 1861. Promoted first lieutenant, March 25, 1862. Mustered out with company, May 28, 1863, at Albany, N.Y. Commissioned second lieutenant, December 2, 1861, with rank from October 19, 1861, after Mooney was promoted. First lieutenant, October 10, 1862, with rank from March 25, 1862, after Fisher was dismissed. Subsequent service in Co. G, D & B, 43rd New York Infantry.

DENNING, JOHN—Age 27 years. Enlisted October 5, 1861, at Ogdensburg. Mustered in as private, Co. K, same date, to serve unexpired term of two years. Mustered out with company, May 28, 1863, at Albany, N.Y. Subsequent service in Co. C, 14th New York Heavy Artillery, Co. M & A, 1st New York Veteran Cavalry & Co. F, 43rd United States Infantry.

DENNISON, THOMAS—Age 28 years. Enlisted December 9, 1861, at Albany. Mustered in as private, Co. F, same date, to serve unexpired term of two years. Mustered out with company, May 28, 1863, at Albany, N.Y.

DEVOE, DAVID—Age 22 years. Enlisted May 7, 1861, at Albany. Mustered in as private, Co. H, May 17, 1861, to serve two years. Promoted corporal, date not stated. Mustered out with company, May 28, 1863, at Albany, N.Y.

DICKERSON, WILLIAM—Age 20 years. Enlisted May 17, 1861, at Albany. Mustered in as private, Co. I, same date, to serve two years. Mustered out with company, May 28, 1863, at Albany, N.Y.

DILLON, JOHN—Age 19 years. Enlisted April 19, 1861, at Albany. Mustered in as private, Co. I, May 17, 1861, to serve two years. Wounded in thigh, September 14, 1862, at Crampton's Gap, Md. Hospitalized, October 6, 1862, at Camp A General Hospital in Frederick, Md. Returned to regiment, December 26, 1862. Mustered out with company, May 28, 1863, at Albany, N.Y. Subsequent service in Co. L, 13th New York Heavy Artillery.

DILLON, JOHN—Age 23 years. Enlisted May 2, 1861, at Schenectady. Mustered in as private, Co. E, May 17, 1861, to serve two years. Detailed as company cook. Absent-without-leave, November 10, 1861, from Camp King, Alexandria, Va. Returned to regiment, November 15, 1861, at Camp King, Alexandria, Va. Court-martialed for absence, January 16, 1862, at Alexandria, Va. Mustered out with company, May 28, 1863, at Albany, N.Y. Subsequent service in Co. "U" 4th New York Heavy Artillery, Co. D, 13th New York Heavy Artillery & Co. L, 6th New York Heavy Artillery.

DINGS, ASHBEL SYKES—Age 18 years. Enlisted October 1, 1861, at Ogdensburg. Mustered in as private, Co. K, same date, to serve unexpired term of two years. Promoted corporal, December 25, 1862. Mustered out with company, May 28, 1863, at Albany, N.Y. Brother of Louis O. Dings.

DINGS, LOUIS OLIAN—Age 16 years, but gave age as 18 years. Enlisted May 12, 1861, at Ogdensburg. Mustered in as private, Co. K, May 17, 1861, to serve two years. Mustered out with company, May 28, 1863, at Albany, N.Y. Subsequent service in Co. A, 16th New York Heavy Artillery & Co. L, 1st New York Mounted Rifles. Brother of Ashbel S. Dings.

DOBSON, THOMAS—Age 27 years. Enlisted May 10, 1861, at Albany. Mustered in as private, Co. B, May 17, 1861, to serve two years. Mustered out with company, May 28, 1863, at Albany, N.Y.

DOLAN, JOHN—Age 19 years. Enlisted April 19, 1861, at Albany. Mustered in as private, Co. F, May 17, 1861, to serve two years. No further record.

DOLAN, JOHN—Age 32 years. Enlisted April 28, 1861, at Schenectady. Mustered in as private, Co. A, May 17, 1861, to serve two years. Mustered out with company, May 28, 1863, at Albany, N.Y. Subsequent service in Co. E, 3rd New York Infantry.

DOLLAR, CONRAD TERWILLIGER—Age 31 years. Enlisted April 19, 1861, at Albany. Mustered in as private, Co. F, May 17, 1861, to serve two years. Mustered out with company, May 28, 1863, at Albany, N.Y. Subsequent service in Co. H, 18th New York Cavalry, Co. M, 10th New York Cavalry & Co. M, 1st New York Provisional Cavalry.

DONOHOE, TIMOTHY—Age 18 years. Enlisted April 19, 1861, at Albany. Mustered in as private, Co. F, May 17, 1861, to serve two years. Deserted, August 18, 1862, at Newport News, Va.

DONOVAN, JEREMIAH—Age 18 years. Enlisted September 2, 1862, at Schenectady. Mustered in as private, Co. C, September 26, 1862, at Albany, to serve three years. Transferred, May 10, 1863, to Co. H, 121st New York Infantry & Co. I, 6th Regiment Veteran Reserve Corps.

DONOVAN, MICHAEL—Age 23 years. Enlisted May 12, 1861, at Ogdensburg. Mustered in as private, Co. K, May 17, 1861, to serve two years. Mustered out with company, May 28, 1863, at Albany, N.Y.

DONOVAN, MICHAEL H.—Age 38 years. Enrolled May 2, 1861, at Albany. Mustered in as captain, Co. F, May 17, 1861, to serve two years. Detailed on recruiting service, November 1861, at Albany, N.Y. Mustered out with company, May 28, 1863, at Albany, N.Y. Commissioned captain, July 4, 1861, with rank from May 2, 1861, original. Subsequent service in 59th New York Infantry.

DOODY, MICHAEL F.—Age 20 years. Enlisted April 19, 1861, at Albany. Mustered in as private, Co. F, May 17, 1861, to serve two years. On ten day furlough, February 1863, in Albany, N.Y. Mustered out with company, May 28, 1863, at Albany, N.Y. Subsequent service in Co. C, 79th New York Infantry, under alias William Crawford.

DOOLY, PETER—Age 19 years. Enlisted May 17, 1861, at Albany. Mustered in as private, Co. I, same date, to serve two years. Mustered out with company, May 28, 1863, at Albany, N.Y.

DOUGHERTY, WILLIAM—Age 16 years. Enlisted May 8, 1861, at Albany. Mustered in as musician, Co. I, May 17, 1861, to serve two years. Reduced to private, date not stated. Deserted, August 29, 1861, at Alexandria, Va.

DOUGLAS, HUGH—Age 19 years. Enlisted May 2, 1861, at Schenectady. Mustered in as private, Co. E, May 17, 1861, to serve two years. Wounded in left shoulder, September 14, 1862, at Crampton's Gap, Md. Hospitalized, October 4, 1862, at Camp A General Hospital in Frederick, Md. Remained in hospital as nurse. Returned to regiment, March 18, 1863. At Convalescent Camp, April 1863, in Alexandria, Va. Mustered out with company, May 28, 1863, at Albany, N.Y.

DOWNING, SYLVANUS B.—Age 24 years. Enlisted April 30, 1861, at Middletown. Mustered in as private, Co. H, May 17, 1861, to serve two years. Promoted corporal, date not stated. Mustered out with company, May 28, 1863, at Albany, N.Y. Subsequent service in Co. L, 15th New York Cavalry.

DOYLE, JAMES—Age 21 years. Enlisted February 17, 1862, at Ogdensburg. Mustered in as private, Co. K, same date, to serve unexpired term of two years. Mustered out with company, May 28, 1863, at Albany, N.Y.

DOYLE, ROBERT J.—Age about 17 years, but gave age as 18 years. Enlisted April 19, 1861, at Albany. Mustered in as private, Co. F, May 17, 1861, to serve two years. Mustered out with company, May 28, 1863, at Albany, N.Y.

DROWN, BENJAMIN F. "Frank"—Age 23 years. Enlisted May 7, 1861, at Albany. Mustered in as private, Co. G, May 17, 1861, to serve two years. Captured, June 27, 1862, at Gaines's Mill, Va. Confined, June 28, 1862, at Richmond, Va. Paroled, September 13, 1862, at City Point, Va. Sent to hospital in Alexandria, Va. in November 1862. Discharged for disability, February 14, 1863, from Camp Parole, near Alexandria, Va. Subsequent service in Co. I, 18th Michigan Infantry & Co. C, 22nd Veteran Reserve Corps.

DUEL, JOHN—Age 19 years. Enlisted April 19, 1861, at Albany. Mustered in as private, Co. F, May 17, 1861, to serve two years. Killed, September 14, 1862, at Crampton's Gap, Md.

DUNKLE, CHARLES WATSON—Age 24 years. Enlisted October 29, 1861, at Canandaigua. Mustered in as private, Co. G, same date, to serve unexpired term of two years. Mustered out with company, May 28, 1863, at Albany, N.Y. Brother of George W. & Lewis F. Dunkle.

DUNKLE, GEORGE W.—Age 19 years. Enlisted November 5, 1861, at Canandaigua. Mustered in as private, Co. G, same date, to serve two years. Died of disease,

April 29, 1862, in hospital at Alexandria, Va. Brother of Charles W. & Lewis F. Dunkle.

DUNKLE, LEWIS F.—Age 23 years. Enlisted May 7, 1861, at Canandaigua. Mustered in as private, Co. G, May 17, 1861, to serve two years. Mustered out with company, May 28, 1863, at Albany, N.Y. Brother of Charles W. & George W. Dunkle.

DUNNIGAN, JOHN—Age 19 years. Enlisted May 17, 1861, at Albany. Mustered in as private, Co. C, same date, to serve two years. Court-martialed for absence, October 17, 1861. Hospitalized sick, June 27–July 2, 1862, at Chickahominy River, near Richmond, Va. Sent sick, July 2, 1862, from Harrison's Landing, Va. Hospitalized, July 4, 1862, at Washington, D.C. No further record.

DUNNING, EZEKIEL PERRY—Age 40 years. Enlisted May 7, 1861, at Albany. Mustered in as private, Co. H, May 17, 1861, to serve two years. Sent sick, May 24, 1862. Hospitalized, June 1862, at City Hall Park Barracks, New York City, N.Y. Deserted from hospital, before October 1862. No further record. Brother of William C. Dunning.

DUNNING, WILLIAM C.—Age 26 years. Enlisted May 7, 1861, at Albany. Mustered in as private, Co. H, May 17, 1861, to serve two years. Died, September 21, 1861, at camp near Alexandria, Va. Brother of Ezekiel P. Dunning.

DURKEE, SHUBAEL—Age 25 years. Enlisted April 23, 1861, at Albany. Mustered in as private, Co. I, May 17, 1861, to serve two years. Mustered out with company, May 28, 1863, at Albany, N.Y. Subsequent service in Co. H, 22nd New York Cavalry.

EARL (Earle), CHARLES L.—Age 18 years. Enlisted May 7, 1861, at Albany. Mustered in as private, Co. G, May 17, 1861, to serve two years. Sent sick, May 11, 1862, from Yorktown, Va., aboard transport *Ocean Queen*, to Ladies General Hospital in New York City, N.Y. Discharged from hospital, May 26, 1862, for furlough to Canandaigua, N.Y. Failed to report to hospital in New York City, N.Y., on June 25, 1862. Discharged by decree of a civil court, August 18, 1862, at Canandaigua, N.Y.

EBEL, HENRY (Heinrich)—Age 36 years. Enlisted January 7, 1862, at Ogdensburg. Mustered in as private, Co. K, same date, to serve unexpired term of two years. Captured, June 27, 1862, at Gaines's Mill, Va. Confined, June 28, 1862, at Richmond, Va. Paroled, August 5, 1862, at City Point, Va. Mustered out with company, May 28, 1863, at Albany, N.Y. Subsequent service in Co. C, 14th New York Heavy Artillery.

EDMESTON, ALEXANDER A.—Age 31 years. Enrolled May 14, 1861, at Albany. Mustered in as assistant surgeon, May 17, 1861, to serve two years. Captured, June 29, 1862, at Savage's Station, Va. Confined, July 5, 1862, at Richmond, Va. Paroled, July 25, 1862, at City Point, Va. Resigned, October 7, 1862. Commissioned assistant surgeon, July 4, 1861, with rank from May 14, 1861, original. Resigned for promotion to surgeon, 92nd New York Infantry, where he received commission to surgeon on September 25, 1862.

ELDRIDGE, FREDERICK A.—Age 27 years. Enlisted April 30, 1861, at Middletown. Mustered in as private, Co. D, May 17, 1861, to serve two years. Mustered out with company, May 28, 1863, at Albany, N.Y.

ELLIOTT, WILLIAM—Age 20 years. Enlisted May 19, 1861, at Albany. Mustered in as private, Co. I, same date, to serve two years. Wounded slightly in head, June 27, 1862, at Gaines's Mill, Va. Mustered out with company, May 28, 1863, at Albany, N.Y. Subsequent service in Co. A, 47th New York Infantry.

ELLIS, GEORGE WHITE—Age 26 years. Enlisted May 7, 1861, at Canandaigua. Mustered in as first sergeant, Co. G, May 17, 1861, to serve two years. Detailed on recruiting service, October & November 1861, at Canandaigua, N.Y. Captured, June 27, 1862, at Gaines's Mill, Va. Confined, July 13, 1862, at Richmond, Va. Paroled, July 17, 1862, at Haxall's Landing, James River, near Richmond, Va. Hospitalized, date not stated, at Fort Hamilton, N.Y. Returned to regiment, November or December 1862. Mustered out with company, May 28, 1863, at Albany, N.Y. Subsequent service in, Co. "U" 175th New York Infantry & Co. K, 2nd New York Cavalry. Brother of William H. Ellis, Jr.

ELLIS, WILLIAM HENRY, Jr.—Age 30 years. Enrolled May 7, 1861, at Canandaigua. Mustered in as second lieutenant, Co. G, May 17, 1861, to serve two years. Detailed on recruiting service, January 20, 1862. Wounded in left thigh, September 14, 1862, at Crampton's Gap, Md. Hospitalized, date not stated, at Burkittsville, Md. Transferred, date not stated, to U.S. Hotel, in Washington, D.C. Furlough for wound, October 4, 1862, at Canandaigua, N.Y. Returned to regiment, November 1, 1862. Resigned on account of wounds, February 9, 1863, at Falmouth, Va. Commissioned second lieutenant, July 4, 1861, with rank from May 7, 1861, original. Brother of George W. Ellis.

ELLISON, WILLIAM A.—Age 22 years. Enlisted April 30, 1861, at Middletown. Mustered in as private, Co. D, May 17, 1861, to serve two years. Fell out of ranks, August 30, 1862, on account of sickness. Hospitalized, September 1, 1862, at 2nd Division General Hospital, at Alexandria, Va. Died of disease, November 5, 1862, at St. Paul's Church General Hospital, in Alexandria, Va.

EMPEROR, JOHN, Jr.—Age 23 years. Enlisted April 24, 1861, at Albany. Mustered in as private, Co. B, May 17, 1861, to serve two years. Mustered out with company, May 28, 1863, at Albany, N.Y. Subsequent service in Co. I & E, 43rd New York Infantry.

ETTS, JOHN H.—Age 20 years. Enlisted May 7, 1861, at Canandaigua. Mustered in as sergeant, Co. G, May 17, 1861, to serve two years. Wounded slightly in finger, June 27, 1862, at Gaines's Mill, Va. Hospitalized, July 1862, at David's Island General Hospital, in New York Harbor, N.Y. Transferred, date not stated, hospital in Philadelphia, Pa. Reduced to private, February 28, 1863. Returned to regiment, April or May 1863. Mustered out with company, May 28, 1863, at Albany, N.Y.

FAGAN, THOMAS—Age 19 years. Enlisted April 22, 1861, at Schenectady. Mustered in as private, Co. A, May 17, 1861, to serve two years. Wounded, September 14, 1862, at Crampton's Gap, Md. Hospitalized,

September 1862, at Columbian College Hospital, at Washington, D.C. Returned to regiment, April or May 1863. Mustered out with company, May 28, 1863, at Albany, N.Y. Subsequent service in Co. H, 16th New York Heavy Artillery.

FAGRET, ADOLPHE—Age 34 years. Enlisted October 18, 1861, at Ogdensburg. Mustered in as private, Co. K, same date, to serve unexpired term of two years. Mustered out with company, May 28 1863, at Albany, N.Y. Subsequent service in 17th United States Infantry & Co. H, 5th Vermont Infantry.

FAILING, ANDREW ROOF "Rufus"—Age 20 years. Enlisted April 28, 1861, at Schenectady. Mustered in as sergeant, Co. A, May 17, 1861, to serve two years. Mustered out with company, May 28, 1863, at Albany, N.Y.

FARR, ALFRED AUGUSTUS—Age 50 years. Enrolled May 14, 1861, at Albany. Mustered in as chaplain, May 17, 1861, to serve two years. On furlough in charge of remains of Colonel Jackson, November 13–19, 1861, at Albany and Schenectady. Resigned, July 31, 1862. Reappointed, November 27, 1862, at Stafford Court House, Va. Mustered out with regiment, May 28, 1863, at Albany, N.Y. Commissioned chaplain, July 4, 1861, with rank from May 14, 1861, original. Again commissioned chaplain, November 10, 1862, with rank from July 31, 1862, reappointed.

FARR, JOHN W.—Age 24 years. Enlisted April 19, 1861, at Albany. Mustered in as private, Co. F, May 17, 1861, to serve two years. Promoted sergeant, September 19, 1861. Promoted first sergeant, date not stated. Mustered in as second lieutenant, March 25, 1862. Mustered out with company, May 28, 1863, at Albany, N.Y. Commissioned second lieutenant, November 10, 1862, with rank from March 25, 1862, after Dempsey was promoted. Subsequent service Co. K & D, 18th New York Cavalry.

FARRELL, PERCY—Age 24 years. Enlisted May 12, 1861, at Ogdensburg. Mustered in as private, Co. K, May 17, 1861, to serve two years. Promoted sergeant, July 12, 1861. Hospitalized, July or August 1862, at Satterlee General Hospital, in West Philadelphia, Pa. Returned to regiment, May 19, 1863. Mustered out with company, May 28, 1863, at Albany, N.Y. Subsequent service in Co. L, 14th New York Heavy Artillery.

FARRELL, ROBERT—Age 18 years. Enlisted May 12, 1861, at Ogdensburg. Mustered in as private, Co. K, May 17, 1861, to serve two years. Mustered out with company, May 28, 1863, at Albany, N.Y.

FARTHING, JAMES A.—Age 19 years. Enlisted April 23, 1861, at Schenectady. Mustered in as private, Co. A, May 17, 1861, to serve two years. Deserted, May or June 1861, before regiment left Albany, N.Y.

FAUROT, HENRY—Age 27 years. Enrolled May 7, 1861, at Canandaigua. Mustered in as captain, Co. G, May 17, 1861, to serve two years. Detailed on recruiting service, October & November 1861, at Canandaigua, N.Y. Resigned on account of disability, July 21, 1862. Commissioned captain, July 4, 1861, with rank from May 7, 1861, original. First Cousin Once Removed of Henry Horace Faurot.

FAUROT, HENRY HORACE—Age 20 years. Enlisted May 7, 1861, at Canandaigua. Mustered in as private, Co. G, May 17, 1861, to serve two years. Detailed on recruiting service, January 20, 1862. Sick while on recruiting service in Manchester, N.Y. Deserted, February 1, 1862, while on recruiting service. Subsequent service in Co. H, 16th New York Heavy Artillery & Co. D & E, 40th New York Infantry. First Cousin Once Removed of Henry Faurot.

FAY, JOHN M.—Age 31 years. Enlisted May 12, 1861, at Ogdensburg. Mustered in as corporal, Co. K, May 17, 1861, to serve two years. Appointed commissary sergeant, June 18, 1861. Promoted commissary sergeant, October 10, 1862, and transferred to non-commissioned staff. Mustered out with regiment, May 28, 1863, at Albany, N.Y.

FIELD, CHARLES H.—Age 18 years. Enlisted May 7, 1861, at Albany. Mustered in as private, Co. H, May 17, 1861, to serve two years. Mustered out with company, May 28, 1863, at Albany, N.Y. Subsequent service in Co. "U" 15th New York Engineers.

FIELD, WILLIAM—Age 34 years. Enlisted October 10, 1861, at Ogdensburg. Mustered in as private, Co. K, same date, to serve unexpired term of two years. Mustered out with company, May 28, 1863, at Albany, N.Y. Subsequent service in Co. I, 13th New York Heavy Artillery.

FINLAYSON, JOHN—Age 23 years. Enlisted May 12, 1861, at Ogdensburg. Mustered in as private, Co. K,

Sgt. Percy Farrell, Company K, died on June 16, 1913, in Virginia (courtesy New York State Military Museum).

May 17, 1861, to serve two years. Discharged for disability, November 20, 1861, at Camp King, Alexandria, Va.

FINN, CALVIN ALVIN—Age 18 years. Enlisted November 14, 1861, at Canandaigua. Mustered in as private, Co. G, same date, to serve unexpired term of two years. Promoted sergeant, February 28, 1862. Mustered out with company, May 28, 1863, at Albany, N.Y. Subsequent service in Co. A, 157th New York Infantry.

Sgt. Calvin A. Finn joined Company G two months after he turned eighteen. He saw the war end where it all started, in Charleston, South Carolina, while in service with the 157th New York. He died on September 27, 1927, in Grants Pass, Oregon (courtesy New York State Military Museum).

FISHER, CONRAD—Age 21 years. Enlisted April 28, 1861, at Schenectady. Mustered in as private, Co. A, May 17, 1861, to serve two years. Deserted, July 30, 1861, from Camp Myers, Alexandria, Va.

FISHER, EDWARD—Age 32 years. Enrolled April 19, 1861, at Albany. Mustered in as first lieutenant, Co. F, May 17, 1861, to serve two years. Dismissed from service, March 25, 1862, by sentence of general court martial. Commissioned first lieutenant, July 4, 1861, with rank from April 22, 1861, original.

FISHER, HIRAM L.—Age 25 years. Enlisted April 19, 1861, at Albany. Mustered in as private, Co. F, May 17, 1861, to serve two years. Promoted sergeant, date not stated. Hospitalized, July or August 1862, at Satterlee General Hospital, in West Philadelphia, Pa. Reported, March 27, 1863, to Fort Columbus, N.Y. Mustered out with company, May 28, 1863, at Albany, N.Y.

FISHER, IRA (Isaac) J.—Age 19 years. Enlisted April 30, 1861, at Middletown. Mustered in as private, Co. D, May 17, 1861, to serve two years. Sent sick, January 19, 1863, to hospital at Windmill Point, Va. Hospitalized, February 13, 1863, at Judiciary Square General Hospital in Washington, D.C. Transferred, date not stated, at David's Island General Hospital, in New York Harbor, N.Y. Returned to regiment, May 16, 1863. Mustered out with company, May 28, 1863, at Albany, N.Y. Subsequent service in Co. G, 2nd New York Mounted Rifles.

FISHER, JOHN—Age 25 years. Enlisted October 28, 1861, at Canandaigua. Mustered in as private, Co. G, same date, to serve unexpired term of two years. Mustered out with company, May 28, 1863, at Albany, N.Y.

FISHER, WILLIAM—Age 23 years. Enlisted October 29, 1861, at Canandaigua. Mustered in as private, Co. G, same date, to serve unexpired term of two years. Mustered out with company, May 28, 1863, at Albany, N.Y.

FISHER, WILLIAM—Age 22 years. Enlisted September 1, 1861, at Albany. Mustered in as private, Co. I, same date, to serve unexpired term of two years. Mustered out with company, May 28, 1863, at Albany, N.Y.

FITCH, JOHN—Age 18 years. Enlisted April 1, 1862, at Middletown. Mustered in as private, Co. H, same date, to serve two years. Mustered out with company, May 28, 1863, at Albany, N.Y.

FIX, JOHN—Age 19 years. Enlisted May 1, 1861, at Albany. Mustered in as private, Co. B, May 17, 1861, to serve two years. Sent sick, May 7, 1862, from Brick House Landing (West Point), Va. Hospitalized, date not stated, at General Hospital, in New York. Returned to regiment, October 18, 1862. Mustered out with company, May 28, 1863, at Albany, N.Y.

FLEETHAM, JOSEPH O.—Age 20 years. Enlisted May 12, 1861, at Ogdensburg. Mustered in as private, Co. K, May 17, 1861, to serve two years. Mustered out with company, May 28, 1863, at Albany, N.Y. Subsequent service in Co. G, 10th Michigan Cavalry.

FLYNN, JAMES—Age 21 years. Enlisted December 19, 1861, at Albany. Mustered in as private, Co. C, same date, to serve unexpired term of two years. Wounded in left hand, June 27, 1862, at Gaines's Mill, Va. Hospitalized, July 18, 1862, in York, Pa. Returned to regiment, May 23, 1863. Mustered out with company, May 28, 1863, at Albany, N.Y. Subsequent service in Co. K, 16th New York Cavalry & Co. M, 3rd New York Provisional Cavalry.

FOGERTY, EDWARD M.—Age 33 years. Enlisted April 19, 1861, at Albany. Mustered in as corporal, Co. I, May 17, 1861, to serve two years. Killed, September 14, 1862, at Crampton's Gap, Md.

FORCE, JOHN MECKER—Age 45 years, but gave age as 43 years. Enlisted April 23, 1861, at Albany. Mustered in as private, Co. C, May 17, 1861, to serve two years. Hospitalized, July or August 1862, at Newport News, Va. Discharged for disability, January 3, 1863, at White Oak Church, Falmouth, Va. Subsequent service in Co. H, 56th New York Infantry.

FORD, JOHN—Age 27 years. Enlisted April 30, 1861, at Middletown. Mustered in as private, Co. H, May 17, 1861, to serve two years. Deserted, August 30, 1862, at Alexandria, Va.

FORSYTH, JAMES—Age 34 years. Enlisted April 24, 1861, at Albany. Mustered in as private, Co. B, May 17, 1861, to serve two years. Hospitalized, May or June 1861, at E Street General Hospital, at Washington, D.C. Mustered out with company, May 28, 1863, at Albany, N.Y. Subsequent service in 3rd New York Infantry.

FORTNER, OLIVER P.—Age 26 years. Enlisted September 8, 1862, at Albany. Mustered in as private, Co. D, same date, to serve three years. Transferred, May 10, 1863, to Co. D, 121st New York Infantry.

FOX, WILLIAM H.—Age 23 years. Enlisted May 7, 1861, at Albany. Mustered in as private, Co. G, May 17, 1861, to serve two years. Hospitalized, September or October 1862, at Hagerstown, Md. Died of disease, January 22, 1863, at hospital in Hagerstown, Md.

FOXIN, JOHN—Age 20 years. Enlisted May 4, 1861, at Albany. Mustered in as private, Co. B, May 17, 1861, to serve two years. Sent sick, August 10, 1862, from Harrison's Landing, Va., to be hospitalized at Satterlee General Hospital, in West Philadelphia, Pa. Returned to regiment, May 15, 1863. Mustered out with company, May 28, 1863, at Albany, N.Y.

FOY, BERNARD—Age 26 years. Enlisted May 9, 1861, at Albany. Mustered in as private, Co. I, May 17, 1861, to serve two years. Hospitalized, July or August 1862, at Satterlee General Hospital, in West Philadelphia, Pa. Returned to regiment, September 12, 1862. Mustered out with company, May 28, 1863, at Albany, N.Y.

FRANCIS, JAMES S.—Age 23 years. Enlisted May 7, 1861, at Canandaigua. Mustered in as private, Co. G, May 17, 1861, to serve two years. Hospitalized, July 12, 1861, at Washington, D.C. Discharged for disability, November 20, 1861, at Camp King, Alexandria, Va. Subsequent service in Co. D & C, 15th New York Cavalry & Co. C, 2nd New York Provisional Cavalry.

FRASIER (Frazier), JAMES—Age 19 years. Enlisted May 12, 1861, at Ogdensburg. Mustered in as private, Co. K, May 17, 1861, to serve two years. Hospitalized, September 9, 1862, at Harewood General Hospital, in Washington, D.C. Died of disease, November 1, 1862, at Harewood General Hospital, in Washington, D.C.

FREER, ROBERT—Age 22 years. Enlisted May 7, 1861, at Canandaigua. Mustered in as private, Co. G, May 17, 1861, to serve two years. Wounded in leg, June 27, 1862, at Gaines's Mill, Va. Captured, June 29, 1862, at Savage's Station, Va. Confined at Richmond, Va. Paroled, July 27, 1862, at City Point, Va. Sent to Alexandria, Va. in November 1862. Hospitalized, date not stated, at Annapolis, Md. Returned to regiment, February 24, 1863. Mustered out with company, May 28, 1863, at Albany, N.Y. Subsequent service in Co. H, 16th New York Heavy Artillery.

FRITZ, MARTIN—Age 42 years. Enlisted August 16, 1862, at Albany. Mustered in as private, Co. C, same date, to serve three years. Hospitalized, March 15, 1862. Died of disease, December 18, 1862, in camp near White Oak Church, near Falmouth, Va.

FULLER, AMASA "Amzy" WOODWARD—Age 23 years. Enlisted April 30, 1861, at Middletown. Mustered in as private, Co. D, May 17, 1861, to serve two years. Promoted corporal, October 12, 1861. Detailed on recruiting service, August 13, 1862, at Middletown, N.Y. Returned to regiment, October 31, 1862. Mustered out with company, May 28, 1863, at Albany, N.Y. Brother of Stephen D. Fuller.

FULLER, STEPHEN D.—Age 21 years. Enlisted April 30, 1861, at Middletown. Mustered in as private, Co. D, May 17, 1861, to serve two years. Hospitalized for sickness, April 16, 1862, at Alexandria, Va. Discharged for disability, July 1, 1862, at Alexandria, Va. Subsequent service in Co. I, 168th New York Infantry & Co. "U" 63rd New York Infantry. Brother of Amasa W. Fuller.

FULLERTON, PETER MILLS—Age 23 years. Enlisted April 27, 1861, at Middletown. Mustered in as private, Co. D, May 17, 1861, to serve two years. Promoted corporal, December 1, 1861. Wounded slightly in left shoulder, September 14, 1862, at Crampton's Gap, Md. Hospitalized, date not stated. Returned to regiment after September 17, 1862. Mustered out with company, May 28, 1863, at Albany, N.Y. First Cousin of Henry C. Mills & William B. Mills.

FURNISS, GEORGE CAPRON—Age 19 years. Enlisted May 12, 1861, at Ogdensburg. Mustered in as private, Co. K, May 17, 1861, to serve two years. Hospitalized for sickness, about July 1, 1862. Transferred, August 17, 1862, to Fort Hamilton, N.Y. Discharged for disability, October 8, 1862, at hospital, Fort Hamilton, N.Y. Died of disease, August 20, 1863, at Parishville, N.Y.

GALE, JOHN H.—Age 28 years. Enlisted April 22, 1861, at Schenectady. Mustered in as private, Co. A, May 17, 1861, to serve two years. Died, June 28, 1861, accidentally shot by Alonzo Richardson, at Camp Harris, Washington, D.C.

GARRISON, SYLVESTER TUTTLE—Age 19 years. Enlisted April 30, 1861, at Middletown. Mustered in as private, Co. D, May 17, 1861, to serve two years. Mustered out with company, May 28, 1863, at Albany, N.Y. Subsequent service in Co. M, 15th New York Heavy Artillery.

GARRITY, JAMES—Age 21 years. Enlisted January 6, 1862, at Albany. Mustered in as private, Co. C, same date, to serve unexpired term of two years. Mustered out with company, May 28, 1863, at Albany, N.Y. Subsequent service in Co. I & C, 7th New York Heavy Artillery.

GARRITY, JAMES—Age 29 years, but gave age as 26 years. Enlisted January 24, 1862, at Ogdensburg. Mustered in as private, Co. K, same date, to serve unexpired term of two years. Wounded in back and buttocks from shell, September 14, 1862, at Crampton's Gap, Md. Hospitalized, October 3, 1862, at Camp A General Hospital at Frederick, Md. Returned to regiment, January 17, 1863. Discharged on account of such wounds, February 3, 1863, at White Oak Church, Falmouth, Va.

GARRITY, JOHN—Age 27 years. Enlisted April 23,

1861, at Albany. Mustered in as private, Co. C, May 17, 1861, to serve two years. Court-martialed for disobedience, October 17, 1861. Deserted, August 24, 1862, from camp, near Alexandria, Va.

GARRITY, MICHAEL—Age 19 years. Enlisted April 29, 1861, at Albany. Mustered in as private, Co. I, May 17, 1861, to serve two years. Mustered out with company, May 28, 1863, at Albany, N.Y.

GARVEY, ERASTUS R.—Age 20 years. Enlisted May 2, 1861, at Albany. Mustered in as private, Co. I, May 17, 1861, to serve two years. Wounded, September 14, 1862, at Crampton's Gap, Md. Hospitalized, October 3, 1862, at Camp A General Hospital at Frederick, Md. Returned to regiment, January 17, 1863. Mustered out with company, May 28, 1863, at Albany, N.Y. Subsequent service in Co. L, 7th New York Heavy Artillery.

GARVEY, JAMES—Age 29 years. Enlisted December 19, 1861, at Schenectady. Mustered in as private, Co. C, same date, to serve eighteen months. Wounded in right leg, June 27, 1862, at Gaines's Mill, Va. Right leg amputated. Captured, June 29, 1862, at Savage's Station, Va. Confined, July 1, 1862, at Richmond, Va. Paroled, August 5, 1862, at City Point, Va. Hospitalized, September 21, 1862, at City Hospital in New York City, N.Y. Transferred, November 6, 1862, to Central Park Hospital in New York City, N.Y. Discharged on account of such wounds, March 24, 1863, at New York City, N.Y. Subsequent service in 2nd Battalion, Veteran Reserve Corps.

GARWOOD, WILLIAM M.—Age 19 years. Enlisted May 7, 1861, at Canandaigua. Mustered in as private, Co. G, May 17, 1861, to serve two years. Mustered out with company, May 28, 1863, at Albany, N.Y. Subsequent service in Co. C, 15th New York Cavalry & Co. C, 2nd New York Provisional Cavalry.

GEARY, THOMAS—Age 21 years. Enlisted April 22, 1861, at Schenectady. Mustered in as private, Co. A, May 17, 1861, to serve two years. Court-martialed at regimental level, September or October 1861. Captured, June 30, 1862, at Chickahominy River, near Richmond, Va. Confined, June 30, 1862, at Richmond, Va. Paroled, August 5, 1862, at City Point, Va. Mustered out with company, May 28, 1863, at Albany, N.Y. Subsequent service in Co. "U" 16th New York Heavy Artillery.

GETMAN, ALBERT N.—Age 22 years. Enlisted May 2, 1861, at Schenectady. Mustered in as private, Co. E, May 17, 1861, to serve two years. Mustered out with company, May 28, 1863, at Albany, N.Y.

GETTY, CHARLES ALBERT—Age 16 years, but gave age as 19 years. Enlisted May 12, 1861, at Ogdensburg. Mustered in as private, Co. K, May 17, 1861, to serve two years. Wounded in breast, June 27, 1862, at Gaines's Mill, Va. Hospitalized, July 2, 1862, to Fort Monroe, Va. Returned to regiment, April 7, 1863. Mustered out with company, May 28, 1863, at Albany, N.Y. Subsequent service in Co. I, 26th New York Cavalry.

GEYWITS, BYRON—Age 22 years. Enlisted April 28, 1861, at Schenectady. Mustered in as corporal, Co. A, May 17, 1861, to serve two years. Promoted sergeant, October 21, 1861. Detailed on recruiting service, August 13, 1862, in Schenectady, N.Y. Mustered out with company, May 28, 1863, at Albany, N.Y., as Byron Gewint or Geywinto.

GIFFEN (Griffen), JOHN F.—Age 30 years. Enlisted May 17, 1861, at Albany. Mustered in as drum major, same date, to serve two years. Detailed on recruiting service, November 1861. Deserted, August 5, 1862, at Alexandria, Va. Reported, March 31, 1863, at Fort Columbus, N.Y. Returned to regiment, May 14, 1863, at Washington, D.C. Mustered out with regiment, May 28, 1863, at Albany, N.Y.

GILCHRIST, JAMES—Age 24 years. Enlisted December 23, 1861, at Albany. Mustered in as private, Co. F, same date, to serve unexpired term of two years. Mustered out with company, May 28, 1863, at Albany, N.Y. Subsequent service in Co. C, 13th New York Heavy Artillery & Co. K, 6th New York Heavy Artillery.

GILCHRIST, JOHN—Age 18 years. Enlisted April 19, 1861, at Albany. Mustered in as private, Co. F, May 17, 1861, to serve two years. Mustered out with company, May 28, 1863, at Albany, N.Y. Subsequent service in Co. I, 7th New York Heavy Artillery.

GILL, LAWRENCE R.—Age 23 years. Enlisted April 22, 1861, at Schenectady. Mustered in as sergeant, Co. A, May 17, 1861, to serve two years. Promoted first sergeant, November 1, 1862. Mustered out with company, May 28, 1863, at Albany, N.Y. Subsequent service in Co. E, 1st Veteran Reserve Corps.

GILLAN, PATRICK—Age 29 years. Enlisted May 1, 1861, at Albany. Mustered in as private, Co. B, May 17, 1861, to serve two years. No further record.

GILLETT, CHARLES R., Jr.—Age 21 years. Enlisted April 30, 1861, at Middletown. Mustered in as private, Co. D, May 17, 1861, to serve two years. Hospitalized, July 22, 1861, at General Hospital, in Alexandria, Va. Transferred to hospital in Annapolis, Md. in July or August 1861. Retained as hospital attendant, January 3, 1862, at General Hospital, in Annapolis, Md. Returned to regiment, May 18, 1863. Mustered out with company, May 28, 1863, at Albany, N.Y.

GILLIGAN, EDWARD—Age 27 years. Enlisted May 2, 1861, at Albany. Mustered in as private, Co. F, May 17, 1861, to serve two years. Hospitalized, May 11, 1862, at Seminary Hospital, at Hampton, Va. Hospitalized, May 14, 1862, at Chesapeake General Hospital, in Fort Monroe, Va. Retained at hospital as nurse, November 1, 1862, to February 7, 1863, at Chesapeake General Hospital, in Fort Monroe, Va. Returned to regiment, on or about February 14, 1863. Mustered out with company, May 28, 1863, at Albany, N.Y. Subsequent service in Co. H, 64th New York Infantry.

GILLSON, GEHIEL—Age 26 years. Enlisted April 30, 1861, at Middletown. Mustered in as private, Co. D, May 17, 1861, to serve two years. Hospitalized, June 25, 1861, at E Street General Hospital, in Washington, D.C. Transferred, July 22, 1861, at General Hospital, in Annapolis, Md. Returned to regiment, August 10, 1861. Captured, June 27, 1862, at Gaines's Mill, Va. Confined, June 28, 1862, at Richmond, Va. Paroled, August 5, 1862, at City Point, Va. Mustered out with company, May 28,

1863, at Albany, N.Y. Subsequent service in Co. K, 142nd New York Infantry & Co. I, 169th New York Infantry.

GILMORE (Gilmour), JOSEPH (John)—Age 22 years. Enlisted May 2, 1861, at Albany. Mustered in as private, Co. B, May 17, 1861, to serve two years. Mustered out with company, May 28, 1863, at Albany, N.Y.

GIRVAN, JOHN—Age 27 years. Enlisted April 19, 1861, at Albany. Mustered in as private, Co. F, May 17, 1861, to serve two years. Mustered out with company, May 28, 1863, at Albany, N.Y.

GOLDEN, ALVAH, Jr.—Age 29 years. Enlisted April 19, 1861, at Albany. Mustered in as private, Co. F, May 17, 1861, to serve two years. Detached on western gunboat service in United States Navy aboard Gunboat *Benton* and Gunboat *Clara Dolsen*. Served in Navy until discharged, August 26, 1863, at Albany, N.Y.

GOODE, THOMAS—Age 27 years. Enlisted October 8, 1861, at Ogdensburg. Mustered in as private, Co. K, same date, to serve unexpired term of two years. Promoted corporal, November 1, 1862. Mustered out with company, May 28, 1863, at Albany, N.Y.

GOODNO, GEORGE NELSON—Age 41 years. Enlisted October 1, 1861, at Ogdensburg. Mustered in as sergeant, Co. K, same date, to serve unexpired term of two years. Detailed on recruiting service, December 1861 & January 1862, in Ogdensburg, N.Y. Hospitalized, July or August 1862, at Satterlee General Hospital, in West Philadelphia, Pa. Promoted second lieutenant, Co. B, October 24, 1862. Returned to regiment, December 23, 1862. Mustered out with company, May 28, 1863, at Albany, N.Y. Commissioned second lieutenant, January 22, 1863, with rank from October 24, 1862, after Norton resigned. Brother of Horatio G. Goodno & Uncle of George W. R. Goodno.

GOODNO, GEORGE WASHINGTON RINGOLD—Age 15 years. Enlisted November 1, 1861, at Alexandria, Va. Mustered in as drummer, Co. K, same date, to serve unexpired term of two years. Captured but escaped, June 27, 1862, at Gaines's Mill, Va. Hospitalized, July or August 1862. Deserted, January 25, 1863. Son of Horatio G. Goodno & Nephew of George N. Goodno.

GOODNO, HORATIO GATES—Age 50 years. Enrolled May 12, 1861, at Malone. Mustered in as second lieutenant, Co. K, May 17, 1861, to serve two years. Promoted first lieutenant, August 4, 1861. Detailed on recruiting service, October & November 1861. Wounded in mouth, captured but escaped, June 27, 1862, at Gaines's Mill, Va. Hospitalized, July 4, 1862, to Washington, D.C. Hospitalized at Douglas Hospital, in Washington, D.C. Placed on furlough, July 18, 1862, at Ogdensburg, N.Y. Returned to regiment, September 7, 1862. Hospitalized, September 10, 1862, in Washington, D.C. Promoted captain, October 1, 1862. Returned to regiment, October 26, 1862. Resigned, January 19, 1863, at Washington, D.C. Commissioned second lieutenant, July 4, 1861, with rank from May 12, 1861, original. First lieutenant, August 27, 1861, with rank from August 4, 1861, original. Captain, November 10, 1862, with rank from October 1, 1862, after Seely resigned. Father of George W. R. Goodno & Brother of George N. Goodno.

GOODRICH, ALLEN—Age 31 years. Enlisted April 19, 1861, at Albany. Mustered in as private, Co. F, May 17, 1861, to serve two years. Wounded in right shoulder, September 14, 1862, at Crampton's Gap, Md. Hospitalized, October 5, 1862, to Camp A General Hospital, in Frederick, Md. Died on account of such wounds and disease, December 11, 1862, at Camp A General Hospital, in Frederick, Md. Brother of Theodore Goodrich.

GOODRICH, THEODORE—Age 36 years. Enlisted May 12, 1861, at Albany. Mustered in as private, Co. F, May 17, 1861, to serve two years. Mustered out with company, May 28, 1863, at Albany, N.Y. Subsequent service in Co. L, 7th New York Heavy Artillery. Brother of Allen Goodrich.

GOULAY, JOHN—Age 20 years. Enlisted May 7, 1861, at Albany. Mustered in as private, Co. H, May 17, 1861, to serve two years. Mustered out with company, May 28, 1863, at Albany, N.Y. Subsequent service in Co. C, 13th New York Heavy Artillery & Co. K, 6th New York Heavy Artillery.

GOWAN, JOHN—Age 41 years. Enlisted May 12, 1861, at Ogdensburg. Mustered in as private, Co. K, May 17, 1861, to serve two years. Discharged for disability, July 8, 1861, at Washington, D.C. Died of disease, January 19, 1862, in Crysler, Ontario, Canada.

GRACE, JAMES—Age 26 years. Enlisted December 7, 1861, at Albany. Mustered in as private, Co. F, same date, to serve unexpired term of two years. No further record.

GRACEY, JOHN, Sr.—Age 43 years, but gave age as 42 years. Enlisted April 23, 1861, at Albany. Mustered in as private, Co. C, May 17, 1861, to serve two years. Detailed for detached duty, November 1861, with Division Quartermaster. Detailed for detached duty, December 1861–January 1862, as Brigade Wagon Master. Detailed for detached duty, July or August 1862–May 1863. Mustered out with regiment, May 28, 1863, at Albany, N.Y. Subsequent service in Co. F, 115th New York Infantry.

GRAHAM, PATRICK—Age 19 years. Enlisted April 23, 1861, at Fishkill. Mustered in as private, Co. C, May 17, 1861, to serve two years. Mustered out with company, May 28, 1863, at Albany, N.Y. Subsequent service in Co. "U" 15th New York Cavalry.

GRANT, ARTHUR MORRIS—Age 21 years. Traded to this regiment on June 24, 1861, from the 16th New York Infantry, swapped for David C. J. Russell. Mustered in as private, Co. K, to serve two years. Promoted sergeant, June 27, 1862. Mustered in as second lieutenant, December 9, 1862. Mustered out with company, May 28, 1863, at Albany, N.Y. Commissioned second lieutenant, November 10, 1862, with rank from June 27, 1862, after Tilley resigned. Brother of Ralph R. Grant.

GRANT, RALPH ROLLO—Age 19 years. Enlisted May 12, 1861, at Ogdensburg. Mustered in as corporal, Co. K, May 17, 1861, to serve two years. Reduced to private, August 12, 1861. Promoted corporal, November 13, 1861. Mustered out with company, May 28, 1863, at Albany, N.Y. Brother of Arthur M. Grant.

GRAVELINE, WILLIAM B.—Age 20 years. Enlisted June 17, 1861, at Albany. Mustered in as private, Co. A, same date, to serve two years. Discharged for disability, September 24, 1861, at Alexandria, Va. Subsequent service in Co. A, 25th New York Militia National Guard.

GRAVES, FRANCIS "Frank" STANLEY—Age 20 years. Enlisted June 17, 1861, at Albany. Mustered in as private, Co. A, same date, to serve two years. Promoted sergeant, November 1, 1862. Mustered out with company, May 28, 1863, at Albany, N.Y. Discharged, June 17, 1863, at Albany, N.Y.

GRAY, DAVID HENRY—Age 33 years. Enlisted May 12, 1861, at Ogdensburg. Mustered in as private, Co. K, May 17, 1861, to serve two years. Discharged for disability, August 8, 1861, at Alexandria, Va.

GREEN, ALPHONSO—Age 22 years. Enlisted May 2, 1861, at Schenectady. Mustered in as private, Co. E, May 17, 1861, to serve two years. Deserted, January 20, 1863. Returned to regiment, January 25, 1863. Absent-without-leave, January 20, 1863, from Camp Russell, White Oak Church, Falmouth, Va. Returned to regiment, January 24, 1863, same place. Court-martialed for absence and cowardice, February 21, 1863, at same place. Sent to Rip Raps, March 4, 1863. Arrived to Fort Jefferson, Dry Tortugas, Fl. on April 10, 1863. Released and dishonorably discharged, July 15, 1863.

GREEN, CLARK—Age 29 years. Enlisted August 28, 1862, at Albany. Mustered in as private, Co. E, same date, to serve three years. Transferred, May 10, 1863, to Co. H, 121st New York Infantry.

GREEN, GEORGE J.—Age 18 years. Enlisted May 17, 1861, at Albany. Mustered in as private, Co. C, same date, to serve two years. Promoted corporal, September 14, 1862. Mustered out with company, May 28, 1863, at Albany, N.Y.

GREEN, ISAAC SUTHERLAND—Age 31 years, but gave age as 26 years. Enlisted May 7, 1861, at Albany. Mustered in as private, Co. G, May 17, 1861, to serve two years. Promoted fife major for regiment, same date. Transferred, promoted, and mustered in as first lieutenant, Co. G, September 30, 1861. Appointed Signal Officer, December 26, 1861. Resigned, August 8, 1862. Commissioned first lieutenant, November 2, 1861, with rank from September 30, 1861, after Morgan resigned. Subsequent service in Co. F & B, 16th New York Heavy Artillery.

GREEN, SAMUEL—Age 23 years. Enlisted April 23, 1861, at Albany. Mustered in as private, Co. C, May 17, 1861, to serve two years. Promoted corporal, date not stated. Hospitalized, September or October 1862, at Hagerstown, Md. Died of disease, November 1, 1862, at Hammond General Hospital, in Hagerstown, Md.

GREEN, WILLIAM R.—Age 35 years. Enlisted April 23, 1861, at Fishkill. Mustered in as corporal, Co. C, May 17, 1861, to serve two years. Promoted first sergeant, date not stated. Hospitalized and retained as nurse, September 23, 1862, at Harewood General Hospital, in Washington, D.C. Transferred, November or December 1862, at Brooklyn City Hospital, in Brooklyn, N.Y. Reduced to private, December 1, 1862. Hospitalized, March 1863, at General Hospital, in Brooklyn, N.Y. Deserted, date not stated. Arrested, March 21, 1863, and confined at Fort Columbus, N.Y. Forwarded, April 2, 1863, to Washington, D.C. Mustered out with company, May 28, 1863, at Albany, N.Y.

GREGORY, ORVILLE—Age 23 years. Enlisted April 22, 1861, at Schenectady. Mustered in as private, Co. A, May 17, 1861, to serve two years. Wounded in left arm, June 27, 1862, at Gaines's Mill, Va. Sent off, July 2, 1862, from Harrison's Landing, Va. Hospitalized, July 4, 1862, at Carver General Hospital, in Washington, D.C. Hospitalized, September or October 1862, at David's Island General Hospital, in New York Harbor, N.Y. Retained as guard, January 1, 1863, at David's Island General Hospital, in New York Harbor, N.Y. Returned to regiment, May 16, 1863, at Albany, N.Y. Mustered out with company, May 28, 1863, at Albany, N.Y. Subsequent service in Co. "U" 16th New York Heavy Artillery.

GREWELL, JOHN H.—Age 22 years. Enlisted May 17, 1861, at Albany. Mustered in as private, Co. C, same date, to serve two years. No further record since the regiment left Albany, June 18, 1861. Also born as John R. Grewell.

GRIDLEY, JOSEPH WALTER—Age 16 years, but gave age as 18 years. Enlisted May 1, 1861, at Schenectady. Mustered in as private, Co. A, May 17, 1861, to serve two years. Promoted corporal, September 1, 1861. Captured, June 27, 1862, at Gaines's Mill, Va. Confined, June 28, 1862, at Richmond, Va. Paroled, August 5, 1862, at City Point, Va. Mustered out with company, May 28, 1863, at Albany, N.Y. Subsequent service in Co. H, 19th Maine Infantry, Co. H, 1st Maine Heavy Artillery & the United States Marine Corps (post war). First Cousin of Nathaniel P. T. Gridley & William S. Gridley.

GRIDLEY, NATHANIEL (Nate) (Nathan) PETER TALMATE—Age 19 years. Enlisted April 22, 1861, at Schenectady. Mustered in as private, Co. A, May 17, 1861, to serve two years. Killed, June 27, 1862, at Gaines's Mill, Va. Brother of William S. Gridley & First Cousin of Joseph W. Gridley.

GRIDLEY, WILLIAM SEWARD—Age 22 years. Enrolled April 22, 1861, at Schenectady. Mustered in as captain, Co. A, May 17, 1861, to serve two years. On furlough, January 1862, in Schenectady, N.Y. Promoted major, August 14, 1862. On ten day furlough, about March 2, 1863, in Schenectady, N.Y. Returned to regiment, about March 13, 1863. Mustered out with regiment, May 28, 1863, at Albany, N.Y. Commissioned captain, July 4, 1861, with rank from April 22, 1861, original. Commissioned major, October 11, 1862, with rank from August 14, 1862, after Meginnis was promoted. Brother of Nathaniel P. T. Gridley & First Cousin of Joseph W. Gridley.

GRIEPE, HARMON—Age 23 years. Enlisted April 29, 1861, at Schenectady. Mustered in as private, Co. A, May 17, 1861, to serve two years. Court-martialed at regimental level, September or October 1861. Hospitalized, May or June 1862. Captured, June 29, 1862, while sick at Savage's Station, Va. Died of disease, June 30, 1862, at Savage's Station, Va.

GRIFFIN, DENNIS—Age 26 years. Enlisted May 15, 1861, at Albany. Mustered in as private, Co. F, May

17, 1861, to serve two years. Deserted, September 7, 1861, at Alexandria, Va.

GRIFFIN, PATRICK—Age 18 years. Enlisted May 16, 1861, at Albany. Mustered in as private, Co. B, May 17, 1861, to serve two years. Discharged, May 23, 1861, by writ of Habeas Corpus, at Albany, N.Y.

GROAT (Groot), JOHN—Age 22 years. Enlisted April 22, 1861, at Schenectady. Mustered in as private, Co. A, May 17, 1861, to serve two years. Wounded in right leg, June 27, 1862, at Gaines's Mill, Va. Captured, June 30, 1862, at Chickahominy River, near Richmond, Va. Confined, July 13, 1862, Richmond, Va. Paroled, July 27, 1862, at City Point, Va. Hospitalized, July 30, 1862, to Chesapeake General Hospital, at Fort Monroe, Va. Mustered out with company, May 28, 1863, at Albany, N.Y.

GROFFMAN (Gruffman), ERNEST "Ernie" (Aaron)—Age 22 years. Enlisted May 2, 1861, at Schenectady. Mustered in as private, Co. E, May 17, 1861, to serve two years. Detailed on recruiting service, January 21, 1862. Deserted and captured, December 13, 1862, at Fredericksburg, Va. Paroled, December 17, 1862, at Fredericksburg, Va. No further record.

GROOM, AMOS, Jr.—Age 23 years. Enlisted May 7, 1861, at Albany. Mustered in as private, Co. G, May 17, 1861, to serve two years. Sent sick, August 10, 1862, from Harrison's Landing, Va., to be hospitalized at Satterlee General Hospital, in West Philadelphia, Pa. Returned to regiment, May 2, 1863. Mustered out with company, May 28, 1863, at Albany, N.Y.

GROOT, EDWARD W.—Age 19 years. Enrolled April 22, 1861, at Schenectady. Mustered in as second lieutenant, Co. A, May 17, 1861, to serve two years. Wounded in left hand, July 17, 1861, near Fairfax Court House, Va. Discharged for disability, December 14, 1861. Commissioned second lieutenant, July 4, 1861, with rank from April 22, 1861, original. Subsequent service in 134th New York Infantry.

GUNDERMAN, JAMES E.—Age 21 years. Enlisted May 7, 1861, at Albany. Mustered in as private, Co. G, May 17, 1861, to serve two years. Promoted corporal, date not stated. Mustered out with company, May 28, 1863, at Albany, N.Y. Subsequent service in Co. M, 1st New Jersey Cavalry.

GUYER, JAMES—Age 25 years. Enlisted May 7, 1861, at Albany. Mustered in as private, Co. H, May 17, 1861, to serve two years. Promoted corporal, date not stated. Wounded slightly in breast, June 27, 1862, at Gaines's Mill, Va. Mustered out with company, May 28, 1863, at Albany, N.Y.

GUYETTE, EDWARD—Age 21 years. Enlisted May 12, 1861, at Ogdensburg. Mustered in as corporal, Co. K, May 17, 1861, to serve two years. Mustered out with company, May 28, 1863, at Albany, N.Y.

HABERMYER, URIC (Ulrich)—Age 26 years. Enlisted April 30, 1861, at Middletown. Mustered in as private, Co. D, May 17, 1861, to serve two years. Wounded slightly in face, June 27, 1862, at Gaines's Mill, Va. Mustered out with company, May 28, 1863, at Albany, N.Y. Subsequent service in Co. G, 15th New York Heavy Artillery.

HADDEN, WILLIAM J.—Age 24 years. Enlisted April 23, 1861, at Albany. Mustered in as private, Co. C, May 17, 1861, to serve two years. Promoted corporal, same date. Promoted sergeant, in May 1862. Mustered out with company, May 28, 1863, at Albany, N.Y.

HAGERMAN, JOHN, Sr.—Age 29 years. Enlisted April 24, 1861, at Albany. Mustered in as private, Co. B, May 17, 1861, to serve two years. Wounded in right side of groin, June 27, 1862, at Gaines's Mill, Va. Captured, June 29, 1862, at Savage's Station, Va. Confined at Richmond, Va. Paroled, July 27, 1862, at City Point, Va. Hospitalized, July 30, 1862, to Chesapeake General Hospital, at Fort Monroe, Va. Transferred, August 24, 1862, to hospital in Annapolis, Md. Transferred, September 25, 1862, to hospital in Washington, D.C. Mustered out with company, May 28, 1863, at Albany, N.Y.

HALE, WINFIELD SCOTT—Age 15 years, but gave age as 18 years. Enlisted October 9, 1861, at Ogdensburg. Mustered in as private, Co. K, same date, to serve unexpired term of two years. Mustered out with company, May 28, 1863, at Albany, N.Y.

HALL, ISAAC F.—Age—years. Enlisted May 17, 1861, at Albany. Mustered in as sergeant, Co. F, same date, to serve two years. Killed, June 27, 1862, at Gaines's Mill, Va.

HALL, WILLIAM H.—Age 27 years. Enlisted November 2, 1861, at Albany. Mustered in as private, Co. F, same date, to serve unexpired term of two years. Mustered out with company, May 28, 1863, at Albany, N.Y. Subsequent service in Co. I, 91st New York Infantry. Son-in-law of Joshua Pangburn.

HAMILTON, GEORGE—Age 26 years. Enlisted October 15, 1861, at Ogdensburg. Mustered in as private, Co. K, same date, to serve unexpired term of two years. Discharged for disability, January 3, 1863, at White Oak Church, Falmouth, Va.

HAMILTON, SAMUEL—Age 21 years. Enlisted April 30, 1861, at Middletown. Mustered in as private, Co. H, May 17, 1861, to serve two years. Mustered out with company, May 28, 1863, at Albany, N.Y. Subsequent service in Co. K, 15th New York Cavalry & Co. K, 2nd New York Provisional Cavalry.

HANFORD, AUGUSTUS EMMET—Age 19 years. Enlisted April 30, 1861, at Middletown. Mustered in as corporal, Co. D, May 17, 1861, to serve two years. Promoted sergeant, October 12, 1861. Mustered out with company, May 28, 1863, at Albany, N.Y. First Cousin of Edward M. Hanford.

HANFORD, EDWARD M.—Age 20 years. Enlisted April 30, 1861, at Middletown. Mustered in as private, Co. D, May 17, 1861, to serve two years. Sent sick, May 7, 1862, from Brick House Landing (West Point), Va. to New York City, N.Y. Returned to regiment, August 7, 1862. Mustered out with company, May 28, 1863, at Albany, N.Y. Subsequent service in Co. "U" 7th New York Heavy Artillery. First Cousin of Augustus E. Hanford.

HANLEY, MICHAEL—Age 38 years. Enlisted April 22, 1861, at Schenectady. Mustered in as private, Co. A, May 17, 1861, to serve two years. Mustered out with company, May 28, 1863, at Albany, N.Y. Subsequent service in Co. H, 16th New York Heavy Artillery.

Pvt. Edward M. Hanford, Company D, survived two enlistments, and died on November 10, 1890, at the age of fifty (courtesy Mary Helen Crans Lockwood album, family collection).

HANNA, RICHARD L.—Age 33 years. Enlisted December 14, 1861, at Albany. Mustered in as private, Co. C, same date, to serve unexpired term of two years. Discharged for disability, May 19, 1862, at Alexandria, Va.

HARDEN (Hardin), JOHN—Age about 52 years, but gave age as 43. Enlisted October 14, 1861, at Ogdensburg. Not mustered in. Deserted, October 16, 1861, at Watertown, N.Y. Reported, June 26, 1863, to Fort Columbus, N.Y. Discharged July 4, 1863, at Fort Columbus, N.Y.

HARDICK, STEPHEN—Age 18 years. Enlisted March 4, 1862, at Port Jervis. Mustered in as private, Co. B, same date, to serve unexpired term of two years. Discharged for disability, March 12, 1863, at White Oak Church, Falmouth, Va. Died of disease, March 20, 1863, at Washington, D.C.

HARDING, ELISHA C.—Age 46 years, but gave age as 40 years. Enlisted February 26, 1862, at Port Jervis. Mustered in as private, Co. B, same date, to serve unexpired term of two years. Discharged for disability, May 26, 1862, at Mechanicsville, Va.

HARE, ADAM—Age 23 years. Enlisted November 30, 1861, at Albany. Mustered in as private, Co. F, same date, to serve unexpired term of two years. Captured, June 27, 1862, at Gaines's Mill, Va. Confined, June 28, 1862, at Richmond, Va. Paroled, August 5, 1862, at City Point, Va. Wounded in right leg, September 14, 1862, at Crampton's Gap, Md. Hospitalized, October 3, 1862, at Camp A General Hospital, in Frederick, Md. Returned to regiment, February 17, 1863. Mustered out with company, May 28, 1863, at Albany, N.Y.

HARGREAVE, JAMES—Age—years. Enlisted April 30, 1861, at Middletown. Mustered in as private, Co. D, term of service or muster-in not stated. No further record.

HARKNESS, JOHN—Age 21 years. Enlisted April 19, 1861, at Albany. Mustered in as private, Co. F, May 17, 1861, to serve two years. Promoted corporal, September 19, 1861. Wounded in right arm, June 27, 1862, at Gaines's Mill, Va. Promoted sergeant, July 1, 1862. Hospitalized, November 1, 1862, at Harewood General Hospital, in Washington, D.C. Discharged, November 6, 1862, at Washington, D.C., by reason of enlistment in Regular Army, in Co. C, 5th United States Cavalry.

HARMAN, GUILFORD "Gill" D.—Age 19 years. Enlisted May 2, 1861, at Schenectady. Mustered in as private, Co. E, May 17, 1861, to serve two years. Mustered out with company, May 28, 1863, at Albany, N.Y.

HARPER, WILLIAM H.—Age 30 years. Enlisted May 17, 1861, at Albany. Mustered in as private, Co. E, same date, to serve two years. Promoted corporal, October 11, 1861. Served as corporal of color guard. Mustered out with company, May 28, 1863, at Albany, N.Y.

HARRIGAN, JOHN—Age 21 years. Enlisted April 24, 1861, at Albany. Mustered in as private, Co. B, May 17, 1861, to serve two years. Mustered out with company, May 28, 1863, at Albany, N.Y.

HARRIGAN, THOMAS—Age 22 years. Enlisted April 19, 1861, at Albany. Mustered in as private, Co. I, May 17, 1861, to serve two years. Promoted corporal, March 1, 1862. Hospitalized, August 10, 1862, at Satterlee General Hospital, in West Philadelphia, Pa. Returned to regiment, January 10, 1863. Mustered out with company, May 28, 1863, at Albany, N.Y. Subsequent service in Co. I, 93rd New York Infantry.

HARRIGAN, WILLIAM—Age 35 years. Enlisted August 21, 1862, at Albany. Mustered in as private, Co. C, September 26, 1862, to serve three years. Transferred, May 10, 1863, to Co. K, 121st New York Infantry.

HARRINGTON, ABLE J.—Age 28 years. Enlisted May 2, 1861, at Schenectady. Mustered in as private, Co. E, May 17, 1861, to serve two years. Mustered out with company, May 28, 1863, at Albany, N.Y.

HARRINGTON, JEREMIAH "Jerry"—Age 24 years. Enlisted May 12, 1861, at Ogdensburg. Mustered in as private, Co. K, May 17, 1861, to serve two years. Promoted corporal, November 13, 1861. Promoted sergeant, December 25, 1862. Mustered out with company, May 28, 1863, at Albany, N.Y. Subsequent service in Co. A, 16th New York Light Artillery, Co. M, 1st New York Mounted Rifles & Co. M, 4th New York Provisional Cavalry.

HARRIS, DAVID—Age 17 years, but gave age as 18 years. Enlisted May 12, 1861, at Ogdensburg. Mustered in as private, Co. K, May 17, 1861, to serve two years. Discharged for disability, March 22, 1862, at Camp Jackson, Alexandria, Va. Re-enlisted September 30, 1862, at Ogdensburg. Mustered in as private, Co. K, October 13, 1862, at Albany, to serve three years. Transferred, May 10, 1863, to Co. A, 121st New York Infantry & Co. L, 26th New York Cavalry.

HARRIS, WILLIAM HENRY—Age 18 years. Enlisted May 2, 1861, at Schenectady. Mustered in as private, Co. E, May 17, 1861, to serve two years. Promoted corporal, October 11, 1861. Captured, June 29, 1862, while sick at Savage's Station, Va. Confined, July 1, 1862, at Libby Prison, Richmond, Va. Paroled, August 5, 1862, at City Point, Va. Hospitalized, August 1862, at David's Island General Hospital, in New York Harbor, N.Y. Never reported to hospital and listed as deserted. Arrested, date not stated. Confined, date not stated, at Fort Columbus, N.Y. Mustered out, August 28, 1863, at Albany, N.Y.

HART, JOHN—Age 55 years, but gave age as 30 years. Enlisted April 22, 1861, at Schenectady. Mustered in as private, Co. A, May 17, 1861, to serve two years. Mustered out with company, May 28, 1863, at Albany, N.Y.

HASKIN, JOEL—Age 28 years. Enlisted October 15, 1861, at Ogdensburg. Mustered in as private, Co. K, October 30, 1861, at Camp Williams, Va., to serve two years. Mustered out with company, May 28, 1863, at Albany, N.Y.

HASLAM, WILLIAM H.—Age 19 years. Enlisted May 19, 1861, at Albany. Mustered in as private, Co. A, same date, to serve two years. Hospitalized, November & December 1861, at Alexandria, Va. Wounded in right shoulder, June 27, 1862, at Gaines's Mill, Va. Aboard Steamer *Daniel Webster* and hospitalized, July 7, 1862, at Catharine Street General Hospital, in Philadelphia, Pa. Discharged on account of such wounds, January 28, 1863, from Catharine Street General Hospital, in Philadelphia, Pa.

HASTINGS, JOHN "Captain Jack"—Age 36 years. Enrolled April 24, 1861, at Albany. Mustered in as captain, Co. B, May 17, 1861, to serve two years. Furlough to Albany for pulmonary hemorrhage, on or about October 18, 1861, from Camp King, Alexandria, Va. Returned to regiment, November 18, 1861. Mustered out, to date, September 8, 1862, to accept promotion as lieutenant colonel of 113th New York Infantry. Commissioned captain, July 4, 1861, with rank from April 24, 1861, original. The 113th New York Infantry became the 7th New York Heavy Artillery.

HATCH, FREDERICK PERRY—Age 22 years. Enlisted May 7, 1861, at Albany. Mustered in as private, Co. G, May 17, 1861, to serve two years. Hospitalized, August 1861, in Alexandria, Va. Mustered out with company, May 28, 1863, at Albany, N.Y.

HAVENS, WILLIAM S.—Age 21 years. Enlisted May 12, 1861, at Ogdensburg. Mustered in as private, Co. K, May 17, 1861, to serve two years. Hospitalized, November 1862, at Harewood General Hospital, in Washington, D.C. Transferred, date not stated, to General Hospital, in Portsmouth Grove, R. I. Returned to regiment, February 5, 1863. Mustered out with company, May 28, 1863, at Albany, N.Y. Subsequent service in Co. A, 14th New York Heavy Artillery.

HAWLEY, EDMUND BURKE—Age 21 years. Enlisted April 22, 1861, at Schenectady. Mustered in as musician, Co. A, May 17, 1861, to serve two years. Promoted corporal, May 17, 1861. Killed, September 14, 1862, at Crampton's Gap, Md.

HAYDEN, HENRY—Age 18 years. Enlisted April 30, 1861, at Middletown. Mustered in as private, Co. D, May 17, 1861, to serve two years. Captured, August 29, 1861, at Bailey's Crossroads, Va. Confined, September 7, 1861, at Richmond, Va. Relocated, September 25, 1861, to New Orleans, La. Paroled, May 28, 1862, at Salisbury, N.C. Sent to Washington, D.C., on September 27, 1862. Released, October 10, 1862, for thirty-day furlough. Returned to regiment, November 7, 1862. Mustered out with company, May 28, 1863, at Albany, N.Y. Subsequent service in Co. G & D, 7th New York Heavy Artillery.

HAYTHORNE, MAURICE E.—Age 18 years. Enlisted April 23, 1861, at Fishkill. Mustered in as private, Co. C, May 17, 1861, to serve two years. Killed, September 14, 1862, at Crampton's Gap, Md.

HEALD, CHARLES WESLEY—Age 42 years. Enrolled April 20, 1861, at Albany. Mustered in as second lieutenant, Co. I, May 17, 1861, to serve two years. Resigned, November 5, 1861. Commissioned second lieutenant, July 4, 1861, with rank from April 20, 1861, original. Subsequent service in 11th Independent Battery New York (Veteran) Light Artillery & Co. F, 2nd New York Heavy Artillery.

HEALY, JAMES—Age 22 years. Enlisted May 17, 1861, at Albany. Mustered in as private, Co. C, same date, to serve two years. Court-martialed at regimental level for absence without leave, September or October 1861. Deserted, August 24, 1862, from camp at Alexandria, Va.

HECK, SAMUEL—Age 15 years, but gave age as 19 years. Enlisted May 25, 1861, at Albany. Mustered in as private, Co. K, same date, to serve two years. Mustered out with company, May 28, 1863, at Albany, N.Y.

HEINTZ, JACOB—Age 35 years. Enlisted, August 22, 1862, at Albany. Mustered in as private, Co. C, same date, to serve three years. Transferred, May 10, 1863, to Co. H, 121st New York Infantry.

HELMS, CHARLES V.—Age 19 years. Enlisted April 30, 1861, at Middletown. Mustered in as private, Co. H, May 17, 1861, to serve two years. Hospitalized, August 10, 1862, at Fairfax Seminary General Hospital, in Alexandria, Va. Transferred, September 5, 1862, to General Hospital, in Newark, N.J. Returned to duty, October 23, 1862, but detailed as nurse at General Hospital, in Newark, N.J. Deserted, November 1, 1862, from General Hospital, in Newark, N.J. Enlisted, November 1, 1862, to the 176th New York Infantry, at Wallkill. Deserted, December 21, 1862, from the 176th. Arrested, August 27, 1863, at Southfields, N.Y., as a deserter. Transferred, same date, to Fort Columbus, New York Harbor, N.Y. Transferred, September 5, 1863, to Washington, D.C. No further record.

HENNESSY, DAVID—Age 23 years. Enlisted May 7, 1861, at Albany. Mustered in as private, Co. I, May 17, 1861, to serve two years. Hospitalized, July or August 1862, at Satterlee General Hospital, in West Philadelphia, Pa. Returned to regiment, September 12, 1862. Mustered out with company, May 28, 1863, at Albany, N.Y.

HENNESSY, RICHARD—Age 19 years. Enlisted May 17, 1861, at Albany. Mustered in as private, Co. B, same date, to serve two years. Killed, September 14, 1862, at Crampton's Gap, Md.

HENRY, JAMES—Age 22 years. Enlisted April 30,

1861, at Middletown. Mustered in as private, Co. H, May 17, 1861, to serve two years. Mustered out with company, May 28, 1863, at Albany, N.Y. Subsequent service in Co. B, 16th New York Heavy Artillery.

HENYON, PETER B.—Age 43 years. Enlisted April 30, 1861, at Middletown. Mustered in as sergeant, Co. H, May 17, 1861, to serve two years. Deserted, June 9, 1861, at Albany Barracks, Albany, N.Y. Arrested, March 31, 1864, at Goshen, N.Y. Sent, April 14, 1864, to Fort Columbus, N.Y.

HERBERT, JOHN—Age 51 years, but gave age as 35 years. Enlisted May 2, 1861, at Albany. Mustered in as private, Co. F, May 17, 1861, to serve two years. Discharged for disability, March 31, 1862, at Camp Jackson, Alexandria, Va.

HEUSTIS, NICHOLAS—Age 24 years. Enlisted May 17, 1861, at Albany. Mustered in as private, Co. C, same date, to serve two years. Deserted, May or June 1861, before regiment left Albany, N.Y.

HEWITT, DAVID FOSTER—Age 19 years. Enlisted April 19, 1861, at Albany. Mustered in as corporal, Co. I, May 17, 1861, to serve two years. Promoted sergeant, February 8, 1862. Hospitalized for sickness, September 10, 1862, at Union Hotel General Hospital, at Georgetown, Washington, D.C. Returned to duty, October 6, 1862. Discharged for disability, November 13, 1862, at Convalescent Camp, Alexandria, Va. Subsequent service in the United States Navy on the USS *Vermont*, *A.D. Vance*, *Baltic*, *Estrella* & *Ft. Donelson*.

HICKEY, JOHN—Age 23 years. Enlisted May 17, 1861, at Albany. Mustered in as private, Co. A, same date, to serve two years. Deserted, August 4, 1861, from Camp Myers, Alexandria, Va.

HIPP, HENRY—Age 22 years. Enlisted April 26, 1861, at Schenectady. Mustered in as private, Co. A, May 17, 1861, to serve two years. Court-martialed at regimental level, September or October 1861. Deserted, November 24, 1861, from Camp King, Alexandria, Va.

HODGKINS, SAMUEL—Age 21 years. Enlisted May 12, 1861, at Ogdensburg. Mustered in as private, Co. K, May 17, 1861, to serve two years. Sent sick, August 7, 1862, onboard Steamer *State of Maine* at Harrison's Landing, Va. Hospitalized, August 1862, at Satterlee General Hospital, in West Philadelphia, Pa. Returned to regiment, November 10, 1862, at New Baltimore, Va. Mustered out with company, May 28, 1863, at Albany, N.Y. Subsequent service in Co. C, 14th New York Heavy Artillery.

HOEY, JOHN J.—Age 18 years. Enlisted April 19, 1861, at Albany. Mustered in as private, Co. F, May 17, 1861, to serve two years. Court-martialed at regimental level, October 17, 1861. Court-martialed for disobedience, March 7, 1862, at Alexandria, Va. Mustered out with company, May 28, 1863, at Albany, N.Y.

HOFFMAN, GEORGE ADAM—Age 21 years. Enlisted May 2, 1861, at Schenectady. Mustered in as private, Co. E, May 17, 1861, to serve two years. Mustered out with company, May 28, 1863, at Albany, N.Y. Subsequent service in Co. F & D, 13th New York Heavy Artillery & Co. L, 6th New York Heavy Artillery.

HOGAN, PETER—Age 33 years. Enrolled May 7, 1861, at Albany. Mustered in as captain, Co. H, May 17, 1861, to serve two years. Resigned, November 6, 1861. Commissioned captain, July 4, 1861, with rank from May 7, 1861, original.

HOGEBOOM, STEPHEN—Age 40 years. Enlisted May 8, 1861, at Albany. Mustered in as private, Co. I, May 17, 1861, to serve two years. Hospitalized, September 21, 1861, at Seminary General Hospital, at Washington, D.C. Discharged for disability, September 22, 1861, at Alexandria, Va. Died of disease, October 16, 1861, at Washington, D.C.

HOLD, ANTHONY—Age about 40 years, but gave age as 34 years. Enlisted April 26, 1861, at Schenectady. Mustered in as private, Co. A, May 17, 1861, to serve two years. Hospitalized, May 11, 1862, at Seminary Hospital, at Hampton, Va. Sent sick, on or about May 24, 1862, from White House Landing, Va., to New York. Returned to regiment, date not stated. Hospitalized, October 28, 1862, in hospital, at Alexandria, Va. Hospitalized, November or December 1862, at General Hospital, in Fort Schuyler, New York Harbor, N.Y. Returned to duty, January 14, 1863. Hospitalized, January or February 1863, at 2nd Division General Hospital, in Alexandria, Va. Transferred, March 27, 1863, to Central Park General Hospital, in New York City. Returned to regiment, May 28, 1863. Mustered out with company, May 28, 1863, at Albany, N.Y.

HOLDEN, THOMAS M.—Age 26 years. Enlisted April 19, 1861, at Albany, to serve two years, as first sergeant, Co. F. Mustered in as sergeant-major, May 17, 1861. Promoted second lieutenant, Co. C, November 1, 1861. Court-martialed for absent-without-leave, neglect of duty, and breach of arrest, March 25, 1862, at Alexandria, Va. Deserted, March 27, 1862. Dismissed, July 22, 1862, by order of the Secretary of War. Commissioned second lieutenant, December 2, 1861, with rank from October 9, 1861, after Leith resigned.

HOLLY, RICHARD ALLISON, Jr.—Age 20 years. Enlisted April 30, 1861, at Middletown. Mustered in as sergeant, Co. D, May 17, 1861, to serve two years. Promoted first sergeant, December 9, 1862. Mustered out with company, May 28, 1863, at Albany, N.Y. Second Cousin of Lewis R. McCoy & William B. McCoy.

HOMAN, GEORGE EDGAR—Age 19 years. Enlisted May 17, 1861, at Albany. Mustered in as private, Co. H, same date, to serve two years. Killed, June 27, 1862, at Gaines's Mill, Va.

HOOPER, JOHN—Age 19 years. Enlisted April 19, 1861, at Albany. Mustered in as private, Co. I, May 17, 1861, to serve two years. Wounded slightly in head, June 27, 1862, at Gaines's Mill, Va. Mustered out with company, May 28, 1863, at Albany, N.Y. Subsequent service in Co. C, 18th New York Cavalry.

HORSFALL, WILLIAM "Billy"—Age 45 years. Enrolled May 2, 1861, at Schenectady. Mustered in as first lieutenant, Co. E, May 17, 1861, to serve two years. Promoted captain, December 27, 1861. On seven day furlough, January 17, 1862, in Schenectady, N.Y. Returned to regiment, January 24, 1862. Killed, September 14,

First Sgt. Richard A. Holly, Jr., Company D, moved to Scranton, Pennsylvania, after the war. He was a member of GAR Post 139, and died on Feb. 11, 1921 (United States Army Heritage and Education Center, Carlisle, Pennsylvania).

1862, at Crampton's Gap, Md. Commissioned first lieutenant, July 4, 1861, with rank from May 2, 1861, original. Captain, January 3, 1862, with rank from December 27, 1861, after Truax was promoted.

HORSFALL, WILLIAM VAN VRANKEN—Age 37 years. Enrolled May 14, 1861, at Albany. Mustered in as regimental quartermaster, May 17, 1861, to serve two years. Resigned, September 16, 1861. Commissioned quartermaster, July 4, 1861, with rank from May 14, 1861, original.

HORTON, JAMES H.—Age 23 years. Enlisted May 12, 1861, at Ogdensburg. Mustered in as private, Co. K, May 17, 1861, to serve two years. Captured, June 27, 1862, at Gaines's Mill, Va. Confined, June 28, 1862, at Richmond, Va. Paroled, August 5, 1862, at City Point, Va. Wounded slightly, September 14, 1862, at Crampton's Gap. Detached as nurse, September 16, 1862, by order of General McClellan. Hospitalized, January or February 1863, at Jarvis General Hospital, in Baltimore, Md. Returned to regiment, May 19, 1863, at Albany, N.Y. Mustered out with company, May 28, 1863, at Albany, N.Y.

HORTON, WALTER M.—Age 22 years. Enlisted April 23, 1861, at Albany. Mustered in as private, Co. C, May 17, 1861, to serve two years. Deserted, October 31, 1862, from camp at Crampton's Gap, Md.

HOTALING, LEONARD—Age 29 years. Enlisted May 7, 1861, at Albany. Mustered in as private, Co. H, May 17, 1861, to serve two years. Discharged, June 18, 1861, by writ of Habeas Corpus, at Albany, N.Y. Subsequent service in Co. F, 14th New York Heavy Artillery.

HOTCHKISS, ALBERT—Age 45 years, but gave age as 44 years. Enlisted May 7, 1861, at Canandaigua. Mustered in as private, Co. G, May 17, 1861, to serve two years. Sick, remained at home, Bristol, N.Y. when regiment left state. Discharged for disability, August 25, 1861. Brother-in-law of Charles Orson Ingraham.

HOUGHKIRK, WILLIAM H.—Age 21 years. Enlisted April 19, 1861, at Albany. Mustered in as private, Co. I, May 17, 1861, to serve two years. Hospitalized, July or August 1862, at Satterlee General Hospital, in West Philadelphia, Pa. Returned to regiment, May 8, 1863. Mustered out with company, May 28, 1863, at Albany, N.Y. Subsequent service in Co. D & H, 7th New York Heavy Artillery.

HOUGHTALING (Hotaling), CORNELIUS—Age 14 years, but gave age as 18 years. Enlisted April 24, 1861, at Albany. Mustered in as private, Co. B, May 17, 1861, to serve two years. Mustered out with company, May 28, 1863, at Albany, N.Y. Subsequent service in Co. "U" 14th New York Heavy Artillery, Co. H, 13th New York Heavy Artillery & Co. L, 6th New York Heavy Artillery.

HOUGHTALING, JOHN H.—Age 36 years. Enlisted December 20, 1861, at Albany. Mustered in as private, Co. F, same date, to serve unexpired term of two years. Rejected, December 31, 1861, at Camp King, Alexandria, Va. Subsequent service in Co. F, 91st New York Infantry.

HOUSE, GEORGE—Age 21 years. Enlisted June 14, 1861, at Albany. Mustered in as private, Co. D, same date, to serve two years. Captured, August 29, 1861, at Bailey's Crossroads, Va. Confined, September 7, 1861, at Richmond, Va. Relocated, September 25, 1861, to New Orleans, La. Paroled, May 28, 1862, at Salisbury, N.C. Arrived to New York, June 9, 1862, aboard Steamer *Guide*. Sent to Washington, D.C., on September 27, 1862. Released, October 8, 1862, for thirty-day furlough. Returned to regiment, November 7, 1862. Mustered out, June 15, 1863. Subsequent service in the United States Navy.

HOWARD, FRANCIS W. (Thomas F. Quigley)—Age 28 years. Enlisted April 19, 1861, at Albany. Mustered in as private, Co. F, May 17, 1861, to serve two years. Promoted corporal, July 1, 1862. Deserted, August 18, 1862, at Newport News, Va.

HOWD, SAMUEL—Age 24 years. Enlisted May 2, 1861, at Schenectady. Mustered in as private, Co. E, May 17, 1861, to serve two years. Detailed as brigade butcher. Mustered out with company, May 28, 1863, at Albany, N.Y. Subsequent service in Co. E, 16th New York Heavy Artillery.

HOYT, FRANK (Frances) C.—Age 21 years. Enlisted September 18, 1862, at Albany. Mustered in as private, Co. D, October 13, 1862, to serve three years. Detailed as teamster, March 6, 1863. Transferred, May 10, 1863, to Co. H, 121st New York Infantry.

HOYT, GEORGE MILFORD—Age 22 years. Enlisted April 22, 1861, at Albany. Mustered in as private, Co. I, May 17, 1861, to serve two years. Hospitalized, July 10, 1862, at 4th & George Streets General Hospital, in Philadelphia, Pa. Transferred, October or November 1862, at Satterlee General Hospital, in West Philadel-

Pvt. Samuel Howd left his job as a butcher and joined Company A on May 2, 1861. He was soon after detailed as the brigade butcher (courtesy New York State Military Museum).

phia, Pa. Returned to regiment, May 2, 1863. Mustered out with company, May 28, 1863, at Albany, N.Y. Subsequent service in Co. K, 46th New York Infantry.

HOYT, HEZEKIAH W.—Age 17 years, but gave age as 18 years. Enlisted October 14, 1862, at Wallkill. Mustered in as private, Co. D, October 25, 1862, to serve three years. Transferred, May 10, 1863, to Co. F, 121st New York Infantry. Brother of Isaac Hoyt.

HOYT, ISAAC—Age 18 years. Enlisted April 30, 1861, at Middletown. Mustered in as sergeant, Co. D, May 17, 1861, to serve two years. Detailed on recruiting service, September & October 1861. Detailed in Ambulance Corps, November 1862. Reduced to private, May 31, 1862. Promoted corporal, July 1, 1862. Mustered out with company, May 28, 1863, at Albany, N.Y. Brother of Hezekiah W. Hoyt.

HULLIGAN, MICHAEL—Age 21 years. Enlisted May 12, 1861, at Ogdensburg. Mustered in as sergeant, Co. K, May 17, 1861, to serve two years. Detailed on recruiting service, August 13, 1862, in Middletown, N.Y. Reduced to private, December 25, 1862. Promoted sergeant, December 28, 1862. Mustered out with company, May 28, 1863, at Albany, N.Y. Subsequent service in Co. E, 142nd New York Infantry & Co. K, 169th New York Infantry.

HUNGERFORD, CHARLES—Age 20 years. Enlisted April 26, 1861, at Schenectady. Mustered in as private, Co. A, May 17, 1861, to serve two years. Mustered out with company, May 28, 1863, at Albany, N.Y. Subsequent service in Co. F, 2nd New York Heavy Artillery.

HUNT, JOHN M.—Age 19 years. Enlisted April 23, 1861, at Albany. Mustered in as private, Co. C, May 17, 1861, to serve two years. Mustered out with company, May 28, 1863, at Albany, N.Y. Subsequent service in Co. "U," 5th New York Veteran Infantry & Co. D, 18th New York Cavalry.

HUNT, JOSEPH G. W.—Age 21 years. Enlisted May 10, 1861, at Albany. Mustered in as private, Co. B, May 17, 1861, to serve two years. Promoted sergeant, July 1, 1861. Discharged for disability, September 25, 1861, at Camp King, Alexandria, Va. Subsequent service in Co. G, 18th New York Cavalry & Co. G, 17th United States Infantry.

HUNTER, JOHN—Age 18 years. Enlisted May 6, 1861, at Albany. Mustered in as private, Co. B, May 17, 1861, to serve two years. Wounded, December 13, 1862, at Fredericksburg, Va. Mustered out with company, May 28, 1863, at Albany, N.Y.

HUNTINGTON, FREEMAN FARNUM—Age 20 years. Enlisted May 12, 1861, at Ogdensburg. Mustered in as sergeant, Co. K, May 17, 1861, to serve two years. Promoted first sergeant, July 12, 1861. Accidentally shot off a portion of index finger on right hand, July 21, 1861, near Centreville, Va. Injured shoulder from musket fall from a wounded comrade, June 27, 1862, at Gaines's Mill, Va. Attached, December 1, 1862, to Camp A General Hospital, in Frederick, Md. Returned to regiment, January 17, 1863. Mustered in as first lieutenant, February 1, 1863. Mustered out with company, May 28, 1863, at Albany, N.Y. Commissioned first lieutenant, November 10, 1862, with rank from October 1, 1862, after H. G. Goodno was promoted. Subsequent service in Co. A, 16th New York Heavy Artillery.

HUSON, ROBERT—Age 37 years. Enlisted December 18, 1861, at Albany. Mustered in as private, Co. F, same date, to serve unexpired term of two years. Sent sick, August 7, 1862, onboard Steamer *State of Maine* at Harrison's Landing, Va. Hospitalized, August 10, 1862, at Satterlee General Hospital, in West Philadelphia, Pa. Died of disease, August 12, 1862, at Satterlee General Hospital, in West Philadelphia, Pa.

HUSTON, CHARLES WILLIAM—Age 30 years. Enlisted October 15, 1861, at Ogdensburg. Mustered in as private, Co. K, October 30, 1861, at Camp Williams, Va., to serve two years. Mustered out with company, May 28, 1863, at Albany, N.Y. Subsequent service in Co. A, 16th New York Heavy Artillery.

HUTCHINS, HENRY T.—Age about 52 years, but gave age as 38 years. Enlisted May 17, 1861, at Albany. Mustered in as private, Co. I, same date, to serve two years. Detailed as teamster, August 19, 1861. Discharged for disability, January 15, 1863, at White Oak Church, Falmouth, Va. Subsequent service in Co. K, 2nd Veteran Reserve Corps.

HYER, JOSEPH F.—Age 26 years. Enlisted April 22, 1861, at Albany. Mustered in as private, Co. I, May 17, 1861, to serve two years. Mustered out with company, May 28, 1863, at Albany, N.Y. Subsequent service in Co. K, 2nd Veteran Reserve Corps.

ICKLIN, JOHN JAMES—Age 33 years. Enlisted May 17, 1861, at Albany. Mustered in as private, Co. C, same date, to serve two years. Wounded in right breast, June 8, 1862, by an enemy picket on the Chickahominy River, Va. Hospitalized, on or about July 2, 1862, to Fort Monroe, Va. Hospitalized, date not stated, in Baltimore, Md. Returned to regiment, on or about October 1, 1862. Mustered out with company, May 28, 1863, at Albany, N.Y. Subsequent service the Co. A, 16th Regiment, Veteran Reserve Corps & 2nd Independent Company, Veteran Reserve Corps.

INGALLS, PETER—Age 26 years. Enlisted May 6, 1861, at Albany. Mustered in as private, Co. I, May 17, 1861, to serve two years. Detailed as teamster, August 19, 1861. Mustered out with company, May 28, 1863, at Albany, N.Y. Subsequent service in Co. A, 169th New York Infantry.

INGRAHAM, CHARLES "Charley" ORSON—Age 20 years. Enlisted May 7, 1861, at Canandaigua. Mustered in as private, Co. G, May 17, 1861, to serve two years. Hospitalized, May 11, 1862, at Seminary Hospital, at Hampton, Va. Returned to regiment, date not stated. Mustered out with company, May 28, 1863, at Albany, N.Y. Subsequent service in Co. E, 1st New York Veteran Cavalry. Brother-in-law of Albert Hotchkiss.

INSSE, GREGOIRE, Jr.—Age 21 years. Enlisted May 17, 1861, at Albany. Mustered in as corporal, Co. G, May 17, 1861, to serve two years. Promoted sergeant, November 30, 1861. Hospitalized, July or August 1862, at Satterlee General Hospital, in West Philadelphia, Pa. Mustered out with company, May 28, 1683, at Albany, N.Y. Subsequent service in Co. H, 16th New York Heavy Artillery.

IRELAND, GEORGE—Age 37 years. Enlisted April 23, 1861, at Albany. Mustered in as private, Co. C, May 17, 1861, to serve two years. Mustered out with company, May 28, 1863, at Albany, N.Y. Subsequent service in Co. G & C, 52nd New York Infantry & Co. H, 14th Infantry Regiment, Veteran Reserve Corps.

IRELAND, WILLIAM C.—Age 23 years. Enlisted April 23, 1861, at Albany. Mustered in as private, Co. C, May 17, 1861, to serve two years. Deserted, September 21, 1861, from Camp King, Alexandria, Va. Arrested, September 23, 1861, at Alexandria, Va. Court-martialed, October 9, 1861, at Camp Williams, Va., and drummed out of service. Confined at District of Columbia Penitentiary for two years. Released and dishonorably discharged, January 23, 1862. Subsequent service in Co. I, 15th New York Cavalry.

IRWIN, HENRY—Age 16 years. Enlisted November 9, 1861, at Canandaigua. Mustered in as musician, Co.

Pvt. Charles O. Ingraham, Company G, was wounded in 1864 during his second enlistment with the 1st New York Veteran Cavalry. He died on April 1, 1908, in Utica, New York (courtesy New York State Military Museum).

G, November 9, 1861, at Elmira, N.Y., to serve unexpired term of two years. Mustered out with company, May 28, 1863, at Albany, N.Y.

IVES, JOSEPH—Age 18 years. Enlisted May 17, 1861, at Albany. Mustered in as private, Co. C, same date, to serve two years. Deserted, May or June 1861, before regiment left Albany, N.Y. Subsequent service in Co. B & D, 65th New York Infantry & Co. I, 158th New York Infantry.

JACKSON, JOSEPH DERVIS—Age 24 years. Enlisted April 30, 1861, at Middletown. Mustered in as private, Co. D, May 17, 1861, to serve two years. Mustered out with company, May 28, 1863, at Albany, N.Y. Subsequent service in Co. K, 124th New York Infantry.

JACKSON, WILLIAM—Age 18 years. Enlisted April 24, 1861, at Albany. Mustered in as private, Co. B, May 17, 1861, to serve two years. Mustered out with company, May 28, 1863, at Albany, N.Y.

JACKSON, WILLIAM AYRAULT—Age 29 years. Enrolled May 14, 1861, at Albany. Mustered in as colonel, May 17, 1861, to serve two years. On seven day furlough, August 25, 1861, in Schenectady, N.Y. Died of disease, November 11, 1861, at Washington, D.C. Commissioned colonel, June 18, 1861, with rank from May 13, 1861, original.

JACKSON, WILLIAM HENRY—Age 21 years. Enlisted April 30, 1861, at Middletown. Mustered in as private, Co. H, May 17, 1861, to serve two years. Wounded slightly in head, June 27, 1862, at Gaines's Mill, Va. Hospitalized, date not stated, at Fairfax Seminary General Hospital, at Alexandria, Va. Transferred, September 1, 1862, to Hammond General Hospital, in Point Lookout, Md. Retained as nurse at same hospital, November 1, 1862. Returned to regiment, May 15, 1863. Mustered out with company, May 28, 1863, at Albany, N.Y. Subsequent service in Co. F & K, 22nd New York Cavalry.

JAPHET, CHARLES—Age 34 years. Enlisted May 7, 1861, at Albany. Mustered in as private, Co. G, May 17, 1861, to serve two years. Mustered out with company, May 28, 1863, at Albany, N.Y.

JAQUES, CHRISTIAN—Age 40 years. Enlisted May 12, 1861, at Ogdensburg. Mustered in as private, Co. K, May 17, 1861, to serve two years. Hospitalized, and discharged after refusal to take the oath, May 17, 1861, at Albany, N.Y.

JAYCOX, JOHN WEBLEY—Age 19 years. Enlisted May 17, 1861, at Albany. Mustered in as private, Co. C, same date, to serve two years. Court-martialed for neglect of duty, deserting post, and conduct prejudicial to military discipline, January 22, 1862, at Alexandria, Va. Wounded in left leg, September 14, 1862, at Crampton's Gap, Md. Hospitalized, September 1862, at Camp B General Hospital, in Frederick, Md. Transferred, October 24, 1862, in Camp A General Hospital, in Frederick, Md. Transferred and hospitalized, March 10, 1863, to McKim's Mansion General Hospital, in Baltimore, Md. Returned to regiment, May 20, 1863. Mustered out with company, May 28, 1863, at Albany, N.Y.

JENNER, JOHN—Age 30 years. Enlisted May 2, 1861, at Schenectady. Mustered in as private, Co. E, May 17, 1861, to serve two years. Mustered out with company, May 28, 1863, at Albany, N.Y. Subsequent service in Co. F & A, 95th New York Infantry.

JOHNSON, BENJAMIN H.—Age 24 years. Enlisted September 19, 1862, at Schenectady. Mustered in as private, unassigned, same date, to serve three years. Deserted, September 21, 1862.

JOHNSTON, JOHN—Age 16 years. Enlisted November 20, 1861, at Albany. Mustered in as musician, Co. A, December 7, 1861, at Albany, to serve two years. Reduced to private, March or April 1862. Mustered out with company, May 28, 1863, at Albany, N.Y. Subsequent service in Co. D, 91st New York Infantry.

JONES, ALONZO D.—Age 22 years. Enlisted May 17, 1861, at Albany. Mustered in as private, Co. H, same date, to serve two years. Deserted, May 20, 1861, at Albany, N.Y.

JONES, EZRA CURTIS—Age 24 years. Enlisted May 7, 1861, at Albany. Mustered in as private, Co. G, May 17, 1861, to serve two years. Hospitalized, June 1861, at Washington, D.C. Discharged for disability, September 24, 1861, at Alexandria, Va. Subsequent service in Co. E, 147th New York Infantry.

Pvt. John Johnston was a sixteen-year-old baker when he enlisted as a musician for Company A (courtesy New York State Military Museum).

JONES, GEORGE—Age 22 years. Enlisted May 17, 1861, at Albany. Mustered in as private, Co. C, same date, to serve two years. Deserted, May or June 1861, before regiment left Albany, N.Y.

JONES, JOHN P.—Age 18 years. Enlisted May 10, 1861, at Albany. Mustered in as private, Co. B, May 17, 1861, to serve two years. Mustered out with company, May 28, 1863, at Albany, N.Y.

JONES, JOSEPH C.—Age 21 years. Enlisted May 7, 1861, at Albany. Mustered in as musician, Co. G, May 17, 1861, to serve two years. Reduced to private, June 18, 1861. Detailed in Ambulance Corps, November 1862. Mustered out with company, May 28, 1863, at Albany, N.Y. Subsequent service in Co. H, 4th New York Heavy Artillery.

JORALEMON, LEONARD (Lansing Isaac)—Age 20 years. Enlisted May 17, 1861, at Albany. Mustered in as private, Co. H, same date, to serve two years. Deserted, May 20, 1861, at Albany, N.Y. Subsequent service in Co. F, 3rd New York Infantry & the United States Navy aboard Gunboats *Saratoga*, *North Carolina* & *Princeton*.

JORDAN, SAMUEL PATRICK—Age 28 years. Enlisted May 7, 1861, at Albany. Mustered in as private, Co. H, May 17, 1861, to serve two years. Deserted, August 29, 1862. Arrested and returned to regiment, March 27, 1863. Mustered out with company, May 28, 1863, at Albany, N.Y. Subsequent service in Co. I, 31st Pennsylvania Infantry (Emergency) Militia.

KALFELS, JOSEPH—Age 39 years. Enlisted April 23, 1861, at Schenectady. Mustered in as private, Co. A, May 17, 1861, to serve two years. Discharged for disability, November 20, 1861, at Camp King, Alexandria, Va.

KANE, JOHN—Age 26 years. Enlisted April 28, 1861, at Schenectady. Mustered in as private, Co. A, May

17, 1861, to serve two years. Discharged for disability, September 24, 1861, at Alexandria, Va.

KEAGAN, THOMAS—Age 18 years. Enlisted June 13, 1861, at Albany. Mustered in as private, Co. B, same date, to serve two years. Mustered out, June 13, 1863. Subsequent service in Co. D, 16th New York Heavy Artillery.

KEARNS (Kerrins), THOMAS—Age about 23 years. Enlisted May 30, 1861, at Albany. Mustered in as private, Co. K, same date, to serve two years. Transferred to Co. F, June 17, 1861, in place of Truman Stoddard. Promoted corporal, September 19, 1861. Served as corporal of color guard. Wounded in head and both legs, June 27, 1862, at Gaines's Mill, Va. Hospitalized, July 1, 1862, Mill Creek General Hospital, near Fort Monroe, Va. Transferred, August 2, 1862, to Casparis General Hospital, in Washington, D.C. Transferred, February 21, 1863, to Turner's Lane General Hospital, in Philadelphia, Pa. Transferred, April 21, 1863, to Fort Schuyler, N.Y. Returned to regiment, May 18, 1863, at Albany, N.Y. Mustered out with company, May 28, 1863, at Albany, N.Y. Subsequent service in Co. E, 175th New York Infantry.

KEENAN, PATRICK—Age 31 years. Enlisted August 25, 1862, at Albany. Mustered in as private, Co. C, same date, to serve three years. Transferred, May 10, 1863, to Co. C, 121st New York Infantry.

KEENAN, THOMAS—Age 31 years. Enlisted May 1, 1861, at Albany. Mustered in as private, Co. B, May 17, 1861, to serve two years. No further record.

KELLER, JACOB—Age 17 years, but gave age as 19 years. Enlisted May 7, 1861, at Albany. Mustered in as private, Co. G, May 17, 1861, to serve two years. Discharged for disability, October 31, 1862, at hospital, in New York City, N.Y. Subsequent service in Co. C, 15th New York Cavalry & Co. C, 2nd New York Provisional Cavalry.

KELLER, LEONARD—Age 36 years. Enlisted April 22, 1861, at Schenectady. Mustered in as private, Co. A, May 17, 1861, to serve two years. Deserted, May or June 1861, before regiment left Albany, N.Y.

KELLY, ABRAHAM L.—Age 23 years. Enlisted April 23, 1861, at Albany. Mustered in as private, Co. C, May 17, 1861, to serve two years. Discharged for disability, September 24, 1861, at Camp King, Alexandria, Va.

KELLY, BERNARD—Age 28 years. Enlisted May 7, 1861, at Albany. Mustered in as private, Co. H, May 17, 1861, to serve two years. Hospitalized, June 2, 1863. Mustered out, June 20, 1863. Subsequent service in Co. I, 13th New York Heavy Artillery.

KELLY, CHARLES—Age 30 years. Enlisted September 23, 1862, at Albany. Mustered in as private, Co. C, same date, to serve three years. No further record.

KELLY, ROBERT B.—Age 19 years. Enlisted April 24, 1861, at Albany. Mustered in as private, Co. B, May 17, 1861, to serve two years. Discharged for disability, September 24, 1861, at Camp King, Alexandria, Va. Subsequent service in Co. I, 115th New York Infantry.

KENNEDY, ALEXANDER—Age 38 years. Enlisted April 24, 1861, at Albany. Mustered in as private, Co. B, May 17, 1861, to serve two years. Mustered out with company, May 28, 1863, at Albany, N.Y. Subsequent service in Co. E, 3rd New York Infantry.

KENNY, DAVID—Age 35 years. Enlisted May 17, 1861, at Albany. Mustered in as private, Co. G, same date, to serve two years. Transferred to another company. No further record.

KENNY, DENNIS—Age 21 years. Enlisted April 22, 1861, at Schenectady. Mustered in as private, Co. A, May 17, 1861, to serve two years. Deserted, May or June 1861, before regiment left Albany, N.Y.

KENT, CHARLES—Age 18 years. Enlisted April 19, 1861, at Albany. Mustered in as corporal, Co. F, May 17, 1861, to serve two years. Reduced to private, September 19, 1861. Detailed as nurse in regimental hospital, November 27, 1862, until May 1863. Mustered out with company, May 28, 1863, at Albany, N.Y. Subsequent service in Co. "U" 13th New York Heavy Artillery.

KERR, JAMES—Age 24 years. Enlisted May 17, 1861, at Albany. Mustered in as private, Co. I, same date, to serve two years. Deserted, August 6, 1861, at Meridian Hill, Washington, D.C.

KERR, PATRICK—Age 47 years. Enlisted August 30, 1862, at Albany. Mustered in as private, unassigned, September 2, 1862, to serve three years. Rejected. No further record.

KETCHAM, HENRY EDWIN—Age 19 years. Enlisted April 30, 1861, at Middletown. Mustered in as private, Co. D, May 17, 1861, to serve two years. Promoted corporal, December 9, 1862. Mustered out with company, May 28, 1863, at Albany, N.Y. Brother of Thomas J. Ketcham.

KETCHAM, THOMAS JEFFERSON—Age 20 years. Enlisted April 30, 1861, at Middletown. Mustered in as private, Co. D, May 17, 1861, to serve two years. Wounded slightly in face, September 14, 1862, at Crampton's Gap, Md. Mustered out with company, May 28, 1863, at Albany, N.Y. Subsequent service in Co. K, 15th New York Cavalry. Brother of Henry E. Ketcham.

KETTLE, JAMES—Age 44 years. Enlisted May 2, 1861, at Albany. Mustered in as private, Co. E, May 17, 1861, to serve two years. Hospitalized, June 7, 1861, at hospital in New York City, N.Y. Discharged for disability, September 1, 1861, from hospital in New York City, N.Y.

KIDDER, SAMUEL RICHARDSON—Age 27 years. Enlisted August 28, 1862, at Albany. Mustered in as private, Co. H, September 26, 1862, to serve three years. Joined regiment, February 24, 1863. Transferred, May 10, 1863, to Co. C, 121st New York Infantry.

KILBOURN, GEORGE—Age 44 years. Enlisted August 18, 1862, at Albany. Mustered in as private, unassigned, same date, to serve three years. Deserted, August 25, 1862.

KILROE (Kilroy), MARTIN—Age 22 years. Enlisted April 19, 1861, at Albany. Mustered in as corporal, Co. F, May 17, 1861, to serve two years. Reduced to private, July 10, 1861. Detailed with Pioneer Corps, November 1862. Mustered out with company, May 28, 1863, at Albany, N.Y.

KIMBALL, EBENEZER ABNER—Age 23 years.

Enlisted May 7, 1861, at Albany. Mustered in as private, Co. H, May 17, 1861, to serve two years. Promoted corporal, August 15, 1861. Promoted sergeant, November 6, 1861. Mustered out with company, May 28, 1863, at Albany, N.Y.

KING, ALFRED—Age 19 years. Enlisted April 19, 1861, at Albany. Mustered in as private, Co. F, May 17, 1861, to serve two years. Wounded in left hand, June 27, 1862, at Gaines's Mill, Va. Mustered out with company, May 28, 1863, at Albany, N.Y. Subsequent service in Co. I, 29th Michigan Infantry.

KING, GARDINER—Age 22 years. Enlisted May 7, 1861, at Albany. Mustered in as private, Co. G, May 17, 1861, to serve two years. Killed, June 27, 1862, at Gaines's Mill, Va.

KING, JOHN SMITH—Age 19 years. Enlisted April 30, 1861, at Middletown. Mustered in as sergeant, Co. D, May 17, 1861, to serve two years. Promoted first sergeant, December 1, 1861. Mustered in as first lieutenant, June 28, 1862. On ten day furlough, March 1–10, 1863, in Middletown, N.Y. Mustered out with company, May 28, 1863, at Albany, N.Y. Commissioned first lieutenant, November 10, 1862, with rank from June 27, 1862, after Sayer was promoted. Subsequent service in Co. K, 124th New York Infantry.

KINGSLAND, KINSLEY E.—Age 17 years, but gave age as 18 years. Enlisted April 23, 1861, at Albany. Mustered in as private, Co. C, May 17, 1861, to serve two years. Discharged for disability, November 20, 1861, at Camp King, Alexandria, Va. Subsequent service in Co. D, 74th New York Infantry & Co. "U" 16th New York Heavy Artillery.

KINGSLEY, JOSEPH—Age 20 years. Enlisted May 7, 1861, at Albany, N.Y. Mustered in as private, Co. G, May 17, 1861, to serve two years. Mustered out with company, May 28, 1863, at Albany, N.Y.

KIRK, JAMES FRANCIS—Age 16 years, but gave age as 18 years. Enlisted May 12, 1861, at Ogdensburg. Mustered in as private, Co. K, May 17, 1861, to serve two years. Mustered out with company, May 28, 1863, at Albany, N.Y.

KIRKPATRICK, THOMAS—Age 36 years. Enlisted December 26, 1861, at Albany. Mustered in as private, Co. B, January 20, 1862, to serve two years. Promoted corporal, July 1, 1862. Mustered out with company, May 28, 1863, at Albany, N.Y.

KIRKWOOD, ANDREW W.—Age 15 or 16 years, but gave age as 20 years. Enlisted September 20, 1861, at Middletown. Mustered in as private, Co. D, October 21, 1861, at Camp King, Alexandria, Va., to serve two years. Mustered out with company, May 28, 1863, at Albany, N.Y.

KLINE, FRANCIS "Frank" W.—Age 23 years. Enlisted April 19, 1861, at Albany. Mustered in as private, Co. F, May 17, 1861, to serve two years. Promoted corporal, December 8, 1862. Mustered out with company, May 28, 1863, at Albany, N.Y.

KNAPP, ELIAS PATTEE—Age 19 years. Enlisted May 7, 1861, at Albany. Mustered in as private, Co. G, May 17, 1861, to serve two years. Hospitalized, July 1861, at hospital, in Washington, D.C. Captured, June 29, 1862, at Savage's Station, Va. Confined, July 13, 1862, at Richmond, Va. Paroled, September 13, 1862, at City Point, Va. Sent, September 26, 1862, to Washington, D.C. Mustered out with company, May 28, 1863, at Albany, N.Y.

KNIGHT, WARREN P.—Age 18 years. Enlisted May 7, 1861, at Albany. Mustered in as private, Co. H, May 17, 1861, to serve two years. Discharged for disability, May 18, 1861, at Albany, N.Y.

KNOWLES, LEWIS A.—Age 29 years. Enlisted May 7, 1861, at Canandaigua. Mustered in as corporal, Co. G, May 17, 1861, to serve two years. Hospitalized, June 1861, at E Street General Hospital, in Washington, D.C. Discharged for disability, September 7, 1861, at Alexandria, Va.

KNOX, ANDREW G.—Age 17 years, but gave age as 18 years. Enlisted April 30, 1861, at Middletown. Mustered in as private, Co. D, May 17, 1861, to serve two years. Wounded in right leg, September 14, 1862, at Crampton's Gap, Md. Right thigh amputated. Hospitalized, September 18, 1862, at General Hospital Number 1, in Frederick, Md. Retained as nurse at same hospital, September 22, 1862. Secondary amputation of right thigh, December 12, 1862. Discharged on account of such wounds, January 14, 1863, at Frederick, Md.

KNOX, DAVID M.—Age 18 years. Enlisted May 12, 1861, at Ogdensburg. Mustered in as private, Co. K, May 17, 1861, to serve two years. Hospitalized, June 1861, at E Street General Hospital, in Washington, D.C., discharged for disability, July 8, 1861, at Washington, D.C. Subsequent service in Co. G, 98th New York Infantry.

KNOX, VALENTINE—Age 22 years. Enlisted April 29, 1861, at Schenectady. Mustered in as private, Co. A, May 17, 1861, to serve two years. Detailed as cook for regimental hospital, November 1, 1862, to May 1863. Mustered out with company, May 28, 1863, at Albany, N.Y.

KRUG, JOHN FREDERIC—Age 21 years. Enlisted December 2, 1861, at Albany. Mustered in as private, Co. F, same date, to serve two years. Wounded in left leg, June 27, 1862, at Gaines's Mill, Va. Captured, June 29, 1862, at White Oak Swamp, Va. Confined, June 29, 1862, at Richmond, Va. Paroled, August 5, 1862, at City Point, Va. Deserted, September 7, 1862, at Alexandria, Va.

LACKEY, MAJOR J.—Age 16 years, but gave age as 18 years. Enlisted April 14, 1861, at Albany. Mustered in as private, Co. B, May 17, 1861, to serve two years. Detailed on recruiting service, December 1861. Detailed to Ambulance Corps, August 12, 1862. Returned to regiment, May 13, 1863. Mustered out with company, May 28, 1863, at Albany, N.Y. Subsequent service in Co. I & D, 7th New York Heavy Artillery.

LAMERS, BERNHART (Barney)—Age 26 years. Enlisted April 23, 1861, at Schenectady. Mustered in as private, Co. A, May 17, 1861, to serve two years. Sent sick, August 7, 1862, onboard Steamer *State of Maine* at Harrison's Landing, Va., and hospitalized, in West Philadelphia, Pa. Deserted, September 4, 1862, from hospital in N.Y.

LAMSON, JAMES—Age 24 years. Enlisted September 24, 1861, at Albany. Mustered in as private, Co. A, October 21, 1861, at Camp King, Alexandria, Va., to serve two years. Discharged, February 24, 1862, by reason of transfer to western gunboat service in the United States Navy aboard Gunboat *Pittsburgh* and served in Navy beyond regimental muster-out. Subsequent service in Co. M, 9th West Virginia Light Artillery.

LAMSON, WILLIAM H.—Age 29 years. Enlisted June 17, 1861, at Albany. Mustered in as private, Co. A, same date, to serve two years. Deserted to work in hospital, May 19, 1862, at White House Landing, Va. Captured, June 29, 1862, at Savage's Station, Va. Confined at Richmond, Va. Paroled, July 27, 1862, at City Point, Va. Hospitalized, date not stated, in Chester, Pa. Listed as deserter, October 14, 1862. Returned to regiment, December 9, 1862, near Fredericksburg, Va. Court-martialed for desertion, February 21, 1863, at White Oak Church, Falmouth, Va. Mustered out with company, May 28, 1863, at Albany, N.Y. Discharged, June 17, 1863, at Albany, N.Y.

LANDASSA, FREDERICK—Age 34 years. Enlisted April 25, 1861, at Schenectady. Mustered in as private, Co. A, May 17, 1861, to serve two years. Deserted, May or June 1861, before regiment left Albany, N.Y.

LANE, THOMAS S.—Age 22 years. Enlisted April 30, 1861, at Middletown. Mustered in as first sergeant, Co. H, May 17, 1861, to serve two years. Promoted second lieutenant, November 6, 1861. Promoted first lieutenant, July 16, 1862. On ten day furlough, February of 1863, in Middletown, N.Y. Mustered out with company, May 28, 1863, at Albany, N.Y. Commissioned second lieutenant, December 2, 1861, with rank from November 6, 1861, after Carmichael was promoted. Commissioned first lieutenant, November 10, 1862, with rank from July 16, 1862, after Carmichael resigned.

LANG, JOSEPH—Age 19 years. Enlisted May 7, 1861, at Canandaigua. Mustered in as private, Co. G, May 17, 1861, to serve two years. Hospitalized, November or December 1862, at 6th Corps Hospital, in Hagerstown, Md. Died of disease, May 5, 1863, at General Hospital Number 1, in Frederick, Md.

LANGDON, THEODORE—Age 25 years. Enlisted May 6, 1861, at Albany. Mustered in as private, Co. B, May 17, 1861, to serve two years. Killed, June 27, 1862, at Gaines's Mill, Va.

LAQUE, JOHN B.—Age 20 years. Enlisted May 1, 1861, at Schenectady. Mustered in as private, Co. A, May 17, 1861, to serve two years. Injured by kick from horse, July 16, 1861, near Alexandria, Va. Mustered out with company, May 28, 1863, at Albany, N.Y.

LARABY, ROSWELL J.—Age 57 years, but gave age as 51 years. Enlisted September 15, 1862, at Ogdensburg. Mustered in as private, Co. K, same date, to serve three years. Discharged for disability, December 23, 1862, at White Oak Church, Falmouth, Va.

LARKIN, JAMES MARSDALE—Age 15 years, but gave age as 19 years. Enlisted May 7, 1861, at Albany. Mustered in as private, Co. H, May 17, 1861, to serve two years. Wounded in right knee, June 27, 1862, at Gaines's Mill, Va. Captured, June 29, 1862, at Savage's Station, Va. Confined at Richmond, Va. Paroled, July 27, 1862, at City Point, Va. Hospitalized, July 30, 1862, to Chesapeake General Hospital, at Fort Monroe, Va. Transferred, August 29, 1862, to hospital in Annapolis, Md. Hospitalized, September 1, 1862, at General Hospital, in Annapolis, Md. Returned to regiment, December 18, 1862. Hospitalized for sickness, December 23, 1862, at Fairfax Seminary General Hospital, in Alexandria, Va. Discharged for disability, January 8, 1863, at Fairfax Seminary, Va.

LARKIN (Larkins), JOHN—Age 18 years. Enlisted April 19, 1861, at Albany. Mustered in as private, Co. I, May 17, 1861, to serve two years. Mustered out with company, May 28, 1863, at Albany, N.Y. Subsequent service in Co. B, 21st Veteran Reserve Corps.

LARKIN, JOHN J.—Age 17 years. Enlisted November 20, 1861, at Albany. Mustered in as musician, Co. H, December 9, 1861, at Albany, to serve two years. Mustered out with company, May 28, 1863, at Albany, N.Y. Subsequent service in Co. D, 7th New York Heavy Artillery.

LARKINS (Larkin), DAVID HENRY—Age 28 years. Enlisted May 2, 1861, at Schenectady. Mustered in as private, Co. E, May 17, 1861, to serve two years. Deserted, June 2, 1861, at Albany, N.Y. Arrested, July 23, 1863, at Baltimore, Md. Subsequent service in Co. F, 134th New York Infantry & Co. D, 21st Veteran Reserve Corps.

LARUE, SAMUEL C.—Age about 26 years. Enlisted April 22, 1861, at Schenectady. Mustered in as private, Co. A, May 17, 1861, to serve two years. Absent-without-leave, January 20, 1863, from Camp Russell, White Oak Church, Falmouth, Va. Returned to regiment, January 24, 1863, same place. Court-martialed for absence and disobedience, February 23, 1863, at same place. Mustered out with company, May 28, 1863, at Albany, N.Y. Subsequent service in Co. B, 2nd New York Veteran Cavalry.

LASHER, CHARLES W.—Age 25 years. Enlisted May 17, 1861, at Schenectady. Mustered in as private, Co. A, same date, to serve two years. Deserted, May or June 1861, before regiment left Albany, N.Y.

LAWLESS, JOHN—Age about 30 years. Enrolled April 22, 1861, at Albany. Appointed captain, Co. F, to serve two years. Not mustered in, and out of service, April 30, 1861. Not commissioned. Subsequent service in Co. R, 25th New York Militia National Guard.

LAWRENCE, THOMAS HENRY D.—Age 25 years. Enlisted April 30, 1861, at Middletown. Mustered in as private, Co. D, May 17, 1861, to serve two years. Never participated in any engagement. Mustered out with company, May 28, 1863, at Albany, N.Y. Subsequent service in Co. "U" 7th New York Heavy Artillery.

LEACH, LUCIUS—Age 25 years. Enlisted May 19, 1861, at Albany. Mustered in as private, Co. I, same date, to serve two years. Discharged for disability, January 20, 1863, at White Oak Church, Falmouth, Va.

LEARY, JEREMIAH—Age 31 years. Enlisted April 19, 1861, at Albany. Mustered in as sergeant, Co. I, May 17, 1861, to serve two years. Wounded in hand, September 14, 1862, at Crampton's Gap, Md. Hospitalized, October

6, 1862, at Camp A General Hospital, in Frederick, Md. Returned to regiment, January 17, 1863. Mustered out with company, May 28, 1863, at Albany, N.Y. Subsequent service in Co. H, 91st New York Infantry & the United States Navy, aboard *Roanoke*.

LEARY, MORRIS—Age 25 years. Enlisted April 19, 1861, at Albany. Mustered in as private, Co. I, May 17, 1861, to serve two years. Mustered out with company, May 28, 1863, at Albany, N.Y.

LECOMPTE, CHARLES THOMAS—Age 21 years. Enlisted April 30, 1861, at Middletown. Mustered in as private, Co. D, May 17, 1861, to serve two years. Sent sick, August 7, 1862, onboard Steamer *State of Maine* at Harrison's Landing, Va. and hospitalized at Satterlee General Hospital, in West Philadelphia, Pa. Forwarded to Washington, D.C., August 27, 1862. Returned to regiment, August 31, 1862. Mustered out with company, May 28, 1863, at Albany, N.Y.

LEE, DANIEL F.—Age 21 years. Enlisted May 12, 1861, at Ogdensburg. Mustered in as private, Co. K, May 17, 1861, to serve two years. Mustered out with company, May 28, 1863, at Albany, N.Y.

LEFLEUR, JOHN—Age 30 years. Enlisted April 30, 1861, at Albany. Mustered in as private, Co. I, May 17, 1861, to serve two years. Mustered out with company, May 28, 1863, at Albany, N.Y. Subsequent service in Co. E, 2nd United States Infantry.

LEHNING, WILLIAM H.—Age 23 years. Enlisted April 27, 1861, at Middletown. Mustered in as private, Co. D, May 17, 1861, to serve two years. Hospitalized, June 15, 1861, for tonsillitis. Returned to duty, July 8, 1861. Wounded in left forearm, June 27, 1862, at Gaines's Mill, Va. Hospitalized, July 5, 1862, at Fort Monroe, Va. Discharged on account of such wounds, October 17, 1862, at Fort Hamilton, N.Y. Subsequent service in Co. G, 2nd New York Cavalry.

LEITH, SAMUEL—Age 21 years, but gave age as 30 years. Enrolled April 25, 1861, at Albany. Mustered in as second lieutenant, Co. C, May 17, 1861, to serve two years. Resigned, October 9, 1861, at Alexandria, Va., but continued service until November 29, 1861, when paperwork was received. Commissioned second lieutenant, July 4, 1861, with rank from April 25, 1861, original. Subsequent service in Co. E, 53rd New York Infantry & Co. B & H, 132nd New York Infantry.

LEMAIRE, ALFRED A.—Age 22 years. Enlisted April 23, 1861, at Fishkill. Mustered in as drummer, Co. C, May 17, 1861, to serve two years. Discharged for disability, January 6, 1862, at Camp King, Alexandria, Va.

LEVISON, HENRY—Age 17 years, but gave age as 18 years. Enlisted April 29, 1861, at Schenectady. Mustered in as private, Co. A, May 17, 1861, to serve two years. Discharged, May 19, 1861, by writ of Habeas Corpus, at Albany, N.Y.

LEWIS, JESSE—Age 32 years, but gave age as 25 years. Enlisted April 22, 1861, at Albany. Mustered in as private, Co. I, May 17, 1861, to serve two years. Discharged for disability, September 11, 1861, at Alexandria, Va. Subsequent service in Co. D, 4th New York Heavy Artillery.

LILLY, SAMUEL—Age 19 years. Enlisted June 17, 1861, at Albany. Mustered in as private, Co. A, same date, to serve two years. Killed, June 27, 1862, at Gaines's Mill, Va.

LINKLETTER, WILLIAM H.—Age 23 years. Enlisted November 6, 1861, at Canandaigua. Mustered in as private, Co. G, November 15, 1861, at Elmira, N.Y., to serve two years. Wounded and captured, June 27, 1862, at Gaines's Mill, Va. Confined, June 30, 1862, at Richmond, Va. Paroled, July 27, 1862, at City Point, Va. Died of disease, August 1, 1862, at Episcopal General Hospital, in Philadelphia, Pa.

LITCHFIELD, ELISHA C.—Age 29 years. Enlisted May 7, 1861, at Albany. Mustered in as private, Co. H, May 17, 1861, to serve two years. Deserted, July 25, 1861, from Camp Myers, Alexandria, Va.

LITCHULT, JOHN, Jr.—Age 22 years. Enlisted November 9, 1861, at Canandaigua. Mustered in as private, Co. G, November 15, 1861, at Elmira, N.Y., to serve two years. Wounded in breast, September 14, 1862, at Crampton's Gap, Md. Died on account of such wounds, September 22, 1862, in hospital at Hagerstown, Md.

LOBER, JOHN—Age 27 years. Enlisted September 30, 1861, at Albany. Mustered in as private, Co. Unassigned, October 21, 1861, at Camp King, Alexandria, Va. Deserted while on the way to join the regiment.

LOGAN, JAMES—Age 26 years. Enlisted April 25, 1861, at Schenectady. Mustered in as private, Co. A, May 17, 1861, to serve two years. Court-martialed at regimental level, date not stated. Wounded in right arm, September 14, 1862, at Crampton's Gap, Md. Hospitalized, October 4, 1862, at Camp A General Hospital, in Frederick, Md. Returned to regiment, January 5, 1863. Mustered out with company, May 28, 1863, at Albany, N.Y.

LOONEY (Luny), MICHAEL "Mike"—Age 42 years. Enlisted April 24, 1861, at Albany. Mustered in as private, Co. B, May 17, 1861, to serve two years. Wounded in right arm, June 27, 1862, at Gaines's Mill, Va. Right arm amputated. Hospitalized, date not stated, at General Hospital, in Annapolis, Md. Discharged on account of such wounds, September 14, 1862, at Annapolis, Md. Subsequent service in Unassigned Veteran Reserve Corps & 129th Co. 2nd Battalion Veteran Reserve Corps.

LOVETT, ISAAC G.—Age 21 years. Enlisted May 2, 1861, at Schenectady. Mustered in as private, Co. E, May 17, 1861, to serve two years. Mustered out with company, May 28, 1863, at Albany, N.Y.

LUCIUS, CHRISTIAN W.—Age 43 years. Enlisted September 17, 1862, at Albany. Mustered in as private, Co. C, same date, to serve three years. Transferred, May 10, 1863, to Co. H & F, 121st New York Infantry.

LUFFMAN, ERASTUS R.—Age 22 years. Enlisted January 16, 1862, at Camp King, Alexandria, Va. Mustered in as private, Co. E, same date, to serve unexpired term of two years. Mustered out with company, May 28, 1863, at Albany, N.Y. Subsequent service in Co. D, 16th New York Heavy Artillery.

LUTZSINGER, BALTHAZAR—Age 38 years. Enlisted May 2, 1861, at Schenectady. Mustered in as private, Co. A, May 17, 1861, to serve two years. Deserted,

May or June 1861, before regiment left Albany, N.Y. Subsequent service in Co. A, 58th New York Infantry.

LYNE, WILLIAM H.—Age 31 years. Enlisted April 23, 1861, at Albany. Mustered in as private, Co. C, May 17, 1861, to serve two years. Wounded in left leg, June 27, 1862, at Gaines's Mill, Va. Mustered out with company, May 28, 1863, at Albany, N.Y. Subsequent service in Co. B, 45th United States Infantry, Co. H, 14th United States Infantry, Co. C, 21st Veteran Reserve Corps & United States Navy.

MACKEY, EDWARD (Edwin) E.—Age 27 years. Enlisted April 30, 1861, at Middletown. Mustered in as musician, Co. H, May 17, 1861, to serve two years. Reduced to private, November or December 1861. Mustered out with company, May 28, 1863, at Albany, N.Y.

MACKNEY, JOHN—Age 19 years. Enlisted April 30, 1861, at Middletown. Mustered in as private, Co. H, May 17, 1861, to serve two years. Sent sick from camp near Bakersville, Md., and hospitalized, October 30, 1862, at 2nd Division General Hospital, in Alexandria, Va. Transferred, January or February 1863, at General Hospital, in Portsmouth Grove, R. I. Returned to regiment, March 26, 1863. Mustered out with company, May 28, 1863, at Albany, N.Y.

MACROW, JOSEPH—Age 29 years. Enlisted October 5, 1861, at Ogdensburg. Mustered in as private, Co. K, October 30, 1861, at Camp Williams, Alexandria, Va., to serve unexpired term of two years. Mustered out with company, May 28, 1863, at Albany, N.Y. Subsequent service in Co. C, 6th New Hampshire Infantry & Co. C, 11th New Hampshire Infantry.

MADDEN, EDWARD JAMES—Age 33 years. Enlisted May 12, 1861, at Ogdensburg. Mustered in as private, Co. K, May 17, 1861, to serve two years. Promoted corporal, August 12, 1861. Reduced to private, November 13, 1861. Detailed, August 12, 1862–March 10, 1863, as ambulance driver. Mustered out with company, May 28, 1863, at Albany, N.Y.

MADDEN, WILLIAM—Age 22 years. Enlisted April 19, 1861, at Albany. Mustered in as corporal, Co. F, May 17, 1861, to serve two years. Reduced to private, August 1, 1861. Deserted, August 10, 1861, from Camp Myers, Alexandria, Va.

MADILL, JAMES ALBERT—Age 16 years, but gave age as 18 years. Enlisted May 12, 1861, at Ogdensburg. Mustered in as private, Co. K, May 17, 1861, to serve two years. Wounded in heel, June 27, 1862, at Gaines's Mill, Va. Hospitalized, July or August 1862, at Satterlee General Hospital, in West Philadelphia, Pa. Returned to regiment, December 2, 1862. Mustered out with company, May 28, 1863, at Albany, N.Y. Subsequent service in Co. E & A, 16th New York Heavy Artillery.

MAGUIRE, EDWARD—Age 22 years. Enlisted April 24, 1861, at Albany. Mustered in as private, Co. B, May 17, 1861, to serve two years. Deserted, April 17, 1862, from Camp Jackson, Alexandria, Va.

MAHAR, JOHN—Age 16 years. Enlisted, October 28, 1861, at Albany. Mustered in as musician, Co. H, November 20, 1861, to serve unexpired term of two years. Mustered out with company, May 28, 1863, at Albany, N.Y.

MAHER, JEREMIAH "Jerry"—Age 40 years. Enlisted May 2, 1861, at Schenectady. Mustered in as private, Co. E, May 17, 1861, to serve two years. Absent-without-leave, January 20, 1863, from Camp Russell, White Oak Church, Falmouth, Va. Returned to regiment, January 24, 1863, same place. Court-martialed for absence, February 20, 1863, at same place. Mustered out with company, May 28, 1863, at Albany, N.Y. Subsequent service in Co. B, 2nd New York Veteran Cavalry.

MAJOR, EDWARD—Age 51 years, but gave age as 43 years. Enlisted May 12, 1861, at Ogdensburg. Mustered in as private, Co. K, May 17, 1861, to serve two years. Discharged for disability, August 30, 1861, at Washington, D.C.

MALLEN (Mellon), THOMAS—Age 28 years. Enlisted April 23, 1861, at Albany. Mustered in as private, Co. C, May 17, 1861, to serve two years. Captured, June 27, 1862, at Gaines's Mill, Va. Confined, June 28, 1862, at Richmond, Va. Paroled, September 13, 1862, at City Point, Va. Sent to Washington, D.C., on September 26, 1862. Mustered out with company, May 28, 1863, at Albany, N.Y.

MALLOY, WILLIAM—Age 17 years, but gave age as 19 years. Enlisted April 19, 1861, at Albany. Mustered in as private, Co. F, May 17, 1861, to serve two years. Mustered out with company, May 28, 1863, at Albany, N.Y. Subsequent service in Battery D, 4th New Jersey Light Artillery & Unassigned Maryland Infantry, under alias James Anderson.

MALONE, ROBERT ARMSTRONG—Age 23 years. Enlisted April 30, 1861, at Middletown. Mustered in as first sergeant, Co. D, May 17, 1861, to serve two years. Promoted second lieutenant, November 11, 1861. Detailed on recruiting service, August 13, 1862, in Middletown, N.Y. Promoted captain, Co. B, September 8, 1862. Returned to regiment after recruiting service, on or about October 31, 1862. Mustered out with company, May 28, 1863, at Albany, N.Y. Commissioned second lieutenant, December 2, 1861, with rank from November 11, 1861, after Barry was promoted. Captain, November 10, 1862, with rank from September 8, 1862, after Hastings was promoted. Subsequent service in Co. K, 124th New York Infantry.

MANN, SIMEON H.—Age 30 years. Enlisted August 25, 1862, at Albany. Mustered in as private, Co. C, September 26, 1862, to serve three years. Transferred, May 10, 1863, to Co. G, 121st New York Infantry. Prior service in Co. C, 22nd New York Infantry.

MANTLINE, JOHN W.—Age 25 years. Enlisted May 17, 1861, at Albany. Mustered in as private, Co. I, same date, to serve two years. On seven day furlough, February 1862, in Albany, N.Y. Deserted, February 19, 1862, at expiration of furlough. Detained on account of sickness, July or August 1862. Mustered out with company, May 28, 1863, at Albany, N.Y. Subsequent service in Co. I, 4th New York Cavalry & Co. E, 9th New York Cavalry.

MARCEAU, ALFRED J.—Age 18 years. Enlisted May 12, 1861, at Ogdensburg. Mustered in as private, Co. K, May 17, 1861, to serve two years. Wounded slightly,

September 14, 1862, at Crampton's Gap, Md. Mustered out with company, May 28, 1863, at Albany, N.Y.

MARCELLUS, GEORGE H.—Age 33 years. Enlisted May 2, 1861, at Schenectady. Mustered in as private, Co. E, May 17, 1861, to serve two years. Promoted sergeant, October 7, 1861. Reduced to private, January or February 1862. Left in hospital, August 24, 1862, in Alexandria, Va. Transferred, October 22, 1862, at Patent Office General Hospital, in Washington, D.C. Transferred, November 24, 1862, to Baltimore, Md. Discharged for disability, March 7, 1863, at hospital in Baltimore, Md. Subsequent service in Co. E & G, 13th New York Heavy Artillery & Co. M, 6th New York Heavy Artillery.

MARLETT, GILES—Age 20 years. Enlisted May 2, 1861, at Schenectady. Mustered in as private, Co. E, May 17, 1861, to serve two years. Hospitalized, March or April 1862, at Alexandria, Va. Detailed as nurse, June 19, 1862, at 3rd Division General Hospital, at Alexandria, Va. Returned to regiment, May 1863. Mustered out with company, May 28, 1863, at Albany, N.Y.

MARLETTE, GEORGE W.—Age 18 years. Enlisted August 22, 1861, at Schenectady. Mustered in as private, Co. E, October 21, 1861, at Camp King, Alexandria, Va., to serve unexpired term of two years. Mustered out with company, May 28, 1863, at Albany, N.Y.

MARTIN, ALFRED A.—Age 21 years. Enlisted May 10, 1861, at Albany. Mustered in as private, Co. I, May 17, 1861, to serve two years. Promoted corporal, June 30, 1861. Detailed as blacksmith, December 1861–January 1862, at Division Headquarters. Reduced to private, March or April 1862. Mustered out with company, May 28, 1863, at Albany, N.Y.

MARTIN, EDWIN A.—Age 20 years. Enlisted May 7, 1861, at Albany. Mustered in as private, Co. G, May 17, 1861, to serve two years. Wounded in head, June 27, 1862, at Gaines's Mill, Va. Captured, June 29, 1862, at Savage's Station, Va. Died of such wounds, July 4, 1862, at Savage's Station, Va.

MARTIN, GEORGE—Age 34 years. Enlisted May 6, 1861, at Albany. Mustered in as private, Co. B, May 17, 1861, to serve two years. Killed, September 14, 1862, at Crampton's Gap, Md.

MARTIN, JOHN—Age 21 years. Enlisted September 30, 1861, at Albany. Mustered in as private, Co. A, October 21, 1861, at Camp King, Alexandria, Va., to serve two years. Mustered out with company, May 28, 1863, at Albany, N.Y.

MARTIN, MICHAEL—Age 27 years. Enlisted May 7, 1861, at Albany. Mustered in as private, Co. H, May 17, 1861, to serve two years. Accidentally shot left hand by self, October 1, 1861. Discharged on account of such wound, December 23, 1861, at Camp King, Alexandria, Va. Subsequent service in Co. E, 61st New York Infantry.

MARVIN, JOHN HENRY—Age 27 years. Enlisted April 19, 1861, at Albany. Mustered in as corporal, Co. I, May 17, 1861, to serve two years. Mustered out with company, May 28, 1863, at Albany, N.Y. Commissioned second lieutenant, May 30, 1863, with rank from January 15, 1863, after Chalmers was promoted. Not mustered. Subsequent service in Co. G, 2nd New York Veteran Cavalry.

MATHEWS, JOHN J.—Age 34 years. Enlisted May 12, 1861, at Albany. Mustered in as private, Co. F, May 17, 1861, to serve two years. Captured, June 27, 1862, at Gaines's Mill, Va. Confined, June 28, 1862, at Richmond, Va. Paroled, August 5, 1862, at City Point, Va. Promoted sergeant, December 8, 1862. Mustered out with company, May 28, 1863, at Albany, N.Y. Subsequent service in Co. B, 13th New York Heavy Artillery.

MATHEWS, WILLIAM—Age 20 years. Enlisted April 23, 1861, at Albany. Mustered in as private, Co. C, May 17, 1861, to serve two years. Hospitalized sick, June 27–July 2, 1862, at Chickahominy River, near Richmond, Va. Sent sick, July 2, 1862, from Harrison's Landing, Va. Hospitalized, July 4, 1862, at Carver General Hospital, in Washington, D.C. Transferred, September or October 1862, to General Hospital, in Portsmouth Grove, R. I. Deserted, December 30, 1862.

MATHISE, HENRY—Age 38 years. Enlisted August 28, 1862, at Albany. Mustered in as private, Co. A, same date, to serve three years. Transferred, May 10, 1863, to Co. H, 121st New York Infantry.

MATTESON, WILLIAM "Billy" HENRY H.—Age 20 years. Enlisted May 7, 1861, at Albany. Mustered in as private, Co. G, May 17, 1861, to serve two years. Promoted corporal, January 1, 1863. Mustered out with company, May 28, 1863, at Albany, N.Y. Subsequent service in Co. L, 50th New York Engineers.

MATTIMORE, FRANK J.—Age 28 years. Enrolled August 11, 1862, at Albany. Mustered in as assistant surgeon, August 18, 1862, to serve three years. Detached in hospital, September 14, 1862, at Burkittsville, Md. Returned to regiment, October 20, 1862. Absent on sick leave, March 15, 1863, at Washington, D.C. Returned to regiment, May 15, 1863. Mustered out with regiment, May 28, 1863, at Albany, N.Y. Died of disease, October 11, 1863, in Albany, N.Y. commissioned assistant surgeon, August 18, 1862, with rank from August 11, 1862, original.

MAXWELL, LEGRANT—Age 25 years. Enlisted April 28, 1861, at Schenectady. Mustered in as private, Co. A, May 17, 1861, to serve two years. Mustered out with company, May 28, 1863, at Albany, N.Y. Subsequent service in Co. E, 2nd New York Veteran Cavalry.

MAYETTE, WILLIAM HENRY—Age 16 years, but gave age as 19 years. Enlisted May 12, 1861, at Ogdensburg. Mustered in as private, Co. K, May 17, 1861, to serve two years. Promoted corporal, August 12, 1861. Promoted first sergeant, November 12, 1862. Mustered out with company, May 28, 1863, at Albany, N.Y.

MCALLISTER, JOHN—Age 42 years, but gave age as 38 years. Enlisted April 23, 1861, at Albany. Mustered in as private, Co. C, May 17, 1861, to serve two years. Hospitalized, August 10, 1862, at Satterlee General Hospital, in West Philadelphia, Pa. Hospitalized, October 4, 1862, at Convalescent Camp, in Alexandria, Va. Transferred, December 8, 1862, to King Street General Hospital, in Alexandria, Va. Transferred, December 12, 1862, to 5th and Buttonwood Streets General Hospital, in

Philadelphia, Pa. Transferred, January 15, 1863, to Mower General Hospital, in Philadelphia, Pa. Discharged for disability, March 13, 1863, at Mower General Hospital in Philadelphia, Pa.

MCANESPY, JAMES—Age 25 years. Enlisted June 6, 1861, at Albany. Mustered in as private, Co. A, same date, to serve two years. Mustered out, June 6, 1863.

MCCABE, MICHAEL—Age 21 years. Enlisted April 30, 1861, at Middletown. Mustered in as private, Co. H, May 17, 1861, to serve two years. Deserted, March 1, 1862, from Camp Jackson, Alexandria, Va.

MCCABE, THOMAS—Age 22 years. Enlisted December 13, 1861, at Albany. Mustered in as private, Co. F, same date, to serve two years. Mustered out with company, May 28, 1863, at Albany, N.Y.

MCCAFFREY, PATRICK—Age 29 years. Enlisted April 19, 1861, at Albany. Mustered in as corporal, Co. I, May 17, 1861, to serve two years. Promoted sergeant, June 30, 1861. Mustered out with company, May 28, 1863, at Albany, N.Y.

MCCALL, THOMAS—Age 35 years. Enlisted May 7, 1861, at Albany. Mustered in as private, Co. G, May 17, 1861, to serve two years. Deserted, September 21, 1861, from camp, near Alexandria, Va. Arrested, September 1, 1864, at Washington, D.C.

MCCALL, WILLIAM N.—Age 21 years. Enlisted April 30, 1861, at Middletown. Mustered in as private, Co. D, May 17, 1861, to serve two years. Promoted drummer, November or December 1861. Reduced to private, July or August 1862. Promoted to musician, October 1, 1862. Mustered out with company, May 28, 1863, at Albany, N.Y. Subsequent service in Co. K, 15th New York Cavalry & Co. K, 2nd New York Provisional Cavalry.

MCCANN, JOHN—Age 19 years. Enlisted April 22, 1861, at Schenectady. Mustered in as private, Co. A, May 17, 1861, to serve two years. Mustered out with company, May 28, 1863, at Albany, N.Y.

MCCARTHY, PATRICK—Age 28 years. Enlisted May 12, 1861, at Ogdensburg. Mustered in as private, Co. K, May 17, 1861, to serve two years. Mustered out with company, May 28, 1863, at Albany, N.Y.

MCCARTY, JAMES—Age 30 years. Enlisted April 22, 1861, at Schenectady. Mustered in as private, Co. A, May 17, 1861, to serve two years. Wounded, on or about May 3, 1863, near Fredericksburg, Va. Joined regiment, June 2, 1863, at Albany, N.Y. Mustered out, June 2, 1863, at Albany, N.Y.

MCCARTY, MICHAEL—Age 29 years. Enlisted May 7, 1861, at Albany. Mustered in as private, Co. G, May 17, 1861, to serve two years. Mustered out with company, May 28, 1863, at Albany, N.Y.

MCCLINCH, DANIEL, Jr.—Age 19 years. Enlisted May 13, 1861, at Albany. Mustered in as private, Co. I, May 17, 1861, to serve two years. Hospitalized, July or August 1862, at Satterlee General Hospital, in West Philadelphia, Pa. Returned to regiment, May 8, 1863. Mustered out with company, May 28, 1863, at Albany, N.Y. Son of Daniel McClinch, Sr.

MCCLINCH, DANIEL, Sr.—Age 43 years. Enlisted August 30, 1862, at Albany. Mustered in as private, Co. I, September 26, 1862, at Albany, to serve three years. Transferred, May 10, 1863, to Co. F, 121st New York Infantry. Father of Daniel McClinch, Jr.

MCCLURE, WILLIAM—Age 19 years. Enlisted October 1, 1861, at Middletown. Mustered in as private, Co. D, October 21, 1861, at Camp King, Alexandria, Va., to serve two years. Mustered out with company, May 28, 1863, at Albany, N.Y.

MCCOLLUM, ROBERT—Age 18 years. Enlisted September 1, 1861, at Albany. Mustered in as private, Co. H, October 21, 1861, at Camp King, Alexandria, Va., to serve two years. Discharged for disability, December 23, 1861, at Camp King, Alexandria, Va.

MCCORMICK, EDWARD M.—Age 21 years. Enlisted September 27, 1861, at Middletown. Mustered in as private, Co. D, October 21, 1861, at Camp King, Alexandria, Va., to serve two years. Sent sick, May 7, 1862, from Brick House Landing (West Point), Va. Hospitalized, May 7, 1862, at Chesapeake General Hospital, at Fort Monroe, Va. Hospitalized, May 11, 1862, at Seminary Hospital, at Hampton, Va. Discharged for disability, December 24, 1862, at Fort Monroe, Va.

MCCORMICK, THOMAS—Age 25 years. Enlisted May 2, 1861, at Schenectady. Mustered in as private, Co. E, May 17, 1861, to serve two years. Hospitalized, August 15, 1862, at General Hospital, near Harrison's Landing, Va. Returned to regiment, August or September 1862. Mustered out with company, May 28, 1863, at Albany, N.Y.

MCCOY, LEWIS ROE—Age 22 years. Enlisted February 20, 1862, at Middletown. Mustered in as private, Co. D, same date, to serve three years. Captured, June 29, 1862, while sick at Savage's Station, Va. Confined, June 30, 1862, at Richmond, Va. Paroled, September 13, 1862, at City Point, Va. Sent to Washington, D.C., on September 25, 1862. Hospitalized and retained as nurse, November 15, 1862, at Camp Banks Hospital, in Alexandria, Va. Mustered out with company, May 28, 1863, at Albany, N.Y. Brother of William B. McCoy & Second Cousin of Richard A. Holly, Jr.

MCCOY, WILLIAM B.—Age 19 years. Enlisted February 20, 1862, at Middletown. Mustered in as private, Co. D, same date, to serve two years. Captured, June 30, 1862, near James River, near Richmond, Va. Confined, July 13, 1862, at Richmond, Va. Paroled, August 5, 1862, at City Point, Va. Hospitalized, August 1862, at Broad and Cherry Streets General Hospital, in Philadelphia, Pa. Transferred, August 1862, to Satterlee General Hospital, in West Philadelphia, Pa. Detailed as provost guard, December 2, 1862, in Philadelphia, Pa. Returned to regiment, April or May 1863. Mustered out with company, May 28, 1863, at Albany, N.Y. Subsequent service in the United States Navy. Brother of Lewis R. McCoy & Second Cousin of Richard A. Holly, Jr.

MCCREA, WILLIAM R.—Age 26 years. Enlisted April 30, 1861, at Middletown. Mustered in as private, Co. D, May 17, 1861, to serve two years. Left sick, June 18, 1861, at Albany hospital when regiment left state. Deserted, July 1, 1861, at New York City, N.Y. Arrested, December 28, 1863, at Middletown, N.Y. Sent to Fort Columbus, N.Y. on December 29, 1863.

MCDERMOTT, EDWARD—Age 36 years. Enlisted December 26, 1861, at Albany. Mustered in as private, Co. B, January 2, 1862, at Albany, to serve two years. Hospitalized, October or December 1, 1862, at Camp A General Hospital, in Frederick, Md. Transferred, date not stated, to hospital in Baltimore and Hagerstown, Md. Returned to regiment, May 19, 1863. Mustered out with company, May 28, 1863, at Albany, N.Y. Subsequent service in Co. H, 7th New York Heavy Artillery.

MCDONALD, ARCHIBALD J.—Age 21 years. Enlisted October 12, 1861, at Ogdensburg. Mustered in as private, Co. K, October 30, 1861, at Camp Williams, Va., to serve two years. Mustered out with company, May 28, 1863, at Albany, N.Y.

MCDONALD, NELSON—Age 24 years. Enlisted May 2, 1861, at Schenectady. Mustered in as private, Co. E, May 17, 1861, to serve two years. Wounded in right hand, September 14, 1862, at Crampton's Gap, Md. Amputation of two fingers. Hospitalized, October 4, 1862, at Camp A General Hospital, in Frederick, Md. Transferred, March 6, 1863, to General Hospital Number 1, in Frederick, Md. Returned to regiment, March 19, 1863. Discharged on account of such wounds, April 4, 1863, at Convalescent Camp, Alexandria, Va. Subsequent service in Co. B, 2nd New York Veteran Cavalry.

MCDONALD, PATRICK—Age 26 years. Enlisted September 1, 1861, at Albany. Mustered in as private, Co. B, October 21, 1861, at Camp King, Alexandria, Va., to serve unexpired term of two years. Promoted corporal, July 1, 1862. Mustered out with company, May 28, 1863, at Albany, N.Y.

MCELROY, CHARLES D.—Age 19 years. Enlisted April 30, 1861, at Middletown. Mustered in as private, Co. D, May 17, 1861, to serve two years. Sent sick, August 7, 1862, onboard Steamer *State of Maine*, at Harrison's Landing, Va. Hospitalized, August 10, 1862, at Satterlee General Hospital, in West Philadelphia, Pa. Discharged for disability, September 11, 1862, at Philadelphia, Pa.

MCFALL, JOHN W.—Age 19 years. Enlisted May 12, 1861, at Ogdensburg. Mustered in as private, Co. K, May 17, 1861, to serve two years. Wounded in fingers, June 27, 1862, at Gaines's Mill, Va. Mustered out with company, May 28, 1863, at Albany, N.Y. Subsequent service in Co. A, 16th New York Heavy Artillery.

MCFETRISH, JAMES A.—Age 19 years. Enlisted May 10, 1861, at Albany. Mustered in as private, Co. I, May 17, 1861, to serve two years. Captured, June 27, 1862, at Gaines's Mill, Va. Confined, June 28, 1862, at Richmond, Va. Paroled, August 5, 1862, at City Point, Va. Mustered out with company, May 28, 1863, at Albany, N.Y. Subsequent service in Co. L, 7th New York Heavy Artillery. Brother of Robert McFetrish.

MCFETRISH, ROBERT—Age 18 years. Enlisted June 5, 1861, at Albany. Mustered in as private, Co. K, July 1, 1861, at Washington, D.C., to serve two years. Wounded in back, September 17, 1862, at Sharpsburg, Md. Mustered out with company, May 28, 1863, at Albany, N.Y. Brother of James A. McFetrish.

MCGILL, JOHN—Age 15 years. Enlisted October 29, 1861, at Ogdensburg. Mustered in as drummer, Co. K, same date, to serve two years. Deserted August 31, 1862, at Alexandria, Va.

MCGOVERN, JOHN—Age 40 years. Enlisted April 19, 1861, at Albany. Mustered in as private, Co. F, May 17, 1861, to serve two years. Straggled or deserted, September 7, 1862, at Alexandria, Va. Hospitalized, September 23, 1862, at Epiphany General Hospital, in Washington, D.C. Returned to regiment, November 18, 1862. Hospitalized, December 8, 1862, at 2nd Division General Hospital, in Alexandria, Va. Returned to regiment, February 10 or March 13, 1863. Mustered out with company, May 28, 1863, at Albany, N.Y. Subsequent service in Co. L, 2nd New York Veteran Cavalry.

MCGOWAN, THEODORE S.—Age 18 years. Enlisted April 19, 1861, at Albany. Mustered in as private, Co. F, May 17, 1861, to serve two years. Mustered out with company, May 28, 1863, at Albany, N.Y.

MCGRAW, EDWARD D.—Age 25 years. Enlisted May 2, 1861, at Schenectady. Mustered in as private, Co. E, May 17, 1861, to serve two years. Mustered out with company, May 28, 1863, at Albany, N.Y. Subsequent service in Co. F, 2nd New York Heavy Artillery.

MCGRAW, MICHAEL—Age 20 years. Enlisted May 7, 1861, at Albany. Mustered in as private, Co. G, May 17, 1861, to serve two years. Detailed in Ambulance Corps, November 1862. Mustered out with company, May 28, 1863, at Albany, N.Y. Subsequent service in Co. H & L, 24th New York Cavalry.

MCGUINNESS, EDWARD—Age 18 years. Enlisted April 23, 1861, at Albany. Mustered in as private, Co. C, May 17, 1861, to serve two years. Court-martialed for disobedience, January 31, 1862, at Alexandria, Va. Mustered out with company, May 28, 1863, at Albany, N.Y.

MCINTOSH, WILLIAM H. H.—Age 25 years. Enlisted June 8, 1861, at Albany. Mustered in as private, Co. A, same date, to serve two years. Deserted, September 20, 1861, at Camp King, Alexandria, Va. Returned to regiment, January or February 1862. Deserted, December 13, 1862, at Fredericksburg, Va. Returned to regiment, December 16, 1862. Court-martialed for cowardice, February 23, 1863. Sentenced to hard labor at Rip Raps, Fort Jefferson, Dry Tortugas, Fl. Dishonorably discharged for cowardice, March 10, 1863, near Falmouth, Va.

MCINTYRE, CHARLES—Age 22 years. Enlisted May 17, 1861, at Albany. Mustered in as private, Co. E, same date, to serve two years. Hospitalized, May 11, 1862, at Seminary Hospital, at Hampton, Va. Returned to regiment, date not stated. Sent sick, September 1, 1862, aboard transport *Kennebec*, from Alexandria, Va., and hospitalized at U.S. General Hospital, in Portsmouth Grove, R.I. Returned to regiment, date not stated. Mustered out with company, May 28, 1863, at Albany, N.Y.

MCKEON, THOMAS—Age 25 years. Enlisted May 7, 1861, at Albany. Mustered in as corporal, Co. G, May 17, 1861, to serve two years. Reduced to private, July 14, 1861. Hospitalized, May 11, 1862, at Seminary Hospital, at Hampton, Va. Sent sick, on or about May 24, 1862, from White House Landing, Va., to New York. Returned to regiment, date not stated. Promoted corporal, January 1, 1863. Mustered out with company, May 28, 1863, at

Albany, N.Y. Subsequent service in Co. L, 21st New York Cavalry.

MCKINLEY, HUGH—Age 34 years. Enlisted May 12, 1861, at Ogdensburg. Mustered in as private, Co. K, May 17, 1861, to serve two years. Wounded in thigh and captured, July 17, 1861, near Fairfax Court House, Va. Confined at Richmond, Va. Paroled, January 3, 1862, at Fort Monroe, Va. Returned to regiment, January 17, 1862, at Camp King, Alexandria, Va. Placed on thirty day furlough. Discharged, February 3, 1862.

MCKINNEY, DENNIS—Age 21 years. Enlisted September 9, 1861, at Schenectady. Mustered in as private, Co. E, October 21, 1861, at Camp King, Alexandria, Va., to serve two years. Captured, June 27, 1862, at Gaines's Mill, Va. Confined, June 28, 1862, at Richmond, Va. Paroled, September 13, 1862, at City Point, Va. Absent-without-leave, January 20, 1863, from Camp Russell, White Oak Church, Falmouth, Va. Returned to regiment, January 24, 1863, same place. Court-martialed for absence, February 23, 1863, at same place. Mustered out with company, May 28, 1863, at Albany, N.Y. Subsequent service in Co. C, 13th New York Heavy Artillery & Co. K, 6th New York Heavy Artillery. Brother of Patrick McKinney.

MCKINNEY, PATRICK—Age 18 years. Enlisted May 2, 1861, at Schenectady. Mustered in as private, Co. E, May 17, 1861, to serve two years. Mustered out with company, May 28, 1863, at Albany, N.Y. Subsequent service in Co. "U" 16th New York Heavy Artillery & Co. F & C, 1st New York Mounted Rifles. Brother of Dennis McKinney.

MCKINNEY, WILLIAM H.—Age 20 years. Enlisted May 2, 1861, at Schenectady. Mustered in as private, Co. E, May 17, 1861, to serve two years. Mustered out with company, May 28, 1863, at Albany, N.Y. Subsequent service in Co. D, 16th New York Heavy Artillery.

MCKOON, HORACE WILLIAM—Age 19 years. Enlisted April 30, 1861, at Middletown. Mustered in as corporal, Co. H, May 17, 1861, to serve two years. Discharged for disability, August 5, 1861, at Alexandria, Va. Subsequent service in Co. L, 56th New York Infantry.

MCLANE, PATRICK—Age 39 years. Enlisted May 2, 1861, at Albany. Mustered in as private, Co. F, May 17, 1861, to serve two years. Deserted, September 17, 1862, at Sharpsburg, Md.

MCLEAN, ROBERT L.—Age 41 years. Enlisted January 27, 1862, at Ogdensburg. Mustered in as private, Co. K, same date, to serve unexpired term of two years. Wounded in hip, June 27, 1862, at Gaines's Mill, Va. Hospitalized, date not stated, at hospital in Annapolis, Md. Discharged for disability, January 19, 1863, at Fairfax Seminary, Va. Subsequent service in Co. I, 142nd Illinois Infantry.

MCMANNUS, BARNEY—Age 39 years. Enlisted May 1, 1861, at Albany. Mustered in as private, Co. B, May 17, 1861, to serve two years. Deserted, June 16, 1861, at Albany, N.Y.

MCNEAL (McNeil), JOHN—Age 21 years. Enlisted April 22, 1861, at Schenectady. Mustered in as private, Co. A, May 17, 1861, to serve two years. Deserted, December 13, 1862, at Fredericksburg, Va. Returned to regiment, December 16, 1862. Court-martialed for cowardice, February 23, 1863. Sentenced to hard labor at Rip Raps, Fort Jefferson, Dry Tortugas, Fl. Dishonorably discharged for cowardice, March 10, 1863, near Falmouth, Va. Sentence expired, August 10, 1863, at Rip Raps, Fort Jefferson, Dry Tortugas, Fl.

MCNEIL, JAMES—Age 22 years. Enlisted May 2, 1861, at Schenectady. Mustered in as private, Co. E, May 17, 1861, to serve two years. Court-martialed at regimental level, September or October 1861. Promoted corporal, August 12, 1862. Mustered out with company, May 28, 1863, at Albany, N.Y. Subsequent service in 17th United States Infantry.

MEAD, CHARLES E.—Age 18 years. Enlisted May 2, 1861, at Schenectady. Mustered in as private, Co. E, May 17, 1861, to serve two years. Deserted, August 4, 1861, from Camp Myers, Alexandria, Va.

MEAD, MICHAEL—Age 20 years. Enlisted May 17, 1861, at Albany. Mustered in as private, Co. C, same date, to serve two years. Mustered out with company, May 28, 1863, at Albany, N.Y.

MEGINNIS, JOHN C.—Age 33 years. Enlisted April 27, 1861, at Middletown. Enrolled May 17, 1861, at Albany. Mustered in as captain, Co. D, same date, to serve two years. Detailed on recruiting service, December 1861, in Middletown, N.Y. Promoted major, November 11, 1861. On seven day furlough, January 31, 1862. Promoted lieutenant colonel, August 14, 1862. On ten day furlough, January 31, 1863, in Middletown, N.Y. Mustered out with regiment, May 28, 1863, at Albany, N.Y. Commissioned captain, July 4, 1861, with rank from May 17, 1861, original, major, December 2, 1861, with rank from November 11, 1861, after Myers was promoted. Lieutenant colonel, October 11, 1862, with rank from August 14, 1862, after Myers was promoted. Brother of Samuel G. Meginnis.

MEGINNIS, SAMUEL G.—Age 22 years. Enlisted April 30, 1861, at Middletown. Mustered in as private, Co. D, May 17, 1861, to serve two years. Promoted corporal, October 12, 1861. Reduced to private, May 31, 1862. Hospitalized, July 9, 1862. Died of disease, July 22, 1862, at Brooklyn City Hospital, at Brooklyn, N.Y. Brother of John C. Meginnis.

MELANY, MICHAEL—Age 25 years. Enlisted May 2, 1861, at Schenectady. Mustered in as private, Co. E, May 17, 1861, to serve two years. Deserted, April 10, 1862, from Bristoe Station, Va.

MERRON (Marrion), PATRICK—Age 38 years. Enlisted May 12, 1861, at Ogdensburg. Mustered in as private, Co. K, May 17, 1861, to serve two years. Mustered out with company, May 28, 1863, at Albany, N.Y. Subsequent service in Co. C, 13th New York Heavy Artillery & Co. K, 6th New York Heavy Artillery.

MESSENGER, WILLIAM H.—Age 24 years. Enlisted September 20, 1862, at Wallkill. Mustered in as private, Co. D, October 25, 1862, at Albany, to serve three years. Hospitalized, January 4, 1863, at Harewood General Hospital, in Washington, D.C. Discharged for disability, February 20, 1863, at Harewood General Hospital, in Washington, D.C.

MIDDAUGH, CARSON S.—Age 25 years. Enlisted April 30, 1861, at Middletown. Mustered in as private, Co. D, May 17, 1861, to serve two years. Never participated in any engagement. Mustered out with company, May 28, 1863, at Albany, N.Y.

MILLAR, ROBERT J.—Age 24 years. Enlisted April 22, 1861, at Schenectady. Mustered in as private, Co. A, May 17, 1861, to serve two years. Promoted corporal, June 1, 1861. Promoted sergeant, November or December 1861. Mustered out with company, May 28, 1863, at Albany, N.Y.

MILLARD, DAVIS—Age 29 years. Enlisted May 17, 1861, at Albany. Mustered in as drummer, Co. E, same date, to serve two years. Reduced to private, September 25, 1861. Mustered out with company, May 28, 1863, at Albany, N.Y.

MILLARD, ROBERT A.—Age 19 years. Enlisted May 17, 1861, at Albany. Mustered in as private, Co. K, same date, to serve two years. Deserted, May 19, 1861, at Albany, N.Y. Subsequent service in Co. G, 106th New York Infantry.

MILLER, JOHN—Age 25 years. Enlisted April 19, 1861, at Albany. Mustered in as private, Co. F, May 17, 1861, to serve two years. Absent-without-leave, February 7, 1862, from Camp King, Alexandria, Va. Returned to regiment, February 12. Court-martialed for absence, February 26, 1862, at Alexandria, Va. Wounded in right leg, June 27, 1862, at Gaines's Mill, Va. Captured, June 29, 1862, at Savage's Station, Va. Confined, July 13, 1862, at Richmond, Va. Paroled, July 25, 1862, at City Point, Va. Hospitalized, date not stated, at General Hospital, in Chester, Pa. Forwarded to regiment, August 27, 1862, from Philadelphia, Pa. Wounded in left breast, September 14, 1862, at Crampton's Gap, Md. Hospitalized, October 4, 1862, at Camp A General Hospital, in Frederick, Md. Died of such wound, November 16, 1862, at Camp A General Hospital, in Frederick, Md.

MILLER, REUBEN—Age 34 years. Enlisted September 19, 1862, at Albany. Mustered in as private, Co. D, October 13, 1862, at Albany, to serve three years. Transferred, May 10, 1863, to Co. H, 121st New York Infantry.

MILLER, RICHARD—Age 20 years. Enlisted April 24, 1861, at Albany. Mustered in as private, Co. B, May 17, 1861, to serve two years. Deserted, May 23, 1861, at Albany, N.Y.

MILLER, WILLIAM W.—Age 39 years. Enlisted April 19, 1861, at Albany. Mustered in as private, Co. I, May 17, 1861, to serve two years. Deserted, August 10, 1861, at Alexandria, Va.

MILLIKEN, EDWARD ALEXANDER, Jr.—Age 20 years. Enlisted May 7, 1861, at Canandaigua. Mustered in as private, Co. G, May 17, 1861, to serve two years. Detailed to Ambulance Corps, November 1862. Mustered out with company, May 28, 1863, at Albany, N.Y. Subsequent service in Co. H, 4th New York Heavy Artillery.

MILLS, ARTHUR WESLEY—Age 43 years, but gave age as 40 years. Enlisted May 14, 1861, at Albany. Mustered in as private, Co. B, May 17, 1861, to serve two years. Detailed as regimental hospital steward, May 17, 1861. Discharged for disability, September 24, 1861, at Camp King, Alexandria, Va. Subsequent service in Co. D, 3rd New York Infantry, 22nd United States Colored Troops Infantry & United States Marine Corps, under alias Adam Milton.

MILLS, FRANKLIN LEWIS—Age 24 years. Enlisted May 17, 1861, at Albany. Mustered in as private, Co. I, May 17, 1861, to serve two years. Detailed to Ambulance Corps, November 1862. Mustered out with company, May 28, 1863, at Albany, N.Y.

MILLS, HENRY CLAY—Age 26 years. Enlisted June 14, 1861, at Middletown. Mustered in as private, Co. D, same date, to serve two years. Hospitalized, July 1, 1861, at Finley Hospital, in Washington, D.C. Retained as nurse, July 15, 1861, at E Street General Hospital, in Washington, D.C. Transferred as nurse, February 1, 1862, to Eckington General Hospital, in Washington, D.C. Transferred as nurse, March or April 1863, to Finley General Hospital, in Washington, D.C. Returned to regiment, May 16, 1863. Mustered out with company, May 28, 1863, at Albany, N.Y. Brother of William B. Mills & First Cousin of Peter M. Fullerton.

MILLS, JAMES H.—Age 17 years, but gave age as 18 years. Enlisted May 12, 1861, at Ogdensburg. Mustered in as private, Co. K, May 17, 1861, to serve two years. Captured, June 27, 1862, at Gaines's Mill, Va. Confined, June 28, 1862, at Richmond, Va. Paroled, September 13, 1862, at City Point, Va. On duty at parole camp, at Alexandria, Va. Returned to regiment, January 25, 1863. Mustered out with company, May 28, 1863, at Albany, N.Y. Subsequent service in Co. C, 24th New York Cavalry.

MILLS, WILLIAM BRONSON—Age 24 years. Enlisted April 30, 1861, at Middletown. Mustered in as private, Co. D, May 17, 1861, to serve two years. Detailed as Adjutant Clerk, March 1, 1863. Mustered out with company, May 28, 1863, at Albany, N.Y. Brother of Henry C. Mills & First Cousin of Peter M. Fullerton.

MINIX, THOMAS—Age 16 years, but gave age as 18 years. Enlisted December 20, 1861, at Alexandria, Va. Mustered in as private, Co. K, same date, to serve two years. Mustered out with company, May 28, 1863, at Albany, N.Y. Subsequent service in Co. K, 1st New York Engineers.

MITCHELL, ANDREW BARCLAY—Age 21 years. Enlisted May 2, 1861, at Schenectady. Mustered in as musician, Co. E, May 17, 1861, to serve two years. Promoted first lieutenant, Co. C, June 16, 1861. Promoted captain, October 19, 1861. Detailed on recruiting service, December 1861, in Schenectady, N.Y. Returned to regiment, on or about January 10, 1862. On ten day furlough, February of 1863, in Schenectady, N.Y. Mustered out with company, May 28, 1863, at Albany, N.Y. Commissioned first lieutenant, July 4, 1861, with rank from June 16, 1861, original. Captain, November 11, 1861, with rank from October 19, 1861, after Wiltse was dismissed.

MONAHAN, PATRICK—Age 18 years. Enlisted May 16, 1861, at Albany. Mustered in as private, Co. F,

May 17, 1861, to serve two years. Mustered out with company, May 28, 1863, at Albany, N.Y. Subsequent service in Co. D, 13th New York Heavy Artillery & Co. L, 6th New York Heavy Artillery.

MONK, CHARLES WILLIAM—Age 21 years. Enlisted May 12, 1861, at Ogdensburg. Mustered in as private, Co. K, May 17, 1861, to serve two years. Detailed as Waggoner, June 30, 1861. Returned to company, September 1, 1861. Mustered out with company, May 28, 1863, at Albany, N.Y.

MONTIETH, RICHARD "Dick" (James Byron)— Age 24 years. Enlisted May 12, 1861, at Ogdensburg. Mustered in as first sergeant, Co. K, May 17, 1861, to serve two years. Reduced to private, July 12, 1861. Detailed as orderly, December 1861. Detailed as servant, January 1862. Mustered out with company, May 28, 1863, at Albany, N.Y. Subsequent service in Co. K, 7th Pennsylvania Cavalry, under alias Samuel D. Byerly.

MOODIE, JAMES—Age 19 years. Enlisted April 19, 1861, at Albany. Mustered in as private, Co. F, May 17, 1861, to serve two years. Promoted corporal, September 19, 1861. Reduced to private, November 3, 1861. Hospitalized, August 10, 1862, at Satterlee General Hospital, in West Philadelphia, Pa. Discharged for disability, November 28, 1862, at Satterlee General Hospital, in West Philadelphia, Pa.

MOONEY, FRANK (Francis)—Age 23 years. Enlisted April 22, 1861, at Schenectady. Mustered in as private, Co. A, May 17, 1861, to serve two years. Deserted, August 4, 1861, from Camp Myers, Alexandria, Va. Returned to regiment, September 1, 1861. Captured, June 27, 1862, at Gaines's Mill, Va. Confined, June 28, 1862, at Richmond, Va. Paroled, August 5, 1862, at City Point, Va. Promoted corporal, date not stated. Absent-without-leave, January 20, 1863, from Camp Russell, White Oak Church, Falmouth, Va. Returned to regiment, January 24, 1863, same place. Court-martialed for absence, February 20, 1863, at same place. Reduced to private, February, 20, 1863. Mustered out with company, May 28, 1863, at Albany, N.Y. Subsequent service in Co. E, 2nd New York Veteran Cavalry.

MOONEY, JOHN—Age 31 years. Enrolled April 19, 1861, at Albany. Mustered in as second lieutenant, Co. F, May 17, 1861, to serve two years. Promoted first lieutenant, Co. C, October 19, 1861. Detailed as officer in charge of recruiting service, August 13, 1862, in Albany, N.Y. Promoted captain, Co. H, April 1, 1863. Mustered out with company, May 28, 1863, at Albany, N.Y. Commissioned second lieutenant, July 4, 1861, with rank from April 22, 1861, original. First lieutenant, December 2, 1861, with rank from October 19, 1861, after Mitchell was promoted. Captain, March 23, 1863, with rank from June 27, 1862, after Rogers died. Subsequent service in Co. M, 7th New York Heavy Artillery.

MOORE (Morr), CHARLES A.—Age 23 years. Enlisted June 14, 1861, at Middletown. Mustered in as private, Co. D, same date, to serve two years. Mustered out with company, May 28, 1863, at Albany, N.Y. Son of Jacob A. Moore.

MOORE (Morr), JACOB A.—Age 43 years. Enlisted April 30, 1861, at Middletown. Mustered in as private, Co. D, May 17, 1861, to serve two years. Discharged for disability, October 9, 1861, at Camp King, Alexandria, Va. Father of Charles A. Moore.

MOORE, JAMES—Age 24 years. Enlisted May 17, 1861, at Albany. Mustered in as private, Co. C, same date, to serve two years. Deserted, May or June 1861, before regiment left Albany, N.Y.

MOORE, THOMAS—Age 28 years. Enlisted August 18, 1862, at Albany. Mustered in as private, unassigned, same date, to serve three years. Reported deserted, October 25, 1862.

MORGAN, JAMES H.—Age 23 years. Enrolled May 7, 1861, at Canandaigua. Mustered in as first lieutenant, Co. G, May 17, 1861, to serve two years. Resigned, September 30, 1861. Commissioned first lieutenant, July 4, 1861, with rank from May 7, 1861, original. Subsequent service in Co. M, 7th New York Heavy Artillery.

MORGAN, JOHN T.—Age 31 years. Enlisted April 19, 1861, at Albany. Mustered in as first sergeant, Co. I, May 17, 1861, to serve two years. Deserted, July 8, 1861, at Washington, D.C.

MORSE, JAMES H.—Age 33 years. Enlisted April 24, 1861, at Albany. Mustered in as sergeant, Co. B, May 17, 1861, to serve two years. Resigned to the rank of private, October 1, 1861. Discharged for disability, May 4, 1862, at General Hospital in Alexandria, Va.

MOWATT, AUGUSTUS WAKEMAN—Age 19 years. Enlisted April 23, 1861, at Fishkill. Mustered in as sergeant, Co. C, May 17, 1861, to serve two years. Promoted first sergeant, December 1, 1862. Mustered out with company, May 28, 1863, at Albany, N.Y.

MULFORD, CHARLES M.—Age 20 years. Enlisted September 20, 1861, at Middletown. Mustered in as private, Co. D, October 21, 1861, at Camp King, Alexandria, Va., to serve unexpired term of two years. Captured, June 27, 1862, at Gaines's Mill, Va. Confined, June 28, 1862, at Richmond, Va. Paroled, August 5, 1862, at City Point, Va. Mustered out with company, May 28, 1863, at Albany, N.Y.

MULLEN, JAMES—Age 19 years. Enlisted November 20, 1861, at Albany. Mustered in as private, Co. F, same date, to serve unexpired term of two years. Hospitalized, July or August 1862, at Hammond General Hospital, in Point Lookout, Md. Discharged for disability, November 1, 1862, at Hammond General Hospital, in Point Lookout, Md. Subsequent service in the United States Navy.

MULLEN, PATRICK—Age 18 years. Enlisted May 16, 1861, at Albany. Mustered in as private, Co. F, May 17, 1861, to serve two years. Wounded slightly in head, June 27, 1862, at Gaines's Mill, Va. Mustered out with company, May 28, 1863, at Albany, N.Y.

MUNGER, HENRY "Harry" ELIAS—Age 20 years. Enlisted November 1, 1861, at Albany. Mustered in as sergeant, Co. A, December 1, 1861, to serve unexpired term of two years. Promoted second lieutenant, December 14, 1861. Promoted first lieutenant, August 14, 1862. Mustered out with company, May 28, 1863, at Albany, N.Y. Commissioned second lieutenant, December 26,

Shown here as a member of GAR Post 48 in Beacon, New York, the former first sergeant for Company C, Augustus W. Mowatt was a lifelong member. He died on November 17, 1911, in Fishkill, New York (courtesy Stephanie Graves).

1861, with rank from December 14, 1861, after Groot resigned. First lieutenant, November 10, 1862, with rank from August 14, 1862, after Daley was promoted. Acting Adjutant at muster-out.

MURPHY, PATRICK—Age 18 years. Enlisted May 12, 1861, at Ogdensburg. Mustered in as private, Co. K, May 17, 1861, to serve two years. Mustered out with company, May 28, 1863, at Albany, N.Y.

MURPHY, WILLIAM H.—Age 26 years. Enlisted April 30, 1861, at Middletown. Mustered in as drummer, Co. D, May 17, 1861, to serve two years. Killed, June 27, 1862, at Gaines's Mill, Va.

MURRAY, JOHN H.—Age 21 years. Enlisted April 19, 1861, at Albany. Mustered in as private, Co. F, May 17, 1861, to serve two years. Promoted corporal, September 19, 1861. Deserted, July 1, 1862, at Harrison's Landing, Va.

MYERS, ANDREW (Georg) (Andreas) J.—Age 29 years. Enlisted September 30, 1861, at Albany. Mustered in as private, Co. A, October 21, 1861, at Camp King, Alexandria, Va., to serve unexpired term of two years. Absent-without-leave, January 20, 1863, from Camp Russell, White Oak Church, Falmouth, Va. Returned to regiment, January 24, 1863, same place. Court-martialed for absence, February 23, 1863, at same place. Mustered out with company, May 28, 1863, at Albany, N.Y. Subsequent service in the Veteran Reserve Corps. Brother of Philip Myers.

MYERS, AUGUSTUS J.—Age 25 years. Enlisted April 28, 1861, at Schenectady. Mustered in as private, Co. A, May 17, 1861, to serve two years. Promoted corporal, December 1, 1861. Mustered out with company, May 28, 1863, at Albany, N.Y.

MYERS, GEORGE RANNEY—Age 23 years. Enrolled May 14, 1861, at Albany. Mustered in as major, May 17, 1861, to serve two years. Promoted lieutenant colonel, November 11, 1861. On furlough as escort for remains of Colonel Jackson, November 13–19, 1861, at Albany and Schenectady. Sent sick, on or about July 9, 1862, from Harrison's Landing, Va., to New York on for fifteen-day furlough. Returned to regiment, August 1862. Promoted colonel, December 9, 1862. Mustered out with regiment, May 28, 1863, at Albany, N.Y. Commissioned major, June 18, 1861, with rank from May 13, 1861, original. Lieutenant colonel, November 15, 1861, with rank from November 11, 1861, after Young was promoted. Colonel, September 24, 1862, with rank from August 14, 1862, after Young resigned. Brevet brigadier general, March 13, 1865.

MYERS, HENRY L.—Age 23 years. Enlisted, April 30, 1861, at Middletown. Mustered in as private, Co. H, May 17, 1861, to serve two years. Left sick, June 18, 1861, at Albany hospital when regiment left state. Returned to regiment, date not stated. Wounded, June 27, 1862, at Gaines's Mill, Va. Captured, June 29, 1862, at Savage's Station, Va. Paroled, July 27, 1862, at City Point, Va. Sent to Washington, D.C., on September 29, 1862. Returned to regiment, November 10, 1862. Mustered out with company, May 28, 1863, at Albany, N.Y. Subsequent service in Co. "U" 13th New York Heavy Artillery.

MYERS, JOHN, Jr.—Age 24 years. Enlisted April 30, 1861, at Middletown. Mustered in as private, Co. H, May 17, 1861, to serve two years. Discharged for disability, August 5, 1861, at Alexandria, Va. Subsequent service in Co. G, 143rd New York Infantry.

MYERS, PHILIP H.—Age 24 years. Enlisted June 17, 1861, at Albany. Mustered in as private, Co. A, same date, to serve two years. Promoted corporal, December 1, 1861. Detailed as brigade butcher, November 1862. Mustered out with company, May 28, 1863, at Albany, N.Y. Discharged, June 17, 1863., at Albany, N.Y. Brother of Andrew J. Myers.

MYERS, ROBERT—Age 21 years. Enlisted May 2, 1861, at Schenectady. Mustered in as private, Co. E, May 17, 1861, to serve two years. Mustered out with company, May 28, 1863, at Albany, N.Y.

NAUMAN, CHARLES H.—Age 34 years. Enlisted May 10, 1861, at Albany. Mustered in as private, Co. B, May 17, 1861, to serve two years. Discharged for disability, January 20, 1863, at White Oak Church, Falmouth, Va.

NEWELL, GEORGE S.—Age 25 years. Enlisted October 29, 1861, at Canandaigua. Mustered in as private, Co. G, November 15, 1861, at Elmira, N.Y., to serve unexpired term of two years. Mustered out with company, May 28, 1863, at Albany, N.Y. Subsequent service in Co. C, 15th New York Cavalry & Co. C, 2nd New York Provisional Cavalry.

NOBLE, JOHN—Age 21 years. Enlisted April 27, 1861, at Middletown. Mustered in as private, Co. D, May 17, 1861, to serve two years. Detailed, March 31, 1863, as nurse in regimental hospital. Mustered out with company, May 28, 1863, at Albany, N.Y. Subsequent service in Co. K, 1st New York Engineers.

NOLAN, JOHN—Age 18 years. Enlisted May 13, 1861, at Albany. Mustered in as private, Co. I, May 17, 1861, to serve two years. Detailed as servant, December 1861 & January 1862. Mustered out with company, May 28, 1863, at Albany, N.Y. Subsequent service in Co. C, 14th New York Heavy Artillery.

NOLAN, MICHAEL A.—Age about 28 years. Enrolled, April 20, 1861, at Albany. Appointed first lieutenant, Co. I, to serve two years. Not mustered in, and out of service, April 29, 1861. Not commissioned. Subsequent service in Co. R, 25th New York Militia National Guard.

NOLAN, PATRICK—Age 23 years. Enlisted April 19, 1861, at Albany. Mustered in as private, Co. I, May 17, 1861, to serve two years. Promoted corporal, September 14, 1862. Mustered out with company, May 28, 1863, at Albany, N.Y. Subsequent service in Co. E, 3rd New York Infantry.

NOONAN, FRANCIS—Age 32 years. Enlisted April 19, 1861, at Albany. Mustered in as private, Co. F, May 17, 1861, to serve two years. Wounded in right leg, September 14, 1862, at Crampton's Gap, Md. Right leg amputated. Hospitalized for ulcer of right leg, January 2, 1863, at Frederick, Md. Hospitalized, February 28, 1863, at Camp B General Hospital, at Frederick, Md. Transferred, March 4, 1863, to General Hospital Number 1, at Frederick, Md. Died from amputation and pneumonia, August 8, 1863, at General Hospital Number 1 in Frederick, Md.

NORRIS, CHARLES "Charlie" EDWARD—Age 21 years. Enlisted April 30, 1861, at Middletown. Mustered in as private, Co. D, May 17, 1861, to serve two years. Promoted corporal, April 28, 1863. Mustered out with company, May 28, 1863, at Albany, N.Y.

NORRIS, JAMES "Jimmie" S.—Age 18 years. Enlisted August 25, 1862, at Albany. Mustered in as private, Co. C, same date, to serve three years. Transferred, May 10, 1863, to Co. H, 121st New York Infantry.

NORTON, MORTIER LAFAYETTE—Age 33 years. Enrolled April 24, 1861, at Albany. Mustered in as second lieutenant, Co. B, May 17, 1861, to serve two years. Sent sick, August 10, 1862, from Harrison's Landing, Va., aboard transport *Vanderbilt*, to David's Island General Hospital, in New York Harbor, N.Y. Returned to regiment, on or about October 15, 1862. Resigned for disability, October 24, 1862. Commissioned second lieutenant, July 4, 1861, with rank from April 24, 1861, original. Subsequent service in 14th Regiment, 2nd Battalion, Veteran Reserve Corps & 1st Veteran Reserve Corps.

NUGENT, EDWARD—Age 18 years. Enlisted April 19, 1861, at Albany. Mustered in as private, Co. I, May 17, 1861, to serve two years. Killed, June 27, 1862, at Gaines's Mill, Va.

NUGENT, HENRY—Age 54 years, but gave age as 36 years. Enlisted February 17, 1862, at Wallkill. Mustered in as private, Co. H, March 22, 1862, to serve two years. Joined regiment, April 29, 1862, at Ship Point, Va. Hospitalized, April or May 1862. Rejoined regiment, March 19, 1863, at White Oak Church, Falmouth, Va. Discharged for disability, March 28, 1863, at White Oak Church, Falmouth, Va.

NUTTING, THOMAS W.—Age 22 years. Enlisted April 30, 1861, at Middletown. Mustered in as private, Co. D, May 17, 1861, to serve two years. Mustered out with company, May 28, 1863, at Albany, N.Y.

O'BRIEN, JOHN—Age 19 years. Enlisted May 7, 1861, at Albany. Mustered in as private, Co. H, May 17, 1861, to serve two years. Mustered out with company, May 28, 1863, at Albany, N.Y. Subsequent service in Co. A, 13th New York Heavy Artillery & Co. H, 6th New York Heavy Artillery.

O'BRIEN, PATRICK—Age 19 years. Enlisted April 22, 1861, at Schenectady. Mustered in as private, Co. A, May 17, 1861, to serve two years. Promoted corporal, December 1, 1861. Mustered out with company, May 28, 1863, at Albany, N.Y. Subsequent service in Co. C, 14th New York Heavy Artillery.

O'BRIEN, PATRICK—Age 24 years. Enlisted May 7, 1861, at Albany. Mustered in as private, Co. G, May 17, 1861, to serve two years. Hospitalized, August 1862, at Satterlee General Hospital, in West Philadelphia, Pa. Returned to regiment, April or May 1863. Mustered out with company, May 28, 1863, at Albany, N.Y.

O'CONNELL, JAMES—Age 19 years. Enlisted May 2, 1861, at Schenectady. Mustered in as private, Co. E, May 17, 1861, to serve two years. Mustered out, June 2, 1863, at Albany, N.Y.

O'DELL (Odell), WILLIAM HENRY—Age 26 years. Enlisted April 23, 1861, at Fishkill. Mustered in as private, Co. C, May 17, 1861, to serve two years. Deserted, September 21, 1861, from Camp King, Alexandria, Va. Arrested, September 23, 1861, at Alexandria, Va. Court-martialed, October 8, 1861, at Camp Williams, Va., and drummed out of service. Confined at District of Columbia Penitentiary for two years. Released and dishonorably discharged, January 23, 1862. Subsequent service in Co. L & B, 11th New York Cavalry.

O'HARA, JOHN—Age 21 years. Enlisted February 11, 1862, at Albany. Mustered in as private, Co. K, March 29, 1862, at Albany, to serve unexpired term. Wounded slightly in back, June 27, 1862, at Gaines's Mill, Va. Reported absent, sick in 1st Division Sixth Corps Hospital, Potomac Creek, Va., at muster-out of company. Died of disease, June 2, 1863, at 1st Division Sixth Corps Hospital, Potomac Creek, Va.

O'LARNEY (Larinan), MICHAEL—Age 16 years, but gave age as 19 years. Enlisted April 22, 1861, at Schenectady. Mustered in as private, Co. A, May 17, 1861, to serve two years. Mustered out with company, May 28, 1863, at Albany, N.Y. Subsequent service in Co. "U" 150th New York Infantry.

O'NEIL, PATRICK—Age 22 years. Enlisted April 24, 1861, at Albany. Mustered in as private, Co. B, May

17, 1861, to serve two years. Mustered out with company, May 28, 1863, at Albany, N.Y.

O'NEILS, FRANKLIN L.—Age 24 years. Enlisted May 17, 1861, at Albany. Mustered in as private, Co. D, same date, to serve two years. Mustered out with company, May 28, 1863, at Albany, N.Y.

OPEMAN (Oakman), FRANK—Age 19 years. Enlisted April 30, 1861, at Middletown. Mustered in as private, Co. H, May 17, 1861, to serve two years. Sent sick, August 8, 1862, from Harrison's Landing, Va. Hospitalized, August 10, 1862, at Satterlee General Hospital, in West Philadelphia, Pa. Returned to regiment, March 31, 1863. Mustered out with company, May 28, 1863, at Albany, N.Y.

ORMSBY, JAMES K. POLK—Age 18 years. Enlisted May 12, 1861, at Ogdensburg. Mustered in as private, Co. K, May 17, 1861, to serve two years. Mustered out with company, May 28, 1863, at Albany, N.Y.

OTIS, JAMES—Age 19 years. Enlisted May 2, 1861, at Schenectady. Mustered in as private, Co. E, May 17, 1861, to serve two years. Mustered out with company, May 28, 1863, at Albany, N.Y.

OTT, CHARLES—Age 35 years. Enlisted April 23, 1861, at Fishkill. Mustered in as private, Co. C, May 17, 1861, to serve two years. Detailed with Pioneer Corps, November 1862. Mustered out with company, May 28, 1863, at Albany, N.Y. Subsequent service in Co. D, 51st New York Infantry.

OVERTON, JOHN BURDETTE—Age 19 years. Enlisted April 30, 1861, at Middletown. Mustered in as private, Co. H, May 17, 1861, to serve two years. Mustered out with company, May 28, 1863, at Albany, N.Y. Subsequent service in Co. G, 2nd New York Mounted Rifles.

PAGE, CHARLES W.—Age 22 years. Enlisted May 7, 1861, at Canandaigua. Mustered in as private, Co. G, May 17, 1861, to serve two years. Court-martialed at regimental level, September or October 1861. Hospitalized as sick, June 27, 1862, at Savage's Station, Va. Captured, June 29, 1862, while sick at Savage's Station, Va. Confined, July 13, 1862, at Richmond, Va. Paroled, July 25, 1862, at City Point, Va. Hospitalized, July 27, 1862, at Chesapeake General Hospital, at Fort Monroe, Va. Transferred and detailed as cook, September 1, 1862, at Fort Hamilton, N.Y. Detailed as provost guard, January 17, 1863, at Fort Hamilton, N.Y. Returned to regiment, May 1863. Mustered out with company, May 28, 1863, at Albany, N.Y. Subsequent service in Co. I & B, 2nd New York Mounted Rifles.

PALIN, ROBERT—Age 27 years. Enlisted October 5, 1861, at Ogdensburg. Mustered in as private, Co. K, October 30, 1861, at Camp Williams, Va., to serve unexpired term of two years. Mustered out with company, May 28, 1863, at Albany, N.Y.

PANGBURN, JOSHUA—Age about 44 years, but gave age as 41 years. Enlisted December 9, 1861, at Albany. Mustered in as private, Co. F, same date, to serve unexpired term of two years. Discharged for disability, July 18, 1862, at Harrison's Landing, Va. Father-in-law of William H. Hall.

PAQUET, JOSEPH—Age 19 years. Enlisted April 19, 1861, at Albany. Mustered in as private, Co. F, May 17, 1861, to serve two years. Promoted corporal, July 1, 1862. Mustered out with company, May 28, 1863, at Albany, N.Y.

PARSHALL, JESSE—Age 24 years. Enlisted May 7, 1861, at Albany. Mustered in as private, Co. G, May 17, 1861, to serve two years. Discharged for disability, September 23, 1862, from hospital at Fort Wood, N.Y. Subsequent service in the United States Navy on Gunboat *Ceres, Allegheny* & *North Carolina*. Brother-in-law of Charles H. Brandow.

PATTERSON, HENRY A.—Age 21 years. Enlisted April 19, 1861, at Albany. Mustered in as private, Co. I, May 17, 1861, to serve two years. Deserted, June 12, 1861, at Albany Barracks, Albany, N.Y.

PATTERSON, JAMES—Age 20 years. Enlisted April 19, 1861, at Albany. Mustered in as private, Co. I, May 17, 1861, to serve two years. Deserted, September 5, 1861, at Alexandria, Va.

PATTERSON, JOHN—Age 24 years. Enlisted April 19, 1861, at Albany. Mustered in as private, Co. I, May 17, 1861, to serve two years. Deserted, June 12, 1861, at Albany Barracks, Albany, N.Y.

PATTERSON, NATHAN—Age 21 years. Enlisted April 30, 1861, at Middletown. Mustered in as private, Co. D, May 17, 1861, to serve two years. Discharged for disability, November 20, 1861, at Camp King, Alexandria, Va.

PATTERSON, WILLIAM—Age 44 years. Enlisted May 17, 1861, at Albany. Mustered in as private, Co. K, same date, to serve two years. Discharged for disability, July 15, 1861, at Alexandria, Va.

PAYNE, JOSEPH—Age 29 years. Enlisted September 18, 1861, at Albany. Mustered in as private, Co. A, same date, to serve unexpired term of two years. Wounded in left arm, June 27, 1862, at Gaines's Mill, Va. Absent-without-leave, January 20, 1863, from Camp Russell, White Oak Church, Falmouth, Va. Returned to regiment, January 24, 1863, same place. Court-martialed for absence and disobedience, February 23, 1863, at same place. Mustered out with company, May 28, 1863, at Albany, N.Y.

PECK, MYRON—Age 26 years. Enlisted April 30, 1861, at Middletown. Mustered in as private, Co. D, May 17, 1861, to serve two years. Detailed as driver in Ambulance Corps, August 16, 1861. Remained as driver in Ambulance Corps for remainder of service. Mustered out with company, May 28, 1863, at Albany, N.Y.

PECKHAM, CHARLES W.—Age 31 years. Enlisted April 13, 1861, at Albany. Mustered in as private, Co. I, May 17, 1861, to serve two years. Detailed as orderly, January 1, 1862, in the Signal Corps, at Washington, D.C. Returned to regiment, May 4, 1863. Mustered out with company, May 28, 1863, at Albany, N.Y. Subsequent service in Co. B, 17th New York Veteran Infantry.

PERCELL, PATRICK—Age 21 years. Enlisted April 30, 1861, at Middletown. Mustered in as private, Co. H, May 17, 1861, to serve two years. Deserted while on the march, July 12, 1861, from Camp Harris, Washington, D.C.

PERRY, FRANK C.—Age 19 years. Enlisted April 22, 1861, at Schenectady. Mustered in as private, Co. A, May 17, 1861, to serve two years. Mustered out with company, May 28, 1863, at Albany, N.Y. Subsequent service in Co. B, 2nd New York Veteran Cavalry.

PETERS, CHRISTOPHER—Age 21 years. Enlisted May 2, 1861, at Schenectady. Mustered in as private, Co. E, May 17, 1861, to serve two years. Hospitalized, November 1861, at Alexandria, Va. Discharged for disability, November 20, 1861, at Camp King, Alexandria, Va.

PETERSON, CHARLES—Age 49 years, but gave age as 44 years. Enlisted May 9, 1861, at Albany. Mustered in as private, Co. B, May 17, 1861, to serve two years. Accidentally shot in right arm, July 29, 1861, at Alexandria, Va. Hospitalized, date not stated, at General Hospital, in Alexandria, Va. Returned to regiment, December 3, 1861. Discharged for disability, December 30, 1861, at Camp King, Alexandria, Va.

PETERSON, FREDERICK—Age 44 years, but gave age as 39 years. Enlisted May 9, 1861, at Albany. Mustered in as private, Co. B, May 17, 1861, to serve two years. Hospitalized, March 1, 1862, at Fairfax Seminary Hospital, in Alexandria, Va. Returned to regiment, January 28, 1863. Mustered out with company, May 28, 1863, at Albany, N.Y.

PETERSON, JOSEPH—Age 44 years. Enlisted August 20, 1862, at Albany. Mustered in as private, Co. C, September 26, 1862, at Albany, to serve three years. Transferred, May 10, 1863, to Co. K, 121st New York Infantry.

PHILLIPS, JOHN DANIEL—Age 17 years, but gave age as 18 years. Enlisted May 17, 1861, at Albany. Mustered in as private, Co. I, same date, to serve two years. Promoted sergeant, October 1, 1861. Reduced to private, February 8, 1862. Wounded, June 27, 1862, at Gaines's Mill, Va. Captured, June 29, 1862, at Savage's Station, Va. Paroled, July 3, 1862, at City Point, Va. On furlough, July 24 to August 27, 1862. Captured, May 3 or 4, 1863, at Fredericksburg, Va. Confined, May 9, 1863, at Richmond, Va. Paroled, May 15, 1863, at City Point, Va. Mustered out with company, May 28, 1863, at Albany, N.Y. Subsequent service in Co. I, 61st New York Infantry.

PICQUET, JAMES—Age 18 years. Enlisted April 19, 1861, at Albany. Mustered in as private, Co. F, May 17, 1861, to serve two years. Mustered out with company, May 28, 1863, at Albany, N.Y. Subsequent service in Co. "U" 16th New York Cavalry.

PIERCE, HENRY—Age 19 years. Enlisted May 12, 1861, at Ogdensburg. Mustered in as private, Co. K, May 17, 1861, to serve two years. Hospitalized with confirmed lameness, May 25, 1861, at Albany, N.Y. Discharged for disability, June 18, 1861, by writ of Habeas Corpus, at Albany, N.Y.

PIERCE, RICHARD—Age 26 years. Enlisted October 15, 1861, at Ogdensburg. Mustered in as private, Co. K, October 30, 1861, at Camp Williams, Va., to serve unexpired term of two years. Mustered out with company, May 28, 1863, at Albany, N.Y.

PINSON, WILLIAM H.—Age 20 years. Enlisted April 29, 1861, at Albany. Mustered in as corporal, Co. B, May 17, 1861, to serve two years. Promoted sergeant, July 1, 1861. Promoted first sergeant, July 1, 1862. Mustered out with company, May 28, 1863, at Albany, N.Y. Subsequent service in Co. G, 18th New York Cavalry.

PITTENGER, MORTON P.—Age 19 years. Enlisted May 7, 1861, at Albany. Mustered in as private, Co. G, May 17, 1861, to serve two years. Hospitalized, August 1861, at Alexandria, Va. Discharged for disability, December 21, 1861, at Camp King, Alexandria, Va.

PLACE, DAVID—Age 19 years. Enlisted May 7, 1861, at Albany. Mustered in as private, Co. G, May 17, 1861, to serve two years. Discharged for disability, January 24, 1862, at Alexandria, Va. Died, January 28, 1862, in Naples, N.Y.

POLLARD, JOHN H.—Age 18 years. Enlisted May 2, 1861, at Schenectady. Mustered in as private, Co. E, May 17, 1861, to serve two years. Captured, June 27, 1862, at Gaines's Mill, Va. Confined, June 28, 1862, at Richmond, Va. Paroled, August 5, 1862, at City Point, Va. Mustered out with company, May 28, 1863, at Albany, N.Y.

POLLOCK, GEORGE WASHINGTON—Age 17 years, but gave age as 21 years. Enlisted April 30, 1861, at Middletown. Mustered in as private, Co. D, May 17, 1861, to serve two years. Detailed as teamster, November or December 1861 to July or August 1862. Mustered out with company, May 28, 1863, at Albany, N.Y. Subsequent service in Co. K, 15th New York Cavalry.

PORTER, CHARLES O.—Age 20 years. Enlisted May 17, 1861, at Albany. Mustered in as corporal, Co. B, same date, to serve two years. Deserted, September 20, 1861, from Camp King, Alexandria, Va.

POST, BEVERLY—Age 22 years. Enlisted April 27, 1861, at Middletown. Mustered in as private, Co. D, May 17, 1861, to serve two years. Mustered out with company, May 28, 1863, at Albany, N.Y. Subsequent service in Co. A, 7th New York Heavy Artillery.

POST, JOSEPH D.—Age 21 years. Enlisted April 30, 1861, at Middletown. Mustered in as private, Co. D, May 17, 1861, to serve two years. Hospitalized, August 11, 1862, at General Hospital, in Craney Island, Va. Returned to regiment, September 21, 1862. Mustered out with company, May 28, 1863, at Albany, N.Y.

POST, WILLIAM H.—Age 20 years. Enlisted April 30, 1861, at Middletown. Mustered in as private, Co. H, May 17, 1861, to serve two years. Captured, August 30, 1862, near Manassas, Va. Paroled, September 1, 1862, at Vienna, Va. Transferred, date not stated, to Camp Sangster, Annapolis, Md. Transferred, November 1862, to Alexandria, Va. Returned to duty, December 31, 1862. Returned to regiment, May 14, 1863. Mustered out with company, May 28, 1863, at Albany, N.Y. Subsequent service in Co. C, 18th New York Cavalry.

POTTER, CALVIN BRITTAIN—Age 24 years. Enlisted June 18, 1861, at Albany. Mustered in as private, Co. B, same date, to serve unexpired term of two years. Captured, July 17, 1861, near Fairfax Court House, Va. Confined, July 23, 1861, at Libby Prison, Richmond, Va. Paroled, January 3, 1862, at Fort Monroe, Va. Returned to regiment, January 17, 1862, at Camp King, Alexandria,

Va. Placed on thirty day furlough. Hospitalized, on or about September 6, 1862, at Alexandria, Va. Returned to regiment, on or about September 19, 1862. Mustered out with company, May 28, 1863, at Albany, N.Y. Discharged June 18, 1863. Subsequent service in Co. D, 52nd New York Infantry & Co. E, 45th United States Colored Troops Infantry.

POTTS, WILLIAM H.—Age 19 years. Enlisted April 19, 1861, at Albany. Mustered in as private, Co. I, May 17, 1861, to serve two years. Deserted, October 6, 1861, near Alexandria, Va.

POWERS, JOHN—Age 26 years. Enlisted May 17, 1861, at Albany. Mustered in as private, Co. E, same date, to serve two years. Promoted corporal, July 15, 1861. Promoted sergeant, February 4, 1862. Mustered out with company, May 28, 1863, at Albany, N.Y.

POWIEKIEL, EDWARD—Age 40 years. Enlisted April 24, 1861, at Albany. Mustered in as private, Co. B, May 17, 1861, to serve two years. No further record.

PRATT, GEORGE CHAUNCEY—Age 20 years. Enlisted April 30, 1861, at Middletown. Mustered in as private, Co. H, May 17, 1861, to serve two years. Hospitalized, June 19, 1861, in City Hospital, in New York City, N.Y. Discharged for disability, August 17, 1861, at City Hospital, in New York City, N.Y. Subsequent service in Co. H, 56th New York Infantry.

PRESTON, THOMAS—Age 19 years. Enlisted June 3, 1861, at Albany. Mustered in as private, Co. F, same date, to serve two years. Detailed with Pioneer Corps, November 1862. Mustered out with company, May 28, 1863, at Albany, N.Y. Discharged, June 4, 1863. Subsequent service in Co. "U" 91st New York Infantry.

PRESTON, WHITLEY—Age 21 years. Enlisted April 23, 1861, at Fishkill. Mustered in as private, Co. C, May 17, 1861, to serve two years. Court-martialed for neglect of duty, deserting post, and conduct prejudicial to military discipline, January 21, 1862, at Alexandria, Va. Mustered out with company, May 28, 1863, at Albany, N.Y.

PRICE, WILLARD—Age 38 years. Enlisted November 1, 1861, at Canandaigua. Mustered in as private, Co. G, November 15, 1861, at Elmira, N.Y., to serve two years. Discharged for disability, February 24, 1862, at Camp Jackson, Alexandria, Va.

PRYME, JAMES W.—Age 18 years. Enlisted May 2, 1861, at Schenectady. Mustered in as private, Co. E, May 17, 1861, to serve two years. Hospitalized, August 1862, at Cliffburne General Hospital, in Washington, D.C. Retained as nurse at Cliffburne General Hospital, in Washington, D.C. Discharged for disability, September 14, 1862, at hospital, in Washington, D.C.

PURDY, WILLIAM B.—Age 21 years. Enlisted April 24, 1861, at Albany. Mustered in as sergeant, Co. B, May 17, 1861, to serve two years. Promoted first sergeant, July 1, 1861. Mustered in as first lieutenant, July 19, 1862. Mustered out with company, May 28, 1863, at Albany, N.Y. Commissioned first lieutenant, November 10, 1862, with rank from July 18, 1862, after Wands resigned. Subsequent service in Co. E, 8th United States Veteran Volunteer Infantry.

PUTMAN, JOHN A.—Age 18 years. Enlisted April 26, 1861, at Schenectady. Mustered in as private, Co. A, May 17, 1861, to serve two years. Wounded in fingers, June 27, 1862, at Gaines's Mill, Va. Amputation of three fingers. Discharged on account of such wounds, August 11, 1862, from Mount Pleasant General Hospital at Washington, D.C.

PUTNAM, WILLIS E.—Age 19 years. Enlisted May 7, 1861, at Albany. Mustered in as private, Co. G, May 17, 1861, to serve two years. Promoted corporal, November 30, 1861. Promoted sergeant, February 28, 1863. Mustered out with company, May 28, 1863, at Albany, N.Y.

PYERS, JOHN WESLEY—Age 21 years. Enlisted April 23, 1861, at Albany. Mustered in as private, Co. C, May 17, 1861, to serve two years. Discharged for disability, November 20, 1861, at Camp King, Alexandria, Va. Subsequent service in Co. I, 2nd New York Veteran Cavalry.

RADCLIFF, THOMAS J.—Age 40 years. Enrolled May 10, 1861, at Albany. Mustered in as captain, Co. I, May 17, 1861, to serve two years. Dismissed from service, January 13, 1862, by sentence of general court martial. Reinstated as captain, June 14, 1862. Wounded in leg, June 27, 1862, at Gaines's Mill, Va. Mustered out with company, May 28, 1863, at Albany, N.Y. Commissioned captain, July 4, 1861, with rank from May 10, 1861, original. Again commissioned captain, June 14, 1862, with rank of same date.

RADLEY, CHARLES—Age 18 years. Enlisted April 19, 1861, at Albany. Mustered in as private, Co. F, May 17, 1861, to serve two years. Wounded in left side near thigh, September 14, 1862, at Crampton's Gap, Md. Hospitalized, October 1862, at Camp A General Hospital, in Frederick, Md. Deserted hospital, December 26, 1862. Mustered out with company, May 28, 1863, at Albany, N.Y.

RAINES, JOSEPH SADLER—Age 24 years. Enlisted May 7, 1861, at Canandaigua. Mustered in as private, Co. G, May 17, 1861, to serve two years. Detailed as teamster for brigade headquarters, November 1862. Mustered out with company, May 28, 1863, at Albany, N.Y.

RANKIN, THOMAS M.—Age 30 years. Enlisted April 19, 1861, at Albany. Mustered in as private, Co. F, May 17, 1861, to serve two years. Hospitalized, July or August 1862, at Satterlee General Hospital, in West Philadelphia, Pa. Returned to duty, September 20, 1862. Mustered out with company, May 28, 1863, at Albany, N.Y. Subsequent service in Co. I, 13th New York Heavy Artillery.

RARICK, PATRICK—Age 29 years. Enlisted May 7, 1861, at Albany. Mustered in as private, Co. H, May 17, 1861, to serve two years. Mustered out with company, May 28, 1863, at Albany, N.Y. Subsequent service in Co. D, 18th New York Cavalry.

RAYMOND, LEONARD—Age 22 years. Enlisted April 23, 1861, at Albany. Mustered in as private, Co. C, May 17, 1861, to serve two years. Detailed as nurse, August 1, 1861. Returned to company, March 18, 1862. Sent sick, on or about June 6, 1862, from White House Landing, to Fort Monroe, Va. Wounded in both legs, September 14, 1862, at Crampton's Gap, Md. Hospitalized, October 4, 1862, and retained as nurse at Camp A General Hospital, in Frederick, Md. Returned to regiment, February 16, 1863. Mustered out with company, May 28, 1863, at Albany, N.Y.

REDFIELD, GEORGE—Age 19 years. Enlisted May 7, 1861, at Canandaigua. Mustered in as private, Co. G, May 17, 1861, to serve two years. Mustered out with company, May 28, 1863, at Albany, N.Y.

REDIKER, JOHN H.—Age 19 years. Enlisted April 19, 1861, at Albany. Mustered in as private, Co. F, May 17, 1861, to serve two years. Deserted, May 2, 1862, at Ship Point, Va. Enlisted in Co. A, 17th United States Infantry. Arrested and returned to regiment, August 4, 1862, at Harrison's Landing while serving with 17th United States Infantry. Court-martialed for desertion, February 20, 1863, at White Oak Church, Falmouth, Va. Mustered out with company, May 28, 1863, at Albany, N.Y. Subsequent service in Co. M, 4th New York Heavy Artillery.

REDINGTON, JOHN CALVIN OWEN—Age 23 years. Enlisted May 12, 1861, at Ogdensburg. Mustered in as private, Co. K, May 17, 1861, to serve two years. Detailed as clerk at Fifth Division Headquarters, July 14, 1861. On thirty day furlough, August 3, 1861, at Ogdensburg, N.Y. Recruited for Co. K while at Ogdensburg, August 12, 1861, and became captain of Co. C, 60th New York Infantry, September 13, 1861. Officially discharged, March 25, 1862, by General Order No. 91.

REDMAN (Redmond), JOHN—Age 35 years. Enlisted May 12, 1861, at Ogdensburg. Mustered in as private, Co. K, May 17, 1861, to serve two years. Promoted corporal, November 13, 1861. Mustered out with company, May 28, 1863, at Albany, N.Y. Subsequent service in Co. E & A, 16th New York Heavy Artillery.

REED, CHARLES H.—Age 21 years. Enlisted April 30, 1861, at Middletown. Mustered in as private, Co. D, May 17, 1861, to serve two years. Sent sick, August 7, 1862, onboard Steamer *State of Maine*, from Harrison's Landing, Va. Hospitalized, August 10, 1862, at Satterlee General Hospital, in West Philadelphia, Pa. Died of disease, October 15, 1862, at Satterlee General Hospital, in West Philadelphia, Pa.

REED, DAVID FREDERICK—Age 19 years. Enlisted May 2, 1861, at Schenectady. Mustered in as private, Co. E, May 17, 1861, to serve two years. Mustered out with company, May 28, 1863, at Albany, N.Y. Subsequent service in Co. H, 16th New York Heavy Artillery. Brother of William H. Reed.

REED, GEORGE—Age 37 years. Enlisted January 31, 1862, at Albany. Mustered in as private, Co. K, April 9, 1862, at Albany, to serve unexpired term of two years. Wounded in arm, June 27, 1862, at Gaines's Mill, Va. Wounded slightly in right side, September 14, 1862, at Crampton's Gap, Md. Hospitalized, October 24, 1862, at Frederick, Md. Returned to regiment, December 18, 1862. Mustered out with company, May 28, 1863, at Albany, N.Y. Subsequent service in Co. A, 16th New York Heavy Artillery.

REED, ROBERT—Age 23 years. Enlisted May 12, 1861, at Ogdensburg. Mustered in as private, Co. K, May 17, 1861, to serve two years. Mustered out with company, May 28, 1863, at Albany, N.Y. Subsequent service in Co. F, 2nd New York Veteran Cavalry.

REED, THOMAS J.—Age 18 years. Enlisted November 11, 1861, at Canandaigua. Mustered in as private, Co. G, November 15, 1861, at Elmira, N.Y., to serve unexpired term of two years. Wounded slightly in right foot, June 27, 1862, at Gaines's Mill, Va. Mustered out with company, May 28, 1863, at Albany, N.Y. Subsequent service in Co. C, 15th New York Cavalry & Co. C, 2nd New York Provisional Cavalry.

REED, WILLIAM HENRY—Age 26 years, but gave age as 19 years. Enlisted May 2, 1861, at Schenectady. Mustered in as private, Co. E, May 17, 1861, to serve two years. Hospitalized, August 6, 1862, at David's Island General Hospital, in New York Harbor, N.Y. Returned to regiment, May 16, 1863, in New York City, N.Y. Mustered out with company, May 28, 1863, at Albany, N.Y. Subsequent service in Co. A, 61st New York Infantry. Brother of David F. Reed.

REEVES, FLOYD S.—Age 18 years. Enlisted April 30, 1861, at Middletown. Mustered in as private, Co. D, May 17, 1861, to serve two years. Mustered out with company, May 28, 1863, at Albany, N.Y. Subsequent service in Co. K, 1st New York Engineers.

REID, MICHAEL J.—Age 25 years. Enlisted June 18, 1861, at Albany. Mustered in as private, Co. B, same date, to serve unexpired term of two years. Sent sick, August 10, 1862, onboard transport *Vanderbilt*, from Harrison's Landing, Va., hospitalized, on or about August 12, 1862, at David's Island General Hospital, in New York Harbor, N.Y. Returned to regiment, May 20, 1863. Mustered out with company, May 28, 1863, at Albany, N.Y. Discharged, June 18, 1863.

REMER, THEODORE L.—Age 22 years. Enlisted December 9, 1861, at Albany. Mustered in as private, Co. F, same date, to serve unexpired term of two years. Promoted corporal, July 1, 1862. Promoted sergeant, September 1, 1862. Promoted first sergeant, January 14, 1863. Mustered out with company, May 28, 1863, at Albany, N.Y.

REXMAN, AUGUSTUS—Age 25 years. Enlisted April 22, 1861, at Schenectady. Mustered in as private, Co. A, May 17, 1861, to serve two years. Court-martialed at regimental level, September or October 1861. Detailed as ambulance driver, December 1861. Mustered out with company, May 28, 1863, at Albany, N.Y. Subsequent service in Co. A, 13th New York Cavalry.

REYNOLDS, CHARLES BIRNEY—Age 16 years, but gave age as 19 years. Enlisted May 10, 1861, at Albany. Mustered in as private, Co. B, May 17, 1861, to serve two years. Mustered out with company, May 28, 1863, at Albany, N.Y. Subsequent service in Co. C, 80th New York Infantry.

REZNOR, LOT—Age 22 years. Enlisted May 7, 1861, at Albany. Mustered in as sergeant, Co. G, May 17, 1861, to serve two years. Hospitalized, July or August 1862, at Satterlee General Hospital, in West Philadelphia,

Pa. Returned to regiment, December 23, 1862. Mustered out with company, May 28, 1863, at Albany, N.Y. Subsequent service in Co. D & C, 15th New York Cavalry.

RICE, DANIEL G.—Age 33 years. Enlisted May 12, 1861, at Ogdensburg. Mustered in as private, Co. K, May 17, 1861, to serve two years. Hospitalized, November or December 1862, at Satterlee General Hospital, at West Philadelphia, Pa. Returned to regiment, February 4, 1863. Mustered out with company, May 28, 1863, at Albany, N.Y. Subsequent service in Co. I, 13th New York Heavy Artillery.

RICE, JAMES—Age 16 years, but gave age as 18 years. Enlisted May 15, 1861, at Albany. Mustered in as private, Co. B, May 17, 1861, to serve two years. Accidentally killed, November 4, 1861, by Richard Hennessy, while on picket, at Little River Turnpike, near Alexandria, Va.

RICE, MILTON H.—Age 19 years. Enlisted May 7, 1861, at Canandaigua. Mustered in as private, Co. G, May 17, 1861, to serve two years. Wounded slightly in shoulder, June 27, 1862, at Gaines's Mill, Va. Mustered out with company, May 28, 1863, at Albany, N.Y. Subsequent service in the United States Marine Corps.

RICE, NATHAN PAYSON—Age 32 years. Enrolled August 19, 1861, at Alexandria, Va. Mustered in as surgeon, same date, to serve two years. On furlough as escort for remains of Colonel Jackson, November 13–19, 1861, at Albany and Schenectady. Mustered out with regiment, May 28, 1863, at Albany, N.Y. Commissioned surgeon, July 4, 1861, with rank from April 25, 1861, original. Subsequent service as assistant surgeon of volunteers, August 7, 1863. Surgeon in volunteers, September 2, 1863. Brevet lieutenant colonel, August 15, 1865.

RICHARDS, HENRY—Age 32 years. Enlisted October 16, 1861, at Malone. Mustered in as private, Co. K, October 30, 1861, at Camp Williams, Va., to serve unexpired term of two years. Mustered out with company, May 28, 1863, at Albany, N.Y. Subsequent service in Co. F, 16th New York Cavalry & Co. B, 3rd New York Provisional Cavalry.

RICHARDSON, ALONZO—Age 19 years. Enlisted April 19, 1861, at Albany. Mustered in as private, Co. F, May 17, 1861, to serve two years. Straggled from regiment, September 6, 1862, and confined in the Washington Penitentiary. Returned to regiment, January 22, 1863. Court-martialed for absence without leave, February 20, 1863, at Camp Russell, White Oak Church, Falmouth, Va. Mustered out with company, May 28, 1863, at Albany, N.Y. Subsequent service in Co. E & B, 13th New York Heavy Artillery & Co. I, 6th New York Heavy Artillery.

RICHARDSON, DAVID—Age 26 years. Enlisted April 19, 1861, at Albany. Mustered in as private, Co. I, May 17, 1861, to serve two years. Promoted corporal, September 29, 1862. Mustered out with company, May 28, 1863, at Albany, N.Y. Subsequent service in the Veteran Reserve Corps.

RICHARDSON, JOHN M.—Age 21 years. Enlisted September 23, 1862, at Wallkill. Mustered in as private, Co. D, October 25, 1862, at Albany, to serve three years. Transferred, May 10, 1863, to Co. C, 121st New York Infantry.

RICHFORD, JAMES—Age 18 years. Enlisted April 19, 1861, at Albany. Mustered in as private, Co. I, May 17, 1861, to serve two years. Mustered out with company, May 28, 1863, at Albany, N.Y. Subsequent service in Co. I, 2nd New York Cavalry.

Born in Kildare, Ireland, Pvt. James Richford of Company I, died in Albany on August 4, 1878 (courtesy Bob Richford).

RICHMOND, HIRAM R.—Age 51 years, but gave age as 38 years. Enlisted May 7, 1861, at Canandaigua. Mustered in as private, Co. G, May 17, 1861, to serve two years. Discharged for disability, September 24, 1861, Alexandria, Va. Subsequent service in Co. K, 126th New York Infantry.

RIELY, JAMES—Age 39 years. Enlisted May 9, 1861, at Albany. Mustered in as private, Co. B, May 17, 1861, to serve two years. Deserted, June 12, 1861, at Albany Barracks, Albany, N.Y.

RIGNEY, BERNARD "Barney"—Age 40 years, but gave age as 35 years. Enlisted May 7, 1861, at Albany. Mustered in as private, Co. H, May 17, 1861, to serve two years. Hospitalized from camp near Bakersville, Md., October 30, 1862, at 6th Corps General Hospital, at Hagerstown, Md. Returned to regiment, January 4, 1863. Mustered out with company, May 28, 1863, at Albany, N.Y. Subsequent service in Co. C, 21st New York Cavalry.

RILEY, EDMOND—Age 23 years. Enlisted May 9, 1861, at Albany. Mustered in as private, Co. B, May 17, 1861, to serve two years. Mustered out with company,

May 28, 1863, at Albany, N.Y. Subsequent service in Co. K, 29th Michigan Infantry.

RILEY (Raleigh), JOHN G.—Age 22 years. Enlisted May 12, 1861, at Ogdensburg. Mustered in as private, Co. K, May 17, 1861, to serve two years. Wounded in right arm, June 27, 1862, at Gaines's Mill, Va. Aboard Steamer *Daniel Webster* and hospitalized, July 7, 1862, at Satterlee General Hospital, in West Philadelphia, Pa. Left hospital, May 8, 1863, and returned to regiment, May 16, 1863. Mustered out with company, May 28, 1863, at Albany, N.Y. Subsequent service in Co. A, 14th New York Heavy Artillery.

RILEY, SIMON G.—Age 22 years. Enlisted May 2, 1861, at Schenectady. Mustered in as private, Co. E, May 17, 1861, to serve two years. Promoted corporal, November 11, 1861. Mustered out with company, May 28, 1863, at Albany, N.Y.

RIQUER, THOMAS—Age 21 years. Enlisted May 12, 1861, at Ogdensburg. Mustered in as drummer, Co. K, May 17, 1861, to serve two years. Discharged for disability, March 23, 1862, at Camp Jackson, Alexandria, Va.

RITZENTHALER, REINOLD—Age 23 years. Enlisted May 7, 1861, at Canandaigua. Mustered in as private, Co. G, May 17, 1861, to serve two years. Wounded in right arm, June 27, 1862, at Gaines's Mill, Va. Right arm amputated. Captured. Paroled, July 19, 1862, at City Point, Va. Discharged on account of wound, September 6, 1862, in N.Y.

ROACH, JAMES—Age 20 years. Enlisted May 2, 1861, at Schenectady. Mustered in as private, Co. E, May 17, 1861, to serve two years. Promoted corporal, September 20, 1862. Mustered out with company, May 28, 1863, at Albany, N.Y. Subsequent service in Co. F, 13th New York Heavy Artillery.

ROACH, JOHN—Age 25 years. Enlisted April 30, 1861, at Middletown. Mustered in as private, Co. H, May 17, 1861, to serve two years. Detailed as teamster, January 1862. Mustered out with company, May 28, 1863, at Albany, N.Y. Subsequent service in Co. "U" 16th New York Heavy Artillery.

ROBINSON, SETH K.—Age 41 years. Enlisted September 18, 1862, at Albany. Mustered in as private, Co. D, October 13, 1862, at Albany, to serve three years. Hospitalized, January 19, 1863, at Windmill Point, Va. Discharged for disability, February 25, 1863, at White Oak Church, Falmouth, Va. Subsequent service in Co. L, 15th New York Cavalry & Co. L, 2nd New York Provisional Cavalry.

ROCKEFELLER, RICHARD—Age 21 years. Enlisted May 17, 1861, at Canandaigua. Mustered in as private, Co. G, same date, to serve two years. Promoted corporal, January or February 1862. Deserted, September 1862, from Fort Monroe, Va. Reduced to private, February 28, 1863. Arrested, December 18, 1863, at Albany, N.Y. Transferred, December 23, 1863, to Fort Columbus, N.Y.

ROCKWELL, JOSEPH NAPOLEON—Age 13 years. Enlisted November 20, 1861, at Albany. Mustered in as drummer, Co. A, January 28, 1862, at Camp King, Alexandria, Va., to serve two years. Discharged for disability, July 18, 1862, at Harrison's Landing, Va. Subsequent service in Co. C, 93rd New York Infantry.

ROGERS, HARVEY LEROY—Age 42 years, but gave age as 40 years. Enlisted April 19, 1861, at Albany. Mustered in as sergeant, Co. F, May 17, 1861, to serve two years. Discharged for disability, August 30, 1861, at Alexandria, Va. Subsequent service in Co. F & K, 152nd New York Infantry.

ROGERS, THEODORE CALDWELL—Age 21 years. Enrolled May 7, 1861, at Albany. Mustered in as first lieutenant, Co. H, May 17, 1861, to serve two years. Promoted captain, November 6, 1861. On ten day furlough, January 1862. Killed, June 27, 1862, at Gaines's Mill, Va. Commissioned first lieutenant, July 4, 1861, with rank from May 7, 1861, original. Captain, December 2, 1861, with rank from November 6, 1861, after Hogan resigned.

ROOSEVELT, CORNELIUS—Age 30 years. Enlisted May 17, 1861, at Albany. Mustered in as private, Co. C, same date, to serve two years. Deserted, June 1861, before regiment left Albany, N.Y.

ROPER, JOHN BERNARD—Age 23 years. Enlisted May 7, 1861, at Canandaigua. Mustered in as private, Co. G, May 17, 1861, to serve two years. Promoted sergeant, November 30, 1861. Captured, June 29, 1862, while sick at Savage's Station, Va. Confined, July 13, 1862, at Richmond, Va. Paroled, September 13, 1862, at City Point, Va. Sent to Washington, D.C., on September 26, 1862. Mustered out with company, May 28, 1863, at Albany, N.Y.

ROTHERBILLER, JOSEPH—Age 25 years. Enlisted April 26, 1861, at Schenectady. Mustered in as private, Co. A, May 17, 1861, to serve two years. Discharged for disability, September 24, 1861, at Alexandria, Va. Subsequent service in Co. F, 1st Maryland Cavalry.

ROWE, DAVID N.—Age 21 years. Enlisted May 12, 1861, at Ogdensburg. Mustered in as private, Co. K, May 17, 1861, to serve two years. Deserted, June 17, 1861, at Albany, N.Y.

ROYCE, GEORGE W.—Age 19 years. Enlisted May 7, 1861, at Canandaigua. Mustered in as private, Co. G, May 17, 1861, to serve two years. Wounded in left arm, June 27, 1862, at Gaines's Mill, Va. Hospitalized sick, on or about November 1, 1862, in Hagerstown, Md. Died of disease while on furlough, November 30, 1862, at Canandaigua, N.Y.

RUDE, DAVID L.—Age 18 years. Enlisted April 30, 1861, at Middletown. Mustered in as private, Co. D, May 17, 1861, to serve two years. Wounded through left side, September 14, 1862, at Crampton's Gap, Md. Hospitalized, October 4, 1862, at Camp A General Hospital, in Frederick, Md. Returned to regiment, December 27, 1862. Mustered out with company, May 28, 1863, at Albany, N.Y.

RUSAW (Rosseau), DAVID—Age 23 years. Enlisted May 12, 1861, at Ogdensburg. Mustered in as private, Co. K, May 17, 1861, to serve two years. Detailed as blacksmith to the Ambulance Corps, from August 21, 1862, to October 20, 1862. Detailed as ambulance driver,

January or February 1863. Mustered out with company, May 28, 1863, at Albany, N.Y. Subsequent service in Co. A, 16th New York Heavy Artillery, Co. L & D, 1st New York Mounted Rifles & Co. D, 4th New York Provisional Cavalry. Brother of Joseph Rusaw.

RUSAW (Rosseau), JOSEPH—Age 18 years. Enlisted May 12, 1861, at Ogdensburg. Mustered in as private, Co. K, May 17, 1861, to serve two years. Mustered out with company, May 28, 1863, at Albany, N.Y. Subsequent service in Co. A, 16th New York Heavy Artillery & Co. L, 1st New York Mounted Rifles. Brother of David Rusaw.

RUSSELL, DAVID C. J.—Age 21 years. Enlisted May 12, 1861, at Ogdensburg. Mustered in as private, Co. K, May 17, 1861, to serve two years. Transferred, June 15, 1861, to Co. I, 16th New York Infantry, in place of Arthur M. Grant.

RUSSELL, JOHN—Age 19 years. Enlisted May 12, 1861, at Ogdensburg. Mustered in as private, Co. K, May 17, 1861, to serve two years. Discharged for disability, July 8, 1861, at Alexandria, Va. Subsequent service in Co. E & D, 92nd New York Infantry & Co. M, 14th New York Heavy Artillery.

RUSSELL, JOHN HENRY—Age 24 years. Enrolled May 14, 1861, at Albany. Mustered in as adjutant, May 17, 1861, to serve two years. On furlough as escort for remains of Colonel Jackson, November 13–19, 1861, at Albany and Schenectady. Wounded in left ankle, June 27, 1862, at Gaines's Mill, Va. Hospitalized, July 2, 1862, to Fort Monroe, Va. Transferred aboard Steamer *Daniel Webster* and hospitalized, July 7, 1862, at Philadelphia, Pa. Died of wound and disease, July 28, 1862, in hospital, Philadelphia, Pa. Commissioned adjutant, July 4, 1861, with rank from May 17, 1861, original. Brother of William H. Russell, Jr.

RUSSELL, SOLOMON WRIGHT, Jr.—Age 25 years. Enrolled May 1, 1863, at Fredericksburg, Va. Mustered in as quartermaster, same date, to serve unexpired term of two years. Mustered out with regiment, May 28, 1863, at Albany, N.Y. Previously served in the 7th New York Cavalry. Commissioned first lieutenant, April 24, 1863, with rank from April 22, 1863, after Mooney was promoted. Subsequent service in Co. B & D, 49th New York Infantry.

RUSSELL, WILLIAM H. Jr.—Age 22 years. Enrolled September 21, 1861, place not stated. Mustered in as quartermaster, same date, to serve two years. Aide-de-camp for Fifth Brigade, December 1861. Aide-de-camp for General Newton, April 1862. Resigned for promotion, April 22, 1863. Commissioned quartermaster, September 28, 1861, with rank from September 21, 1861, original. Subsequent service as assistant adjutant general of volunteers, April 15, 1863. Brother of John H. Russell.

RUST, ELISHA CONVERSE—Age 22 years. Enlisted May 2, 1861, at Schenectady. Mustered in as private, Co. E, May 17, 1861, to serve two years. Captured, June 30, 1862, near James River, near Richmond, Va. Paroled, July 25, 1862, at City Point, Va. Hospitalized, July 27, 1862, at Fort Monroe, Va. Sent to Washington, D.C., on September 26, 1862. Mustered out with company, May 28, 1863, at Albany, N.Y. Subsequent service in Co. C, 16th New York Heavy Artillery.

RYAN, EDWARD—Age 24 years. Enlisted May 19, 1861, at Albany. Mustered in as private, Co. I, same date, to serve two years. Deserted, June 18, 1861, at Albany, N.Y. Arrested June 19, 1861, at Albany, N.Y., and placed back in company. Mustered out with company, May 28, 1863, at Albany, N.Y.

RYAN, JEREMIAH—Age 24 years. Enlisted May 10, 1861, at Albany. Mustered in as private, Co. B, May 17, 1861, to serve two years. Wounded in both legs, September 14, 1862, at Crampton's Gap, Md. Hospitalized, September 20, 1862, at Camp A General Hospital, in Frederick, Md. Returned to regiment, January 16, 1863. Mustered out with company, May 28, 1863, at Albany, N.Y. Subsequent service in Co. E, 3rd New York Infantry.

RYAN, JOHN—Age 19 years. Enlisted June 4, 1861, at Albany. Mustered in as private, Co. B, same date, to serve unexpired term of two years. Mustered out with company, May 28, 1863, at Albany, N.Y. Discharged, June 4, 1863. Subsequent service in Co. "U" 193rd New York Infantry.

RYAN, JOHN—Age 18 years. Enlisted November 9, 1861, at Canandaigua. Mustered in as private, Co. G, November 15, 1861, at Elmira, N.Y., to serve unexpired term of two years. Hospitalized for sickness, October 25, 1862, at Hagerstown, Md. Returned to duty, March 25, 1863. Mustered out with company, May 28, 1863, at Albany, N.Y. Subsequent service in Co. E, 28th Pennsylvania Infantry.

RYAN, MARTIN—Age 26 years. Enlisted December 18, 1861, at Albany. Mustered in as private, Co. F, same date, to serve unexpired term of two years. Mustered out with company, May 28, 1863, at Albany, N.Y.

RYAN, MICHAEL (Max Mabeus)—Age 23 years. Enlisted December 26, 1861, at Albany. Mustered in as private, Co. B, January 2, 1862, at Albany, to serve unexpired term of two years. Promoted corporal, July 1, 1862. Reduced to private, date not stated. Mustered out with company, May 28, 1863, at Albany, N.Y. Discharged, June 18, 1863. Subsequent service in Co. E, 91st New York Infantry.

RYAN, MICHAEL J.—Age 19 years. Enlisted April 19, 1861, at Albany. Mustered in as musician, Co. F, May 17, 1861, to serve two years. Reduced to private, September or October 1861. Mustered out with company, May 28, 1863, at Albany, N.Y. Subsequent service in Co. "U" 13th New York Heavy Artillery.

SAGE, GEORGE B.—Age 21 years. Enlisted May 7, 1861, at Canandaigua. Mustered in as private, Co. G, May 17, 1861, to serve two years. Detailed in Ambulance Corps, November 1862. Detailed as division blacksmith, June 1862 to March 1863. Mustered out with company, May 28, 1863, at Albany, N.Y. Subsequent service in Co. E, 1st New York Veteran Cavalry & Co. K, 2nd New York Cavalry.

SALEM, JOHN W.—Age 30 years. Enlisted August 27, 1862, at Albany. Mustered in as private, Co. C, August 30, 1862, to serve three years. Transferred, May 10, 1863, to Co. K, 121st New York Infantry.

SANTAUS, ANDREW (Antoine)—Age 55 years, but gave age as 45 years. Enlisted May 12, 1861, at Ogdensburg. Mustered in as private, Co. K, May 17, 1861, to serve two years. Discharged for disability, August 29, 1861, at Washington, D.C.

SANTAUS, PETER "Pete"—Age 21 years. Enlisted May 12, 1861, at Ogdensburg. Mustered in as private, Co. K, May 17, 1861, to serve two years. On thirty day furlough to New York in care of George Chapman, November 24, 1862, from Stafford Court House, Va. Deserted, December 1862. Arrested, April 10, 1865, in Watertown, N.Y. Mustered out, May 15, 1865, at Elmira, N.Y, under Presidential Proclamation 124.

SAWYER, WASHINGTON IRVING—Age 22 years. Enlisted May 7, 1861, at Albany. Mustered in as private, Co. H, May 17, 1861, to serve two years. Killed, June 27, 1862, at Gaines's Mill, Va.

SAYER, ROSWELL MEAD—Age 22 years. Enrolled April 30, 1861, at Middletown. Mustered in as second lieutenant, Co. D, May 17, 1861, to serve two years. Promoted first lieutenant, November 11, 1861. Detailed on recruiting service, January 20, 1862, at Middletown, N.Y. Returned to regiment after recruiting service, April 24, 1862. Promoted captain, December 9, 1862. Mustered out with company, May 28, 1863, at Albany, N.Y. Commissioned second lieutenant, July 4, 1861, with rank from April 30, 1861, original. First lieutenant, December 2, 1861, with rank from November 11, 1861, after Barry was promoted. Captain, November 10, 1862, with rank from June 27, 1862, after Barry died.

SCANLIN, MICHAEL—Age 21. Enlisted May 17, 1861, at Albany. Mustered in as private, Co. I, May 17, 1861, to serve two years. Deserted, October 6, 1861.

SCHERMERHORN, ELIPHALET NOTT—Age 22 years. Enlisted May 2, 1861, at Schenectady. Mustered in as first sergeant, Co. E, May 17, 1861, to serve two years. Promoted sergeant-major, November 11, 1861. Mustered in as second lieutenant, December 27, 1861. On six day furlough, March 1, 1862, in Schenectady, N.Y. Returned to regiment, March 8, 1862. Promoted adjutant and detached as aide-de-camp on General Stoughton's staff, August 1, 1862. Returned to regiment and promoted first lieutenant, April 9, 1863. Mustered out with regiment, May 28, 1863, at Albany, N.Y. Commissioned second lieutenant, January 3, 1862, with rank from December 27, 1861, after Vedder was promoted. Adjutant, November 10, 1862, with rank from August 1, 1862, after John H. Russell died.

SCHERMERHORN, WILLIAM HENRY "Hank"—Age 25 years. Enlisted May 2, 1861, at Schenectady. Mustered in as corporal, Co. E, May 17, 1861, to serve two years. Promoted sergeant, October 11, 1861. Reduced to private, January or February 1862. Mustered out with company, May 28, 1863, at Albany, N.Y. Subsequent service in Co. B, 2nd New York Veteran Cavalry & Co. H, 16th New York Heavy Artillery.

SCHERRER, CHRISTIAN—Age 22 years. Enlisted June 17, 1861, at Albany. Mustered in as private, Co. A, same date, to serve two years. Hospitalized, March 4, 1862, at Alexandria, Va. Returned to regiment, May 1863, at Albany, N.Y. Mustered out with company, May 28, 1863, at Albany, N.Y. Discharged, June 17, 1863, at Albany, N.Y.

SCHNEIDER, VICTOR—Age 33 years. Enlisted April 23, 1861, at Fishkill. Mustered in as private, Co. C, May 17, 1861, to serve two years. Detailed as acting armourer, July 12, 1861. Hospitalized, July or August 1862, at Satterlee General Hospital, in West Philadelphia, Pa. Returned to regiment, October 2, 1862. Mustered out with company, May 28, 1863, at Albany, N.Y. Subsequent service in Co. C, 98th New York Infantry.

SCHRIMP (Schrempf), JOHN—Age 22 years. Enlisted May 2, 1861, at Schenectady. Mustered in as private, Co. E, May 17, 1861, to serve two years. Hospitalized, April 6, 1862, in Alexandria, Va. Transferred, April 9, 1862, to Old Hallowell General Hospital in Alexandria, Va. Transferred, April 19, 1862, to Carver General Hospital, in Washington, D.C. No further record.

SCHROETER (Sleiter), CHRISTIAN—Age 37 years. Enlisted May 9, 1861, at Albany. Mustered in as musician, Co. B, May 17, 1861, to serve two years. Promoted to fife major, February 1, 1862. Hospitalized, April 9, 1862, at Old Hallowell General Hospital, in Alexandria, Va. Transferred to Washington, D.C., October 28, 1862, from Fort Hamilton, New York Harbor, N.Y. Reduced from fife major, October 31, 1862. Mustered out with company, May 28, 1863, at Albany, N.Y. Subsequent service in Battery K, 1st New York Light Artillery.

SCHUFELDT, EDWARD—Age 23 years. Enlisted May 7, 1861, at Albany. Mustered in as private, Co. H, May 17, 1861, to serve two years. Deserted, July 22, 1861, from Camp Myers, Alexandria, Va. Returned to regiment, April 3, 1863. Mustered out with company, May 28, 1863, at Albany, N.Y. Discharged, June 1, 1863. Subsequent service in Co. D, 1st Iowa Cavalry & Co. C & K, 7th New York Heavy Artillery.

SCHUTTER, LOUIS—Age 20 years. Enlisted May 15, 1861, at Schenectady. Mustered in as private, Co. A, May 17, 1861, to serve two years. Detailed as nurse, December 1861 to January 1862. Detailed as nurse, March 18, 1862, and remained as nurse until expiration. Mustered out with company, May 28, 1863, at Albany, N.Y.

SCHWANTNER, JOHN—Age 34 years. Enlisted April 26, 1861, at Schenectady. Mustered in as private Co. A, May 17, 1861, to serve two years. Wounded in left shoulder and captured, June 27, 1862, at Gaines's Mill, Va. Confined, June 28, 1862, at Richmond, Va. Paroled, July 19, 1862, at City Point, Va. Hospitalized, November 1862, at Alexandria, Va. Discharged on account of wounds, December 24, 1862, at White Oak Church, Falmouth, Va. Subsequent service in 12th Veteran Reserve Corps.

SCOFIELD (Cofield), JAMES—Age 22 years. Enlisted April 23, 1861, at Albany. Mustered in as private, Co. C, May 17, 1861, to serve two years. Mustered out with company, May 28, 1863, at Albany, N.Y.

SCOTLAND, ROBERT—Age 31 years. Enlisted April 22, 1861, at Schenectady. Mustered in as private, Co. A, May 17, 1861, to serve two years. Mustered out with company, May 28, 1863, at Albany, N.Y. Subsequent service in Co. F & G, 21st New York Cavalry.

SCOTT, WILLIAM B.—Age 24 years. Enlisted April 19, 1861, at Albany. Mustered in as private, Co. I, May 17, 1861, to serve two years. Mustered out with company, May 28, 1863, at Albany, N.Y.

SCOUTEN, SIMON SAMUEL—Age 38 years. Enlisted April 23, 1861, at Albany. Mustered in as private, Co. C, May 17, 1861, to serve two years. Mustered out with company, May 28, 1863, at Albany, N.Y. Subsequent service in Co. "U" 16th New York Heavy Artillery.

SCULLY, JOHN—Age 32 years. Enlisted April 22, 1861, at Schenectady. Mustered in as private, Co. A, May 17, 1861, to serve two years. Promoted corporal, October 2, 1861. Reduced to private, November or December 1861. Wounded in right ear, June 27, 1862, at Gaines's Mill, Va. Sent off, August 1862, from Harrison's Landing, Va. Hospitalized, August 1862, at Satterlee General Hospital, in West Philadelphia, Pa. Returned to regiment, December 11, 1862. Absent-without-leave, January 20, 1863, from Camp Russell, White Oak Church, Falmouth, Va. Returned to regiment, January 24, 1863, same place. Court-martialed for absence and disobedience, February 23, 1863, at same place. Mustered out with company, May 28, 1863, at Albany, N.Y. Subsequent service in Co. "U" 14th New York Heavy Artillery & Co. I, 13th New York Heavy Artillery.

SEARS, DAVID E.—Age 30 years. Enlisted April 25, 1861, at Albany. Mustered in as private, Co. I, May 17, 1861, to serve two years. Transferred, September 26, 1862, to Battery D, 2nd United States Artillery. Subsequent service in Co. I, 13th New York Heavy Artillery.

SEDORE, JOHN—Age 22 years. Enlisted April 23, 1861, at Albany. Mustered in as private, Co. C, May 17, 1861, to serve two years. Wounded in arm, September 14, 1862, at Crampton's Gap, Md. Hospitalized, October 6, 1862, at Camp A General Hospital, in Frederick, Md. Returned to regiment, December 26, 1862. Promoted corporal, January 1, 1863. Detailed as nurse with regimental hospital, March 21, 1863. Mustered out with company, May 28, 1863, at Albany, N.Y.

SEELY, ALBERT SYKES—Age 27 years. Enrolled May 12, 1861, at Ogdensburg. Mustered in as first lieutenant, Co. K, May 17, 1861, to serve two years. Promoted captain, August 4, 1861. On eight day furlough, December 26, 1861. Sent sick, August 4, 1862, from Harrison's Landing, Va. to New York. Returned to regiment, on or about September 20, 1862. Resigned, October 1, 1862. Commissioned first lieutenant, July 4, 1861, with rank from May 12, 1861, original. Captain, August 27, 1861, with rank from August 4, 1861, original.

SENFERT, JACOB—Age 26 years. Enlisted June 17, 1861, at Albany. Mustered in as private, Co. A, same date, to serve two years. Mustered out with company, May 28, 1863, at Albany, N.Y. Subsequent service in Co. A, 68th New York Infantry.

SESSAGRANT, WILLIAM—Age 18 years. Enlisted April 24, 1861, at Albany. Mustered in as private, Co. B, May 17, 1861, to serve two years. Promoted corporal, July 1, 1862. Mustered out with company, May 28, 1863, at Albany, N.Y. Subsequent service in Co. K, 18th New York Cavalry.

SEYMORE, FRANKLIN—Age 19 years. Enlisted September 30, 1861, at Middletown. Mustered in as private, Co. D, October 21, 1861, at Camp King, Alexandria, Va., to serve unexpired term of two years. Mustered out with company, May 28, 1863, at Albany, N.Y.

SEYMOUR, FRANKLIN "Frank"—Age 20 years. Enlisted May 2, 1861, at Schenectady. Mustered in as corporal, Co. E, May 17, 1861, to serve two years. Promoted sergeant, October 11, 1861. Wounded in left arm, September 14, 1862, at Crampton's Gap, Md. Hospitalized, October 4, 1862, at Camp A General Hospital, in Frederick, Md. Returned to regiment, March 26, 1863. Mustered out with company, May 28, 1863, at Albany, N.Y. Subsequent service in Co. A, 1st New York Veteran Cavalry.

SHAKELL, WILLIAM—Age 21 years. Enlisted April 30, 1861, at Middletown. Mustered in as private, Co. H, May 17, 1861, to serve two years. Hospitalized, November 15, 1862, at Washington, D.C. Discharged for disability, February 14, 1863, at Convalescent Camp, Alexandria, Va.

SHANNON, GEORGE E.—Age 17 years, but gave age as 18 years. Enlisted April 22, 1861, at Schenectady. Mustered in as private, Co. A, May 17, 1861, to serve two years. Discharged, May 21, 1861, by writ of Habeas Corpus, at Albany, N.Y. Subsequent service in Co. G, I, & M, 1st New York Mounted Rifles & Co. M, 4th New York Provisional Cavalry.

SHAUGHNESSY, JOHN H.—Age 21 years. Enlisted May 20, 1861, at Albany. Mustered in as private, Co. I, same date, to serve two years. Died of disease, April 19, 1862, at 3rd Division General Hospital in Alexandria, Va.

SHAW, CHESTER (Charles) C.—Age 18 years. Enlisted May 7, 1861, at Albany. Mustered in as corporal, Co. H, May 17, 1861, to serve two years. Captured, July 17, 1861, near Fairfax Court House, Va. Confined at Richmond, Va. Promoted sergeant, August 15, 1861. Paroled, January 3, 1862, at Fort Monroe, Va. Returned to regiment, January 9, 1862, at Camp King, Alexandria, Va. On thirty day furlough. Wounded in left arm, June 27, 1862, at Gaines's Mill, Va. Hospitalized, July 1862, at General Hospital, in York, Pa. Deserted hospital, July 20, 1862. Mustered out with company, May 28, 1863, at Albany, N.Y. Subsequent service in Co. H, 61st New York Infantry.

SHAW, WILLIAM ANSEN—Age 50 years, but gave age as 42 years. Enlisted March 26, 1862, at Wallkill. Mustered in as private, Co. H, same date. Wounded slightly in head, June 27, 1862, at Gaines's Mill, Va. Died of disease, August 4, 1862, at Harrison's Landing, Va.

SHAY (Shea), JOHN R.—Age 19 years. Enlisted September 24, 1861, at Albany. Mustered in as private, Co. A, October 21, 1861, at Camp King, Alexandria, Va., to serve unexpired term of two years. Mustered out with company, May 28, 1863, at Albany, N.Y. Subsequent service in Co. C, 7th New York Heavy Artillery.

SHAY, PATRICK—Age 24 years. Enlisted May 17, 1861, at Albany. Mustered in as private, Co. H, same date, to serve two years. Mustered out with company, May 28, 1863, at Albany, N.Y.

SHEA, JOHN F.—Age 41 years. Enlisted November 19, 1861, at Albany. Mustered in as private, Co. F, same date, to serve unexpired term of two years. Wounded in head, June 27, 1862, at Gaines's Mill, Va. Hospitalized, date not stated, at Harewood General Hospital, in Washington, D.C. Returned to regiment, April or May 1863. Mustered out with company, May 28, 1863, at Albany, N.Y. Subsequent service in Co. I, 13th New York Heavy Artillery.

SHEA, WILLIAM, Sr.—Age 49 years. Enlisted May 17, 1861, at Albany. Mustered in as corporal, Co. C, same date, to serve two years. Promoted sergeant, September 15, 1861. Detailed on recruiting service, November and December 1861, at Albany, N.Y. Detached from regiment as guard at recruitment depot, July 1862, at Albany, N.Y. Reduced to private, December 31, 1862, at recruitment depot hospital, in Albany, N.Y. Remained at recruitment depot until expiration. Returned to regiment, May 1863, at Albany, N.Y. Mustered out with company, May 28, 1863, at Albany, N.Y. Father of William B. Shea, Jr.

SHEA, WILLIAM B., Jr.—Age 14 or 15 years. Enlisted November 20, 1861, at Albany. Mustered in as musician, Co. C, same date, to serve eighteen months. Mustered out with company, May 28, 1863, at Albany, N.Y. Son of William Shea, Sr.

SHEEHAN (Shean), PETER—Age 42 years, but gave age as 31 years. Enlisted May 12, 1861, at Malone. Mustered in as private, Co. K, May 17, 1861, to serve two years. Discharged for disability, August 29, 1861, at Washington, D.C.

SHEIL, JACOB—Age 22 years. Enlisted April 30, 1861, at Middletown. Mustered in as private, Co. H, May 17, 1861, to serve two years. Wounded in left hand, December 13, 1862, at Fredericksburg, Va. Hospitalized, December 1862, at Satterlee General Hospital, in West Philadelphia, Pa., where middle finger was amputated. Returned to regiment, May 2, 1863. Mustered out with company, May 28, 1863, at Albany, N.Y. Subsequent service in Co. A, 25th New York Cavalry.

SHELDON, DAVID D.—Age 22 years. Enlisted September 1, 1861, at Albany. Mustered in as private, Co. F, same date, to serve two years. Promoted sergeant, September 19, 1861. Reduced to private, April 17, 1862. Wounded, September 14, 1862, at Crampton's Gap, Md. Mustered out with company, May 28, 1863, at Albany, N.Y. Subsequent service in Co. K & I, 192nd New York Infantry.

SHELDON, GRIFFIN—Age 25 years. Enlisted April 30, 1861, at Middletown. Mustered in as private, Co. D, May 17, 1861, to serve two years. Promoted corporal, October 12, 1861. Hospitalized, July 9, 1862. Died of disease, July 19, 1862, onboard transport *Vanderbilt* at Harrison's Landing, Va.

SHERAN, JOHN—Age 21 years. Enlisted April 19, 1861, at Albany. Mustered in as private, Co. I, May 17, 1861, to serve two years. Mustered out with company, May 28, 1863, at Albany, N.Y. Subsequent service in Co. E, 3rd New York Infantry.

SHIRLEY (Shirly), JOHN—Age 42 years. Enlisted May 7, 1861, at Canandaigua. Mustered in as private, Co. G, May 17, 1861, to serve two years. Discharged for disability, September 24, 1861, at Alexandria, Va. Subsequent service in Co. I, 97th New York Infantry.

SHOOK, GEORGE W.—Age 28 years. Enlisted April 19, 1861, at Albany. Mustered in as corporal, Co. F, May 17, 1861, to serve two years. Discharged for disability, September 24, 1861, at Alexandria, Va.

SHULTZ, JOHN—Age 26 years. Enlisted April 22, 1861, at Schenectady. Mustered in as private, Co. A, May 17, 1861, to serve two years. Wounded, June 27, 1862, at Gaines's Mill, Va. Deserted, December 13, 1862, at Fredericksburg, Va. Returned to regiment, December 16, 1862. Court-martialed for cowardice, February 23, 1863. Sentenced to hard labor at Rip Raps, Fort Jefferson, Dry Tortugas, Fl. Dishonorably discharged for cowardice, March 10, 1863, near Falmouth, Va. Sentence expired, August 10, 1863, at Rip Raps, Fort Jefferson, Dry Tortugas, Fl.

SICKLER, PETER EDWARD—Age 33 years. Enlisted June 13, 1861, at New York City, N.Y. Mustered in as private, Co. H, same date, to serve two years. Transferred to regimental hospital and promoted hospital steward, June 16, 1861. Mustered in as hospital steward, June 19, 1861, at Jersey City, N.J. Reduced to ranks, October 31, 1861. Discharged, November 15, 1861. Subsequent service in 8th New York Cavalry, 10th New York Cavalry, 47th New York Infantry & 48th New York Infantry.

SILSBY (Selvy), WILLIAM—Age 19 years. Enlisted May 17, 1861, at Albany. Mustered in as musician, Co. B, same date, to serve two years. Absent, date not stated. Returned to regiment, March 25, 1863. Mustered out with company, May 28, 1863, at Albany, N.Y. Subsequent service in Co. I & D, 13th New York Heavy Artillery & Co. L, 6th New York Heavy Artillery.

SINGLER, JOHN, Jr.—Age 21 years. Enlisted April 30, 1861, at Middletown. Mustered in as private, Co. D, May 17, 1861, to serve two years. Sent sick, May 7, 1862, from Brick House Landing (West Point), Va. to a New York hospital. Returned to regiment, September 30, 1862. Mustered out with company, May 28, 1863, at Albany, N.Y. Discharged, June 1, 1863.

SKELLY, EDWARD S.—Age 35 years. Enlisted May 2, 1861, at Schenectady. Mustered in as private, Co. E, May 17, 1861, to serve two years. Mustered out with company, May 28, 1863, at Albany, N.Y.

SKELTON, STEPHEN—Age 29 years. Enlisted April 24, 1861, at Albany. Mustered in as sergeant, Co. B, May 17, 1861, to serve two years. Reduced to private, July 1, 1861. Promoted corporal, May 1, 1862. Promoted sergeant, July 1, 1862. Mustered out with company, May 28, 1863, at Albany, N.Y. Subsequent service in Co. E & G, 21st New York Cavalry.

SLATTERY, JAMES S.—Age 21 years. Enlisted April 19, 1861, at Albany. Mustered in as private, Co. F, May 17, 1861, to serve two years. Wounded, June 27, 1862, at Gaines's Mill, Va. Hospitalized, date not stated, at General Hospital, in Annapolis, Md. Returned to regiment, July or August 1862. Mustered out with company, May 28, 1863, at Albany, N.Y.

SLITER, ERASMUS DALY—Age 19 years. Enlisted May 17, 1861, at Albany. Mustered in as private, Co. I, same date, to serve two years. Detailed with medical department, November 1861–November 1862. Mustered out with company, May 28, 1863, at Albany, N.Y.

SMITH, HENRY B.—Age 30 years. Enlisted June 4, 1861, at Albany. Mustered in as private, Co. G, same date, to serve two years. Hospitalized, July 1861, at Washington, D.C. Deserted, September 1, 1861, at Union General Hospital, in Georgetown, Washington, D.C.

SMITH, HENRY F.—Age 18 years. Enlisted April 19, 1861, at Albany. Mustered in as private, Co. F, May 17, 1861, to serve two years. Mustered out with company, May 28, 1863, at Albany, N.Y.

SMITH, JOHN H.—Age 38 years. Enlisted September 10, 1861, at Schenectady. Mustered in as private, Co. E, October 21, 1861, at Camp King, Alexandria, Va., to serve unexpired term of two years. Promoted corporal, November 21, 1861. Mustered out with company, May 28, 1863, at Albany, N.Y.

SMITH, JOHN W.—Age 22 years. Enlisted April 24, 1861, at Albany. Mustered in as private, Co. B, May 17, 1861, to serve two years. Promoted corporal, July 1, 1862. Mustered out with company, May 28, 1863, at Albany, N.Y. Subsequent service in Co. G, 18th New York Cavalry.

SMITH, MARTIN V.—Age 20 years. Enlisted April 30, 1861, at Middletown. Mustered in as private, Co. D, May 17, 1861, to serve two years. Discharged, September 25, 1862. Subsequent service in Co. B, 179th Pennsylvania "Drafted Militia" Infantry & Co. B, 56th Pennsylvania Infantry.

SMITH, NATHANIEL—Age 20 years. Enlisted April 24, 1861, at Albany. Mustered in as private, Co. B, May 17, 1861, to serve two years. Promoted corporal, October 1, 1861. Reduced to private, date not stated. Deserted, August 28, 1862, at Alexandria, Va. Arrested, February 29, 1864, in Washington, D.C. Arrested, March 31, 1864, at Castleton, N.Y. Transferred, April 6, 1864, to Fort Columbus, New York Harbor, N.Y. Deserted, April 1864, from Camp Distribution in Alexandria, Va. Arrested, February 6, 1865, at Castleton, N.Y. Transferred, March 7, 1865, to Prince Street Military Prison, at Alexandria, Va. Discharged for disability, March 19, 1865, at Alexandria, Va.

SMITH, PERCIVAL R.—Age 26 years. Enlisted November 5, 1861, at Canandaigua. Mustered in as private, Co. G, November 15, 1861, at Elmira, N.Y., to serve two years. Died of disease, June 26, 1862, at regimental camp, Fair Oaks, Va.

SMYTH, ANDREW JACKSON—Age 23 years. Enlisted October 29, 1861, at Canandaigua. Mustered in as private, Co. G, November 15, 1861, at Elmira, N.Y., to serve unexpired term of two years. Detailed December 26, 1861, as aid for Isaac S. Green, regimental signal officer, at Washington, D.C. Returned to regiment, May 1863. Mustered out with company, May 28, 1863, at Albany, N.Y.

SNELL, WILLIAM—Age 40 years. Enlisted May 17, 1861, at Albany. Mustered in as private, Co. H, same date, to serve two years. Sent sick, August 8, 1862, from Harrison's Landing, Va. Hospitalized, August 10, 1862, at Satterlee General Hospital, in West Philadelphia, Pa. Died of disease, September 5, 1862, at Satterlee General Hospital, in West Philadelphia, Pa.

SNIDER, GEORGE—Age 17 years. Enlisted November 1, 1861. Not mustered in. Deserted, November 8, 1861, at Camp King, Alexandria, Va.

SNOOK, GEORGE—Age 18 years. Enlisted April 30, 1861, at Middletown. Mustered in as private, Co. D, May 17, 1861, to serve two years. Mustered out with company, May 28, 1863, at Albany, N.Y.

SNYDER, CHARLES—Age 42 years. Enlisted April 19, 1861, at Albany. Mustered in as private, Co. I, May 17, 1861, to serve two years. Hospitalized, July or August 1862, at Satterlee General Hospital, in West Philadelphia, Pa. Discharged for disability, January 16, 1863, at Satterlee General Hospital, in West Philadelphia, Pa.

SNYDER, JOSEPH—Age 25 years. Enlisted April 25, 1861, at Albany. Mustered in as private, Co. F, May 17, 1861, to serve two years. Killed, June 27, 1862, at Gaines's Mill, Va.

SNYDER, THOMPSON (Thomas) "Tom" H.—Age 22 years. Enlisted April 19, 1861, at Albany. Mustered in as private, Co. F, May 17, 1861, to serve two years. Killed, June 27, 1862, at Gaines's Mill, Va.

SOLOMON, PETER—Age 43 years. Enlisted April 28, 1861, at Schenectady. Mustered in as private, Co. A, May 17, 1861, to serve two years. Promoted musician, September or October 1861. Mustered out with company, May 28, 1863, at Albany, N.Y. Subsequent service in Co. B, 2nd New York Veteran Cavalry.

SOULE, PERRIE (Peter) CLEMENT—Age 16 years, but gave age as 18 years. Enlisted September 1, 1861, at Albany. Mustered in as private, Co. B, October 21, 1861, at Camp King, Alexandria, Va., to serve unexpired term of two years. Mustered out with company, May 28, 1863, at Albany, N.Y. Subsequent service in Co. I, 5th New York Cavalry.

SOULS, JOHN W.—Age 31 years. Enlisted May 1, 1861, at Albany. Mustered in as private, Co. B, May 17, 1861, to serve two years. Mustered out with company, May 28, 1863, at Albany, N.Y.

SOUTHARD, JOHN JAMES—Age 23 years. Enlisted April 30, 1861, at Middletown. Mustered in as private, Co. H, May 17, 1861, to serve two years. Promoted corporal, November 6, 1861. Wounded in left hand, June 27, 1862, at Gaines's Mill, Va. Two fingers amputated. Sent sick, July 2, 1862, from Harrison's Landing, Va. Hospitalized, July 4, 1862, at Seminary General Hospital, in Georgetown, Washington, D.C. Discharged for disability, November 3, 1862, at Providence, R. I.

SPAWN, LEWIS (Louis)—Age 19 years. Enlisted April 19, 1861, at Albany. Mustered in as private, Co. F, May 17, 1861, to serve two years. Captured, August 30, 1862, at Centerville, Va. Paroled, September 2, 1862, at Paw Paw, Md. Sent to Annapolis, Md. Sent to regiment, February 24, 1863. Returned to regiment, February 27, 1863. Mustered out with company, May 28, 1863, at Albany, N.Y. Subsequent service in Co. H, 2nd New York Veteran Cavalry, under alias John Williams.

SPEENBURGH, WILLIAM—Age 22 years. Enlisted May 7, 1861, at Albany. Mustered in as private, Co. H, May 17, 1861, to serve two years. Sent sick, May 11, 1862, from Yorktown, Va., aboard transport *Ocean Queen*, to New York Harbor, N.Y. Died of disease, May 11, 1862, on transport *Ocean Queen*, near Ship Point, Va.

STALKER, HENRY (John)—Age 17 years, but gave age as 18 years. Enlisted April 22, 1861, at Albany. Mustered in as private, Co. B, May 17, 1861, to serve two years. Killed, June 27, 1862, at Gaines's Mill, Va.

STALL, HENRY B.—Age 29 years. Enlisted April 22, 1861, at Schenectady. Mustered in as sergeant, Co. A, May 17, 1861, to serve two years. Captured, July 21, 1861, while sick at abandoned hospital, Centreville, Va. Confined, July 23, 1861, at Richmond, Va. Paroled, January 3, 1862, at Fort Monroe, Va. Promoted sergeant-major, January 6, 1862. Placed on thirty day furlough. Hospitalized, August 10, 1862, at Satterlee General Hospital, in West Philadelphia, Pa. Returned to regiment, May 17, 1863. Mustered out, June 30, 1863, at Albany, N.Y.

STANTON, WILLIAM H.—Age 21 years. Enlisted April 22, 1861, at Schenectady. Mustered in as corporal, Co. A, May 17, 1861, to serve two years. Reduced to private, June 1, 1861. Absent-without-leave, January 20, 1863, from Camp Russell, White Oak Church, Falmouth, Va. Returned to regiment, January 24, 1863, same place. Court-martialed for absence and disobedience, February 23, 1863, at same place. Mustered out with company, May 28, 1863, at Albany, N.Y. Subsequent service in Co. "U" 13th New York Heavy Artillery.

STERNBERG, JOHN F.—Age 18 years. Enlisted April 19, 1861, at Albany. Mustered in as private, Co. F, May 17, 1861, to serve two years. Discharged for disability, August 15, 1861, at Alexandria, Va.

STEVENS (Sterns), HENRY (Henry "Harry" Conger)—Age 18 years. Enlisted May 17, 1861, at Albany. Mustered in as private, Co. K, same date, to serve two years. Deserted, May 19, 1861, at Albany, N.Y. Reenlisted, October 2, 1862, at Oswegatchie. Mustered in as private, Co. K, October 13, 1862, at Albany, to serve three years. Transferred, May 10, 1863, to Co. A, 121st New York Infantry.

STEVENS (Sterns), JEHIEL J., Jr.—Age 23 years. Enlisted May 12, 1861, at Ogdensburg. Mustered in as private, Co. K, May 17, 1861, to serve two years. Wounded slightly from shell in left leg, June 27, 1862, at Gaines's Mill, Va. Hospitalized for sickness, August 10, 1862, from Harrison's Landing, Va. and sent to Satterlee General Hospital, in West Philadelphia, Pa. Transferred, September 21, 1862, to Race Street General Hospital, in Philadelphia, Pa. Transferred, April 3, 1863, to McClellan General Hospital, in Philadelphia, Pa. Transferred, February 1863, to Crown Street Hospital, in Philadelphia, Pa. Transferred, May 8, 1863, to Convalescent General Hospital, at Filbert Street, Philadelphia, Pa. Returned to regiment, May 14, 1863. Mustered out with company, May 28, 1863, at Albany, N.Y. Subsequent service in Woodward's Independent Battery, Pennsylvania Light Artillery.

STEVENSON, SINCLAIR L.—Age 18 years. Enlisted April 23, 1861, at Albany. Mustered in as private, Co. C, May 17, 1861, to serve two years. Promoted corporal, February 3, 1862. Served as corporal of color guard. Wounded in back of neck, June 27, 1862, at Gaines's Mill, Va. Hospitalized, July 3, 1862, at Hampton, Va. Transferred, date not stated, to Annapolis, Md. Returned to duty, July or August 1862. Mustered out with company, May 28, 1863, at Albany, N.Y. Subsequent service in Co. "U" 1st New York Engineers.

STILLWELL (Stilwell), DANIEL D.—Age 23 years. Enlisted April 19, 1861, at Albany. Mustered in as private, Co. F, May 17, 1861, to serve two years. Hospitalized for sickness, April 9, 1862, at Washington Street General Hospital, in Alexandria, Va. Returned to regiment, May 2, 1862. Served as corporal of color guard. Mustered out with company, May 28, 1863, at Albany, N.Y. Subsequent service in Co. C, 7th New York Heavy Artillery. Brother of William Stillwell.

STILLWELL, WILLIAM—Age 21 years. Enlisted September 10, 1861, at Albany. Mustered in as private, Co. I, October 21, 1861, at Camp King, Alexandria, Va., to serve two years. Discharged for disability, November 24, 1861, at Camp King, Alexandria, Va. Subsequent service in Co. C, 7th New York Heavy Artillery. Brother of Daniel D. Stillwell.

STODDARD, TRUMAN—Age 38 years. Enlisted April 19, 1861, at Albany. Mustered in as private, Co. F, May 17, 1861, to serve two years. Transferred to Co. K, June 17, 1861, in place of Thomas Kearns. Hospitalized, November 20, 1862, at Continental General Hospital, in Baltimore, Md. Transferred, November or December 1862, at Steuart's Mansion Hospital, in Baltimore, Md. Discharged for disability, January 1, 1863, at Steuart's Mansion Hospital, in Baltimore, Md.

STORMS, WILLIAM J.—Age 19 years. Enlisted May 17, 1861, at Albany. Mustered in as private, Co. C, same date, to serve two years. Killed, September 14, 1862, at Crampton's Gap, Md.

STORY, JAMES P.—Age 21 years. Enlisted April 22, 1861, at Schenectady. Mustered in as private, Co. A, May 17, 1861, to serve two years. Deserted, May or June 1861, before regiment left Albany, N.Y.

STORY, WILLIAM—Age 19 years. Enlisted May 17, 1861, at Albany. Mustered in as private, Co. C, same date, to serve two years. Deserted, May or June 1861, before regiment left Albany, N.Y.

STRATHERN, JAMES K.—Age 18 years. Enlisted May 17, 1861, at Albany. Mustered in as private, Co. K, same date, to serve two years. Died of disease, January 31, 1862, at Camp King, Alexandria, Va.

STRUNK, JOSEPH—Age 16 or 17 years, but gave age as 19 years. Enlisted April 22, 1861, at Schenectady. Mustered in as sergeant, Co. A, May 17, 1861, to serve two years. Promoted first sergeant, April 15, 1862. Promoted second lieutenant, August 14, 1862. Mustered out with company, May 28, 1863, at Albany, N.Y. Commissioned second lieutenant, November 10, 1862, with rank from August 14, 1862, after Munger was promoted. Subsequent service in Co. B, 2nd New York Veteran Cavalry.

STUART (Plumer), WILLIAM—Age 30 years. Enlisted May 7, 1861, at Albany. Mustered in as private, Co. H, May 17, 1861, to serve two years. Promoted corporal, November 6, 1861. Sent sick, August 8, 1862, from Harrison's Landing, Va. Hospitalized, August 10, 1862, at Satterlee General Hospital, in West Philadelphia, Pa. Reduced to ranks, October 1, 1862. Returned to regiment, May 12, 1863. Mustered out with company, May 28, 1863, at Albany, N.Y. Subsequent service in Co. G, 3rd Battalion 12th United States Infantry, Co. G, 30th United States Infantry, Co. B, 9th United States Infantry & Co. I, 11th United States Infantry.

SULLIVAN, ANTHONY—Age 22 years. Enlisted April 19, 1861, at Albany. Mustered in as private, Co. I, May 17, 1861, to serve two years. Wounded in right shoulder, June 27, 1862, at Gaines's Mill, Va. Hospitalized, July 2, 1862, at Fort Monroe, Va. Transferred aboard Steamer *Daniel Webster* and hospitalized, July 7, 1862, at 22nd and Wood Streets General Hospital, in Philadelphia, Pa. Discharged on account of such wounds, February 7, 1863, at Philadelphia, Pa. Subsequent service in 5th Independent Company, Veteran Reserve Corps.

SULLIVAN, CHARLES—Age 24 years. Enlisted May 17, 1861, at Albany. Mustered in as private, Co. E, same date, to serve two years. Court-martialed at regimental level, September or October 1861. Sent off, July 2, 1862, from Harrison's Landing, Va. Hospitalized, July 4, 1862, at Washington, D.C. Returned to regiment, date not stated. Captured, August 18, 1862, at Charles City Court House, Va. Confined, August 23, 1862, at Richmond, Va. Paroled, September 13, 1862, at City Point, Va. Mustered out with company, May 28, 1863, at Albany, N.Y.

SULLIVAN, THOMAS—Age 17 years, but gave age as 19 years. Enlisted April 23, 1861, at Albany. Mustered in as private, Co. C, May 17, 1861, to serve two years. Mustered out with company, May 28, 1863, at Albany, N.Y. Subsequent service in Co. G, 13th New York Cavalry, Co. B, 3rd New York Provisional Cavalry & Co. D, B, & F, 17th United States Infantry.

SUPPLEE, ABNER—Age 17 years, but gave age as 18 years. Enlisted November 9, 1861, at Canandaigua. Mustered in as a musician, Co. G, November 15, 1861, at Elmira, N.Y., to serve unexpired term of two years. Mustered out with company, May 28, 1863, at Albany, N.Y.

SUTHERLAND, IRA (Isaac)—Age 28 years. Enlisted May 10, 1861, at Albany. Mustered in as private, Co. I, May 17, 1861, to serve two years. Mustered out with company, May 28, 1863, at Albany, N.Y. Subsequent service in Co. C, 18th New York Cavalry, Co. I & M, 1st New York Mounted Rifles & Co. M, 4th New York Provisional Cavalry.

SUTTER (Shuter), CHARLES—Age 38 years. Enlisted September 15, 1862, at Schenectady. Mustered in as private, Co. E, October 13, 1862, at Albany, to serve three years. Transferred May 10, 1863, to Co. E, 121st New York Infantry & Co. F, 1st Regiment, Veteran Reserve Corps.

SWARTHOUT, LEVI—Age 36 years. Enlisted June 4, 1861, at Albany. Mustered in as private, Co. B, June 14, 1861, to serve unexpired term of two years. Killed, June 27, 1862, at Gaines's Mill, Va.

SWIFT, HENRY J.—Age 18 years. Enlisted April 30, 1861, at Middletown. Mustered in as private, Co. H, May 17, 1861, to serve two years. Discharged for disability, September 23, 1861, at Alexandria, Va.

SWIMM, SYLVANUS L.—Age 15 years, but gave age as 18 years. Enlisted April 23, 1861, at Albany. Mustered in as private, Co. C, May 17, 1861, to serve two years. Court-martialed, on or about January 24, 1862, at Alexandria, Va. Wounded in right foot, June 27, 1862, at Gaines's Mill, Va. Hospitalized, July or August 1862, at Douglas General Hospital, in Washington, D.C. Mustered out with company, May 28, 1863, at Albany, N.Y. Subsequent service in Co. B, 17th New York Veteran Infantry.

TALMADGE, JAMES W.—Age 18 years. Enlisted May 7, 1861, at Albany. Mustered in as private, Co. H, May 17, 1861, to serve two years. Deserted, July 10, 1861, from Camp Harris, Washington, D.C.

TAYLOR, HENRY W.—Age 19 years. Enlisted May 7, 1861, at Canandaigua. Mustered in as private, Co. G, May 17, 1861, to serve two years. Killed, June 27, 1862, at Gaines's Mill, Va.

TAYLOR, JOSEPH—Age 26 years. Enlisted April 30, 1861, at Middletown. Mustered in as private, Co. H, May 17, 1861, to serve two years. Wounded with skull fracture, September 14, 1862, at Crampton's Gap, Md. Mustered out with company, May 28, 1863, at Albany, N.Y. Subsequent service in Co. "U" 13th New York Heavy Artillery.

TAYLOR, SAMUEL V.—Age 19 years. Enlisted April 23, 1861, at Albany. Mustered in as private, Co. C, May 17, 1861, to serve two years. Mustered out with company, May 28, 1863, at Albany, N.Y. Subsequent service in Co. I, 7th New York Heavy Artillery.

TAYLOR, WILLIAM—Age 18 years. Enlisted October 24, 1861, at Ogdensburg. Mustered in as private, Co. K, same date, to serve unexpired term of two years. Mustered out with company, May 28, 1863, at Albany, N.Y.

TELLER, HENRY K.—Age 20 years. Enlisted May 2, 1861, at Schenectady. Mustered in as private, Co. E, May 17, 1861, to serve two years. Deserted, June 2, 1861, at Albany, N.Y. TERRIT, THOMAS—Age 39 years. Enlisted May 12, 1861, at Ogdensburg. Mustered in as private, Co. K, May 17, 1861, to serve two years. Discharged for disability, December 18, 1861, at Alexandria, Va. Subsequent service in Co. G, 78th New York Infantry & Co. E, 14th New York Heavy Artillery.

TERWILLIGER, HENRY W.—Age 19 years. Enlisted April 23, 1861, at Fishkill. Mustered in as private, Co. C, May 17, 1861, to serve two years. Discharged for disability, September 24, 1861, at Camp King, Alexandria, Va.

THOMPSON, ARTHUR—Age 29 years. Enlisted May 4, 1861, at Albany. Mustered in as private, Co. I, May 17, 1861, to serve two years. Detailed as hospital cook, June 17, 1861. Returned to ranks, November 2, 1862. Detailed as ambulance driver, November 1862. Mustered out with company, May 28, 1863, at Albany,

N.Y. Subsequent service in Co. I & C, 7th New York Heavy Artillery.

THOMPSON, CHARLES H.—Age 25 years. Enlisted April 24, 1861, at Albany. Mustered in as private, Co. B, May 17, 1861, to serve two years. Promoted corporal, July 1, 1861. Killed, August 12, 1861, by provost guard, at Alexandria, Va.

THOMPSON, GEORGE W.—Age 18 years. Enlisted May 7, 1861, at Canandaigua. Mustered in as private, Co. G, May 17, 1861, to serve two years. Promoted corporal, January 1, 1863. Mustered out with company, May 28, 1863, at Albany, N.Y. Subsequent service in Co. L, 50th New York Engineers.

THOMPSON, JAMES H.—Age 19 years. Enlisted August 19, 1862, at Albany. Mustered in as private, Co. C, September 20, 1862, at Albany, to serve two years. Transferred, May 10, 1863, to Co. H, 121st New York Infantry.

THOMPSON, JOHN—Age 23 years. Enlisted April 23, 1861, at Albany. Mustered in as private, Co. C, May 17, 1861, to serve two years. Court-martialed for absence without leave, October 17, 1861. Deserted, December 15, 1861, from Camp King, Alexandria, Va. Returned to regiment, December 21, 1861, at Camp King, Alexandria, Va. Court-martialed for desertion, January 30, 1862, at Alexandria, Va. Wounded in left shoulder, June 27, 1862, at Gaines's Mill, Va. Sent sick, July 2, 1862, from Harrison's Landing, Va. and hospitalized at Fort Monroe, Va. Deserted, July 1862, from hospital, at Annapolis, Md.

THOMPSON, SAMUEL—Age 26 years. Enlisted April 22, 1861, at Schenectady. Mustered in as private, Co. A, May 17, 1861, to serve two years. Deserted, May or June 1861, before regiment left Albany, N.Y.

THOMPSON, WILLIAM H.—Age 25 years. Enlisted April 30, 1861, at Middletown. Mustered in as private, Co. D, May 17, 1861, to serve two years. Killed, June 27, 1862, at Gaines's Mill, Va.

THOMY, CHARLES A.—Age 16 years, but gave age as 18 years. Enlisted May 2, 1861, at Schenectady. Mustered in as private, Co. E, May 17, 1861, to serve two years. Mustered out with company, May 28, 1863, at Albany, N.Y.

THORN, DANIEL—Age 18 years. Enlisted April 24, 1861, at Albany. Mustered in as private, Co. B, May 17, 1861, to serve two years. Deserted, September 20, 1861, from Camp King, Alexandria, Va.

TICEHURST, DAVID L.—Age 18 years. Enlisted May 17, 1861, at Albany. Mustered in as private, Co. C, same date, to serve two years. Discharged for disability, September 24, 1861, at Camp King, Alexandria, Va. Subsequent service in Co. E, 19th New York Militia National Guard.

TIFFANY, PATRICK—Age 19 years. Enlisted April 19, 1861, at Albany. Mustered in as private, Co. F, May 17, 1861, to serve two years. Deserted, August 10, 1861, from Camp Myers, Alexandria, Va.

TILLEY, EDWARD MUNRO—Age 26 years. Enlisted May 12, 1861, at Ogdensburg. Mustered in as private, Co. K, May 17, 1861, to serve two years. On one week furlough, August 3, 1861. Promoted second lieutenant, August 4, 1861. Commissioned second lieutenant, August 4, 1861, with rank from July 16, 1861. Appointed quartermaster, November 9, 1861. Discharged for promotion to captain and assistant quartermaster in Quartermaster's Department Regiment United States Volunteers, June 9, 1862. Resigned, April 13, 1864.

TIMMINS, EDWARD—Age 20 years. Enlisted April 23, 1861, at Albany. Mustered in as private, Co. C, May 17, 1861, to serve two years. Court-martialed for disobedience, January 25, 1862, at Alexandria, Va. Mustered out with company, May 28, 1863, at Albany, N.Y.

TIMMINS, WILLIAM—Age 20 years. Enlisted May 12, 1861, at Albany. Mustered in as private, Co. F, May 17, 1861, to serve two years. Deserted, August 10, 1861, from Camp Myers, Alexandria, Va.

TIPLADY, JOHN—Age 24 years. Enlisted April 23, 1861, at Albany. Mustered in as private, Co. C, May 17, 1861, to serve two years. Captured, June 29, 1862, at Savage's Station, Va. Confined, June 30, 1862, at Richmond, Va. Paroled, September 13, 1862, at City Point, Va. Sent to Washington, D.C., on September 26, 1862. Mustered out with company, May 28, 1863, at Albany, N.Y.

TITSWORTH, HENRY—Age about 16 years, but gave age as 21 years. Enlisted April 30, 1861, at Middletown. Mustered in as private, Co. H, May 17, 1861, to serve two years. Promoted corporal, May or June 1862. Wounded slightly in back left of head, June 27, 1862, at Gaines's Mill, Va. Hospitalized for sickness, October 30, 1862, from camp near Bakersville, Md., and hospitalized at Smoketown General Hospital, near Hagerstown, Md. Returned to regiment, March 19, 1863, at White Oak Church, Falmouth, Va. Mustered out with company, May 28, 1863, at Albany, N.Y.

TOMPKINS, MILTON—Age 18 years. Enlisted April 30, 1861, at Middletown. Mustered in as private, Co. H, May 17, 1861, to serve two years. Mustered out with company, May 28, 1863, at Albany, N.Y. Subsequent service in the 28th Independent Battery New York Light Artillery.

TOMPKINS, WILLIAM H.—Age 19 years. Enlisted May 7, 1861, at Albany. Mustered in as private, Co. H, May 17, 1861, to serve two years. Discharged for disability, September 23, 1861, at Alexandria, Va.

TONKINS, JOSEPH—Age 29 years. Enlisted October 15, 1861, at Ogdensburg. Mustered in as private, Co. K, October 30, 1861, at Camp Williams, Va., to serve unexpired term of two years. Mustered out with company, May 28, 1863, at Albany, N.Y.

TOWNSEND, HEZEKIAH E.—Age 20 years. Enlisted May 7, 1861, at Canandaigua. Mustered in as private, Co. G, May 17, 1861, to serve two years. Sick, remained at home, Bristol, N.Y. when regiment left state. Never returned to regiment, listed as a deserter. Subsequent service in Co. G, 148th New York Infantry.

TRABILCOX, THOMAS C.—Age 24 years. Enlisted April 19, 1861, at Albany. Mustered in as private, Co. F, May 17, 1861, to serve two years. Promoted sergeant, July 1, 1862. Mustered out with company, May 28, 1863, at Albany, N.Y.

TRAINOR, ROBERT T.—Age 35 years. Enlisted

May 7, 1861, at Albany. Mustered in as private, Co. H, May 17, 1861, to serve two years. Deserted, June 18, 1861, at Albany, N.Y.

TROWBRIDGE, W. R.—Age—years. Appointed surgeon, no date. Resigned, October 3, 1862, by order of Maj. Gen. E. D. Morgan, per Special Order No. 43. Not commissioned.

TRUAX, ALFRED—Age 30 years. Enlisted May 2, 1861, at Schenectady. Mustered in as sergeant, Co. E, May 17, 1861, to serve two years. Promoted orderly sergeant, November 11, 1861. Promoted first sergeant, November 14, 1861. Mustered in as first lieutenant, September 20, 1862. On ten day furlough, April 3–13, 1863, in Schenectady, N.Y. Mustered out with company, May 28, 1863, at Albany, N.Y. Commissioned first lieutenant, December 9, 1862, with rank from September 20, 1862, after Vedder resigned. Son of Stephen Truax.

TRUAX, STEPHEN—Age 52 years. Enrolled May 2, 1861, at Schenectady. Mustered in as captain, Co. E, May 17, 1861, to serve two years. On thirty day furlough, August 6, 1861, in Schenectady, N.Y. Resigned, December 27, 1861. Commissioned captain, July 4, 1861, with rank from May 2, 1861, original. Father of Alfred Truax.

TRUE, WILLIAM J.—Age 15 years. Enlisted November 20, 1861, at Albany. Mustered in as drummer, Co. D, December 7, 1861, at Camp King, Alexandria, Va., to serve two years. Deserted, August 24, 1862. Returned to regiment, December 21, 1862. Mustered out with company, May 28, 1863, at Albany, N.Y. Subsequent service in Co. C, 18th New York Cavalry.

TUBBS, LUTHER TAYLOR—Age 43 years, but gave age as 38 years. Enlisted May 7, 1861, at Canandaigua. Mustered in as private, Co. G, May 17, 1861, to serve two years. Sick, remained at home, Bristol, N.Y. when regiment left state. Never returned to regiment, listed as a deserter.

TUCKER, EDWARD C.—Age 22 years. Enlisted May 7, 1861, at Albany. Mustered in as private, Co. H, May 17, 1861, to serve two years. Deserted, May 18, 1861, at Albany, N.Y.

TURNBULL, JAMES—Age 34 years, but gave age as 28 years. Enlisted September 29, 1862, at Rotterdam. Mustered in as private, Co. E, October 13, 1862, at Albany, to serve two years. Transferred, May 10, 1863, to Co. E, 121st New York Infantry.

TURNER, JAMES—Age 22 years. Enlisted April 30, 1861, at Middletown. Mustered in as private, Co. H, May 17, 1861, to serve two years. Deserted, June 12, 1861, at Albany Barracks, Albany, N.Y.

TURNER (McNamee), JOSEPH—Age 20 years. Enlisted April 30, 1861, at Middletown. Mustered in as private, Co. H, May 17, 1861, to serve two years. Hospitalized, June 1861, at E Street General Hospital, in Washington, D.C. Mustered out with company, May 28, 1863, at Albany, N.Y. Subsequent service in Co. C, 56th New York Infantry & United States Navy.

TUTTLE, WILLIAM—Age 23 years. Enlisted September 9, 1862, at Albany. Mustered in as private, Co. D, October 13, 1862, at Albany, to serve three years. Transferred, May 10, 1863, to Co. E, 121st New York Infantry.

UNDERHILL, DANIEL—Age 34 or 28 years. Enlisted April 23, 1861, at Albany. Mustered in as private, Co. C, May 17, 1861, to serve two years. Hospitalized, July or August 1862, at Blackwell's Island, in New York City, N.Y. Transferred, September of October 1862, to Convalescent Camp, in Alexandria, Va. Returned to regiment, November or December 1862. Mustered out with company, May 28, 1863, at Albany, N.Y.

UNDERHILL, FRANKLIN "Frank" K.—Age 17 years, but gave age as 18 years. Enlisted May 2, 1861, at Schenectady. Mustered in as private, Co. E, May 17, 1861, to serve two years. Absent-without-leave, January 20, 1863, from Camp Russell, White Oak Church, Falmouth, Va. Returned to regiment, January 24, 1863, same place. Court-martialed for absence, February 19, 1863, at same place. Discharged for disability, March 28, 1863, at White Oak Church, Falmouth, Va. Died of disease, May 1, 1863, at Charlton, N.Y. Brother of James K. Underhill.

UNDERHILL, GEORGE T.—Age 31 years. Enlisted April 23, 1861, at Albany. Mustered in as private, Co. C, May 17, 1861, to serve two years. Hospitalized, date not stated, at Harewood General Hospital, in Washington, D.C. Returned to regiment, November 1, 1861. Mustered out with company, May 28, 1863, at Albany, N.Y.

UNDERHILL, JAMES KIPP—Age 23 years. Enlisted May 2, 1861, at Schenectady. Mustered in as private, Co. E, May 17, 1861, to serve two years. Sent sick, August 14, 1862, from camp near Harrison's Landing, Va. and hospitalized at Satterlee General Hospital, in West Philadelphia, Pa. Returned to regiment, May 12, 1863. Mustered out with company, May 28, 1863, at Albany, N.Y. Subsequent service in Co. F, 13th New York Heavy Artillery & Co. F, 6th New York Heavy Artillery. Brother of Franklin K. Underhill.

VAN AUKEN, WILLIAM—Age 24 years. Enlisted April 23, 1861, at Albany. Mustered in as private, Co. C, May 17, 1861, to serve two years. Discharged for disability, September 24, 1861, at Camp King, Alexandria, Va. Subsequent service in the 11th New York Cavalry.

VAN BENTHUYSEN, FRANCIS—Age 58 years, but gave age as 40 years. Enlisted April 24, 1861, at Albany. Mustered in as private, Co. B, May 17, 1861, to serve two years. Discharged for disability, November 20, 1861, at Camp King, Alexandria, Va.

VAN BRAMER, JAMES L.—Age 22 years. Enlisted April 30, 1861, at Middletown. Mustered in as private, Co. D, May 17, 1861, to serve two years. Mustered out with company, May 28, 1863, at Albany, N.Y. Subsequent service in Co. A, 7th New York Heavy Artillery.

VAN BUEREN, JOHN—Age 27 years. Enlisted May 17, 1861, at Albany. Mustered in as private, Co. A, same date, to serve two years. Killed, September 14, 1862, at Crampton's Gap, Md.

VANCE, BOYD—Age 21 years. Enlisted May 18, 1861, Albany. Mustered in as private, Co. A, same date, to serve two years. Discharged for disability, September 24, 1861, at Alexandria, Va. Subsequent service in Co. E, 177th New York Infantry, Co. A, 25th New York Militia National Guard, Co. "U" 91st New York Infantry & 110th New York Infantry.

VAN DUSEN, FREDRICK—Age 19 years. Enlisted May 20, 1861, at Albany. Mustered in as private, Co. G, same date, to serve two years. Hospitalized, May 11, 1862, at Seminary Hospital, at Hampton, Va. Sent sick, on or about May 24, 1862, from White House Landing, Va., to New York. Returned to regiment, date not stated. Mustered out with company, May 28, 1863, at Albany, N.Y. Subsequent service in Co. A, 192nd New York Infantry.

VAN EVERA, WILLIAM H.—Age 34 years. Enlisted September 2, 1862, at Albany. Mustered in as private, Co. A, same date, to serve three years. Transferred, May 10, 1863, to Co. G, 121st New York Infantry & Co. A, 6th New York Heavy Artillery.

VAN HOESEN, PETER—Age 28 years. Enlisted April 24, 1861, at Albany. Mustered in as private, Co. B, May 17, 1861, to serve two years. Promoted corporal, October 1, 1861. Reduced to private, May or June 1862. Deserted, September 6, 1862, at Alexandria, Va. Arrested, July 2, 1863, at New Scotland, N.Y. Deserted, July 5, 1863, at Albany. Subsequent service in Co. H, 7th Connecticut Infantry & the United States Navy, under alias James Sullivan, aboard the USS *Agawam*.

VAN HOUSEN, CHARLES—Age 25 years. Enlisted September 25, 1862, at Rotterdam. Mustered in as private, Co. E, October 13, 1862, at Albany, to serve three years. Transferred, May 10, 1863, to Co. H, 121st New York Infantry.

VAN INGEN, JAMES LUCAS—Age 43 years. Enrolled May 14, 1861, at Albany. Mustered in as surgeon, May 17, 1861, to serve two years. Resigned, August 4, 1861, at Alexandria, Va. Commissioned surgeon, July 4, 1861, with rank from May 14, 1861, original. Subsequent service in the 5th New York Infantry.

VAN KUREN, ISAAC H.—Age 28 years. Enlisted May 7, 1861, at Canandaigua. Mustered in as private, Co. G, May 17, 1861, to serve two years. Killed, June 27, 1862, at Gaines's Mill, Va. Brother of Simon & William H. Van Kuren.

VAN KUREN, SIMON P.—Age 21 years. Enlisted May 7, 1861, at Canandaigua. Mustered in as private, Co. G, May 17, 1861, to serve two years. Discharged for disability, September 24, 1861, at Alexandria, Va. Subsequent service in the United States Navy on the USS *Great Western*, *Collier* & *Red Rover*. Brother of Isaac & William H. Van Kuren.

VAN KUREN, WILLIAM H.—Age 19 years. Enlisted May 7, 1861, at Canandaigua. Mustered in as private, Co. G, May 17, 1861, to serve two years. Wounded, June 27, 1862, at Gaines's Mill, Va. Deserted, November 1, 1862. Arrested, date not stated. Confined at Fort Columbus, N.Y. Transferred, November 25, 1863, to Alexandria, Va. Transferred, January 29, 1864, to Co. F, 146th New York Infantry. Brother of Isaac & Simon P. Van Kuren.

VANNESS, JOHN N.—Age 22 years. Enlisted April 30, 1861, at Middletown. Mustered in as private, Co. D, May 17, 1861, to serve two years. Mustered out with company, May 28, 1863, at Albany, N.Y.

VAN STEINBERG, CHARLES—Age 24 years. Enlisted June 13, 1861, at Albany. Mustered in as private, Co. B, same date, to serve unexpired term of two years. Hospitalized, September 3, 1862, at General Hospital in Philadelphia, Pa. Died of disease, November 14, 1862, at Broad & Cherry Streets General Hospital, in Philadelphia, Pa.

VAN STRANDER, SAMUEL FLOYD—Age 19 years. Enlisted April 23, 1861, at Albany. Mustered in as private, Co. C, May 17, 1861, to serve two years. Mustered out with company, May 28, 1863, at Albany, N.Y. Subsequent service in the 28th Independent Battery New York Light Artillery.

VAN VOAST, WALTER—Age 19 years. Enlisted May 2, 1861, at Schenectady, as private, Co. E, to serve two years. No further record.

VAN VORT (Van Voort) (Van Vert), CHARLES W.—Age 16 years, but gave age as 18 years. Enlisted April 23, 1861, at Fishkill. Mustered in as private, Co. C, May 17, 1861, to serve two years. Wounded in left knee, June 27, 1862, at Gaines's Mill, Va. Hospitalized, July 4, 1862, at Columbian College Hospital, in Washington, D.C. Returned to regiment, September or October 1862. Mustered out with company, May 28, 1863, at Albany, N.Y. Subsequent service in Co. H, 128th New York Infantry.

VAN VRANKEN, ELEAZOR C.—Age 23 years. Enlisted May 2, 1861, at Schenectady. Mustered in as private, Co. E, May 17, 1861, to serve two years. Discharged for disability, September 24, 1861, at Camp King, Alexandria, Va.

VAN WIE, LEVI—Age 41 years. Enlisted May 3, 1861, at Schenectady. Mustered in as private, Co. A, May 17, 1861, to serve two years. Hospitalized, July or August 1861, at hospital, in Annapolis, Md. Transferred, September 1861, to hospital, in Washington, D.C. Returned to regiment, September 27, 1861. Court-martialed, February 1863, at White Oak Church, Falmouth, Va. Mustered out with company, May 28, 1863, at Albany, N.Y. Subsequent service in Co. D, 13th New York Heavy Artillery & Co. L, 6th New York Heavy Artillery.

VAN ZANDT, HENRY—Age 21 years. Enlisted April 24, 1861, at Albany. Mustered in as private, Co. B, May 17, 1861, to serve two years. Mustered out with company, May 28, 1863, at Albany, N.Y.

VEDDER, BARNEY M.—Age 21 years. Enlisted May 2, 1861, at Schenectady. Mustered in as private, Co. E, May 17, 1861, to serve two years. Absent-without-leave, January 20, 1863, from Camp Russell, White Oak Church, Falmouth, Va. Returned to regiment, January 24, 1863, same place. Court-martialed for absence and disrespect, February 20, 1863, at same place. Sent to Rip Raps, March 4, 1863. Arrived to Fort Jefferson, Dry Tortugas, Fl. on April 10, 1863. Released and dishonorably discharged, July 15, 1863.

VEDDER, JOHN—Age about 27 years. Enrolled May 2, 1861, at Schenectady. Mustered in as second lieutenant, Co. E, May 17, 1861, to serve two years. Promoted first lieutenant, December 27, 1861. Promoted captain, September 20, 1862. On ten day furlough, March 1, 1863, in Schenectady, N.Y. Returned to regiment, March 12, 1863. Mustered out with company, May 28, 1863, at

Albany, N.Y. Commissioned second lieutenant, July 4, 1861, with rank from May 2, 1861, original. First lieutenant, January 3, 1862, with rank from December 27, 1861, after Horsfall was promoted. Captain, December 9, 1862, with rank from September 20, 1862, after Horsfall died.

VEDDER, RODNEY STILES—Age 19 years. Enlisted May 2, 1861, at Schenectady. Mustered in as private, Co. E, May 17, 1861, to serve two years. Promoted regimental commissary-sergeant, October 17, 1861. Mustered in as second lieutenant, Co. H, July 16, 1862. Detailed as quartermaster, December 9, 1862. Mustered out with regiment, May 28, 1863, at Albany, N.Y. Commissioned second lieutenant, November 10, 1862, with rank from July 16, 1862, after Lane was promoted. Subsequent service as assistant paymaster at Washington, D.C.

VINCENT, LEVI D.—Age 21 years. Enlisted May 7, 1861, at Albany. Mustered in as sergeant, Co. H, May 17, 1861, to serve two years. Reduced to private, August 15, 1861. Deserted, January 15, 1862, from Camp King, Alexandria, Va.

VINCENT, MORTIMER—Age 21 years. Enlisted May 7, 1861, at Canandaigua. Mustered in as private, Co. G, May 17, 1861, to serve two years. Discharged for disability, September 24, 1861, at Alexandria, Va. Subsequent service in Co. M, 10th New York Cavalry.

VOSBURGH, CHARLES H.—Age 19 years. Enlisted May 2, 1861, at Schenectady. Mustered in as corporal, Co. E, May 17, 1861, to serve two years. Reduced to private, September 25, 1861. Mustered out with company, May 28, 1863, at Albany, N.Y.

VREDENBURGH, WILLET (Willis)—Age 38 years. Enlisted April 23, 1861, at Albany. Mustered in as corporal, Co. C, May 17, 1861, to serve two years. Detailed as carpenter, January or February 1863, for brigade headquarters. Mustered out with company, May 28, 1863, at Albany, N.Y. Subsequent service in Co. C, 98th New York Infantry.

WADSWORTH, JOSEPH—Age 21 years. Enlisted April 23, 1861, at Fishkill. Mustered in as sergeant, Co. C, May 17, 1861, to serve two years. Captured, June 29, 1862, while sick at Savage's Station, Va. Confined, July 1, 1862, at Richmond, Va. Paroled, August 5, 1862, at City Point, Va. Mustered out with company, May 28, 1863, at Albany, N.Y.

WAGONER, JOHN G.—Age 30 years. Enlisted May 17, 1861, at Albany. Mustered in as private, Co. A, same date, to serve two years. Mustered out with company, May 28, 1863, at Albany, N.Y. Discharged, June 1, 1863. Subsequent service in Co. A, 7th New York Heavy Artillery.

WALDEN, ISAAC B.—Age 19 years. Enlisted April 19, 1861, at Albany. Mustered in as private, Co. F, May 17, 1861, to serve two years. Died of disease, February 2, 1862, at Camp King, Alexandria, Va.

WALKER, RICHARD N.—Age 24 years. Enlisted April 19, 1861, at Albany. Mustered in as private, Co. F, May 17, 1861, to serve two years. Wounded in right arm, September 14, 1862, at Crampton's Gap, Md. Hospitalized, September 1862, at Camp B General Hospital, in Frederick, Md. Detailed as nurse, December 17, 1862, at Camp B General Hospital, in Frederick, Md. Transferred, March 9, 1863, to Jarvis General Hospital, in Baltimore, Md. Mustered out with company, May 28, 1863, at Albany, N.Y. Subsequent service in Co. H & B, 7th New York Heavy Artillery.

WALKER, STEPHEN—Age 29 years. Enlisted August 31, 1862, at Albany. Mustered in as private, Co. C, September 26, 1862, at Albany, to serve three years. Transferred, May 10, 1863, to Co. C, 121st New York Infantry.

WALL, JOHN—Age 30 years. Enlisted April 23, 1861, at Fishkill. Mustered in as private, Co. C, May 17, 1861, to serve two years. Discharged for disability, November 20, 1861, at Camp King, Alexandria, Va.

WALLACE, ALEXANDER M.—Age 21 years. Enlisted April 29, 1861, at Schenectady. Mustered in as private, Co. A, May 17, 1861, to serve two years. Accidentally wounded by self, July 28, 1861. Hospitalized, August 1861, at hospital, in Alexandria, Va. Discharged on account of accidental gunshot wounds, January 3, 1862, at Camp King, Alexandria, Va. Subsequent service in the 6th Independent Company, Veteran Reserve Corps & Co. F, 42nd United States Infantry.

WALLACE, JAMES—Age 27 years. Enlisted April 19, 1861, at Albany. Mustered in as private, Co. I, May 17, 1861, to serve two years. Mustered out with company, May 28, 1863, at Albany, N.Y.

WALLEY, CHARLES CHAUNCEY—Age 20 years. Enlisted May 2, 1861, at Schenectady. Mustered in as private, Co. E, May 17, 1861, to serve two years. Promoted corporal, October 11, 1861. Promoted sergeant, November 14, 1861. Detailed on recruiting service, August 13, 1862, in Schenectady, N.Y. Promoted first sergeant, September 20, 1862. Mustered out with company, May 28, 1863, at Albany, N.Y.

WANDS, ALEXANDER HAMILTON—Age 23 years. Enrolled April 24, 1861, at Albany. Mustered in as first lieutenant, Co. B, May 17, 1861, to serve two years. Hospitalized, November 1861, in Alexandria, Va. Detailed on recruiting service, December 1861 & January 1862, in Albany, N.Y. Resigned, July 18, 1862. Commissioned first lieutenant, July 4, 1861, with rank from April 24, 1861, original. Subsequent service in 1st Independent Company, Veteran Reserve Corps, 10th Regiment, Veteran Reserve Corps, & 36th U.S Infantry. Brother of Robert J. Wands.

WANDS, ROBERT J.—Age 26 years. Enlisted May 17, 1861, at Albany. Mustered in as quartermaster-sergeant, same date, to serve two years. Mustered out with regiment, May 28, 1863, at Albany, N.Y. Brother of Alexander H. Wands.

WARDEN, WARREN—Age 20 years. Enlisted February 17, 1862, at Port Jervis. Mustered in as private, Co. B, same date, to serve unexpired term of two years. Deserted, September 6, 1862, at Alexandria, Va.

WARFIELD, ANNIAH NEWTON—Age 21 years. Enlisted May 7, 1861, at Canandaigua. Mustered in as private, Co. G, May 17, 1861, to serve two years. Mustered out with company, May 28, 1863, at Albany, N.Y. Subsequent service in Co. C, 15th New York Cavalry. Brother of John J. Warfield.

WARFIELD, JOHN "Johnny" JAMES—Age 17 years, but gave age as 18 years. Enlisted November 1, 1861, at Canandaigua. Mustered in as private, Co. G, November 15, 1861, at Elmira, N.Y., to serve two years. Died of disease, January 19, 1862, at Camp King, Alexandria, Va. Brother of A. Newton Warfield.

WARNER, JOHN—Age 31 years. Enlisted April 23, 1861, at Fishkill. Mustered in as private, Co. C, May 17, 1861, to serve two years. Deserted, May or June, before regiment left Albany, N.Y.

WATERBURY, PETER LEWIS—Age 23 years. Enlisted April 30, 1861, at Middletown. Mustered in as private, Co. D, May 17, 1861, to serve two years. Hospitalized, June 1, 1861, at Albany. Left sick, June 18, 1861, at Albany hospital when regiment left state. Returned to regiment, November 12, 1861. Discharged for disability, December 23, 1861, at Camp King, Alexandria, Va. Subsequent service in Co. E, 143rd New York Infantry.

WATERSON, JOHN—Age 22 years. Enlisted June 17, 1861, at Albany. Mustered in as private, Co. A, same date, to serve two years. Promoted sergeant, date not stated. Wounded in thigh, July 17, 1861, near Fairfax Court House, Va. Hospitalized, July 18, 1861, at General Hospital in Washington, D.C. Died of such wounds, July 23, 1861, at E Street General Hospital, in Washington, D.C.

WATSON, HENRY—Age 33 years. Enlisted April 19, 1861, at Albany. Mustered in as private, Co. I, May 17, 1861, to serve two years. Mustered out with company, May 28, 1863, at Albany, N.Y.

WEATHERWAX, WALTER WILSON—Age 18 years. Enlisted May 2, 1861, at Schenectady. Mustered in as private, Co. E, May 17, 1861, to serve two years. Mustered out with company, May 28, 1863, at Albany, N.Y. Subsequent service in Co. E, 1st New York Veteran Cavalry & Co. K, 2nd New York Cavalry.

WEBSTER, AURELIUS—Age 24 years. Enlisted April 29, 1861, at Albany. Mustered in as private, Co. I, May 17, 1861, to serve two years. Detailed on recruiting service, August 13, 1862, in Middletown, N.Y. Mustered out with company, May 28, 1863, at Albany, N.Y.

WEED, CHARLES A.—Age 26 years. Enlisted May 12, 1861, at Ogdensburg. Mustered in as private, Co. K, May 17, 1861, to serve two years. Captured, July 2, 1862, near the James River, near Richmond, Va. Confined, July 4, 1862, at Richmond, Va. Paroled, August 5, 1862, at City Point, Va. Mustered out with company, May 28, 1863, at Albany, N.Y.

WEED, WILLIAM G.—Age 38 years. Enrolled to serve two years, and appointed captain, Co. I, April 19, 1861. Not mustered in, and out of service, May 10, 1861. Not commissioned.

WELSH, JOHN—Age 28 years. Enlisted September 1, 1861, at Albany. Mustered in as private, Co. B, October 21, 1861, at Camp King, Alexandria, Va., to serve unexpired term of two years. Sent sick, August 10, 1862, from Harrison's Landing, Va., aboard transport *Vanderbilt*, to David's Island General Hospital, in New York Harbor, N.Y. Discharged, December 31, 1862, at David's Island General Hospital, in New York Harbor, N.Y.

WELSH (Walsh), THOMAS—Age 34 years. Enlisted November 26, 1861, at Albany. Mustered in as private, Co. F, same date, to serve unexpired term of two years. Wounded in right shin, June 27, 1862, at Gaines's Mill, Va. Captured, June 29, 1862, at Savage's Station, Va. Confined, July 13, 1862, at Richmond, Va. Paroled, July 25, 1862, at City Point, Va. Hospitalized, July 27, 1862, at General Hospital at Newport News, Va. Hospitalized, August 10, 1862, from Harrison's Landing, Va. Sent to Washington, D.C., on September 26, 1862. Discharged for disability, December 31, 1862, at David's Island General Hospital, in New York Harbor, N.Y. Subsequent service in Co. A & B, 17th New York Veteran Infantry & Co. C, 44th United States Infantry (post war).

WESTFALL, JOHN S., Jr.—Age 19 years. Enlisted September 1, 1861, at Albany. Mustered in as private, Co. I, October 21, 1861, at Camp King, Alexandria, Va., to serve unexpired term of two years. Detailed in Ambulance Corps, November 1862. Mustered out with company, May 28, 1863, at Albany, N.Y. Subsequent service in Co. K, 7th New York Heavy Artillery.

WEYMER, MICHAEL—Age 24 years. Enlisted April 30, 1861, at Middletown. Mustered in as private, Co. D, May 17, 1861, to serve two years. Wounded in left elbow, June 27, 1862, at Gaines's Mill, Va. Hospitalized, July 4, 1862, at Columbian College Hospital, in Washington, D.C. Transferred, March 27, 1863, Central Park General Hospital in New York City, N.Y. Returned to regiment, May 22, 1863. Mustered out with company, May 28, 1863, at Albany, N.Y.

WHEELER, WILLIAM WIRT—Age 18 years. Enlisted May 7, 1861, at Canandaigua. Mustered in as sergeant, Co. G, May 17, 1861, to serve two years. Left sick, June 18, 1861, at Albany hospital when regiment left state. Deserted, July 1861, at hospital, Albany, N.Y.

WHITBECK, JOHN V.—Age 18 years. Enlisted May 10, 1861, at Albany. Mustered in as private, Co. I, May 17, 1861, to serve two years. Mustered out with company, May 28, 1863, at Albany, N.Y. Subsequent service in Co. "U" 21st New York Cavalry. Brother of Samuel McKay Whitbeck.

WHITBECK, SAMUEL MCKAY—Age 16 years, but gave age as 18 years. Enlisted May 7, 1861, at Albany. Mustered in as private, Co. H, May 17, 1861, to serve two years. Promoted corporal, March 1, 1863. Mustered out with company, May 28, 1863, at Albany, N.Y. Subsequent service in Co. M, 6th New York Cavalry & Co. M, 2nd New York Provisional Cavalry. Brother of John V. Whitbeck.

WHITCOMB, WILLIAM PITT—Age 31 years. Enlisted May 12, 1861, at Ogdensburg. Mustered in as drum-major, May 17, 1861, to serve two years. Deserted, June 5, 1861, at Albany, N.Y. Subsequent service in the Company Band, 28th Pennsylvania Infantry.

WHITE, JACOB—Age 25 years. Enlisted May 17, 1861, at Albany, mustered in as private, Co. H, same date, to serve two years. Deserted, July 25, 1861, from Camp Myers, Alexandria, Va. Arrested, August 17, 1863, at Albany, N.Y. Sent to Fort Columbus, N.Y. on August 20, 1863.

WHITE, WILLIAM HENRY, Jr.—Age 17 years, but gave age as 18 years. Enlisted April 23, 1861, at Fishkill. Mustered in as private, Co. C, May 17, 1861, to serve two years. Wounded in left leg and hand, September 14, 1862, at Crampton's Gap, Md. Hospitalized, October 4, 1862, at Camp A General Hospital, in Frederick, Md. Returned to regiment, February 10, 1863. Mustered out with company, May 28, 1863, at Albany, N.Y.

WHITNEY, CHARLES CLINTON—Age 17 years, but gave age as 19 years. Enlisted November 8, 1861, at Canandaigua. Mustered in as private, Co. G, November 15, 1861, at Elmira, N.Y., to serve unexpired term of two years. Mustered out with company, May 28, 1863, at Albany, N.Y. Subsequent service in Co. H, 16th New York Heavy Artillery.

WHITNEY, EDWARD HENRY—Age 19 years. Enlisted August 27, 1862, at Albany, mustered in as private, Co. K, September 26, 1862, at Albany, to serve two years. Detailed as nurse, January 5, 1863. Transferred, May 10, 1863, to Co. H, 121st New York Infantry & Co. K, 4th Massachusetts Cavalry.

WHITTEMORE, NATHANIEL GREEN—Age 24 years. Enlisted May 10, 1861, at Albany. Mustered in as private, Co. I, May 17, 1861, to serve two years. Promoted sergeant, November 5, 1861. Promoted first sergeant, October 1, 1862. Mustered out with company, May 28, 1863, at Albany, N.Y. First Cousin of Alfred M. Chesmore.

WILBUR, HENRY D.—Age 16 years, but gave age as 18 years. Enlisted April 23, 1861, at Albany. Mustered in as private, Co. C, May 17, 1861, to serve two years. Deserted, June 1861, before regiment left Albany, N.Y. Arrested, September 3, 1862, at Hudson, N.Y. Detached as guard for depot of recruits, September or October 1862, at Albany, N.Y. Detailed as cook, January or February 1863, at Lincoln General Hospital, in Washington, D.C., and remained at hospital as cook, March and April 1863. No further record. Subsequent service in Co. H, 128th New York Infantry, Co. I, 150th New York Infantry, & Co. I, 60th New York Infantry.

WILLE, FREDERICK—Age 23 years. Enlisted May 2, 1861, at Schenectady. Mustered in as private, Co. E, May 17, 1861, to serve two years. Mustered out with company, May 28, 1863, at Albany, N.Y.

WILLETTE (Millard), GABRIEL, Jr.—Age 25 years. Enlisted May 12, 1861, at Ogdensburg. Mustered in as private, Co. K, same date, to serve two years. Hospitalized, August 3, 1861, at Washington, D.C. Detailed as regimental teamster, November 1862. Mustered out with company, May 28, 1863, at Albany, N.Y. Discharged, June 9, 1863.

WILLIAMS, JAMES—Age 32 years. Enlisted August 18, 1862, at Albany. Mustered in as private, unassigned, same date, to serve three years. No further record.

WILLIAMS, JOHN—Age 32 years. Enlisted May 1, 1861, at Albany. Mustered in as private, Co. B, May 17, 1861, to serve two years. Mustered out with company, May 28, 1863, at Albany, N.Y.

WILLIAMS, JOHN—Age 22 years. Enlisted May 2, 1861, at Schenectady. Mustered in as private, Co. E, May 17, 1861, to serve two years. Mustered out with company, May 28, 1863, at Albany, N.Y.

WILLIAMS, MILLARD FILLMORE—Age 18 years. Enlisted May 17, 1861, at Canandaigua. Mustered in as private, Co. G, same date, to serve two years. Wounded in neck, June 27, 1862, at Gaines's Mill, Va. Mustered out with company, May 28, 1863, at Albany, N.Y.

WILLIAMS, NICHOLAS—Age 33 years. Enlisted April 19, 1861, at Albany. Mustered in as private, Co. I, May 17, 1861, to serve two years. Wounded, June 27, 1862, at Gaines's Mill, Va. Mustered out with company, May 28, 1863, at Albany, N.Y. Subsequent service in Co. C, 7th New York Heavy Artillery.

WILLIAMS, WILLIAM H.—Age 20 years. Enlisted April 23, 1861, at Albany. Mustered in as private, Co. C, May 17, 1861, to serve two years. Captured, July 2, 1862, at James River, near Richmond, Va. Confined, July 2, 1862, at Richmond, Va. Paroled, August 5, 1862, at City Point, Va. Mustered out with company, May 28, 1863, at Albany, N.Y.

WILLIS, JESSE—Age 18 years. Enlisted April 24, 1861, at Albany. Mustered in as private, Co. B, May 17, 1861, to serve two years. Discharged for disability, July 12, 1861, at Washington, D.C.

WILSON, CHARLES—Age 15 years. Enlisted February 3, 1862, at Albany, mustered in as drummer, Co. E, same date, to serve unexpired term of two years. Mustered out with company, May 28, 1863, at Albany, N.Y. Subsequent service in Co. D, 39th New Jersey Infantry.

WILSON, JACOB H.—Age 24 years. Enlisted May 12, 1861, at Ogdensburg. Mustered in as private, Co. K, May 17, 1861, to serve two years. Detailed as driver in Ambulance Corps, January or February 1863. Mustered out with company, May 28, 1863, at Albany, N.Y. Subsequent service in Co. C, 60th New York Infantry.

WILSON, JAMES—Age 14 years. Enlisted January 28, 1862, at Camp King, Alexandria, Va. Mustered in as drummer, Co. H, same date, to serve sixteen months. Mustered out with company, May 28, 1863, at Albany, N.Y.

WILSON, SAMUEL C.—Age 22 years. Enlisted April 30, 1861, at Middletown. Mustered in as private, Co. H, May 17, 1861, to serve two years. Promoted corporal, date not stated. Captured, July 3, 1862, at James River, near Richmond, Va. Confined, July 4, 1862, at Richmond, Va. Paroled, August 5, 1862, at City Point, Va. Hospitalized, August 11, 1862, at General Hospital at Harrison's Landing, Va. No further record.

WILSON, WALTER—Age 25 years. Enlisted April 30, 1861, at Middletown. Mustered in as private, Co. D, May 17, 1861, to serve two years. Mustered out with company, May 28, 1863, at Albany, N.Y.

WILTSE, HENRY, Jr.—Age 27 years. Enrolled April 25, 1861, at Fishkill. Mustered in as captain, Co. C, May 17, 1861, to serve two years. Dismissed, October 19, 1861, at Alexandria, Va. Died of disease, May 7, 1862, at

Washington, D.C. Commissioned captain, July 4, 1861, with rank from April 25, 1861, original.

WISEMAN, ROBERT—Age 23 years. Enlisted April 24, 1861, at Albany. Mustered in as corporal, Co. B, May 17, 1861, to serve two years. Reduced to private, July 1, 1861. Promoted sergeant, October 1, 1861. Wounded in left arm, June 27, 1862, at Gaines's Mill, Va. Hospitalized, July 8, 1862, at General Hospital, in York, Pa. Sent to Fort McHenry, Baltimore, Md., August 1862. Reduced to private, date not stated. Discharged of account of such wound, January 9, 1863, at Fort McHenry, Baltimore, Md.

WOLFF, MARK—Age 23 years. Enlisted April 19, 1861, at Albany. Mustered in as private, Co. I, May 17, 1861, to serve two years. Detailed, July 7, 1861, as personal attendant for Colonel Jackson. On furlough as escort for remains of Colonel Jackson, November 13–19, 1861, at Albany and Schenectady. Returned to regiment, on or about November 27, 1861. Detailed as servant, December 1861 and January 1862. Detailed as nurse, May 20, 1862. Captured, June 29, 1862, at Savage's Station, Va. Confined, July 13, 1862, at Richmond, Va. Paroled, July 25, 1862, at City Point, Va. Hospitalized, July 27, 1862, at Fort Monroe, Va. Returned to regiment, July 28, 1862. Discharged for disability, August 2, 1862, at Harrison's Landing, Va. Subsequent service in Co. I, 3rd New York Infantry.

WOOD, ALBERT—Age 41 years. Enlisted April 24, 1861, at Albany. Mustered in as private, Co. B, May 17, 1861, to serve two years. Deserted, June 11, 1861, at Albany, N.Y.

WOOD, CHARLES—Age 30 years. Enlisted May 17, 1861, at Albany. Mustered in as private, Co. A, same date, to serve two years. Detailed as regimental nurse, August 1, 1861, and remained until discharged. Discharged for disability, May 26, 1862, at Chickahominy River, near Richmond, Va.

WOOD, EDWARD G.—Age 18 years. Enlisted April 19, 1861, at Albany. Mustered in as private, Co. F, May 17, 1861, to serve two years. Detached to ambulance corps, July 1862, and remained until discharged. Mustered out with company, May 28, 1863, at Albany, N.Y. Subsequent service in Co. I, 13th New York Heavy Artillery.

WOOD, SPENCER—Age 32 years. Enlisted November 12, 1861, at Canandaigua. Mustered in as private, Co. G, November 25, 1861, at Elmira, N.Y., to serve two years. Captured, June 27, 1862, at Gaines's Mill, Va. Confined at Richmond, Va. Paroled, September 13, 1862, at City Point, Va. Sent to Alexandria, Va. on November 1862. Discharged for disability, February 19, 1863, at Camp Parole, near Alexandria, Va.

WOODROW (Woodruff), HENRY—Age 18 years. Enlisted January 6, 1862, at Albany. Mustered in as drummer, Co. K, same date, to serve unexpired term of two years. Discharged for disability, May 22, 1862, at Ship Point, Va. Subsequent service in Co. E, 142nd New York Infantry & Co. I, 9th Veteran Reserve Corps.

WOODWORTH, HEZEKIAH "Hal" F.—Age 44 years. Enlisted November 30, 1861, at Albany. Mustered in as private, Co. F, December 23, 1861, at Albany, to serve unexpired term of two years. Discharged for disability, January 1, 1862, at Camp King, Alexandria, Va. Subsequent service in Co. E, 145th New York Infantry.

YEOMANS, WILLIAM HENRY—Age 21 years. Enlisted April 30, 1861, at Middletown. Mustered in as private, Co. D, May 17, 1861, to serve two years. Straggled from regiment, August 28, 1862. Hospitalized, September 1, 1862, at Columbian College Hospital, in Washington, D.C. Transferred, September 13, 1862, to Hammond General Hospital, in Point Lookout, Md. Returned to regiment, December 9, 1862. Mustered out with company, May 28, 1863, at Albany, N.Y.

YOUNG, DAVID W.—Age 18 years. Enlisted March 1, 1862, at Camp Jackson, Alexandria, Va. Mustered in as private, Co. K, same date, to serve unexpired term of two years. Hospitalized, May 11, 1862, at Seminary Hospital, at Hampton, Va. Sent sick, on or about May 24, 1862, from White House Landing, Va., to New York. Discharged for disability, August 1, 1862, at New York City, N.Y. Subsequent service in Co. B, 21st Veteran Reserve Corps. Son of William Henry Young.

YOUNG, THOMAS—Age 28 years. Enlisted April 23, 1861, at Albany. Mustered in as musician, Co. C, May 17, 1861, to serve two years. Deserted, May or June 1861, before regiment left Albany, N.Y.

YOUNG, WILLIAM—Age 30 years. Enlisted April 23, 1861, at Albany. Mustered in as musician, Co. C, May 17, 1861, to serve two years. Deserted, May or June 1861, before regiment left Albany, N.Y.

YOUNG, WILLIAM HENRY—Age 37 years. Enrolled May 14, 1861, at Albany. Mustered in as lieutenant colonel, May 17, 1861, to serve two years. Promoted colonel, November 11, 1861. On ten day furlough, December 9, 1861, in Schenectady, N.Y. Returned to regiment, December 20, 1861. Sent sick, on or about May 24, 1862, from White House Landing, Va., to New York on furlough. Returned to regiment, July 15, 1862. Resigned, August 14, 1862. Commissioned lieutenant colonel, June 18, 1861, with rank from May 13, 1861, original. Colonel, November 15, 1861, with rank from November 11, 1861, after Jackson died. Father of David W. Young.

ZINDLE, JONAS—Age 21 years. Enlisted April 30, 1861, at Middletown. Mustered in as private, Co. D, May 17, 1861, to serve two years. Wounded slightly in elbow, June 27, 1862, at Gaines's Mill, Va. Mustered out with company, May 28, 1863, at Albany, N.Y. Subsequent service in Co. I, 158th New York Infantry & Co. I, 100th New York Infantry.

Chapter Notes

The following abbreviations are used in the notes.

AG of SNY	New York State Adjutant General's Office, *Annual Report of the Adjutant General of the State of New York, Transmitted to the Legislature January 15, 1862*
AG Report	New York State Adjutant General's Office, *Annual Report of the Adjutant General of the State of New York, for the Year 1899*, Eighteenth Infantry, 959–1083
F.A.R.	New York State Bureau of Military Statistics, *First Annual Report of the Chief of the Bureau of Military Statistics*
LLMVC	Louisiana and Lower Mississippi Valley Collections, LSU Libraries, Baton Rouge, Louisiana
NYSMM	New York State Military Museum and Veterans Research Center, Saratoga Springs
NARA	National Archives and Records Administration, Washington, D.C.
NYPL	New York Public Library, New York
NYSA	New York State Archives, Albany
NYSL	New York State Library,
OR	*The War of the Rebellion: A Compilation of the Official Records of the Union and Confederate Armies*
USAHEC	U.S. Army Heritage and Education Center, Carlisle, Pennsylvania
WLC	William L. Clements Library, University of Michigan, Ann Arbor, Michigan

Chapter 1

1. Samuel Hodgkins, *Autobiography of Samuel Hodgkins* (Minneapolis, MN: Carrie E. Chatfield, 1923), 9.
2. Ibid.
3. Ibid.
4. Ibid.
5. Ibid., 6 and 9.
6. Ibid., 9–10.
7. U.S. War Department, *War of the Rebellion: Official Records of the Union and Confederate Armies* (Washington, D.C.: Government Printing Office, 1880–1901), ser 1, vol. 1, 305 (hereinafter cited as OR).
8. James A. Rawley, *Edwin D. Morgan, 1811–1883: Merchant in Politics* (New York: Columbia University Press, 1955), 134–135; New York State Adjutant General's Office, *Annual Report of the Adjutant General of the State of New York, Transmitted to the Legislature January 15, 1862* (Albany, NY: Van Benthuysen, Printer, 1862), 6 (hereinafter cited as *AG of SNY*).
9. Rawley, *Edwin D. Morgan*, 140–142; *AG of SNY*, 6 and 9.
10. Ethel B. Gage, *Orange County in the Civil War* (Goshen, NY: Orange County Community of Museums and Galleries, no date), 5; Franklin B. Williams, *Middletown: A Biography* (Middletown, NY: L.A. Toepp, 1928), 52–53 and 58.
11. Williams, *Middletown*, 58–59.

12. *Middletown Mercury*, April 19, 1861; Gage, *Orange County*, 5; *The Whig Press*, December 4, 1861; Williams, *Middletown*, 59.
13. Gage, *Orange County*, 3 and 5; *The Orange County Press*, September 2, 1881.
14. *The Whig Press*, December 4, 1861.
15. *Middletown Mercury*, April 26, 1861; *The New York Times*, June 26, 1854; National Archives and Records Administration (NARA), Pension Records, John C. Meginnis; Brotherhood of Locomotive Engineers, "In Railroad Service from 1855 to 1901," *Locomotive Engineers Journal* 42, no. 1 (1908): 314.
16. *Middletown Mercury*, April 26, 1861.
17. *The Whig Press*, April 24, 1861, and May 1, 1861; *Middletown Mercury*, April 26, 1861, and May 3, 1861; New York State Adjutant General's Office, *Annual Report of the Adjutant General of the State of New York for the Year 1899, Registers of the Twelfth, Thirteenth, Fourteenth, Sixteenth, Seventeenth, Seventeenth Veteran, and Eighteenth Regiments of Infantry* (Albany, NY: J.B. Lyon, 1900), no. 19, 959–1083 (hereinafter cited as *AG Report*); *The Whig Press*, December 4, 1861; *AG of SNY*, 711; NARA—Pension Records, Samuel G. Meginnis, widow Elizabeth Keller.
18. *Middletown Mercury*, May 3, 1861, and May 10, 1861; *The Whig Press*, April 24, 1861, and May 8, 1861; Williams, *Middletown*, 57 and 59; *Middletown Daily Press*, April 14, 1881, and April 22, 1881; *The Whig Press*, December 4, 1861; NARA—Pension Records, Roswell M. Sayer.
19. *Middletown Mercury*, May 3, 1861, and May 10, 1861; *The Whig Press*, May 8, 1861; Williams, *Middletown*, 59; *Middletown Daily Press*, April 14, 1881, and April 22, 1881.
20. *Ogdensburg Advance*, April 12, 1861; James H. Smith, *History of Duchess County, New York* (Syracuse, NY: Mason and Co., 1882), 143–144, 149, 505–506 and 512.
21. Smith, *History of Duchess County*, 511–512.
22. J.H. Beers, *Commemorative Biographical Record of the Counties of Dutchess and Putnam, New York* (Chicago: J.H. Beers and Co., 1897), 348–349; *AG Report*.
23. Smith, *History of Duchess County*, 511–512; *AG Report*; Henry Wiltse, Jr., papers, Rutgers University Biographical Files: Alumni (Class of 1850), Special Collections and University Archives, Rutgers University Libraries, Rutgers University, New Brunswick, N.J.; John H. Raven, *Catalogue of the Officers and Alumni of Rutgers College in New Brunswick, N.J. 1776 to 1916* (Trenton, NJ: State Gazette Publishing, 1916), 110; *AG of SNY*, 710; Beers, *Commemorative Biographical Record*, 349. Leith was eventually reimbursed by the state for his expenditure, seventeen years later.
24. Newton Martin Curtis, *From Bull Run to Chancellorsville* (New York: G.P. Putnam's Sons, 1906), 3.
25. Ibid., 3–4.
26. P.S. Garand, *The History of the City of Ogdensburg* (Ogdensburg, NY: M.J. Belleville, 1927), 212–213; *Ogdensburg Advance*, April 26, 1861.
27. *Ogdensburg Advance*, March 11, 1861, March 25, 1861, and April 26, 1861; Winifred Bartlett, *Bartlett-Randles History*, Bartlett family file, at Ogdensburg Public Library, Ogdensburg, NY; Hodgkins, *Autobiography*, 10; *The Ogdensburg Journal*, October 13, 1893.
28. *Ogdensburg Advance*, April 26, 1861.
29. *St. Lawrence Republican*, April 30, 1861; NARA— *1860 U.S. Census, Population Schedule*, Ogdensburg, Saint Lawrence County, NY, for Albert Seely, roll M653_854, 209; *Ogdensburg Advance*, March 8, 1888.
30. Hodgkins, *Autobiography*, 10; *Ogdensburg Advance*, May 3, 1861; *The Atlas & Argus*, May 2, 1861.
31. Hodgkins, *Autobiography*, 10.
32. Ibid.; *St. Lawrence Republican*, May 21, 1861.
33. Austin A. Yates, *Schenectady County, New York ...* (place of publication not identified: New York History, 1902), 175; Myron F. Westover, *Schenectady Past and Present: Historical Papers* (Strasburg, VA: Shenandoah Publishing House, 1931), 39; *Schenectady Weekly Republican*, February 22, 1861.
34. Charles W. Howgate, Gridley family genealogical information, descendent of William S. Gridley; *History of Jackson County* (Chicago: Inter-State Publishing, 1881), 636; *Albany Evening Journal*, July 29, 1839; William Henry Seward papers, *General Correspondence*, Letter from William Henry Seward to Reuben Gridley, dated July 24, 1839, River Campus Libraries, University of Rochester, Rochester, NY.
35. Charles W. Howgate, Gridley family genealogical information, descendent of William S. Gridley; *History of Jackson County*, 636.
36. Charles W. Howgate, Gridley family genealogical information, descendent of William S. Gridley; *History of Jackson County*, 636; *Schenectady Union-Star*, March 7, 1950; NARA—*1860 U.S. Census, Population Schedule*, Schenectady Ward 4, Schenectady County, NY, for William S. Gridley, roll M653_858, 213.
37. NARA—*U.S. Military Academy Cadet Application Papers*, 1857, File #101-207, William Seward Gridley.
38. *History of Jackson County*, 636; *Schenectady City and County Directory, 1860–1861* (Schenectady, NY: W.M. Colborne, 1860), 12; William Henry Seward papers, *General Correspondence*, Letter from William Seward Gridley, dated October 15, 1860, River Campus Libraries, University of Rochester, Rochester, NY.
39. *History of Jackson County*, 636; *Schenectady Union-Star*, April 26, 1955; George Rogers Howell and John H. Munsell, *History of the County of Schenectady, N.Y. from 1662 to 1886* (New York: W.W. Munsell and Co., 1886), 42.
40. *Schenectady Union-Star*, March 7, 1950, and April 26, 1955; Yates, *Schenectady County, New York*, 176; Howell and Munsell, *History of the County of Schenectady*, 42; *AG of SNY*, 709; The "Seward Volunteer Zouaves" was merely a short-lived moniker, as they had no uniforms or special drill routines at this time, and the name was all but forgotten by the time they became Company A.
41. *Schenectady Weekly Republican*, April 19, 1861; *Schenectady Daily Union*, April 19, 1881; Yates, *Schenectady County, New York*, 177; Stephen Truax diary, 1861–1863, Special Collections and Archives, Auburn University Library, Auburn University, Auburn, AL; *Union University Quarterly*, May 1904, no. 1, 318; NARA— *1860 U.S. Census, Population Schedule*, Schenectady Ward 4, Schenectady County, NY, for Stephen Truax, Roll M653_858, 215; *Schenectady City and County Directory, 1860–1861*, 68; Howell and Munsell, *History of the County of Schenectady*, 41; *AG of SNY*, 712.
42. *The Atlas & Argus*, April 22, 1861.
43. George Rogers Howell and Jonathan Tenney, *Bi-Centennial History of Albany* (New York: W.W. Munsell and Co., 1886), 461.

44. *Albany Evening Journal*, April 15, 1861, April 16, 1861, April 17, 1861, and April 19, 1861; *Albany Directory, for the Year 1861* (Albany, NY: Adams, Sampson and Co., 1861), 83; NARA—Pension Records, Edward Fisher, widow Margaret E. Fisher; *AG of SNY*, 709. Malta Saloon was located at 28 Maiden Lane, in Albany, NY.

45. A.W. Bowen, *Progressive Men Of... Idaho* (Chicago: A.W. Bowen and Co., 1904), 383; *AG Report*.

46. *The Atlas & Argus*, August 14, 1862; *Albany Evening Journal*, April 22, 1861, and June 7, 1902; *AG Report*; *AG of SNY*, 710.

47. *Albany Evening Journal*, April 19, 1861, and April 22, 1861; Albany Rural Cemetery, in Menands, NY, William G. Weed plot; NARA—*1860 U.S. Census, Population Schedule*, Albany Ward 7, Albany County, NY, for William G. Weed, roll M653_719, 774.

48. *Albany Evening Journal*, April 20, 1861, August 18, 1899 and May 3, 1906; *The Atlas & Argus*, April 25, 1861, and June 19, 1861; *AG Report*; Rufus W. Clark, *The Heroes of Albany: A Memorial of the Patriot-Martyrs* (Albany, NY: S.R. Gray, 1866), 524. Donovan's recruiting station was located at Barney Kavenaugh's, located on Broadway Street, between North Lansing Street and DeWitt Street.

49. *AG Report*; Clark, *The Heroes of Albany*, 525; New York State Legislature Assembly 85th Session, *Documents of the Assembly of the State of New York, Eighty-Fifth Session* (Albany, NY: Van Benthuysen, Printer, 1862),vol. 2, no. 15, *Communication*, 70–71.

50. George Chapman, Enlistment Paper for New York State Militia, Chapman family genealogical information and George Chapman diary, Jill Palmer, descendent of George Chapman, family possession; *The Rockford Daily Register-Gazette*, June 11, 1898 and November 10, 1922; *Amsterdam Evening Recorder and Daily Democrat*, September 14, 1907; NARA—*1850 U.S. Federal Census, Population Schedule*, Amsterdam, Montgomery County, NY, for George Chapman, roll M432_532, 123B.

51. Clark, *The Heroes of Albany*, 454–455.

52. NARA—*1860 U.S. Census, Population Schedule*, Canandaigua, Ontario County, NY, for Henry Faurot, roll M653_832, 1004; Joseph C. Jones, *What a Boy Saw in the Army*, Julie Jones O'Leary, descendent of Joseph C. Jones, family possession; W.H. McIntosh, *History of Ontario County, New York* (Philadelphia: Everts, Ensign and Everts, 1878), 46 and 115.

53. *The Atlas & Argus*, April 26, 1861; *Ontario Republican Times*, May 10, 1861; McIntosh, *History of Ontario County*, 82; *AG of SNY*, 712; *AG Report*; NARA—Compiled Service Records; Clark, *The Heroes of Albany*, 542–543. Morgan's time in the regiment was short, as exposure and fatigue after the Bull Run campaign sapped his health. He resigned in September, but served again two years later in the 7th New York Heavy Artillery, and died as a prisoner of war in 1864.

54. *The Whig Press*, May 15, 1861; Hodgkins, *Autobiography*, 10; Henry C. Lyon, *Desolating This Fair Country: The Civil War Diary and Letters of Lt. Henry C. Lyon, 34th New York* (Jefferson, NC: McFarland, 1999), 22.

55. *The New York Times*, April 30, 1861.

56. Augustus W. Mowatt transcribed diary, Susanne Armentrout, descendent of Augustus W. Mowatt, family possession.

57. Truax diary.

58. *Ibid.*

59. *The Whig Press*, May 15, 1861; The Spirit of '76, "Empire State, S.A.R.'S First Thousand Members," *The Spirit of '76*, 2, no. 13, September 1896, 337.

60. *The Whig Press*, May 15, 1861; *Ogdensburg Advance*, May 23, 1861; Hodgkins, *Autobiography*, 10.

61. Hodgkins, *Autobiography*, 10–11.

62. *Ibid.*; *The Atlas & Argus*, May 27, 1861; *Ogdensburg Advance*, May 23, 1861, the correspondent "X" is stated by the author to be John C. O. Redington.

63. Curtis, *From Bull Run to Chancellorsville*, 18.

64. *Ibid.*, 18–19.

65. *Ibid.*, 19–20; *Ogdensburg Advance*, May 23, 1861.

66. Curtis, *From Bull Run to Chancellorsville*, 20–21.

67. *Ibid.*, 21–22; *St. Lawrence Republican*, May 21, 1861.

68. Curtis, *From Bull Run to Chancellorsville*, 9–10; *The Atlas & Argus*, May 16, 1861; *Ogdensburg Advance*, May 23, 1861.

69. *Ogdensburg Advance*, May 17, 1861, and May 24, 1861; *St. Lawrence Republican*, May 21, 1861; *The Atlas & Argus*, May 16, 1861, and May 17, 1861.

70. *AG Report*.

71. *Ibid.*; *The Whig Press*, May 15, 1861, May 22, 1861, and December 4, 1861.

72. *The Whig Press*, May 15, 1861, and December 4, 1861; Caroline Halstead Royce, *Bessboro: A History of Westport, Essex Co., N.Y.* (Elizabethtown, NY: n.p., 1904), 510.

73. *Albany Sunday Press*, August 24, 1879; *AG of SNY*, 712.

74. Clark, *The Heroes of Albany*, 395–396; *The Rev. E.P. Rogers, D.D.: Pastor of the South Reformed Church, Fifth Avenue and Twenty-First St., New York* (New York: Harvard College Library, 1882), 7–9.

75. Lyon, *Desolating This Fair Country*, 22; Hodgkins, *Autobiography*, 10; Bell Irvin Wiley, *The Life of Billy Yank* (Baton Rouge: Louisiana State University, 1978), 249–251; Clark, *The Heroes of Albany*, 525; Truax diary; Mowatt diary.

76. *Ogdensburg Advance*, May 31, 1861.

77. Mowatt diary; *Documents of the Assembly of the State of New York, Eighty-Fifth Session*, vol. 2, no. 15, *Communication*, 88.

Chapter 2

1. *St. Lawrence Republican*, May 21, 1861. Tweedle Hall was located on the corner of State and North Pearl Street.

2. *Ibid.*; *AG Report*; *AG of SNY*, 422–424.

3. *St. Lawrence Republican*, May 21, 1861; *AG Report*.

4. Joel Munsell, *Memoir of William A. Jackson, a Member of the Albany Bar and Colonel of the 18th Regiment, N.Y. Volunteers, Who Died at the City of Washington, November 11, 1861* (Albany, NY: Albany Bar and Joel Munsell, 1862), 3.

5. *Ibid.*; Wayne Somers, *Encyclopedia of Union College History* (Schenectady, NY: Union College Press, 2003), 410; M. John Lubetkin, *Union College's Class of 1868: The Unique Experiences of Some Average Americans* (McLean, VA: M. John Lubetkin and Union College, 1995), 116–117. As a testament to the iconic importance the garden held to Union College is the fact that the

institution still provides perpetual care to the garden that retains its original name.

6. Jackson Family Committee, *Record of the Jackson Family*, 1878, Schaffer Library Union College, Schenectady, NY; Clark, *The Heroes of Albany*, 129; William A. Jackson, *Commonplace Book*, 1850, Special Collections, Schaffer Library Union College, Schenectady, NY, 57–73.

7. Munsell, *Memoir of William A. Jackson*, 3–4; *Evening Star and Times*, November 13, 1861.

8. Munsell, *Memoir of William A. Jackson*, 4; *Evening Star and Times*, November 13, 1861; Thomas H. Fearey, *Union College Alumni in the Civil War, 1861–1865* (Schenectady, NY: Union University, Graduate Council, 1915), 24; Clark, *The Heroes of Albany*, 129.

9. Munsell, *Memoir of William A. Jackson*, 4–5.

10. John Meredith Read papers, 1870–1907, Box 3, *General William Ayrault Jackson*, River Campus Libraries, University of Rochester, Rochester, NY.

11. Munsell, *Memoir of William A. Jackson*, 6.

12. Read, *General William Ayrault Jackson*.

13. *Evening Star and Times*, November 13, 1861; James H. Manning, *Albany Zouave Cadets, Esto Vigilans, Fifty Years Young* (Albany, NY: Weed-Parsons Printing, 1910), 8–15, 23, 33–34, 55 and 238.

14. Munsell, *Memoir of William A. Jackson*, 5–7.

15. Ibid., 7–8.

16. *The Atlas & Argus*, September 4, 1861; Isaac W. Jackson, *Documents Relative to an Attack Upon the Character of the Late Col. Wm. A. Jackson* (Schenectady, NY: n.p., 1862), 13.

17. *The Atlas & Argus*, September 4, 1861.

18. Ibid.; Mark Wilson, *The Business of Civil War: Military Mobilization and the State, 1861–1865* (Baltimore: Johns Hopkins University Press, 2006), 24.

19. *The Atlas & Argus*, September 4, 1861.

20. Ibid.; Wilson, *The Business of Civil War*, 24; Fred A. Shannon, *The Organization and Administration of the Union Army, 1861–1865* (Cleveland, OH: Arthur H. Clark, 1928), 58; Jackson, *Documents Relative to an Attack*, 4–16.

21. *The Atlas & Argus*, May 15, 1861; *St. Lawrence Republican*, May 21, 1861; Jackson, *Documents Relative to an Attack*, 13 and 17.

22. Homer Eaton, *Memorial of Colonel William H. Young* (Albany, NY: Geo. C. Riggs, 1876), 5.

23. Ibid., 5 and 20. Birth and death dates of Young's children was provided by Brian Cooke, a Young descendent.

24. *Schenectady Reflector*, June 20, 1856; *Schenectady Daily Union*, November 1, 1876; Howell and Munsell, *History of the County of Schenectady, N.Y.*, 41.

25. Eaton, *Memorial of Colonel William H. Young*, 6.

26. Methodist Episcopal Church, *Minutes of the Troy Annual Conference of the Methodist Episcopal Church, for 1874* (Troy, NY: Brainerd and Brown, 1874), 40–42.

27. Samuel W. Durant and Henry B. Peirce, *History of St. Lawrence Co., New York* (Philadelphia: L.H. Everts and Co., 1878), 188; Ogdensburg Cemetery, Ogdensburg, NY, George R. Myers plot.

28. Francis B. Heitman, *Historical Register and Dictionary of the United States Army 1789–1903* (Washington, D.C.: Government Printing Office, 1903), vol. 1, 739; NARA—*Register of Cadet Applicants, 1819–1867*, no. 27, 1854–1855, George R. Myers; NARA—*U.S. Military Academy Cadet Application Papers, 1805–1866*, 1855, file #092–169, George R. Myers; NARA—*1860 U.S. Census, Population Schedule*, Ogdensburg, St. Lawrence County, NY, for George R. Myers, roll M653_854, 254.

29. Durant and Peirce, *History of St. Lawrence Co.*, 188.

30. Curtis, *From Bull Run to Chancellorsville*, 18–19; *The Atlas & Argus*, November 25, 1861; Manning, *Albany Zouave Cadets*, 41–42 and 44; NARA—Pension Records, George R. Myers.

31. *AG Report*; *St. Lawrence Republican*, May 21, 1861; Clark, *The Heroes of Albany*, 381; Manning, *Albany Zouave Cadets*, 36–37, 42 and 56.

32. *AG Report*; *Ontario Republican Times*, May 31, 1861; NARA—Pension Records, William V. Horsfall, minor William J. Horsfall, and Isaac S. Green; *Elmira Telegram*, February 26, 1899.

33. *AG Report*; Thomas P. Lowry and Jack D. Welsh, *Tarnished Scalpels, The Court-Martials of Fifty Union Surgeons* (Mechanicsburg, PA: Stackpole Books, 2000), 153; Fearey, *Union College Alumni*, 12; *Schenectady City and County Directory, 1860–1861*, 70; Howell and Munsell, *History of the County of Schenectady, N.Y.*, 41.

34. *AG Report*; *Transactions of the Medical Society of the County of Albany* (Albany, NY: Burdick and Taylor, 1883), vol. 3, 856.

35. *St. Lawrence Republican*, May 21, 1861.

36. *AG Report*; NARA—Compiled Service Records.

37. *AG Report*; NARA—Compiled Service Records; Pleasant Ridge Cemetery, Lincoln County, OK; Forest Hill Cemetery, Utica, NY, Cornelius Hotaling plot; United States Army, 18th New York Infantry Descriptive Book, 1863, accessed at William L. Clements Library, University of Michigan, Ann Arbor (hereinafter cited as WLC).

38. *AG Report*; NARA—Compiled Service Records; WLC. Shannon later served in the 1st NY Mounted Rifles and 4th NY Provisional Cavalry.

39. NARA—Compiled Service Records; NARA—Pension Records, Samuel C. LaRue.

40. WLC; NARA—Compiled Service Records; NYSA—*Civil War Muster Roll Abstracts of New York State Volunteers*, 18th Infantry, Box #76. A database of this information was compiled by the author based on numerous sources when birth place, height, age, and other particulars could be determined.

41. *The Atlas & Argus*, August 14, 1862; *Albany Evening Journal*, April 22, 1861, and October 7, 1902; WLC; NARA—Compiled Service Records; Albany Rural Cemetery, in Menands, NY, John Hastings plot; NYSA—*Civil War Muster Roll Abstracts*, 18th Infantry, Box #76. A database of this information was compiled by the author based on numerous sources when birth place, height, age, and other particulars could be determined.

42. *The Atlas & Argus*, August 14, 1862; *Albany Evening Journal*, April 22, 1861, and October 7, 1902; WLC; NARA—Compiled Service Records; NYSA—*Civil War Muster Roll Abstracts*, 18th Infantry, Box #76; William Henry Seward papers, *General Correspondence*, Letter from William Seward Gridley, dated October 15, 1860, River Campus Libraries, University of Rochester, Rochester, NY. A database of this information was compiled by the author based on numerous sources when birth place, height, age, and other particulars could be determined.

43. *The Atlas & Argus*, August 14, 1862; *Albany Eve-

ning Journal, April 22, 1861, and October 7, 1902; WLC; NARA—Compiled Service Records; NYSA—*Civil War Muster Roll Abstracts*, 18th Infantry, Box #76. A database of this information was compiled by the author based on numerous sources when birth place, height, age, and other particulars could be determined.

44. Company K Descriptive Roll, Eighteenth New York Infantry, at the St. Lawrence County Historical Association, Canton, NY.

45. Clark, *The Heroes of Albany*, 766.

46. Coye Cemetery, South Bristol, NY, John Bernard Roper plot.

47. NARA—Pension Records, Alexander Abercrombie.

48. *The Atlas & Argus*, August 14, 1862; *Albany Evening Journal*, April 22, 1861, and October 7, 1902; WLC; NYSA—*Civil War Muster Roll Abstracts*, 18th Infantry, Box #76; NARA—Compiled Service Records; NARA—Pension Records, Henry Clay, widow Irene Clay. A database of this information was compiled by the author based on numerous sources when birth place, height, age, and other particulars could be determined.

49. NYSA—*Town Clerks' Registers*, Thomas Snyder, Schoharie, NY; NARA—*1860 U.S. Census, Population Schedule*, Schoharie, Schoharie County, NY, for Thomas Snyder, roll M653_860, 634; George H. Warner, *Military Records of Schoharie County Veterans of Four Wars* (Albany, NY: Weed, Parsons and Co., 1891), 202–203; NARA—Pension Records, Thompson H. Snyder, mother Diana Snyder.

50. Company K Descriptive Roll; *Ogdensburg Advance*, July 5, 1861; NARA—Pension Records, John Redmond, widow Margaret D. Redmond, Samuel C. LaRue, Arthur W. Mills (alias Adam Milton), widow Mary Ann Mills, John Shirley, John Giffen, widow Mary Giffen, and Peter Shean, widow Sarah Sheehan.

51. Curtis, *From Bull Run to Chancellorsville*, 10; *St. Lawrence Republican*, May 27, 1861; NARA—Compiled Service Records.

52. *AG Report*; *Wands War Record: War Record of Five Brothers*, Jeff Sauter collection; *Albany Evening Journal*, November 30, 1863; *Biographical History of La Crosse, Monroe, and Juneau Counties, Wisconsin* (Chicago: Lewis Publishing Co., 1892), 905; Whittemore family genealogical information, David Griffith, descendent of Nathaniel G. Whittemore; NARA—*1860 U.S. Census, Population Schedule*, Schenectady Ward 4, Schenectady County, NY, for Alfred Truax, roll M653_858, 233; NARA—Tenth Census of the United States, 1880, Nassau, Rensselaer County, NY, for William H. Hall.

53. *Ogdensburg Advance*, May 24, 1861; *St. Lawrence Republican*, May 21, 1861; *The Ogdensburg Journal*, October 30, 1905; NARA—Pension Records, John C. O. Redington, widow Emma S. Redington; Redington family genealogical information, Nancy Webster, descendent of John C. O. Redington.

54. *Middletown Mercury*, May 17, 1861; *The Whig Press*, May 15, 1861.

55. *Middletown Mercury*, May 17, 1861; *The Whig Press*, May 15, 1861, and May 22, 1861.

56. *Schenectady Weekly Republican*, May 17, 1861.

57. *Ogdensburg Advance*, May 31, 1861; Hodgkins, *Autobiography*, 11; Frederick Phisterer, *New York in the War of the Rebellion: 1861 to 1865* (Albany, NY: J.B. Lyon, 1912), vol. 3, 1,946.

58. *AG Report*; *Ogdensburg Advance*, May 24, 1861, and May 31, 1861; Hodgkins, *Autobiography*, 11; New York State Bureau of Military Statistics, *First Annual Report of the Chief of the Bureau of Military Statistics* (New York: Horatio Seymour, 1864), 42 (hereinafter cited as *F.A.R.*).

59. *Ogdensburg Advance*, May 31, 1861; *Ontario Republican Times*, May 31, 1861; *St. Lawrence Republican*, June 18, 1861; Lyon, *Desolating This Fair Country*, 23; Mowatt diary.

60. Lyon, *Desolating This Fair Country*, 23; Hodgkins, *Autobiography*, 12; *St. Lawrence Republican*, May 27, 1861; Mowatt diary.

61. *Ontario Republican Times*, May 31, 1861; Lyon, *Desolating This Fair Country*, 24; Mowatt diary; Newspaper account from the files of the NYSMM and Veterans Research Center, NYS Division of Military and Naval Affairs, untitled and undated.

62. Mowatt diary; Hodgkins, *Autobiography*, 12; Truax diary; *Ontario Republican Times*, May 31, 1861.

63. Mowatt diary; Truax diary.

64. *Ogdensburg Advance*, May 31, 1861.

65. *The Atlas & Argus*, August 6, 1861; Hodgkins, *Autobiography*, 12.

66. *Ogdensburg Advance*, May 31, 1861; *St. Lawrence Republican*, June 4, 1861.

67. *Ogdensburg Advance*, May 31, 1861; *St. Lawrence Republican*, May 27, 1861.

68. *Ogdensburg Advance*, May 31, 1861; *The Atlas & Argus*, May 24, 1861; *Ontario Republican Times*, May 31, 1861; *St. Lawrence Republican*, May 27, 1861; *Arms and Equipment of the Union* (Alexandria, VA: Time-Life Books, 1991), 125; Hodgkins, *Autobiography*, 11; *F.A.R.*, 43. Based on the Board of Uniforms for the State of New York, the blanket issued was most likely the double Mackinaw blanket.

69. *Ogdensburg Advance*, May 31, 1861; *Ontario Republican Times*, May 31, 1861.

70. Clark, *The Heroes of Albany*, 396–399.

71. *Ontario Republican Times*, May 31, 1861; Munsell, *Memoir of William A. Jackson*, 8; Jones, *What a Boy Saw*.

72. Jones, *What a Boy Saw*.

73. *Ogdensburg Advance*, June 7, 1861; *St. Lawrence Republican*, June 4, 1861; *The Whig Press*, July 3, 1861; *Albany Evening Journal*, June 11, 1861; *Arms and Equipment*, 188; Truax diary; Margaret Leech, *Reveille in Washington: 1860–1865* (New York: New York Review Books, 2011), 88–89.

74. *Ogdensburg Advance*, May 31, 1861, and June 7, 1861; *St. Lawrence Republican*, June 11, 1861; Truax diary.

75. *Ogdensburg Advance*, May 31, 1861.

76. Ruth P. Randall, *Colonel Elmer Ellsworth* (Toronto: Little, Brown and Co., 1960), 257–259.

77. Ibid., 264–267; *The Atlas & Argus*, May 28, 1861.

78. *The Atlas & Argus*, May 28, 1861; *Ogdensburg Advance*, June 7, 1861; Hodgkins, *Autobiography*, 13–14.

79. *St. Lawrence Republican*, June 4, 1861; *Ogdensburg Advance*, June 7, 1861; *Ontario Republican Times*, May 31, 1861; Manning, *Albany Zouave Cadets*, 38.

80. *St. Lawrence Republican*, June 4, 1861, and June 18, 1861; *The Atlas & Argus*, May 30, 1861, and May 31, 1861; *Ogdensburg Advance*, June 7, 1861.

81. *St. Lawrence Republican*, June 11, 1861; *Ogdensburg Advance*, June 7, 1861, and June 21, 1861; Truax diary; Mowatt diary. Camp Bethlehem, located along

Normanskill Creek, would later adopt the name of Camp Morgan.

82. *St. Lawrence Republican*, June 11, 1861, and June 18, 1861; Mowatt diary.

83. Franklin B. Hough, *Franklin B. Hough Papers, 1840–1885* [SC7009], Series 4: Civil War Papers, 1861–1865, Box 22, Folder 4, Notes on 18th NY S. V., Manuscripts and Special Collections, New York State Library, Albany, NY (NYSL), ; *The Atlas & Argus*, May 31, 1861, and June 3, 1861; *Daily National Intelligencer*, June 22, 1861; Phisterer, *New York in the War of the Rebellion: 1861 to 1865*, vol. 1, 110; F.A.R., 42–43 and 181–182; New York State Bureau of Military Statistics, *Presentation of Flags of New York Volunteer Regiments and Other Organizations, to His Excellency, Governor Fenton, in Accordance with a Resolution of the Legislature, July 4, 1865; Published Under Direction of the Chief of Bureau of Military Records* (Albany, NY: Weed, Parsons, and Company, Printers, 1865), 45. Separate sources state that the inscription says, "Rally Around Them." The flag is currently housed in the State Capitol in Albany. The 18th never received nor used any guidons.

84. *The Atlas & Argus*, June 3, 1861.

85. *St. Lawrence Republican*, June 11, 1861; Mowatt diary; Truax diary.

86. Jones, *What a Boy Saw*; *Ogdensburg Advance*, June 7, 1861.

87. *St. Lawrence Republican*, June 4, 1861.

88. Jones, *What a Boy Saw*.

89. *St. Lawrence Republican*, June 11, 1861; *Ogdensburg Advance*, June 7, 1861.

90. *St. Lawrence Republican*, June 11, 1861, and June 18, 1861; Truax diary; NYSA—*Civil War Muster Roll Abstracts*, 18th Infantry, Box #76.

91. *St. Lawrence Republican*, June 18, 1861; *Ogdensburg Advance*, June 21, 1861.

92. *St. Lawrence Republican*, June 18, 1861.

93. Ibid.

94. Ibid.; *AG Report*.

95. *St. Lawrence Republican*, June 18, 1861; *Albany Evening Journal*, June 14, 1861.

96. *St. Lawrence Republican*, June 18, 1861; *Ogdensburg Advance*, June 21, 1861, author states correspondent "X" is John C. O. Redington.

97. *The Atlas & Argus*, June 15, 1861.

98. *The Atlas & Argus*, September 4, 1861; *Ogdensburg Advance*, June 7, 1861; Jackson, *Documents Relative to an Attack*, 1–3 and 11; *New York Tribune*, April 24, 1862. The search for blame by state officials resurfaced later in the war, but poignantly after the death of Jackson. With Jackson's voice silent, his father, Isaac, had to defend his dead son's character when officials tried to pin the blame on him. They accused Jackson of using his influence as Inspector General to grant Brooks Brothers the sole contract of uniforms with a kickback of a personally tailored suit and dress uniform. The committee agreed to let all fault lie with Jackson and rest the case, but luckily his father would not allow his dead son to be their scapegoat. He published a pamphlet of unedited reports and additional testimonies from those closest to the former Inspector General to stand as his defense. Isaac even included a receipt for the uniform his son was accused of receiving as a gift which showed he was charged at full price, a debt that the elder Jackson had paid for himself. Brooks Brothers corroborated the receipt with their copy of the bill of sales which showed Jackson never received any such gifts for free. The father's persistence paid off and the matter eventually faded from discussion.

99. *Ogdensburg Advance*, May 31, 1861; *AG Report*; Phisterer, *New York in the War of the Rebellion: 1861 to 1865*, vol. 3, 1, 951. Bartlett's son, Francis, would later serve in a different hometown regiment and died from disease in 1863.

100. *The Atlas & Argus*, June 18, 1861; *Ogdensburg Advance*, June 21, 1861; *St. Lawrence Republican*, June 18, 1861; *Albany Evening Journal*, June 17, 1861; *AG Report*. Whitcomb enlisted into the Company Band of the 28th Pennsylvania Infantry on July 20, 1861, and deserted them on October 1, 1861.

101. *AG Report*; Fearey, *Union College Alumni*, 63; NARA—Pension Records, A. Barclay Mitchell, widow Frederica Mitchell; Beers, *Commemorative Biographical Record*, 349.

102. *AG Report*; Captain John Vedder Ledger, Grems-Doolittle Library, Schenectady County Historical Society, Schenectady, NY.

103. Mowatt diary.

104. Ibid.; *Schenectady Weekly Republican*, June 28, 1861; *Ogdensburg Advance*, July 5, 1861; Hodgkins, *Autobiography*, 12.

105. *The Atlas & Argus*, June 18, 1861; *Schenectady Weekly Republican*, June 28, 1861; Newspaper account from the files of the NYSMM and Veterans Research Center, NYS Division of Military and Naval Affairs, untitled and undated; *Ogdensburg Advance*, July 5, 1861, author states correspondent "X" is John C. O. Redington.

106. *Ogdensburg Advance*, July 5, 1861; *Schenectady Weekly Republican*, June 28, 1861; Mowatt diary; Hodgkins, *Autobiography*, 12; Newspaper account from the files of the NYSMM, from an untitled newspaper, June 20, 1861.

107. *The Atlas & Argus*, June 20, 1861.

Chapter 3

1. *St. Lawrence Republican*, June 18, 1861, and July 2, 1861; *Ogdensburg Advance*, July 5, 1861; *Schenectady Weekly Republican*, June 28, 1861; Mowatt diary; Hodgkins, *Autobiography*, 12.

2. *Schenectady Weekly Republican*, June 28, 1861; *Albany Evening Journal*, June 20, 1861; Mowatt diary; Hodgkins, *Autobiography*, 12.

3. *St. Lawrence Republican*, June 18, 1861, and July 2, 1861; *Schenectady Weekly Republican*, June 28, 1861; *The Whig Press*, July 3, 1861; *Albany Evening Journal*, June 20, 1861; Mowatt diary; Hodgkins, *Autobiography*, 12; *Arms and Equipment*, 38; *AG of SNY*, 11; *The New York Times*, June 21, 1861.

4. *Ogdensburg Advance*, July 5, 1861; *St. Lawrence Republican*, July 2, 1861; *Philadelphia Inquirer*, June 21, 1861; Jones, *What a Boy Saw*.

5. *Schenectady Weekly Republican*, June 28, 1861; *The Whig Press*, July 3, 1861; *St. Lawrence Republican*, July 2, 1861.

6. *St. Lawrence Republican*, July 2, 1861.

7. Ibid.; *Ogdensburg Advance*, July 5, 1861.

8. Jones, *What a Boy Saw*.

9. *St. Lawrence Republican*, July 2, 1861; *Ogdensburg*

Advance, July 5, 1861; *Schenectady Weekly Republican*, June 28, 1861; *The Whig Press*, July 3, 1861; Mowatt diary; *Philadelphia Inquirer*, June 21, 1861.

10. *St. Lawrence Republican*, July 2, 1861; *Ogdensburg Advance*, July 5, 1861; *Schenectady Weekly Republican*, June 28, 1861; *The Whig Press*, July 3, 1861; *Sunday Dispatch*, May 23, 1880; Mowatt diary; Hodgkins, *Autobiography*, 12; Frank H. Taylor, *Philadelphia in the Civil War, 1861–1865* (Philadelphia: City of Philadelphia, 1913), 210 and 212; Samuel B. Fales, *Union Volunteer Refreshment Saloon Papers*, Collection 1580, Boxes 11–12 and Collection 2074, Box 1, Historical Society of Pennsylvania, Philadelphia. The Union Volunteer Refreshment Saloon was located on the southwest corner of Washington Avenue and Swanson Street, in South Philadelphia.

11. *St. Lawrence Republican*, July 2, 1861.

12. Ibid.; *Ogdensburg Advance*, July 5, 1861; *Schenectady Weekly Republican*, June 28, 1861; Mowatt diary.

13. OR, ser. 1, vol. 2, 7–8; George William Brown, *Baltimore and the Nineteenth of April, 1861* (Baltimore: N. Murray, 1887), 49–53.

14. *Ogdensburg Advance*, July 5, 1861; *St. Lawrence Republican*, July 2, 1861; *Schenectady Weekly Republican*, June 28, 1861.

15. *Ogdensburg Advance*, July 5, 1861; *St. Lawrence Republican*, July 2, 1861; *Schenectady Weekly Republican*, June 28, 1861.

16. *Ogdensburg Advance*, July 5, 1861; Mowatt diary; Hodgkins, *Autobiography*, 12; *American and Commercial Advertiser*, June 21, 1861; Jones, *What a Boy Saw*.

17. *Ogdensburg Advance*, July 5, 1861; *Schenectady Weekly Republican*, June 28, 1861; *The Whig Press*, July 3, 1861; Jones, *What a Boy Saw*.

18. *Ogdensburg Advance*, July 5, 1861; Jones.

19. *St. Lawrence Republican*, July 2, 1861; *Ogdensburg Advance*, July 5, 1861; *Schenectady Weekly Republican*, June 28, 1861; *The Whig Press*, July 3, 1861; Hodgkins, *Autobiography*, 12–13; *American and Commercial Advertiser*, June 21, 1861.

20. *Ogdensburg Advance*, July 5, 1861; *The Whig Press*, July 3, 1861; *Schenectady Weekly Republican*, June 28, 1861; *National Republican*, June 21, 1861; Mowatt diary; Vedder Ledger; *F.A.R.*, 43.

21. *St. Lawrence Republican*, July 2, 1861; *Ogdensburg Advance*, July 5, 1861; Robert K. Krick, *Civil War Weather in Virginia* (Tuscaloosa: University of Alabama Press, 2007), 28.

22. *Schenectady Weekly Republican*, June 28, 1861; *The Whig Press*, July 17, 1861; Leech, *Reveille in Washington*, 6–7.

23. *Daily National Intelligencer*, June 22, 1861; *Schenectady Weekly Republican*, June 28, 1861; *Ogdensburg Advance*, July 5, 1861; Mowatt diary; Truax diary; *F.A.R.*, 43.

24. *St. Lawrence Republican*, July 9, 1861; *The Whig Press*, July 3, 1861; Truax diary; *F.A.R.*, 43.

25. *Schenectady Weekly Republican*, June 28, 1861; Mowatt diary.

26. *Schenectady Weekly Republican*, June 28, 1861; *the Whig Press*, July 3, 1861; Mowatt diary; Hodgkins, *Autobiography*, 13.

27. *Schenectady Weekly Republican*, June 28, 1861; Hodgkins, *Autobiography*, 13.

28. *Schenectady Weekly Republican*, June 28, 1861; *the Whig Press*, July 3, 1861; Mowatt diary.

29. *St. Lawrence Republican*, July 9, 1861; Mowatt diary; Truax diary; Paul Taylor, *Glory Was Not Their Companion: The Twenty-Sixth New York Volunteer* (Jefferson, NC: McFarland, 2005), 16; George Blake, Letter, June 24, 1861, author's collection.

30. Mowatt diary; Taylor, *Glory Was Not Their Companion*, 16; Blake, Letter, June 24, 1861, author's collection.

31. Blake, Letter, June 24, 1861, author's collection.

32. Ibid.; *St. Lawrence Republican*, July 9, 1861; Truax diary.

33. Blake, Letter, June 24, 1861, author's collection.

34. Ibid.; *St. Lawrence Republican*, July 9, 1861; Mowatt diary.

35. *Ogdensburg Advance*, July 5, 1861; *AG Report*; NARA—Compiled Service Records; NARA—Pension Records, Peter Shean, widow Sarah Sheehan.

36. *Ogdensburg Advance*, July 5, 1861; *AG Report*; NARA—Compiled Service Records. Buckley was discharged on July 2, 1861.

37. Leech, *Reveille in Washington*, 93; *The Whig Press*, July 3, 1861.

38. Leech, *Reveille in Washington*, 93.

39. *Ogdensburg Advance*, July 5, 1861; *The Whig Press*, July 3, 1861; *Albany Evening Journal*, July 3, 1861; *Evening Star and Times*, July 5, 1861; *AG Report*; Mowatt diary; Arlington National Cemetery, Arlington, Virginia, John H. Gale plot.

40. *Ogdensburg Advance*, July 5, 1861; *St. Lawrence Republican*, July 9, 1861; *The Whig Press*, July 3, 1861; Mowatt diary.

41. *St. Lawrence Republican*, July 9, 1861; *The Whig Press*, July 17, 1861; Truax diary.

42. *St. Lawrence Republican*, July 9, 1861; Mowatt diary; Krick, *Civil War Weather*, 28; *The Whig Press*, July 3, 1861; George Blake, Letter, July 5, 1861, author's collection; Leech, *Reveille in Washington*, 89.

43. *St. Lawrence Republican*, July 9, 1861; *The Whig Press*, July 3, 1861.

44. Mowatt diary; Krick, *Civil War Weather*, 28.

45. *The Whig Press*, July 3, 1861, July 17, 1861.

46. *St. Lawrence Republican*, July 9, 1861.

47. *Harper's Weekly*, July 27, 1861; Mowatt diary.

48. *Ogdensburg Advance*, July 12, 1861.

49. *Ogdensburg Advance*, July 12, 1861; *Harper's Weekly*, July 27, 1861; *The Whig Press*, July 17, 1861; Mowatt diary; Truax diary; Taylor, *Glory Was Not Their Companion*, 16.

50. *Ogdensburg Advance*, July 12, 1861.

51. George Blake, Letter, July 4, 1861, author's collection.

52. Ibid., July 5, 1861; Vedder Ledger; *AG Report*.

53. *AG Report*; NARA—Compiled Service Records; NARA—Pension Records, Jessie Gowan widow of John Gowan.

54. *New York Daily Tribune*, July 21, 1861.

55. United States Sanitary Commission Records, Ser. 7, Statistical Bureau Archives, Camp Inspection Reports, b.28 f.23 18th New York Infantry 1861 July 11—14th Street, Washington, D.C. Robert Tomes. Reel 28-frames 0292–0298, NYPL.

56. *Evening Star and Times*, July 20, 1861; Mowatt diary; Curtis, *From Bull Run to Chancellorsville*, 33; *Ogdensburg Advance*, July 26, 1861, author states correspondent "X" is John C. O. Redington.

57. *Evening Star and Times,* July 20, 1861; *Ogdensburg Advance,* July 26, 1861; Mowatt diary; Curtis, *From Bull Run to Chancellorsville,* 33; *Utica Daily Observer,* July 16, 1861; NARA—Compiled Service Records.

Chapter 4

1. *Ogdensburg Advance,* July 26, 1861, author states correspondent "X" is John C. O. Redington; *Evening Star and Times,* July 20, 1861.
2. *Ogdensburg Advance,* July 26, 1861, author states correspondent "X" is John C. O. Redington; *Evening Star and Times,* July 20, 1861.
3. *Ogdensburg Advance,* July 26, 1861; *Evening Star and Times,* July 20, 1861; *Schenectady Weekly Republican,* September 27, 1861; Mowatt diary; Hough (NYSL).
4. *Evening Star and Times,* July 20, 1861.
5. Ibid.
6. Phisterer, *New York in the War of the Rebellion: 1861 to 1865,* vol. 3, 1,946; Curtis, *From Bull Run to Chancellorsville,* 13–14; *Report of the Committee on the Conduct of the War,* 1863, vol. 2, 38, McDowell in testimony to the Committee on the Conduct of the War.
7. *Ogdensburg Advance,* July 26, 1861; *Evening Star and Times,* July 20, 1861; William C. Davis, *Battle of Bull Run* (Garden City, NY: Doubleday and Co., 1977), 45; Kent Masterson Brown, *Cushing of Gettysburg, The Story of a Union Artillery Commander* (Lexington: University Press of Kentucky, 1993), 59.
8. *Evening Star and Times,* July 20, 1861.
9. Mowatt diary.
10. Vedder Ledger; *Evening Star and Times,* July 20, 1861; *Schenectady Weekly Republican,* August 2, 1861.
11. *Evening Star and Times,* July 20, 1861; *Schenectady Weekly Republican,* August 2, 1861; *OR,* ser. 1, vol. 2, 343.
12. *Ogdensburg Advance,* July 26, 1861; *Schenectady Weekly Republican,* August 2, 1861; *Ogdensburg Republican Journal,* June 30, 1916; Mowatt diary.
13. *Schenectady Weekly Republican,* August 2, 1861; *The Whig Press,* July 31, 1861; *Ontario Republican Times,* August 2, 1861, and August 9, 1861; *OR,* ser. 1, vol. 2, 303–304; Mowatt diary.
14. NARA—Pension Records, John B. LaQue.
15. *Schenectady Weekly Republican,* August 2, 1861; *Ontario Republican Times,* August 9, 1861.
16. *Evening Star and Times,* July 20, 1861; *Ogdensburg Advance,* July 26, 1861; *The Atlas & Argus,* July 20, 1861; *Schenectady Weekly Republican,* August 2, 1861; *Ontario Republican Times,* August 2, 1861; Curtis, *From Bull Run to Chancellorsville,* 38; *OR,* ser. 1, vol. 2, 423; *F.A.R.,* 44; Mowatt diary; Hodgkins, *Autobiography,* 14; Hough (NYSL).
17. *Ontario Republican Times,* August 9, 1861.
18. *Ogdensburg Advance,* July 26, 1861; *The Atlas & Argus,* July 20, 1861; *Schenectady Weekly Republican,* August 2, 1861; Curtis, *From Bull Run to Chancellorsville,* 38; *OR,* ser. 1, vol. 2, 423; Mowatt diary.
19. *The Atlas & Argus,* July 20, 1861; *Evening Star and Times,* July 20, 1861, and July 22, 1861; *Ogdensburg Advance,* July 26, 1861; *The Whig Press,* July 31, 1861; *Schenectady Weekly Republican,* July 26, 1861; *Ontario Republican Times,* August 9, 1861; *OR,* ser. 1, vol. 2, 423, 433 and 459–460; Mowatt diary.
20. *The Atlas & Argus,* July 20, 1861; *Ogdensburg Advance,* July 26, 1861, August 2, 1861, and August 16, 1861; *OR,* ser. 1, vol. 2, 423; NYSA—*Town Clerks' Registers,* John Seymour Allen.
21. *The Atlas & Argus,* July 20, 1861; *Evening Star and Times,* July 22, 1861; *Ogdensburg Advance,* July 26, 1861; *OR,* ser. 1, vol. 2, 423; NARA—*Special Schedules of the Eleventh Census (1890) Enumerating Union Veterans and Widows of Union Veterans of the Civil War,* Petoskey, Emmet County, Michigan, for Hugh McKinley; *AG Report*; NARA—Compiled Service Records.
22. *The Atlas & Argus,* July 20, 1861; *Evening Star and Times,* July 22, 1861; *Ogdensburg Advance,* July 26, 1861; *Evening Star and Times,* July 20, 1861; *Schenectady Weekly Republican,* August 2, 1861; *OR,* ser. 1, vol. 2, 423; *AG Report*.
23. *The Atlas & Argus,* July 20, 1861; *Ogdensburg Advance,* July 26, 1861, and August 16, 1861; *Ontario Republican Times,* August 9, 1861.
24. *Ogdensburg Advance,* August 2, 1861; *Ontario Republican Times,* August 9, 1861; *OR,* ser. 1, vol. 2, 433 and 460.
25. *AG Report*; NARA—Compiled Service Records; *Schenectady Weekly Republican,* October 1861; William H. Jeffrey, *Richmond Prisons, 1861–1862* (St. Johnsbury, VT: Republican Press, 1893), 200; *New York Daily Tribune,* October 19, 1861; *Albany Evening Journal,* October 17, 1861; *OR,* ser. 1, vol. 2, 460.
26. *OR,* ser. 1, vol. 2, 433; *The Whig Press,* July 31, 1861.
27. *OR,* ser. 1, vol. 2, 423 and 433; *The Whig Press,* July 31, 1861.
28. *The Whig Press,* July 31, 1861.
29. Ibid.; *OR,* ser. 1, vol. 2, 423 and 433; Mowatt diary; Curtis, *From Bull Run to Chancellorsville,* 38; *Evening Star and Times,* July 20, 1861; *The Atlas & Argus,* July 20, 1861; *Ogdensburg Advance, July 26, 1861;* *Schenectady Weekly Republican,* July 26, 1861, and August 2, 1861; *Ontario Republican Times,* August 9, 1861.
30. *OR,* ser. 1, vol. 2, 305–306 and 422; Mowatt diary; *The Atlas & Argus,* July 20, 1861; NARA—Compiled Service Records; Hough (NYSL).
31. *OR,* ser. 1, vol. 2, 305–306; Mowatt diary; *The Atlas & Argus,* July 20, 1861; *Ogdensburg Advance,* July 26, 1861.
32. *Ogdensburg Advance,* July 26, 1861; *Evening Star and Times,* July 20, 1861.
33. *OR,* ser. 1, vol. 2, 307; Truax diary; Mowatt diary; *Schenectady Weekly Republican,* August 2, 1861; *The Whig Press,* July 31, 1861.
34. *Ogdensburg Advance,* July 26, 1861, author states correspondent "X" is John C. O. Redington.
35. *OR,* ser. 1, vol. 2, 313; *The Whig Press,* July 31, 1861; Clark, *The Heroes of Albany,* 526.
36. *OR,* ser. 1, vol. 2, 307 and 317; Mowatt diary; R.H. Beatie, *Road to Manassas* (New York: Cooper Square Publishers, 1961), 127; *Ogdensburg Advance,* July 26, 1861, author states correspondent "X" was John C. O. Redington; *Schenectady Weekly Republican,* August 2, 1861; *The Whig Press,* July 31, 1861; *Ontario Republican Times,* August 9, 1861.
37. *OR,* ser. 1, vol. 2, 313 and 461–462; Mowatt diary; *Ogdensburg Advance,* July 26, 1861; *Schenectady Weekly Republican,* August 2, 1861; *The Whig Press,* July 31, 1861.
38. *OR,* ser. 1, vol. 2, 317–318; *Evening Star and Times,* August 16, 1861.

39. *Ogdensburg Advance,* July 26, 1861.
40. *The Atlas & Argus,* July 27, 1861; *Schenectady Weekly Republican,* August 2, 1861; Mowatt diary.
41. *Ogdensburg Advance,* July 26, 1861; *The Whig Press,* July 31, 1861.
42. *Schenectady Weekly Republican,* August 2, 1861; *OR,* ser. 1, vol. 2, 317; Mowatt diary; *Albany Evening Journal,* July 29, 1861.
43. *OR,* ser. 1, vol. 2, 318 and 424.
44. Ibid.; *Albany Evening Journal,* July 29, 1861.
45. *OR,* ser. 1, vol. 2, 326, 335, 424 and 429; Beatie, *Road to Manassas,* 178–179; Curtis, *From Bull Run to Chancellorsville,* 42; F.A.R., 44; *Schenectady Weekly Republican,* August 2, 1861; *Albany Evening Journal,* July 29, 1861; Munsell, *Memoir of William A. Jackson,* 12.
46. *St. Lawrence Republican,* July 30, 1861; *Ogdensburg Advance,* August 2, 1861; NARA—Pension Records, Freeman F. Huntington, widow Ellen R. Huntington. His wound was not severe enough to require a discharge from the service, and he stayed with the 18th for its entirety.
47. *OR,* ser. 1, vol. 2, 319.
48. Ibid., 326; Hodgkins, *Autobiography,* 14.
49. *OR,* ser. 1, vol. 2, 326 and 4219; F.A.R., 44; Beatie, *Road to Manassas,* 179; Curtis, *From Bull Run to Chancellorsville,* 42; *Schenectady Weekly Republican,* August 2, 1861.
50. *OR,* ser. 1, vol. 2, 429.
51. Ibid., 423–425 and 429; Beatie, *Road to Manassas,* 179–180; *Schenectady Weekly Republican,* August 2, 1861; *The Whig Press,* July 31, 1861.
52. *OR,* ser. 1, vol. 2, 335, 424–425 and 429–430.
53. Ibid., 430; *The Whig Press,* July 31, 1861.
54. *OR,* ser. 1, vol. 2, 320 and 430.
55. *AG Report; Ogdensburg Advance,* August 2, 1861, author states correspondent "X" is John C. O. Redington; John C. O. Redington letter, *Letter to Friends of the Mission School,* July 27, 1861, Charles T. Creekman, Jr. Collection, Military Era Collections, Box No. 2, St. Lawrence County Historical Association, Canton, NY. Redington had quickly demonstrated innate leadership unlike other privates, and the officers of the 18th felt the same way. Redington was sent home two weeks after the battle to recruit for the regiment, but he did so well, he amassed enough men to make up a company, and the officers of the 18th allowed him to be discharged to accept a commission as captain of the 60th New York Infantry.
56. *OR,* ser. 1, vol. 2, 378–379, 425 and 430; Curtis, *From Bull Run to Chancellorsville,* 43; *Ogdensburg Advance,* August 2, 1861; *Evening Star and Times,* August 16, 1861.
57. *OR,* ser. 1, vol. 2, 436–437; *Schenectady Weekly Republican,* August 2, 1861; *St. Lawrence Republican,* July 30, 1861; *The National Tribune,* July 13, 1893.
58. *OR,* ser. 1, vol. 2, 375, 378–379, 425 and 430–431 and 541; Curtis, *From Bull Run to Chancellorsville,* 43; *The Whig Press,* July 31, 1861; *St. Lawrence Republican,* July 30, 1861.
59. *The Whig Press,* July 31, 1861.
60. *OR,* ser. 1, vol. 2, 378–379, 430–431, 538–539 and 541; *St. Lawrence Republican,* July 30, 1861.
61. *OR,* ser. 1, vol. 2, 375, 378–379, 425, 430–431 and 538–539; Curtis, *From Bull Run to Chancellorsville,* 43; *St. Lawrence Republican,* July 30, 1861.
62. *OR,* ser. 1, vol. 2, 430; *The Whig Press,* July 31, 1861; *Schenectady Weekly Republican,* August 2, 1861; *Albany Evening Journal,* July 29, 1861.
63. *OR,* ser. 1, vol. 2, 431; *Schenectady Weekly Republican,* August 2, 1861; *The Whig Press,* July 31, 1861; *Albany Evening Journal,* July 29, 1861.
64. *Schenectady Weekly Republican,* August 2, 1861; *Albany Evening Journal,* July 29, 1861.
65. *The National Tribune,* July 27, 1893. The dog's name was originally "Bull Run" but shortened to Bull, and sometimes, Old Bull.
66. *Albany Evening Journal,* July 29, 1861.
67. *OR,* ser. 1, vol. 2, 365–366 and 431; Mowatt diary; *The Whig Press,* July 31, 1861; F.A.R., 45; Munsell, *Memoir of William A. Jackson,* 12; NARA—Compiled Service Records.
68. *OR,* ser. 1, vol. 2, 321; Beatie, *Road to Manassas,* 189; *Evening Star and Times,* August 16, 1861; *Schenectady Weekly Republican,* August 2, 1861; *The Whig Press,* July 31, 1861.
69. *The National Tribune,* July 27, 1893.
70. F.A.R., 45; *Middletown Mercury,* July 26, 1861; *The Whig Press,* July 31, 1861; *Albany Evening Journal,* July 29, 1861; NARA—Pension Records, Harvey L. Rogers.
71. *AG Report;* NARA—Compiled Service Records.
72. F.A.R., 45; Mowatt diary; *Schenectady Weekly Republican,* August 2, 1861; *The Whig Press,* July 31, 1861; Munsell, *Memoir of William A. Jackson,* 12; *Albany Evening Journal,* July 29, 1861.
73. *St. Lawrence Republican,* July 30, 1861; *Schenectady Weekly Republican,* August 2, 1861; *Ogdensburg Advance,* August 2, 1861; *AG Report;* NARA—Compiled Service Records.
74. *Ontario Republican Times,* August 2, 1861, and August 9, 1861.
75. Mowatt diary; *St. Lawrence Republican,* August 6, 1861; Hough (NYSL). The Garibaldi Guards were the 39th New York Infantry.
76. *OR,* ser. 1, vol. 2, 299–300, 649–650 and 652; Truax diary; *St. Lawrence Republican,* July 2, 1861; Clark, *The Heroes of Albany,* 455.
77. Truax diary; Mowatt diary; *Schenectady Weekly Republican,* August 9, 1861; *Ontario Republican Times,* August 9, 1861.
78. James A. McPherson, *Battle Cry of Freedom: The Civil War Era* (New York: Oxford University Press, 1988), 355–356.
79. *AG Report;* NARA—Compiled Service Records; Albany Rural Cemetery, in Menands, NY, John Waterson plot. Waterson's burial record states his death differently, to have taken place on July 24, 1861.
80. *Evening Star and Times,* July 22, 1861; *AG Report.* Edward Groot enlisted as a First Lieutenant in the 134th New York Infantry on July 28, 1862.
81. *Ogdensburg Advance,* July 26, 1861, and August 16, 1861; Preston King, *Preston King Papers, 1834–1865,* Letter to E.B. Allen, August 19, 1861, ODY Special Collections, St. Lawrence University, Canton, NY.
82. *Ogdensburg Advance,* August 2, 1861, and August 16, 1861; *St. Lawrence Republican,* August 13, 1861; *Daily National Intelligencer,* August 10, 1861; *AG Report;* Curtis, *From Bull Run to Chancellorsville,* 38; Preston King, Letter to E.B. Allen, August 19, 1861.
83. *Daily National Intelligencer,* August 10, 1861; *AG Report;* Curtis, *From Bull Run to Chancellorsville,* 38;

Preston King, Letter to E.B. Allen, August 19, 1861; NARA—Pension Records, John S. Allen, widow Mary Anne Allen. Allen was buried at the Soldiers Home Cemetery in Washington, D. C. After the following winter, his father, Elijah B. Allen, visited the cemetery and had the body disinterred and buried in the Allen family plot in Ogdensburg Cemetery, in Ogdensburg, NY, on March 2, 1862.

84. *Democrat & Reflector*, August 8, 1861.
85. *Albany Evening Journal*, July 29, 1861.
86. Clark, *The Heroes of Albany*, 526.
87. *OR*, ser. 1, vol. 2, 327; *Evening Star and Times*, August 16, 1861.
88. *AG Report*; *OR*, ser. 1, vol. 2, 327; *Ogdensburg Advance*, August 2, 1861.
89. *The National Tribune*, July 27, 1893.

Chapter 5

1. Heitman, *Historical Register and Dictionary of the United States Army 1789–1903*, vol. 1, 656; *OR*, ser. 1, vol. 2, 766; Stephen W. Sears, *To the Gates of Richmond* (New York: Ticknor and Fields, 1992), 3–4.
2. *OR*, ser. 1, vol. 2, 315, 439 and ser. 1, vol. 5, 15; *The Union Army: A History of Military Affairs in the Loyal States 1861–1865* (Wilmington, NC: Broadfoot Publishing, 1997), vol. 2, 61; Mark A. Snell, *From First to Last: The Life of Major General William B. Franklin* (New York: Fordham University Press, 2002), 9; Phisterer, *New York in the War of the Rebellion: 1861 to 1865*, vol. 3, 1,946; *F.A.R.*, 46.
3. *AG Report*; NARA—Compiled Service Records; *Ogdensburg Advance*, May 24, 1861.
4. *Evening Star and Times*, September 2, 1861; *The Whig Press*, July 17, 1861, and August 28, 1861; Lowry and Welsh, *Tarnished Scalpels*, 149–154.
5. *AG Report*; NARA—Compiled Service Records; *The Whig Press*, August 28, 1861; Lowry and Welsh, *Tarnished Scalpels*, 149–154.
6. *AG Report*; the *Whig Press*, August 28, 1861; Harvard Graduates' Magazine Association, *Harvard Graduates' Magazine*, vol. 9, 1901, 393. In 1858, Dr. Nathan P. Rice authored *Trials of a Public Benefactor as Illustrated in the Discovery of Etherization*.
7. Mowatt diary.
8. *Ibid.*; *AG Report*; NARA—Compiled Service Records; NARA—Pension Records, Charles Peterson, widow Sarah Peterson; Alexandria National Cemetery, Alexandria, Virginia, Charles H. Thompson plot. Thompson was originally buried in Penny Hill Cemetery in Alexandria, but was later removed and interred at the National Cemetery.
9. Mowatt diary.
10. *Ibid.*; Wiley, *The Life of Billy Yank*, 48–49.
11. John Mooney, Letter, undated, Collection of Letters and Documents of Lieutenant John Mooney, 18th New York Volunteer Infantry, Jeff Sauter Collection.
12. NARA—Court Martial Records, Record Group 153, Edward Adams, Walter Allen, Alonzo Richardson, James Slattery, and Daniel Stillwell, August 1861.
13. *Ibid.*
14. *Daily Courier & Union*, August 19, 1861.
15. NARA—Compiled Service Records.
16. NARA—Court Martial, Dixon S. Miles, August–October 1861; *OR*, ser. 1, vol. 2, 439; Davis, *Battle of Bull Run*, 257; Paul R. Teetor, *A Matter of Hours: Treason at Harper's Ferry* (Rutherford, NJ: Farleigh Dickinson University Press, 1982), 29–34.
17. NARA—Court Martial, John Lafloy [Lefleur], September 1861.
18. Mowatt diary; *F.A.R.*, 46.
19. Mowatt diary; Letters to John A. Barhydt, Andrew D. Barhydt Letter, August 18, 1861, Mss 8979-L, Albert and Shirley Small Special Collections Library, University of Virginia, Charlottesville.
20. United States Sanitary Commission Records, Series 7, Statistical Bureau Archives, Camp Inspection Reports, b.11 f.1-7-#2—18th NY Infantry—August 20, 1861—Near Alexandria, VA, Reel 15, NYPL.
21. Mowatt diary.
22. *Ibid.*; *The Whig Press*, August 7, 1861; Barhydt, Letter, August 18, 1861.
23. *Evening Star and Times*, September 2, 1861; Hodgkins, *Autobiography*, 15; Mowatt diary.
24. *Evening Star and Times*, September 2, 1861; Barhydt, Letter, August 18, 1861.
25. NARA—Compiled Service Records; NARA—Pension Records, Peter Shean, widow Sarah Sheehan.
26. Truax diary; NARA—Pension Records, Stephen Truax, widow Marilla Truax.
27. Mowatt diary; *Evening Star and Times*, September 2, 1861.
28. United States Sanitary Commission Records, Series 7, Statistical Bureau Archives, Camp Inspection Reports, b.11 f.1-7-#2—18th NY Infantry—August 20, 1861—Near Alexandria, VA, Reel 15, NYPL; Mowatt diary.
29. *Evening Star and Times*, September 6, 1861; Mowatt diary; Vedder Ledger; *F.A.R.*, 46.
30. *Evening Star and Times*, September 6, 1861; *Schenectady Weekly Republican*, August 30, 1861; Mowatt diary; George Blake, Letter, September 18, 1861, author's collection.
31. *The New York Times*, August 29, 1861; *St. Lawrence Republican*, September 24, 1861; *Harper's Weekly*, October 5, 1861.
32. *The New York Times*, August 29, 1861; *Schenectady Weekly Republican*, September 27, 1861.
33. *The Whig Press*, September 11, 1861; *Harper's Weekly*, October 5, 1861; *Schenectady Weekly Republican*, September 27, 1861.
34. *The Whig Press*, September 11, 1861; *The New York Times*, August 29, 1861; *Schenectady Weekly Republican*, September 27, 1861; Fearey, *Union College Alumni*, 71; *Cambridge Chronicle*, September 21, 1861.
35. *The Whig Press*, September 11, 1861; *AG Report*; NARA—Compiled Service Records; Jeffrey, *Richmond Prisons*, 200.
36. *Evening Star and Times*, September 6, 1861; Mowatt diary; *St. Lawrence Republican*, September 24, 1861; *Harper's Weekly*, October 5, 1861; *Schenectady Weekly Republican*, September 27, 1861.
37. *St. Lawrence Republican*, September 24, 1861; James Longstreet, *From Manassas to Appomattox: Memoirs of the Civil War in America* (Philadelphia: J.B. Lippincott, 1908), 59–60; *Cambridge Chronicle*, September 21, 1861.
38. *St. Lawrence Republican*, September 10, 1861, and September 24, 1861.

39. Snell, *From First to Last*, 70–71; Heitman, *Historical Register and Dictionary of the United States Army 1789–1903*, vol. 1, 434, 641 and 746; *F.A.R.*, 46; *St. Lawrence Republican*, September 24, 1861.
40. *Evening Star and Times*, September 6, 1861.
41. Mowatt diary.
42. *Ibid.*; William J. Miller, *The Men of Fort Ward: Defenders of Washington* (Alexandria, VA: Friends of Fort Ward, 1989), 5; *Schenectady Weekly Republican*, September 27, 1861.
43. Mowatt diary; *Evening Star and Times*, September 6, 1861; *St. Lawrence Republican*, September 24, 1861; *Schenectady Weekly Republican*, September 27, 1861.
44. Mowatt diary; *Schenectady Weekly Republican*, September 27, 1861.
45. *Ogdensburg Advance*, February 28, 1862; *F.A.R.*, 46; Miller, *The Men of Fort Ward*, 5. Fort Ward was named after Commander James Harmon Ward, who was the first Union naval officer to die in the Civil War.
46. *Evening Star and Times*, September 2, 1861; *Schenectady Weekly Republican*, September 27, 1861.
47. *Ogdensburg Advance*, August 30, 1861; Mowatt diary; *St. Lawrence Republican*, September 24, 1861; *Schenectady Weekly Republican*, September 27, 1861.
48. *Schenectady Weekly Republican*, September 27, 1861.
49. *Ibid.*; *St. Lawrence Republican*, September 24, 1861.
50. Miller, *The Men of Fort Ward*, 5 and 11; *Cambridge Chronicle*, September 21, 1861.
51. NARA—Court Martial, Phillip Cullen, December 1861; NYSA—*Civil War Muster Roll Abstracts*, 18th Infantry, Box #76, Phillip Cullen.
52. Mowatt diary; *Schenectady Weekly Republican*, September 27, 1861.
53. Mowatt diary; *The Union Army*, vol. 2, 58; Phisterer, *New York in the War of the Rebellion: 1861 to 1865*, vol. 2, 1,650–1,651 and 1,665. Captain James McQueen of the 15th New York Infantry, died on September 18, 1861.
54. John S. Bantham journal, Joan Bantham Byer and Dave Byer, descendants of John S. Bantham, family possession.
55. *The Whig Press*, September 11, 1861, and October 2, 1861; *Harper's Weekly*, October 5, 1861.
56. *Evening Star and Times*, September 17, 1861.
57. *Ibid.* and September 25, 1861; *St. Lawrence Republican*, September 24, 1861.
58. George Blake, Letter, September 17, 1861, author's collection.
59. *AG Report*; NARA—Compiled Service Records; NARA—Pension Records, Charles H. Brandow, widow Juliet C. Brandow.
60. *The Whig Press*, September 4, 1861, and September 11, 1861; *Philadelphia Inquirer*, August 27, 1861; *AG Report*; NARA—Compiled Service Records; NARA—Pension Records, William V. Horsfall, minor William J. Horsfall.
61. *AG Report*; Clark, *The Heroes of Albany*, 381; Manning, *Albany Zouave Cadets*, 42, 44 and 99.
62. Mowatt diary; Bantham journal.
63. Mowatt diary; Bantham journal.
64. NARA—Court Martial, John Thompson, February 1862.
65. *AG Report*; NARA—Compiled Service Records.
66. NARA—Court Martial, William C. Ireland and William H. Odell [O'Dell], September 1861; NARA—Pension Records, William H. Odell, widow Olivia Odell. O'Dell and Ireland both enlisted again in 1864 in separate cavalry regiments, but Ireland deserted again after just five months of service.
67. NYSA—*Civil War Muster Roll Abstracts*, 18th Infantry, Box #76.
68. Mowatt diary.
69. Longstreet, *From Manassas to Appomattox*, 60–61; *The New York Times*, September 29, 1861; *St. Lawrence Republican*, September 24, 1861, and October 15, 1861; Shelby Foote, *The Civil War, a Narrative: Fort Sumter to Perryville* (New York: Random House, 1958), 103–104.

Chapter 6

1. Mowatt diary.
2. *Ibid.*; *St. Lawrence Republican*, October 15, 1861.
3. Mowatt diary.
4. NARA—Compiled Service Records.
5. *OR*, ser. 1, vol. 5, 237; Mowatt diary. This forgettable incident has appeared in some regimental descriptions of actions and engagements as the Skirmish at Springfield Station.
6. Mowatt diary; *St. Lawrence Republican*, October 15, 1861.
7. Mowatt diary; Vincent Colyer, *Report of the Christian Mission to the United States Army* (New York: G.A. Whitehorne, 1862), 8, letter from A.A. Farr, dated October 25, 1861.
8. NARA—Court Martial, August Heiss, 31st NYSV, September 1861. Heiss would later be killed in battle on May 7, 1862, at Brick House Landing (West Point), Virginia.
9. *St. Lawrence Republican*, October 15, 1861, and November 5, 1861; Blake, Letter, September 17, 1861, author's collection; Andrew Carroll, *War Letters: Extraordinary Correspondence from American Wars* (New York: Scribner, 2001), 73; NARA—Compiled Service Records.
10. *Albany Evening Journal*, October 17, 1861; *New York Daily Tribune*, October 19, 1861; Michigan Pioneer and Historical Society, *Historical Collections: Collections and Researched Made by the Michigan Pioneer and Historical Society* (Lansing, MI: Robert Smith and Co., 1892) issue 17, 403; NARA—Pension Records, Calvin B. Potter, widow Julia A. Potter.
11. United States Sanitary Commission Records, Series 7, Statistical Bureau Archives, Camp Inspection Reports, b.12 f.1–7–#142—18th NY Infantry—October 10, 1861—Camp King, Alexandria, VA, Reel 16, NYPL.
12. *St. Lawrence Republican*, October 15, 1861, and November 5, 1861; Mowatt diary; George Blake Letters, October 30, 1861, Mss 2449, Louisiana and Lower Mississippi Valley Collections, LSU Libraries, Baton Rouge, LA (LLMVC).
13. Charles M. Evans, *The War of the Aeronauts: A History of Ballooning During the Civil War* (Mechanicsburg, PA: Stackpole Books, 2002), 130–135; *St. Lawrence Republican*, October 15, 1861.
14. *AG Report*; NARA—Compiled Service Records; NARA—Pension Records, Henry Carbino, widow Adella Carbino and minor Otto Bryan.
15. *AG Report*; NARA—Compiled Service Records;

NARA—Pension Records, William E. Dunning, father, Shadrach Dunning. Records within his pension also state William E. Dunning could have died September 21, 22, or 23, 1861.

16. *AG Report*; NARA—Compiled Service Records; *Fishkill Standard*, May 15, 1862; *Middletown Mercury*, May 16, 1862.

17. *AG Report*; NARA—Compiled Service Records; Beers, *Commemorative Biographical Record*, 349. Samuel Leith enlisted into Co. F, of the 53rd NY Infantry on August 22, 1862, at New York City. He was commissioned as a First Lieutenant on August 22, 1862. He was later transferred to Co. B, of the 132nd NY Infantry on September 10, 1862, and remained with the regiment until the end of the war, mustering out on June 29, 1865, at Salisbury, NC.

18. *AG Report*; Clark, *The Heroes of Albany*, 525–526.

19. *AG Report*.

20. *Ibid.*; *St. Lawrence Republican*, September 24, 1861; *Ogdensburg Advance*, October 11, 1861; *Ontario Republican Times*, October 30, 1861.

21. *Ogdensburg Advance*, November 8, 1861.

22. *Ibid.*; *AG Report*; NARA—Compiled Service Records; Brundage Plot in Tioga Point Cemetery, Athens, PA.

23. *St. Lawrence Republican*, October 15, 1861; Mowatt diary.

24. *AG Report*; NARA—Compiled Service Records.

25. Mowatt diary.

26. *Ibid.*; *Schenectady Weekly Republican*, November 8, 1861; Blake Letters, October 30, 1861 (LLMVC).

27. Mowatt diary; John D. Billings, *Hardtack and Coffee: The Unwritten Story of Army Life* (Boston: George M. Smith and Co., 1888), 381. The abatis "is a row of the large branches of trees, sharpened and laid close together, points outward, with the butts pinned to the ground."

28. Mowatt diary; Blake Letters, October 29, 1861 (LLMVC).

29. *Schenectady Weekly Republican*, November 8, 1861.

30. George N. Galloway, *The Ninety-Fifth Pennsylvania Volunteers (Gosline's Pennsylvania Zouaves), in the Sixth Corps* (Philadelphia: Collins, 1884), 8, 18–19; *St. Lawrence Republican*, November 19, 1861.

31. *Schenectady Weekly Republican*, November 8, 1861; Mowatt diary.

32. *St. Lawrence Republican*, November 5, 1861.

33. Blake Letters, October 30, 1861 (LLMVC).

34. Mowatt diary.

35. *Ibid.*; *AG Report*; *St. Lawrence Republican*, November 19, 1861; NARA—Compiled Service Records; Clark, *The Heroes of Albany*, 827.

36. Mowatt diary.

37. *St. Lawrence Republican*, November 19, 1861; NARA—Court Martial, Adams, Allen, Richardson, Slattery, and Stillwell, August 1861.

38. NARA—Court Martial, Thomas Radcliffe [Radcliff], October 1861. The court case outlined that he was to be dismissed from that date, November 7, 1861, yet Adjutant General Reports give a date of dismissal of January 13, 1862. Either way, Radcliff went on a successful letter campaign to General McClellan and was reinstated on June 13, 1862, and served as Company I's commander until the regiment's expiration.

39. Mowatt diary; *St. Lawrence Republican*, November 19, 1861; Billings, *Hardtack and Coffee*, 48–49.

40. *St. Lawrence Republican*, November 19, 1861; Mowatt diary; Vedder Ledger.

41. *AG Report*; NARA—Compiled Service Records; Clark, *The Heroes of Albany*, 454–455.

42. *AG Report*; NARA—Compiled Service Records; Clark, *The Heroes of Albany*, 395.

43. Munsell, *Memoir of William A. Jackson*, 13–15; NARA—Compiled Service Records; *Evening Star and Times*, November 19, 1861; *F.A.R.*, 46; *The Atlas & Argus*, November 12, 1861; *Democrat & Reflector*, November 14, 1861. Jackson was quartered at the home of the widowed Maria Turpin, at 485 12th Street West, three doors down from F Street, in Washington.

44. *Evening Star and Times*, November 19, 1861; Mowatt diary.

45. Munsell, *Memoir of William A. Jackson*, 15; Mowatt diary; *The Atlas & Argus*, November 14, 1861: *AG Report*; NARA—Compiled Service Records; *Daily National Intelligencer*, November 13, 1861; Jackson, *Documents Relative to an Attack*, 17.

46. *The Atlas & Argus*, November 13, 1861; *Evening Star and Times*, November 14, 1861; NARA—Compiled Service Records.

47. *The Atlas & Argus*, November 13, 1861; *Evening Star and Times*, November 14, 1861; Manning, *Albany Zouave Cadets*, 56.

48. *Evening Star and Times*, November 14, 1861; Clark, *The Heroes of Albany*, 136; Cuyler Reynolds, *Hudson-Mohawk Genealogical and Family Memoirs* (New York: Lewis Historical Publishing, 1911), vol. 4, 1,741; Vale Cemetery, Schenectady, NY, Jackson grave is located in Section X, Union College Plot, Lot 10.

49. Mowatt diary; *Evening Star and Times*, November 19, 1861.

50. Mowatt diary; *Evening Star and Times*, November 19, 1861; *The Local News*, November 15, 1861; Galloway, *The Ninety-Fifth Pennsylvania*, 42.

51. *AG Report*; *The Atlas & Argus*, November 30, 1861; *The Whig Press*, July 3, 1861; *Albany Evening Journal*, November 21, 1861.

52. *AG Report*; NARA—Compiled Service Records.

53. *AG Report*; NARA—Compiled Service Records.

54. NARA—Compiled Service Records.

55. NARA—Court Martial, John Dillon, January 1862.

56. Mowatt diary.

57. *Ibid.*; Curtis, *From Bull Run to Chancellorsville*, 80; James H. Stevenson, *Boots and Saddles: A History of the First Volunteer Cavalry of the War* (Harrisburg: Patriot Publishing, 1879), 63.

58. Curtis, *From Bull Run to Chancellorsville*, 80–81; Mowatt diary; Stevenson, *Boots and Saddles*, 63–64.

59. Curtis, *From Bull Run to Chancellorsville*, 81–82; Mowatt diary; Stevenson, *Boots and Saddles*, 64–65; Hodgkins, *Autobiography*, 16; Leech, *Reveille in Washington*, 142; *Daily National Intelligencer*, November 21, 1861.

60. Mowatt diary; Vedder Ledger.

61. *AG Report*; NARA—Compiled Service Records.

62. Mowatt diary; Vedder Ledger; *The New York Times*, October 3, 1861.

63. United States Sanitary Commission Records, Series 7, Statistical Bureau Archives, Camp Inspection Reports, b.14 f.1-7-#328—18th NY Infantry—November 29, 1861—Camp King, VA, Reel 17, NYPL.

64. *Ontario Republican Times*, December 11, 1861.

65. Mowatt diary; Vedder Ledger.
66. Mowatt diary; Truax diary.
67. Mowatt diary; Truax diary; Billings, *Hardtack and Coffee*, 49, 54–55.
68. Mowatt diary; Blake Letters, December 18, 1861 (LLMVC).
69. Mowatt diary; Vedder Ledger; NARA—Compiled Service Records.
70. Mowatt diary; Truax diary; *Ogdensburg Advance*, December 20, 1861; *The New York Times*, December 14, 1861.
71. William H. Beach, *The First New York (Lincoln) Cavalry* (New York: Lincoln Cavalry Association, 1902), 67–68; William B. Westervelt, *Lights and Shadows of Army Life: From Bull Run to Bentonville* (Shippensburg, PA: Burd Street Press, 1998), 24; Stevenson, *Boots and Saddles*, 68.
72. Beach, *The First New York*, 68; Stevenson, *Boots and Saddles*, 68–69; Truax diary.
73. Beach, *The First New York*, 68–69; Stevenson, *Boots and Saddles*, 69; *The New York Times*, December 14, 1861.
74. Beach, *The First New York*, 68–69; Stevenson, *Boots and Saddles*, 69–70; Westervelt, *Lights and Shadows*, 24; Jones, *What a Boy Saw*; *The New York Times*, December 14, 1861; Snell, *From First to Last*, 75.

Chapter 7

1. Mowatt diary; Vedder Ledger.
2. Truax diary; Methodist Episcopal Church, *Minutes of the Troy Annual Conference of the Methodist Episcopal Church, for 1874* (Troy, NY: Brainerd and Brown, 1874), 41; *Ontario Republican Times*, February 5, 1862; Clark, *The Heroes of Albany*, 866.
3. Mowatt diary.
4. *Ontario Republican Times*, December 4, 1861, and December 18, 1861.
5. NARA—Court Martial, John Hastings, December 1861.
6. NARA—Court Martial, John Thompson, February 1862.
7. NARA—Court Martial, W. Preston, John Jaycox. Urbind Concling [Urband Conkling], January 1862.
8. NARA—Court Martial, William Burt, January 1862.
9. Ibid.
10. NARA—Court Martial, W. Preston, John Jaycox. Urbind Concling [Urband Conkling], January 1862.
11. NARA—Compiled Service Records; NARA—Court Martial, W. Preston, John Jaycox. Urbind Concling [Urband Conkling], William Burt, January 1862.
12. *AG Report*; NARA—Compiled Service Records; *Schenectady Weekly Republican*, December 27, 1861; *Evening Star and Times*, December 20, 1861; *Albany Evening Journal*, January 13, 1862; *Ogdensburg Advance*, December 20, 1861. The 60th NY Infantry was mustered in Ogdensburg on October 30, 1861, and was heavily recruited by a former member of the 18th, John C. O. Redington.
13. *AG Report*; NARA—Compiled Service Records; NARA—Tenth Census of the United States, 1880, Nassau, Rensselaer County, NY, for William H. Hall.
14. *Evening Star and Times*, December 20, 1861; *The Atlas & Argus*, December 19, 1861; *Springfield Weekly Republican*, December 28, 1861; *Elmira Daily Advertiser*, December 19, 1861.
15. *AG Report*; NARA—Compiled Service Records.
16. AG Report; NARA—Compiled Service Records.
17. *AG Report*; NARA—Compiled Service Records; NARA—Pension Records, Stephen Truax, widow Marilla Truax; Truax diary; Barhydt, Letter, August 18, 1861.
18. Vedder Ledger; Truax diary; Mowatt diary.
19. Mowatt diary; Truax diary; Charles B. Fairchild, *History of the 27th Regiment New York Volunteers* (Binghamton, NY: Carl and Matthews, Printers, 1888), 26.
20. Mowatt diary, Vedder Ledger.
21. Mowatt diary, Vedder Ledger.
22. Mowatt diary; Vedder Ledger.
23. *Ontario Republican Times*, February 5, 1862.
24. NARA—Court Martial, Edward Timmins, January 1862, Edward McGinnis, February 1862.
25. Mowatt diary; Truax diary; *New York Herald-Tribune*, January 31, 1862.
26. *AG Report*; NARA—Compiled Service Records; *Dispatch*, August 17, 1861; *The Atlas & Argus*, January 6, 1862.
27. Mowatt diary; Truax diary; *Ogdensburg Advance*, February 14, 1862; *St. Lawrence Republican*, February 18, 1862.
28. Mowatt diary; Truax diary.
29. *Ogdensburg Advance*, February 14, 1862; Mowatt diary.
30. *Ogdensburg Advance*, February 14, 1862.
31. Mowatt diary; NARA—Compiled Service Records; *Ogdensburg Advance*, February 28, 1862;
32. *AG Report*; NARA—Compiled Service Records.
33. *AG Report*; NARA—Compiled Service Records; *Ontario Republican Times*, February 5, 1862; *St. Lawrence Republican*, February 18, 1862; Clifton Springs Village Cemetery, in Manchester, NY, Warfield plot; NARA—Pension Records, John J. Warfield, father Lewis B. Warfield.
34. *AG Report*; NARA—Compiled Service Records; *St. Lawrence Republican*, February 18, 1862; Albany Rural Cemetery, in Menands, NY, Strathern; NARA—Pension Records, James K. Strathern, sister Annie W. Strathern; NARA-*Famine Irish Entry Project, 1846–1851*.
35. *AG Report*; NARA—Compiled Service Records; West Hollow Cemetery, Naples, NY, Place plot.
36. *AG Report*; NARA—Compiled Service Records; *Ontario Republican Times*, February 12, 1862.
37. Mowatt diary; Truax diary; *Ogdensburg Advance*, February 28, 1862; *The Whig Press*, March 12, 1862; *F.A.R.*, 46; *The Whig Press*, March 12, 1862; Blake Letters, February 16, 1862 (LLMVC). The Daingerfield was mentioned to be owned by a farmer named John Gillen.
38. Blake Letters, February 16, 1862 (LLMVC); Clark, *The Heroes of Albany*, 399.
39. Mowatt diary; Truax diary; *Ogdensburg Advance*, March 7, 1862; *The Whig Press*, March 12, 1862.
40. United States Sanitary Commission Records, Series 7, Statistical Bureau Archives, Camp Inspection Reports, b.19 f.1-7-#816—18th NY Infantry—February 24, 1862—Camp Jackson, VA, Reel 21, NYPL.
41. Mowatt diary; Vedder Ledger; *Ogdensburg Advance*, March 7, 1862.

42. *Ogdensburg Advance*, March 7, 1862; *St. Lawrence Republican*, February 18, 1862; Stevenson, *Boots and Saddles*, 79–80.
43. *AG Report*; NARA—Compiled Service Records; *Ogdensburg Advance*, February 28, 1862.
44. *AG Report*; NARA—Compiled Service Records; NARA—Court Martial, Michael Daniels, February 1862.
45. *AG Report*; NARA—Compiled Service Records; NARA—Pension Records, Horace Faurot. He later served in the 16th New York Heavy Artillery and 40th New York Infantry.
46. *AG Report*; NARA—Compiled Service Records; *The Whig Press*, July 30, 1862.

Chapter 8

1. Mowatt diary; *Ogdensburg Advance*, February 14, 1862; F.A.R., 46.
2. Mowatt diary.
3. *OR*, ser. 1, vol. 5, 18.
4. NARA—Court Martial, T. M. Holden, March 1862.
5. Sears, *To the Gates of Richmond*, 16.
6. Mowatt diary; Vedder Ledger.
7. Mowatt diary; NARA—Court Martial, T. M. Holden, March 1862; NARA—Pension Records, William E. Carmichael, widow, Katharine Carmichael.
8. Mowatt diary; F.A.R., 47.
9. Mowatt diary; Vedder Ledger.
10. Mowatt diary; Truax diary.
11. NARA—Court Martial, T. M. Holden, March 1862.
12. Mowatt diary; Truax diary; Hough (NYSL).
13. NARA—Court Martial, T. M. Holden, March 1862.
14. *Ibid.*
15. Mowatt diary; Truax diary; F.A.R., 47.
16. NARA—Court Martial, T.M. Holden, March 1862.
17. Sears, *To the Gates of Richmond*, 16–19.
18. *Ibid.*, 21; *The New York Times*, March 16, 1862.
19. Mowatt diary; Truax diary.
20. NARA—Court Martial, T.M. Holden, March 1862.
21. Mowatt diary; Vedder Ledger; Hough (NYSL).
22. NARA—Court Martial, T.M. Holden, March 1862; NARA—Compiled Service Records; *AG Report*. The same day as Holden's ousting, First Lieutenant Edward Fisher of Company F went through a trial that similarly cost him his job. The details of Fisher's court-martial and dismissal is not known, other than it occurred the same day as Holden's case.
23. Nathaniel G. Whittemore, Letter, April 2, 1862, Marguerite (Whittemore) Griffith, descendent of Nathaniel G. Whittemore, family possession.
24. Mowatt diary; Truax diary; Hough (NYSL).
25. Mowatt diary; Truax diary; *Evening Star and Times*, April 16, 1862; Hough (NYSL).
26. Mowatt diary; Truax diary; Hough (NYSL).
27. United States Sanitary Commission Records, Series 7, Statistical Bureau Archives, Camp Inspection Reports, b.19 f.1-7-#865—18th NY Infantry—April 1, 1862—Camp Jackson, VA, Reel 22, NYPL.

Chapter 9

1. Mowatt diary; Vedder Ledger; *Evening Star and Times*, April 16, 1862; Sears, *To the Gates of Richmond*, 40; Snell, *From First to Last*, 92.
2. Mowatt diary; Truax diary; *Evening Star and Times*, April 16, 1862; F.A.R., 47.
3. Mowatt diary; Truax diary; *Evening Star and Times*, April 16, 1862; F.A.R., 47.
4. Mowatt diary; Truax diary; F.A.R., 47.
5. *AG Report*; NARA—Compiled Service Records.
6. Mowatt diary; Vedder Ledger; *AG Report*; NARA—Pension Records, George R. Myers; Nathaniel G. Whittemore, Letter, April 14, 1862, Marguerite (Whittemore) Griffith, descendent of Nathaniel G. Whittemore, family possession.
7. Mowatt diary; *Evening Star and Times*, April 16, 1862.
8. *Evening Star and Times*, April 16, 1862.
9. Sears, *To the Gates of Richmond*, 42–43.
10. *OR*, ser. 1, vol. 11, part 3, 71, 73–74 and 90.
11. Mowatt diary; Truax diary; *Evening Star and Times*, April 16, 1862; F.A.R., 47; Hough (NYSL).
12. Mowatt diary; Truax diary; *Evening Star and Times*, April 16, 1862; F.A.R., 47.
13. Mowatt diary; Truax diary; *Evening Star and Times*, April 16, 1862; F.A.R., 47.
14. Mowatt diary; Truax diary; *Evening Star and Times*, April 16, 1862.
15. Mowatt diary; Truax diary; *Evening Star and Times*, April 16, 1862; Hough (NYSL); Hodgkins, *Autobiography*, 16.
16. Mowatt diary.
17. Vedder Ledger; *AG Report*; NARA—Compiled Service Records; F.A.R., 47.
18. Mowatt diary; *AG Report*; NARA—Compiled Service Records.
19. Mowatt diary; *Evening Star and Times*, May 2, 1862; *Ontario Republican Times*, April 30, 1862; F.A.R., 47; Andre Trudeau, Bryce A. Suderow, and Noah Hewett, eds., *Supplement to the Official Records of the Union and Confederate Armies* (Wilmington, NC: Broadfoot Publishing, 1994–2001), vol. 43, 261–268; Hodgkins, *Autobiography*, 16; Nathaniel G. Whittemore, Letter, April 21, 1862, Marguerite (Whittemore) Griffith, descendent of Nathaniel G. Whittemore, family possession; Hough (NYSL).
20. Mowatt diary; *Evening Star and Times*, May 2, 1862; *The Whig Press*, April 30, 1862; F.A.R., 47; Whittemore, Letter, April 21, 1862.
21. Vedder Ledger; *Evening Star and Times*, May 2, 1862; *Ontario Republican Times*, April 30, 1862; Gregoire Insse, Letter, April 27, 1862, *Telesphor Insse Papers*, Special Collections Research Center, Syracuse University Library, Syracuse University, Syracuse, NY.
22. Vedder Ledger; Truax diary; *Evening Star and Times*, May 2, 1862; *Ontario Republican Times*, April 30, 1862; Snell, *From First to Last*, 96; Hough (NYSL).
23. *Evening Star and Times*, May 2, 1862; Insse, Letter, April 27, 1862; Truax diary; Hough (NYSL).
24. NARA—Compiled Service Records; NARA—Union Provost Marshals' File of Papers Relating to Individual Civilians, 1861–1867, Edward W. Groot.
25. NARA—Compiled Service Records; NARA—Union Provost Marshals' File of Papers Relating to Individual Civilians, 1861–1867, Edward W. Groot.

26. NARA—Compiled Service Records; NARA—Union Provost Marshals' File of Papers Relating to Individual Civilians, 1861–1867, Edward W. Groot.

27. Yates, *Schenectady County, New York*, 92; Fearey, *Union College Alumni*, 58; Richard Schermerhorn, *Schermerhorn Genealogy and Family Chronicles* (New York: T.A. Wright, 1914), 105–106 and 123–124; NARA—Compiled Service Records. John Crane Schermerhorn often dropped his New York surname in the South, but kept it when he served in Company D, 8th Alabama Infantry as a first lieutenant. He resigned on January 27, 1862. After the war he returned to the family in Schenectady and stayed until his death.

28. NARA—Compiled Service Records; NARA—Union Provost Marshals' File of Papers Relating to Individual Civilians, 1861–1867, Edward W. Groot. He joined the 134th New York Infantry as their adjutant on July 28, 1862.

29. Vedder Ledger; *The Whig Press*, April 30, 1862; NYSA-*Town Clerks' Registers*, Thomas Alexander.

Chapter 10

1. Truax diary; *OR*, ser. 1, vol. 11, part 1, 614–615; *F.A.R.*, 47–48; *The Whig Press*, May 21, 1862.
2. Duane H. Hurd, *History of Clinton and Franklin Counties, New York* (Philadelphia: J.W. Lewis and Co., 1880), 65; *The Whig Press*, May 21, 1862.
3. *The Whig Press*, May 21, 1862; *OR*, ser. 1, vol. 11, part 1, 137 and 615.
4. Truax diary; Hough (NYSL); *The Whig Press*, May 14, 1862, and May 21, 1862; *OR*, ser. 1, vol. 11, part 1, 137 and 615; Sears, *To the Gates of Richmond*, 85.
5. *The Whig Press*, May 14, 1862, and May 21, 1862; Hurd, *History of Clinton and Franklin Counties*, 65.
6. Sears, *To the Gates of Richmond*, 85.
7. *The Whig Press*, May 14, 1862, and May 21, 1862; *OR*, ser. 1, vol. 11, part 1, 615; *F.A.R.*, 48.
8. *The Whig Press*, May 21, 1862; *Evening Star and Times*, June 5, 1862; Hough (NYSL); Fairchild, *History of the 27th*, 33.
9. *The Whig Press*, May 21, 1862; *Evening Star and Times*, June 5, 1862; *OR*, ser. 1, vol. 11, part 1, 615.
10. *Evening Star and Times*, June 5, 1862.
11. *Ibid.*; *F.A.R.*, 48.
12. *Evening Star and Times*, June 5, 1862.
13. *OR*, ser. 1, vol. 11, part 1, 615 and 623.
14. *The Whig Press*, May 21, 1862.
15. *OR*, ser. 1, vol. 11, part 1, 626–627; Sears, *To the Gates of Richmond*, 85.
16. *OR*, ser. 1, vol. 11, part 1, 616, 623 and 627.
17. *Ibid.*, 616, 623–625 and 629; *The Whig Press*, May 14, 1862; *F.A.R.*, 48; Hurd, *History of Clinton and Franklin Counties*, 65.
18. *OR*, ser. 1, vol. 11, part 1, 138, 618–621 and 625; *F.A.R.*, 48.
19. *The Whig Press*, May 14, 1862, and May 21, 1862.
20. *The Whig Press*, May 21, 1862; *Evening Star and Times*, May 23, 1862; *F.A.R.*, 48; George W. Bicknell, *History of the Fifth Regiment Maine Volunteers* (Portland: Hall L. Davis, 1871), 93.
21. *OR*, ser. 1, vol. 11, part 1, 625, 627–628 and 630.
22. *Ibid.*, 624, 627 and 629–630; Francis E. Pinto, *History of the 32nd Regiment, New York Volunteers, in the Civil War, 1861–1863, and Personal Recollection During That Period* (Brooklyn: publisher not identified, 1895), 57; *F.A.R.*, 48.
23. *The Whig Press*, May 21, 1862; *Daily City Press*, June 26, 1866.
24. *OR*, ser. 1, vol. 11, part 1, 625; *The Whig Press*, May 21, 1862; *St. Lawrence Republican*, May 20, 1862; *Evening Star & Times*, May 23, 1862; Curtis, *From Bull Run to Chancellorsville*, 97–98.
25. Truax diary; *F.A.R.*, 48.
26. *St. Lawrence Republican*, May 20, 1862.
27. *The Whig Press*, May 21, 1862.
28. *Ibid.*; Vedder Ledger; Truax diary; *F.A.R.*, 48; Hough (NYSL); Sears, *To the Gates of Richmond*, 98; Bicknell, *History of the Fifth Regiment Maine Volunteers*, 95.
29. Vedder Ledger; *F.A.R.*, 48; Hough (NYSL).
30. Vedder Ledger; *Fishkill Journal*, June 26, 1862; *F.A.R.*, 48; Hough (NYSL).
31. *Fishkill Journal*, June 26, 1862; Sears, *To the Gates of Richmond*, 104.
32. Sears, *To the Gates of Richmond*, 104; Curtis, *From Bull Run to Chancellorsville*, 105.
33. *Fishkill Journal*, June 26, 1862; *F.A.R.*, 48; Hodgkins, *Autobiography*, 16; Sears, *To the Gates of Richmond*, 104.
34. *AG Report*; NARA—Compiled Service Records; NARA—Pension Records, Coradon A. Dawley, archived with William T. Carpenter pension.
35. *AG Report*; NARA—Compiled Service Records; NARA—Pension Records, George W. Dunkle, mother Melinda Dunkle.
36. *AG Report*; NARA—Compiled Service Records; Clark, *The Heroes of Albany*, 833–834; *New York Herald-Tribune*, May 13, 1862; *The New York Times*, May 17, 1862. Speenburgh was originally buried at Cypress Hills National Cemetery, in Brooklyn, but was later removed to Coeymans Hollow Cemetery, in Coeymans Hollow, NY.
37. *Evening Star and Times*, June 5, 1862; *St. Lawrence Republican*, June 3, 1862; *Albany Evening Journal*, May 26, 1862; NARA—Compiled Service Records; *F.A.R.*, 48–49; Hough (NYSL).
38. *Fishkill Journal*, June 26, 1862.
39. *OR*, ser. 1, vol. 11, part 3, 181; Sears, *To the Gates of Richmond*, 106–107 and 383–384.
40. Fairchild, *History of the 27th*, 3, 13 and 237.
41. *Fishkill Journal*, June 26, 1862.
42. *Ibid.*; Vedder Ledger; *F.A.R*, 49.
43. Truax diary; *Fishkill Journal*, June 26, 1862; Mowatt diary; *F.A.R*, 49.
44. Vedder Ledger; *Fishkill Journal*, June 26, 1862; Mowatt diary; *F.A.R.*, 49; Sears, *To the Gates of Richmond*, 109 and 213.
45. *Fishkill Journal*, June 26, 1862; Mowatt diary; *F.A.R.*, 49.
46. *Fishkill Journal*, June 26, 1862; Mowatt diary; Sears, *To the Gates of Richmond*, 125–126; Hough (NYSL).
47. *Fishkill Journal*, June 26, 1862; Mowatt diary; *Evening Star and Times*, June 5, 1862; *F.A.R.*, 49; Hodgkins, *Autobiography*, 16; Hough (NYSL).
48. *Fishkill Journal*, June 26, 1862; Mowatt diary; *F.A.R.*, 49; Sears, *To the Gates of Richmond*, 112–113.
49. *Fishkill Journal*, June 26, 1862; Mowatt diary; Sears, *To the Gates of Richmond*, 113–117.

50. Truax diary; *Fishkill Journal*, June 26, 1862; Mowatt diary; Hough (NYSL).
51. Mowatt diary.
52. NARA—Compiled Service Records.
53. *Fishkill Journal*, June 26, 1862; Mowatt diary.
54. *Fishkill Journal*, June 26, 1862; Mowatt diary; Sears, *To the Gates of Richmond*, 120.
55. Sears, *To the Gates of Richmond*, 118–120 and 124.
56. *Fishkill Journal*, June 26, 1862; Mowatt diary.
57. Sears, *To the Gates of Richmond*, 138–140 and 145.
58. *Ibid.*, 144; *Fishkill Journal*, June 26, 1862; Mowatt diary.
59. Vedder Ledger; *Fishkill Journal*, June 26, 1862; Mowatt diary.
60. *Fishkill Journal*, June 26, 1862; Mowatt diary; *F.A.R.*, 49.
61. Vedder Ledger; *Fishkill Journal*, June 26, 1862; Mowatt diary; Sears, *To the Gates of Richmond*, 109.
62. *Fishkill Journal*, June 26, 1862.
63. *Ibid.*; Truax diary; Mowatt diary; *F.A.R.*, 49; Hough (NYSL).
64. Truax diary; *Fishkill Journal*, June 26, 1862; Mowatt diary; *F.A.R.*, 49; NARA—Pension Records, John J. Icklin.
65. Truax diary; *Fishkill Journal*, June 26, 1862, and July 10, 1862; Mowatt diary.
66. Truax diary; *Fishkill Journal*, June 26, 1862, and July 10, 1862; Mowatt diary; Blake Letters, June 10, 1862 (LLMVC); Hough (NYSL).
67. *Fishkill Journal*, July 10, 1862.
68. *Ibid.*; *F.A.R.*, 49–50; Hough (NYSL).
69. *Fishkill Journal*, July 10, 1862; *F.A.R.*, 50.
70. *AG Report*; NARA—Compiled Service Records; NARA—*1860 U.S. Census, Population Schedule*, Albany (Ward 8), Albany County, NY, for John Cullen, roll M653_720, 63; Sears, *To the Gates of Richmond*, 163.
71. NARA—Compiled Service Records; *OR*, ser. 1, vol. 11, part 2, 457–458.
72. NARA—Compiled Service Records; WLC.
73. *Fishkill Journal*, July 10, 1862; Vedder Ledger.
74. *Fishkill Journal*, July 10, 1862.
75. *Ibid.*; Vedder Ledger.
76. Sears, *To the Gates of Richmond*, 184–189.
77. *OR*, ser. 1, vol. 11, part 2, 429; *Fishkill Journal*, July 10, 1862; Vedder Ledger; *F.A.R.*, 50.
78. *AG Report*; NARA—Compiled Service Records; *Ontario Republican Times*, July 9, 1862; *Fishkill Journal*, July 10, 1862.
79. Sears, *To the Gates of Richmond*, 195, 199–201 and 208.
80. Truax diary; Edmund B. Hawley, Letter, July 14, 1862, Manuscript Archive, USAHEC.
81. *OR*, ser. 1, vol. 11, part 2, 429; Truax diary; *The Whig Press*, July 23, 1862; *F.A.R.*, 50.
82. Clark, *The Heroes of Albany*, 527–528.

Chapter 11

1. Sears, *To the Gates of Richmond*, 210.
2. *Ibid.*, 210–211 and 214.
3. *OR*, ser. 1, vol. 11, part 2, 457–458; NARA—Compiled Service Records; *The Whig Press*, July 23, 1862.
4. NARA—Pension Records, Samuel Hodgkins.
5. *The Whig Press*, July 23, 1862; *Middletown Mercury*, August 1, 1862; *F.A.R.*, 50; Bantham journal.
6. *OR*, ser. 1, vol. 11, part 2, 429; Vedder Ledger; *The Whig Press*, July 23, 1862; *F.A.R.*, 50; Sears, *To the Gates of Richmond*, 213; Bantham journal.
7. *OR*, ser. 1, vol. 11, part 2, 458; Vedder Ledger; *Fishkill Journal*, July 17, 1862; *The Whig Press*, July 23, 1862; Clark, *The Heroes of Albany*, 528; Hough (NYSL); Bantham journal.
8. *OR*, ser. 1, vol. 11, part 2, 458; Vedder Ledger; *Fishkill Journal*, July 17, 1862; *The Whig Press*, July 23, 1862; *F.A.R.*, 50; Clark, *The Heroes of Albany*, 528; Hough (NYSL); *AG Report*; NARA—Compiled Service Records; Bantham journal.
9. *OR*, ser. 1, vol. 11, part 2, 458; Vedder Ledger; *Fishkill Journal*, July 17, 1862; *The Whig Press*, July 23, 1862; Clark, *The Heroes of Albany*, 528; Hough (NYSL); Robert U. Johnson and Clarence C. Buel, eds., *Battles and Leaders of the Civil War* (New York: Castle Books, 1991), vol. 2, 367; Bantham journal.
10. Sears, *To the Gates of Richmond*, 214–215 and 223–224.
11. *Ibid.*, 224; *OR*, ser. 1, vol. 11, part 2, 429, 432, 456 and 458; Bantham journal; *Fishkill Journal*, July 17, 1862; *The Whig Press*, July 23, 1862; NARA—Pension Records, George R. Myers; *F.A.R.*, 50; Clark, *The Heroes of Albany*, 528.
12. *OR*, ser. 1, vol. 11, part 2, 429 and 458; *Fishkill Journal*, July 17, 1862; *The Whig Press*, July 23, 1862; Hawley, Letter, July 14, 1862; Sears, *To the Gates of Richmond*, 224.
13. Hawley, Letter, July 14, 1862.
14. *Ibid.*; *OR*, ser. 1, vol. 11, part 2, 432, 456–458; *Fishkill Journal*, July 17, 1862; *F.A.R.*, 50.
15. *OR*, ser. 1, vol. 11, part 2, 458 and 460; *The Whig Press*, July 23, 1862; Clark, *The Heroes of Albany*, 528; Sears, *To the Gates of Richmond*, 233; Hawley, Letter, July 14, 1862.
16. *OR*, ser. 1, vol. 11, part 2, 458; *Fishkill Journal*, July 17, 1862.
17. *OR*, ser. 1, vol. 11, part 2, 458; Bantham journal.
18. *OR*, ser. 1, vol. 11, part 2, 458; *The Whig Press*, July 23, 1862; Hawley, Letter, July 14, 1862; NARA—Pension Records, Thomas Kearns.
19. *OR*, ser. 1, vol. 11, part 2, 457–458; Bantham journal; *Fishkill Journal*, July 17, 1862; Hawley, Letter, July 14, 1862; *The National Tribune*, February 26, 1891.
20. *Albany Evening Journal*, September 3, 1862.
21. Clark, *The Heroes of Albany*, 381–383.
22. Hawley, Letter, July 14, 1862; *Schenectady Gazette*, August 13, 1929; *AG Report*; NARA—Compiled Service Records; WLC; Hough (NYSL); NARA—Pension Records, John Hagerman, widow Annie M. Hagerman, John Blackwell, widow Mary Blackwell, James Flynn, widow Mary E. Flynn and Jehiel J. Stevens; *The Medical and Surgical History of the Civil War* (Wilmington, NC: Broadfoot Publishing, 1992), vol. 10, 890.
23. *AG Report*; NARA—Compiled Service Records; NARA—Pension Records, George E. Homan and James E. Homan, father Mordecai Homan.
24. Sears, *To the Gates of Richmond*, 233–234.
25. *OR*, ser. 1, vol. 11, part 2, 458; *The Whig Press*, July 16, 1862, and July 23, 1862; *Middletown Mercury*, August 1, 1862; NARA—Compiled Service Records; NARA—Pension Records, George R. Myers.

26. *Ontario Republican Times,* July 16, 1862; NARA—Compiled Service Records; NARA—Pension Records, Henry Faurot and George W. Ellis.

27. *AG Report;* NARA—Compiled Service Records; NYSA—*Civil War Muster Roll Abstracts,* 18th Infantry, Box #76, Theodore Langdon; NARA—*1860 U.S. Census, Population Schedule,* Watervliet, Albany County, NY, for Theodore Langdon, roll M653_722, 384; *The Medical and Surgical History,* vol. 12, 559; NARA—Pension Records, William H. Thompson, minor Henry M. Thompson.

28. Grand Army of the Republic, *Department of New York, Personal War Sketches, Presented to General Lyon Post No. 266, Middletown,* 65, Historical Society of Middletown and the Wallkill Precinct, Inc. Middletown, NY; NARA—Compiled Service Records; NARA—Pension Records, Thomas Kearns.

29. *OR,* ser. 1, vol. 11, part 2, 459; *The Whig Press,* July 23, 1862; *F.A.R.,* 50.

30. Sears, *To the Gates of Richmond,* 236–237.

31. *OR,* ser. 1, vol. 11, part 2, 458; *The Whig Press,* July 23, 1862.

32. *OR,* ser. 1, vol. 11, part 2, 458; *The Whig Press,* July 16, 1862, and July 23, 1862; Grand Army of the Republic, *Lyon Post No. 266,* 20.

33. *The Whig Press,* May 28, 1862, July 16, 1862, and July 23, 1862; *Middletown Mercury,* July 4, 1862; NARA—Pension Records, George Barry, mother Mary Barry.

34. *OR,* ser. 1, vol. 11, part 2, 459; *The Whig Press,* July 16, 1862, and July 23, 1862; Grand Army of the Republic, *Lyon Post No. 266,* 20.

35. *OR,* ser. 1, vol. 11, part 2, 459; Bantham journal.

36. *F.A.R.,* 51; *The Whig Press,* July 23, 1862; Bantham journal.

37. *F.A.R.,* 51; *The Whig Press,* July 23, 1862; *Middletown Mercury,* August 1, 1862; Bantham journal; NARA—Pension Records, Thomas Kearns; *OR,* ser. 1, vol. 11, part 2, 459.

38. NARA—Pension Records, Thomas Kearns.

39. Ibid.

40. *AG Report;* NARA—Compiled Service Records; NYSA—*Civil War Muster Roll Abstracts,* 18th Infantry, Box #76, Anson A. Shaw; *The Whig Press,* August 27, 1862.

41. *OR,* ser. 1, vol. 11, part 2, 459.

42. Clark, *The Heroes of Albany,* 399–401; *Middletown Mercury,* August 1, 1862; *the Whig Press,* July 23, 1862.

43. Clark, *The Heroes of Albany,* 399–401; *New York Observer and Chronicle,* March 12, 1863. The location of Rogers' burial is unknown, and more than likely remains unmarked somewhere on the battlefield.

44. *OR,* ser. 1, vol. 11, part 2, 459; *AG Report; The Whig Press,* July 23, 1862; NARA—Pension Records, William E. Carmichael, widow, Katharine Carmichael.

45. *OR,* ser. 1, vol. 11, part 2, 459; *Fishkill Journal,* July 17, 1862; *The Whig Press,* July 23, 1862; Clark, *The Heroes of Albany,* 528.

46. *Fishkill Journal,* July 17, 1862; *The Whig Press,* July 23, 1862; *Ontario Republican Times,* July 16, 1862; NARA—Compiled Service Records; Hough (NYSL); NARA—Pension Records, Henry Faurot; Hawley, Letter, July 14, 1862. Hawley shared a tent with Lilly, Gridley, and Putman.

47. *OR,* ser. 1, vol. 11, part 2, 459; *The Whig Press,* July 23, 1862; *AG Report;* NYSA—*Town Clerks' Registers,* James Daley.

48. *St. Lawrence Republican,* July 15, 1862; NARA—Pension Records, Thomas Kearns; Curtis, *From Bull Run to Chancellorsville,* 21 and 363–365.

49. Sears, *To the Gates of Richmond,* 246–247.

50. Bantham journal.

51. *AG Report;* NARA—Compiled Service Records; *Evening Star and Times,* August 16, 1862.

52. *AG Report;* NARA—Compiled Service Records; *The Medical and Surgical History,* vol. 10, 757.

53. *OR,* ser. 1, vol. 11, part 2, 459; *The Whig Press,* July 23, 1862; *F.A.R.,* 50.

54. *OR,* ser. 1, vol. 11, part 2, 71; *F.A.R.,* 50; Hodgkins, *Autobiography,* 16; NARA—Pension Records, Thomas Kearns.

55. *OR,* ser. 1, vol. 11, part 2, 459.

56. Ibid., 71 and 459; *F.A.R.,* 51; *The Whig Press,* July 23, 1862.

57. Sears, *To the Gates of Richmond,* 249.

58. *OR,* ser. 1, vol. 11, part 2, 434; *Fishkill Journal,* July 17, 1862; Hodgkins, *Autobiography,* 16.

59. *AG Report;* NARA—Compiled Service Records; Royce, *Bessboro,* 510; NYSA—*Civil War Muster Roll Abstracts,* 18th Infantry, Box #76, John (Henry) Stalker; WLC.

60. *AG Report;* NARA—Compiled Service Records; NYSA—*Town Clerks' Registers,* Thomas Snyder; NARA—*1860 U.S. Census, Population Schedule,* Schoharie, Schoharie County, NY, for Thomas Snyder, roll M653_860, 634; WLC; *Schoharie Republican,* December 4, 1862; Warner, *Military Records of Schoharie County Veterans,* 202–203.

61. *AG Report;* NARA—Compiled Service Records; *Evening Star and Times,* July 9, 1862, October 6, 1862, and December 1, 1862; NYSA—*Civil War Muster Roll Abstracts,* 18th Infantry, Box #76, Nathaniel P.T. Gridley.

62. *AG Report;* NARA—Compiled Service Records; NARA—Pension Records, Isaac Van Kuren, mother Netty Van Kuren.

63. *AG Report;* NARA—Compiled Service Records.

64. Clark, *The Heroes of Albany,* 528–529.

65. *AG Report;* NARA—Compiled Service Records.

66. NARA—Pension Records, Samuel Hodgkins.

67. NARA—Compiled Service Records; Hodgkins, *Autobiography,* 17; NARA—Pension Records, Edwin Martin, widow Elva A. Martin.

68. NARA—Compiled Service Records; NYSA—*Town Clerks' Registers,* Charles Albert Getty, James Albert Madill, Millard F. Williams; NARA—Pension Records, James M. Larkin, widow Margaret F. Larkin and Robert Courtney.

69. Sears, *To the Gates of Richmond,* 254.

70. Ibid.; Hillside Cemetery, Westport, NY, Washington Irving Sawyer plot; WLC.

Chapter 12

1. *OR,* ser. 1, vol. 11, part 2, 76 and 434; *The Whig Press,* July 23, 1862; *F.A.R.,* 51; Trudeau, Suderow, Hewett, eds., *Supplement to the Official Records,* vol. 43, 265; Hough (NYSL).

2. Clark, *The Heroes of Albany,* 382.

3. *OR,* ser. 1, vol. 11, part 2, 76 and 434; Vedder

Ledger; *The Whig Press*, July 23, 1862; *F.A.R.*, 51; Sears, *To the Gates of Richmond*, 260; Hough (NYSL).

4. Sears, *To the Gates of Richmond*, 254.

5. Ibid.; NARA—Compiled Service Records; *Evening Star and Times*, March 10, 1863; *The Medical and Surgical History*, vol. 10, 765 and vol. 12, 466.

6. NARA—Pension Records, Thomas Kearns.

7. *OR*, ser. 1, vol. 11, part 3, 272; Sears, *To the Gates of Richmond*, 260.

8. *OR*, ser. 1, vol. 11, part 2, 434–435; Johnson and Buel, eds., *Battles and Leaders*, vol. 2, 370.

9. Sears, *To the Gates of Richmond*, 264; *AG Report*; NARA—Compiled Service Records; NARA—Court Martial, W.A. Lamson, February 1863; Clark, *The Heroes of Albany*, 382–383.

10. Sears, *To the Gates of Richmond*, 264; *AG Report*; NARA—Compiled Service Records; *Dispatch*, July 12, 1862; *The Whig Press*, July 23, 1862; *St. Lawrence Republican*, July 15, 1862; *The Ogdensburg Advance and St. Lawrence Weekly Democrat*, March 14, 1918; *The Medical and Surgical History*, part 3, vol. 2, 466; NARA—Pension Records, Thomas Welsh.

11. *OR*, ser. 1, vol. 11, part 2, 435–436, 789–790, 797; *The Whig Press*, July 23, 1862; *F.A.R.*, 51.

12. *OR*, ser. 1, vol. 11, part 2, 435–436, 789–790; *The Whig Press*, July 23, 1862; *F.A.R.*, 51.

13. *The Whig Press*, July 23, 1862.

14. Ibid.; *OR*, ser. 1, vol. 11, part 2, 435–436, 798 and 981; NARA—Compiled Service Records; NYSA—*Town Clerks' Registers*, Julius Becking; NARA—Pension Records, Julius Becking, widow Mary E. Becking; Sears, *To the Gates of Richmond*, 307.

15. Johnson and Buel, eds., *Battles and Leaders*, vol. 2, 381.

16. *OR*, ser. 1, vol. 11, part 2, 436; *F.A.R.*, 51; *The Whig Press*, July 23, 1862; Hodgkins, *Autobiography*, 17.

17. *OR*, ser. 1, vol. 11, part 2, 436; *The Whig Press*, July 23, 1862; Sears, *To the Gates of Richmond*, 310; *Middletown Mercury*, July 11, 1862.

18. Sears, *To the Gates of Richmond*, 310, 312–313, 318–321 and 335.

19. *OR*, ser. 1, vol. 11, part 2, 436; *The Whig Press*, July 23, 1862.

20. *OR*, ser. 1, vol. 11, part 2, 436; *The Whig Press*, July 23, 1862; Hodgkins, *Autobiography*, 17; Vedder Ledger.

21. *OR*, ser. 1, vol. 11, part 2, 436; *The Whig Press*, July 23, 1862; *F.A.R.*, 51; Truax diary; Benjamin F. Cooling, *Counter-Thrust, from the Peninsula to the Antietam* (Lincoln: University of Nebraska, 2007), 2; Sears, *To the Gates of Richmond*, 338; Trudeau, Suderow, Hewett, eds., *Supplement to the Official Records*, vol. 43, 265; *AG Report*; NARA—Compiled Service Records.

22. *The Whig Press*, July 23, 1862; Truax diary; *F.A.R.*, 52.

23. *The Whig Press*, July 23, 1862; Truax diary.

24. Vedder Ledger; *F.A.R.*, 52; Hough (NYSL).

25. *F.A.R.*, 52.

26. *OR*, ser. 1, vol. 11, part 2, 459.

27. *The Whig Press*, July 9, 1862, and July 23, 1862.

28. *The Whig Press*, July 2, 1862, July 9, 1862, and July 16, 1862; *The New York Times*, July 3, 1862; *Evening Star and Times*, July 3, 1862, and July 9, 1862; *The Atlas & Argus*, July 4, 1862, and July 8, 1862; *Ontario Republican Times*, July 9, 1862; *Middletown Mercury*, July 4, 1862, and July 18, 1862.

29. *Fishkill Journal*, June 26, 1862, and July 17, 1862; *Ontario Republican Times*, July 16, 1862, and August 6, 1862.

30. NARA—Pension Records, Jehiel J. Stevens; *St. Lawrence Herald*, June, undated, 1903.

31. *The New York Times*, July 6, 1862.

32. NARA—Compiled Service Records; *Albany Evening Journal*, July 9, 1862.

33. *Middletown Mercury*, August 1, 1862; *the Whig Press*, July 23, 1862.

34. NARA—Compiled Service Records.

35. Ibid.; *Evening Star and Times*, August 16, 1862.

36. NARA—Compiled Service Records.

37. NARA—Compiled Service Records; *Albany Evening Journal*, July 22, 1862.

38. *Evening Star and Times*, August 16, 1862; *St. Lawrence Republican*, August 19, 1862; *AG Report*; NARA—Compiled Service Records; NARA—Pension Records, William Harris, minor Mary R. Pope. City Point was also called Aiken's Landing.

39. Vedder Ledger; *The Whig Press*, July 23, 1862; Hawley, Letter, July 14, 1862.

40. NARA—Court Martial, John H. Radeker [Rediker], February 1863.

41. Hawley, Letter, July 14, 1862; NARA—Compiled Service Records; *Middletown Mercury*, August 1, 1862.

42. *AG Report*; NARA—Compiled Service Records; Clark, *The Heroes of Albany*, 381–383.

43. *AG Report*; NARA—Compiled Service Records; NYSA—*Civil War Muster Roll Abstracts*, 18th Infantry, Box #76, Anson A. Shaw; *The Whig Press*, August 27, 1862; *Middletown Mercury*, August 29, 1862. Shaw is buried in Glendale National Cemetery, in Richmond, VA.

44. *AG Report*; NARA—Compiled Service Records; NARA—Pension Records, William Snell and Robert Huson.

45. *AG Report*; NARA—Compiled Service Records; *The Medical and Surgical History*, vol. 3, 116.

46. NARA—Pension Records, George C. Furniss.

47. *AG Report*; NARA—Compiled Service Records; *The Atlas & Argus*, August 6, 1862; Newspaper account from the files of the NYSMM, untitled and undated newspaper.

48. *AG Report*; NARA—Compiled Service Records; *The Whig Press*, July 23, 1862; NARA—Pension Records, William E. Carmichael, widow, Katharine Carmichael.

49. *AG Report*; NARA—Compiled Service Records; *Ontario Republican Times*, July 16, 1862, and July 30, 1862.

50. *AG Report*; NARA—Compiled Service Records; *Ontario Republican Times*, July 16, 1862.

51. *AG Report*: *The Atlas & Argus*, August 14, 1862; NARA—Pension Records, Catharine Mattimore, mother of Frank J. Mattimore; Mattimore family genealogical information, Gerard Mattimore, descendent of Frank J. Mattimore; *Transactions of the Medical Society of the County of Albany*, vol. 3, 365–366.

52. *OR*, ser. 1, vol. 11, part 1, 78–79; Sears, *To the Gates of Richmond*, 354; Hough (NYSL); Vedder Ledger.

53. Hough (NYSL); Vedder Ledger.

54. *AG Report*; NARA—Compiled Service Records; *Evening Star and Times*, August 16, 1862; Ogdensburg Cemetery, Ogdensburg, NY, Myers plot.

55. Vedder Ledger; *F.A.R.*, 52; Hough (NYSL).
56. *OR*, ser. 1, vol. 11, part 2, 90; Vedder Ledger; Cooling, *Counter-Thrust*, 34; *F.A.R.*, 52; NARA—Compiled Service Records; Fairchild, *History of the 27th*, 83–84.
57. *AG Report*; *Albany Evening Journal*, September 3, 1862.
58. Vedder Ledger; *F.A.R.*, 52; Hough (NYSL); Fairchild, *History of the 27th*, 84.
59. *Albany Evening Journal*, September 3, 1862.
60. Truax Diary; Cooling, *Counter-Thrust*, 34; *F.A.R.*, 52; Hough (NYSL); *Evening Star and Times*, November 24, 1862.
61. Truax Diary; Cooling, *Counter-Thrust*, 34; *F.A.R.*, p. 52; Hough (NYSL); Fairchild, *History of the 27th*, 85.

Chapter 13

1. Vedder Ledger; *F.A.R.*, 52; Frank J. Mattimore, diary, 1862, NYSMM; Hough (NYSL); *OR*, ser. 1, vol. 12, part 3, 651 and 676.
2. *AG Report*; NARA—Compiled Service Records; *Albany Evening Journal*, September 3, 1862.
3. *AG Report*; NARA—Compiled Service Records.
4. *AG Report*; NARA—Compiled Service Records; *Middletown Mercury*, August 22, 1862; *The Whig Press*, September 3, 1862; Mooney, Letter, August 22, 1862, Jeff Sauter Collection.
5. *AG Report*; *The Whig Press*, September 3, 1862.
6. *AG Report*; NARA—*1860 U.S. Census, Population Schedule*, Auburn Ward 4, Cayuga County, NY, for Oliver P. Fortner, roll M653_727, 247; NYSA—*Executive Pardons, 1856–1931*, ser. B0042, July 10, 1862, for Oliver P. Fortner; NYSA—*Registers of Commitments to Prisons, 1842–1908*, ser. A0603, vol. 2, Pre-1875, Auburn Prison, for Oliver P. Fortner.
7. *Evening Star and Times*, September 10, 1862.
8. NARA—Compiled Service Records; NYSA—*Civil War Muster Roll Abstract*, 18th Infantry, Box #76, Henry Wilbur and 128th Infantry, Box #526, Henry D. Wilbur.
9. *OR*, ser. 1, vol. 19, part 1, 24; Cooling, *Counter-Thrust*, 108.
10. Truax diary; Mattimore diary; *F.A.R.*, 52; Hough (NYSL); *OR*, ser. 1, vol. 11, part 1, 97.
11. *OR*, ser. 1, vol. 11, part 1, 97–98 and vol. 12, part 3, 710 and 740.
12. Cooling, *Counter-Thrust*, 121–123; *OR*, ser. 1, vol. 12, part 3, 710.
13. Truax diary; Mattimore diary; Cooling, *Counter-Thrust*, 140; *F.A.R.*, 53; Hough (NYSL).
14. *AG Report*; NARA—Compiled Service Records.
15. Truax diary; Mattimore diary; *F.A.R.*, 53; Hough (NYSL).
16. *OR*, ser. 1, vol. 19, part 1, 25.
17. Cooling, *Counter-Thrust*, 148 and 150; *The Atlas & Argus*, August 14, 1862; Mattimore diary.
18. Cooling, *Counter-Thrust*, 151; Vedder Ledger; Mattimore diary; Hough (NYSL); *OR*, ser. 1, vol. 19, part 1, 378.
19. Vedder Ledger; *F.A.R.*, 53; *OR*, ser. 1, vol. 19, 378; *Evening Star and Times*, October 13, 1862; Hough (NYSL); George T. Stevens, *Three Years in the Sixth Corps* (Albany, NY: S.R. Gray, 1866), 134–135.
20. *Evening Star and Times*, September 10, 1862. Fort Pennsylvania was renamed in 1863 to Fort Reno.
21. Horatio G. Goodno, Letter, September 10, 1862, Jeff Sauter Collection.
22. Vedder Ledger; Mattimore diary; *F.A.R.*, 53; *OR*, ser. 1, vol. 19, part 1, 38; *OR*, ser. 1, vol. 19, part 1, 378; Ezra A. Carman, *The Maryland Campaign of September 1862*, ed. Joseph Pierro (New York: Routledge Press, 2008), 83–84; Hough (NYSL).
23. NARA—Compiled Service Records; *AG Report*; Truax diary; Mattimore diary; NARA—Pension Records, James Sullivan, alias Peter Van Hoesen. Service Records for Van Hoesen show a possible desertion date of January 18, 1863, from Falmouth, VA.
24. NARA—Court Martial, Alonzo Richardson, February 1863.
25. Truax diary; Mattimore diary; *F.A.R.*, 53; Carman, *The Maryland Campaign*, 86–88.
26. Vedder Ledger; Mattimore diary; *OR*, ser. 1, vol. 19, 378.
27. NARA—Compiled Service Records; *AG Report*; *Middletown Mercury*, October 10, 1862.
28. NARA—Compiled Service Records; *AG Report*; *Daily City Press*, June 26, 1866; Hough (NYSL).
29. NARA—Compiled Service Records; *AG Report*.
30. *Evening Star and Times*, September 23, 1862.
31. Vedder Ledger; Mattimore diary; *OR*, ser. 1, vol. 19, part 1, 378 and 380.
32. *OR*, ser. 1, vol. 19, part 1, 44–46.

Chapter 14

1. *OR*, ser. 1, vol. 19, part 1, 374; *The Whig Press*, October 8, 1862.
2. *OR*, ser. 1, vol. 19, part 1, 46, 374, 380 and 388; *Evening Star and Times*, October 13, 1862.
3. *OR*, ser. 1, vol. 19, part 1, 374–375; *Evening Star and Times*, October 13, 1862; *The Whig Press*, September 24, 1862, and October 8, 1862.
4. Stephen W. Sears, *Landscape Turned Red: The Battle of Antietam* (New Haven, CT: Ticknor and Fields, 1983), 146–147; *OR*, ser. 1, vol. 19, part 1, 826–827.
5. *The National Tribune*, December 19, 1889; *The Whig Press*, October 8, 1862.
6. *OR*, ser. 1, vol. 19, part 1, 375; Pinto, *History of the 32nd Regiment*, 97.
7. *The Whig Press*, September 24, 1862, and October 8, 1862.
8. *OR*, ser. 1, vol. 19, part 1, 375; *The Whig Press*, October 8, 1862.
9. *OR*, ser. 1, vol. 19, part 1, 380 and 397.
10. Ibid., 380 and 388–389; *The Whig Press*, September 24, 1862, and October 8, 1862.
11. *OR*, ser. 1, vol. 19, part 1, 380; Timothy J. Reese, *Sealed with Their Lives: The Battle for Crampton's Gap, Burkittsville, Maryland, September 14, 1862* (Baltimore: Butternut and Blue, 1998), 75.
12. *OR*, ser. 1, vol. 19, part 1, 375, 389 and 397; *St. Lawrence Republican*, September 23, 1862; *the Whig Press*, October 8, 1862.
13. NYSA—*Town Clerks' Registers*, Vincent H. Clark.
14. *Evening Star and Times*, December 1, 1862; Hough (NYSL).
15. NARA—Compiled Service Records.

16. *The Whig Press*, October 8, 1862.
17. *Ibid.*; *OR*, ser. 1, vol. 19, part 1, 390, 396 and 398.
18. *OR*, ser. 1, vol. 19, part 1, 390; *Evening Star and Times*, September 23, 1862, and October 13, 1862; Reese, *Sealed with Their Lives*, 87; *AG Report*; NARA—Compiled Service Records; NARA—Pension Records, Francis Noonan, minor Mary Ann Noonan.
19. *OR*, ser. 1, vol. 19, part 1, 389.
20. *Ibid.*, 389–390, 396 and 398; *Evening Star and Times*, October 13, 1862.
21. *OR*, ser. 1, vol. 19, part 1, 382–383 and 389; Reese, *Sealed with Their Lives*, 128–129.
22. *OR*, ser. 1, vol. 19, part 1, 398; NARA—Compiled Service Records.
23. *OR*, ser. 1, vol. 19, part 1, 375 and 398; Reese, *Sealed with Their Lives*, 143 and 145; *The Whig Press*, October 8, 1862; Yates, *Schenectady County, New York*, 92; *Evening Start and Times*, September 23, 1862; NARA—Compiled Service Records; NYSA—*Town Clerks' Registers*, Abram Blaisdell; WLC; Clark, *The Heroes of Albany*, 843; *AG Report*; NARA—Pension Records, William J. Storms, Edward Fogerty, George Martin and Abraham Blaisdell.
24. NARA—Compiled Service Records; WLC; Clark, *The Heroes of Albany*, 843; *Albany Evening Journal*, May 19, 1894. Robert Bullent served in the 32nd NY Infantry and survived the war.
25. *OR*, ser. 1, vol. 19, part 1, 398; *AG Report*; *Evening Star and Times*, September 20, 1862, September 23, 1862, September 27, 1862, and October 11, 1862; *The Atlas & Argus*, September 26, 1862; *Democrat & Reflector*, September 20, 1862.
26. *Evening Star and Times*, October 13, 1862.
27. *OR*, Series 1, Vol. 19, Part 1, p. 398; *The Daily Evening Star*, March 17, 1866, October 18, 1866, October 20, 1866; *AG Report*; NARA—Compiled Service Records; NARA—Pension Records, Daniel Daily.
28. Clark, *The Heroes of Albany*, 766–767.
29. *OR*, ser. 1, vol. 19, part 1, 398; *AG Report*; NARA—Compiled Service Records; NARA—Pension Records, William H. Ellis, Jr.; Whittemore, Letter, September 16, 1862, Marguerite (Whittemore) Griffith, descendent of Nathaniel G. Whittemore, family possession.
30. *OR*, ser. 1, vol. 19, part 1, 380–381 and 389; *The Whig Press*, October 8, 1862.
31. *OR*, ser. 1, vol. 19, part 1, 375, 380–381 and 826–827; *The Whig Press*, October 8, 1862.
32. *The Whig Press*, October 8, 1862.
33. *The National Tribune*, December 19, 1889.
34. *The Whig Press*, September 24, 1862, and October 8, 1862.
35. *OR*, ser. 1, vol. 19, part 1, 396–398; *St. Lawrence Republican*, September 23, 1862; *The Whig Press*, September 24, 1862; *Evening Star and Times*, September 26, 1862, and October 13, 1862; *AG Report*.
36. *OR*, ser. 1, vol. 19, part 1, 394, 398; *The Whig Press*, September 24, 1862, and October 8, 1862; Clark, *The Heroes of Albany*, 527.
37. *St. Lawrence Republican*, September 23, 1862.
38. *AG Report*; NARA—Compiled Service Records; NYSA—*Civil War Muster Roll Abstracts*, 18th Infantry, Box #76, Richard Hennessy.
39. *AG Report*; NARA—Compiled Service Records; *Evening Star and Times*, September 23, 1862.
40. *AG Report*: NARA—Compiled Service Records; *Evening Star and Times*, September 20, 1862, and September 24, 1862; *Fishkill Journal*, June 26, 1862; Fairview Cemetery, Beacon, NY, William H. White plot; NYSA—*Town Clerks' Registers*, William Henry White; *Ontario Republican Times*, October 8, 1862; *The Whig Press*, October 8, 1862; NARA—Pension Records, Thomas J. Ketcham; *Daily City Press*, June 29, 1866; Terry Reimer, *One Vast Hospital: The Civil War Hospital Sites in Frederick, Maryland After Antietam: With Detailed Hospital Patient List* (Frederick, MD: The National Museum of Civil War Medicine, 2001), unpaged hospital patient list; *OR*, ser. 1, vol. 19, part 1, 827.
41. NARA—Pension Records, Alexander Abercrombie.
42. *The Whig Press*, September 24, 1862; Reese, *Sealed with Their Lives*, 297–304.
43. *OR*, ser. 1, vol. 19, 381.
44. Curtis, *From Bull Run to Chancellorsville*, 172–174.
45. *Ibid.*, 174; F.A.R., 55; *St. Lawrence Republican*, September 23, 1862.
46. *Evening Star and Times*, September 26, 1862; *Middletown Mercury*, October 10, 1862; NARA—Pension Records, Peter M. Fullerton, widow Katharine A. Fullerton.
47. *Evening Star and Times*, September 26, 1862, and October 13, 1862; *The Whig Press*, October 8, 1862; Mattimore diary; *The Medical and Surgical History*, vol. 11, 227, 308 and vol. 12, 508.
48. *AG Report*; NARA—Compiled Service Records; WLC; *Ontario Republican Times*, October 8, 1862; *The Medical and Surgical History*, vol. 12, 508; NARA—Pension Records, Allen Goodrich and Isaac DeBaum, widow Rachel DeBaum; Hough (NYSL).
49. *AG Report*; NARA—Compiled Service Records; NARA—Pension Records, Francis Noonan, minor Mary Ann Noonan. Originally buried in Frederick, Maryland, Noonan was eventually removed and interred at the Antietam National Cemetery, in Sharpsburg, MD, in Grave 175, and incorrectly identified as "Newman" instead of Noonan.
50. *Evening Star and Times*, October 13, 1862.
51. *OR*, ser. 1, vol. 19, part 1, 391, 394–395 and 398; Reese, *Sealed with Their Lives*, 167.
52. *OR*, ser. 1, vol. 19, part 1, 389; *The Whig Press*, October 8, 1862.

Chapter 15

1. *The Whig Press*, September 24, 1862; Whittemore, Letter, September 16, 1862.
2. Isaac O. Best, *History of the 121st New York State Infantry* (Chicago: J.H. Smith, 1921), 21; NARA—Pension Records, George Martin.
3. Clark, *The Heroes of Albany*, 767.
4. Hawley, Letter, July 14, 1862; NARA—Pension Records, Edward B. Hawley, minors Elizabeth Hawley and Lewis Marcus Hawley.
5. Vedder Ledger; *Evening Star and Times*, September 25, 1862, and September 27, 1862; Hough (NYSL); *Schenectady Weekly Republican*, October 3, 1862.
6. *The Whig Press*, October 8, 1862; Best, *History of the 121st New York*, 21–22; Hough (NYSL).
7. *OR*, ser. 1, vol. 19, part 1, 47.
8. Sears, *Landscape Turned Red*, 153.

9. Ibid.; *AG Report*; NARA—Compiled Service Records; NARA—Pension Records, Hiram R. Richmond, widow Catharine Richmond.
10. *The Whig Press*, October 8, 1862; *OR*, ser. 1, vol. 19, part 1, 47.
11. *F.A.R.*, 55; *The Whig Press*, October 8, 1862; *OR*, ser. 1, vol. 19, part 1, 376.
12. Sears, *Landscape Turned Red*, 186.
13. *F.A.R.*, 55; *The Whig Press*, October 8, 1862.
14. Sears, *Landscape Turned Red*, 256–257; *OR*, ser. 1, vol. 19, part 1, 134 and 377.
15. *The Whig Press*, October 8, 1862.
16. Ibid.; *F.A.R.*, 55; *Evening Star and Times*, September 30, 1862; *OR*, ser. 1, vol. 19, part 1, 402.
17. *F.A.R.*, 55; Sears, *Landscape Turned Red*, 180–181.
18. *F.A.R.*, 55; *Evening Star and Times*, September 30, 1862; *The Whig Press*, October 8, 1862; Pierre C. Soule papers, D.136, Box 1, *Lincoln's Dream: Foreboding His Assassination*, 3, River Campus Libraries, University of Rochester, Rochester, NY.
19. Sears, *Landscape Turned Red*, 271–273; Snell, *from First to Last*, 194–195; *OR*, ser. 1, vol. 19, part 1, 377.
20. *Evening Star and Times*, September 30, 1862; *Middletown Mercury*, October 10, 1862; *The Whig Press*, October 8, 1862.
21. *F.A.R.*, 55; *Evening Star and Times*, September 30, 1862; *The Whig Press*, October 8, 1862; *OR*, ser. 1, vol. 19, part 1, 195, 377 and 382.
22. NARA—Pension Records, Walter Weatherwax.
23. *F.A.R.*, 55; *AG Report*; NARA—Compiled Service Records; *Evening Star and Times*, September 30, 1862; Hough (NYSL); *OR*, ser. 1, vol. 19, part 1, 195.
24. *Evening Star and Times*, September 30, 1862; *The Whig Press*, October 8, 1862; Soule, *Lincoln's Dream*, 3.
25. *OR*, ser. 1, vol. 19, part 1, 200; Sears, *Landscape Turned Red*, 296.
26. Soule, *Lincoln's Dream*, 4–5; Gideon T. Ridlon, *A Contribution to the History, Biography and Genealogy of the Families Named Sole, Solly, Soule, Sowle, Soulis* (Lewiston, ME: Journal Press, 1926), vol. 2, 707.
27. Soule, *Lincoln's Dream*, 5; *Evening Star and Times*, September 30, 1862.
28. *The Whig Press*, October 8, 1862.
29. *Evening Star and Times*, September 30, 1862; Vedder Ledger.
30. *The Whig Press*, October 8, 1862.
31. Soule, *Lincoln's Dream*, 6.
32. *Evening Star and Times*, September 30, 1862; Vedder Ledger; *F.A.R.*, 55; *The Whig Press*, October 8, 1862; *OR*, ser. 1, vol. 19, part 1, 378; Hough (NYSL).
33. *Evening Star and Times*, September 30, 1862; Vedder Ledger; *F.A.R.*, 55–56; Hough (NYSL).
34. *F.A.R.*, 56; Stevens, *Three Years in the Sixth Corps*, 156.
35. Sears, *Landscape Turned Red*, 324; Vedder Ledger.
36. Sears, *Landscape Turned Red*, 324; Vedder Ledger; Hough (NYSL); Stevens, *Three Years in the Sixth Corps*, 156.
37. Charles E. Slocum, *The Life and Services of Major-General Henry Warner Slocum* (Toledo, OH: Arthur H. Clark, 1928), 54.
38. *AG Report*; NARA—Compiled Service Records; Tioga Point Cemetery, Athens, Pa., John L. Brundage plot; NYSA—*Town Clerks' Registers*, Hezekiah W. Hoyt and Isaac Hoyt.

39. *AG Report*; NARA—Compiled Service Records; *Ogdensburg Advance*, February 14, 1862; *St. Lawrence Republican*, October 14, 1862.
40. *AG Report*; NARA—Compiled Service Records.
41. Truax diary.
42. Ibid.
43. Vedder Ledger; Hough (NYSL); Stevens, *Three Years in the Sixth Corps*, 158.
44. Vedder Ledger; Mattimore diary; Hough (NYSL).
45. *OR*, ser. 1, vol. 19, part 2, 512; Truax diary; Mattimore diary; *F.A.R.*, 56; *AG Report*; Hough (NYSL); Stevens, *Three Years in the Sixth Corps*, 162–163.

Chapter 16

1. Fairchild, *Record of the 27th*, 110; Truax diary.
2. *OR*, ser. 1, vol. 19, part 1, 87.
3. *Ibid.* 86–87; Truax diary; Mattimore diary; *F.A.R.*, 56; Hough (NYSL).
4. Truax diary; Mattimore diary; *F.A.R.* 56; Hough (NYSL); *OR*, ser. 1, vol. 19, part 1, 88.
5. Truax diary.
6. Ibid.; Mattimore diary; *F.A.R.* 56.
7. Truax diary; Mattimore diary; Curtis, *From Bull Run to Chancellorsville*, 215.
8. Truax diary; Mattimore diary; *F.A.R.*, 56; *Evening Star and Times*, November 24, 1862; Francis Augustín O'Reilly, *The Fredericksburg Campaign: Winter War on the Rappahannock* (Baton Rouge: Louisiana State University Press, 2003), 17–18.
9. O'Reilly, *The Fredericksburg Campaign*, 24.
10. *OR*, ser. 1, vol. 21, 59–60; Heitman, *Historical Register and Dictionary of the United States Army 1789–1903*, vol. 1, 904; Snell, *From First to Last*, 57.
11. *OR*, ser. 1, vol. 21, 59–60.
12. Ibid., 59; Heitman, *Historical Register and Dictionary of the United States Army 1789–1903*, vol. 1, 852.
13. *OR*, ser. 1, vol. 19, part 1, 403 and vol. 21, 59; Stevens, *Three Years in the Sixth Corps*, 160.
14. *Middletown Daily Times*, August 31, 1916; *AG Report*.
15. Vedder Ledger; *Evening Star and Times*, November 24, 1862.
16. Vedder Ledger; Mattimore diary; *F.A.R.*, 56; O'Reilly, *The Fredericksburg Campaign*, 27.
17. Truax diary; Mattimore diary.
18. *AG Report*; Columbia University, *Catalogue of Officers and Graduates of Columbia University*, 16th ed., 1916, 336; Society of Colonial Wars in the State of New York, *Year Book for 1920–1921*, no. 29, 124; Terry Reimer, *One Vast Hospital*, 14 and 23.
19. *AG Report*; NARA—Compiled Service Records; Jeffrey, *Richmond Prisons*, 200.
20. *AG Report*; NARA—Compiled Service Records; NARA—Pension Records, William A. Ellison, mother Eliza Ellison and Charles Van Steinburgh, mother Hannah Vansteinburgh; NARA—*Registers of Deaths of Volunteers, Compiled 1861–1865*, Aaron Chapman.
21. *AG Report*; NARA—Compiled Service Records; *Ontario Republican Times*, December 3, 1862.
22. *F.A.R.*, 56; Vedder Ledger; Hough (NYSL).
23. *F.A.R.*, 56; Vedder Ledger; Mattimore diary.
24. Vedder Ledger; Mattimore diary.
25. Vedder Ledger.

26. Truax diary; *AG Report*; NARA—Compiled Service Records; *St. Lawrence Republican*, February 3, 1863; *Evening Star and Times*, December 20, 1862. Bell was originally buried at Fletcher's Chapel, but was later removed for final interment into the Fredericksburg and Spotsylvania National Military Park, Fredericksburg, VA, Grave 4756.
27. Truax diary.
28. *OR*, ser. 1, vol. 21, 87–88.
29. Ibid., 448 and 523; Truax diary; Mattimore diary; O'Reilly, *The Fredericksburg Campaign*, 73 and 76; NARA—Court Martial, John Baker, March 1863.
30. *OR*, ser. 1, vol. 21, 88–89, 449, 523, 526 and 536; Truax diary; O'Reilly, *The Fredericksburg Campaign*, 99–100.
31. *OR*, ser. 1, vol. 21, 523 and 526–527; *F.A.R.*, 56; Truax diary.
32. Hough (NYSL).
33. *OR*, ser. 1, vol. 21, 523.
34. NARA—Pension Records, Malcolm E. Colby.
35. *F.A.R.*, 56; Truax diary.
36. *OR*, ser. 1, vol. 21, 89.
37. Ibid., 527–528; Hough (NYSL).
38. NARA—Compiled Service Records; NARA—Court Martial, William H. McIntosh, John McNeal, John Schultz [Shultz], February 1863.
39. *OR*, ser. 1, vol. 21, 91–93; Snell, *From First to Last*, 228.
40. *OR*, ser. 1, vol. 21, 526–528.
41. *AG Report*; NARA—Compiled Service Records; NARA—Pension Records, John Hunter and Jacob Sheil, widow Mary K. Sheil.
42. Vedder Ledger; NARA—Compiled Service Records.
43. Jones, *What a Boy Saw*.
44. *F.A.R.*, 57; Truax diary; Vedder Ledger; Mattimore diary; Hough (NYSL).
45. *F.A.R.*, 57; Vedder Ledger; NARA—Compiled Service Records. Fritz was originally buried in Bray's farm in Stafford County, VA, but was later removed for final interment into the Fredericksburg and Spotsylvania National Military Park, Fredericksburg, VA, Grave 5795.
46. Vedder Ledger; *AG Report*; Mattimore diary; *St. Lawrence Republican*, February 3, 1863.
47. Truax diary; Mattimore diary.

Chapter 17

1. Truax diary; *St. Lawrence Republican*, February 3, 1863; Chapman diary.
2. Chapman diary.
3. Ibid.
4. Ibid.; *AG Report*; *The Rockford Daily Register-Gazette*, June 13, 1898.
5. Chapman diary.
6. Vedder Ledger; Hough (NYSL).
7. O'Reilly, *The Fredericksburg Campaign*, 473–475.
8. NARA—Court Martial, Thomas E. Atkinson, Wilhelmus L. Bink, Patrick Conway, William A. Cooley, Samuel LaRue, Andrew Meyers, Frank Mooney, Joseph Payne, John Scully, William H. Stanton, Francis Underhill, February 1863.
9. Fairchild, *History of the 27th*, 134; *F.A.R.*, 57; O'Reilly, *The Fredericksburg Campaign*, 476.
10. NARA—Court Martial, Alexander [Alphonso] Green, Jeremiah Mayher, Dennis McKinney, Barney M. Vedder, February 1863.
11. *F.A.R.*, 57; Truax diary; Vedder Ledger; Hough (NYSL); Fairchild, *History of the 27th*, 134–135; *OR*, ser. 1, vol. 21, 69.
12. *F.A.R.*, 57; Truax diary; Hough (NYSL); Fairchild, *History of the 27th*, 135; *OR*, ser. 1, vol. 21, 69 and 752.
13. *F.A.R.*, 57; Truax diary; Hough (NYSL); NARA—Pension Records, William Elliott.
14. O'Reilly, *The Fredericksburg Campaign*, 480–481.
15. Ibid., 483; *OR*, ser. 1, vol. 21, 69.
16. NARA—Court Martial, Alonzo Richardson, February 1863.
17. O'Reilly, *The Fredericksburg Campaign*, 478 and 488; *F.A.R.*, 57; Truax diary; Hough (NYSL).
18. NARA—Court Martial, Thomas E. Atkinson, Wilhelmus L. Bink, Patrick Conway, William A. Cooley, Alexander [Alphonso] Green, Samuel LaRue, Jeremiah Mayher, Dennis McKinney, Andrew Meyers, Frank Mooney, Joseph Payne, John Scully, William H. Stanton, Francis Underhill, Barney M. Vedder, February 1863.
19. Truax diary.
20. O'Reilly, *The Fredericksburg Campaign*, 489–491; *OR*, ser. 1, vol. 21, 1004–1005; Snell, *From First to Last*, 251.
21. Stevens, *Three Years in the Sixth Corps*, 178–179; Heitman, *Historical Register and Dictionary of the United States Army 1789–1903*, vol. 1, 540.
22. Stevens, *Three Years in the Sixth Corps*, 179.
23. Snell, *From First to Last*, 252; Heitman, *Historical Register and Dictionary of the United States Army 1789–1903*, vol. 1, 872; Sears, *Landscape Turned Red*, 222 and 227; Sears, *Chancellorsville* (New York: Houghton Mifflin, 1996), 66.
24. Samuel P. Bates, *History of the Pennsylvania Volunteers, 1861–65* (Harrisburg: B. Singerly, State Printer, 1869–1871), vol. 1, 1236 and 1238–1239 and vol. 4, 1–2; Robert S. Westbrook, *History of the 49th Pennsylvania Volunteers* (Altoona, PA: Altoona Times Print, 1898), 137.
25. Sears, *Chancellorsville*, 72; Fairchild, *History of the 27th*, 140–141.
26. Sears, *Chancellorsville*, 73; Jones, *What a Boy Saw*.
27. Stevens, *Three Years in the Sixth Corps*, 179; Jones, *What a Boy Saw*.
28. Truax diary; NARA—Pension Records, Catharine Mattimore, mother of Frank J. Mattimore.
29. Vedder Ledger; *St. Lawrence Republican*, February 3, 1863; Gregoire Insse, Letter, March 5, 1863, *Telesphor Insse Papers*, Special Collections Research Center, Syracuse University Library, Syracuse University, Syracuse, NY.
30. Vedder Ledger.
31. Ibid.; NARA—Pension Records, Catharine Mattimore, mother of Frank J. Mattimore.
32. Insse, Letter, March 5, 1863.
33. *OR*, ser. 1, vol. 25, part 2, 77–78; *AG Report*; Sears, *Chancellorsville*, 70.
34. Sears, *Chancellorsville*, 70.
35. Ibid.; *OR*, ser. 1, vol. 25, part 2, 52; *AG Report*; NARA—Compiled Service Records; NARA—Court Martial, John Allen, February 1863.
36. NARA—Court Martial, Thomas E. Atkinson,

Wilhelmus L. Bink, Patrick Conway, William A. Cooley, Alexander [Alphonso] Green, Samuel LaRue, Jeremiah Mayher, Dennis McKinney, Andrew Meyers, Frank Mooney, Joseph Payne, John Scully, William H. Stanton, Francis Underhill, Barney M. Vedder, February 1863.

37. NARA—Court Martial, John Baker, March 1863.
38. Ibid.; *OR*, ser. 1, vol. 25, part 2, 70; Sears, *Chancellorsville*, 70; *AG Report*.
39. *OR*, ser. 1, vol. 25, part 2, 11.
40. Vedder Ledger; Pinto, *History of the 32nd Regiment*, 130; Blake Letters, March 16, 1863 (LLMVC); Gregoire Insse, Letter, March 21, 1863, *Telesphor Insse Papers*, Special Collections Research Center, Syracuse University Library, Syracuse University, Syracuse, NY.
41. Vedder Ledger; *F.A.R.*, 57; Westbrook, *History of the 49th Pennsylvania Volunteers*, 142.
42. Noah Brooks, "Glimpses of Lincoln in War Time," *The Century Magazine*, November 1894, 457–458; Sears, *Chancellorsville*, 115; Robert G. Carter, *Four Brothers in Blue* (Washington, D.C.: Press of Gibson Bros., 1913), 367–368; *F.A.R.*, 57; Westbrook, *History of the 49th Pennsylvania Volunteers*, 142.
43. Truax diary; Blake Letters, April 10, 1863 (LLMVC); Sears, *Chancellorsville*, 103.
44. John Sedgwick, *Correspondence of John Sedgwick, Major General* (New York: Carl Stoeckel, 1903), vol. 2, 91, letter dated April 20, 1863.
45. Insse, Letter, March 5, 1863.
46. Truax diary; Blake Letters, April 9, 1863 (LLMVC).
47. Blake Letters, April 10, 1863 (LLMVC).
48. *AG Report*; NARA—Compiled Service Records.
49. *AG Report*; NARA—Compiled Service Records.
50. *AG Report*; NARA—Compiled Service Records; NARA—Pension Records, Malcolm E. Colby; Truax diary.
51. *AG Report*; NARA—Compiled Service Records.
52. *AG Report*; NARA—Compiled Service Records.
53. *AG Report*; NARA—Compiled Service Records; NARA—Pension Records, Catharine Mattimore, mother of Frank J. Mattimore; Amasa J. Parker, *Landmarks of Albany County, New York* (Syracuse, NY: D. Mason & Co., 1897), part I, 180.
54. NARA—Compiled Service Records; WLC.
55. NARA—Compiled Service Records.
56. Ibid.; NARA—Court Martial, Francis Underhill, February 1863; Nathaniel B. Sylvester, *History of Saratoga County, New York* (Philadelphia: Everts and Ensign, 1878), 323.
57. Blake Letters, April 10, 1863 (LLMVC).
58. Truax diary; *F.A.R.*, 57.
59. Truax diary; *F.A.R.*, 57; Westbrook, *History of the 49th Pennsylvania Volunteers*, 142.
60. Vedder Ledger; *AG Report*; NARA—Court Martial, John Baker, March 1863.

Chapter 18

1. Vedder Ledger; *F.A.R.*, 57; George N. Galloway, *The Ninety-Fifth Pennsylvania Volunteers (Gosline's Pennsylvania Zouaves), in the Sixth Corps* (Philadelphia: Collins, 1884), 47–48 and 51; Hough (NYSL).
2. Sears, *Chancellorsville*, 140–141 and 154.
3. Galloway, *The Ninety-Fifth Pennsylvania*, 51; Westbrook, *History of the 49th Pennsylvania Volunteers*, 143.
4. *AG Report*; NARA—Compiled Service Records; NYSA—*Town Clerks' Registers*, Vincent H. Clark and Sanford S. Clauson; *Daily City Press*, June 26, 1866.
5. Galloway, *The Ninety-Fifth Pennsylvania*, 51; Fairchild, *History of the 27th*, 156.
6. Galloway, *The Ninety-Fifth Pennsylvania*, 51; Westbrook, *History of the 49th Pennsylvania Volunteers*, 143; *OR*, ser. 1, vol. 25, part 1, 591.
7. Galloway, *The Ninety-Fifth Pennsylvania*, 51–52; *F.A.R.*, 57.
8. Galloway, *The Ninety-Fifth Pennsylvania*, 52; *OR*, ser. 1, vol. 25, part 1, 591; Hough (NYSL); Sedgwick, *Correspondence of John Sedgwick*, vol. 2, 113, letter dated May 13, 1863.
9. Galloway, *The Ninety-Fifth Pennsylvania*, 53; *OR*, ser. 1, vol. 25, part 1, 591; Sears, *Chancellorsville*, 155.
10. Galloway, *The Ninety-Fifth Pennsylvania*, 52–53; *OR*, ser. 1, vol. 25, part 1, 591.
11. *OR*, ser. 1, vol. 25, part 1, 591; Philip W. Parsons, *The Union Sixth Army Corps in the Chancellorsville Campaign* (Jefferson, NC: McFarland, 2006), 23–24.
12. *OR*, ser. 1, vol. 25, part 1, 591; Galloway, *The Ninety-Fifth Pennsylvania*, 52–53; Westbrook, *History of the 49th Pennsylvania Volunteers*, 144.
13. Sears, *Chancellorsville*, 155.
14. Galloway, *The Ninety-Fifth Pennsylvania*, 54; Westbrook, *History of the 49th Pennsylvania Volunteers*, 144.
15. Galloway, *The Ninety-Fifth Pennsylvania*, 54–55; *OR*, ser. 1, vol. 25, part 1, 566 and 591; Westbrook, *History of the 49th Pennsylvania Volunteers*, 144.
16. Galloway, *The Ninety-Fifth Pennsylvania*, 54–55; *OR*, ser. 1, vol. 25, part 1, 172 and 591; Sears, *Chancellorsville*, 155; *F.A.R.*, 58; Hough (NYSL).
17. *Daily City Press*, June 29, 1866; *F.A.R.*, 58; Hough (NYSL).
18. *OR*, ser. 1, vol. 25, part 1, 566; *F.A.R.*, 58; Parsons, *The Union Sixth Army Corps in the Chancellorsville Campaign*, 25.
19. *OR*, ser. 1, vol. 25, part 1, 591; *F.A.R.*, 58; Hough (NYSL).
20. *OR*, ser. 1, vol. 25, part 1, 591; Hough (NYSL).
21. Westbrook, *History of the 49th Pennsylvania Volunteers*, 144; Hough (NYSL).
22. Westbrook, *History of the 49th Pennsylvania Volunteers*, 144; Hough (NYSL).
23. *AG Report*; NARA—Compiled Service Records; *New York Herald*, July 29, 1865; Fearey, *Union College Alumni*, 75–76.
24. Westbrook, *History of the 49th Pennsylvania Volunteers*, 145; Galloway, *The Ninety-Fifth Pennsylvania*, 57–58.
25. Galloway, *The Ninety-Fifth Pennsylvania*, 57–58.
26. Westbrook, *History of the 49th Pennsylvania Volunteers*, 145; Parsons, *The Union Sixth Army Corps in the Chancellorsville Campaign*, 45–47; Vedder Ledger; Hough (NYSL).
27. Galloway, *The Ninety-Fifth Pennsylvania*, 59; *OR*, ser. 1, vol. 25, part 1, 591–592; Parsons, *The Union Sixth Army Corps in the Chancellorsville Campaign*, 49–50; *F.A.R.*, 59; Hough (NYSL).
28. Parsons, *The Union Sixth Army Corps in the Chancellorsville Campaign*, 52; *OR*, ser. 1, vol. 25, part 1, 559.

29. *OR*, ser. 1, vol. 25, part 1, 592.
30. Parsons, *The Union Sixth Army Corps in the Chancellorsville Campaign*, 76 and 80–81.
31. *OR*, ser. 1, vol. 25, part 1, 592.
32. *F.A.R.*, 59; Hough (NYSL); NARA—Compiled Service Records; *Evening Star and Times*, May 18, 1863. Records again around this time were not tracked correctly, mixed with wounds that were probably too light to be documented, but it had to be here when Private James McCarty of Company A was ambiguously listed in his service records as being wounded somewhere within a time that spanned five days of early May, but lacks further detail. His wounding was severe enough to bring him off the line and hospitalized.
33. *OR*, ser. 1, vol. 25, part 1, 592; *F.A.R.*, 59.
34. Parsons, *The Union Sixth Army Corps in the Chancellorsville Campaign*, 90.
35. *Ibid.*, 99–100 and 107; *OR*, ser. 1, vol. 25, part 1, 581.
36. *OR*, ser. 1, vol. 25, part 1, 568; *F.A.R.*, 59; Camille Baquet, *History of the First Brigade, New Jersey Volunteers, from 1861 to 1865* (Trenton, NJ: MacCrellish and Quigley, state printers, 1910), 248.
37. Galloway, *The Ninety-Fifth Pennsylvania*, 68; Westbrook, *History of the 49th Pennsylvania Volunteers*, 145; Bates, *History of the Pennsylvania Volunteers, 1861–65*, vol. 4, 2; Parsons, *The Union Sixth Army Corps in the Chancellorsville Campaign*, 100 and 108–109.
38. *OR*, ser. 1, vol. 25, part 1, 568 and 592; *F.A.R.*, 59.
39. *OR*, ser. 1, vol. 25, part 1, 568 and 592.
40. *Ibid.*; *F.A.R.*, 59.
41. *OR*, ser. 1, vol. 25, part 1, 568 and 592; *F.A.R.*, 59.
42. Sears, *Chancellorsville*, 424–425; *AG Report*; NARA—Compiled Service Records.
43. Sears, *Chancellorsville*, 425; *OR*, ser. 1, vol. 25, part 1, 592; *F.A.R.*, 59; Vedder Ledger.
44. *F.A.R.*, 59.
45. *Ibid.*; *OR*, ser. 1, vol. 25, part 1, 592; Vedder Ledger.
46. Curtis, *From Bull Run to Chancellorsville*, 367–369.
47. Best, *History of the 121st New York*, 76–77; *F.A.R.*, 60.
48. *AG Report*; Best, *History of the 121st New York*, 76.
49. Curtis, *From Bull Run to Chancellorsville*, 307; *F.A.R.*, 60.
50. *F.A.R.*, 60.
51. *Ibid.*; Hough (NYSL).
52. *F.A.R.*, 60; Hough (NYSL); Newspaper account from the files of the NYSMM, untitled and undated; *The New York Times*, May 16, 1863; Samuel B. Fales, *Union Volunteer Refreshment Saloon Papers*, Collection 1580, Boxes 11–12 and Collection 2074, Box 1, Historical Society of Pennsylvania, Philadelphia. The souvenir square of the flag is within the same Fales records, collection 2074.
53. *AG Report*; NARA—Compiled Service Records; NARA—Pension Records, John J. Icklin.
54. *AG Report*; NARA—Compiled Service Records; NARA—*Registers of Deaths of Volunteers, Compiled 1861–1865*, John O'Hara.
55. *The Atlas & Argus*, May 18, 1863; *Evening Star and Times*, May 18, 1863; *Albany Evening Journal*, May 16, 1863.
56. *The Atlas & Argus*, May 18, 1863; *Evening Star and Times*, May 18, 1863; *The Whig Press*, May 27, 1863; *AG Report*; Hough (NYSL); *Albany Evening Journal*, May 16, 1863; *The National Tribune*, July 27, 1893; Ogdensburg Cemetery, Ogdensburg, NY, Myers plot; NARA—Pension Records, Thomas Kearns.
57. *The Atlas & Argus*, May 18, 1863; *Evening Star and Times*, May 18, 1863; *The Whig Press*, May 27, 1863; *St. Lawrence Republican*, May 19, 1863; *Albany Evening Journal*, May 16, 1863.
58. *The Atlas & Argus*, May 18, 1863; *The Whig Press*, May 27, 1863.
59. *The Atlas & Argus*, May 18, 1863. The national flag from the 18th New York stood in the Capitol's rotunda for decades, along with countless other regimental flags for about 150 years. Preservation efforts required their public display moved for restoration purposes. As of 2016, the flag still remains furled on its staff, awaiting conservation.
60. Hough (NYSL); *The Whig Press*, May 27, 1863; *Evening Star and Times*, May 18, 1863; *The Atlas & Argus*, May 18, 1861; Newspaper account from the files of the NYSMM, untitled and undated.
61. *Evening Star and Times*, May 16, 1863, May 18, 1863, and May 21, 1863; *Democrat & Reflector*, May 21, 1863; Vedder Ledger.
62. *Evening Star and Times*, May 18, 1863; *Democrat & Reflector*, May 21, 1863; Vedder Ledger.
63. *AG Report*; *The Atlas & Argus*, May 18, 1863, and May 23, 1863; *Albany Evening Journal*, May 23, 1863.
64. Vedder Ledger; *The Atlas & Argus*, May 20, 1863; *Evening Star and Times*, May 21, 1863.
65. *Ontario Republican Times*, May 20, 1863.
66. *The Atlas & Argus*, May 26, 1863.
67. *Troy Daily Times*, May 21, 1863; *Albany Evening Journal*, May 23, 1863.
68. *The Atlas & Argus*, May 26, 1863; WLC; Newspaper account from the files of the NYSMM, untitled and undated.
69. *AG Report*; NARA—Compiled Service Records.
70. *AG Report*; NARA—Compiled Service Records.
71. *AG Report*; NARA—Compiled Service Records; *Evening Star and Times*, May 18, 1863.
72. *AG Report*; NARA—Compiled Service Records.
73. *AG Report*; NARA—Compiled Service Records.
74. *AG Report*; NARA—Compiled Service Records; *The Atlas & Argus*, May 18, 1863; *Evening Star and Times*, May 18, 1863.
75. *The Atlas & Argus*, May 28, 1863.
76. *The Atlas & Argus*, June 1, 1863; *Evening Star and Times*, June 2, 1863; NARA—Pension Records, Calvin B. Potter, widow Julia A. Potter.
77. *The Atlas & Argus*, June 1, 1863; *Evening Star and Times*, June 2, 1863; *Ontario Republican Times*, June 3, 1863, and June 10, 1863.
78. *The Atlas & Argus*, May 26, 1863, and June 1, 1863; *Evening Star and Times*, June 2, 1863.
79. *The Whig Press*, June 10, 1863.
80. *Ibid.*; *Middletown Daily Press*, April 14, 1881, and April 22, 1881. The flag of the Wallkill Guards is still in possession of the city, and can be viewed at the Historical Society of Middletown and Wallkill Precinct, in Middletown, NY.
81. *The Whig Press*, June 10, 1863.
82. *Fishkill Journal*, May 28, 1863, and June 11, 1863; Newspaper account from the files of the NYSMM, untitled and undated.

Epilogue

1. *AG Report*; Best, *History of the 121st New York*, 76–77.
2. Best, *History of the 121st New York*, 76–77 and 88–89; *AG Report*; NARA—Court Martial, Charles Van Husen, December 4, 1863.
3. *AG Report*.
4. *OR*, ser. 1, vol. 36, part 1, 665–668; Phisterer, *New York in the War of the Rebellion: 1861 to 1865*, vol. 4, 3,424.
5. Best, *History of the 121st New York*, 127; Phisterer, *New York in the War of the Rebellion: 1861 to 1865*, vol. 4, 3, 424; *AG Report*; NARA—Pension Records, Stephen Walker, widow Mary Walker; *National Tribune*, May 26, 1887.
6. *AG Report*; NARA—Pension Records, Robert Bradshaw; NYSA—*Civil War Muster Roll Abstract*, 121st Infantry, Box #502, Robert Bradshaw; NARA—*Selected Records of the War Department Commissary General of Prisoners Relating to Federal Prisoners of War Confined at Andersonville, GA, 1864–65*, Record Group 249, Microfilm Roll M1303_1, Robert Bradshaw.
7. Best, *History of the 121st New York*, 162 and 181; Phisterer, *New York in the War of the Rebellion: 1861 to 1865*, vol. 4, 3, 424.
8. Best, *History of the 121st New York*, 192–199; *AG Report*.
9. NARA—Pension Records, Charles R. Arnold, widow Hattie Arnold.
10. Best, *History of the 121st New York*, 203, 208–211; Phisterer, *New York in the War of the Rebellion: 1861 to 1865*, vol. 4, 3, 424; *AG Report*.
11. Best, *History of the 121st New York*, 214–216; *AG Report*.
12. *AG Report*; NYSA—*Civil War Muster Roll Abstract*, 18th Infantry, Box #76, Jacob Heitz; NARA—*Registers of Deaths of Volunteers, Compiled 1861–1865*, Jacob Heintz and Reuben Miller; NARA—Pension Records, Jacob Heintz, minors Frederick and William Heintz.
13. *AG Report*.
14. NYSA—*Civil War Muster Roll Abstract*, 13th Cavalry, Box #873, August Rixman.
15. *The Chatham Courier*, June 6, 1889; New York State Adjutant General's Office, *Annual Report of the Adjutant General of the State of New York for the Year 1897, Registers of the Seventh Artillery and Eighth Artillery in the War of the Rebellion* (Albany, NY: Wynkoop Hallenbreck Crawford Co., 1898), 1–407.
16. Clark, *The Heroes of Albany*, 529–538.
17. *AG Report*. These calculations come from the author's research through Adjutant General Reports for over 160 different regiments that 18th veterans served in.
18. *Albany Evening Journal*, November 30, 1863; *Evening Star and Times*, December 1, 1863; New York State Adjutant General's Office, *Annual Report of the Adjutant General of the State of New York for the Year 1894, Registers of the Eighty-Eight, Eighty-Ninth, Ninetieth, Ninety-First, Ninety-Second, and Ninety-Third Regiments of Infantry* (Albany, NY: J.B. Lyon, 1902), 1088; NARA—Pension Records, Richard A. Burn, widow Jane E. Burn.
19. NARA—Pension Records, James Sullivan, alias Peter Van Hoesen; NARA—Compiled Service Records, which also show a possible desertion from regiment as January 18, 1863, from Falmouth, VA; Coeymans Hollow Cemetery, Coeymans Hollow, NY, Van Hoesen plot; Committee on Veterans' Affairs United States Senate, *Medal of Honor Recipients: 1863–1978: In the Name of the Congress of the United States* (Washington: U.S. Govt. Printing, 1979), 230.
20. *AG Report*; New York State Adjutant General's Office, *Annual Report of the Adjutant General of the State of New York for the Year 1894, Registers of the 20th, 21st, 22d, 23d, 24th, 25th and 26th Regiments of Cavalry, New York Volunteers in War of the Rebellion* (Albany, NY: J.B. Lyon, 1895), 471–720; *OR*, ser. 1, vol. 46, part 1, 509; NARA—Pension Records, Christopher Bruton; NARA—Compiled Service Records; H.C. Bradsby, *History of Bureau County, Illinois* (Chicago: World Publishing Co., 1885), 468–469; Committee on Veterans' Affairs United States Senate, *Medal of Honor Recipients: 1863–1978*, 44; Saint Patricks Cemetery, in Caledonia, Michigan, Bruton plot.
21. Manning, *Albany Zouave Cadets*, 67–71.
22. Hodgkins, *Autobiography*, 23.
23. *Albany Evening Journal*, July 5, 1865; *The Atlas & Argus*, June 3, 1861.
24. Heitman, *Historical Register and Dictionary of the United States Army 1789–1903*, vol. 1, 854; George A. Otis, *A Report of Surgical Cases Treated in the Army of the United States from 1865–1871* (Washington, D.C.: Government Printing Office, 1871), 51; Albany Rural Cemetery, Menands, NY, John H. Russell and William H. Russell plot.
25. Heitman, *Historical Register and Dictionary of the United States Army 1789–1903*, vol. 1, 1,000; Frances C. Carrington, *My Army Life and the Fort Phil. Kearney Massacre with an Account of the Celebration of "Wyoming Opened"* (Philadelphia and London: J.B. Lippincott, 1910), 74, 79–81 and 132; *San Francisco Bulletin*, August 27, 1887.
26. NARA—Pension Records, Walter Allen and William Allen. He died in Albany on October 26, 1892, at the age of fifty.
27. Heitman, *Historical Register and Dictionary of the United States Army 1789–1903*, vol. 1, 827; *Harvard Graduate's Magazine*, Vol. IX, 1900–1901, 393; NARA—Pension Records, Nathan P. Rice, widow Hattie P. Rice and Milton Thompkins (Tompkins), widow Harriet Thompkins (Tompkins); *Troy Daily Times*, June 7, 1876.
28. Parker, *Landmarks of Albany County, New York*, 180; *AG Report*; Julius F. Miner, *Buffalo Medical and Surgical Journal* (Buffalo, NY: Baker, Jones & Co., 1871), vol. 10, 365–369; *Transactions of the Medical Society of the County of Albany* (Albany: Burdick and Taylor, 1883), vol. 3, 856; *Albany Evening Journal*, April 6, 1871; Albany Rural Cemetery, in Menands, NY, Edmeston plot.
29. Methodist Episcopal Church, *Minutes of the Troy Annual Conferences of the Methodist Episcopal Church, for 1874* (Troy, NY: Brainerd and Brown, 1874), 40–42; *Albany Evening Journal*, November 6, 1874.
30. *AG Report*; Eaton, *Memorial of Colonel William H. Young*, 5–6. Birth and death dates of his children was provided by Brian Cooke, a descendent of Young.
31. *The National Tribune*, July 27, 1893.
32. Eaton, *Memorial of Colonel William H. Young*, 7; *Albany Evening Journal*, November 1, 1876; *Schenectady Daily Union*, November 1, 1876; *Albany Daily Evening Times*, November 1, 1876.

33. Eaton, *Memorial of Colonel William H. Young*, 9–12, 18 and 21; *Albany Evening Journal*, November 4, 1876; *Schenectady Reflector*, November 9, 1876.

34. *The Ogdensburg Advance and St. Lawrence Weekly Democrat*, June 8, 1905, May 14, 1891; *The Daily Journal*, November 7, 1864.

35. NARA—Pension Records, George R. Myers; *St. Lawrence Republican*, June 7, 1905; *The Ogdensburg Advance and St. Lawrence Weekly Democrat*, June 8, 1905, December 29, 1881 and January 5, 1882; *The Daily Journal*, June 6, 1905; Ogdensburg Cemetery, Ogdensburg, NY, Myers Plot.

36. *The Daily Journal*, January 16, 1865; NARA—Pension Records, John C. Meginnis, widow Lizzie S. Meginnis.

37. *Denver Daily Tribune*, September 10, 1878; NARA—Pension Records, John C. Meginnis, widow Lizzie S. Meginnis.

38. *Evening Star & Times*, September 9, 1863, and December 30, 1863; *Schenectady Daily Evening Star and Times*, October 13, 1866; William Henry Seward papers, *General Correspondence*, Letter from William Seward Gridley to William Henry Seward, dated January 20, 1864, and letter from Mrs. William Seward Gridley to William Henry Seward, dated October 21, 1867, River Campus Libraries, University of Rochester, Rochester, NY; *History of Jackson County* (Chicago: Inter-State Publishing, 1881), 637; Rosehill Cemetery, in Chicago, Il, William S. Gridley plot; *Chicago Tribune*, June 30, 1940.

39. *Albany Evening Journal*, April 27, 1888, September 14, 1888, September 15, 1888; *The Schenectady Daily Union*, September 15, 1888.

40. *The Evening Star*, September 16, 1889.

41. *Albany Evening Journal*, September 15, 1890; *The Daily Union*, September 16, 1890.

42. *The Naples Daily Record*, September 9, 1891; *Ontario County Journal*, September 9, 1891; *The Phelps Citizen*, September 17, 1891; *Albany Evening Journal*, August 18, 1899; Albany Rural Cemetery, in Menands, NY, Michael H. Donovan plot.

43. Grand Army of the Republic, *Roster of the Department of New York, Grand Army of the Republic* (Albany, NY: J.B. Lyon, 1915), 4 and 13.

44. *Washington Post*, September 18, 1904.

45. NARA—Pension Records, John W. Farr.

46. *Middletown Daily Times*, February 24, 1894, February 26, 1894 and March 15, 1894.

47. NARA—Pension Records, Julius Becking, widow Mary E. Becking; *Philadelphia Inquirer*, February 23, 1901, December 4, 1901, January 26, 1902, January 27, 1902 and February 4, 1902.

48. NARA—Pension Records, Edward Riley.

49. NARA—Pension Records, Robert Farrell; *Daily Evening Bulletin*, July 25, 1884, and October 12, 1885; *The Evening Bulletin*, May 11, 1896, and November 9, 1896; *Chicago Sunday Tribune*, May 10, 1896.

50. New York, State Board of Charities, *Census of Inmates in Almshouses and Poorhouses*, admission year 1885, Wayne County, NY; Lyons Rural Cemetery, Lyons, NY; *The Ogdensburg Journal*, September 1, 1870, September 26, 1871, February 7, 1872, April 24, 1872, April 19, 1877, April 26, 1881, May 2, 1882, June 24, 1882 and May 21, 1895; *Seattle Post-Intelligencer*, June 4, 1899.

51. *AG Report*; NARA—Pension Records, Henry E. Munger, widow Anne Gilbert Munger; Elodie Pritchartt, Munger family history, descendent of Henry E. Munger; Stranger's Rest Cemetery (Frost Cemetery), Lufkin, Texas, Harry E. Munger mention on marker.

52. *The Arizona Republican*, March 18, 1906, March 20, 1906; Rosedale Cemetery, Phoenix, Arizona, Joseph S. Raines Plot; *The New York Times*, December 16, 1909.

53. Michigan Pioneer and Historical Society, *Historical Collections: Collections and Researches Made by the Michigan Pioneer and Historical Society* (Lansing, Mi.: Robert Smith and Co., 1892) 17, 403; NARA—Pension Records, Calvin B. Potter, widow Julia A. Potter; *Salt Lake Telegram*, August 19, 1902.

54. Hodgkins, *Autobiography*, 19 and 23–25; *Watertown Daily Times*, July 10, 1916; *Ogdensburg Republican Journal*, July 10, 1916.

55. NARA—Pension Records, John B. LaQue; Comrade John B. Laque and his Model T Ford, Souvenir card, author's collection; Library of Congress, Motion Picture, Broadcasting and Recorded Sound Division, *Original Amateur Hour Collection Preservation Tape*, LWO 5799 R26, *Major Bowes Amateur Hour* (NBC), February 16, 1936; *Albany Times Union*, May 3, 1938; *Schenectady Gazette*, August 13, 1929, August 13, 1930, August 13, 1931, August 15, 1935, May 27, 1937, and May 2, 1938.

Bibliography

Primary Sources

Manuscripts and Related Materials

PRIVATE COLLECTIONS

Susanne Armentrout
    Augustus W. Mowatt Diary
Joan (Bantham) Byer and Dave Byer Collection
    John S. Bantham Journal
Brian Cooke Collection
    Young Family Genealogical Information
Ryan A. Conklin Collection
    George Blake Letters
    Comrade John B. Laque and His Model T Ford Souvenir Card
David Griffith and Marguerite (Whittemore) Griffith Collection
    Nathaniel G. Whittemore Letters
    Whittemore Family Genealogical Information
Charles W. Howgate and Margaret-Ann (Howgate) Bamberg Collection
    Gridley Family Genealogical Information
Gerard Mattimore Collection
    Mattimore Family Genealogical Information
Julie Jones O'Leary Collection
    Joseph C. Jones *What a Boy Saw in the Army* Manuscript
Jill Palmer Collection
    Chapman Family Genealogical Information
    George Chapman Diary
    George Chapman New York State Militia Enlistment Papers and Company I Muster Roll
Elodie Pritchartt Collection
    Munger Family Genealogical Information
Jeff Sauter Collection
    Horatio G. Goodno Letter
    John Mooney Letters
    Wands War Record: War Record of Five Brothers
Nancy Webster Collection
    Redington Family Genealogical Information

ARCHIVAL COLLECTIONS

Auburn University, Auburn University Library, Auburn, Alabama
    Stephen Truax Papers, Special Collections and Archives, Record Group 301
Historical Society of Middletown and the Wallkill Precinct, Inc., Middletown, New York
    Ethel B. Gage, *Orange County in the Civil War*, no date, Goshen, N.Y., Orange County Community of Museums and Galleries
    Grand Army of the Republic, *Department of New York, Personal War Sketches Presented to General Lyon Post No. 266*, Middletown, 1897
    The Old Battle Flag, April 1881, newspaper clippings regarding flag of Wallkill Guards
Historical Society of Pennsylvania, Philadelphia, Pennsylvania
    Samuel B. Fales, *Union Volunteer Refreshment Saloon Papers*, Collection 1580, Boxes 11–12, and Collection 2074, Box 1
Library of Congress, Motion Picture, Broadcasting and Recorded Sound Division, Madison Building, Washington, D.C.
    Original Amateur Hour Collection Preservation Tape, LWO 5799 R26, *Major Bowes Amateur Hour* (NBC)—February 16, 1936
Louisiana State University, LSU Libraries, Baton Rouge, Louisiana (LLMVC)
    George Blake Letters, Mss 2449, Louisiana and Lower Mississippi Valley Collections
National Archives and Records Administration, Washington, D.C. (NARA)
    1850 U.S. Federal Census, Population Schedule, Microfilm Publication M432, 1,009 rolls, Records of the Bureau of the Census, Record Group 29
    1860 U.S. Federal Census, Population Schedule, Microfilm Publication M653, 1,438 rolls

Compiled Services Records for Individuals in the 18th N.Y.S.V.
Court Martial Records, Record Group 153
Famine Irish Entry Project, 1846–1851
Pension Records for Individuals in the 18th N.Y.S.V., Record Group 15
Register of Cadet Applicants, 1819–1867, Records of the Adjutant General's Office, 1780s-1917, Microfilm Serial M2037, 3 rolls, Record Group 94
Registers of Deaths of Volunteers, Compiled 1861–1865, Records of the Adjutant General's Office, 1780's–1917, Record Group 94
Selected Records of the War Department Commissary General of Prisoners Relating to Federal Prisoners of War Confined at Andersonville, Ga, 1864–65, Microfilm Publication M1303, 6 rolls, Records of the Commissary General of Prisoners, Record Group 249
Special Schedules of the Eleventh Census (1890) Enumerating Union Veterans and Widows of Union Veterans of the Civil War, Microfilm Publication M123, 118 rolls, Records of the Department of Veterans Affairs, Record Group 15
Tenth Census of the United States, 1880, Records of the Bureau of the Census, Record Group 29
U.S. Military Academy Cadet Application Papers, 1805–1866, Records of the Adjutant General's Office, 1780s–1917, Microfilm Publication M688, 1 roll, Record Group 94
Union Provost Marshals' File of Papers Relating to Individual Civilians, 1861–1867, Microfilm publication M0345, 300 rolls, Record Group 109
New York Public Library, Manuscripts and Archives Division, New York, New York (NYPL)
United States Sanitary Commission Records, Astor, Lenox, and Tilden Foundations Series 7: Statistical Bureau Archives, Camp Inspection Reports, 1861–1864
New York State Archives, Albany, New York (NYSA)
Census of Inmates in Almshouses and Poorhouses, 1835–1921, New York State Board of Charities, Series A1978, Microfilm, 225 rolls
Civil War Muster Roll Abstracts of New York State Volunteers, United States Sharpshooters, and United States Colored Troops [Ca. 1861–1900], Series 13775, Microfilm, 1185 rolls, 18th Infantry, Box 76, 121st Infantry, Box 502, 128th Infantry, Box 526 & 13th Cavalry, Box 873
Executive Pardons, 1799–1846, 1856–1931. 10 vols., Series B0042, July 10, 1862, for Oliver P. Fortner
Registers of Commitments to Prisons, 1842–1908, Series A0603, vol. 2, pre–1875, Auburn Prison, for Oliver P. Fortner
Town Clerks' Registers of Men Who Served in the Civil War, Ca 1865–1867, Series 13774–83, Microfilm, 37 rolls
New York State Library, Albany, New York (NYSL)
Franklin B. Hough Papers, 1840–1885 [SC7009], Series 4: Civil War Papers, 1861–1865, Box 22, Folder 4, Notes on 18th N.Y.S.V.
New York State Military Museum and Veterans Research Center, Saratoga Springs, New York (NYSMM)
Frank J. Mattimore Diary
18th Regiment, N.Y. Volunteer Infantry Civil War Newspaper Clippings
Ogdensburg Public Library, Ogdensburg, New York
Winifred Bartlett, Bartlett-Randles History, Bartlett Family File
Rutgers University, Rutgers University Libraries, New Brunswick, New Jersey
Henry Wiltse, Jr., Papers, Rutgers University Biographical Files: Alumni (Class of 1850), Special Collections and University Archives
St. Lawrence County Historical Association, Canton, New York
Company K Descriptive Roll, Eighteenth New York Infantry
John C. O. Redington Letter, Military Era Collections, Box No. 2
Letter to Friends of the Mission School, Charles T. Creekman, Jr. Collection
St. Lawrence University, Canton, New York
Preston King Papers, 1834–1865, Letter to E.B. Allen, August 19, 1861, ODY Special Collections, Mss. Coll. No. 013
Schenectady County Historical Society, Grems-Doolittle Library, Schenectady, New York
John Vedder Ledger, 973.74 C, Cabinet 14
Syracuse University, Syracuse University Library, Syracuse, New York
Telesphor Insse Papers, Special Collections Research Center, Box 1, Correspondence from Gregoire Insse
Union College, Schaffer Library, Schenectady, New York
William A. Jackson, *Commonplace Book*, Special Collections
Jackson Family Committee, *Record of the Jackson Family*, 1878
United States Army Heritage and Education Center, Carlisle, Pennsylvania (USAHEC)
Edmund Hawley Letter
University of Michigan, William L. Clements Library, Ann Arbor, Michigan (WLC)
U.S. Army, 18th New York Infantry Descriptive Book, ca 1863, 1900, vol. 1, Manuscripts Division
University of Rochester, River Campus Libraries, Department of Rare Books, Special Collections and Preservation, Rochester, New York
John Meredith Read Papers 1870–1907, Box 3, Miscellaneous Typewritten Manuscripts, *General William Ayrault Jackson*
William Henry Seward Papers, General Correspondence, Letters from Reuben Gridley and William Seward Gridley
Perrie C. Soule Papers, D.136, Box 1, *Lincoln's Dream: Foreboding His Assassination*
University of Virginia, Albert and Shirley Small Special Collections Library, Charlottesville, Virginia
Letters to John A. Barhydt, Andrew D. Barhydt Letters, Mss 8979-L

Newspapers

Albany Daily Evening Times—Albany, New York
Albany Evening Journal—Albany, New York
Albany Sunday Press—Albany, New York
Albany Times Union—Albany, New York
American and Commercial Advertiser—Baltimore, Maryland
Amsterdam Evening Recorder and Daily Democrat—Amsterdam, New York
The Arizona Republican—Phoenix, Arizona
The Atlas & Argus—Albany, New York
Cambridge Chronicle—Cambridge, Massachusetts
The Chatham Courier—Chatham, New York
Chicago Sunday Tribune—Chicago, Illinois
Chicago Tribune—Chicago, Illinois
Daily City Press—Newburgh, New York
Daily Courier & Union—Syracuse, New York
Daily Evening Bulletin—Maysville, Kentucky
The Daily Evening Star—Schenectady, New York
The Daily Journal—Ogdensburg, New York
Daily National Intelligencer—Washington, D.C.
The Daily Union—Schenectady, New York
Democrat & Reflector—Schenectady, New York
Denver Daily Tribune—Denver, Colorado
Dispatch—Richmond, Virginia
Elmira Daily Advertiser—Elmira, New York
Elmira Telegram—Elmira, New York
The Evening Bulletin—Maysville, Kentucky
The Evening Star—Schenectady, New York
Evening Star and Times—Schenectady, New York
Fishkill Journal—Fishkill, New York
Fishkill Standard—Fishkill, New York
Harper's Weekly—New York City, New York
The Local News—Alexandria, Virginia
Middletown Daily Press—Middletown, New York
Middletown Daily Times—Middletown, New York
Middletown Mercury—Middletown, New York
The Naples Daily Record—Naples, New York
National Republican—Washington, D.C.
The National Tribune—Washington, D.C.
New York Daily Tribune—New York City, New York
New York Herald-Tribune—New York City, New York
New York Observer & Chronicle—New York City, New York
The New York Times—New York City, New York
Ogdensburg Advance—Ogdensburg, New York
The Ogdensburg Advance and St. Lawrence Weekly Democrat—Ogdensburg, New York
The Ogdensburg Journal—Ogdensburg, New York
Ogdensburg Republican Journal—Ogdensburg, New York
Ontario County Journal—Canandaigua, New York
Ontario Republican Times—Canandaigua, New York
The Orange County Press—Middletown, New York
The Phelps Citizen—Phelps, New York
Philadelphia Inquirer—Philadelphia, Pennsylvania
The Rockford Daily Register-Gazette—Rockford, Illinois
St. Lawrence Herald—Potsdam, New York
St. Lawrence Republican—Ogdensburg, New York
Salt Lake Telegram—Salt Lake City, Utah.
San Francisco Bulletin—San Francisco, California
Schenectady Daily Evening Star and Times—Schenectady, New York
The Schenectady Daily Union—Schenectady, New York
Schenectady Gazette—Schenectady, New York
Schenectady Reflector—Schenectady, New York
Schenectady Union-Star—Schenectady, New York
Schenectady Weekly Republican—Schenectady, New York
Schoharie Republican—Schoharie, New York
Seattle Post-Intelligencer—Seattle, Washington
Springfield Weekly Republican—Springfield, Massachusetts
Sunday Dispatch—Philadelphia, Pennsylvania
Troy Daily Times—Troy, New York
Utica Daily Observer—Utica, New York
Washington Post—Washington, D.C.
Watertown Daily Times—Watertown, New York
The Whig Press—Middletown, New York

Books

Baquet, Camille. *History of the First Brigade, New Jersey Volunteers, from 1861 to 1865*. Trenton, NJ: MacCrellish and Quigley, state printers, 1910.
Bates, Samuel P. *History of the Pennsylvania Volunteers, 1861–65*, 5 vols. Harrisburg: B. Singerly, State Printer, 1869–1871.
Beach, William H. *The First New York-Lincoln-Cavalry*. New York: Lincoln Cavalry Association, 1902.
Best, Isaac O. *History of the 121st New York State Infantry*. Chicago: J.H. Smith, 1921.
Bicknell, George W. *History of the Fifth Regiment Maine Volunteers*. Portland: Hall L. Davis, 1871.
Billings, John D. *Hardtack and Coffee, the Unwritten Story of Army Life*. Boston: George M. Smith and Co., 1888.
Carman, Ezra A. *The Maryland Campaign of September 1862*, ed. Joseph Pierro. New York: Routledge, 2008.
Carrington, Frances C. *My Army Life and the Fort Phil. Kearney Massacre with an Account of the Celebration of "Wyoming Opened."* Philadelphia and London: J.B. Lippincott, 1910.
Colyer, Vincent. *Report of the Christian Mission to the United States Army*. New York: G.A. Whitehorne, 1862.
Curtis, Newton Martin. *From Bull Run to Chancellorsville*. New York: G.P. Putnam's Sons, 1906.
Fairchild, Charles B. *History of the 27th Regiment New York Volunteers*. Binghamton, NY: Carl and Matthews, Printers, 1888.
Galloway, George N. *The Ninety-Fifth Pennsylvania Volunteers (Gosline's Pennsylvania Zouaves), in the Sixth Corps*. Philadelphia: Collins, 1884.
Heitman, Francis B. *Historical Register and Dictionary of the United States Army, 1789–1903*. 2 vols. Washington, D.C.: Government Printing Office, 1903.
Hodgkins, Samuel. *Autobiography of Samuel Hodgkins*. Minneapolis, MN: Carrie E. Chatfield, 1923.
Jackson, Isaac W. *Documents Relative to an Attack Upon the Character of the Late Col. Wm. A. Jackson*. Schenectady, NY: n.p., 1862.

Jeffrey, William H. *Richmond Prisons, 1861–1862*. St. Johnsbury, VT: Republican Press, 1893.

Longstreet, James. *From Manassas to Appomattox: Memoirs of the Civil War in America*. 2d ed. Philadelphia: J.B. Lippincott, 1908.

Lyon, Henry C. *Desolating This Fair Country: The Civil War Diary and Letters of Lt. Henry C. Lyon, 34th New York*, ed. Emily N. Radigan. Jefferson, NC: McFarland, 1999.

Methodist Episcopal Church. *Minutes of the Troy Annual Conference of the Methodist Episcopal Church, for 1874*. Troy, NY: Brainerd and Brown, 1874.

Munsell, Joel. *Memoir of William A. Jackson, a Member of the Albany Bar and Colonel of the 18th Regiment, N.Y. Volunteers, Who Died at the City of Washington, November 11, 1861*. Albany, NY: Albany Bar and Joel Munsell, 1862.

New York State Adjutant General's Office. *Annual Report of the Adjutant General of the State of New York for the Year 1894. Registers of the 20th, 21st, 22d, 23d, 24th, 25th and 26th Regiments of Cavalry, New York Volunteers in War of the Rebellion*. Albany, NY: J.B. Lyon, 1895.

_____. *Annual Report of the Adjutant General of the State of New York for the Year 1897. Registers of the Seventh and Eighth Artillery in the War of the Rebellion*. Albany, NY: Wynkoop Hallenbeck Crawford Co., 1898.

_____. *Annual Report of the Adjutant General of the State of New York, for the Year 1899. Registers of the Twelfth, Thirteenth, Fourteenth, Sixteenth, Seventeenth, Seventeenth Veteran, and Eighteenth Regiments of Infantry*. Albany, NY: J.B. Lyon, 1900.

_____. *Annual Report of the Adjutant General of the State of New York, for the Year 1901. Registers of the Eighty-Eight, Eighty-Ninth, Ninetieth, Ninety-First, Ninety-Second, and Ninety-Third Regiments of Infantry*. Albany, NY: J.B. Lyon, 1902.

_____. *Annual Report of the Adjutant General of the State of New York, Transmitted to the Legislature January 15, 1862*. Albany, NY: C. Van Benthuysen, Printer, 1862.

New York State Bureau of Military Statistics. *First Annual Report of the Chief of the Bureau of Military Statistics*. New York: Horatio Seymour, 1864.

_____. *Presentation of Flags of New York Volunteer Regiments and Other Organizations, to His Excellency, Governor Fenton, in Accordance with a Resolution of the Legislature, July 4, 1865; Published Under Direction of the Chief of Bureau of Military Records*. Albany, NY: Weed, Parsons, and Company, Printers, 1865.

New York State Legislature Assembly 85th Session. *Documents of the Assembly of the State of New York, Eighty-Fifth Session, 1862*. vol. 2, Communication. Albany, NY: Van Benthuysen, Printer, 1862.

Otis, George A. *A Report of Surgical Cases Treated in the Army of the United States from 1865–1871*. Washington, D.C.: Government Printing Office, 1871.

Phisterer, Frederick. *New York in the War of the Rebellion: 1861 to 1865*. 3rd ed. 5 vols. Albany, NY: J.B. Lyon, 1912.

Pinto, Francis E. *History of the 32nd Regiment, New York Volunteers, in the Civil War, 1861–1863, and Personal Recollection During That Period*. Brooklyn: publisher not identified, 1895.

Report of the Committee on the Conduct of the War: Reports. 8 vols. Washington, D.C. 1863–1866.

The Rev. E.P. Rogers, D.D.: Pastor of the South Reformed Church, Fifth Avenue and Twenty-First St., New York. New York: Privately Printed for Harvard College Library, 1882.

Sedgwick, John. *Correspondence of John Sedgwick, Major General*. 2 vols. New York: Carl Stoeckel, 1903.

Stevens, George T. *Three Years in the Sixth Corps*. Albany, NY: S.R. Gray, 1866.

U.S. War Department. *The War of the Rebellion: A Compilation of the Official Records of the Union and Confederate Armies*. 128 vols. Washington, D.C.: Government Printing Office, 1880–1901.

Westbrook, Robert S. *History of the 49th Pennsylvania Volunteers*. Altoona, PA: Altoona Times Print, 1898.

Secondary Sources

Books and Pamphlets

Albany Directory, for the Year 1861. Albany, NY: Adams, Sampson and Co., 1861.

Arms and Equipment of the Union. Alexandria, VA: Time-Life Books, 1991.

Beatie, R.H. *Road to Manassas*. New York: Cooper Square Publishers, 1961.

Beers, J.H. *Commemorative Biographical Record of the Counties of Dutchess and Putnam, New York*. Chicago: J.H. Beers and Co., 1897.

Biographical History of La Crosse, Monroe, and Juneau Counties, Wisconsin. Chicago: Lewis Publishing Co., 1892.

Bowen, A.W., and Co. *Progressive Men of Bannock, Bear Lake, Bingham, Fremont and Oneida Counties, Idaho*. Chicago: A.W. Bowen and Co., 1904.

Bradsby, H.C., ed. *History of Bureau County, Illinois*. Chicago: World Publishing Co., 1885.

Brown, George William. *Baltimore and the Nineteenth of April, 1861*. Baltimore: N. Murray, 1887.

Brown, Kent Masterson. *Cushing of Gettysburg, the Story of a Union Artillery Commander*. Lexington: University Press of Kentucky, 1993.

Carroll, Andrew. *War Letters: Extraordinary Correspondence from American Wars*. New York: Scribner, 2001.

Carter, Robert G. *Four Brothers in Blue, or, Sunshine and Shadows of the War of the Rebellion: A Story of the Great*

Civil War from Bull Run to Appomattox. Washington, D.C.: Press of Gibson Bros., 1913.

Clark, Rufus W. *The Heroes of Albany: A Memorial of the Patriot-Martyrs of the City and County of Albany Who Sacrificed Their Lives During the Late War in Defence of Our Nation, 1861–1865*. Albany, NY: S.R. Gray, 1866.

Cooling, Benjamin F. *Counter-Thrust, from the Peninsula to the Antietam*. Lincoln: University of Nebraska, 2007.

Committee on Veterans' Affairs United States Senate. *Medal of Honor Recipients, 1863–1978: In the Name of the Congress of the United States*. Washington: U.S. Govt. Printing, 1979.

Davis, William C. *Battle of Bull Run*. Garden City, NY: Doubleday and Co., 1977.

Durant, Samuel W., and Henry B. Peirce. *History of St. Lawrence Co., New York*. Philadelphia: L.H. Everts and Co., 1878.

Eaton, Homer. *Memorial of Colonel William H. Young*. Albany, NY: Geo. C. Riggs, 1876.

Evans, Charles M. *The War of the Aeronauts: A History of Ballooning During the Civil War*. Mechanicsburg, PA: Stackpole Books, 2002.

Fearey, Thomas H. *Union College Alumni in the Civil War, 1861–1865*. Schenectady, NY: Union University, Graduate Council, 1915.

Foote, Shelby. *The Civil War, a Narrative: Fort Sumter to Perryville*. New York: Random House, 1958.

Garand, P. S. *The History of the City of Ogdensburg*. Ogdensburg, NY: M.J. Belleville, 1927.

Grand Army of the Republic. *Roster of the Department of New York, Grand Army of the Republic*. Albany, NY: J.B. Lyon, 1915.

History of Jackson County, Michigan. Chicago: Inter-State Publishing, 1881.

Howell, George Rogers, and John H. Munsell. *History of the County of Schenectady, N.Y. from 1662 to 1886*. New York: W.W. Munsell and Co., 1886.

Howell, George Rogers, and Jonathan Tenney. *Bi-Centennial History of Albany*. New York: W.W. Munsell and Co., 1886.

Hurd, Duane H. *History of Clinton and Franklin Counties, New York*. Philadelphia: J.W. Lewis and Co., 1880.

Johnson, Robert U., and Clarence C. Buel, eds. *Battles and Leaders of the Civil War*, vol. 2, *The Struggle Intensifies*. New York: Castle Books, 1991.

Krick, Robert K. *Civil War Weather in Virginia*. Tuscaloosa: University of Alabama Press, 2007.

Leech, Margaret. *Reveille in Washington: 1860–1865*. New York: New York Review Books, 2011.

Lowry, Thomas P., and Jack D. Welsh. *Tarnished Scalpels: The Court-Martials of Fifty Union Surgeons*. Mechanicsburg, PA: Stackpole Books, 2000.

Lubetkin, M. John. *Union College's Class of 1868: The Unique Experiences of Some Average Americans*. McLean, VA: M. John Lubetkin and Union College, 1995.

Manning, James H. *Albany Zouave Cadets, Esto Vigilans Fifty Years Young*. Albany, NY: Weed-Parsons Printing, 1910.

McIntosh, W.H. *History of Ontario County, New York*. Philadelphia: Everts, Ensign and Everts, 1878.

McPherson, James M. *Battle Cry of Freedom: The Civil War Era*. New York: Oxford University Press, 1988.

The Medical and Surgical History of the Civil War. 15 vols. Reprint, Wilmington, NC: Broadfoot Publishing, 1992. Originally published in 1883 as *Medical and Surgical History of the War of the Rebellion*.

Miller, William J. *The Men of Fort Ward: Defenders of Washington*. Alexandria, VA: Friends of Fort Ward, 1989.

O'Reilly, Francis Augustín. *The Fredericksburg Campaign: Winter War on the Rappahannock*. Baton Rouge: Louisiana State University Press, 2003.

Parker, Amasa J., ed. *Landmarks of Albany County, New York*. Syracuse, NY: D. Mason & Co., 1897.

Parsons, Philip W. *The Union Sixth Army Corps in the Chancellorsville Campaign*. Jefferson, NC: McFarland, 2006.

Randall, Ruth P. *Colonel Elmer Ellsworth*. Toronto: Little, Brown and Co., 1960.

Raven, John H. *Catalogue of the Officers and Alumni of Rutgers College in New Brunswick, N.J. 1776 to 1916*. Trenton, NJ: State Gazette Publishing, 1916.

Rawley, James A. *Edwin D. Morgan, 1811–1883: Merchant in Politics*. New York: Columbia University Press, 1955.

Reese, Timothy J. *Sealed with Their Lives: The Battle for Crampton's Gap, Burkittsville, Maryland, September 14, 1862*. Baltimore: Butternut and Blue, 1998.

Reimer, Terry. *One Vast Hospital: The Civil War Hospital Sites in Frederick, Maryland After Antietam: With Detailed Hospital Patient List*. Frederick, MD: National Museum of Civil War Medicine, 2001.

Reynolds, Cuyler. *Hudson-Mohawk Genealogical and Family Memoirs: A Record of Achievements of the People of the Hudson and Mohawk Valleys in New York State*, vol. 4. New York: Lewis Historical Publishing, 1911.

Ridlon, Gideon T. *A Contribution to the History, Biography and Genealogy of the Families Named Sole, Solly, Soule, Sowle, Soulis*, vol. 2. Lewiston, ME: Journal Press, 1926.

Royce, Caroline Halstead. *Bessboro: A History of Westport, Essex Co., N.Y.* Elizabethtown, NY: n.p., 1904.

Schenectady City and County Directory, 1860–1861. Schenectady, NY: W.M. Colborne, 1860.

Schermerhorn, Richard. *Schermerhorn Genealogy and Family Chronicles*. New York: T.A. Wright, 1914.

Sears, Stephen W. *Chancellorsville*. New York: Houghton Mifflin, 1996.

———. *Landscape Turned Red: The Battle of Antietam*. New Haven, CT: Ticknor and Fields, 1983.

———. *To the Gates of Richmond: The Peninsula Campaign*. New York: Ticknor and Fields, 1992.

Shannon, Fred A. *The Organization and Administration of the Union Army, 1861–1865*. Cleveland, OH: Arthur H. Clark, 1928.

Slocum, Charles E. *The Life and Services of Major-General Henry Warner Slocum*. Toledo, OH: Slocum Publishing, 1913.

Smith, James H. *History of Duchess County, New York*. Syracuse, NY: D. Mason and Co., 1882.

Snell, Mark A. *From First to Last: The Life of Major General*

William B. Franklin. New York: Fordham University Press, 2002.
Somers, Wayne. *Encyclopedia of Union College History.* Schenectady, NY: Union College Press, 2003.
Stevenson, James H. *Boots and Saddles: A History of the First Volunteer Cavalry of the War.* Harrisburg: Patriot Publishing, 1879.
Sylvester, Nathaniel Bartlett. *History of Saratoga County, New York.* Philadelphia: Everts and Ensign, 1878.
Taylor, Frank H. *Philadelphia in the Civil War, 1861–1865.* Philadelphia: City of Philadelphia, 1913.
Taylor, Paul. *Glory Was Not Their Companion: The Twenty-Sixth New York Volunteer Infantry in the Civil War.* Jefferson, NC: McFarland, 2005.
Teetor, Paul R. *A Matter of Hours: Treason at Harper's Ferry.* Rutherford, NJ: Farleigh Dickinson University Press, 1982.
Transactions of the Medical Society of the County of Albany, 1870–1880, with Biographical Sketches of Deceased Members, vol. 3, ed. Medical Society of the County of Albany. Albany, NY: Burdick and Taylor, 1883.
Trudeau, Andre, Bryce A. Suderow, and Noah Hewett, eds. *Supplement to the Official Records of the Union and Confederate Armies.* 100 vols. Wilmington, NC: Broadfoot Publishing, 1994–2001.
The Union Army: A History of Military Affairs in the Loyal States, 1861–1865. 8 vols. Wilmington, NC: Broadfoot Publishing, 1997. Originally published in 1908 by Federal Publishing.
Warner, George H. *Military Records of Schoharie County Veterans of Four Wars.* Albany, NY: Weed, Parsons and Co., 1891.
Westervelt, William B. *Lights and Shadows of Army Life: From Bull Run to Bentonville,* ed. George S. Maharay. Shippensburg, PA: Burd Street Press, 1998.
Westover, Myron F. *Schenectady Past and Present: Historical Papers.* Strasburg, VA: Shenandoah Publishing House, 1931.
Wiley, Bell Irvin. *The Life of Billy Yank.* Baton Rouge: Louisiana State University, 1978.
Williams, Franklin B. *Middletown: A Biography.* Middletown, NY: Lawrence A. Toepp, 1928.
Wilson, Mark. *The Business of Civil War: Military Mobilization and the State, 1861–1865.* Baltimore: Johns Hopkins University Press, 2006.
Yates, Austin A. *Schenectady County, New York: Its History to the Close of the Nineteenth Century.* Place of publication not identified: New York History, 1902.

Magazines, Journals, and Periodicals

Brooks, Noah. "Glimpses of Lincoln in War Time." *The Century Magazine,* November 1894.
Brotherhood of Locomotive Engineers. "In Railroad Service from 1855 to 1901." *Locomotive Engineers Journal* 42, no. 1, January 1908.
Columbia University. *Catalogue of Officers and Graduates of Columbia University,* 16th ed., 1916.
Harvard Graduates' Magazine Association. *The Harvard Graduates' Magazine,* 9, 1901.
Michigan Pioneer and Historical Society. *Historical Collections: Collections and Researches Made by the Michigan Pioneer and Historical Society,* 17. Lansing, MI: Robert Smith and Co., 1892.
Miner, Julius F., ed.: *Buffalo Medical and Surgical Journal,* vol. X, 1871. Buffalo, NY: Baker, Jones & Co., 1871.
Society of Colonial Wars in the State of New York. *Year Book For 1920–1921,* no. 29, May 1921.
The Spirit of '76. "Empire State, S.A.R.'S First Thousand Members." *The Spirit of '76* 2, no. 13, September 1896.
Union University. *Union University Quarterly* 1, no. 1, May 1904.

Electronic Sources

New York State Military Museum. 18th Regiment, NY Volunteer Infantry: Civil War Newspaper Clippings. Available at https://dmna.ny.gov/historic/reghist/civil/infantry/18thInf/18thInfCWN.htm.

Cemeteries

Albany Rural Cemetery, Menands, New York
    Michael H. Donovan Plot
    Alexander A. Edmeston Plot
    John Hastings Plot
    John H. Russell and William H. Russell Plot
    James K. Strathern Plot
    John Waterson Plot
    William G. Weed Plot
Alexandria National Cemetery, Alexandria, Virginia
    Charles H. Thompson Plot
Arlington National Cemetery, Arlington, Virginia
    John H. Gale Plot
Clifton Springs Village Cemetery, Manchester, New York
    John James Warfield, Jr. Plot
Coeymans Hollow Cemetery, Coeymans, New York
    William Speenburgh Plot
    Peter Van Hoesen Plot
Coye Cemetery, South Bristol, New York
    John Bernard Roper Plot
Fairview Cemetery, Beacon, New York
    William H. White Plot
Forest Hill Cemetery, Utica, New York
    Cornelius Hotaling Plot
Fredericksburg and Spotsylvania National Military Park, Fredericksburg, Virginia
    Gleason C. Bell Plot
    Martin Fritz Plot
Glendale National Cemetery, Richmond, Virginia
    William A. Shaw Plot
Hillside Cemetery, Westport, New York
    Washington Irving Sawyer Plot
Lyons Rural Cemetery, Lyons, New York
    Shubael Durkee Plot
Ogdensburg Cemetery, Ogdensburg, New York
    George Ranney Myers Plot
Pleasant Ridge Cemetery, Lincoln County, Oklahoma
    William Henry Mayette Plot
Rosedale Cemetery, Phoenix, Arizona

Joseph S. Raines Plot
Rosehill Cemetery, Chicago, Illinois
   William S. Gridley Plot
St. Agnes Cemetery, Menands, New York
   Frank J. Mattimore Plot
St. Patricks Cemetery, Caledonia, Michigan
   C. C. Bruton Plot
Stranger's Rest Cemetery (Frost Cemetery), Lufkin, Texas
   Henry "Harry" E. Munger Plot
Tioga Point Cemetery, Athens, Pennsylvania
   John L. Brundage Plot
Vale Cemetery, Schenectady, New York
   William Horsfall Plot
   William Ayrault Jackson Plot
West Hollow Cemetery, Naples, New York
   David Place Plot

Index

Numbers in ***bold italics*** indicate pages with photographs.

Abercrombie, Alexander 45, 280
Adams, Edward J. 111, 143
Adams House 26–30, 32–33, 37, 46, 48–50
aeronautics 135, 200
USS *Agawam* (gunboat) 365
Alabama troops: 4th Infantry 188; 5th Infantry 85–88; 8th Infantry 185
Albany, N.Y. 14, 19, 22–28, 30–34, 36–37, 42, 45, 48–51, 53–54, 58, 60–61, 103, 134, 146–147, 159, 166, 244, 250–251, 256, 271–272, 275, 295, 330, 348, 350–357, 364–367, 369–372, 374–377
Albany Brigade Band 51, 55, 354
Albany Burgesses Corps 24, 36
Albany City Volunteers 24
Albany Law School 17, 25, 134
Albany Medical College 42, 251
Albany Zouave Cadets 36–37, 41–42, 50, 54, 56, 60, 127, 146
Aldrich, Daniel H. 330–331
Alexander, Thomas 7, 185–187, 190–194, 209–210, 213, 215, 219, 221–222, 228, 239–240, 246
Alexander's Bridge 214
Alexandria, Va. 53, 77, 79–80, ***80***, 90, 99, 101, 112–114, 120–122, 126, 129, 135–136, 138, 140, 142–144, 146, 149, 151–152, 157, 162, 166, 170, 172–183, 195, 197, 254–255, 257, 259, 261, 306, 321, 356
Allen, John 325
Allen, John S. 85–86, 103–104
Allen, Walter 111, 143, 369
Andersonville Prison 362
Antietam (Sharpsburg), Battle of 287–291
Ardill, Robert T. 261
Armstrong, William R. 312–313
Army of Northeastern Virginia 81, 83, 101
Army of the Potomac 106, 111, 121, 129, 139, 142, 150–153, 165, 171, 174–175, 178, 180, 194, 197–198, 207–209, 228, 236, 242–243, 251, 253, 257, 262, 281, 287, 291, 295, 299–302, 305–306, 311, 314–315, 318, 321–323, 325, 328, 333, 344, 348, 362
Army of Virginia 257
Arnold, Charles R. 363
Atkinson, Thomas E. 319
The Atlas & Argus 244
Austin, Thomas 355

Bailey's Crossroads 116–119, ***118***, 124–126, 132, 150
Baker, John 309, 326, 332
Baker, Joseph 105
Bakersville, Md. 295, 298
Ball, Lucius W.H. 247
USS *Baltimore* (steamer) 78
Baltimore, Md. 66–67, 138, 164, 349, 356
Banks's Ford 318, 320–321, 345–348
Bantham, John S. 128, 211, 222, 227, ***227***
Barhydt, Andrew D. 48, 113, 115, 161, 179, 354
Barhydt, Anna A. 39
Barhydt, G. Dallas 161
Barhydt, J.A. 354
Barringer, Alvin 101
Barron, James 76
Barry, George 47, 148, 184, 221, 233, 244, 250
Barry, Samuel 47, 221
Barry, William F. ***196***
Bartholf, John H. 305–306, ***306***, 319, 330
Bartlett, David L. 18–19, ***18***, 28–30, 33–34, 53, 59, 103, 106
Bartlett, Joseph J. ***196***, 266–270, 276, 288
Beaver Dam Creek *see* Mechanicsville (Beaver Dam Creek)
Becking, Julius 240, 379

Bell, Gleason C. 308
Bendine, Frederick 151
Benham, Henry W. 336–337
USS *Benton* (gunboat) 169
Benton's Tavern 163, 165, 168
Berlin, Md. 300, ***301***
Bicknell, George W. 192
Bink (Binck), Wilhelmus L. 319
Bird, Peter 280
Birmingham, John W. 16, 60
Blackburn's Ford 89–91, 111, 181
Blackwell, John 218
Blaisdell, Abraham 271–272
Blake, George 70–71, 76, 106, 126, 133, 139–142, 153, 168, 206, 231, 329
Board of Uniforms Committee 37
Bovee, John N. 236–237
Boyle, Frank 261
Bradshaw, Robert 362
Brandow, Charles H. 126–127
Brick House Landing (West Point), Battle of 188–193
Brick House Point 187–188, 194
Bristoe Station 179–180
Brooks, Noah 328
Brooks, William T.H. 298, 303–305, ***304***, 310, 312, 323, 336, 343–346
Brooks Brothers (Brooks & Company) 38, 59
Brown, James 193
Brownell, Francis 53–54
Browning, John W. 86, 164
Brundage, Albert 295
Brundage, John L. 139, 295
Bruton, Christopher C. 365–366, ***366***
Buckley, Thomas H. 71–72
Bulchey, John 161
Bulson, George 242
Bull Run (creek) 90, 93–94, 181; *see also* Bull Run (Manassas)
Bull Run (Manassas), Battle of 91–100, 111–112, 134, 164, 181

481

482 Index

"Bull" the dog 99–100, 105, 111, 371
Bullent, Anthony C. 216, 253, 255, 272, **273**, 281
Burkittsville, Md. 262, 264, 266–267, 281–282, 284–285, 299–300
Burn, Christopher G. 47, 364–365
Burn, Richard A. 47, 365
Burns, John 280
Burnside, Ambrose 302, 308–310, 312, 314–315, 318, 320, 322
Burt, William G. 158–159
Burton, Myron 229

Cake, Henry L. 278, 282–283
Callan, John 207
Camp Harris 69–77, 139
Camp Jackson 167–169, **167**, 172–173, 175, 181–182
Camp King 116–117, **117**, 120–121, 123, 130, 132, **133**, 134–135, 138–139, **140**, 141, 144–147, 151, 153–154, 160, 164–168, 259
"Camp Misery" 113–115, 179, 181
Camp Myers 79–83, 101–103, 105, 108–109, 113–114
Camp Russell 315
Canandaigua, N.Y. 26, 45, 138, 152, 157, 245, 307, 357, 376, 381
Carbino, Henry 135
Carmichael, William E. **69**, 172–173, 225, 250
Cassidy, Matthew 182
Catlett's Station 180, 305
Centreville, Va. 89–91, 93–94, 96–99, 101–102, 172, 181, 258–259
Chadderdon, Elijah L. 351, **352**
Chalmers, James 25, 145, 231, 316–317
Chamberlain, Smith 44
Chancellorsville, Battle of 338–348
Chancellorsville, Va. 333, 341, 343–344
Chancellorsville campaign 333–348
Chantilly (Ox Hill), Battle of 258–259
Chapman, Aaron 306
Chapman, George 25, **25**, 316–318, **317**
Charles City Crossroads (Glendale), Battle of 238–241
Chesmore, Alfred M. 47, 231, 275–276, **275**, 356
Chickahominy fever 207, 246, 250, 331
Chickahominy River 200–204, 206–209-211, 214, 228–229, 232, 234–235, 246, 250, 252
Christian, William L. 250
Christiance, Francis 133, 134
Clark, Vincent (Vinson) H. 119, 125, 268, 334
Clarke, Ephraim C. 161

Clauson, Sanford S. 334
Clay, Henry 46, 246
Cleary, Thomas 21
Cleary's Saloon 21–22, **21**, 256
Cobb, Howell 276
Cochrane, Charles W. 169
Colby, Malcolm E. 311, 330
Cold Harbor, Va. 198–199
Cole, Samuel B. 281–282
Collard, Samuel 204
USS *Columbia* (steamer) 182
Conaty, Francis J. 377–378
Conklin, Robert 1–2, **394**
Conkling, Alfred 36
Conkling, Urband 158–159
Connecticut troops: 7th Infantry 365
Connors, John 58
Conway, Patrick 319
Cooley, William A. 319
Cooper, Wesley 179
Cooper Shop Refreshment Saloon 64
Corbally, Edward 379
Cordell, Charles T. 249
corduroy roads 201–202, **201**, 204, 207
corps badges 323
Courtney, Robert 232
Craig, George 128
Craig, John R. 128
Crampton's Gap 262, 266, 282–283, 287, 299
Crampton's Gap, Battle of 264–282
Crimean War 46, 221
Crist, Ernest J. 354
Crowley, John 151
Crozier, Abram 86, 164
Cullen, Philip 124–125
Culver, George W. 166–167
Cumberland Landing 194, **195**
Cunnihine, James 289
Curry, Thomas 278, 359

Dailey, James 125, 226
Daingerfield, Edward 167
Daley, Daniel H. 22, 80–81, **81**, 124, 141, 180, 230, 252, 274–275, **274**, 317
USS *Daniel Webster* (steamer) 182, 253
Daniels, Michael 111, 170
Daniels, William H. **230**
Davies, Thomas A. 29, 81, **82**, 91, 93–94, 97–100, 112
Davis, Jefferson 41, 203
Dawley, Corydon A. 196
Deanstatt, John 44
DeBaum, Isaac 225, 244, 282
Dee, Mathew 330
De Joinville, Prince 148
Delaney, John 348
Delavan House 27–28, 351–352
Dempsey, John M. 24, 33, 104, 110, 136–137, **137**, 231, **231**, 278, 364

Denning Guards 16, 359–360
Dillon, John 149
Dings, Ashbel 311
Donohoe, Timothy 252
Donovan, Michael H. 24, 34, 109–111, **110**, 128, 136, 173, 213, 228, 236, 270, 321, 372, 375–376
Downing, Sylvanus B. 159
Dunker Church 288–289, 291, **293**, 294
Dunkle, Charles W. 47
Dunkle, George W. 47, 197
Dunkle, Lewis F. 47
Dunning, William C. 136
Durkee, Shubael 380

Early, Jubal 341, 363, 365
Ebel, Henry 380
Edmeston, Alexander A. 42–43, **43**, 99, **140**, 165, 237, 247, 297, 369
Edwards, John 93–94, 97
Eldridge, Frederick 13
Elliott, William 321
Ellis, George W. 219, 225, 245, 247
Ellis, William H., Jr. 219, 225, 245, 250, 275
Ellison, William A. 306
Ellmaker, Peter C. 346
Ellsworth, Elmer E. 36, 53–54, 79, 147
Eltham, Va. 187–188, 192, 194
Eltham's Landing, Battle of *see* Brick House Landing (West Point)
USS *Emperor* (steamer) 186
Enfield musket 57, 62–63, 73, 97, 138, 204
Erie Station (Middletown, N.Y.) **15**, 16
Evening Star and Times 133, 160, 236, 244, 308

Fair Oaks *see* Seven Pines (Fair Oaks)
Fairfax Court House 83, 85, 87–88, 99, 100, 172–174, 181, 259
Fairfax Seminary 116, **116**, 154, 259
Falmouth, Va. 315–316, 319, 321, 328, 331, 334, 348–349
Farr, the Rev. A.A. 40, **40**, 71, 82, 99, 108, 132, **140**, 144, 146–147, 151, 156, 172, 216, 234, 250, 286, 306, 308, 369–371, **370**
Farr, John W. 378, **378**
Farrell, Percy **400**
Farrell, Robert 379–380
Faurot, Henry 26, 34, 138, 152, 157, 161, 219, 225, 244, 250
Faurot, Henry Horace 170
Fay, John M. 268
female soldier 160
Finn, Calvin A. **401**
Fisher, Edward 23, 46
Fisher, Hiram L. 170

Fisher, Ira J. 125
Fishkill, N.Y. 16–17, 245, 256, 359–360
Fishkill Journal 245
Fishkill Landing, N.Y. 16, 359–360
Fitzhugh's Crossing 334
Flynn, James 218, 244
Fogerty, Edward M. 271
Fogliardi, Augusto 332
Fort Columbus 326
Fort Dahlgren 113
Fort Ellsworth 113, 121, 255, 257
Fort Jefferson 326
Fort Monroe 54, 164, 196, 245, 369
Fort Pennsylvania 260
Fort Sumter 9, 11, 17, 19
Fort Ward 121–125, 131, 139, 142, 148, 154, 165, 167–168, 176
Fort Washington 182
Fortner, Oliver P. 256, **257**
Fox, William H. 330
Fox's Gap 262
Franklin, William B. 106, **107**, 121, 131, 148, 150, 153–155, 159, 161–162, 169, 176, 178, 180, 183, 187–188, 190–191, 193–194, **196**, 198, 213, 241, 246, 255, 258, 261–266, 286–289, 295, 302, 307, 309–310, 312, 322
Franklin's Crossing 334–335, **340**, 341, 343
Frasier, James 306
Frederick, Md. 262, 282, 306, 351, 356
Fredericksburg, Battle of 309–314
Fredericksburg, Va. 300, 302, 309, 318, 333–335, 343–346
Fredericksburg campaign 307–315
Frémont, John C. 62
Fritz, Martin 314
Fuller, Amasa 256
Fullerton, Peter M. 281
Furniss, George C. 250

Gaines, William G. 199–200, 211, 232
Gaines's Mill 200, 211
Gaines's Mill, Battle of 210–233, 243–244
Gale, John H. 72–73
Garland, Samuel 224–225
Garrity, James 268–269
Garvey, James 220, 236
USS *George Washington* (steamer) 164
Georgia troops: 10th Infantry 266
Getty, Charles A. 232
Geywits, Byron 256
Giffen, John F. 46, 326
USS *Gipsey* (steamer) 182
Givens Hotel 21, 354
Glendale, Battle of *see* Charles City Crossroads (Glendale)
Glendale, Va. 236–239; *see also*

Charles City Crossroads (Glendale)
Gloucester Point 183–184, 186
Golden, Alvah, Jr. 169
Goodman farm 271, 284–285
Goodno, George N. 160, 297
Goodno, George W.R. 226, 237, 324, 330, 373
Goodno, Horatio G. 18, 28–29, 41, 48, 83, 115, 179, 223, 226, **226**, 237, 255, 260, 297, 311, 317, 324, 330, 372–373
Goodrich, Allen 282
Gosline, John M. 141
Gothic Hall 12–14, **12**, 48
Gowan, John 76
Gracey, John 245
Grand Army of the Republic 372, 376–377, 383
Grant, Arthur M. 59
Grant, Ralph R. 59
Grant, U.S. 367
Graves, Frank 260
Gray, David H. 46
Green, Alphonso 319, 326
Green, George J. 195, 197, 201, 203–204, 206, 208, 216, 225
Green, Isaac S. 42, 219, 250–251
Green, Samuel 306
Green, William R. 158, 326
Greene, Oliver D. 81, 97–98, 181
Greene's Battery (Battery G, 2nd U.S. Artillery) 81, 91, 96–99; *see also* 2nd United States Artillery
Gridley, Eleanor 374
Gridley, Henry S. 19–21
Gridley, Joseph W. 47, 230
Gridley, Nathaniel P.T. 20–21, 47, 230, 244, 285
Gridley, William S. 19–22, **20**, 34, 47–48, 80–81, 83, 102, 125, 141, 157, 176, 189–190, 197, 210, **212**, 216, 228, 230, 244, 252, 271, 273–274, 280, 284–285, 289, 291–292, **292**, 294, 353–354, 374
Griepe, Harmon 237
Groffman, Ernest 314
Groom, Amos 340
Groot, Edward W. 22, 79, 86, 88, 103, 126, 183–185, 304

Hagerman, John 217–218
Hagerstown, Md. 298, 306–307, 330
"Hail Columbia" 75, 359
"Hail to the Chief" 148, 150, 302
Hale, Winfield S. 48
Hall, Isaac F. 229
Hall, William H. 48, 160
Hamilton, Edward D. 160
Hampton's Legion 192
Hanford, Augustus E. 13, **13**
Hanford, Edward M. **407**
Hanover Court House, Battle of 202, 204

Harden, John 138–139
Hardick, Stephen 330–331
Harpers Ferry, W.V. 112, 263, 286–287, 295, 300
Harrigan, William 363
Harris, Ira 69, 74
Harris, William H. 123, 248
Harrison's Landing 242–245, 248–252, 255
Harvard University 108
Hastings, John 24, 34, 44–45, 132, **133**, 146, 157, 262, 364, 366
havelocks 53, 58, 73–74
Hawley, Edmund B. 48, 214, 216, 225, 234, 249, 285
Hayden, Henry 119, 202, 306
Haythorne, Maurice 271
Heald, Charles W. 25, 102, 113, 144–145
Heintz, Jacob 363
Hennessy, David 317
Hennessy, Richard 143, 279
Hewitt, David 25
Hill, Edward B. 99
Hipp, Henry 151
Hodgkins, Samuel 9–10, 19, 28, 51, 54, 65, 70, 93, 115, 151, 181–182, 201, 211, 228–229, 232, 241, 367, 382
Hogan, Peter **31**, 31–32, 34, 46, **69**, 145
Hogeboom, Stephen 136
Holden, Thomas M. 70, 158, 173–176
Holly, Richard A., Jr. **410**
Homan, George E. **218**, 219
Hood, John B. 188
Hooker, Joseph 322–323, 325–326, 328, 333, 338, 341, 344, 346–347
Horsfall, William 23, 161, **162**, 260, 272–274, **273**, 285–286, 377
Horsfall, William V. 42, 73, 127
Horton, Walter 299
Houghtaling, Cornelius 43–44, 291–292
Houghtaling, John H. 160
House, George 119, 202, 306
Howard, Francis W. 252
Howd, Samuel **411**
Hoyt, George M. 340
Hoyt, Hezekiah W. 295–296, 359
Hoyt, Isaac 295–296, 359
Huger, Benjamin 238
Hulligan, Michael 256
Hunter, John 313
Hunting Creek 79–80, 102
Huntington, Freeman F. 76, 92, 105, 149, 218, 356
Huson, Robert 250
Huston, Charles W. 138, 165, 171

Icklin, John J. 205, 350–351
Industrial School Barracks 30, 33, 49–51, 55–56, 58, 60, 353
Ingraham, Charles O. **412**

484 Index

Insse, Gregoire, Jr. 157, 178, 183, 316, 324–325, 329
Ireland, William C. 128–129

Jackson, Isaac W. 35, 76–77, 145–146
Jackson, James W. 53
Jackson, Thomas J. "Stonewall" 209–210, 219, 222, 240–241, 286, 288, 341, 343
Jackson, William A. 5, 35–39, **35**, 42, 49, 51–52, 55–60, 63, 66–68, 70–72, 74, 76, 87, 91, 97–99, 101–102, 108–112, 114–115, 127, 133, 136, **140**, 145–148, 181, 377
James, Amaziah B. 29
James River 164, 236, 240–242, 248, 253
Jaycox, John W. 158–159, 245, **279**, 280
Jenner, John 311
Jersey City, N.J. 62–63, 350
Johnson, Pres. Andrew 367
Johnson, William H. 153–155
Johnston, John **413**
Johnston, Joseph E. 188, 191, 203
Jones, Joseph C. 52, 56–57, 63–64, 67, 154–155, 314, 323
Jordan, Samuel 326
Judd, Schuyler F. 18
Judson, E.Z.C. 19

Kearns, Thomas 222–223, 236
Kearny, Philip 154
USS *Kent* (steamer) 182
Ketcham, Thomas J. 48
King, Gardiner 218–219
King, John S. 27–28, 67–68, 72–74, 83, 87, 90, 97, 264, 267–269, **268**, 271, 278, 286, 292, 294
King, Preston 103, 116
Kingsland, Kinsley E. 101
Knapp, Elias P. 237
Knickerbocker 24, 45
Knox, Andrew G. 281–282
Krug, John F. 261

Ladies' Aid Society (Canandaigua, N.Y.) 152
Ladies Association (Middletown, N.Y.) 53, 74
Ladies of Albany 53, 55
Ladies of Middletown 14–15, 359
Ladies of Ogdensburg 48
Ladies of Schenectady 53
La Mountain, John 135
Lamson, James 169
Lamson, William H. 237
Lane, Thomas S. 223–224, 244, 249–250, 331
Lang, Joseph 351
Langdon, Theodore 220
LaQue, John B. 83–84, 217, 382–383, **382**
Laraby, Roswell J. 295

Larkin, James M. 232
LaRue, Samuel C. 44, 46, 319
Lawless, John 23–24
Leary, Daniel 173–175
Lee, Cassius 122
Lee, Robert E. 122, 195, 203, 208–209, 229, 241, 258–259, 291, 294, 318, 346–347
Lee, William H.F. 195
LeFleur, John 112–113
Leith, Samuel 16–17, 136, **137**
LeMaire, Alfred 166
Levison, Henry 44
Libby Prison 134, 164, 247
Lilly, Samuel 229, 244
Lincoln, Pres. Abraham 9, 11, 19, 54, 58, 68, 75, 81, 102, 135, 151, 174, 178, 180, 243, 251, 291, 295, **296**, 301–302, 318, 322, 326, 328, 366–367, 374, 379
Linkletter, William H. 227, 247
Litchult, John, Jr. 282
USS *Long Branch* (steamer) 183
Longstreet, James 89, 117, 120–121
Looney, Michael 236
USS *Louisiana* (steamer) 182–184
Lowe, Thaddeus S.C. 135, 200, 202

Maguire, Edward 182
Maher, Jerry 319
Mahone, William 238–241
Maine troops: 5th Infantry 123, 191–192, 194, 267, 269; 6th Infantry 349
Major Bowes Amateur Hour 383
Malone, Robert A. 68, 73, 75, 107, 148, 221, 256, 262, 304, **305**
Malvern Hill 240–242, 251
Manassas, Battle of *see* Bull Run (Manassas)
Manassas, Va. 83, 90, 102, 172, 174, 178–179, 181, 257
Mann, Simeon H. 362
Mansfield, Joseph K.F. 68, 72, 108
Martin, Edwin 232, 237
Martin, George 271–272
Martin, Michael 131
Marye's Heights 314, 343–344
Maryland campaign 259–300
Mason's Hill 129, 139
Massachusetts troops: 6th Militia 66; 7th Infantry 303
Matheson, Roderick 215–216, **215**, 219, 221–222, 225, 276
Mathise, Henry 362
Matteson, William H.H. 57
Mattimore, Frank J. 251, 259, 282, 300, 305, 324–325, 330
Mayette, William H. 44, 79, 311
McClellan, George B. 106, 113–115, 119–121, 126–127, 129–130, 142–144, 148, 150–151, 154, 172, 174–176, 178, 180, 183, 187, 194–198, 202, 206–210, 213, 219, 228–229, 236–237, 242–243, 251, 257, 260, 262–264, 286, 288–289, 291, 295, **296**, 300–302, 325
McClinch, Daniel, Jr. 355
McCollum, Robert 139
McCormick, Thomas 280
McCoy, Lewis R. 170
McCoy, William B. 170
USS *McDonald* (steamer) 61
McDonald, Nelson 270
McDowell, Irvin 81, 84, 88–91, 93–95, 99, 106, 171, 176, 178, 180
McFetrish, James A. 364
McGuinness, Edward 163
McIntosh, William H. 312
McKinley, Hugh 86, 164
McKinney, Dennis 319
McKinney, William H. 109, 280
McLane, Patrick 289
McLean's Ford 93–94
McNeal, John 312
McQuoid, Charles C. 15, 333, 359
McRae, Duncan 224
Mechanicsville (Beaver Dam Creek), Battle of 209
Medal of Honor 365–366
Meginnis, John C. 9, 13–15, 30–31, 34, 120, 148, 188–190, 197, 210, 213–214, 216, 219, 221–223, 225, 228, 243, 245–246, 249–252, 271, 276, 278, 282, 321, 359, 373–374
Meginnis, Samuel G. 14, 125
Melany, Michael 179
Meridian Hill 69–70, 74–75, 77
USS *Metamora* (steamer) 349
Mexican War 31, 46, 106, 303
Michigan troops: 2nd Infantry 118–119, 126
Middaugh, Carson S. 338
Middletown, N.Y. 11–16, 27, 30, 45, 48–49, 127, 139, 170, 185, 219, 244, 250, 256, 262, 304, 357–359
Middletown Brass Band 14
Middletown Light Guards 13
Miles, Dixon S. 81, **82**, 84, 87–89, 91, 93–94, 96–99, 112, 263, 286–287
Miller, John 282
Miller, Reuben 363, **363**
Mills, Arthur W. 46
Mills, Henry C. 48
Mills, W. Bronson 235, 239–242, **240**, 261, 289
Minix, Thomas 160
Mississippi troops: 17th Infantry 97; 18th Infantry 97
Mitchell, A. Barclay 60, 126, 128, 157, 159, 274, 360
Montieth, Richard 76
Mooney, Frank 319
Mooney, John 109–110, 136, 157, 159, 256, 331
Moore, Jacob A. 379
Morgan, Gov. Edwin D. (N.Y.) 11,

27–28, 37–39, 53–54, 57–58, 60, 63, 146, 151, 153, 256
Morgan, James H. 26
Morgan, John T. 76
Mount Vernon 141
Mowatt, Augustus W. 50, 82, 109, 122–123, 139, 143, 158, 162, 168, 171–172, 202, **425**
Mud March 318–322, **320**
Munford, Thomas 266, 276
Munger, Henry E. 141, 340, 356, **357**, 380–381
Munson's Hill 117, 119–122, 124–125, 129–130, 150
Murphy, William H. 226
Murray, John H. 242
mustering in 49
mustering out 355–357
Myers, Andrew 319
Myers, Charles G. 29, 37, 41, 48, 58–59, 80, 372
Myers, George R. 29, **41**, 41–42, 54, 58, 83, 100, **100**, 105, 111, 127, 132, **140**, 145–148, 153, 179, 182, 184, 197, 207, 210, 213–214, 216, 219, 245–246, 252–253, 267, 269–271, **271**, 274, 277–278, 282–283, 297, 304, 318, 324, 326, 331, 335, 338, 347, **347**, 349, 351–353, 372–373, **373**, 375–376
Myers, Robert 380
USS *Mystic* (steamer) 182

USS *Nantasket* (steamer) 182–183
New Baltimore, Va. 302, 304
New Jersey troops: 1st Infantry 163; 1st Light Artillery 194, 220; 2nd Infantry 203; 4th Infantry 226; 15th Infantry 312
New York Times 244
New York Tribune 48, 244
New York troops: 1st (Lincoln) Cavalry 106, 153–154; 3rd Infantry 22, 49, 63; 5th Infantry 108, 215; 7th Cavalry 339; 11th Infantry (1st New York Fire Zouaves) 53–54, 79; 13th Cavalry 364; 14th Heavy Artillery 367; 14th Infantry 50, 54–55, 58, 60, 63, 70, 77; 15th Infantry (Engineers) 106, 113, 117, 123–125, 141–142, 335; 16th Heavy Artillery 374; 16th Infantry 29, 33, 41, 46, 52, 55, 59, 62, 77, 81, 86–88, 93–94, 97–99, 112, 124, 191, 193–194, 226, 267, 269, 271, 278, 310, 345, 348–349; 17th Infantry 129; 22nd Cavalry 365–366; 25th Militia National Guard 146; 26th Infantry 143; 26th Militia 39, 42; 27th Infantry 164, 188, 191, 198, 267, 310, 349; 28th Infantry 55, 352–353; 29th Infantry 80; 31st Infantry 81, 93–94, 97–99, 106, 117, 119, 123, 131–132, 182, 191, 193, 198, 215, 220, 259, 267, 303, 311, 323, 341, 349; 32nd Infantry 81, 91, 94, 98–99, 106, 117, 123–124, 191, 193, 198, 215–216, 220, 253, 258, 266–272, 276, 278, 303, 311, 323, 327, 335, 337, 343–344, 346, 349; 39th Infantry 123, 134; 40th Infantry 123; 43rd Infantry 364; 50th Engineers 252; 71st Militia 78; 80th Infantry 112; 92nd Infantry 297, 369; 93rd Infantry 365; 113th Infantry (7th Heavy Artillery) 262, 364, 366; 121st Infantry 262, 267, 298, 346, 349, 361–363; 126th Infantry 287; 128th Infantry 256; 134th Infantry 304
Newport News, Va. 252–253
Newton, John 121, **121**, 139, 141, 154, 162, 173, 188, 190–193, **196**, 198, 213–215, 219, 230, 237, 246, 266–268, 270, 289, 303, 305
Nolan, Michael A. 24–25
Noonan, Francis 111, 270, 282
Norris, Charles E. 221
Norris, James 363
North Carolina troops: 5th Infantry 224; 13th Infantry 227
CSS *Northampton* (steamer) 164
Norton, Mortier L. **133**, 134, 220, 297, **297**, 366
Nugent, Edward 213
Nugent, Henry 170
Nutting, Thomas W. 74

Oak Grove, Battle of 208
USS *Ocean Queen* (steamer) 182, 197
O'Dell, William H. 128–129
Ogdensburg, N.Y. 10, 17–19, 30, 45, 103, 107, 138, 160, 297, 372–373, 380
Ogdensburg Volunteer Aid Association 53
O'Hara, John 225, 351
Ontario Republican Times 138
Ormsby, James K.P. 48
Oswegatchie, N.Y. 9
Ox Hill *see* Chantilly (Ox Hill)

Pamunkey River 187, 194–195
Pangburn, Joshua 48, 160
Parham, William 266
Parshall, Jesse 126–127
Patriotic Christians of Albany 53
Payne, Joseph 232, 319
Peninsula campaign 174, 180, 182–254
Pennsylvania troops: 11th Infantry 226; 49th Infantry 323, 335, 337–338, 344, 346; 95th Infantry 141–142, 146, 148, 156, 179, 181, 191, 198, 215, 267, 303, 311, 323, 335, 337, 344–346, 349; 96th Infantry 267, 270–271, 278; 119th Infantry 323, 335, 344–346
Percell, Patrick 77
Peterson, Charles 108
USS *Philadelphia* (steamer) 78
Philadelphia, Pa. 64–65, 138, 141–142, 245, 247–250, 297, 306, 313, 323, 350, 356
Phillips, John D. 247, 348
USS *Pioneer* (steamer) 186
Pittenger, Morton P. 56–57, 160–161
USS *Pittsburgh* (gunboat) 169
Place, David 166
Pollard, John H. 227, 247
Pollock, George W. 48
Pomeroy, Elizabeth 35
Pope, John 257–258
Poquoson River 183, 186
Porter, Fitz John 197, 202, 209–211, **211**, 213–215, 219, 229, 241, 258
Post, William H. 258
Potomac River 78–79, 117, 146, 182, 254, 258–259, 287, 294, 298, 300, 349
Potter, Calvin B. 86, 134, 164, 361, 381–382, **381**
Potts, William H. 129
Price, Willard 149
Pronk, James N. 15
Purdy, William B. 76, 262, 284, 304
Putman, John A. 218

"Quaker Gun" 130, **130**, 174

Radcliff, Thomas J. 25, 34, 112, 143–144, 207, 231, 316–317
Raines, John 381
Raines, Joseph S. 381
Ranney, Frances 41, 372–373
Rappahannock River 302, 309, 314, 318–319, 333–335, 337, 343, 346
Rarick, Patrick 159
Raymond, Leonard 280
Read, George 36
Read, John M. 36
Rediker, John H. 248
Redington, John C.O. 34, 48, 58, 60, 77, 79, 89, 95–96, **96**, 372
Redman, John 46, 149
Reed, Charles H. 250
Reed, George 282
Rexman, Augustus 364
Reznor, Lot 102
Rice, James 143, 279
Rice, Nathan P. 108, 136, 139, **140**, 145–149, 152, 157, 160–161, 165, 167, 169, 172, 176, 219, 228, 237, 240, 245–246, 250, 275, 321, 330–331, 369
Richardson, Alonzo 72–73, 111, 143, 321
Richardson, Israel B. 91, 93, 97–98

Richford, James **431**
Richmond, Hiram R. 287
Richmond, Va. 164, 174, 180, 188, 198–203, 209, 227–229, 237–238, 246–248, 252, 262, 300, 302, 333, 348
Riley, Edmond 355, 379
Riquer, Thomas 67
Ritzenthaler, Reinold 227, 245, 247
Rockwell, Joseph N. 43, 149
Rogers, Harvey L. 23–24, 101
Rogers, Theodore C. 31–32, **32**, 52, **69**, 145, 168, 223–225, **223**, 244, 250
"Rogue's March" 58
Roper, John B. 45
Royce, George W. 52, 84–85, 88–89, 102, 306–307
Rude, David L. 281
Russell, David A. 303, **303**, 312, 315, 323, 332, 334–337, 340, 343–346, 348–349, 362
Russell, David C.J. 59
Russell, John H. **42**, 42, 76, 90–91, 99–101, **100**, 104, 112, 127–128, **140**, 146–147, 175, 216, 234, 237, 249–250
Russell, Solomon W., Jr. 339–340, **341**
Russell, William H., Jr. 127–128, **127**, **140**, 191, 237, 368, **368**
Ryan, Edward 61
Ryan, Jeremiah 355

St. Lawrence Republican 324
Salem Church, Battle of 344–345, 348–349
Salisbury Prison 202, 306, 363
Sanford, Charles 75
Santaus, Peter 317
Savage's Station 232, 234–237, **235**, 243–245, 247
Sawyer, Washington Irving 31, 229, 233
Sayer, Roswell M. 15–16, 148, 221, 244, 317, 344, 348
Scanlin, Michael 129
Schenectady, N.Y. 19, 21–23, 39, 45, 49, 115, 124, 127, 133, 141, 145, 147, 159, 161, 184–185, 244, 252, 256, 260, 273–275, 285–286, 304, 308, 353–355, 357, 371–372, 374–377, 383
Schenectady City Artillery 22, 39
Schenectady Washington Continentals 22–23, 273, 286
Schermerhorn, E. Nott 184–185, 192–193, 249, 260, 271–273, 279, 285, 354
Schermerhorn, Henry 79, 311
Schermerhorn, Jonathan Crane 184–185
Schufeldt, Edward 101, 326
Schwantner, John 227–228, 247
Scott, Winfield 75

Scully, John 149, 319
Second Fredericksburg *see* Marye's Heights
Second Manassas (Bull Run), Battle of 257–258
Sedgwick, John 323, 329, 334, 338, 341, 343–344, 347
Seely, Albert S. 18, 28–30, 107, **107**, 123, 166, 296–297
Semmes, Paul 266
Seven Days' battles 208–242
Seven Pines (Fair Oaks), Battle of 203, 207–208
Seward, William H. 19, 68, 151, 374
Seward Volunteer Zouaves 22
Seymour, Franklin (Frank) 87, 90, 96, 98, 100, 104, 183, 264, 269, 274, **277**, 278, 281–282
Seymour, Gov. Horatio (N.Y.) 352–353
Shannon, George E. 44
Sharpsburg, Battle of *see* Antietam (Sharpsburg)
Sharpsburg, Md. 287, 292, 294; *see also* Antietam (Sharpsburg)
Shaughnessy, John H. 197
Shaw, Chester C. 86, 164
Shaw, William A. 223, 249
Sheehan, Peter 46, 71, 115
Sheil, Jacob 313, 340
Sheldon, David D. 216
Sheldon, Griffin 249
Shepherdstown, W.V. 294
Ship Point, Va. 182–184, 186
Shirley, John 46
Shook, George W. 90, 135–136
Shultz, John 312
Shuter's Hill 113
Sickler, Peter E. 157
Slattery, James S. 111, 143
Slocum, Henry W. 154, 162, **196**, 198, **198**, 211, 213–214, 229, 235–242, 266–267, 270, 278, 281, 288–289, 295
Smith, Percival R. 208–209
Smith, William F. 198, 266, 288, 302–303, **303**, 309–311, 321–323
Smyth, Andrew J. 48
Snell, William 250
Snyder, Joseph 218
Snyder, Thompson H. 46, 229–230
Soule, Perrie 291–292, **291**, 294
South Carolina troops: 5th Infantry 97
Southard, John J. 218
Spawn, Lewis 101, 229, 258
Speenburgh, William 197
Springfield musket 204
Springfield Station 131–132, 178
Stafford Court House 305–307
Stalker, Henry 229
Stall, Henry B. 99, 164
Stanton, William H. 319
"Star-Spangled Banner" 13, 48, 75

Stevens, Henry 362
Stevens, Jehiel J. 105, 218, **218**, 245, 351, 371
Stevenson, Sinclair L. 220
Stillwell, Daniel D. 111, 143, 233
Stivers, Moses D. 359
Storms, William J. 271
Strathern, James K. 166
Strong, Richard M. 36
Strunk, Joseph 190, 322
Stuart, J.E.B. 120, 298
Sullivan, Charles 252
Sumner, Edwin 219, 228, 287–289, 322
Swartout, Levi 229
Swimm, Sylvanus L. 158–159

Taylor, Henry W. 218
Taylor, Joseph 280
Territ, Thomas 86
Thompson, Charles H. 108
Thompson, John 128, 157
Thompson, William H. 220, **220**
Tilley, Edward M. 50, 55, 57–58, 62–63, 65, 67–68, 71, 74, 90, 101, 120, 124, 126, 130, 132–133, 135, 142–143, 156, 165, 169, 173, 278
Timmins, Edward 163
Torbert, Alfred T.A. 267, 270
Townsend, Frederick 36–37, 49, 63
Trabilcox, Thomas 226
Truax, Alfred 47, 374
Truax, Stephen 22–23, 27, 34, 45, 49, 60, 70, 115, 123, 161, 286
True, William J. 315
Turkey Hill 211, 214, 228
Turnbull, James 363
Turner's Gap 262–263

Underhill, Frank K. 319, 326, 331
Union College 19, 35–36, 42, 60, 77, 119, 147, 184, 340
Union Volunteer Refreshment Saloon 64–65, **64–65**, 138, 350
United States Christian Commission 132
United States Military Academy (West Point) 21, 41, 106, 121, 198, 302–303, 322–323
United States Sanitary Commission 77, 113–114, 134, 151–152, 168–169, 177, 194, 281
United States troops: 1st Artillery 93, 99; 2nd Artillery 81, 106, 165, 239, 311, 321, 338, 343–344; 2nd Infantry 81; 4th Cavalry 368; 7th Cavalry 369; 10th Infantry 46; 17th Infantry 248; 18th Infantry 368
Upton, Emory 362
Upton's Battery (Battery D, 2nd U.S. Artillery) 214; *see also* 2nd United States Artillery
Upton's Hill 129

Vale Cemetery 147, 286, 372
Van Benthuysen, Francis 43
Van Bueren, John 45, 275, 284–285
USS *Vanderbilt* (steamer) 249
Van Hoesen, Peter 261, 365
Van Housen, Charles 363
Van Ingen, James L. 42, 107–108
Van Kuren, Isaac H. 47, 230–231
Van Kuren, Simon P. 47, 230
Van Kuren, William H. 47, 230–231
Van Santvoord, John 259–260
Van Steinberg, Charles 306
Vedder, Barney M. 319, 326
Vedder, John 102, 123–124, 253, 268, **269**, 304, 314, 317, 319, 322, 326
Vedder, Rodney S. 119–120, 123–124, 131, 146
Veterans Reserve Corps 366, 368
Virginia Theological Seminary *see* Fairfax Seminary
Virginia troops: 2nd Cavalry 266, 280; 5th Infantry 126; 6th Infantry 266, 271; 12th Cavalry 266; 12th Infantry 266, 271; 16th Infantry 266

Walden, Isaac B. 166
Walker, Stephen 362
Wallace, Alexander M. 108
Walley, Charles C. 256
Wands, Alexander H. 47–48, **47**, 132, 159, 184, 234, 368–369, **368**

Wands, Robert J. 47, **47**
Warden, Warren 261
Warfield, John J. 166
Warrenton, Va. 302, 307
Washington, D.C. 53, 58, 67–70, 72–73, 75–77, 86, 88, 93, 99, 101, 103, 113, 117, 120–121, 125, 136, 142, 145–146, 151, 162, 166, 172, 174, 177–178, 180, 182, 245, 251, 253, 256–260, 301, 306, 316, 321–322, 330, 349, 356, 367, 376, 379
Waterson, John 86, 103
Weatherwax, Walter W. 289
Webster, Aurelius 256, 355
Weed, William G. 24
Werner, Jacob I. 55–56
West Point (academy) *see* United States Military Academy (West Point)
West Point, Battle of *see* Brick House Landing (West Point)
West Point, Va. 187; *see also* Brick House Landing (West Point)
Weymer, Michael 218
Wheaton, Frank 49
The Whig Press 27, 127, 244
Whitcomb, William P. 59
White, William H. 280
White House (Washington D.C.) 54, 68, 75
White House, Va. 195–198, 232
White Oak Church 308, **308**, 314–316, 319, 321, 328–330, 332, 348–349

White Oak Swamp 236
Whiting, William H.C. 191–193
Whitley, Preston 158–159
Whittemore, Nathaniel G. 47, 179, 284
Wilbur, Henry D. 256–257
Wilcox, Cadmus 345
Willette, Gabriel 317
Williams, Millard F. 48
Williamsburg, Va. 253
Williamsport, Md. 294–295, 298
Wiltse, Henry, Jr. 16–17, 27, 34, 112, 136
Wisconsin troops: 5th Infantry 349
Wiseman, Robert 218
Wolff, Mark 146, 237
Wood, Spencer 231
Woodbury's Bridge 204–206, **205**, 211

York River 182, 186–187, 192
Yorktown, Va. 180, 183, 185–187, 191, 253
Young, David W. 48, 170, 173, 175, 197, **247**, 372, 375
Young, William H. **39**, 39–40, 48, 51, 57, 70, 74, 84, 87, 91, 93, 99, 101, 108, 115–116, **140**, 145–148, 151, 153, 161, 167–168, 172–173, 175–176, 182–184, 190–191, 193, 197, 207, 246, **247**, 251–252, 271, 366, 370–372, **370**

www.ingramcontent.com/pod-product-compliance
Lightning Source LLC
Chambersburg PA
CBHW080752300426
44114CB00020B/2709